THE NORM SMITH MEDALLISTS

The Slattery Media Group
Level 39/385 Bourke Street, Melbourne
Victoria, Australia, 3000
Visit *slatterymedia.com*

Text © Dan Eddy, 2018

First published by the Slattery Media Group, 2018.

All rights reserved. No part of this publication may be reproduced, stored in a retrieval system or transmitted in any form by any means without the prior permission of the copyright owner. Inquiries should be made to the publisher.

Cover Image of Norm Smith Medal © AFL Photos.

Back Cover Images: (Top) The evolution of the Norm Smith Medal; (Bottom) Norm Smith as a young Melbourne full-forward. This photo formed the basis of the image on the Medal.

Images throughout © AFL Photos unless otherwise marked.

 A catalogue record for this book is available from the National Library of Australia

Group Publisher: Geoff Slattery
Editor: Geoff Slattery
Assistant Editor: Russell Jackson
Proofing: Mick Ellis
Art Director: Kate Slattery
Designer: Gabrielle Storrs

Cover design: Kate Slattery

Printed and bound in Australia by Griffin Press

www.slatterymedia.com

THE NORM SMITH MEDALLISTS

THE PLAYERS WHO DELIVERED ON FOOTBALL'S GRANDEST STAGE

Dan Eddy

About the author

Dan Eddy is a storyteller with a passion for the history of sport, especially Australian football. Since producing his first book—*King Richard: The Story of Dick Reynolds, Essendon Legend* (in 2014)—he has been prolific. *The Norm Smith Medallists* is his tenth book (five as author, and five as a co-author). He lives in Leongatha, in country Victoria, with his son Ernie, and their sidekick, Dennis, the border collie. They all barrack for Essendon.

Other books by Dan Eddy
Author:
Skills of Australian Football (2016)
Larrikins & Legends: The Untold Story of Carlton's Greatest Era (2017)
Always Striving: The Key Moments That Have Made the Essendon Football Club (2017)

Co-Author
The Will to Fly [co-author with Lydia Lassila and Andrew Clarke, 2016]
Champions: Conversations with Great Players and Coaches of Australian Football [co-author with Ben Collins, 2016]
The Shinboners: The Complete History of the North Melbourne Football Club [co-author with Nick Bowen and Andrew Gigacz, 2017]
Grand Finals Volume III [co-author with Nick Bowen and Andrew Gigacz, 2018]
Nova: Finding my Voice [co-author with Nova Peris, 2018]

THE NORM SMITH MEDALLISTS

Contents

Publisher's Introduction 7
Foreword 11
1979 Wayne Harmes 15
1980 Kevin Bartlett 25
1981 Bruce Doull 39
1982 Maurice Rioli 49
1983 Colin Robertson 65
1984 Bill Duckworth 77
1985 Simon Madden 91
1986, 1988 Gary Ayres 101
1987 David Rhys-Jones 119
1989 Gary Ablett 135
1990 Tony Shaw 155
1991 Paul Dear 175
1992 Peter Matera 185
1993 Michael Long 203
1994 Dean Kemp 223
1995 Greg Williams 239
1996 Glenn Archer 255
1997, 1998 Andrew McLeod 275
1999 Shannon Grant 295
2000 James Hird 309
2001 Shaun Hart 327
2002 Nathan Buckley 345
2003 Simon Black 361
2004 Byron Pickett 375
2005 Chris Judd 385
2006 Andrew Embley 399
2007 Steve Johnson 413
2008, 2014 Luke Hodge 423
2009 Paul Chapman 441
2010 Lenny Hayes 461
2010 Scott Pendlebury 475
2011 Jimmy Bartel 489
2012 Ryan O'Keefe 505
2013 Brian Lake 515
2015 Cyril Rioli 535
2016 Jason Johannisen 549
2017 Dustin Martin 561
Acknowledgements 574

PUBLISHER'S INTRODUCTION

A Proud Chapter of The Game's History

Dan Eddy has a rare capacity to draw information from those he interviews. He showed that ability clearly with his first book for the Slattery Media Group, the biography of the Essendon champion Dick Reynolds (*King Richard*, 2014), which also highlighted his exhaustive approach to research.

Those skills made him the ideal candidate when we looked to publish the history of the Norm Smith Medal, in the words of the winners. The medal, originally called the Norm Smith Memorial Medal, was struck in 1979 to recognise the best player in the VFL Grand Final. Unlike its cousin, the Brownlow Medal, the Norm Smith is based on the votes of administrators and media figures and takes no account of the "fairest" element so integral to the Brownlow. That said, none of the winners can be considered as anything but fair players, at least in their Grand Final triumphs!

The original medal was little more than a Big V—the logo of the Victorian Football League—surrounded by the words Norm Smith Memorial Medal. At the end of the 2000 season, during a meeting of the

← **LEGEND:** Norm Smith was the ultimate football hero: a champion full-forward for Melbourne, pocketing four Premierships, and then a legendary coach at the Demons, leading the club to six flags. His legacy is highlighted on Grand Final day with the Norm Smith Medal presented to the best player on the ground.

THE NORM SMITH MEDAL

AFL's Football Operations Department, then led by Andrew Demetriou, I pointed out that the League's medals looked sub-standard when compared to the medals handed out at the Sydney Olympics. Demetriou was never one to be running second in anything, and enthusiastically embraced the concept of updating the design of all the League's medals. Even the Brownlow was changed—not in looks, but in weight. If the Brownlow winners from around 1980 to 2000 balanced their medals against those that came after, they would notice a substantial difference. The latter medals included real gold, as had been the edict of the League when the Brownlow was first struck, in 1924.

The Norm Smith change was less subtle: out went the League's logo, and in came the image of Smith—not pictured on the medal as the renowned coach, but as the four-time Premiership player, and champion spearhead for Melbourne. Smith was a dominant full-forward in the Demons' first glorious era (1939-41), kicking 7.3 in the club's 1940 win over Richmond, reversing his 3.7 return in the Preliminary Final. Would he have won his own medal in that match? Percy Taylor, writing in *The Argus*, was non-committal on the best player, naming "five who deserved most credit". He wrote of Smith, "Norman Smith's seven goals tell the whole story. He frequently raced away to mark in front of (George) Smeaton and kicked more accurately than he did in the last match."

In *The Red Fox*, Ben Collins's biography of Smith,[1] Collins wrote that Smith was believed to have actually kicked eight goals, with one incorrectly recorded to Ron Baggott. In an interview with Collins, Baggott said, "Although I would never want to deny Smithy his due, I wouldn't want to rob myself of a goal in a Grand Final, either."

Until 2018 Australian Football Hall of Fame inductee David Neitz (631 goals) came along, Smith was Melbourne's leading goalkicker with 546 from his 210 games. Just as importantly, he was the ultimate team player, often playing as a decoy, leading up the ground to allow teammates like Baggott, Jack Mueller and Fred Fanning easy access.

The AFL's decision to name the medal after Norm Smith, for the best player on Grand Final day was rather quirky, as Smith's real claim to immortality was as a coach (six premierships), but quirky decisions are

---

[1] Ben Collins, *The Red Fox: The Biography of Norm Smith* (2nd Ed.), Slattery Media Group, 2017.

not inconsistent with AFL policy. When the League changed the rules regarding elevation of an inductee to Legend in the Australian Football Hall of Fame in 2007, allowing coaches to achieve that honour, Smith, who had been named Coach of the Century in the AFL Team of the Century, announced in 1996, was *not* the first coach to be elevated. That honour went to Jock McHale. Since 2001, McHale is also honoured on Grand Final Day with the Premiership coach receiving the Jock McHale Medal.

Quirky in a different way—fate, perhaps—was the choice of Carlton's dynamic midfielder/forward Wayne Harmes, Smith's great-nephew, as the first recipient of the Norm Smith Medal. Harmes is the grandson of Norm's brother Len, and the first medal was presented by Marj Smith, Norm's widow.

Dan Eddy's work has not only brought back to life the marvellous performances of the players who have taken home the Norm Smith Medal, it has drawn from their formative years, influences and great moments in their careers. Not all the winners wished to be interviewed, certainly their prerogative, and in those cases Eddy talked to many who played with, or against, or perhaps recruited these players, providing a wonderful insight into their careers, and their moments in the sun. Sadly, Maurice Rioli died in 2010, before this book was considered. He is one of just four players to have won the medal in losing teams (Richmond 1982; the others are Gary Ablett in 1989, Nathan Buckley in 2002, and Chris Judd in 2005).

In each interview/profile, the player's career statistics have been listed, and, where available, the voting panel and vote breakdown. Unfortunately, the League has retained these details only since 2003. In the period from 1979 to 2002, Eddy has included votes from various newspaper experts to highlight those who won, and to illustrate those who may have missed narrowly.

This book is a marvellous record of not just the superb winners, but also how the game has evolved from a semi-amateur pursuit to today's ultra-professional era. I am proud to include it in our growing list of books that record the game's great history.

Geoff Slattery,
Publisher,
July 2018.

FOREWORD
BY GREG WILLIAMS

A Dream Comes True, Eventually

Grand Final day holds a special place for me and my family. For it was on that day, 30 September 1995, that I finally achieved my dream of playing in a Premiership team—it only took me three clubs and 219 games to get there! That it was my 32nd birthday, and I was awarded the Norm Smith Medal for best on the ground, ensured it became a day that the Williams family would never forget.

Growing up in Essendon, I recall being in awe of the players who performed on Grand Final day. My hero was Hawthorn's Leigh Matthews, and 'Lethal' seemed to be in the Grand Final every year. I remember always hoping to one day emulate his deeds and play in a final on the MCG. Matthews never won a Norm Smith Medal, but he was a big-game performer who rose to the occasion time and again. He was inspiring to an eager young kid like me.

That desire to play at the highest level increased for me when we moved to Bendigo when I was 10, for Bendigo was Carlton's recruiting zone.

← **PREMIERS** Greg Williams, (below, left of the Premiership Cup) celebrates with his teammates after Carlton's 1995 Premiership. From Williams's right, clockwise, are Fraser Brown, Matt Clape, Brett Ratten, Brad Pearce, Justin Madden, Stephen Kernahan, Glenn Manton, Ang Christou, Scott Camporeale, Dean Rice, Stephen Silvagni, Craig Bradley and Matthew Hogg.

THE NORM SMITH MEDAL

The Blues were dominant during the 1970s and 1980s (winning the 1970, 1972, 1979 and 1981-82 Premierships), and a number of their Grand Final heroes, such as Peter McConville, came from my club Golden Square. You can imagine my disappointment when the Blues rejected me when I first trained with the club in 1982 and 1983. Certainly, I could never have envisaged back then that I would win my only Premiership with the Blues—of all clubs—more than a decade later.

My journey to Grand Final day instead began at Geelong (1984-85), then took me to Sydney (1986-91), but other than two Semi-Finals with the Swans in 1986 and '87, I was nowhere near achieving my ultimate dream. Fortunately, at the end of 1991, an opportunity arose to play with Carlton, thus changing the course of my career and setting me on a path to Grand Final glory.

In 1993 we played Essendon in the Grand Final—my worst day in football. Nothing went right that day. The Bombers opened up a five-goal lead by quarter-time; we were unable to peg them back, and I was tagged closely by Sean Denham. The 'Baby Bombers' were too good for us, but it made me even more determined to get back to Grand Final day and experience the joy that the Essendon players felt that day.

We stuffed up in 1994. It had been a great year personally, winning my second Brownlow Medal to go with my 1986 Brownlow that I shared with Hawthorn's Robert DiPierdomenico, but after we finished second on the ladder, come finals time we blew a great opportunity by losing both finals. At 30 years old and with ageing legs, I admit to having doubts that I was going to claim the one medallion I coveted above all others—the Premiership Medal.

Our 1995 season was something special. Coach David Parkin had entrusted more responsibility on to the players, which enabled us to control our own destiny. As a consequence, we lost just two games during the season, then won all three of our finals. When the siren sounded at the end of the Preliminary Final, and we were 62 points ahead of North Melbourne, it was a sense of relief that we had booked our place in another Grand Final. After lowering my colours in 1993, I was more determined than ever to perform at my optimum in my second crack at it.

A DREAM COMES TRUE, EVENTUALLY

I remember certain moments from the Grand Final against Geelong, including how nervous I was at the start. The pressure applied by teammates Dean Rice and Matt Clape stood out, and I was able to find space repeatedly across half-forward. I knew we had won when we were 10 goals in front at three-quarter time, and the last few minutes of the match were the most enjoyable of my career. When the siren sounded I remember feeling relieved and satisfied to have finally achieved my dream of playing in a winning Grand Final. Did I think I would win the Norm Smith Medal? Well, yeah, I did! I knew I had played well and kicking five goals would certainly have captured the attention of the judging panel. But it's not until your name is called out that it sinks in you've won it.

How does it feel to be known as a Norm Smith medallist? I won many individual awards during my career, but there is something unique about the Norm Smith. It's different from the Brownlow, although both are fantastic to win. It's a bit like choosing your favourite child—you can't separate them, they are as special as each other, albeit unique in their own ways.

This book by Dan Eddy is a fitting tribute to all of us who experienced the highs and lows of Grand Final day. There are some wonderful insights into each medallist and what stands out for me is how we have all come from very different backgrounds yet we now share a unique piece of history for what we did on Grand Final day. And it is something my children, Jye, Jake, Samantha and Charly, can look back on with pride; that their old man lived his dream and tasted the ultimate success on the game's biggest stage.

Greg Williams,
1995 Norm Smith medallist
July 2018

Wayne Harmes

Wayne Harmes was a superb player in a super team. He had power—teammates recall that he was the strongest man in the weights room at Carlton—and he could also leap his own height. Harmes was explosive and versatile. Indeed, the latter quality led to him receiving the first Norm Smith Medal, awarded after the Blues' five-point victory over Collingwood in the 1979 Grand Final. After the Magpies had established a five-goal lead, Harmes moved from the back pocket into the centre, where he swung the momentum with some dynamic play. He contributed 17 disposals (12 kicks, five handballs and three marks) and a goal, but also one remarkable solo feat in the final quarter, when a desperate dive kept the ball in play, leading to a Ken Sheldon goal. It is one of the most iconic moments in Grand Final history, and haunts Magpie supporters to this day.

Len Smith was my grandfather, Norm my great-uncle. I was seven when Len passed away, and I had had a lot more to do with Len than I did Norm. I can remember being taken around to Len's place in Essendon, and he had beautiful couch grass in the backyard. What Len used to do was hang me from the Hills Hoist, wind me up as high as he could, and when he said, "Let go," I had to let go and he'd throw the footy at me. And he'd keep putting me up there until I kept

← **DYNAMO** Wayne Harmes, Norm Smith's great nephew, was a fitting winner of the first Medal in 1979.

marking it! Then, when I had caught three in a row, he would have a footy and my dad would have a footy and when they said, "Let go," I'd have to catch both of them.

Len taught me about tactics.[1] He had a split-level house, and down the bottom was a billiards room with a billiards table. He had a chest of drawers with six drawers on each side, and in each drawer there were 20 soldiers which were all painted in the different club colours. The cover of the billiards table was a football ground, and every Thursday night the Richmond players would all come to Len's place and Mum and Dad would take me around there so I could lay out all the 'players' on the table for him. It was there that he first taught me about the full-back line and half-back line and so forth. I would stand all the soldiers up and then I'd get to go and open the door for all the Richmond players.

Norm, on the other hand, was scary.[2] But I never had a lot to do with him growing up. Personally, I believe Len was the leader of the two in the way he could see where football was going. I have a copy of his famous notes, they are amazing! In 1966, he was talking about having a centre square where only four players on either side were allowed in.[3] He also spoke about having a time clock for the players to see how long there was to go in the quarter; things we take for granted these days. People say that he was 25-30 years ahead of his time, and I know that great coaches like Kevin Sheedy and Allan Jeans used Len's notes when they were coaching. Len was talking about things like the footballer's brain, and how he dissects it into various parts. He was out on his own, in my opinion, and his notes are a terrific read.

I left school after third form [year nine]. I told myself that I was going to play footy, and the teacher said: "You'll never make it." But I couldn't stay at school, I'd had enough; it wasn't my thing. Funnily enough, a few years

---

1 Len Smith is credited with having introduced the idea that handball could be used as an attacking weapon. Before this time, handball was used sparingly, as a means to get out of trouble, rather than to move the ball quickly and offensively. He played 19 games for Melbourne (1934-35), and 76 for Fitzroy (1937-43), but it was as a coach at Fitzroy (1958-62, 92 games) and Richmond (1964-65, 15 games) where he made his greatest contribution. Smith died suddenly of a heart attack, aged just 55, on 23 July 1967.
2 In 1996, Norm Smith was named coach of the VFL/AFL Team of the Century. He played 210 games for Melbourne (1935-48, four Premierships), kicking 546 goals, and was named full-forward in the club's Team of the Century. He also played 17 games, as captain-coach, for Fitzroy (1949-50), before becoming non-playing coach (1951). The following year he returned to Melbourne as coach, and led the club through one of the greatest eras in history. Melbourne played in every Grand Final from 1954 to 1960, winning five Premierships, and claimed a sixth flag—its most recent—in 1964. After falling out with the MCC committee, which then oversaw the football club, Smith later coached at South Melbourne (1969-72), leading the club into its first finals appearance (1970) since 1945. In all, Smith coached 452 games for a winning percentage of 56.75. Norm always praised Len for his coaching nous and innovative thinking. Inducted into the Australian Football Hall Of Fame in 1996, Norm Smith was elevated to Legend status in 2007.
3 The VFL introduced a centre diamond in 1973, and the diamond became a square in 1975.

ago I was driving and I noticed this guy walking his dog: it was my old English teacher, John Wright. I pulled over and introduced myself, and I said "I remember one day you said..." and he jumped in straight away and said: "I apologise!" We had a good laugh about it.

When I first left school I wanted to play golf, that was my ambition. But, a month later, I received the invitation to go and train with Carlton's under-19s. Footy became my thing after that. In fact, it changed my life. The club had some great people who supported us during that period. People like Ian Rice and Richard Pratt, for example. Richard gave me a job at Visy when I was just a brick cleaner; I was only ever educated enough to clean bricks. When Richard gave me that job, in 1977, it all opened up for me from there. He taught me to smarten up. I thought that if I can't learn something from a billionaire, who can I learn from? Richard gave a lot of blokes a start in life.

I went to Carlton as a 14-year-old. I played with the under-19s from 1974-1976, then played with the Reserves in 1977, and I was given one senior game at the end of '77. So, up until 1978, I was away from the main bunch, and it was around then that all these other young guys started coming into the club. Guys like Wayne Johnston, Peter McConville and Jim Buckley for example. A lot came from the Bendigo way. We knew that the Bendigo area was a good breeding ground because we had guys like Rod Ashman and Trevor Keogh who had come from up there.

Our side was tough in that era. We had guys like Buckley, Johnston and Ashman who were hard and nasty. They were three guys who would stand up when we needed them to. You knew you were always safe, and if something happened you knew there were 19 guys around you who were as thick as thieves and who would do anything for their teammates.

Mateship drove us to achieve great things as a football team. We had such a talented group of small players during that period. We also had a sprinkling of metropolitan and regional players, and we all remain close mates to this day. If someone gets into trouble, it only takes a phone call and we are there to help out. We would train three days a week together, we'd play on Saturdays together, then we'd go out on Saturday nights together; we'd always be together. And partners, too. We never held back after a game. But, in saying that, we'd all front up on the Sunday morning, which wasn't pleasant, but we did it because of that closeness.

There was no one who stood out among the group. If 20 of us wanted to do something, and two didn't, it only took a quick look in their direction and we soon had 22.

Alex Jesaulenko scared us into the 1979 Premiership, because his training drills were just horrific. But we just had to do it. I remember one night, we'd been beaten by Geelong for our third loss of the year, and on the Tuesday night we did 10 by 100s, 10 by 200s, 10 by 400s, 10 by 800s and five 1500s. We started at five o'clock and we got off the track at 20 to 11! After the running, we did one-on-one contesting work, and some of those pairings went for 20 minutes. What Jezza used to do at three-quarter time—if we were behind—was, he would just walk up and say, "Think of Tuesday night..." If you go through the record books we could be six goals down at three-quarter time and we'd win by four, because we were all shit-frightened. We were too scared to lose!

You had to be tough to survive. Jezza would put us up against somebody in our own position, and they were the most dangerous games of footy you've ever seen. There'd be blokes running past swinging elbows, and fights going on, because that guy wanted your position in the team. We all knew that we were match-hardened. We would play Saturday, Tuesday, Saturday—we'd play three games in a week! Nowadays, they talk about guys needing a rest for seven days. Turn it up!

Bruce Doull gave me my first kick in League footy. He had it all planned. We played a night game and I stood Richmond's Kevin Bartlett at Waverley. I was that nervous before the game! I started in a back pocket, and Doully walked up and said to me, "If the ball's kicked out of the middle by the opposition, I'll get it and I want you to run." Well, bugger me dead—the ball's kicked out of the middle by Richmond and Doully's marked it. He just stood there; I forgot to run! He turned around with the ball and nodded at me, and I realised I'd better run. So, I did, and he gave me the ball. He was a genius, an absolute genius. He actually played four years in the Reserves before he got a senior game. What a marvel.

I had a fear of stuffing up on the big stage, which I almost did in 1979. What ultimately drove me on Grand Final day was knowing there were millions of people inside and outside of the ground who were watching it. You just run on adrenalin, and maybe it makes you run a bit quicker or jump a bit higher—I don't know. Your parents are there watching too, so you're always keen to impress. But, I'd like to think I played a lot of good home and away games as well.

If Trevor Keogh did not whack Russell Ohlsen in the second quarter, Russell would have won the Norm Smith Medal. I know for a fact that Russell still holds a grudge to this day because of that. He stayed on the ground after the hit, and at one stage he tackled his own teammate because he was concussed. Up until that hit, Russell had been hot. He was someone who was slow, but in those heavier conditions where he could be hard and tough, they suited him perfectly. The hit was a beauty. In fact, I heard it from 30 metres away.

I chased *that* ball in the last quarter because I was embarrassed at stuffing up the kick. Before I picked the ball up on the wing, I saw Ken Sheldon out of the corner of my eye running down the middle of the field. I had decided that I was going to kick it to my left where Kenny was 40 metres clear, and he'd be able to run in and kick an open goal. The kick was shit, and, I don't know why, but I chased after it. I think it was out of fear more than anything; I'd made a horrible blunder late in the final quarter of a Grand Final.

Maybe I just knew that there was a Toyota advertisement coming 30 years down the track that would pay off my house![4] No, fear is what drove me to chase that ball. Bob Barker was the goal umpire, and his positioning for the incident was perfect. He stood on the point post with his arms behind his back. He later told me that they didn't want you umpiring after you turned 50, and he was 49 at that stage. The boundary umpire was well back from the play, and after the game the umpiring fraternity told Bob, "If you hadn't have paid that decision as you called it, you would not have seen out your umpiring career until you were 50." They had been sitting right in front of it and they would

---

4   The Wayne Harmes Toyota Memorable Moment can be viewed here: http://tinyurl.com/y8oj3psk.

have made the same decision as Bob did—that the ball was in play when I whacked it.

Amazingly, nobody followed Kenny as he ran towards goal. He was sitting in the goal square thinking to himself, "What have I done all this running for?" I probably ran 60 or 70 metres to tap it back, so I wasn't all that tired after the play. It was just one of those things that wasn't planned. The easiest plan was to kick it across my body to Kenny and let him do the work. But it was a shit kick in shit conditions. You don't get those types of Grand Finals now with the mud.

Was the ball in or out? That depends on who you barrack for. If they're a Carlton supporter, I tell them it was in. But if they support Collingwood I tell them it was in the Jolimont rail yards! And if you're neutral? I say, "Does it really matter?"

People think I went into the middle early in the Grand Final. But I didn't go in until Jezza went down with a broken ankle in the last quarter.[5] When I tapped that famous ball back late in the final quarter, I was still playing in the back pocket. I stayed back most of the day. It was only when Jezza went down that I was moved. If you watch the last centre bounce, you had Peter Moore versus Mike Fitzpatrick in the ruck and so I stood behind 'Fitzy', knowing full well that Moore would win the tapout. I was left there by myself, and Moore went up and hit the ball straight down my throat! I grabbed it, shit myself, and turned straight to the Members' stand and kicked it end over end. I was yelling, "Get out, get out!" Thankfully, not long after that the game ended.

I should not have been in the top 10 in the Norm Smith Medal voting. I would have had Peter Francis (21 disposals, one goal) as best on the ground, with Wayne Johnston (21 disposals) not far behind him. Then you had guys like Billy Picken, who played a ripper for Collingwood, as did Mark Maclure for us. But it was the first time the Norm Smith Medal had been awarded, he was my great-uncle, and they knew that—of course they did. For a bloke who had just 17 touches in a Grand Final to be

---

5   Our memories can deceive us. In *Larrikins & Legends*, the author found supporting evidence that Harmes was moved up from the back pocket during the second quarter. Before the move Harmes had failed to have a disposal; after the move he altered the course of the game. See 'What's Better Than Beating Collingwood by 10 Goals?' in Dan Eddy, *Larrikins & Legends: The Untold Story of Carlton's Greatest Era*, (Slattery Media Group, 2017), pp. 66-85.

awarded the Norm Smith Medal, of course they had to have known the connection. I'm certainly happy to have it, and I won't give it back, but I'm a little bit embarrassed at times to have it. It was more than a shock when I found out that I had won it. I keep my Medal at the National Sports Museum at the MCG. My three Premiership medallions are also held there.

When I was presented with the Norm Smith by my great-aunt Marj (Norm Smith's widow), we said nothing. We just looked at each other and cried. I gave her a kiss and we cried, and that was because she was Aunty Marj. They called for me to come back and say a few words, but I couldn't because I was a mess. I went and saw Marj about a week after celebrating, and we sat down and had a chat about it. Norm could be intimidating, but Marj was a gorgeous lady. Their son, Peter, has presented a Norm Smith Medal as well (1981), and I was lucky enough to win one, so it's a great thing for our family. And it's great now, because you have somebody standing up on that podium each year who joins your little club.

We were invited to The Lodge after winning the 1981 and 1982 Grand Finals. The Prime Minister, Malcolm Fraser, was a Carlton supporter, so he told us if we won he'd invite us to The Lodge. I've still got salt and pepper shakers and some cutlery that I stole from there! We knocked off golf balls, and I even walked out with his golf driver down the side of my pants leg. I was sure that the Federal Police were going to ring me and demand all their stuff back. The first time we went there we were a disgrace! Why he would want us back again in '82, I don't know! I think we had to go back the second time to appreciate the honour. The second time around we walked the gardens, which we hadn't done the first time, and we had a good look around.

Of all the coaches I had, and there were probably as many as eight, David Parkin had the most influence on me. He was educated, fair, and he had good rapport with the players. Carlton had a lot of talent during that period—very good on the field, and very good off the field—and David changed the off-field to an extent. Not fully, but what he doesn't know won't hurt him! I remember him walking in that first day and seeing a couple of us having a drink and a smoke. I know who they were:

I was one of them, and Des English was the other! He immediately stamped it right on the head. Then what he did was, he gave everyone a footy. And he said: "God help you if you pull up at the traffic lights and a friend of mine pulls up next to you, and you're not sitting there playing with your footy." We realised that we had somebody who was really professional. It was his professionalism that turned us around after missing out in 1980.

I'm still pissed off that we didn't win four Grand Finals in a row. We missed out in 1980. Jezza had walked out on the club along with the president, George Harris, and Percy Jones took over for the year. It took Parkin to get us back on track. If we had have won all four, we'd be ranked up there with the greatest teams of all time. Since us, we have seen what Hawthorn (2012-2016, three Premierships), Geelong (2007-2011, three Premierships) and Brisbane (2001-2004, three Premierships) have done: all great achievements. But yeah, we could have, and *should* have, won four in a row.

—— Statistics ——

BORN: 9 February 1960
GAMES PLAYED (1977-88): 169
GOALS: 86
FINALS PLAYED: 19
FINALS GOALS: 16
GRAND FINALS: 4
PREMIERSHIPS: 1979, 1981, 1982
NORM SMITH MEDAL: 1979 (presented by Marjorie Smith)

WAYNE HARMES

— Norm Smith Voting —

(**JUDGES:** Jack Hamilton, Allen Aylett, Alf Brown, Ron Barassi and Lou Richards.)

The Sun **votes: Lou Richards:** 3 Jim Buckley, 2 Billy Picken, 1 Mike Fitzpatrick;
Tom Prior: 3 Wayne Harmes, 2 Picken, 1 Buckley;
Jack Dunn: 3 Buckley, 2 Peter Francis, 1 Wayne Johnston;
Peter Simunovich: 3 Robbert Klomp, 2 Picken, 1 Johnston;
Tony Peek: 3 Klomp, 2 Francis, 1 Picken;
Michael Davis: 3 Picken, 2 Harmes, 1 Johnston;
Greg Baum: 3 Picken, 2 Francis, 1 Harmes.

The Sun **TOTALS:** Picken 13, Buckley 7, Harmes 6, Francis 6, Klomp 6, Johnston 3.

Kevin Bartlett

Kevin Bartlett was the beating heart of a champion Richmond team that won five Premierships between 1967 and 1980, one of just two players (along with Francis Bourke) to play in all five of the Tigers' winning Grand Finals during that period. Bartlett grew up just a few kicks from Punt Road Oval, debuting for the Tigers as an 18-year-old in 1965. Two years later he kicked the sealing goal against Geelong to end a 24-year Premiership drought; by the time he claimed his second flag (1969), the speedy Bartlett was one of the competition's premier rovers. He won five Richmond best and fairest awards (1967-68, 1973-74, 1977), three of which came in Premiership years. He was also a four-time leading goalkicker (1974-75, 1977, 1983), represented Victoria 20 times, captained the Tigers (1979) and, in 1983, became the first man to play 400 League games. He was later named rover in the club's Team of the Century. Bartlett returned to coach Richmond during its darkest hour (1988-91), a period in which the club was forced to rattle tins to stave off extinction. Barlett's sacking in 1991 put him at loggerheads with the club's administration for many years, but he returned in 2007, and there were few prouder men than Bartlett when the club broke a 37-year drought to win the 2017 Grand Final. In his Norm Smith Medal performance, in the 1980 Grand Final against Collingwood, Bartlett had 20 kicks and one handball, took nine marks and kicked 7.4.

← **SUPER** Kevin Bartlett's 1980 Grand Final performance was one of the best of all time.

THE NORM SMITH MEDAL

I never, in a million years, imagined I would have a statue outside the MCG. I was very humbled when it was unveiled in 2017. It is a great honour. I went to the MCG regularly as a kid, although I followed Footscray in those days. We lived in Lennox St, Richmond, when I first started playing with the Tigers in the early 1960s, so I was in the shadows of the great stadium from a young age. It has always played a big part in my career. I played my first game there, plus my last game, all of my seven Grand Finals were there, my 400th game was there, then I coached my first and last games there, so the MCG has had a massive impact on my life. I still hold the record for most games at the ground (200).

I was at the 1954 Grand Final. I was going on seven-and-a-half years old. My mum and grandparents came from Footscray and my godparents came from Yarraville. My mother was a Bulldogs supporter. Every time we went to the MCG we always sat right in the middle of the ground in the Southern Stand, Bay 9. I can remember seeing Charlie Sutton lead the team out with a big bandage on his thighs. Herb Henderson was my favourite player. I can remember my mum crying and my godparents were so happy.[1]

Every night after school you would come home, see your mum and then you would just go straight across to a park and play there until six o'clock. Kids would just meet there. Sometimes I had a football. We used to play a lot of paper football where you make it out of paper and rubber bands and you could kick it a fair way.[2]

I actually won the best and fairest and the goalkicking for the [Richmond] under-17s. They had an end-of-season night at Café Kanis on Bridge Road. Bill [Boromeo] organised it and Des Rowe and Ron Branton were there and presented trophies to us. I won the best and fairest the next year, under-19s (in 1963). I still could have played in the under-17s. Michael Green came down from Assumption College and played in the under-19s. He has been a life-long friend.[3] I can remember Graeme Richmond coming to me as the secretary and saying, "There are great opportunities at this club, we are looking for rovers, so train hard and be conscientious."

---

1 Rhett Bartlett, *Richmond FC: 'The Tigers', A Proud History of a Great Club*, Slattery Media Group, 2012, p. 187.
2 *Richmond FC: 'The Tigers'*, p. 187
3 *Richmond FC: 'The Tigers'*, p. 188.

KEVIN BARTLETT

In 1965, I played in some of the reserve-type practice matches. I played in the first couple of early games and I must have done well—I was coming home from work and I was sitting on the tram reading the paper; on the back page it started off by saying "Tiger young recruit could be shock selection" and I started reading this thinking, "Who could this be?" and then it read: "Under-19s player Kevin Bartlett is going to be rushed into the last practice game," and I got quite a shock.[4]

1967 was certainly a big year for me, because I had just turned 20, we won the Premiership and I won the best and fairest at the club. In 1968 I was a very warm favourite to win the Brownlow Medal, which I didn't—Bob Skilton won that year. In 1969, I was four votes away. In 1970, I was runner-up in the best and fairest. In 1973-74, I won the best and fairest.[5]

1974 was an extraordinary year, there were 12 or 13 major awards and I think I won every one of them but one. There was a motorcar from *World of Sport*, and a caravan, trips and money. I was an extra hot favourite to win the Brownlow but Keith Greig won.[6]

We lost some good players by the mid-1970s. Having won Premierships in 1967, '69 and 1973-74 (and a losing Grand Final in 1972), we then lost to North Melbourne in the 1975 Preliminary Final (by 17 points) and missed the finals altogether in 1976. There had been a big core of players who started around 1967 and who took us to extraordinary success over an eight-year period. But after '74 there was a transitional period at the club.

Tom Hafey resigned after we missed the finals in 1976. He was actually reappointed as coach for 1977, but Tommy felt he didn't have the full support of the board and so he resigned. That was a big blow for the club, because Tommy had been there since 1966 and had led the team to four Premierships. My former teammate Barry Richardson took over, which was a tough job to do after Tommy's impact. But Barry did a terrific job in his first year and we made it back into the finals. We won the first final (by 34 points over South Melbourne), then lost our second one (by 57 points to North Melbourne). But we missed out again in 1978

---

4   Richmond FC: 'The Tigers', p. 190.
5   Richmond FC: 'The Tigers', p. 191.
6   Richmond FC: 'The Tigers', p. 191.

and Barry was removed as coach. It was a turbulent period. Another of my former teammates in Tony Jewell came in for 1979, we won in 1980, then we missed again in 1981 and Tony was sacked. Francis Bourke then came in for '82 and we made the Grand Final again. We missed in '83 and he was sacked. If you didn't win the Grand Final at Richmond—immediately—you were sacked! It was a nonsensical time for the Richmond Football Club after Tommy left.

I had a number of clubs speak to me [at the end of 1979]. My first thought was if I am going to leave I am going to play under Tommy [at Collingwood]. That would have been the way for me to finish my career. And I spoke to Tommy and Ron Richards, who was the chairman of selectors at Collingwood. We talked a number of times, but Tommy felt it would be wrong for me to leave because he felt my name was synonymous with the Tigers.[7] I spoke to Essendon and in fact I signed a letter of agreement that I would play for the Bombers. I told Tommy about that and he again thought it was the wrong thing to do. So he swayed me to initiate a truce through Michael Green, my great friend and solicitor. Michael went to the club and instigated my return. So I went back.[8]

By 1980, I was starting to wonder whether I would play in another Grand Final. Between 1967 and 1974 we regularly played in and, at times, dominated finals. We also won Australian championships against the premier teams of other states. But by 1980 I was 33 years old, Francis Bourke was the same age; we were getting towards the end of our careers and the last time we'd played in a Premiership was six seasons earlier. My thinking was, maybe we've had our good luck, and maybe that's going to be the end of our Premiership success. That's why 1980 was such a satisfying year for me, and I'm sure for Francis as well. Because right at the end of our careers we were able to play in another Premiership—and with another group of players. Only David Cloke had played in the '74 Premiership with us.

There had been some good signs in 1979. Even though we didn't make

---

7   Richmond FC: 'The Tigers', p. 192.
8   Richmond FC: 'The Tigers', p. 192.

the finals, some young players came into the side and were starting to develop. Then, at the start of 1980, we had a young, emerging Mark Lee in the ruck, a young and emerging Dale Weightman as a rover, an emerging 100-goal forward in Michael Roach, David Cloke was a mature, experienced guy by then but was still relatively young; there was Jimmy Jess, Geoff Raines… these guys had all evolved. We were also able to recruit Robert Wiley, who was an absolute star, from Western Australia. Stephen Mount, who came across from Tasmania, was another. We had a lot of firepower. Barry Rowlings came across from Hawthorn, another experienced player. We also picked up Peter Welsh from the Hawks who would go on to star during the finals series. Then we had the older players such as myself and Francis who added valuable experience. We had a bit of everything in 1980.

Tony Jewell coached magnificently that year. He had the right blend. He knew how to get the best out of the older players, and would look after us at training. But he also had the right blend of mixing with the younger players. He certainly trained us hard, but he coached magnificently. One of his big strengths was his honesty; he was a very, very honest coach. There were no frills with Tony, he was always straight down the line. He was very supportive of his players, even though he had a tough exterior. Being an ex-player, he understood the ups and downs of the game. And I think he had a good gut feeling for coaching.

An example of Tony's gut instinct was in the way he used Peter Welsh during the finals of 1980. In the last game of the year we played South Melbourne, at Lakeside Oval, and we were beaten. The loss knocked us off top position, meaning we finished third and had to play the Qualifying Final rather than have a week's rest. Peter had had injuries that year, and from memory he was a reserve in the reserves that day—19th man in the reserves. Going into that first final, Tony's gut feeling was that Peter was quick, a great competitor and was a thumping kick, and he just had this inkling that Peter should be in our side, that we needed his attributes. Plus, Peter was a very exuberant player, and a well-liked player. He was a great clubman. People loved him. Tony recognised that it was an ingredient we needed in September. He selected him in that first final. Peter starred against Carlton, then against Geelong, then he played a terrific game for us in the Grand Final. It was a stroke of genius on Tony's part, and that was one of his real strengths as a coach.

Me moving to the half-forward line happened in 1979. In those days, communication wasn't as great as what it is these days. We all still listened to the radio to find out if we were in the side! Things were a bit cold-blooded in those days: you play here, or you play there, no questions asked. I was disappointed initially, because I had played my whole career as a rover and I was an on-baller. In those days, playing on a half-forward flank was called playing at "starvation corner": you were out there, somewhere, and told not to get in the way. That was the thinking, which sounds crazy these days, but that's how it was. I had to convince myself that I could be of value there. Don't forget, too, I was nearing the end of my career by that stage. So, I envisaged that positional move as me being on the way out. I'd played 15 years predominantly as an on-baller, but they were going to put me at half-forward for a year or two before waving goodbye. It was that sort of thinking. But it gave me a new challenge to try and play a role that I hadn't played before. And it turned out to be successful in my latter years.

By the Grand Final, I had quietly satisfied myself that I could play a role; that I could still play at the highest level and still be a damaging player. I felt I was still able to contribute to the side. That finals series, everything clicked for me. I kicked six goals in the Qualifying Final against Carlton, then eight goals against Geelong in the second Semi-Final. So I felt confident entering the Grand Final.

I was not a nervous player. I never really suffered from pre-game nerves; I was pretty calm. I used to like playing the game over in my head during the week before each game. I would visualise certain aspects of the game. When you are visualising, you're always dominating, getting the ball, taking the mark or kicking the goal, because it's all about positive visualisation. So, I used to like doing that as part of my preparation, giving myself some self-confidence that I could play well on the weekend. But I was never nervous before the game. I was excited! I loved playing. And I loved playing against the best players and the best sides.

It was always a real challenge, and if you could play well against certain players and certain sides, there was a great deal of satisfaction in that.

The opening of a Grand Final can be intense. It's a one-off game, which is different to a lot of other major sports in that we don't play best of three, or best of five, or even best of seven. So you are always wanting to get away to a good start, knowing what's on the line. You can never get away from the fact of knowing there's a big prize at the end. You don't want to make a mistake; I always wanted to do something good early in the game. All players are up for the contest on Grand Final day, because of the stakes.

I wasn't worried about what the opposition were doing. Being a small forward, and having the likes of Roach, Jess and Cloke up forward, my role was to make certain that when they got to a contest, I, too, was at the contest. I wanted to be at every contest, so that if they didn't mark the ball, or they needed support, there was a smaller, quicker player at their feet. We were a long-kicking side. We were instructed to kick it long, allowing our key forwards to contest strongly and either mark or bring the ball to the ground. Then it was the role of the smaller players, such as myself, to be there to help out. If for some reason the ball hit the ground, I wanted to pounce on it.

It's always a great thrill to kick an early goal in a Grand Final. I had played well in our first two finals, so I was hopeful that my form would continue. As an opportunist forward, if you can kick a goal early it's great for your own confidence. It can also knock the confidence of your opponent, which can be equally important. If you've been in good form, had a couple of good lead-in matches, then all of a sudden you kick an early goal, it puts doubt in their minds. So it has a two-fold effect. To score a goal early in that first quarter was a big bonus for me.

It was a windy day. Collingwood played well early in the game but, unfortunately for them, didn't kick very straight. They were a bit unlucky. From memory, their captain, Ray Shaw, hit the post twice, and another Magpie hit the post as well. They missed several shots at goal which, had they scored them and had the scoreboard been ticking over, they might have gained in confidence. They blew their opportunities by not kicking straight, then we would go down the other end and kick a goal. Collingwood had their window of opportunity early in the game, and when that wasn't taken, from that point it became a struggle for them.

It was about halfway through the second quarter when the Tigers really started getting on top. We were getting the ball quickly into our forward line, and if you get it in quickly it's very, very difficult for defenders. I played on Kevin Morris, my old Premiership teammate (1973-74), who was a tremendous player. But when the ball was coming in so quickly so often, the forward has the best opportunity of making his move and finding a spot to receive the ball. And if the ball is delivered correctly, it doesn't matter how good a defender you are, or how conscious you are of your opponent, it's pretty hard to stop him. Plus, I was able to kick straight in that second quarter. Between our good play bringing the ball forward, and me finding the right spots, I was able to capitalise on my opportunities and kick three goals.

Stan Magro was moved on to me late in that second quarter. Stan was more of a close-checking player than Kevin. Kevin had won a best and fairest at Richmond and was a very talented player who could play forward, back or in the midfield. He was much more attacking than Stan. I had played on Stan before and he was very tough, very strong and a very determined opponent. But, as the game wore on, I would have hated to have been a Collingwood defender. We were dominating through Raines in the centre, Weightman, Wiley, Lee was also doing a terrific job in the ruck, Mervyn Keane was good, too. They were pumping the ball down our way, and I was glad I was playing for Richmond with the amount of ball coming into our forward line.

We were a great attacking side, but our defence was equally as important to our success. Francis went to full-back after having played half-forward in the first final against Carlton. We had Emmett Dunne back there, and Mount played a cracking game at centre half-back. Terry Smith and Keane were rotating off half-back, and Greg Strachan was solid as a rock. Our backline all year had been very, very good. They worked really hard together. Mick Malthouse was part of that, too. We didn't make many changes back there to key personnel. So that was a real strength of ours, and they made life a lot easier for us guys playing on the forward line.

We'd also had the week's rest, whereas Collingwood had played a Preliminary Final. So as the game went on, I think the long season began to take a toll on them. And look, to be perfectly honest, I think the talent that was in the Richmond side that day was far superior to the overall talent in the Collingwood side. Tommy had done a terrific job in getting the Magpies to the Grand Final. He brought in some players from other clubs that weren't stars, but he was able to mould them into valuable parts of the team. Tommy had a team that he was getting the absolute maximum out of, whereas Richmond had a team of really talented players. And once you got the maximum out of the really talented players, that proved too much in the end.

The videotape will show that I handballed to Rowlings in the last quarter and he kicked a goal. But I think that must have been Photoshopped, because I can't recall firing off that handball—that wasn't my thing! I'm assuming it's been Photoshopped just to make fun of me. But I certainly got plenty of help from my teammates that day, so I owed them one.

My seventh and final goal was a memorable one. Daryl Freame had come off the bench, he won the ball and I led towards him. His kick landed just in front of me and I was close to the boundary line. I was able to gather it, but Stan was a very close-checking defender and I could feel him, hear him and even smell his breath—that's how close he was! The way the ball bounced enabled me to take it and, at the same time, side-step one way then turn and go the other way. That gave me the space I needed to get away from Stan. I ran around the boundary line, took a couple of bounces and probably should have been looking to my left but the adrenalin was flowing. If I was playing in the modern day, I would be expected to centre that ball, but we are talking 1980 here. I felt confident I could kick it so I decided to have a crack at it, and it went straight through.

I get asked about that goal a lot. It gets replayed often, so I suppose it sticks in the minds of people more than any of the other 777 goals I kicked. But in terms of kicking big goals in finals, while it's certainly one of my favourites, it's not my absolute favourite. My favourite was in my first Grand Final, in 1967 against Geelong, when I kicked the last goal of the game. I backed out of the pack to kick that goal at a crucial moment, and that's why it's my favourite. It was significant because that helped Richmond win their first Premiership since 1943; we were only three points up when I kicked it, so it remains very special (the Tigers won by nine points). The goal in 1980 is my second favourite though.

A lot of people ask me what my reaction was to winning a Grand Final. My reaction in all five of the winning Grand Finals I played in was relief. When the final siren went, it was just relief; that overrode any excitement initially. I was relieved that we had achieved what we set out to do. We had played together the whole year, trained together the whole year, and luck had it that when the final siren went we were in front. It was like a load had been taken from your shoulders; just relief that it was done and dusted. I also played in two losing Grand Finals (1972 and 1982), and the feeling is the opposite. There's great disappointment because you had put so much into the season, but everything you had done together seemed to dissipate because of the result of that one losing game.

With Premierships, there is a lot of excitement on the day for supporters, but as a player it's relief at the start because you have won and you don't have to go through the disappointment of losing. The satisfaction comes as each year goes by. It's then you truly realise that with a select group of teammates you were able to achieve something that few people actually achieve. There's a bond there because you all came together at a certain stage in your lives. You remain friends for life because of that. It's all held together by the fact that you played in a Premiership, or Premierships, as a group. For me, the thrill and satisfaction of playing in a Premiership gets stronger each year. The longer time goes on, the more I appreciate them.

There was no thought of Norm Smith Medals when I came off the ground. In all the previous Grand Finals I had played in, there was no such thing as a Norm Smith Medal; it had only come in the year before, in 1979, when Wayne Harmes won. So, being just the second year that the Norm Smith Medal was being awarded, it wasn't in the forefront of anyone's mind. Not like these days, where they talk about who's going to win it before the game has even started. There was none of that in 1980.

I felt very fortunate to win it. We had some very good players on the day, a lot of really good players. I was thrilled to win it, and it soon became part of the history of the game, which made it even more special. I had it presented to me by Ron Barassi, which was a fantastic thrill. From a personal point of view, it fulfilled the whole occasion of the Grand Final: playing, playing well, kicking a few goals, then, all of a sudden, I'm presented with the Norm Smith Medal as well. That was a terrific acknowledgment of how I had contributed to that day. So, on that note it finished on a high.

All players like to play well in important games. You can't do it all the time, but you like to hope that on a consistent basis, in big games against good opponents, particularly finals and Grand Finals, that you can play at your best. Reputations are enhanced and made in those games. If you don't play well, consistently, it can hang around your neck as a weight for the rest of your life. People tend to be very, very harsh when someone has struggled in a particular game, no matter how well they have played in other matches. If you can play and perform well in the big games, it gives you a great deal of satisfaction. I played in seven Grand Finals and lost two of them. But I think that, in all seven, I contributed in some way for my team.

The most important key to longevity is luck with injuries. I hardly had an injury during my career, which allowed me to play 403 games. I never had hamstring issues, or tore my calf muscle. I also never suffered a debilitating knee injury, or ankle or shoulder injuries, so luck played a big role in my longevity. It can happen so easily: you turn one way and someone falls across your leg, sudden you've done an ACL. Or you back out of a pack, someone hits you in the head and breaks your jaw, then suddenly you're out for 10 weeks. These things happen to players all the time, which is one of the downsides of the game. But I was fortunate in that sense. I can only put my longevity down to luck. Maybe some reflexes and a bit of speed and awareness, but mainly luck that I was able to play my career virtually unscathed.

I was always aware that coaching was going to be tough. And I knew it only ever ends one way: you get sacked. Particularly in that period, coaching at Richmond, there was only one way it was going to end; no matter how successful you were or weren't, you would end up sacked. So I was aware of what the final circumstances would be. But the state of the Richmond Football Club was something I was not aware of: the financial position the club was in and the ability for the club to even exist. That only became evident once I was appointed coach.

We pressed on regardless. They were a tough four years because it was mainly about survival. The club was officially broke, couldn't recruit players, and we had to offload players just to keep the club afloat, which is not ideal. It was the early days of drafting, so a lot of kids were drafted without much infrastructure at the time in regards to systems. Bringing in school kids with the hope that they would come good in the future was a gamble, plus football wasn't yet full-time. So that was a tough period for a club that had no money. We ran the "Save Our Skins" campaign which ultimately kept the club afloat. That's one of the nice things that's happened. Sometimes you look back and don't have great memories of those types of events. But the best thing to come out of all of it—no matter how many of us got sacked, or how broke the club was—is that the club did ultimately survive. You like to think that the efforts of all the people involved, including your own, paved the way for the club to hang on, even if it was by its fingernails. And that those efforts, no matter how small, helped the club get to where they are now where they have one of the biggest membership figures of any AFL club. Hopefully those hard yards helped to contribute to the euphoria experienced after the 2017 Premiership. That's why a lot of us got so much enjoyment out of the side winning in 2017, because so many people after 1980 never experienced a successful Richmond side. And for all the CEOs and presidents and board members over that 37 years who did it tough, they were able to sit back and, in some small way, know that they helped contribute to the club getting to where they are now.

You need new heroes all the time in this game. That's what Richmond needed during that long time between Premierships. People need a new bunch of heroes to follow, because you can only watch the videos of 1980 so many times. There's now a new Premiership DVD they can watch, which is great for the club and its supporters.

[NOTE: Kevin Bartlett's recollections from his early years are sourced from his interview with son Rhett for *Richmond FC: "The Tigers", A Proud History of a Great Club*. All other quotes are sourced from an interview with Dan Eddy in January 2018.]

—— Statistics ——

BORN: 6 March 1947
GAMES PLAYED (1965-1983): 403
GOALS: 778
FINALS PLAYED: 27
FINALS GOALS: 62
GRAND FINALS: 7
PREMIERSHIPS: 1967, 1969, 1973, 1974, 1980
NORM SMITH MEDAL: 1980 (presented by Ron Barassi)

— Norm Smith Voting —

(JUDGES: Jack Hamilton, Allen Aylett, Ron Carter, Jack Dyer and Doug Heywood)

The Sun **votes: Tom Prior:** 3 Mark Lee, 2 Kevin Bartlett, 1 Geoff Raines;
Lou Richards: 3 Bartlett, 2 Raines, 1 Mick Malthouse;
Jack Dunn: 3 Lee, 2 Raines, 1 Bartlett;
Peter Simunovich: 3 Lee, 2 Raines, 1 Rob Wiley;
Michael Davis: 3 Raines, 2 Lee, 1 Bartlett;
Neil Kearney: 3 Lee, 2 Bartlett, 1 Raines.
The Sun **TOTALS:** Lee 14, Raines 11, Bartlett 9, Malthouse 1, Wiley 1.

Bruce Doull

Media personality Lou Richards famously dubbed Carlton's 356-game defender Bruce Doull 'The Flying Doormat'. It was an appropriate moniker, encompassing both Doull's flowing locks and his capacity to smother opponents of all shapes and sizes. A notoriously shy man, Doull rarely gave interviews, preferring to let his football speak for him; he has retained that preference throughout his life. By the end of his career, his remarkable consistency led David Parkin to declare him the most "coachable" player he encountered in a 518-game career in the coach's box, and some of his teammates to declare Doull to be the "greatest ever" Blue. In the 1981 Grand Final, the enigmatic defender cast his blanket over arch enemy Collingwood, repeatedly denying the desperate Magpies on his way to a third Premiership. He had 14 kicks, three handballs and took two marks.

Bruce Doull was born in Geelong in 1950, but was living at Jacana, a northern suburb of Melbourne in Carlton's metropolitan zone when he joined the Blues' under-19s squad in 1968, the same year Ron Barassi led the club to its first senior Premiership since 1947. Doull's arrival at Princes Park coincided with one of the greatest recruiting drives in Carlton's history, with Alex Jesaulenko, Brent Crosswell, Robert Walls, Peter Jones, Syd Jackson and David McKay—among others—converging

← **SILENT ASSASSIN** Bruce Doull was one of Carlton's greats in its greatest era.

on the club. These champions would form the nucleus of Carlton's finest era.

Initially tried as a ruck-rover and half-forward, Doull's senior appearances were sporadic during his first three years at the club. He was not selected in the 25-point loss to Richmond in the 1969 Grand Final, nor the victorious 1970 side that came from 44 points down at half-time to defeat Collingwood. But the decision by Barassi midway through 1971 to try Doull as a defender proved a masterstroke. Teaming with new full-back Geoff Southby, along with Vin Waite, Kevin Hall and good mate John O'Connell, Doull became part of one of the most formidable defences in the League. By 1972, now under John Nicholls, who replaced Barassi as coach that year, Carlton's rivalry with Richmond had become brutal. Up until then, Tigers centre half-forward Royce Hart had proven nigh unstoppable, but it was Doull who provided the clamp on the champion key forward, a development that enabled the Blues to defeat Richmond in the 1972 Grand Final. According to Carlton centreman Ian Robertson:

> We couldn't beat Richmond until Bruce Doull started playing in defence. He went to centre half-back on Royce … and it gave us some hope of beating Richmond. Bruce did a fantastic job whenever he played on him.

That year Doull and Hart met on a staggering *eight* occasions: twice during the home and away rounds, in the drawn second Semi-Final and its replay, the Grand Final, then in exhibition matches in London, Athens and Singapore. Ruckman Percy Jones joked that Hart "couldn't get away from him." The following year, however, Hart did turn the tables in the Grand Final, and was named among Richmond's best players in its 30-point victory.

Hart was not the only player to find himself blanketed by Doull. South Melbourne's Peter Bedford and David Rhys-Jones, Geelong's David Clarke and Melbourne's Gerard Healy all conceded they needed to be at their best to earn a disposal against the Blues defender. Healy believes Doull played like a defender of the recent era. "He was very assertive and he had you—as well as the ball—covered at all times." Carlton's centre half-forward, Mark Maclure, marvelled at Doull's unfailing desire to take on the opposition's most dangerous player:

> I remember one day he played against Geelong's Larry Donohoe, who had kicked 100 goals the year before, and he kept Larry to *no* touches. Bruce [only] had about five kicks, but he had about 25 spoils, 10 knock-ons, a couple of handballs—he was easily the best on the ground.

Parkin said, "He played on the best people of that era, and they all hated playing on him." Demon centreman Greg Wells was one of those people. He recalled one occasion where Carlton's No. 11 brought a halt to his own early dominance in a game between Melbourne and Carlton during the 1970s:

> Carlton put 'Jezza' in the centre on me. I'd had 25 touches up to half-time, so that didn't work for them. After half-time, they put Bruce on me. I had four touches after that! I just couldn't go anywhere without him right there next to me. Jezza played more his own game, whereas Doully was there to negate me first and foremost. He could dispossess a player without giving a free kick away better than anyone I've ever seen.

In 1974, Doull won the first of his four best and fairest awards, winning again in 1977, 1980 and 1984. What set Doull apart during those years was his ability to see the game unfold before those around him, which often enabled him to react before his opponents—and his teammates.

Parkin, for one, marvelled at Doull's decision-making when in the air, where, if set to spoil, he could react in a split second and instead mark the ball, or vice versa. When spoiling, Doull had an uncanny ability to direct his punch towards a teammate. He was described by Walls, and other teammates, as "cat-like" for his reflex ability not only to land on his feet but, in the same motion, to instantly take off in pursuit of the loose ball, or provide a handballing option out of defence.

Defender Robbert Klomp explained that Doull "would take two steps back, then take two steps sideways, then he'd glide through the gap." And in a time when handball was less prevalent, Doull's willingness to use his hands to release teammates in better positions became a key component of Carlton's game style. His quick thinking enabled the club's famed 'mosquito fleet' to run teams ragged through fast ball movement. Klomp said:

> He was predictable to us, but not to the opposition. He had almost a sixth sense in regard to the movement of players. When he had his eye on the ball, he still could visualise where the players would end up from the movement he saw when he first went into the contest.

Although Doull may not have accumulated many disposals on the stats sheet, almost every possession was of quality, inevitably bringing his teammates into the play. Carlton's rebound out of defence, as a consequence, regularly caught opposing teams out of position. His willingness to involve his teammates was an attribute that endeared him to the Carlton players. Back pocket Wayne Harmes explained how, in his first game, Doull made the point of ensuring the newcomer got an early disposal. It was a similar story with ruck/defender Geoff Hocking, who said that Doull "gave me three handpasses that I knew he didn't have to give me, just to get me involved in the game."

Doull's consistency was no fluke: he was one of the most dedicated trainers at the club. So good, in fact, that the sight of him making an error was cause for celebration; proof he was human like the rest of them. Ruckman Warren Jones remembered, "Bruce would stuff up a kick at training and everybody would start laughing because he'd made one of his rare mistakes." Fellow ruckman Mike Fitzpatrick said that "by the end of training, the main interest was whether Bruce would make a mistake. More than often we would have to carry over to the next session—he just did not make mistakes." Under captain-coach Jesaulenko, this was fortunate for Doull, as Jesaulenko was ruthless on any player who slipped up, or failed to extend themselves at training and in games.

Rover Vin Catoggio was one of the quickest players in the VFL, but at training even 'Vinny' struggled to get around Doull. "I could dance around a lot of blokes, but Doully was one guy I could never get around," Catoggio said. "He had really long arms and he'd get five metres in front of me and put his arms out, slowly come towards me while watching every step, and he'd always catch me when I'd try to go around him."

Despite his competitive nature, Doull preferred to go about his work quietly, rather than speak up in team meetings. Ironically, Doull once said that the key to a strong defence was "teamwork and talking to let each one know how you're going."[1] Midfielder Tony Pickett recalled:

> We used to have team meetings and you'd sit 20 players around in a circle. You would go around the circle and you'd each mention a few things about the opponent that day. When it got to Doully, the person before him would say something, then it was accepted that Doully would say nothing, and the person on the other side would begin saying something, and on it would go. Even in a closed group of 20 people, he'd still just sit there and say nothing.

He was also less than enthusiastic about receiving messages from the team's runner, as fellow defender (and later club president) Ian Collins explained: "The runner came out to give him a message one day, and he sent him back to tell the coach 'I don't get messages.'"

In a room full of extroverts, the introverted Doull was never going to be captain of the Blues: that duty was reserved for the likes of Walls, Jesaulenko, Fitzpatrick, Johnston and Maclure. He was, however, a spiritual leader, widely respected by all at Princes Park. He may not have said much, but when he did offer advice it was gratefully received. Catoggio said:

> When you're young, you're always hoping one of the superstars will notice you. I'll never forget after I'd played a couple of good games early on, Doully walked past me and he tapped me on the thigh and said "Great game," and just kept walking. I couldn't believe it, so I went and told all my mates about it! It was like someone putting a stamp on you and saying you've been approved by Bruce Doull.

---

[1] This quote was sourced from Doull's appearance on Channel Seven's *World of Sport* the day after the 1981 Grand Final. For the full interview, see: https://www.youtube.com/watch?v=uzAqqk2u6y0.

Hocking, too, received the Doull stamp of approval, something he has never forgotten. "He came up to me after my first game and said, 'Well done, that's a good start, you've got plenty more in front of you yet.' He was always very supportive and encouraging of us young fellows."

In 1979 Doull received his only All-Australian guernsey, and would add a second Premiership medallion to his collection in Carlton's nail-biting five-point victory over Collingwood. When the clubs met again in the 1981 decider, Doull—wearing a navy-blue headband and opposed to Craig Davis—was a calm presence in another riveting encounter.

During a frenetic opening quarter, which saw Collingwood do most of the attacking but take just a two-point lead into quarter-time, Doull had the better of Davis in the air and on the ground; his quick recovery and elusiveness was difficult for the Magpie forward to counter. Doull was one of the few Blues, along with Val Perovic, who provided attacking rebound from defence, also acting as designated kicker whenever Collingwood scored a behind.

Magpie skipper Peter Moore threatened to take control of the second quarter, making himself a target in the forward line. Again the Carlton defence had its work cut out as the tug-of-war between the teams intensified. Davis was forced to venture well upfield to win possessions, and took a fine mark over Doull at centre half-forward. But as the quarter ticked on Doull became more productive; at one point his headband was ripped from his head but, undeterred, he charged out of defence and launched the Blues forward. Perovic and Des English were solid supports down back, and Johnston was playing superbly, but as Doull mopped up another Magpie foray, TV commentator Peter Landy cried, "Where would Carlton be without this guy?"[2]

Doull was superb in the opening minutes of the third quarter, keeping Collingwood at bay. His timing and balance were standouts, as he kept his feet in the greasy conditions. Harmes, too, was pivotal, as the Blues maintained a narrow lead midway through the term. But more questions were soon asked of the Carlton players as the Magpies finally began to hit the scoreboard. By late in the quarter they were threatening to blow the game open.

---

2   1981 VFL Grand Final DVD.

BRUCE DOULL

Collingwood led by 21 points at the 28-minute-mark, Doull later conceding he was "very worried". But, he added, "We were very lucky to get a couple of goals just before three-quarter time…we were in a lot of trouble up to then." Indeed, if not for goals to Rod Ashman then Jim Buckley, just before the siren, the Magpies would have led by more than three goals. Instead, the margin was just nine points and, crucially, Carlton's confidence had been restored. With Fitzpatrick dominant in the ruck, the Blues steamrolled the broken Magpies in the final quarter, kicking 4.7 to just two behinds. As defender Scott Howell recalled, any time their opponents threatened to go forward, the sight of Doull standing firm was reassuring: "I probably had the best standing position in the ground to watch Bruce do what he did. I was in the back pocket and I don't think the ball came down there because our half-back line was really solid."

Carlton won by 20 points, and Doull, with a modest disposal count of 11 kicks, three handballs and two marks but a profound influence, was awarded the Norm Smith Medal. Not surprisingly, he declined to comment when he received his medallion. That night at the club's Premiership function, invited to speak, he muttered, "Um…" and the crowd burst into applause. "I'd like to congratulate all the guys that played today," he added. "It was a hard game, physically and mentally. Collingwood is always hard to beat, especially in a Grand Final."[3]

The following year, against Richmond in another brutal Grand Final, Doull was the centre of attention for a different reason when the naked streaker, Helen D'Amico, made a beeline for the bearded veteran, much to his surprise. Johnston joked that it was remarkable that Doull had drifted into the centre at the same time as D'Amico: "I said to Bruce, 'What are you doing here?' It was the first time he'd been in the centre in his life! Doully had just timed his run so well that he was running through the middle of the ground at that very moment." That 18-point victory earned Doull a fourth Premiership medal; again, he was one of his team's best players.

In round 19, 1983, he became the second Carlton player (behind John Nicholls, 328 games) to reach the 300-game milestone. He broke Nicholls'

---

3   *The Age*, 28 September 1981, p. 39.

club record in round one, 1985, against Footscray at Princes Park. Under his final coach in Walls, and despite being the oldest player on Carlton's list, Doull continued to maintain his dedication to training in his latter years. Walls recalled that, "Many a night—and I trained them hard, really hard—when we were halfway through a gruelling session, I would walk over to Bruce and say, 'You go in.' And he'd say, 'No, I'm not going to.'"

His 356th, and last, VFL match came in his sixth Grand Final: the 1986 decider against Hawthorn. Beaten on the day by emerging full-forward Jason Dunstall (six goals), there was no fairytale finish. The Blues lost by 42 points, with the sight of a muddied and dejected Doull leading his defeated team off the field an enduring image from a truly remarkable career. He had averaged just under 20 games a year over his 17 seasons (1969-86). Entering 2018, his 29 finals as a player sees him ranked fourth for most played, behind Gordon Coventry (Collingwood, 31 finals), Shaun Burgoyne (Port Adelaide/Hawthorn, 33) and Michael Tuck (Hawthorn, 39).

In 1996, a decade after retiring, Doull was named on the half-back flank in the VFL/AFL Team of the Century (and was inducted into the Australian Football Hall of Fame). In 2000, he was named in Carlton's greatest team. Despite continuing to shun the spotlight in his later years, Doull did appear in a Toyota Memorable Moments commercial that enacted an incident in 1983 when Essendon's Cameron Clayton famously removed his headband in a match at Waverley Park.

Doull remains one of Carlton's most beloved players. Harmes is adamant Doull was Carlton's finest ever, saying: "If I was to pick a best side from the guys that I played with, I would have Bruce Doull at number one and 'Johnno' (Wayne Johnston) number two."

Perovic considers it was "an absolute privilege to play beside him. His jumping and his reading of the play was just phenomenal. He was absolutely one of a kind." And Walls concluded that Doull "was modest, he was reliable, and he was just dearly loved by everyone who had anything to do with him. He was the most valuable player for Carlton, in my eyes."

NOTE: Interviews with David Parkin, Ian Robertson, Percy Jones, Mark Maclure, Greg Wells, Robert Walls, Robbert Klomp, Wayne Harmes, Geoff Hocking, Mike Fitzpatrick, Warren Jones, Vin Catoggio, Tony Pickett, Ian Collins, Scott Howell, Wayne Johnston and Val Perovic were conducted by the author.

BRUCE DOULL

Statistics

BORN: 11 September 1950
GAMES PLAYED (1969-86): 356
GOALS: 22
FINALS PLAYED: 29
FINALS GOALS: 1
GRAND FINALS: 6
PREMIERSHIPS: 1972, 1979, 1981, 1982
NORM SMITH MEDAL: 1981 (presented by Peter Smith)

— Norm Smith Voting —

(**JUDGES:** Jack Hamilton, Allen Aylett, Greg Hobbs, Harry Beitzel and Bob Skilton)

Sporting Globe votes: **Greg Hobbs:** 3 Bruce Doull, 2 Mike Fitzpatrick, 1 Billy Picken;
Peter Stone: 3 Doull, 2 Fitzpatrick, 1 Picken;
John Rice: 3 Doull, 2 Fitzpatrick, 1 Mick Twomey;
Michael Lovett: 3 Doull, 2 Fitzpatrick, 1 Picken;
Kevin Bartlett: 3 Doull, 2 Fitzpatrick, 1 Mark Williams;
Fred Cook: 3 Fitzpatrick, 2 Doull, 1 Picken.
Sporting Globe **TOTALS:** Doull 17, Fitzpatrick 13, Picken 4, Twomey 1, Williams 1.

Maurice Rioli

The dynamic West Australian played with a purity of skill and purpose that quickly won universal respect across the VFL, and as he helped propel Richmond back into the finals frame he even displaced star midfielder Geoff Raines from the centre. After storming into the Grand Final, the Tigers fell short of arch rival Carlton, but Rioli became the first Indigenous player to win the Norm Smith Medal, and also the first recipient from the losing team. He had 18 kicks, one handball, one mark and kicked three goals.

When Maurice Rioli arrived at Richmond's headquarters, the Punt Road Oval, at the beginning of 1982, there was no fanfare. Only Phil Egan, the club's sole Indigenous player, was on hand to greet the South Fremantle centreman. The West Australian star was to be a key plank in the Tigers' resurrection plans, yet his arrival was surprisingly inauspicious. Egan recalls:

> It was a strange first meeting with Maurice. If it was done in the '90s or today, there would be 100 press there to greet him. But things were much different in 1982. I knew Maurice was going to pick up an old car: there was a loan car

← **BRILLIANT** Maurice Rioli was a fitting winner of the Medal, and the first to do so in a losing team.

at Richmond for the new players, they called it the "Golden Holden", an old HQ Holden. I was the only one there to meet him. He arrived in the car park via taxi, and I went up and shook his hand and told him who I was—he didn't know me from a bar of soap! I showed him around, and from that day on we became great friends.

After storming to the 1980 Premiership, thrashing Collingwood by 81 points, the Tigers had missed the finals in 1981. Their seventh-placed finish was unacceptable to the club's ruthless administration, which sacked coach and 1967 Premiership player Tony Jewell just 12 months after his Grand Final triumph. Jewell was replaced by former teammate and five-time Premiership champion Francis Bourke, who was expected to return the Tigers to the finals in 1982.

The recruitment of Rioli was integral to their Premiership plans: a proven big-game player who had participated in the previous three WAFL Grand Finals, he had won the Simpson Medal for best afield in the past two. In 1979, Rioli's South Fremantle Bulldogs lost to arch rival East Fremantle, before the Bulldogs defeated Swan Districts in 1980 as Rioli claimed his first Simpson Medal. South then lost to Claremont in the 1981 decider, but Rioli earned a second Simpson Medal (in a tie with the Tigers' Gary Shaw). South coach Mal Brown later said, "Maurice kept us in the match all day."

Rioli was born 1 September 1957 on Melville Island, off the Northern Territory's north coast. By his fourth birthday his family had moved to Darwin, where they remained for more than a decade before returning to the Island. "I spent a fair bit of time playing in the school grounds in Darwin," Rioli said, "and also in the streets after school where we organised to pick teams on most days and learned our skills and our balance, because you were playing on bitumen streets."[1]

Sport was central to Rioli's early life. Along with football he also played rugby league, cricket and did boxing in Darwin. He would also go hunting with his family. "You've got to have the skill to go out hunting and catch your food and be able to develop those skills," Rioli said.

---

[1] Sean Gorman, *Legends: The AFL Indigenous Team of the Century*, Aboriginal Studies Press, 2011, p. 75.

"It takes a particular type of skill and effort to make sure you're not wasting too much effort in capturing your next meal."[2] Those life skills may have contributed to his spatial awareness and timing on the football field—the other major passion for his family. "Football was something that all our family and friends and extended family were involved in," Rioli said:

> When I came back home [to the Islands] my home team at Garden Point were called the Imalu Tigers. Then I went to Darwin and the St Mary's Football Club… Then the main reason I went to South [Fremantle] was Basil Campbell and my brother Sebastian Rioli were in Perth while I was still at school up here in Darwin. They were the first two to make the long trek down to Perth and I followed behind them.[3]

Rioli's nephew Cyril, the Hawthorn champion and 2015 Norm Smith medallist, described South Fremantle as "like a family club for us."[4] Indeed, the club fostered a welcoming environment for its Aboriginal players. Maurice remembered the Bulldogs organisation as being "very professional and made me feel welcome" and, importantly, afforded him "an opportunity to at least have a go at playing in the big time."[5]

It was playing in a practice match against Subiaco when Rioli found himself opposed to Hawthorn's 1971 Premiership captain, David Parkin, that he began to take his football more seriously. Until then, Rioli said, he was just "rolling along gently."[6] Playing on Parkin "it suddenly hit me that I was up against some great players. After wondering what the hell someone like me was doing in the big time, I buckled down and really tried to make it."[7]

Brown—who played 14 games for Richmond in 1974—recalled Rioli being "a wonderful player" who had "a beautiful kick, a wonderful handball, always had time—and he was one of the few left-footers who could turn back on to his right foot." Rioli's ability to use both sides of

---

2   Sean Gorman, *Legends: The AFL Indigenous Team of the Century*, Aboriginal Studies Press, 2011, p. 75.
3   Sean Gorman, *Legends: The AFL Indigenous Team of the Century*, Aboriginal Studies Press, 2011, p. 76.
4   Cyril Rioli quote sourced from a story on the Rioli family, titled "The Rioli Dynasty", which aired on Channel Seven's *Sunrise* program on Sunday 3 September, 2017.
5   *Legends*, pp. 76-77.
6   *The Age*, 3 February 1982, p. 26.
7   *The Age*, 3 February 1982, p. 26.

his body would unsettle the opposition. "He would simply walk around them, back on to his left foot," Brown added. Rioli's boxing training proved an important asset in his football armoury. "I saw him give a bloke a short, sharp jab one day, and the bloke had a black eye for a week," Brown said. "The bloke was about six-foot-five, so Maurice was tough." Moreover, Jock McLeod (father of 1997-98 Norm Smith medallist, Andrew) revealed that so capable was Maurice with his fists when he was at Richmond that if any players chose to participate in boxing at training "no one would get in the ring with him."

Rioli appreciated Brown's coaching methods, saying all players were treated equally. He said that Brown was also a great manager of his players, cautious to never over-train them. "If he felt [we] were looking good on the track he took it on himself to make decisions so players could have an early shower. That was the type of person he was."[8] Brown described Rioli as "very quiet" and "very, very placid", and ranked him in the top couple of players he coached. "I was pretty lucky, because I had Stephen Michael and Maurice Rioli in the same side," Brown said. "To try and say who was the best player of the two would be silly—they were both tremendous."

Rioli had the same silky skills that Cyril later demonstrated, as well as his timing and awareness. But, Brown said, Cyril was quicker than his uncle and a better overhead mark. The two Riolis shared one trait: they were outstanding tacklers. "When Maurice got hold of you, it was like a vice-like grip that you couldn't get out of," Brown said. "And he never made many mistakes. You could give him a blast, or give him a kiss, shake him, cuddle him, and his own internal pride would get him going. If he was down and you gave him a bit of a spray, he always lifted. Always."

Bourke, Rioli's first coach at Richmond, said the key to his tackling technique was his ability to "feint and weave like a boxer," using similar movements a boxer made "when he tries to deceive an opponent about when he is going to punch them." Plus, Bourke added, "Maurice had unbelievable balance."

By the end of 1981, a number of VFL clubs had courted Rioli, among

---

8   *Legends*, p. 77.

them Essendon, Carlton, Footscray, Richmond and Geelong. Brown's influence resulted in Rioli choosing the Tigers for 1982. "I put a lot of trust in Mal Brown," Rioli said. "Mal was getting rather tired of all these calls and he said, 'Look, stuff ya, if anyone else rings me I will tell them to forget about talking to you—you're going to Richmond.'"[9] Brown "had a lot to do with him going to Richmond" because, "I just felt that was the next step he needed to make for his own personal success." Brown met with Richmond president Ian Wilson and mutual friend Brian Coppin "in the Richmond boardroom with the Tiger skin on the table." Brown believes the Tigers paid a transfer fee to South of $5000, and, as Rioli packed his bag and headed east, Brown remembers thinking he never doubted that Rioli would play in the VFL. So highly did the Tigers rate Rioli, they presented him with the club's most famous jumper number: Jack Dyer's No. 17.

From as early as their uneventful first meeting at Richmond, Egan recognised that Rioli was "very self-assured, but very reserved as well. He was like a contradiction in personality." According to Egan, Rioli had an aura about him. "He did not have to say anything, one just sensed there was something special about him." Rioli later conceded he was confident he could make it in the VFL. "I know I came to Richmond with a fairly big reputation," he said. "I thought I handled it fairly well. The fact was I wanted to perform at the highest level, that's what drove me."[10] He compared himself to other former West Australians who had made the switch to Victoria. "I can remember considering Tony Buhagiar. He played for East Fremantle and I used to flog the arse off him—and he was a top player for the Bombers!"[11]

Just two weeks after his arrival, Rioli's new teammate, 1980 Norm Smith medallist Kevin Bartlett, declared in *The Sporting Globe* that "glamour recruit Maurice Rioli already looks a million dollars ... and has made a big impact at Punt Rd."[12]

Although most at Richmond were excited at Rioli's arrival, Premiership centreman Geoff Raines was not so enthused. As one of the League's finest midfielders, Raines was dismayed that his club had recruited

---

9   Rioli, Rhett Bartlett, *Richmond F.C.: "The Tigers", A Proud History of a Great Club* (2nd ed.), Slattery Media Group, 2012, pp. 306-309.
10 *Richmond F.C.: "The Tigers"*, p. 306.
11 *Richmond F.C.: "The Tigers"*, p. 306.
12 *The Sporting Globe*, 2 February 1982, p. 35.

another centreman in what, to him, was a sign he was undervalued in his role as the team's centre-square driving force:

> The rivalry was built up [between us] when he came over in the pre-season. We were having a [practice] game at Portsea and it was all this press build-up, the two best centremen in Australia to play on one another. It didn't sit well with me. I found it strange they would go and get another centreman while they had the state's leading centreman in their team.[13]

Bourke later admitted that it was a big decision to play Rioli in the centre early in the 1982 season. "I went and saw 'Rainesy' and explained to him what my thoughts were and why," Bourke said. "I don't think Rainesy was particularly happy about that, but it was only for a maximum of six weeks of the season. I think Rainesy thinks it was the whole season, but that's not true." After initially playing Rioli in the centre, Bourke moved him to a half-forward flank, changing on the ball as a ruck-rover, with Raines restored to the centre.

An ongoing hamstring complaint that had caused him to miss most of the 1981 WAFL season hindered Rioli's early progress. "I came over with a lot of hamstring injuries," Rioli later said, adding:

> Back in the Territory I had never been told how to prepare myself in the area of prevention of injuries and treatment of injuries. I just ran out and did my best. For me, one hamstring would go and then the next. I had so many problems. When I went to Richmond I knew I had to do something about the constant injuries. Consequently I worked harder than I had in my life. I really had to work hard to keep my hamstrings working. I then hardly missed any games, apart from one or two through knee injuries.[14]

Bourke recognised that he needed to manage Rioli to get him on the park as often as possible. "Maurice didn't need coaching, he basically turned up with his bag and went out and played," Bourke said. "The only thing I had to watch him about was, sometimes, not very often because

---

[13] *Richmond F.C.: "The Tigers"*, pp. 279-280.
[14] Rioli, *Richmond F.C.: "The Tigers"*, p. 306.

he was very durable, if he was struggling to be fit to play, and required a fitness test, I had to watch him because he would play when perhaps he shouldn't have. But, overall, he was a dream to coach."

Egan believes Rioli "knew his limitations" and how much ground he had to cover in games, and he would therefore train according to what his role would be and how his body was feeling. "I'm not going to say he was a hard trainer: he was a responsible trainer," Egan said. "The hard trainers were guys like Trevor Poole and Michael Pickering—they'd bust their guts every single session. Maurice didn't do that, but he certainly trained strongly and smartly." Not noted for his pace, Rioli believed the heavy grounds in Victoria were more beneficial to his game than the harder, sandy surfaces in Western Australia. They may also have aided the management of his hamstring injuries, minimising the toll his body had taken when training and playing on dry grounds.

As with Brown at South Fremantle, Rioli was appreciative of Bourke's coaching approach. According to Egan, Bourke was "fantastic towards us. He was colour-blind and didn't see any issues, he just treated us like anybody else." When told of this later, Bourke said:

> It never actually occurred to me, to be honest, that Phil and Maurice would be mindful of that. It was certainly never an issue for me when I coached them both. I would like to think that they were always treated with respect within the club. In my case with Phil and Maurice, why wouldn't you treat them with respect? They were fine people in their own right, aside from their football talents.

As two of the handful of Indigenous players in the VFL at the time, Rioli and Egan recognised they were champions for their people, a status they did not take lightly. "I was one of many Indigenous players who had set the trend for others," Rioli said. "Before me, I recognised Syd Jackson, [Graham] 'Polly' Farmer and later on Barry Cable. I was proud of the fact that being Indigenous was one of the things that helped me perform at my best."[15]

Egan recalled that they ran many clinics in Aboriginal communities

---

15   *Richmond F.C.: "The Tigers"*, p. 306.

and had "lots of invites to attend events and act as ambassadors." The pair seldom shirked their responsibilities. "We would always do those things together," Egan said. "But, above all, we wanted to be role models to our families; that was a big motivation for us. To know that our family was proud of us was the main thing."

Unfortunately, they were not immune to racist taunts. "Opposition players used racist words to try and slow me down—to put me off my game," Rioli said. But, he added, "I would simply use that in my favour."[16] From as early as his first WAFL game, Rioli had copped abuse from opponents. "As a youngster I was always getting screamed at by the opposition," he said. "Their object is to scare the daylights out of you. But you have to learn to take it."[17] The abuse continued when he started his VFL career. "Trying to establish yourself as a League footballer is harder than a lot of people think," he said. "When you're an Aborigine, it can be even tougher."[18]

Egan said there were "some professional players in the League then who would use the race card to put you off your game. But they would also be the first guys to buy you a beer after it. We'd give it back, too. In those days, you didn't sit back and cop it. If you did that, bad luck, you'd get buried. So we gave it back as good as we got."

If the intention was to put Rioli off balance, it backfired, as he was a sensation in his first VFL season. He had 21 disposals and kicked three goals on debut, against North Melbourne at the MCG. He also had more than 30 disposals in a game twice (in rounds nine and 17 against Footscray and St Kilda respectively), and by season's end had averaged 21.7 disposals a match. He was a key member of a group of exciting Tiger players that Bourke had at his disposal throughout 1982, including Raines, Bartlett, Michael Roach, Jim Jess, Barry Rowlings, Dale Weightman and skipper David Cloke. It was no coincidence then, that Richmond, stormed to the top of the ladder with 18 wins in the home and away rounds. Rioli had 19 disposals in Richmond's 23-point victory over reigning premier Carlton in the second Semi-Final, the win ensuring that the Tigers entered the Grand Final as favourites against the Blues, who had recovered to defeat

---

16   *Richmond F.C.: "The Tigers"*, p. 306.
17   *The Age*, 3 February 1982, p. 26.
18   *The Age*, 3 February 1982, p. 26.

North Melbourne in the Preliminary Final by 31 points.

Rioli felt lucky to play in a Grand Final in his first season, describing it as "every kid's dream."[19] And he had plenty of support, with his father, brothers and in-laws converging on Melbourne from the Northern Territory and Western Australia. "It meant a lot to me to play in the 1982 Grand Final," he said. "The fact I was an Indigenous player, the fact I had a huge following back in the Territory and islands where I am from, and back in the west where I had come from. There was a lot of interest and obviously the pressure was a memorable part of it."[20]

According to Egan, Rioli was "quiet and stuck to himself" before games, then, "in the 10 or 15 minutes before each match he would start to rev up. He knew where he stood; knew that everyone was waiting for him to be ready." On the field, Rioli was directional in his instructions to teammates, "but not overly chatty" with opponents.

The 1982 Grand Final could not have started worse for Richmond: Carlton dominated the centre square clearances and kicked three goals in the first five minutes. As frustrations boiled over, the game became a brutal encounter. Carlton rover Rod Ashman recalls being near Rioli when Richmond "started blueing with us." The pair "were having our own box-on, but it wasn't until later that I realised he was a Golden Gloves champion, or something like that. I thought, 'Shit! I was out of my depth there!'" A big bump by Jess knocked out Ken Hunter, who had started well, and with the Carlton playmaker off the field being attended to, Rioli began to assert himself on the game.

Working up the field to win possessions, Rioli was bringing his teammates into the play. Bartlett goaled a few minutes later, then, at the 16-minute-mark, Rioli kicked a goal from 25 metres out as the Tigers began to wrestle back control. Nine minutes later, a brilliant solo effort by Rioli in the forward pocket—where he sharked the hit-out and, in the same action, snapped the ball around his body for a goal—brought Richmond fans to life. After a shaky start, the Tigers trailed by only four points at quarter-time, with *The Herald*'s Mike Sheahan later declaring: "Richmond would have been in serious bother but for the fine first term by Rioli."[21]

---

19   *Richmond F.C.: "The Tigers"*, p. 306.
20   Rioli, *Richmond F.C.: "The Tigers"*, p. 309.
21   *The Herald*, 25 September 1982, p. 32.

THE NORM SMITH MEDAL

The Tigers appeared to have one hand on the Premiership Cup after dominating the second quarter. They kicked five goals to two and took an 11-point lead into half-time. While Rioli had a quieter second term, the likes of Raines, Rowlings and Merv Keane had led the way through the middle of the ground. But Carlton came out strongly. "It was a strange feeling," Rioli said when reflecting on the third quarter, where the Blues kicked 5.4 to just six behinds. "We were playing well, we were in front at half-time, [then] the next minute they went bang, took the lead and the game was [all but] over."[22]

In an eventful, match-defining third quarter, proceedings were sensationally halted when a streaker, Helen D'Amico, wearing nothing but a Carlton scarf, ran on to the field at the 10-minute-mark. "I was in the centre when the streaker turned up," Rioli said. "I did see her running on to the field and I didn't know where to look. I made sure I didn't catch her eye so she didn't come near me."[23] The Blues led by only one point at the time, and some Richmond supporters still claim that D'Amico's entry brought a halt to their momentum, but Carlton was already controlling the play and the Blues' captain, Mike Fitzpatrick, had kicked a goal moments before. Certainly, Carlton continued to play well after D'Amico was escorted from the field—to a standing ovation from the crowd—so perhaps the Blues did get a boost from her cameo!

In the midst of that third-quarter onslaught, Rioli was undoubtedly his team's best player. He always appeared to have an extra second to dispose of the ball, and his composure in decision-making was a feature of his play. Despite Carlton's dominant quarter, the Tigers trailed by just 17 points at three-quarter time. They then kicked two goals in the first five minutes of the last quarter, cutting the margin to five points. Again, Rioli was the Tigers' best player for the quarter, but his efforts were to no avail as Carlton kicked away to win by 18 points, 14.19 (103) to 12.13 (85), in one of the greatest and most brutal Grand Finals of all time.

"It was obviously a terribly disappointing feeling losing that Grand

---

22   *Richmond F.C.: "The Tigers"*, p. 309.
23   *Richmond F.C.: "The Tigers"*, p. 309.

Final," Rioli said. "However, I felt good in the fact that I did my best. I was more numb than anything; I had no feeling, other than the feeling for my fellow players."[24] Rioli became the first from a losing side to be judged the winner of the Norm Smith Medal. He had 18 kicks, one handball, took one mark and kicked 3.1—the second of five occasions during his 118-game VFL career where he kicked three goals. Egan, for one, was in no doubt that Rioli was a worthy recipient:

> Maurice was sublime in the 1982 Grand Final, clearly the best on ground. He did everything in his power to get us over the line, but we had too many good players go missing. In the third quarter there was this switch in momentum and we went to sleep. Maurice kept going; he really tried. He had this clap of the hands, a motion with his head and upper body to say, "Come on guys, keep going." You could see that right through to the final siren. He put in to the end, but other players couldn't lift their games enough to get us there. It was no surprise when Maurice was named the Norm Smith medallist. The way he carried himself, and how he handled himself that day, was beautiful to watch.

Rioli described winning the medal as "a bitter pill to swallow", admitting that he "felt a little ashamed to have received it, among the disappointment that surrounded the Richmond team."[25] As he walked from the dais he "took the medallion off and tried to hide it."[26] With the passing of time, however, he grew to recognise its significance. In 2010 he said: "Now people talk about me being a Norm Smith medallist. I guess it probably means more now because it is in the record books—the fact that Maurice Rioli is a Norm Smith medallist."[27]

Bourke described Rioli's feat as "a feather in his cap; particularly as he played predominantly on the forward line that day." Parkin, the victorious Carlton coach, said Rioli "absolutely deserved his Norm Smith Medal."

While Rioli played another five seasons at Richmond, the club unravelled after that 1982 defeat. It fell to 10th in 1983, Bourke was

---

24 Richmond F.C.: *"The Tigers"*, p. 309.
25 Richmond F.C.: *"The Tigers"*, p. 309.
26 Richmond F.C.: *"The Tigers"*, p. 309.
27 Richmond F.C.: *"The Tigers"*, p. 309.

sacked and Bartlett retired after a VFL record 403 games; Bryan Wood (Essendon), Cloke (Collingwood) and Raines (still unhappy with Rioli's recruitment, also to Collingwood), all departed at the end of 1982. A bidding war between the Tigers and Magpies almost bankrupted both clubs in the ensuing few seasons. Quickly, the 1982 season became a distant memory.

"The politics affected the players of the club," Rioli recalled. "You can imagine how upsetting it would have been for the club and its stability, and what effect it had on the playing group at that time. In the six seasons I was there, I had four coaches—from Bourke to Mike Patterson (1984) to Paul Sproule (1985), and then Tony Jewell came back (1986-87). I can remember a coach going on a holiday, coming back, and he didn't have a job!"[28]

At the end of 1985, high-flying Sydney Swans owner Geoffrey Edelsten enticed Rioli to leave Richmond and move to the Harbour City. It took the intervention of Egan to convince him to stay at Richmond:

> Edelsten threw cash at his manager, so he moved up to Sydney in the mid 1980s and shacked up in a hotel for a couple of months. Then they hired Tom Hafey as coach, and Tom dragged [Geelong's] Greg Williams there. Hafey made it clear that he didn't want two centremen, so Maurice was on the outer before he even played a game. The Richmond hierarchy sent me up there to bring him back. I flew to Sydney and talked with Maurice and his wife, Robyn, and told them to come back to Richmond. He came back and changed numbers from 17 to 27. Tom should have played Maurice as ruck-rover and Williams in the centre: they would have been unstoppable!

Rioli played in the VFL for only six seasons (1982-87) yet his impact was profound—not only at Richmond, where he won the club's best and fairest in his first two seasons (1982-83) and was twice All-Australian (1983 and 1986), but for Indigenous players throughout Australia. Indeed, he was recognised as a trailblazer who helped to open the door for the influx

---

28   Richmond F.C.: "The Tigers", p. 309.

of Indigenous players who have since graced the game at the highest level. At the end of his VFL career, Rioli returned to South Fremantle and played another three seasons, earning a third All-Australian honour (1988) and playing in the losing 1989 Grand Final against Claremont. He then played and coached in Darwin until 1991, and coached the Indigenous All-Stars in 1994.

In 1993, the 'Year of Indigenous People', he was invited to present the Norm Smith Medal after the Essendon-Carlton Grand Final. Fittingly, the medal went to another Indigenous champion in Essendon's Michael Long, who had been inspired by Rioli's exploits. That the Riolis and Longs are related through marriage only added to the occasion.

By that time, Rioli, having found his voice through football, had entered politics as the Labor member for Arafura in the Northern Territory Legislative Assembly. "In most of the places I've been to, most Indigenous people don't believe they're good enough," Rioli once said:

> We think negatively about our ability and that prevents a lot of Indigenous people from going forward. But if there's a message I can put across to any young Indigenous person it is this: if you have a dream and you believe in the dream, whether it's football, whether it's work, whether it's anything in life, dreaming is what motivates you, dreaming is what your goals are, what you want to be, where you want to be. Football was my first love and I always dreamed about playing in the VFL... Playing with the big guys, like the [Alex] Jesaulenkos, and if you believe it and you work hard enough, you'll achieve your dreams.[29]

After leaving politics in 2001, Rioli continued to work passionately in community service on the Islands. "I used to regularly take students up to the Tiwi Islands for placements at the schools," Egan said. "Maurice would always help me with any research. He really wanted to show leadership up there, to help arrest an alarming number of youth suicides occurring on the Islands."

---

29   *Legends*, p. 80.

Rioli struggled with his health after football. "Maurice battled with his weight," Egan said. "He really blew out after footy, and he had a heart problem as a consequence." Sadly, on Christmas Day 2010, Rioli died suddenly of a heart attack. He was just 53.

Egan ranks Rioli alongside Adelaide's Andrew McLeod as the best Indigenous player he has seen. "When you talk about Maurice and McLeod, you're talking about Patrick Dangerfield and Dustin Martin of today: the cream of the crop, and so consistent. Rarely did they play a bad game, and they performed in the big games—they stood out. [North Melbourne's] Jimmy Krakouer was magical, consistent and hard. Maurice was magical, too, but there was a purity to the way he performed."

Rioli believed that Aboriginal people often disliked being thrust into the public spotlight. He had been shy about meeting people and public speaking until football gave him confidence. He became "very proud of that."[30]

NOTE: Interviews with Phil Egan, Mal Brown, Jock McLeod, Francis Bourke, Rod Ashman and David Parkin were conducted by the author.

—— Statistics ——

BORN: 1 September 1957
DIED: 25 December 2010
VFL GAMES PLAYED (1982-87): 118
GOALS: 80
FINALS PLAYED: 2
FINALS GOALS: 3
GRAND FINALS: 1
NORM SMITH MEDAL: 1982 (presented by Jack Mueller)

---

30   *The Age*, 3 February 1982, p. 26.

MAURICE RIOLI

— Norm Smith Voting —

(**JUDGES:** Jack Hamilton, Allen Aylett, Mike Sheahan, Doug Bigelow and Peter Landy)

Sporting Globe **votes:**
Greg Hobbs: 3 Wayne Johnston, 2 Maurice Rioli, 1 Mike Fitzpatrick;
Geoff Poulter: 3 Val Perovic, 2 Johnston, 1 Alex Marcou;
John Rice: 3 Johnston, 2 Rioli, 1 Fitzpatrick;
Michael Lovett: 3 Rioli, 2 Perovic, 1 Johnston;
Fred Cook: 3 Rioli, 2 Johnston, 1 Marcou;
Ray Jamieson: 3 Rioli, 2 Johnston, 1 Marcou.

Sporting Globe **TOTALS:** Rioli 13, Johnston 13, Perovic 5, Marcou 3, Fitzpatrick 2.

Colin Robertson

Four VFL clubs courted Tasmanian midfielder Colin Robertson before he signed with Hawthorn in 1979. During 116 matches for the Hawks (1980-86), the versatile Robertson was used in all areas of the ground before becoming a valuable tagger for coach Allan Jeans. His outstanding aerobic capacity proved a lethal asset, enabling Robertson to outrun many an opponent. He played in the club's 1983 Premiership side, also in its '84 Grand Final loss, but was dropped for both the '85 (losing) and '86 (winning) Grand Finals. Returning to Tasmania after 1986, Robertson coached Burnie and later Wynyard, and in 2011 was elevated to Legend status in the Tasmanian Football Hall of Fame. In his Norm Smith Medal performance, Robertson had 14 kicks, 15 handballs and took four marks in the Hawks' 83-point victory over Essendon. He became the first, and still the only, Tasmanian to win the medal

I grew up on a farm 25 minutes out of Wynyard on the north-west coast of Tasmania. It's a family farm that we still own. We've had it for almost 80 years. It started out as a dairy farm, then we had beef cattle, and we also grew potatoes. My father, Trevor, has passed away, but my mother, Jean, is in her 90s. Dad played sport and Mum was a school teacher, but I don't know a lot about Mum's history in sport. Dad did

← **HIGH POINT** Colin Robertson produced his best performance on the biggest stage. He received the Norm Smith Medal from 1980 winner Kevin Bartlett. Photo courtesy of the Hawks Museum.

a lot of bike riding, as well as playing football with Yolla.

I've got two brothers, and did have two sisters. My oldest sister, Marian, died when I was about five. She was burnt because of a spark in our fireplace. She was wearing just her nightie at the time and it ignited. She then spent a long time in hospital, suspended from the ceiling due to her burns. She was only 11 when that happened. Then there is Wendy, who is a bit over two years older than me; she's a school teacher. My older brothers are twins, Kelvin and Lee.

It was always competitive because the three boys loved our football. We would mow some grass in the paddock, cut down trees and put them up as goal posts, and then play footy.

We were strong St Kilda supporters, so my idols were guys like Darrel Baldock. I used to wear Baldock-brand boots when I was a kid. Royce Hart, another Legend of the Australian Football Hall of Fame, also came from Tasmania. We didn't have TV at home until I was around eight, so we didn't see much of the VFL before then. We always went and watched the local games though.

I played footy at primary and secondary school in Yolla. I played in the school combined sides, and we would beat all the other schools because we were very strong. Robert 'Scratcher' Neal (Geelong 1974-86, 200 games; St Kilda 1987-88, 20 games) played with me in those sides. We had a lot of good footballers on the north-west coast, and we used to annihilate the other schools in the region, sometimes by as much as 250 points. From there, when I was about 15, I went and played football with Wynyard in the under-17s.

I played mostly on the ball as a rover or wingman. I was always pretty fit, competed in all the sports available in the area, including athletics and cross-country, so I was equally good at sprinting and long distance. My brothers were strong in long distance, too. Wendy represented Tasmania in netball—she was state captain—and was an umpire too.

Sport was everything. It was either football or cricket, but I didn't play a lot of cricket as my love for football was stronger. I went from the under-17s to the under-19s, and played senior football from 16. When

I got my driver's licence, I could play other sports, such as squash and volleyball. I represented Tassie in volleyball and played in the Australian championships. But football was more important to me. I was a champion squash player in Wynyard, and I also played basketball. Some days I would go to footy training, then play squash, then volleyball, then head back to the squash courts into the early hours of the morning.

Dad and Mum were fantastic supports. Dad would always carpool us around to our difference sports; he didn't miss many games. We would kick the footy out in the paddock together; he would run me around as much as he could, and would teach me things like how to kick drop-kicks. He was involved in our development, but us boys did a lot of skill work between ourselves as well. Dad would join in whenever he could. It was the same when I moved to Melbourne. Dad used to fly over and Mum would stay home and milk the cows. Dad would arrive on the Friday and fly home on the Sunday. He was passionate about football and seeing us do well at sport.

In my first year of seniors at Wynyard, 1975, we won the Premiership, then won it again in 1979. We also lost in 1978, so I was used to playing in big games from a young age. I played in Grand Finals in the under-17s and under-19s as well, so if you add in my time at Hawthorn there weren't many years where I wasn't involved in finals footy. I was very fortunate in that way.

Everyone's ambition was to play VFL football. It was every kid's dream to do that, and I was no different. I first went to Melbourne when I was 16 as a guest of North Melbourne. Ron Barassi was coach. It was a scary trip in a way. It was during round 16, 1973, North was playing Collingwood, and at half-time was well behind [25 points]. Barassi had all the players lying down and was physically manhandling them to get his points across—it scared the shit out of me! It was an unlucky weekend for me because I was sick, so I couldn't train with them on the Sunday. But it was a good experience otherwise, watching the likes of Barry Cable drop-kicking balls through a tyre in the changerooms.

North wasn't a realistic option for me at the time. Another guy, Danny Newman, came with me from Wynyard who was six-foot-two, whereas

THE NORM SMITH MEDAL

I was about five-11, and Ron took no notice of me due to my lack of height. Years later I let him know about that. After the '83 Grand Final we went to Noosa to raise money for golfer Jack Newton, who had lost an arm in a plane accident. Barassi was up there as well, so I had a lot of fun telling him about that story and letting him know how wrong he was!

The North experience didn't dim my expectations though. I really wasn't interested in going over at that age: I wanted to wait until I felt I was ready to make an impact. My attitude was that I didn't want to go over and hope I could make it; I wanted to go knowing I was good enough.

I had a lot of VFL clubs come over and see me. After one game there were four club representatives lined up to speak with me. I hadn't even played that well! There were Richmond, Hawthorn, Essendon and Geelong waiting to see me. They all invited me to Melbourne, and took my girlfriend Karen along with me. I refused to go to Richmond, as they tried to force me to sign, and Essendon was similar. It was the latter part of the 1970s, the choice was mine, and Hawthorn stood out, although Geelong were terrific hosts to us both. The Hawks looked after me from day one: not just the people around the club but the players, too. They took us out to dinner and made us feel at home from the start. It was a similar feel to a country footy club, which I was used to. The other clubs just put me in a hotel, took me to training, then dropped me back at the hotel. For me, that wasn't appealing, certainly not in comparison to Hawthorn's approach.

Other clubs offered me more money than Hawthorn did, but I felt that Hawthorn was the right fit. Plus, they had the likes of Michael Tuck, Leigh Matthews, Peter Knights, Kelvin Moore—the list was long. I thought, if I'm going to be any good as a player I want to play alongside these guys.

We missed the finals in my first two years, but from 1982 onwards we played finals every year. Coach David Parkin believed that you had to earn your stripes to play senior footy, which I wasn't all that happy about early on. They sat me on the bench for quite a while, and I was ready to go home after my first year rather than stay on the bench week after week. My first game was against Collingwood in round three, 1980.

I got on in the last quarter and kicked a goal with my first kick, ended with two and had six disposals. After the game I was even given a letter from David thanking me for winning the game! (Hawthorn won by 11 points). Then for the next few weeks I was back to sitting on the bench, which I wasn't happy about. I wanted to go home, but Karen, who I had married before coming over, said, "If you go home, I'm staying here!" She obviously wanted me to stay, so of course I did, and things fortunately improved for me from there.

I struggled big time to cope, initially, with Melbourne life. It was hard coming off the farm, where our next neighbour was a kilometre away. When I first moved to Wynyard, even that felt like I'd moved to a city—and Wynyard has a population of about 5000! So imagine what moving to Melbourne was like! But you got used to it. Having my wife with me made things a lot easier during that transitional period. I never had opportunities to be misled or caught up in doing what young guys do. Mind you, I was 22 when I came over, so I wasn't necessarily a young kid.

I would get a little nervous before games, but it was never over the top. My belief was, if you don't get at least a little nervous you won't play a good game. I had my routine of a Friday night as part of preparing myself for the Saturday. I didn't like to waver from that. Some blokes liked to wear the same underpants each week, but I never had superstitions like that. I just wanted a regular routine each Friday night and Saturday morning. I liked having fish and chips Friday night, then eggs on toast with baked beans or spaghetti before going to the game. I'd then have a few black coffees while at the ground waiting to get ready. That was it.

'Yabby' (coach Allan Jeans), a sergeant of police, was always straight-laced—very hard but fair. In my early days he gave me the confidence to go out and play the game, which was wonderful for me. Throughout my career I was able to play in most positions: midfield, defence and even centre half-forward. But later on, all I seemed to be doing was tagging somebody, which concerned me as I felt I was missing out playing in other positions.

I used to love training more than I did playing. You got to kick the ball more, for one, so I used to love going to training. I always trained hard, and I trained even harder during the off-season, alone by myself. I was a curator at the Ivanhoe golf course, and I would run to work and run home at the end of the day. I would time myself, and try to better my times each day. I also did a lot of push-ups and sit-ups and those types of exercises. I was never a big one on weights, but that wasn't my game anyway. My game was based more around aerobic running.

Yabby wouldn't take me on in a wrestling contest, maybe because I was a bit too fit and too quick. Although, if he'd have grabbed hold of me it might have been a different story! Dipper (Robert DiPierdomenico) and Yabby used to get into those types of things though. They used to do things like that on the Sunday, rather than during the week. Yabby would get on top of them and really give it to them.

Leigh Matthews, our captain, was a legend of the game even then. He was a terrific and inspiring leader. But it wasn't only Leigh, we had a lot of leaders at the club at that time. There was Knights, Moore, Tuck... all those guys were equally fantastic in leading by example. It was inspiring playing with them, as well as people like Gary Ayres, Terry Wallace, Gary Buckenara, David O'Halloran, all of them. And a lot of those guys ended up being coaches as well.[1]

Our momentum and belief slowly built throughout the year. When we realised we could go somewhere, that's when the guys began making sacrifices. It was a transition within the season, more so than an acceptance before the year that we could win the Premiership.

It was wonderful to make it into the 1983 Grand Final. You can't really describe how you feel; you're bursting with energy all week. My wife was so hyped up all week and was questioning why I was calmer than she was. But I told her there was time closer to the game to get myself hyped up—I didn't need to waste all that energy during the week. She was burnt out before the game started!

A lot of the players made commitments leading up to the game. Guys like Russell Greene and Mick Byrne and myself, we would all do extra training, and others gave up things to help in their preparation. I think that

---

[1] Of Hawthorn's Grand Final teams under Allan Jeans (1983–89), eight players later became VFL/AFL senior coaches: Leigh Matthews, Gary Ayres, Peter Schwab, Terry Wallace, Rodney Eade, Gary Buckenara, Peter Knights and Ken Judge.

was why we were so successful in 1983. A lot of players gave up the grog, even though we were allowed to drink in those days. I never touched it anyway, but some guys gave it up for weeks leading into that Grand Final. It wasn't the coach's directive either, just individual decisions. Russell and I used to do a lot of boxing after training. All those little extras gave us added confidence in the way we prepared. We would all go to the club on the Sunday, and take our kids with us. We'd do our running, then get together afterwards, and as a consequence we bonded really closely.

It didn't concern me running out in front of 110,000 people (the official attendance was 110,332) on Grand Final day. We all had our mission to do, and that's what we did from the start. It wasn't until near the end of the game where I started looking up and taking it all in. I know in 1984 I came out and looked around more than in '83, so maybe that's why we lost that year!

My role in the Grand Final was to play as an on-baller, changing out of the back pocket with Russell Greene. I was never told to tag Tim Watson, it was just one of those things I felt I needed to do in-game. Yabby was the type of coach who, before the game, just told you to go out and play football. There weren't specific rules regarding opponents, it was more just "go and do it." He didn't give us a lot of instructions, those came throughout the year mainly. So I had the freedom to make decisions like that, and I took it upon myself as Tim was in the middle when I was in there and was looking dangerous. I chose to stay with him for most of the day.

I've got no problems with what I did to Tim, even though I received death threats over it later on. I wasn't happy with the fallout from it, because everybody made me out to be this thug who king-hit Tim. But it was simpler than that. The ball went out to the far wing and Tim was out there, so I went over to pick him up. As I got there, he turned around and belted me in the stomach, so I chased after him and jabbed him in the nose! That's all it was—there was no king hit. It was just that my punch was a bit more effective than his. He says he can't remember the incident, but he made a big run not long after I punched him, so it seemed there was nothing wrong with him then.

I received a lot of negative comments from supporters after that, even after I returned to Tasmania in 1987. Everybody assumed I king-hit him, but I had never been that sort of player. It was only a six-inch punch, which maybe all that boxing after training helped me with. Maybe Greeney can take some credit for that! But it was just one of those things that happened. I was booed all day after that incident. In fact, the following year the booing continued. The other clubs felt I had king-hit Tim, so I copped it on the field as well as over the fence.

I received worse feedback from people after I returned to Tassie than when I was in Melbourne. When I was later coaching Burnie Hawks, there was a function at the Hobart Casino. This lady came up to me and said, "I hope God strikes you down," and I didn't even know what she was talking about at first. She added, "When you king-hit Tim Watson..." Those things happened regularly after that game. It was difficult for all my family, too. But at the time it happened, I had the confidence to move on and continue focusing on playing. Even today people still talk to me about it.

At half-time, Greeney was very emotional, even started crying, and I had to tell him it was not over yet even though we were 57 points ahead. By halfway through the last quarter it was obvious we would win, so that made it much more pleasurable. I was all about winning the game, so the Norm Smith Medal didn't enter my mind. Even after the game it took a while to sink in that we'd won. I remember being interviewed in the rooms afterwards, and my father took over most of the interview—he was so proud. Mum and Dad were both there to watch, which was fantastic.

John Kennedy (junior) deserved to win the Norm Smith Medal as much as I did. I was a lucky winner in the end, because he played just as well as me. Funnily enough, he had a moustache like mine and even had his thumb strapped like I did, so we looked very similar out there. It meant that every time he got the ball he got booed as well! Everybody played so well that day. It certainly wasn't a one- or two-person show.

I like to think I'm a humble person. People ask me where my Norm Smith Medal is, and I tell them it's in a cupboard somewhere. I don't gloat about it. Yes, it's a nice feeling to know that I've won one, and you get introduced as a winner of the Medal, which is nice; it gives you a warm feeling. But on game day it didn't mean a cracker because we were all so excited to have won the Premiership. My kids were young in those days (Clint was born in 1982, Matt in 1984), but I think down the years they've become pretty proud of what their dad achieved.

The rivalry with Essendon was so full-on; there was so much hatred between the clubs. I think that hatred was also about respect: wanting to beat each other so badly. We beat them in '83, then they came back in '84 and '85, but they shouldn't have beaten us in '84. Sheedy swung his backs forward and won the game that way, which was disappointing. There were a lot of guys in our team who hadn't played in a losing Grand Final, so we didn't know what it was like to experience that. But even playing Essendon during the home and away season was full-on because, in those days, there were some tough footballers running around; guys like Roger Merrett, Ron Andrews and Merv Neagle, they did dirty things, as did some of our guys. But that was all part of football in those days. I wasn't a hard player, but blokes like 'Dipper', Ayres and Matthews were.

The crowd would get right into it, too. With the atmosphere and the physicality of the game, there was always a lot of pressure out there: whether a final or a home and away match it was all the same. If we were playing at Essendon we couldn't drive our cars there because we knew they would get wrecked. So the team always took buses. You would jog down the race before and after a game and they'd spit at you—it was terrible. And Collingwood was the same. I remember an early game at Essendon where Lyn Parkin, David's then-wife, was hit over the head with an umbrella by an elderly lady!

Because it was such a strong side in 1985, a lot of us got dropped for the Grand Final. There was myself, Rodney Eade, Buckenara and a few others. While I don't know why we all got dropped, we ended up winning the reserves Premiership. I was dropped for the '86 Grand Final, too, which I believe was for one bad kick I made at VFL Park, in the Semi-Final against Carlton. Eade took my place in the Grand Final. I had already announced my retirement in the week leading up to the game, but it wasn't until the Friday after the parade that I found out I was dropped. It's always hard to take, and I hated it at the time, but that's history now.

I coached Burnie Hawks (Tasmanian Football League) for one season, then Wynyard for two. It's always different coaching rather than playing. You either love it or not. It's never easy as you've got to be a father figure to all the players, and everyone's different in their attitude towards the game. It was challenging in understanding how to get different players motivated, but I enjoyed it. I had my own beliefs on how I wanted to coach, with a big focus on fitness. I figured if I couldn't do it, no one else could, so I tried to lead by example at training. But I had a bad achilles and a bad back, so I knew my time was up in Tassie just like it was at Hawthorn.

I still follow the Hawks closely. I don't get to watch them a lot as I work on the wharf in Burnie, but Hawthorn has always been special to me. They gave me an opportunity to play in the VFL. I also won a Tassie Medal for best player in the 1987 interstate carnival. I've had a fortunate life.

—— Statistics ——

BORN: 19 June 1957
GAMES PLAYED (1980-86): 116
GOALS: 62
FINALS PLAYED: 12
FINALS GOALS: 5
GRAND FINALS: 2
PREMIERSHIP: 1983
NORM SMITH MEDAL: 1983 (presented by Kevin Bartlett)

COLIN ROBERTSON

— Norm Smith Voting —

(**JUDGES:** Jack Hamilton, Allen Aylett, Mike Sheahan, Jack Dyer and Ted Whitten)

The Herald votes: **Mike Sheahan:** 3 Colin Robertson, 2 Chris Mew, 1 Leigh Matthews;
Peter Stone: 3 Mew, 2 John Kennedy, 1 Robertson;
Rod Nicholson: 3 Mew, 2 Robertson, 1 Kennedy;
Peter Keenan: 3 Mew, 2 Robertson, 1 Kennedy;
Bill Cannon: 3 Robertson, 2 Kennedy, 1 Michael Tuck;
Michael Lovett: 3 Robertson, 2 Kennedy, 1 Matthews;
Caroline Wilson: 3 Robertson, 2 Mew, 1 Tuck.

The Herald **TOTALS:** Robertson 17, Mew 13, Kennedy 8, Matthews 2, Tuck 2.

Bill Duckworth

It's doubtful that a greater larrikin has won the Norm Smith Medal. Billy Duckworth, a lad from country Western Australia, was one of Essendon's most popular players during the 1980s, for his on-field performances but also for his off-field exploits. However, behind his cheeky exterior—and who can forget the kiss he planted on Hawthorn star Dermott Brereton—lurked a genuine competitive drive. Duckworth gave his all for the Bombers. Known primarily as a defender, he adopted the swingman role for coach Kevin Sheedy whenever a leaking hole needed to be plugged. He played 126 games, kicked 64 goals, played in two Premierships (and also won two pre-season flags), and also represented WA in State of Origin football. In his Norm Smith Medal performance, Duckworth had 11 kicks and eight handballs, took six marks and kicked two timely goals.

I'm the youngest of four kids. My parents saved the best for last! My oldest brother, John, played with Fitzroy (1970, 1974-76, 58 games) and won a Magarey Medal (1979) with Central Districts. Then there's Rodney and my sister, Heather. John is 10 years older than me, so I was probably an after-thought. When I was starting to walk all three were in primary school, then they were in high school when I was at primary school, so we had different lives because of the age gap.

← **VERSATILE** Bill Duckworth was equally at home at both ends of the ground, and was a significant contributor in Essendon's come-from-behind victory over Hawthorn in 1984.

But certainly when the boys came home I would pester them to play cricket with me, or kick the footy. Half the time they had other things to do rather than play with the little brother. But occasionally they would relent and we'd all play together.

John went to Vietnam. I was only nine or 10 years old when he got drafted, so I didn't really understand it at the time. But I'm sure Mum and Dad were pretty worried. His number was called out; it was luck of the draw whether your name came out or not. He didn't get injured, fortunately. We've never really discussed what went on over there. He came back, that's the important thing.

My dad, Arthur, was a Rat of Tobruk. He was also a prisoner of war, but he never told me any stories of his time as a prisoner. He would say, "You don't know how good you've got it. You're not in a prison camp!" I don't recall it affecting him later in life, unless he hid it from us. If they don't tell you, you never know do you. It's like my teammate, Neil 'Nobby' Clarke, at Essendon in the 1980s. We never knew Neil had mental health issues while we were at the club. He always had a smiling face, and was pleasant to be around. It was only later on that I heard about the treatment he was receiving during that period, as well as post-footy. None of us knew. You wish you did, so you could have tried to help him. That was really sad when he took his own life.

My earliest footy memory is of having a kick with Dad on the farm. Then playing for the local C-grade side at Dudinin, running around on a dirt oval with a big hump in the middle of it. Dad had played footy locally, too. When he was a prisoner of war he played soccer in the prison camp. He was a boxer in the camp as well, so he was clearly a good sportsman. My mother, Jess, was a quick runner. She went to school with Shirley Strickland and ran against her. My earliest memories are kicking the footy around the yard at home. We didn't have a lot else to do in Dudinin, to be honest. Like all boys I played footy in winter and cricket in summer. I also played tennis. I loved my sport.

I was a runt of a kid. Most of my junior days were spent in the forward line. I didn't really grow until I was 15-16 years old. I was in the forward pocket in the C-grade. The age group for C-grade was 16 years down to seven or eight. The age group had to be that large, as that's what it took to make a full side. Obviously, the size of someone 16 is much greater than a seven-year-old. It was the only way you could get to play footy though, so you were more than happy to play against the bigger guys so that you got a game.

I was awarded a scholarship, somehow, to attend Narrogin High School. I still don't know what it was for. Maybe they were giving them out in a raffle that I didn't know about! I went to Narrogin for five years, and I played footy with a town called Cuballing, just north of Narrogin. After finishing school, I went and did a TAFE course in Perth for a year. Cuballing were short of numbers, so they offered to pay me to travel down each weekend to play for them. I was 18 and playing with some mates in Perth on a Saturday morning. Then, because Cuballing were giving me $60 a game in 1977, I was happy to drive down there and play on Sundays.

I tried out with the West Perth Colts, but I was living with some mates and I wasn't that dedicated. I was always going back to the farm whenever I could. Mum said I had to go and learn something, so I went and did a wool crafting course for a year. The colts were training three nights a week, but being with my mates from the bush, we'd rather go and play darts and go to the pub—things young blokes like to do in the country. So I wasn't dedicated enough to make it with the colts at the time.

I went back to the farm, and I was playing footy for Kondinin where my brother Rodney coached. It was then that I got an offer to go and train with West Perth. We won a couple of flags at Kondinin in 1978-79, and then I went to West Perth in 1980. Former Fitzroy player and coach Graham Campbell was coaching, and I went down after harvest and started training. It's interesting how I became a backman. Graham said at the start of pre-season, "Who's a forward?" I stood there, and about 60 blokes went over to the forward side, which only left about 10 blokes. So I decided to go over to the backline side. I thought, "Gee, this might be my best chance to get a game!" When I was at Cuballing, I had played a year at full-back. But when I was at Kondinin I played on a half-forward flank and as a ruck-rover under my brother. So I had played in defence a few times, but most of it I just learned as I went along. I managed to make the League team for the first game at West Perth. From there I had a few VFL clubs ring me.

What VFL clubs did to entice you over was invite you to a Grand Final. I'd never been to one, and St Kilda were the first club that rang and invited me. Fitzroy rang me as well, so did Essendon, but I told them I had agreed to go with St Kilda. Essendon kept ringing, and a week before the 1980 VFL Grand Final I hadn't heard from St Kilda, so as Essendon had kept calling me I decided to go with them instead. The next day St Kilda rang me! I told them that because I hadn't heard from them I had agreed to go with Essendon, so they said they would catch up with me while I was in Victoria. But I never caught up with them. I look back and think that my history could have been very different had St Kilda called me back before Essendon did. I went across for both the 1980 and 1981 Grand Finals, then I went over in 1982 to train with Essendon.

I had no aspirations to play in the VFL. Growing up on the farm it was something I just never thought of. It was only that Essendon came and signed me, then in 1980 or '81 they took me on a trip to America with them. I signed a Form Four with them during that period, which tied me to the club for two years. They paid me $12,000, which was good money back then. I was only 19 when I signed the form.

Even though I had signed the Form Four, I still had no real intention of going to Victoria. But coach Kevin Sheedy was fantastic when I look back to that period. He used to come over to Perth and drive up and see me. One time I was supposed to meet him in Perth, but I had a big night the night before. There were no mobile phones then, and having had a big night I couldn't be bothered going to meet him. He rang up home and found out my movements, then he rang the hardware store that I had to go to that day to pick up something for the farm. I got there and there was a message for me saying Sheeds was going to meet me there. He turned up, and I couldn't believe it—they were the lengths he'd go to!

He came over a few times, and would drive up to the farm. I still wasn't going at the end of 1981, but I never heard anything from West Perth. In the end I thought, "Well, I'll just go." I was still contracted to West Perth, but they never rang me to invite me to play with them again in '82. I knew Essendon were still keen on me, so I thought, "Oh well, I'll get in my car and head off!"

I drove to Melbourne. It took me two weeks to get there. Essendon were ringing Mum and saying, "Where is he?" She said, "I don't know, he left a week ago." I went over with a mate, and we had a bit of fun along the way. He had his car, I had mine, and we slowly made our way across. I finally got there after a couple of weeks and I was well and truly overweight.

I never experienced anything like that first pre-season under Kevin Sheedy. See, I had never been in a system where you did a full pre-season. At West Perth I used to go down after we had done the harvest back home. I also played Country Week cricket, and that was usually held at the end of January, so I used to turn up at West Perth after that. I'd never done a pre-season by the time I rocked up at Essendon. I got stuck paired up with Terry Daniher at training; that nearly killed me! I didn't know what had struck me. I'd never run 10 100s, 10 200s or 10 400s in my life. I didn't know *what* I was doing!

To Sheedy's credit—and this is why I admire him—he stuck with me. He could easily have said, "Go home, you're useless." Did I think of going home? Oh, shit yeah. I wasn't getting a kick, I couldn't catch anyone. I was just too unfit compared to them. I had always got by in the past by my natural fitness from working on the farm; I'd never trained like the guys in the VFL trained, so I never had that base fitness to build off. They sent me a program, but I told Sheeds I used to run to the front gate and back which got me fit. He assumed the driveway was a couple of miles, but it was only 400 metres!

I think some of the supporters thought I should have gone home. My first game was against Footscray, and we won by a lot (109 points), so that helped my cause. I kicked a behind that day, but I was playing down back so I don't know how I ran forward to kick it. I couldn't imagine myself running that far at the time! I wouldn't have blamed them if they had have sent me home, but thankfully Sheeds stood by me and gave me a chance to prove myself.

I got kicked out of my first training camp. In my first year at the club I got stuck with Paul Vander Haar and Glenn Hawker—that wasn't good. We had a camp down at Cerberus, on the Mornington Peninsula, and we were all to go down on the bus together. I had become friendly with Hawker when they took me to America, and he asked me to go down with him and Vander instead. I think we eventually arrived at Cerberus about 11pm, after leaving a nearby pub rather inebriated. We got kicked out of the camp. I was just a naïve bloke from the bush, I didn't know any different. My girlfriend at the time had come over, and was going to drive down to Cerberus on the Sunday, but we got kicked out on the Saturday. I couldn't contact her as I didn't know her phone number, so she gets down to Cerberus and is told we're back in Melbourne by that stage. At a pub, of course! I wasn't in her good books for a while. We eventually got married though. She's a very tolerant lady, fortunately.

Playing under Kevin Sheedy was interesting at times. He was hard; he'd train us all night. I didn't like training that much, but it was always interesting. Captain Terry Daniher was very important in binding the group together under Sheeds. Terry loves a chat and he made everyone feel welcome, so he was central to everything that went on during that period.

It was sensational playing at Windy Hill. What I noticed when I first came over was how passionate Victorian people were for their footy. My first game at the MCG, we played Richmond on a public holiday in front of 90,000. I think I played on Brian Taylor. It was exciting, plus a bit nerve wracking, but overall just the thrill of a lifetime to be able to do something like that.

The off-field side of the club helped bring us closer together. There were a lot of country lads there, such as Terry, Merv Neagle, Tim Watson and Roger Merrett. We were a young group, and I was lucky that I got there at the right time. If I came over two years later, I probably wouldn't have got a look in. But getting there in '82 was good for me as the side was still building up at that stage. We all got along well together, and the wives and partners all mixed in with us. I still love going over there and catching up with them all whenever I can.

In the 1983 Preliminary Final, I got into a scrap with the Krakouer brothers. I was playing on Jimmy, we were having a bit of a scrap, and I didn't see Phil come in from the side. He absolutely drove his knee into my thigh, and I had the biggest 'corkie' imaginable. It just bled and bled. Normally you would miss three or four weeks, but Sheeds still named me in the Grand Final team to play Hawthorn. Because I was selected, my mum and dad came over from Western Australia. But I was never going to play. I had to stay in the dressing rooms all through the lead-in to the game, and I couldn't tell anyone I wasn't playing. It was cloak and dagger stuff by Sheeds. In the end I thought, "Bugger this!" and I left and went and sat on the boundary line. It was fairly hard at the time, because it's everyone's dream to run out with the side on Grand Final day. You never know if you're going to get back there again. Instead of going in the motor parade through the city on the Friday, I had to go for a fitness test. But I didn't even bother doing it. I rang up the club and told them I couldn't play. I couldn't even walk, let alone run. It was disappointing to watch on as we lost by such a large margin (83 points). But the positive thing was we had got there. Just getting past that first final was a big step for us after the club had lost five Elimination Finals in the previous 11 seasons.

I just loved playing footy. Whether that was at school, with Dudinin, or with Essendon, I just loved playing. To play with Essendon was special. By 1984 we all believed in our ability. Sheeds had got us to believe, and we played well as a consequence.

I had my set routine. I liked to get to the game early and watch the reserves, even a bit of the under-19s when possible. At half-time of the reserves I would go in and start getting ready, talk to the guys, and get organised in my own way. I don't think you need anyone to motivate you. I just went out and played. That was the best thing ever: going out to play footy, forgetting about life for two hours. I enjoyed it, and I didn't need any motivation from the coach to get me up for a game. I used to get nervous, though. If I hadn't had a kick by quarter-time I'd get even more nervous.

It didn't matter who I was playing against, I just went out and played. Sheeds used to give us all these stats to study, and he would make us answer questions about how many kicks someone had, and things like that. You just hoped he wouldn't ask you any questions. If he did, I'd take a guess. That wasn't me, and it probably wasn't Terry or Vander either. You just go out and play and do your best, it's pretty simple. Probably nowadays, where it's fully professional, they've got time to do that, but we were all working. When I first came over, I worked on a farm for committeeman Jimmy Matthews. After 12 months I drove buses for former ruckman Don McKenzie. I also drove a truck, did a sales rep job that lasted about a week, and a few other odd jobs to supplement my footy income. Playing footy at that time certainly didn't pay you enough to stop working. Anyway, Paul Salmon got all the money that we were supposed to get!

To be honest, money never really came into it for me. I was happy just to be playing the game, wherever it was. We worked during the day, then went to training Monday, Tuesday, Wednesday and Thursday. It was something you just got used to, so it wasn't too hard to fit training in with work. We would have to train Sunday mornings, too, if we had been flogged the day before. But it was just what you did. Normally you would go up to the club Sunday morning for treatment, then they'd have the pleasant Sunday mornings where you'd spend a couple of hours there together and have a beer or two. I enjoyed it immensely.

Grand Final week in 1984 was amazing. But it's probably when you look back that you really appreciate it. At the time, you don't think much different, but that was certainly a special time to be involved. I got to take part in the Grand Final Parade, and I saw people from WA in the crowd yelling out to me. It brings back great memories for me. I was there at the right time, so you could say I was lucky in that sense. It was a nervous week, a very nervous week in fact. But so exciting.

I started on Leigh Matthews and he kicked a goal in the first 20 seconds. I dropped him after that, but he hit me first. He cracked me over the head![1] But Leigh was a privilege to play against: he was a champion player. He never said much on the field, he was just hard at it. He probably copped as many as he gave. As his record suggests, you've got to admire him for what he did as a footballer. I'll admit that, early on, he probably had the better of me that day.

The runner came and said, "Go down to the forward line." I said, "Thank Christ for that!" Leigh had had the better of me, and Sheeds had thrown me forward before. We were struggling up there, so he must have thought, "I'll give Duckworth a crack and see if it works out." I kicked a goal straight away and I got a bit of the ball after that. It all worked out well for us in the end. I wasn't doing much down back, so I knew I had to try and do something when they put me forward. I decided to get involved and bring an energy to the forward line. I wanted to chase the ball; chase anyone really. Whatever I could do to help the team.

Despite a slow start, we didn't think it was going to be a repeat of the year before. We were more confident in 1984. We had played a really good second Semi-Final against them; they only really got us in the last couple of minutes of that game. I had played well that day, so for me personally, and the team overall, I don't think we ever thought that we were out of it. They got that early jump on us, but for the next two quarters the margin stayed the same. We had quite a few scoring shots; if we had have kicked straight we might have been in front a lot earlier.

At three-quarter time Sheeds was really confident. Then we got the first goal and from there we got on a roll. There was no stopping us in that last quarter. He said at that final break that he thought Hawthorn were tired. He said, "Just get the first one, get them on the back foot." We got that first goal and suddenly everyone was pumped up. Things started going our way, the ball started bouncing for us, which it tends to do when you are playing well. We got on a roll after that and the rest, as they say, is history. It was probably one of the most enjoyable quarters of footy I've ever played in. It's still a great thrill to think about it today. What made

---

1   In truth, Bill Duckworth upended Leigh Matthews immediately after the Hawthorn star kicked the opening goal of the Grand Final, then Matthews punched Duckworth in the head during a late 'spoiling' attempt shortly afterwards.

it so special was the fact that Essendon hadn't won one for so long; that was the best thing about it. It was a cracker night that night, I can tell you! Actually, it was more like a cracker week.

I didn't really know the Norm Smith Medal existed. Winning it had not even entered my mind. Friends still joke, "How did you win it?" I laugh and say, "Someone must have thought I played all right." But it could have been Leon Baker who won it, or Darren 'Daisy' Williams. But I was lucky enough to get voted the winner, and I'll certainly accept it. I won't hand it back! It's up on the wall at home. It's probably just something that happened as part of my journey, more so than the pinnacle of my career. Footy has always been an enjoyable game for me. I still wish I could play it. I had never aspired to play in Victoria, and I had never aspired to win a Norm Smith Medal. I was lucky enough to be playing in a VFL Grand Final, and was lucky to get enough votes to win the medal. You certainly accept the accolades now, but at the time it didn't really mean as much as winning the game did. The excitement of winning a Premiership outweighed everything else. Just seeing the joy on people's faces was more satisfying than winning the Norm Smith Medal. But it's something I look back on with pride now that my career is over.

In 1985, we just knew that we would win most games. That wasn't arrogant, we just knew that if we were behind at three-quarter time we would win. We had that belief in ourselves that we would win from any position.

I was lucky to be there on Grand Final day. I had hurt my knee in the first game, against Hawthorn. I did my posterior cruciate and didn't return until round 20. But I never doubted that I wouldn't get back in time for the finals. I just hoped it would heal in time, and I got there in the end. I got asked to win the Norm Smith Medal again in 1985, but I said, "No, give it to Simon because he's ugly and he doesn't have much going for him." In all seriousness, Simon played a fantastic game that day.

We had an intense rivalry with the Hawks during that period (1983-85); they were a pretty good side, and them winning all those flags gave me the shits. I get sick of hearing Dermott crap on about his five day and five night Premierships. It was a good rivalry though, and it probably still goes on today, albeit not as brutal as it was in the 1980s.

I was one of the people who got dropped for the four Danihers in 1990. It was against St Kilda, and Sheeds wanted to play all four brothers in the one game—something that had never happened before. So, I was a casualty of that. I had had a really good pre-season that year. From about 1987 I stayed in Melbourne each off-season, rather than return home to the farm like I had been doing. We won the night Grand Final, but I did my hamstring in that game. After that I was a bit-part player. Sheeds would play me at half-back one week, then another time I would have to go and tag someone like Terry Wallace or Doug Hawkins at Footscray. I was just everywhere that year.

I was going to retire after 1989, but Sheeds said he wanted me to play one more year. He said I would play 15-16 games, and I was quite happy to do that; I'm certainly not upset by how that year panned out. But, when I got dropped for the four Danihers, I knew I wouldn't get back in for the finals; not unless there was a serious injury. It was hard to take at the time. Particularly seeing them run out there on Grand Final day without me. It would have been nice to have played in another Grand Final, but I still wanted them to win. It was great to see some young blokes be given a chance: guys like Darren Bewick (23 years old), Chris Daniher (24), Peter Cransberg (23), David Grenvold (24), Paul Hamilton (23), Peter Somerville (22), Kieran Sporn (24) and Michael Long (21), for example. But I was certainly disappointed to miss out.

I coached North Beach Football Club to 10 Premierships. When I first came back to Perth, I played a couple of years at West Perth and after that I played with North Beach until I was 36; I won the flag with them in 1993. After that, they asked me if I wanted to coach. It was something I wanted to try, and I had a great time. We won 10 flags and I think we were runners-up twice as well, so it was a pretty successful period of my life.

I applied for the West Perth coaching job once, but I probably didn't interview that well. They must not have appreciated my sense of humour!

I wasn't wise enough to have a PowerPoint presentation like some of the others; I just went in and spoke off my own bat. They asked me for my training drills and all that when I left, but I said, "Oh no, I'll wait until I get the job first!" But that's life. I was also asked to be an assistant at Claremont, but I had already committed to North Beach by then. It would have been interesting to have coached at the highest level, but I have no regrets now that it never eventuated. I enjoyed coaching the Amateurs, and my two boys, Michael and Shane, play there still today. Watching them each Saturday is my footy fix for the week. They love their footy like I did at their age. They don't come to me for advice though. I think they think I'm an idiot. I'm the last person they ask. I try giving it to them anyway, but they don't appreciate it for some reason.

Statistics

BORN: 21 February 1959
GAMES PLAYED (1982-90): 126
GOALS: 64
FINALS PLAYED: 10
FINALS GOALS: 6
GRAND FINALS: 2
PREMIERSHIPS: 1984, 1985
NORM SMITH MEDAL: 1984 (presented by Bob Skilton)

BILL DUCKWORTH

— Norm Smith Voting —

(**JUDGES:** Jack Hamilton, Allen Aylett, Jack Dunn, Kevin Bartlett and Geoff Leek)

The Sun votes: **Lou Richards:** 3 Leon Baker, 2 Glenn Hawker, 1 Bill Duckworth;
Peter Simunovich: 3 Duckworth, 2 Baker, 1 Hawker;
Don Scott: 3 Hawker, 2 Terry Wallace, 1 Shane Heard;
Jack Dunn: 3 Wallace, 2 Duckworth, 1 Richard Loveridge;
Michael Davis: 3 Duckworth, 2 Mark Harvey, 1 Paul Weston;
Bruce Matthews: 3 Harvey, 2 Wallace, 1 Heard;
Paul Murphy: 3 Baker, 2 Duckworth, 1 Harvey;
Greg Baum: 3 Duckworth, 2 Harvey, 1 Wallace.

The Sun **TOTALS:** Duckworth 14, Baker 8, Harvey 8, Wallace 8, Hawker 6, Heard 2, Weston 1, Loveridge 1.

Simon Madden

Simon Madden is one of the AFL's greatest and most durable ruckmen. The self-confessed "uncoordinated schoolboy" played 378 games for Essendon and kicked 575 goals (both club records at the time). He captained his club and his state, won four best and fairests, was runner-up in the 1988 Brownlow Medal and third in 1983, was a three-time All-Australian, and, in 2002, was selected at number five among the 25 Champions of Essendon. A key member of the 1984 Premiership side, Madden's Norm Smith Medal-winning performance in the 1985 decider was as dominant as any ruckman in a Grand Final. He had 12 kicks, 10 handballs, took 14 marks and earned 22 hitouts, giving the Bomber midfield first use at most bounces.

I was a terrible footballer as a kid, and was always the last one picked for lunchtime games. When it was wet, we weren't allowed to play on the oval so we just played this game where there was a team down one end and a team down the other end and you took it in turns to kick the ball to each other. If one kid took a mark you got a point, so we were practising our pack marking.

I was big, awkward and dopey, so I didn't do too well. But, in about grade

← **BIG MAN** Simon Madden is rated one of the game's greatest ruckmen. In the 1985 Grand Final he reigned supreme.

five, I started to play in the school side, and it was there that I started to get the hang of it. My brother, Paul, is 18 months older than me, so we played together every second year before he moved into the older age group. We had a big yard at home, so we were always kicking the ball together. There were always lots of kids kicking the footy in the streets in those days, too, so it was just a part of what you did. I played cricket in the summer, but footy was the main passion.

I don't know if I ever actually aimed to play for Essendon. But I can remember my under-15s coach, George Agius, saying to me once, "You can make it, you can play League footy," which came as a surprise. Paul played in a Grand Final in the under-19s for Essendon, at the MCG, and I snuck in with the team to go and watch. He broke his nose and cheekbone that day, and after that he was 'umming' and 'ahhing' about whether to continue playing footy or not.

Des Tuddenham was coaching Essendon at the time, and he and recruiter Jimmy Matthews came to our house to try and convince Paul to play footy again. Paul was unsure, so they turned around to me and said, "Do you want to come to training?" I wasn't even 16 at the time, but the prospect of training at Essendon was rather exciting, so I said "Oh yeah." Jim Matthews picked me up in his white Mercedes and took me down to the Showgrounds, at Ascot Vale, where they were training—I'd never been in a 'Merc' before—and I was expecting to be playing in the under-19s. But they started me off in the seconds, which was hard work, and then later that year I got a few games in the seniors.

Tuddy was as tough as nails. There was one occasion where he had the whole team crawling on our hands and knees around the oval after a poor game. He did it, too, but can you imagine a coach telling his players to do that now? It wouldn't happen! While he lost some of the players after that, I was still only a kid then so I just did what I was told.

I used to play two games each week. I would play school footy at St Bernard's on Wednesdays, then play with Essendon on the Saturday. You think about it now and it just wouldn't happen, but that was what you did back then. There weren't a lot of kids who were 16 and 17, like I was, and playing League footy at the time. Tuddy was a really hard taskmaster. In some ways it was really daunting. But in other ways it was all very exciting because you were playing with and against guys that you had grown up watching.

We weren't a very good side during the 1970s. I don't think we spent a lot of money during the 1970s either, which didn't help. I know a few people who went to the country and got more money to play there. In my first year, 1974, I reckon I cleared about $2000; at the end of my second year I got an advance on my pay so that I could buy a new Kombi van. It's all relative, but to put that in perspective there was nobody I knew at the time who could afford to buy a brand new car of any sort. I was only 17, so as a school kid it was pretty exciting.

I played in the seconds on the day of the Windy Hill brawl. I was watching with my teammates when the brawl broke out in front of the grandstand, and I remember thinking to myself, "And they want me to play *this* game?" During those years, if I had have left my mouthguard at home I would have worried that I would lose teeth. But by my final years if I left it at home I would have been confident that I would get away with it unscathed. That's how much the game changed during my time, in regards to unnecessary roughness. It got harder to play in my latter years, but it was never as rough as it was back in the '70s.

I sat in the forward pocket for three years while Graham Moss won three best and fairests and a Brownlow Medal. To underscore how valuable he was to the club, I remember when any other player got injured we were just expected to cover his absence. But when Mossy got injured one time, the amount of time and effort that the club went to in order to try and get him up for the next game was huge. And that was the first time I got to see first hand what a superstar was. He won the Brownlow Medal in 1976, then he went back home because he got a chance to captain-coach his old club (Claremont). It was a huge loss to our football club. Now yes, him leaving put added pressure on to my shoulders, but at the same time I was 19, and had done a three-year apprenticeship under him, so it was a real opportunity for me to show what I had learned.

THE NORM SMITH MEDAL

I won the best and fairest that first year after Mossy left, but in the last five games it was a real struggle. It's tough on any kid making the step up to League footy to get through a full season, even back then. I tell the young blokes today that it does your body in, but it also does your head in. It really wears you out, because you've got to concentrate so much. I tell players now that they need to have something else away from footy which can give them a mental break from the game.

Kevin Sheedy came along at the right time for us. He coached the club, as well as coaching the players. Tuddy was great for me in the sense that he just threw me in and gave me the opportunity. Bill Stephen (1976-77, 44 games and a winning percentage of 37.50 per cent) was a good development coach after Tuddy, and I won a best and fairest under him. Then we had Barry Davis (1978-80, 67 games for a winning percentage of 45.52 per cent) who, I believe, was ahead of his time. He was talking about concepts that we had no idea about, but you look back now and think, gee, he was ahead of the game. Then Sheeds came along in 1981 and changed the course of history. So it was a real progression through that 1970s period to get to where we got to by the 1980s.

Were ruckmen more important in my day than they are now? It's a very good question and you can debate it until the cows come home. Graham Moss was so important to us, as Gary Dempsey was important to North Melbourne. My first game in the ruck was against St Kilda's Kevin 'Cowboy' Neale, which was scary enough. Then my first full game was against Richmond's Brian 'Whale' Roberts, who was huge like his nickname suggests. If you go back through the history of Grand Finals, it's proven that a team with a dominant ruckman has a much better chance of winning than a team that lacks one. Hawthorn were a great side during the 1980s, but in that 1985 Grand Final they had Chris Langford rucking against me, and he was not suited to that role, nor was he big enough.

I joke that I made Chris Langford's career, because they played him in the ruck and I won the Norm Smith Medal. They then moved him to full-back and he played 300 games! He was a very good player, but he was used in the ruck because they had no one else, and it proved costly on that occasion. It's very much about the midfield, but it all still starts with the ruckman. If you've got a good ruckman in finals, you are a real chance at winning. And that's very much still the case today.

I would challenge anybody from any era to go through what Kevin Sheedy put us through in his first pre-season and not say it was hard. We all had jobs at the time, and he had us doing three hours each of Monday, Wednesday and Friday, then two hours on Tuesday and Thursday. It was an hour of football every night, and an hour of running every night, plus an extra hour of weights on the Monday, Wednesday and Friday. It was really hard work, and so draining.

I don't think I handled the captaincy very well. Nowadays when you're made captain you have a leadership team around you, whereas in my day they basically said, "You're captain, good luck!" I was 21 when they made me captain, and I captained the club at 22, but I didn't know what to do. Ken Fletcher (1967-80, 264 games) was captain before me, and he was a few years older than I was, so here I was thinking I needed to behave like him. But I was so much younger, and wasn't as mature as he was. Then Sheeds came along in 1981, and it's well known that he preferred the tradesmen to people like me, a school teacher. He came to Essendon with no senior coaching experience, and his passion was fantastic, as were his footy smarts. He taught us a lot. But he was a new coach and he made a lot of mistakes, like we all do. I've no doubt he pigeonholed me, and so he sacked me as captain.

My form dropped away. Then during 1982 I found myself on the interchange bench for the seconds. I'd played about 150 games, I was 24, I'd won a couple of best and fairests and represented my state, yet I'd reached rock bottom. I know I could have blamed any excuse for where I was at. But I realised that there were key people at the club whose opinion of my ability was obviously less than my own. So I asked myself, "What am I going to do about it?" I knew I couldn't change their behaviour, but I could change mine. So, at the end of 1982, I told myself that I'll win the best and fairest the next year. I decided to do anything in my power to get myself right for 1983 and give it a real crack.

I did all the training, plus the weights, plus a bit extra. I really wanted to concentrate on my footy a lot more than I had been. My diet changed, I drank less alcohol, my strength improved as did my speed, and my technique got better also. I won the best and fairest that year, and the year after; that's how quickly I turned things around. It was a real indication to me of how you, alone, can control your footy career, to a certain degree. Yes, a number of things you can't control, but commitment and determination are up to you. I firmly believe that you learn the game in the first 50 games, then you understand it in the next 50, and if you reach 100 games you have a really good perspective on the game which should put you in good stead for any games after that.

Sam Newman came in as ruck coach at the end of 1982. Sheeds got him across, and I had played against Sam when he was at Geelong. Now, I was younger than him, taller than him, could leap higher than him, I was more athletic than him, and yet he used to beat me in the ruck. It was frustrating as hell! My idea had been to run in as hard as you could against the other bloke and hope you came off best. Whereas Sam showed me that if you came in from an angle, jumped early, and then palmed a certain way, you stood a much better chance of directing the ball down to your teammate. I remember thinking, "Wow!" All of a sudden, it wasn't 50-50, it was more 70-30 my way, and that made a huge difference to my game. I reckon in those years I was also one of the last to leave the gym after training, and I was working hard on my goalkicking because I was a forward-ruckman. After that I didn't look back.

We'd lost Elimination Finals in 1981 and 1982. Then, in 1983, we finally won one. All of a sudden our whole mindset changed. You realised what everyone had been talking about, and you understood what it took to succeed. Soon we were in a Grand Final. But because it had been such a long period since we had last played in one (1968, a three-point loss to Carlton), I think we as players, and the club as a whole, were just happy to be there. Hawthorn were the best side that year and we got belted by 83 points, and so we had doubts about whether we could ever beat them.

You need to give Kevin Sheedy his dues. We didn't beat Hawthorn in our two home and away meetings during 1984 (a six-point loss in round two, and 47 points in round 12), then we met them in the second Semi-Final, in a game that some say was the greatest of all time. They beat us by eight points, and we could have been devastated by it. But we went into the team meeting afterwards, and Sheeds said to us, "Now boys, they're the best team going around, and we're that far from them," and he held his thumb and index finger close together. We came out of that meeting thinking that he was right. Two weeks later in the Grand Final we had a lot of the play early on but couldn't kick goals. We went in at three-quarter time trailing by 23 points, but knowing that we were a real chance to run over them in the last quarter.

There's an old saying, "It's not what people say, it's not what people do, it's how they make you feel." Sheeds spoke to us about the fact that we had them if we just kept persevering. He told us that the goals would come. Then immediately from the restart, I got the ball to Darren 'Daisy' Williams who pumped it forward to Leon Baker, and he did a blind turn and kicked a goal. Baker was always a really cool customer, and when he kicked that goal he started dancing and cheering and I thought to myself, if he's excited then maybe we can start to get excited, too. We just steamrolled them after that.

By 1985, we were basically unbeatable. In 1983 Hawthorn was the best team; in 1984 we were both vying to be the best, and in 1985 we *were* the best team. We just knew we were the best. In fact, we got to a stage where we would lose a game and say, "I don't want to feel like that anymore," and we were good enough to win most of our matches during that period because of that attitude.

I have had days where I just couldn't get near the ball, but that 1985 Grand Final was a day when the ball just seemed to follow me. I knew that I was up against a makeshift ruckman in Langford, who was a really hard worker and strong player but wasn't a ruckman *per se*. So I was confident enough to back myself in to be able to outruck and outmark anybody. We used to do a lot of competitive marking at training with full body contact, and so technique-wise and fitness-wise I was really at my peak for that Grand Final.

THE NORM SMITH MEDAL

It's great that I won a Norm Smith Medal. I'd rather have it than not have it. But that 1984 Premiership still ranks as my most special day in footy. From where we'd come from in my first 11 seasons, it was just so rewarding.

To play in two Premierships is fantastic. But to be able to say that you played in back-to-back Premierships is a real honour. I am very proud of that, because it's very hard to do. A lot of players don't even get to play in one Grand Final. We got into the 1983 Grand Final and got belted by a record margin, then we were able to meet them again in 1984 and win, and then come back again in 1985 and win comfortably. Looking back on it, I think that we as a group should be really proud of what we achieved in 1984-85, especially after such a belting in 1983. It was a real sign of the character of the group.

When people introduce you at an event they list all your achievements, but they never list the struggles that you also went through along the way. What you achieved is more rewarding because you went through those struggles, whether it be physically, mentally or emotionally. If you don't understand the struggle you won't fully understand the success. Our group during those years all came along together and we all socialised together, and so we all knew each other's strengths and weaknesses, which really helped us as a group.

—— Statistics ——

BORN: 30 December 1957
GAMES PLAYED (1974-92): 378
GOALS: 575
FINALS PLAYED: 20
FINALS GOALS: 13
GRAND FINALS: 4
PREMIERSHIPS: 1984, 1985
NORM SMITH MEDAL: 1985 (presented by Jim Cardwell)

SIMON MADDEN

— Norm Smith Voting —

(**JUDGES:** Scot Palmer, Ian Major and Drew Morphett)

The Sun **votes: Peter Simunovich:** 3 Simon Madden, 2 Dermott Brereton, 1 Leon Baker;
Lou Richards: 3 Roger Merrett, 2 Madden, 1 Brereton;
Michael Davis: 3 Madden, 2 Brereton, 1 Merrett;
Bruce Matthews: 3 Madden, 2 Brereton, 1 Merrett;
Greg Baum: 3 Madden, 2 Brereton, 1 Merrett;
Rohan Connolly: 3 Madden, 2 Brereton, 1 Merrett.

The Sun **TOTALS:** Madden 17, Brereton 11, Merrett 7, Baker 1.

Gary Ayres

Legendary coach Allan Jeans once described his champion defender Gary Ayres as "a good driver in heavy traffic." It was an apt description. Ayres struck fear into opponents whenever he charged out of defence. With his mullet hairdo and chiselled frame, Ayres was nicknamed 'Conan' after Conan the Barbarian, a 1982 movie with a lead character who met adversity with unyielding strength.

But Ayres's legend was truly made in his ability to play well in big games. He played in eight Grand Finals for Hawthorn—1983-89 and 1991—and was among the best players in all five of its Premierships (1983, 1986, 1988-89 and 1991). That the team included the likes of Leigh Matthews, Michael Tuck, John Platten, Jason Dunstall and Dermott Brereton says plenty about Ayres's big-game temperament. In 1986 and 1988 he won the Norm Smith Medal as best player afield, becoming the first to claim the award twice. In '86, Ayres had 17 kicks and six handballs, took five marks and kicked a goal; in '88, it was 18 kicks and four handballs, plus six marks. He captained his club (1992-93) and state (1989), played 269 games (1978-93) and won Hawthorn's best and fairest in a Premiership year (1986). Later Ayres coached Geelong into the 1995 Grand Final, led the Adelaide Crows to a night Premiership in 2003, and took Port Melbourne to the VFA/VFL flag in 2011 and again in 2017.

← **PAIRS** Gary Ayres was rated a "great driver in heavy traffic". He also proved himself a great player in the biggest games, winning two Norm Smith Medals. Here, he receives his 1988 Medal from former Collingwood great Bruce Andrew. Photo courtesy of the Hawks Museum.

I was born into a family that loved their sport. My dad, Jim, played with the Darnum Football Club and mum, Marie, was a very good netballer. I've got three sisters, Kerry, Bernadette and Tracey, plus one younger brother, Christopher, so our parents were the family taxi and took us wherever we had to go to play sport. That is the earliest and most cherished memory of my childhood.

It was competitive in our household growing up. We used to have football games down the corridor. But that only stayed in vogue until Mum and Dad found out that we were bashing into the walls and leaving dints in the plaster! My father, and our friend's father Alf Ridgeway, were two of the local policemen in Drouin and Warragul, and they started the Drouin Junior Football Club. Dad coached the under-12s, Alf coached the under-14s. So footy became a big part of our lives. In the backyard, we'd pull palings off the fence to use as goals, and the occasional window got smashed. With five kids at home, the last thing Mum wanted was all five of us inside, so we spent a lot of our time in the backyard playing sport.

During the 1960s and '70s, the ability to see your VFL heroes on TV was limited. I was playing with a guy whose father was a member at VFL Park. We would have lunch at his pub after our morning game, then he would take us to Waverley in the afternoon. My favourite memory from those trips was, once the senior team had finished playing, you could run out on to the ground and kick the footy on the same ground the VFL guys had just played on. I would imagine I was kicking goals for St Kilda, the club I supported as a boy. If you were lucky enough to be taken to the MCG, running on to the ground there was something else again.

The St Kilda players were like gods to me. Guys like captain Darrel Baldock, an absolute gun; the casual-looking Bob Murray who would bomb torpedo kicks from full-back; also, Ross Smith, an unbelievable player who, when I was later at Hawthorn was our reserves coach for a while. Everyone loved Carl Ditterich as well, because he was rough, would throw the elbows out and loved the biff and bash. Later it was guys like George Young and, of course, the coach Allan Jeans.

Who would have thought that a few years later he would end up coaching me at Hawthorn?

I was at the 1975 VFL Grand Final between North Melbourne and Hawthorn. The MCG was much different back then, with the old Bay 13 standing room area, plus the amenities were rather sub-standard in comparison to today. But, that was such a great experience to witness a Grand Final in person. I remember thinking, wow, what would it be like to play in a Grand Final? You get caught up in all the euphoria, the size of the crowd; it's just a mind-blowing experience. Hard to believe that, eight years later, there I was playing in my first Grand Final on the famous MCG.

It was daunting playing for Warragul against men at 16 years of age. Around the Latrobe Valley you had the potato farmers and the dairy farmers, and if the spuds weren't growing or the cows weren't milking they became pretty aggressive out on the football field! Playing seniors with the Warragul Football Club, I had to evade elbows and other things that were coming my way. Being a skinny teenager it became very much about learning on the run, trying to survive to a degree. And what made it even harder back then was that the quality of player who came back to the country from the VFL was much higher. The financial remuneration in the VFL was not great, and players could return to the country and make more money. So in those days you came up against guys of a very high calibre, which lifted the standard of the game in the country.

Allan Jeans said that I was "a good driver in heavy traffic". I credit that to the fact I had to learn to evade the men while playing with Warragul as a teenager! Hawthorn's recruiters must have been down our way having a look around, because I was playing in Hawthorn's allotted country zone at the time. I signed a Form Four, which tied me to the club for six games, but my father thought I was still too young to be playing in the VFL so I played that year out at Warragul. I turned 17 in 1977, and at the end of that year I first went to Hawthorn's pre-season training.

It was scary doing my first pre-season under David Parkin. I was very nervous! You were put into two groups; the invitees were on one side, and the guys who had been there for a year or more were in the other group.

Later I would look at that group of new recruits and remember back to my first time at the club and how daunting it was. You looked over and saw Don Scott, Peter Knights, Michael Tuck, Leigh Matthews, Kelvin Moore… the list went on and on. There was so much talent there, you were just pinching yourself in disbelief.

I spent most of 1978 in Hawthorn's reserves. We were lucky that there were a lot of young players at the club that year, and we played off in the reserves Grand Final against North before our seniors played their Grand Final against North that afternoon. We were flogged that morning, losing by 52 points. There weren't many people in the stands at the start, but by the last quarter the crowd was flocking in. After the game I was able to go into the senior rooms before they ran out, and it was great to see their preparation. It was the first time I had witnessed Parkin's visualisation techniques that he put the group through pre-game. The players were all lying on the ground, visualising what they were going to do that day. It instilled in me the fact that I wanted to be a part of Grand Final day at senior level. I played two senior games during the year, which gave me a taste of it.

Footy is a great leveller. Just when you think you're going okay, you quickly get brought back down to earth. I kicked three goals in my debut game against Footscray, having only played half a dozen reserves games; it was quite meteoric in that sense. I even kicked a goal with my first kick! But for my second game I was named on the interchange, had nine disposals, was dropped the next week and didn't play seniors again that year.

In 1980, I received a thunderbolt out of the blue: my father was killed in a tractor accident. That was devastating, and knocked me around for a while. I was 18, and trying to come to terms with something of that magnitude was pretty hard. I had one of my sisters in Melbourne with me, but our three younger ones were still at home with Mum. They were there when the accident happened, which would have been extremely traumatic for them. After that I was in and out of the senior side; there was no consistency or stability during that period. In 1981 I got married, at 20, and we had a baby six months later, so there was a lot happening for me at a young age. I also received a bad hamstring injury that season, which I couldn't shake off. I was facing a real mental challenge, as I didn't know whether I was good enough for VFL standard.

I had decided to leave Hawthorn at the end of 1981. Champion full-forward Peter Hudson had been at Hawthorn (1967-74, 1977), and then gone home to Glenorchy in Tasmania, where he was involved with the Glenorchy Football Club. He must have seen that I had a bit of ability in my early time at Hawthorn, so he put an offer to me to move my young family to Glenorchy, working for and playing with the football club. I had committed to go, because my job at the time was going nowhere, and my footy appeared also to be going nowhere. Plus I'd had the death of my father and the marriage and new baby, so it was all weighing on me. I told Allan Jeans, then in his first year as coach of the club, that I had decided to go, and that the footy caper for me in Melbourne was not what I wanted anymore. I told him about Peter's offer, too.

Jeans convinced me to stay at Hawthorn. He had only known me for a few months by then, but he said to me, "I think leaving will be the biggest footy mistake you will ever make." Wow! That hit me between the eyes after virtually making my mind up that I wasn't good enough. He said, "I want you to go away and think about it." I said, "How long do I have?" to which he replied: "Twenty-four hours!" So I changed my mind and decided to knuckle down and do what I needed to do to make a go of it in the VFL.

I felt an immediate connection between myself and Allan. He may or may not have known it, but my father was a policeman like he was, and having lost my dad meant that Allan, certainly in my mind, was manifesting into a father-figure of sorts. There was a big hole there for me, so I stayed at the Hawks, and I'm bloody-well lucky I did, as it turned out. Who was to know that within 12 months I would establish myself in the back pocket and go on to play another 247 games—and be a part of eight Grand Finals?

We could sense that things were starting to change. The club hadn't made the finals from 1979-81, which was remarkable when you consider the group we had. Looking back on that period, it was evident that a lot of those stars from the 1970s had probably played their best footy by that time. As well as some retirements, a number of guys moved on to other clubs, so there was a lot of change during that '79-'81 period. I had gotten myself fitter by 1982, and felt I was earning my place in the team, so my outlook was more positive.

What helped my footy was being able to settle in the one position: the back pocket. Before 1982, I had played on the wing, half-back, half-forward, even full-forward—I was all over the shop and I had no identity as far as a position was concerned. Allan said, "Son, you've played in a lot of positions, but I think you can fit into the back pocket." My role was generally to play on the opposition's 'resting' rovers, negating them and running off them every chance I could.

We were beaten up pretty badly by Carlton in the 1982 Qualifying Final. They had the mosquito fleet of midfielders who were irrepressible; their third quarters alone helped to coin the phrase "premiership quarter". We had a lot of trouble with them in 1982. But the lessons we learned out of playing finals that year were invaluable. We were improving through continually training and playing together as a group. There is no substitute for training. Guys who started when I did were beginning to cement a place in the side after a lengthy apprenticeship in the reserves. Our leaders had a terrific year in 1983, and everything started to come together due to a good blend between senior, middle and younger players.

In my first Grand Final, 1983, I feel I played my role and did my job. I was in the back pocket in a game we were completely in control of, so to have gathered 20 disposals was pretty good when you think about it. For me, though, all that mattered was that I had played in my first VFL Premiership at my first crack at it, and that's what I take away from that game.

The rivalry with Essendon during the mid 1980s was brutal. After we won in 1983, it was about them getting one back on us. From then on, it was really combative, brutal, and the build-up during the week before these matches was always interesting. We could sense that games against Essendon were bigger than normal home and away games, just by Allan

Jeans's temperament and body language at training. He was competitive as it was, but as a group we could sense before Essendon games—as well as Carlton and St Kilda, having been coach of the latter for so long—that Allan tended to be even more intense. Then, before 1984, Kevin Sheedy told the press that we were all on drugs because we used to sniff eucalyptus bottles to clear our airways. Allan, having been in the police force, saw that as a slur on him as a person. The rivalry between the two clubs became quite brutal. But we certainly respected them, and I'm sure they respected us.

We should have put the 1984 Grand Final well and truly to bed by three-quarter time. But we were only 23 points in front. I sensed that it was going to be on in the last quarter. As it turned out, Essendon changed some players and kicked some early goals in that last quarter (9.5 to 2.1), and we couldn't hold them off. They scored a record last-quarter score, but we felt that was one game that got away from us.

We thought that rivalry was going to go on forever. But after beating us again in the 1985 Grand Final, Essendon didn't make another Grand Final again until 1990. All we wanted to do each year was give ourselves a chance by winning enough games to play finals. Then, once we made the finals, our aim was always to make the Grand Final. We were never satisfied with anything less, and it served us well in the late 1980s.

In 1986, some of us took it upon ourselves as individuals to dedicate ourselves in order to get better as a team. I threw in my job, and just did odd jobs while I spent the last three months of 1985 and the first three months of 1986 getting myself as fit as I possibly could. That really helped me go to another level that year, winning my first and only best and fairest. Some guys started training straight after we lost the '85 Grand Final; others gave up the grog for the year. We had a fair degree of internalisation regarding what we should do to get back there and win it in '86. Leigh Matthews retired after '85, and Jason Dunstall became our new focal point up forward. We also brought in a future Brownlow medallist in Johnny Platten. We were rejuvenated entering 1986, after a kick up the backside in '85.

THE NORM SMITH MEDAL

I never had any problems sleeping before a game; I was lucky in that sense. I certainly always had the butterflies in the stomach the day of the game, but my preparation was always based around consistency and routine. I loved that. From how I packed my bag in the morning, to the time I wanted to arrive at the game so that I wasn't rushing, doing my own warm-up, getting a massage: all that was done by routine, week after week, no matter the game. I used to enjoy the Thursday night training sessions, too. I didn't love the running element, but when the footies came out I loved feeling up and about. My routine was integral to me feeling good as we walked down the race and on to the ground each Saturday, whether it was a Grand Final or a regular home and away match.

I was self-motivated on game day. Having said that, I used to love listening to Allan Jeans speak before a game, because he had one of the best voices, and was one of the best speakers I've had the pleasure to listen to. He could adjust his voice up and down with great effect. When you thought he was about to go over the top, he would bring his voice level back down, which kept you fascinated. He could be quite motivating, and it still gives me chills on the back of my neck today to think of Allan giving a pre-game speech.[1]

I nearly didn't make it to the 1986 Grand Final. I'd hurt my hamstring in the Preliminary Final win against Fitzroy. Our captain, Michael Tuck, had suffered a back spasm that day as well. Allan took me off in the last quarter as a precaution. All through Grand Final week I was really concerned. Allan said to me on the Monday: "Just do what you can, get through to Thursday, and we'll have a fitness test on the Friday morning." So Tucky and I did what he asked. I received treatment all week and, on the Friday, Yabby drove us down to Scotch College where we both had a fitness test on the back oval there. To this day Tucky always laughs and says that my test was *slightly* easier to pass than his was. I was just required to roll the ball along the ground and pick it up, then accelerate down the line, whereas his was more one on one, repeated efforts. I remember saying to myself when I was stretching out at top speed, "If it goes, there's nothing I can do about it." Thankfully, I got through,

---

[1] To view a collection of retrospective "pre-game" speeches from Allan Jeans, John Kennedy, Ron Barassi and Tom Hafey, see: http://tinyurl.com/ycrm86aa.

as did Tucky. I got to the ground on the Saturday and marched straight into the doctor's room and said: "What have you got for me, Doc? Just jab the heck out of it!" He whacked a heap of painkiller in my leg, but I started to feel it a bit before half-time, so I got another jab at half-time. I got through the game, but two days after the Grand Final my hamstring was a purply-blue colour as a consequence.

I was told on the Friday that I was playing on David Rhys-Jones. He had been the match-winner in the second Semi-Final against us. Jeansy had left two gaps on the board when he put up his team: the wing and the interchange. I hadn't been named in either, and hadn't played well in the 1985 Grand Final, so I thought he might start me on the bench. Then he said, "Ayresy, you're going to play on the wing. You don't have to be fast, you can read the play. 'Rhys' was a match-winner last time, so we want you to negate his influence in the game." About four minutes in, Rhys's given me a gangster slap on the face and we were wrestling and carrying on. I gave him a little bop on the chin on the way down, but umpire Peter Cameron gave *me* a free kick for it! On that day we seemed like we had wonderful momentum. Gary Buckenara had a great game after having injured his patella tendon in the '83 Grand Final win, and tactically we did some things that upset Carlton. Rodney Eade went on to their key playmaker, Craig Bradley, and we had guys changing off and on the ball in the midfield. I thought we completely outplayed them in the first half, even first three quarters, and the game was won by then. So we were able to erase those bad memories from 1984-85.

How I played that day hadn't entered my mind immediately after the game. All I had focused on was doing something to help the team win after losing the previous two. Winning the Norm Smith Medal was the last thing on my mind. It's a bloody lonely place out on the MCG if you lose, watching the victors go up on the dais and receive their medals. You just want to dig a hole and bury yourself, and not reappear again until the start of next season. A lot of us contributed to the team cause in 1986, and that is always the most important thing in my mind. If I could have hopefully inspired my teammates to be able to do something that would get us near our best, that was always paramount in my mind.

THE NORM SMITH MEDAL

We had to play so many hard games leading into the 1987 Grand Final. We stuffed our chances by losing to Carlton in the second Semi-Final. Dunstall hurt his ankle, and after getting a few goals in front we completely lost our way, losing to the Blues by 15 points. Then we faced Melbourne in the Preliminary Final. The Demons were riding this tidal wave of emotion, having not made it this far since 1964's Premiership. The weather at Waverley could be fickle at the best of times, and that day we kicked into the breeze three out of the four quarters! Chris Mew got knocked out in what was a physically hard game. Then, who could have predicted that we would encounter 32-degree heat on Grand Final day? We stuffed up at the start: we had five in the centre square instead of four; Wayne Johnston then whacked 'Dipper'; Tucky copped one, too. Despite all that, we were still in the game at three-quarter time. But Carlton was fresher, overran us, and our workload just to get to the Grand Final, plus the heat, caught up with us in the last quarter. I think it was the only time I saw Tucky in a short-sleeved jumper!

Jeansy had an aneurism in his brain at the end of 1987, and Alan Joyce stepped in as coach for 1988. His mantra that year was that we were too soft in the '87 Grand Final, and we went from strength to strength as a team that year. Without a doubt, that was the best side I played in. We only lost three games for the season, and smashed Melbourne in the Grand Final.

Dermott, Dipper and myself were given a licence by Joycey to handle any aggressive acts Melbourne tried to dish out on us. On one occasion, Bucky was jostling with Earl Spalding, so I jumped in and gave Earl a couple around the facial region. Peter Schwab came over and said, "That's enough now!" As he said that, Jim Stynes came in and gave me a left hook to the cheekbone. I later said to Schwabby, "Gee, mate, thanks a lot for protecting me back there!" Not long after, I felt this unusual pain in my cheekbone and I knew it wasn't right. At quarter-time I told the physio and doctor that I couldn't open my mouth properly. They couldn't find an issue, but I knew something wasn't right. It was later diagnosed as a depressed fracture of the cheekbone. I was playing on adrenalin for the rest of that game, no doubt. I can certainly explode the myth that Jimmy was the gentleman everyone later thought he was! By the second quarter we had gained control, and that second half was a domination, really.

That was the most enjoyable half of footy I ever played. I remember back to 1983; we were 57 points up at half-time but I wasn't comfortable until the last quarter. In 1988 you could just sense that Melbourne wasn't coming back in the second half. Guys were kicking goals from everywhere, and we knew pretty early on that it was going to be our day. In the last quarter, we could really soak it all in and enjoy it. I was able to look around the grandstands and see so many happy Hawk supporters. Getting another Premiership win, and contributing in some way, was really exciting and really fulfilling.

I had a problem with my quad for much of the second half of 1989. Yabby (who was back as coach after recovering from illness) told me not to kick on my right leg at training, just save it for games. So I was kicking left foot *only* during the week. I was carrying it going into the finals, but had managed to come through each week and it felt okay going into the Grand Final. Just before three-quarter time, I gave a pass to Dunstall and I felt something tear; it was really sore to run and I couldn't accelerate at all. They took me into the rooms and jabbed me, but I could still feel the pain. Yabby told me at three-quarter time to sit on the bench and if he needed me he would call on me. Every time the phone rang I was shouting, "Get me on! Get me on!" Platten was alongside me as he had been knocked out, and we were getting pretty nervous because Geelong was coming and we were just doing enough to stay in front.

It was a brutal Grand Final. There were spot fires everywhere. Dermott Brereton had taken out Geelong's Mark Yeates in round six, when we fell 49 points behind Geelong at half-time but came back to win by eight points. So Yeates took out Dermott at the first bounce of the Grand Final. I just remember watching the ball come out of the centre and Gary Ablett got on the lead, took the mark and kicked the opening goal. I looked back towards the centre and noticed 'Dermie' down in the middle of the ground. After that start we played some unbelievable footy. At three-quarter time we were still six goals ahead, but Geelong had that man

Ablett, and what he did, particularly in the last quarter, was unbelievable. He was taking the ball from the boundary throw-in, snapping it over his shoulder; he single-handedly kept them in that game.

If it had been a draw, a number of us would have missed the replay. We had key injuries to Dipper (punctured lung), Dermott (ribs), Platten (concussion), myself, and Tucky had split the webbing in his hand. None of us would have played the next week. Fortunately, we held on and won. That was big. Jeansy had said to Joycey at the start of 1988: "You win '88 and I'll come back and we'll win again in 1989." It was Hawthorn's belief that we'd blown opportunities in 1984-85, and again in '87. Not only that, but every time we had won a Premiership—1961, '71, '76, '78, '83 and '86—we had failed to repeat the next year. So in '89 we were hellbent on winning back to back and becoming the first Hawthorn team to do it. It drove us throughout 1989.

To have played in every Grand Final from 1983 to 1989 is phenomenal, when you think about it. There was always external talk about getting sick of Hawthorn, but of course we loved it! We knew how good it was to play in Grand Finals, but we also knew how hard it was to keep getting back there. I played in 28 finals; that's a big part of your career in finals alone. I'm really proud of that, and feel fortunate to have been at Hawthorn during such a great era.

We were called too old and too slow by 1991. Joycey had taken over from Jeansy again and we won the night Grand Final, but some of us were getting older, including myself, Tucky, Dipper, Schwabby and John Kennedy jnr. We had some injuries as well, plus some young guys coming in, yet Alan was flogging us at training. It got to a point where we felt we needed to tell him that perhaps we should ease up on the training. We all knew our bodies and we knew how fit we were. We were in games, but were falling away late because we were just too buggered from overtraining. West Coast flogged us at Princes Park in round seven by 82 points, which was very unusual for us. Thankfully, Joycey listened to our conditioning coach, John Kilpatrick, and George Stone, our runner and an active member of match committee. From round 13, through to and including the Grand Final, we won 13 games and lost just once.

We lost to West Coast by 24 points, in Perth, in our third-last game. But it was the first time I felt that if we had to go back to Perth again we were a reasonable chance to beat them. And that permeated through the group. As it turned out, we played the Eagles in the Qualifying Final. We prepared really well and were supremely confident. Everyone played well that day, the kids included. By September we had a great balance between young and old, which carried us through to the Grand Final. The win over the Eagles in Perth was the catalyst.

My chin was the first thing we saw when we ran out for the 1991 Grand Final. Before the game, with Tucky and me captain and vice-captain respectively, the cheer squad told us that the banner was going to have pictures of our faces on it. We were told we had to run through my chin when we burst through it! So out we came, and there's my chin on the banner, and we made a beeline for that. The Eagles started off really well; we were a bit undisciplined. We roughed them up and did a few things we shouldn't have, and they put some early goals on the board. But late in that first quarter we started to take control and by half-time we were going okay. They had a crack in the third quarter, but we had the breeze in the last quarter and were able to run over them.

Of my five Premierships, the 1991 victory ranks right up there with the best of them. I turned 31 on Grand Final day, Tucky was 38, Chris Mew was 30, so it was probably our final chance to experience success. Before the game Joycey had said that if Jason and Dermott kicked 10 goals between them we'd win: they kicked exactly 10! But everyone was terrific that day for us. Dipper (33 years old by Grand Final day), Schwabby (31) and Kennedy (31) had all missed out on selection, so us older guys knew we were probably next out the door. It was terrific to win that year the way we did. We were able to prove everyone wrong.

It all comes to a screaming halt eventually. I was lucky, I had 15 years as a player then moved straight into coaching. Allan Jeans became my mentor after he finished as my coach. I wanted to play on in 1994, but it all became a bit messy. I had signed a new contract at the start of '93, which was for two years, at which time I knew I'd be ready to retire. I played 17 games in '93, but got dropped late in the year, despite being captain.

That was hard to take. Physically and mentally I was feeling okay. The club felt otherwise, and decided I was finished after '93. I got offered a couple of jobs as a playing-coach, and as I was living in the south-eastern suburbs I decided to accept the role at Frankston. I rang Yabby and asked for his opinion, and he said, "If I was you, laddie, I'd take the assistant coaching job at Geelong. That way, you can see if you really want to coach without having the added pressure of still being a player. If you make a mistake as a playing-coach, how do you go off at yourself like you would at another player?" It was great advice, even though I didn't want to retire from playing. As it turned out, 12 months later I was senior coach at Geelong, taking over from Malcolm Blight, at 34 years of age. That's how quickly it happened.

Coaching in a Grand Final is very different to playing in one. When you're a player, you become quite insular about your own preparation and thought process. You train to prepare yourself, albeit in a team environment, and match day is all about what *you're* doing pre-game and what *you* need to specifically do during the game as an individual in order to help the team. When I became coach, I then had that focus times 21! I needed to be sure that all our players were as prepared as they could be. Plus, you had the opposition, which for us in 1995 was Carlton, which had lost only two games all year. I knew we'd had a good preparation, but so had Carlton. I thought, entering the game, "Could this be a fairytale for the club?" given that the Cats had lost three Grand Finals in seven years and had not won a Premiership since 1963.

Deep-rooted scars that I had not even considered were permeating through the minds of the Geelong players. I was a rookie coach at 35, coaching against the great David Parkin, the master coach. Carlton got off to a terrific start; we got off to a terrible start. I couldn't get the match-ups right, and it felt like an avalanche that you had no way of getting out of the way of. I remember thinking later in the day, I wish there was a trapdoor at the back of the coach's box that I could sneak out of. You become quite helpless. I went down at three-quarter time and I felt that all bar one of our players looked transparent—I could see through them. They were shell-shocked. The only player that kept talking was

Grant Tanner, a young bloke in just his 34th game. Everyone else looked gone. That's when it hit me that they were stuffed, mentally. I knew then that we were not going to come back from there.

I took that loss really badly. For a month or so I felt so let down—not by the players, but by me. We didn't play well, and that's on me. Our good players didn't play well, while their opponents did. Carlton had a bloody good side that year, and outplayed us on the field and in the coach's box.

Gary Ablett didn't play well. We always wanted him up and about in the big games. Unfortunately, aside from the nine goals he kicked in the 1989 Grand Final, his Grand Final record wasn't great after that. But you had to take the good with the bad. The good was, he was a superstar and could do things that mere footballing mortals could not. But was he a team player when it mattered? Probably not. It's difficult to coach a player like that. Many a time there were things organised, such as training sessions, where he'd always get leeway because of his age and who he was and what he could do for the team on game day. So it was always a constant battle as coach to accept that he was treated differently. And it affected the side at times, some of the things he did. There were times where he could have been more team-oriented, and he wasn't. And that was difficult for some players to comprehend. But you had to look at the total package with Gary. As great as he was, he never got a Premiership, which speaks volumes.

Footy, I loved it. The best time of my life. I was at League level half my life, from 17 through to 33 as a player alone, and then coaching Geelong and Adelaide until I was 44. The people I met along the way, my teammates, supporters, administrators, it was a wonderful period in my life. Later, in my coaching at Port Melbourne since 2008, the passion and want to assist young people in realising their dreams has been a different challenge again. But I still love it.

If I could wish for two things, they would be: to have my father back, and to play footy again. Footy never leaves me. I love finals time as much today as I did back when I was playing. The weather fines up, you smell the cut grass of the oval, and you know there's a heck of a lot riding on

THE NORM SMITH MEDAL

each game. You can always find a spring in your step. I still get envious when I go to watch the AFL finals. You see guys getting their Premiership medals, and the Norm Smith Medal, then the Cup. It evokes memories of those euphoric feelings I felt whenever Hawthorn won a Premiership. You're king of the world in those moments—you really are.

——— Statistics ———

BORN: 28 September 1960
GAMES PLAYED (1978-93): 269
GOALS: 70
FINALS PLAYED: 28
FINALS GOALS: 2
GRAND FINALS: 8
PREMIERSHIPS: 1983, 1986, 1988, 1989, 1991
NORM SMITH MEDALS: 1986 (presented by Percy Beames) and 1988 (presented by Bruce Andrew)

— Norm Smith Voting —

(**JUDGES:** Peter Simunovich, Ted Whitten and Lou Richards)

1986 *The Age* votes: Ron Carter: 3 Rodney Eade, 2 Gary Ayres, 1 Gary Buckenara;
Patrick Smithers: 3 Eade, 2 Ayres, 1 Chris Langford;
Harvey Silver: 3 Eade, 2 Ayres, 1 Langford;
Leigh Matthews: 3 Eade, 2 Ayres, 1 Peter Schwab;
Martin Blake: 3 Eade, 2 Ayres, 1 Langford;
Martin Flanagan: 3 Eade, 2 Ayres, 1 Chris Mew;
Geoff Slattery: 3 Terry Wallace, 2 Eade, 1 Jason Dunstall;
Hugo Kelly: 3 Langford, 2 Eade, 1 Buckenara;
James Button: 3 Ayres, 2 Eade, 1 Buckenara.
TOTALS: Eade 24, Ayres 15, Langford 6, Buckenara 3, Dunstall 1, Schwab 1.

GARY AYRES

— Norm Smith Voting —

(JUDGES: Ted Whitten, Ross Oakley, Geoff Poulter, Graham Dawson and Malcolm Blight)

1988 *The Sun* votes: Peter Simunovich: 3 Gary Ayres, 2 John Platten, 1 Paul Abbott;
Daryl Timms: 3 Ayres, 2 Dermott Brereton, 1 Andy Collins;
Bruce Matthews: 3 Ayres, 2 Collins, 1 Robert DiPierdomenico;
Michael Stevens: 3 Ayres, 2 Brereton, 1 Platten;
Greg Baum: 3 Ayres, 2 Brereton, 1 Collins;
Michael Davis: 3 Ayres, 2 Brereton, 1 Collins.
TOTALS: Ayres 18, Brereton 8, Collins 5, Platten 3, DiPierdomenico 1, Abbott 1.

David Rhys-Jones

David Rhys-Jones is the most reported player in the game's history, charged 25 times during his 13-year career. When he wasn't sitting on the sidelines, he was an agile and flexible utility who could play forward, on a wing or in defence. He was a larrikin, too, who after 76 games at South Melbourne/Sydney (1980-84) joined Carlton, a club renowned for its players' off-field exploits as much as their on-field successes. After initially struggling to live up to expectations surrounding his lofty contract, Rhys-Jones blossomed under coach Robert Walls. He was a member of the Blues' losing 1986 Grand Final team, then in the 1987 decider was given the task of negating Hawthorn's dangerman, Dermott Brereton. Rhys-Jones's Norm Smith Medal performance included nine kicks, eight handballs and four marks, but more importantly he held Brereton goalless for the only time that season.

I played in the ruck as a kid. I could jump and used to get around the ground well. Certainly there were ruckmen taller than me, but due to my leap I was used in that position regularly during those junior years.

I grew up in a family of six. Peter is a year older than me, Susan a year younger, and Greg is six years younger. My parents, Emrys and Pat,

← **REVENGE** David Rhys-Jones and Carlton reversed their twin disappointments of 1986 with a resounding victory over Hawthorn in 1987, with Rhys-Jones dominating Hawthorn's great Dermott Brereton.

and my siblings all barracked for Carlton, but I went for Richmond. During the late 1960s and early '70s, my older brother wore No. 25 on his back (Alex Jesaulenko), and I'd have No. 4 on mine for Royce Hart. I hated Carlton when I was growing up, and we'd always get out in the backyard and give each other plenty. Living in the Oakleigh area, it was a very strong breeding ground for Richmond, so that and the influence of my mates were the reasons I was drawn towards the Tigers. I was always a bit of a rebel, though, so going against everyone else in the family seemed natural!

Dad played footy and cricket and was apparently pretty good. He was asked to train at South Melbourne because he grew up around Albert Park, near South's ground. It was pretty rough and ready back in those days around there. He was a Carlton supporter, though, so he knocked back South's offer. It was rather ironic that I started my career at South and then finished up at Carlton.

I played under-18s with Oakleigh Districts and won the medal for best player in the then Federal League (now Southern Football League). Barry White was coach; he later coached South Melbourne's under-19s. South had four recruiting areas, and I was in one of their zones. They ran a competition out at Waverley with players from the four zoned areas all competing in a round-robin format. I won the award for most promising player, plus $200, and attracted the attention of South's recruiters.

When I arrived at South Melbourne, coach Ian Stewart asked me where I played. I said, "In the ruck," and he replied, "You won't be playing in the ruck here. Where else can you play?" I said, "In form four of school footy I played on the wing once and did okay there." I regretted saying it after that, because he put me on the wing and I should have said I played in the centre! I didn't mind a smoke and a beer. But, having said that, I was fit enough to play on the wing, so I wasn't too bad. We did plenty of running out there.

It was all a bit of a whirlwind. I turned up to try out with the under-19s, trained just a couple of nights and then they had an internal senior practice match, which they asked me to play in. I did okay in that, then a couple of weeks later I was picked in a practice match against Collingwood at

Hastings. I played a couple of practice games against VFL clubs, then I played the first five games of the 1980 season in the reserves. I was doing okay and so they gave me an opportunity in the seniors.

On debut (round six, 1980) 'Stewie' told me I wouldn't get a run until half-time. When I came on, I kicked a couple of goals and had 19 disposals, and we won the game against Melbourne at the MCG [by 26 points]. Considering South wasn't very successful during that period, and the game was at the famous MCG, it was a memorable debut. Afterwards a bloke walked up to me and shook my hand. When he pulled his hand away there was a $50 note in my hand. I thought, "Gee, how long has *this* been going on?" It was fantastic! I was in the team, had proven I could play, but then in my fourth game [against Fitzroy] I broke my leg and missed the rest of the year.

I broke my femur, cracked it at the bottom. Initially they thought it was a knee problem. South didn't have a club doctor, couldn't afford one. The club put me on crutches after the game. It was at the Junction Oval, and at the after-match we were having a few drinks but I was experiencing some pain. My teammates all took off, and I was stuck there alone so a Fitzroy supporter ended up driving me home. The Carlton club doctor, Richard Ward, would come to South once or twice each week. I was meant to see Richard the next day, but he called and said he couldn't see me. By this time I'm sitting at home in agony, not knowing my leg was broken. I saw him on the Monday. They did some x-rays, and that was when they realised there was a crack in the femur. I was in plaster for eight weeks, but I returned the next season. Later I had a lot of knee trouble, and when I look back on it the rehab I did for my leg in 1980 wasn't the greatest. I probably spent too much time in the local Notting Hill Hotel while I was on crutches! But I returned the next pre-season and was right to go.

Ian Stewart was very supportive, gave me opportunities I probably wouldn't have got at other clubs. In fact, before the season started Ian told me I would go on to play 200 games. I didn't quite get there (182), but for the coach to show such faith in me from the start was tremendous for my confidence. He was one of those players who every supporter idolised—triple Brownlow medallist, dual Premiership player—but it was as a coach that I really admired him for the way he showed such faith in me. 'Stewie' seemed to like blokes who had a bit of devil in them, as well as good skills. He didn't really look at the battling types of player. He obviously saw something in me to give me such opportunities considering I was young and had an immature body.

I was a confident player. I always thought I could compete against anyone and do okay. I seldom doubted myself, and actually thought I should have been selected in the senior team the week before I was! I was getting pissed off that they weren't playing me in the seniors. But I'm sure that was due to my scrawny body.

The drama surrounding South going to Sydney was a distraction for the players. There were so many meetings we had to attend; the VFL would tell us things, the club, too, plus others were saying things. It split the club in half. For example, John Rantall was coaching the South Melbourne party, and Ricky Quade was coaching Sydney. It was a really weird situation in 1982. Plus, that first year in Sydney we flew up each second week to play but we still *lived* in Melbourne. That was a mistake because, for the Sydney people, they were seeing this Victorian team flying up each second week to play a game of football, then flying home again. The next year we moved up and made a more serious go of it. You can't compare it to the new clubs today, because back then the VFL was broke; they didn't have the money to invest into setting the Swans up like they have with the Greater Western Sydney Giants and Gold Coast Suns.

I was young and I swallowed the message we were told. We were a club with a small supporter base moving to the biggest city in Australia, where we would be the only VFL club in the city's market. We wouldn't be competing for sponsorship and membership dollars like we were in Melbourne, where 10 of the other 11 clubs were based. The biggest problem was that the Sydney media focused on rugby league, so we received minimal publicity. We had to generate our own, and I recall doing ads for Toohey's for basically no money, just to help the club out. Today's blokes would laugh at us with the money they make from marketing ventures. We just did it to help the club out… well, I did anyway! It was the days where you rolled up at the airport five minutes before your flight and walked straight on to the plane. You could smoke on the planes, too. Different times.

One of the biggest downsides to moving to Sydney was the lack of information on football. I would read every scrap I could find on the VFL, but we were limited in what was available. That impacted on your knowledge of opponents. We never had a training ground as such, because they wouldn't let us train on the Sydney Cricket Ground. There was an oval nearby that we trained on a little, but during cricket season it was always being used and if the match was at the SCG then that oval was used as a car park. Most days we had to ring the club about 3pm to learn where we would be training that night. One time we got there and the balls were all flat, so Bernie Evans had to throw them in his car and take them down to the local service station to pump them up.

We got paid whenever the club had money, which was generally when they received their dividend from the VFL, the February after the season. The club just didn't have the money, although I'm sure some of the higher profile guys would have received more consistent payments than the rest of us. I signed a three-year contract in 1983, the first time I had signed one. I was to be paid $20,000 in 1983, $30,000 in '84 and $40,000 in '85, which was good money for that time. I also worked in a sports store in Sydney for a while, then in a factory that made plastics and various products. That was full-time, and they would allow you the time off to get to training and play. I wasn't in love with Sydney in my first year up there, but it grew on me by the second year and I was actually quite settled by the end of 1984. So much so that in the third year I was intending to put down a deposit on a house.

At the end of 1984, the VFL stepped in and the club's leaders were gone. Greg Miller (recruiting officer) and Barry Lyons (general manager) were forced out, then Dean Moore (team manager) resigned. They cleared the decks because the club was going nowhere. In their place came Rod Olsson and Don Roach, but the players were a bit pissed off with what had taken place because we went up there in good faith alongside Greg,

THE NORM SMITH MEDAL

Barry, Dean and others. While we didn't always know when we were getting paid, we were all in it together, so it was disappointing when the sackings happened.

Rod and Don called a meeting. They said, "Every player who has a contract with the club that includes an increase next year won't be receiving it. Instead, you will be on the same money you were on in 1984." Afterwards, I said to them, "Are there any exceptions?" They said, "No, across the board, and if you don't like it, then see you later." I said, "Look, I've got a contract and I don't know you blokes from a bar of soap. How do I know I can trust you like I could trust the people we've just let go?" I told them I would turn up to training every day, and they would be paying me what my contract said I was owed.

My accountant had put my contract together for me in 1983. Unbeknown to me he had included a clause that gave me room to leave if the Swans weren't honouring it. The clause said that if I demanded my money after the season finished, and it wasn't paid in 30 days, then it became null and void. I sent them the letter, waited 30 days, and they paid me on the 34th day. The contract was therefore null and void as it was over the 30 days, so I became a free agent.

I had never played finals, and I told my accountant that I wanted to play for a team who played finals regularly. I got him to ring Carlton and Hawthorn. The Blues had the money, and so I made the move to Princes Park for 1985. We spoke with Ian Collins and Keith McKenzie in the morning, then I met with David Parkin that afternoon because I wanted to know whether the coach saw a place for me in his team. We met, everyone was in agreement, and I signed there and then. I wasn't expecting it to happen that quickly. I hadn't even told my then-wife, Donna! I had to make the awkward phone call to tell her we were moving back to Melbourne.

It was tough initially. After about 10 rounds I was regretting the move. I'd never been dropped before. I went to Carlton on the back of what was the highest transfer fee paid between clubs to that time ($135,000). The League was filthy about it. To them, it was the wealthy club robbing a poor club who couldn't afford to keep their player. But it was the League's fault for sacking the guys at Sydney in the first place. As a consequence they stung Carlton with a hefty fine. I remember in the media early days something was written on how I was costing the club $350,000 over three years. That made it sound like I was being paid around $120,000 per year. But they were actually lumping the clearance fee into that figure. It was bullshit, but that type of thing was doing the rounds, and there I was training with triple Premiership players who were on maybe half the money I was on. But that was the landscape then, too, don't forget. To bring in a player from another club during the mid-1980s was starting to cost clubs a lot more money. I knew that was the case, and I accepted it. But then I struggled for form early on. There were times, though, when I knew I was out on my own and nobody would kick it to me. That's just human nature, I suppose, whether it was jealousy or them thinking I needed to earn my stripes.

Parkin dropped me from the seniors, then there was an injury and I was recalled. It was one of the first Friday night games, against North Melbourne at the MCG. That night I thought, "Stuff it! I'll tackle my teammates if I have to tonight, I don't give a shit. My future is on the line." Fortunately, I did okay that night. I just went and got the ball myself. Out of that, I think I won a bit of respect from the playing group and things improved from there.

I knew I was getting well paid, so I wanted to repay Carlton's investment in me. But also, as sportspeople we have pride in our own performance. I didn't need anyone to tell me when I wasn't performing. I got booed countless times during my career. In fact, at Carlton early on, I remember getting up from the bottom of the pack, hearing boos, looking up and seeing Carlton people booing me.

It was easier for me the next year. The club recruited Stephen Kernahan, Craig Bradley, Peter Motley and Mark Naley from South Australia, Jon Dorotich from Western Australia, and my mate Bernie Evans from Sydney. So the focus was off me and on to them. It allowed me to just go out and play footy, and not worry about anything else.

I found the coaching change from Parkin to Robert Walls (after 1985) a refreshing experience. It allowed me to have a clean start after a poor first year. I'm sure Parkin was happy to see the back of me! There wasn't a lot of difference between the two coaches, both were school teachers. They would load us up with all their paperwork before and after games, but most of that stayed in the bottom of my bag. Halfway through the year, I would have to clean my bag out because of all the paper in there! Now, though, I wish I had kept those documents to look back over. But it all went in the bin, most of it unread. 'Parko' had his "In Retrospect" document, which was up to 10 pages long reviewing each game. You would scan through to see if your name was mentioned, then flip to the back where he rated each player's game. You knew if you saw a "poor" after your name you were likely to be running around in the reserves the next week.

'Wallsy' had different game-plans and tactics at kick-ins. After a team would kick a behind often we would take the ball the length of the field and score. That put pressure on the opposition to kick accurately, because they knew if they missed we'd have it down the other end just like that (clicks fingers); no team could combat our plans at kick-ins. He used it with Fitzroy when he coached there (1981-85), but he had more quality players at Carlton to really exploit it and destroy teams.

I enjoyed being flicked around the ground and learning new positions. I didn't go to the backline until 1987, after playing full-forward, forward pocket, wing, half-forward, all over the place. I would have played every position on the ground at some stage of my senior career, except for ruck and rover. I enjoyed the challenge.

We were an inexperienced team during '86 and '87. There was more experience in our reserves team than the seniors, with the likes of Wayne Harmes and Jim Buckley in there. We had a heap in the seniors who would not have played 50 VFL games by then. We played finals in 1985, but were knocked out by North in the Elimination Final (by 19 points). That's why the club went on an aggressive interstate recruiting program between seasons. The old Form Fours were being phased out and the draft coming in, but Carlton was still able to go out and buy players—probably the last time you could build a team via your cheque book, before the salary cap era began. Losing in '85 was disappointing, as was losing in

'86, but we had got there at least. Hawthorn was a much better team than us in '86, but during '87 we were able to peg them back a bit.

I was arguably best on the ground in the 1986 second Semi-Final. So, for the Grand Final, Hawthorn put Gary Ayres on me. I remember rubbing my hands together and thinking, this is perfect, because I'd played on him once before and kicked a few goals going forward. Gary liked to go for his marks, so I thought it would be a good match-up for me in the Grand Final. But Gary and Hawthorn were too good for us.

Gary won the Norm Smith Medal so I can't rate my performance too highly! It was one of those days—maybe it was the occasion—where I was running to where the ball wasn't, as Jack Dyer used to say. I've watched the replay a few times, and I notice little things that didn't go my way. Things like the bounce of the ball; little things that, had they gone in my favour it might have been a different story. But that happens in football. What it did do was make me bloody determined to get stuck into the pre-season and hopefully get another chance to get back there the next year.

We had some big motivational factors driving us in the 1987 Grand Final. Peter Motley was in a serious car accident (and never played again), Des English got leukemia and Bernie Evans got suspended for one week (for striking Hawthorn's Greg Dear in the second Semi-Final) and missed the Grand Final. I don't think anyone would have beaten us—we would have walked over hot coals to do it for the blokes who couldn't be out there with us. So, in comparison to 1986, it was a different feeling going into the '87 decider.

I found out I was playing on Dermott Brereton in the coach's room on the Thursday night after training. I walked in, looked at the board and saw my name was there at centre half-back opposed to Dermott. Everyone looked at me. I shrugged my shoulders, and that was it. Wallsy just said, "Rhys, you've got a big job." There wasn't much in the way of instruction. I spoke to Jon Dorotich about how he had played on him, but I always had confidence in my own ability and didn't think there was a player I played against that I couldn't match and beat. I probably played some of my best footy on those better players. It was generally when I came up against a third- or fourth-best player that I lowered my colours.

I didn't get uptight before games. I was usually in the trainer's room having a joke, mucking around to keep myself loose. But I was always conscious of not intruding on the players who were serious pre-game. I didn't want to distract them in their preparation, and they knew how I needed to prepare. I had my last smoke about 30 minutes before we ran out, so I was pretty relaxed in those minutes before you leave the rooms. I was always on edge and experienced the butterflies in the stomach, but it never consumed me like it might have others.

It was the only Grand Final where they didn't bounce the ball to start the game. Hawthorn had five in the middle (instead of the required four), and Wayne Johnston was outside the square for us but he knew Peter Schwab would follow him in. We took a bloke out of there, Johnno slipped in and they were caught off guard. So one of our tactics worked from the word go. I don't think umpire Ian Robinson was too happy, because he never got to bounce the ball! Johnno took the kick, but it should have gone to our ruckman, Justin Madden. It bamboozled everyone, no one knew what was going on other than Johnno. He was a great big-game player. He says he should have won a couple of Norm Smith Medals, but I might remind him that I was the first player to be given top votes off every judge. Someone told me that after the game.

We got off to a great start, yet the Hawks were in front at quarter-time. I couldn't believe it, as we had dominated the play. It just shows what a great team Hawthorn was. We knew we had to play 100 minutes to beat the Hawks because they would keep coming at us. They were without Jason Dunstall in that game, but they were one of those teams that never gave in. With Dunstall out, John Kennedy jnr stepped up and kicked three goals. That's the sort of side they were.

We had a young backline that day. I was the most experienced player there (25, 132 games)—Tom Alvin (25, 82), Stephen Silvagni (20, 45), Michael Kennedy (23, 28), Ian Aitken (20, 16) and Peter Dean (22, 75) were the others—so there was added responsibility on me as a senior player. But those guys were great to play alongside. Any time I was caught out of position, I knew 'Deany' or 'SOS' (Silvagni) would be there to come across and spoil.

I prided myself on my second and third efforts. I always had a good recovery, it was a key to my game. I could compete in the air then hit the ground and stay in the contest. Greg Miller identified that as a strength of mine before I went to South. He later told me it was one of the main reasons I was recruited to the club.

After half-time Dermie came out with yellow boots on and I thought, "Here we go, it'll be on now." But nothing happened, which was surprising. I expected him to try something because he had great pride in how he played, and I think he'd regret not doing something physical to change the momentum. I've watched a replay of the game back a couple of times since. What stood out was seeing Dermott alone at times, but they didn't get the ball to him. Now luck plays a part in that, and the pressure up the field helped me. It was just a really good team effort.

I didn't have a huge amount of possessions in the Grand Final. You have days where the ball follows you, then other days where you only get the ball 17 times and you've still done your job, which is what I did in 1987. Bobby Skilton was commentating for Channel Seven, and he said at the start, "Rhys-Jones is lining up on Brereton, that will suit Hawthorn," and I think that was the impression of most people when they first saw us together. So rather than trying to just play a great game myself, one of the most rewarding things about it was that I surprised a few people. I didn't get into any body-on-body stuff with Dermott because I knew that he would have been too strong for me, so I played off him and used my strengths on the ground to win the ball and get away from him.

Because it was a hot day, the final siren was a bloody relief. It was such a draining day. Then came the sense of satisfaction; of going out and achieving what you had dreamt of achieving for years, right back to when you were kicking a plastic footy around the backyard as a kid. It helped erase the disappointment of the year before, while winning the Norm Smith Medal was payback for having my opponent win it the year before. I was even.

THE NORM SMITH MEDAL

Dermott didn't have a great day, and I was fortunate to benefit. We didn't say much to each other—it was too hot to talk! I remember at the 15-minute mark of the last quarter, I was yelling instructions to our blokes and Dermott said, "What are you worried about? You've got it." It's funny, even though we led comfortably on the scoreboard (Carlton led by 16 points at three-quarter time) you never believed you'd won until the final siren. That was one of the only things we said to each other all day. Then, after the game when I was walking to my car, Dermott was sitting around a car with some mates, the boot open with an Esky inside it and they were sharing a few beers. So I went and joined them for a beer or two. He's a good bloke, Dermott, and a tough opponent.

If I didn't win the Norm Smith Medal, I'd just be that dickhead who got reported 25 times.[1] At least I can say I was a Norm Smith medallist and performed when it mattered. That sticks with you throughout your life. You pride yourself on playing good in big games, that's the test of all players.

Could I fight? Put it this way: I wouldn't have taken on Collingwood's Denis Banks or Darren Millane in the boxing ring! But I wasn't one to take a backwards step either. I'd put my hands up and do what I could, but there were certainly tougher blokes than me out there. Towards the end of my career, I did some boxing training and the guys there asked me to jump into the ring. But I found it hard enough to hit punching bags that couldn't swing back at me, let alone being in a ring with someone who could fight! I've got a healthy respect for anyone who does, because it's a tough sport.

You live and die by the mistakes you make. I was reported 25 times during my career, but a lot of those were retaliating. I was only found guilty 11 times from those 25 appearances. Yes, I *was* guilty 25 times, but only *found* guilty 11 times! The tribunal was different back then. You would all watch the vision of the incident in the room together, and they could see me retaliating to something somebody had done to me. Sometimes the chairman would say, "Well, what did you expect him to do? Just take it?" That got me off a few times.

---

[1] As of 2018, David Rhys-Jones remained the most reported player in VFL/AFL history. Of his 25 charges, Rhys-Jones was found guilty on 11 occasions and suspended for a total of 22 matches. Other players have received more total suspended matches throughout their careers (for example, Dermott Brereton received 39 games suspension from 17 charges, and Greg Williams 34 games from 19 charges), but none was cited as many times as Rhys-Jones.

Having since coached at North Launceston (1993-95) and Frankston (1996-98), I know how frustrating it would have been to coach a player like me. Sometimes you've got to take the good with the bad. I always thought of myself as a team player, always trying to help the team as best I could. In hindsight, I did some things that didn't help the team, but that wasn't the intention. I was a young, skinny kid playing against men, so I knew I couldn't take a backward step. I quickly got that reputation for being a dirty player, and soon enough coaches were sending players out specifically to get under my skin. They wouldn't get a kick, but neither would I. All we'd do is wrestle our way around the ground all day.

Wallsy said after 1987 that he wanted two Premierships in a row. But it's hard enough to win one. We almost got back there in '88, but we kicked against the wind three times in the Preliminary Final. Melbourne made the most of that advantage and won their way into the Grand Final.

The first VFL Grand Final I went to was 1986 because I was playing in it. I've only been to four in total. Aside from the two I played in, I also went to the 1990 Grand Final when our seconds were playing before the main game. I remember when the brawl started at quarter-time in the seniors between the Essendon and Collingwood players, I said to the blokes next to me, "I don't like the looks of this, Collingwood's going to win. I'm getting out of here, I don't want to be around when it happens." So, we left. And the last one I went to was 1993. I was coaching North Launceston at the time, but I flew over to watch the Blues lose to Essendon that day. I would have gone to 1995, Carlton's last Premiership, but I had just coached North Launy to a Premiership so I was still on the drink with the boys. If Carlton gets in another one I'll probably go along, but that could be a while off yet.

I have millions of regrets—too many to list. But you can't spend time dwelling on them. We all make mistakes, some make more than others. When I later coached, my motto was: "Do as I say, not as I do!" After I finished with Carlton in 1992, I played three more years with North Launy and one with Frankston, but my body was shot by then.

THE NORM SMITH MEDAL

If I could, I'd still be playing now. Peter Dean is still running around these days. I would be too, if I could. In 2017, Deany couldn't make it to our '87 reunion at Carlton because his team, Bullioh (in the Upper Murray League), were playing in the finals. Lucky bugger.

──── Statistics ────

BORN: 16 June 1962

GAMES PLAYED (1980-92): 182 (South Melbourne/Sydney 1980-84, 76 games; Carlton 1985-92, 106)

GOALS: 112 (South/Sydney 39 goals; Carlton 73)

FINALS PLAYED: 9

FINALS GOALS: 1

GRAND FINALS: 2

PREMIERSHIP: 1987

NORM SMITH MEDAL: 1987 (presented by John Beckwith)

DAVID RHYS-JONES

— Norm Smith Voting —

(**JUDGES:** Ted Whitten, Ross Oakley, Jim Main, Bill Jacobs and Tim Lane)

The Herald **votes:**
Geoff Poulter: 3 David Rhys-Jones, 2 Wayne Johnston, 1 Robert DiPierdomenico;
Michael Lovett: 3 Rhys-Jones, 2 Craig Bradley, 1 Justin Madden;
Geoff Slattery: 3 Johnston, 2 Rhys-Jones, 1 Madden;
Ron Reed: 3 Rhys-Jones, 2 Madden, 1 Johnston;
Rod Nicholson: 3 Rhys-Jones, 2 Madden, 1 DiPierdomenico;
Caroline Wilson: 3 Rhys-Jones, 2 Johnston, 1 Chris Langford;
Nick Place: 3 Rhys-Jones, 2 Johnston, 1 DiPierdomenico;
Richard Hinds: 3 Rhys-Jones, 2 Johnston, 1 DiPierdomenico;
Gerard Wright: 3 Rhys-Jones, 2 Mark Naley, 1 Johnston.

The Herald **TOTALS:** Rhys-Jones 26, Johnston 13, Madden 6, DiPierdomenico 4, Bradley 2, Naley 2, Langford 1.

Gary Ablett

Gary Ablett was a once-in-a-generation footballer who drew people to stadiums simply to watch him play. He was a nightmare for opponents, but also an enigma to his coaches, teammates and the media. According to author Garry Linnell, "Even those closest to him used to wonder just what, if anything, made him tick."[1] Ablett's superb performance in the 1989 Grand Final alone remains a part of football folklore: he kicked an equal Grand Final record nine goals against Hawthorn, almost single-handedly leading Geelong to victory. Alas, the Cats fell six points short and Ablett became just the second player to win the Norm Smith Medal in a losing team. Linnell claimed that Ablett "transformed the game" due to his "prodigious ability to do things others could not."[2] No player transcended the sport like Ablett during the late 1980s and early 1990s.

Ablett was born on 1 October 1961, in Drouin, 90km east of Melbourne, in Hawthorn's country recruiting zone. He was one of eight children, five boys and three girls, to parents Alf and Colleen: Lenny, Graham, Geoff, Kevin and Gary, Faye, Julie and Janice.

---

1   Garry Linnell, *Playing God: The Rise and Fall of Gary Ablett*, HarperCollins*Publishers*, 2003, p. 13.
2   *Playing God: The Rise and Fall of Gary Ablett*, p. 13.

← **SUPERSTAR** Gary Ablett almost won the 1989 Grand Final off his own boot, kicking nine goals, one equaling the record of Gordon Coventry, while putting on a display for the ages. It was not enough for the Cats, who lost by six points.

THE NORM SMITH MEDAL

Ablett explained that, "Being the youngest boy I learned how to run very early in life. We were a sporting family with all the boys playing football and the girls being handy at netball."[3] A young Ablett refined his goalkicking craft by kicking balls between trees and telephone poles across the road from his house.

Football was in the bloodlines. Alf Ablett once trained at Carlton, his younger brother, Ronnie, was a fine country footballer, and their cousin, Len, was a 1943 Premiership player for Richmond (1939-43, 70 games). Gary's oldest brother, Lenny, was "a hard, strong player whose firm grip rarely saw him drop a mark."[4] He was invited to train with Geelong, but soon returned home to assist his father in the family's transport business. Graham was tough and imposing but, having been invited to train with Hawthorn, he injured his knee early on and never played a senior game.[5] Geoff and Kevin were both speedsters, while Gary was all of the above, and more.

Geoff played for Hawthorn (1973-82, 202 games, including the 1976 and '78 Premierships), Richmond (1983-84, 16 games) and St Kilda (1985, 11 games), and won the Grand Final sprint three years in a row. Kevin, too, played for the Hawks (1977-80, 31 games) and Tigers (1984, five games), as well as Geelong (1985, two games), but many of his former Hawthorn teammates believe he failed to reach his full potential. Kevin's son Luke (2002-09, 133 games) later played in Sydney's drought-breaking 2005 Premiership side and the losing 2006 Grand Final team. Gary's sons, Gary junior (discussed later in this chapter) and Nathan (2005-07, 32 games) were members of Geelong's drought-breaking 2007 Premiership side, with Gary junior winning a second Grand Final in 2009. Two of Faye's children (with Michael Tuck), Shane (Richmond 2004-13, 174 games) and Travis (Hawthorn 2007-09, 20 games) also played senior footy. As football families go, the Abletts have been one of the finest.

Kevin Ablett remembered seeing Gary play well in an under-14s match for the Nyah school team, despite being only nine years old. "He got a kick on his wrong side (left foot) and screwed it back over his head for a

---

3   Jon Anderson (ed.), *Icons of Australian Sport: Gary Ablett*, HyperActive, 2007, p. 261.
4   *Playing God*, pp. 43-44.
5   Ken Piesse, *Ablett: The Gary Ablett Story*, Wilkinson Books, 1994, p. 10.

goal," Kevin said. "I'd never seen a kid of that age do that before or since and I guess I knew then he was going to became an AFL footballer."[6]

Gary won Drouin's under-12s and under-14s best and fairest awards in 1971 and 1973 respectively. His hero was Hawthorn's 1971 Premiership rover Leigh Matthews.[7] "I was amazed how hard he could hit the packs and come out the other side with the ball," Ablett said. When playing football in the street, Ablett emulated Matthews' heroics. For all Matthews' strengths—and there were plenty—he was not noted for his high marking. This ability, even from a young age, set Ablett apart. Alan Courtney encountered Ablett in a 1974 match between the Koo Wee Rup and Drouin thirds, and one mark remained vivid in his memory some 20 years later:

> I positioned myself against my opponent, ready to take a mark. Suddenly I felt a football boot on either shoulder... My eyes looked above me to see this figure standing in the air and in the next second he had landed as softly as a falling feather on the ground. He then booted the ball 60-odd yards out of the ground. He jogged back to the centre, hunched in the shoulders but very powerful in the thighs and extremely athletic. Even though I was just 11, I knew I had witnessed something special.[8]

Any sport Ablett played, he excelled at. Whether football, athletics, cricket (he scored 100 for Drouin's A-grade team when filling in), hunting (it is claimed he once caught a rabbit with his hands and could "drop" a wild pig with a bullet due to his steady aim and sharp eye),[9] or even walking, he was a standout (he won a Bronze Medal in an under-9 walking race at the state championships). "Some mornings I didn't want to go to Little Aths but Mum made me and I'm glad she did," Ablett said.[10]

As had been the case with two other champion high-flying forwards,

---

6   Kevin Ablett, *Icons of Australian Sport*, p. 23.
7   Matthews (1969-85, 332 games and 915 goals) played in three more Hawthorn Premierships: 1976, 1978 and 1983. He also won eight best and fairest awards (1971-72, 1974, 1976-78, 1980, 1982). Just as with Ablett, many claim that Matthews is the game's greatest ever player.
8   *Herald Sun*, 20 April 1994, p. 99.
9   *Playing God*, p. 18.
10 *Icons of Australian Sport*, p. 15.

Essendon's John Coleman and Carlton and St Kilda's Alex Jesaulenko, Ablett credited the high-jump as helping him improve his marking. "It taught me approach, timing and spring," he said.[11] Ablett's mother had been a fine sprinter at school, setting a number of records; some who saw her run believe that had she received the right coaching, she may well have represented Australia at the Olympic Games.[12] She was also a "natural" footballer, in a time before women had the opportunity to play the sport at the highest level.[13]

Despite her youngest son also being a gifted athlete, Gary gave those other sports away around the age of 15 to concentrate on football. It coincided with a period in his life where he lacked male discipline and direction. His father was regularly absent due to work commitments and Ablett conceded he was "a bit rebellious" as a teenager, in "a family that was a little dysfunctional."[14] This lack of a father figure in his life led to some poor choices; while his physicality was not always channeled in the right way, Ablett's opponents would later say that his strength and balance were keys to his game.

Sport was Ablett's sanctuary, an aspect of his life where he could focus his attention towards something positive. At 16 he played in Drouin's 1978 West Gippsland Football League Premiership team, which defeated Cora Lynn to break an 11-year drought. The following year he won the club's senior best and fairest award. However, in an early sign of what was to come at VFL level, Ablett's attendance at Drouin training was sporadic. Teammate George Budge said that whenever Ablett chose to turn up for games, "we'd all say, 'thank Christ he's here.'"[15]

Ablett's will to win—at any sport—was clear to see. His competitiveness was "what everyone loved about him," Linnell wrote; that and "his unique skills."[16] Ablett could kick goals from any angle, on either foot, something he said he was "grateful to my father for" teaching him. Indeed, Ablett recalled that, from the age of five, Alf "insisted I learn to use both sides of my body."[17] Ablett later taught his own sons the same lesson.

---

11 *Icons of Australian Sport*, p. 15
12 *Playing God*, p. 42.
13 *The Gary Ablett Story*, p. 11.
14 *Icons of Australian Sport*, p. 18.
15 *The Gary Ablett Story*, p. 17.
16 *Playing God*, p. 57.
17 *Playing God*, p. 57.

Ablett first trained with Hawthorn in 1977, as a 15-year-old. He then played three reserves games in 1978, before returning to Drouin. There were another six reserves matches in 1980, but his reluctance to train with the club, or settle in Melbourne, saw him repeatedly return home. During that period, the Hawks went above and beyond in their endeavours to entice Ablett to commit to the club. Hawthorn's former football manager, Tony Farrugia, explained that he would arrive at the Ablett home in Drouin and ask of Gary's whereabouts, only to be told he had gone fishing:

> His parents were very protective of him. We always had trouble getting him to the post. There was never any question of the talent he had. Everyone knew he had more ability in his little finger than most. But football wasn't a big priority in his life.[18]

Although Hawthorn's champion ruck-rover, Michael Tuck, was married to Ablett's sister, Faye, he preferred to stay removed from any attempts to force Ablett to commit. In all, Ablett made just six senior appearances on the wing for the Hawks, all in 1982, the best of which was a 23-disposal performance in round three against Footscray, when he also kicked 2.5. At season's end Ablett walked out on Hawthorn for good:

> I was getting side-tracked living in Drouin. I was keeping [the] wrong company and I started getting into trouble with the law. I knew the only way to move forward was to get out of Melbourne, so I contacted Dad's cousin Len Ablett in Myrtleford to see if I could move up there for a year and play.[19]

Geoff Ablett later defended his brother's decision to leave Hawthorn, saying that "the city can be a lonely place for a youngster coming from the bush."[20] He described Gary as "a lost soul" at Hawthorn who was "better off in the country lifestyle that he loves."[21] On his disjointed years with

---

18 *The Gary Ablett Story*, p. 35.
19 *Icons of Australian Sport*, p. 50.
20 *The Gary Ablett Story*, p. 43.
21 *The Gary Ablett Story*, p. 43

Hawthorn, Gary later conceded, "I wish I had been more committed."[22]

Free from the distractions of Drouin and the all-encompassing environment of Melbourne, Ablett was a star in 1983 with the Ovens & Murray League's Myrtleford Saints, who narrowly lost the Preliminary Final. Having regained his love for football, a rejuvenated Ablett was receptive to giving the VFL another go. "I could have gone to a Melbourne club but Geelong suited me," he said.[23]

The Cats pursued Ablett on the recommendation of recruiter and 1951-52 Premiership ruckman Bill McMaster. Geelong's coach, Tom Hafey, recalled McMaster telling him during 1983: "I've just seen the best country footballer I've ever seen. You could put him in the centre tomorrow against Collingwood and be confident he would be best on ground."[24]

When new teammate Andrew Bews first saw Ablett at the start of 1984, he thought, "How lazy is this bloke? He won't make a good footballer!"[25] Bews felt Ablett was "nonchalant and didn't talk to anyone."[26] For Hafey, a noted fitness fanatic during his previous stints coaching Richmond (1966-76, four Premierships) and Collingwood (1977-1982), Ablett's less-than-ideal training standards were cause for concern. That was until the games started.

> He wasn't a great trainer but as soon as the games began Gary was something else. Most of his talents seemed natural, such as his speed and strength. He didn't do a lot of weights yet he had that power... I've never declared one player the best I've seen and never will, but for pure natural ability, Gary is right there.[27]

Geelong's captain, Michael Turner, was soon impressed with Ablett's potential after being paired with the newcomer in end-to-end contesting work. "I was always pretty confident that I could hold my own when it came to jumping high," Turner said. "Well, Gaz was my partner in one of those early sessions and we contested for a mark about 25 times and the

---

22 *Icons of Australian Sport*, p. 45.
23 *Icons of Australian Sport*, p. 71.
24 Tom Hafey, *Icons of Australian Sport*, p. 59.
25 John Murray, *We Are Geelong: The Story of the Geelong Football Club since 1859*, Slattery Media Group, 2009, p. 212.
26 *We Are Geelong*, p. 212.
27 *Icons of Australian Sport*, p. 59.

only time I beat him was when he fumbled one."[28]

Former Geelong Premiership player and coach Bill Goggin (1958-71, 248 games) remembered that, as had been the case with Hawthorn, the Cats realised they would need to put extra time and effort into helping Ablett to settle in, although some felt he was going to be "too hard to handle."[29] They enlisted Barry Fowler "to look after him all the time."[30] Fowler said he helped Ablett "get into a relaxed frame of mind," recognising that he was "the sort of fella you had to program a week ahead to [get to] do something."[31]

Ablett's arrival coincided with that of another potential champion in Greg Williams. Both were trialled in the centre, opposed to each other, in an intraclub practice game at the start of 1984. In one game, Ablett kicked eight goals in the first three quarters, before the club recognised they needed to hide him from the prying eyes of opposing club scouts and the media. On another occasion, Ablett outplayed highly publicised interstate recruit and former captain Brian Peake (1981-84, 66 games), and afterwards McMaster announced that Ablett "could be the greatest player of all time."[32] That McMaster had played against Coleman, among other champions, added weight to his argument.

After a dispute that eventually saw Geelong pay Hawthorn $60,000 and Myrtleford $5000 to obtain Ablett's clearance, his first game for the club showed everyone that the effort, and the dollars, were worth it.[33] Ablett had 22 disposals and kicked three goals in round one, against Fitzroy at Kardinia Park, while Williams had 38 disposals and kicked a goal. Ablett was also reported by three umpires for striking Garry Wilson, which cost him a three-match suspension. It was quite the debut! By season's end Ablett had won Geelong's best and fairest award, although with Williams having injured his knee in round 12 and missing the rest of the year, the Cats missed the finals.

Playing as a wingman in year one with the Cats, Ablett had played 15 games and kicked 33 goals, with two bags of five. On being crowned best and fairest, he later said: "I didn't appreciate the significance of it

---

28 Michael Turner, *We Are Geelong*, p. 211.
29 *The Gary Ablett Story*, p. 61.
30 *The Gary Ablett Story*, p. 61.
31 *The Gary Ablett Story*, p. 61.
32 *Playing God*, p. 154.
33 *The Gary Ablett Story*, pp. 64-65.

because I didn't know how hard it was to win one."[34] Remarkably, given his achievements, it was to be Ablett's only best player award in his 14-season, 248-game VFL/AFL career.

Ablett also represented Victoria (coached by his former Hawthorn coach Allan Jeans) in a State of Origin clash with Western Australia, at Subiaco. Playing predominantly at half-forward, Ablett kicked eight goals in a four-point loss. Victorian teammate Gerard Healy remembers it being the first time he recognised Ablett's ability to influence games. "I was in the forward pocket and Ablett kept bombing these balls so far over my head I got a sore neck!" Healy said. "That game was really his announcement to the footy world, and he went on to have an amazing career of power, of performance; he was the strongest, most dynamic player, and a brilliant mark."

Geelong missed the finals in each of Hafey's three seasons (1983-85), and he was replaced by John Devine. Ablett said of Devine's three seasons in charge (1986-88), "We had our differences but I now understand where he was coming from." Ablett found Devine to be "a very intense coach" where it was "very much his way or not at all," an approach that Ablett admits he "didn't respond to."[35] Their differences of opinion led to Ablett considering returning to the Hawks. "At the end of 1987 when John and I were fighting I thought about leaving and Hawthorn offered me over $100,000, while Geelong was around $70,000, but John and I worked things out."[36]

It was the arrival of Devine's replacement, Malcolm Blight, at the end of 1988, that skyrocketed Ablett to superstardom. But not before Blight employed some mind games of his own to convince the inconsistent trainer to prove he was committed to the cause. "Before I got to Geelong, I'd heard his training regime left a little bit to be desired, and sure enough he started doing it to me," said Blight. He arranged to meet Ablett at the Balyang Sanctuary, a popular picnic park in Geelong, and employed a little folk medicine on his charge: "There was a little bridge and I said you can either cross the bridge with me or go home and forget about footy. He crossed the bridge with me, went home and got his training gear and

---

34   *Icons of Australian Sport*, p. 67.
35   *Icons of Australian Sport*, p. 88.
36   *Icons of Australian Sport*, p. 90.

trained."[37] Blight won that day, but Ablett was not always as cooperative.

The Cats won 16 of 22 games in the 1989 home and away rounds, finishing third. Ablett kicked 60 goals, including 14 against Richmond in round nine. He then kicked three in the losing Qualifying Final against Essendon. What happened from then on changed Ablett's life, and took Geelong within a whisker of the Premiership. Teammate and 1989 Brownlow medallist, the late Paul Couch told *Icons of Australian Sport*: "I don't care how good Ted Whitten, Leigh Matthews, Wayne Carey and anyone else was, none of them got anywhere near the level of Gary in the last three finals of that series."[38]

Against Melbourne in the first Semi-Final, Ablett kicked 7.7 on a wet MCG in his team's 63-point victory. Couch deems Ablett's performance "extraordinary, given how wet the ground and day was."[39] However, that was only a precursor to Ablett's Preliminary Final effort, against Essendon at Waverley, a game Couch said was "the best individual performance I've seen, or ever will see."[40] Ablett kicked 8.5 in Geelong's 94-point belting of the Bombers. "Many will remember that baulk around Paul Hamilton on the members' boundary before he booted a 50m goal," Couch said. "What they don't know is he actually practised that move against me in the bus on the way up to the game!"[41]

As Geelong prepared for its first Grand Final appearance since 1967, Hawthorn was attempting to win back-to-back Premierships for the first time. Jeans decided to pit 23-year-old defender Scott Maginness one-out against Ablett. "I'd never played on Gary before," Maginness said:

> It was usually Chris Langford or Gary Ayres who got the job on Gary. I played on [Melbourne's] Garry Lyon in the 1988 Grand Final, and I think I did reasonably well on him that day. Allan Jeans's thinking was, if I could nullify Gary it would allow Langford and Ayres to play more attacking roles. They could give us a bit more drive if I could hold Ablett to two or three goals. It was an enormous task, though.

---

37 Malcolm Blight, *We Are Geelong*, p. 212.
38 Paul Couch, *Icons of Australian Sport*, p. 93.
39 Paul Couch, *Icons of Australian Sport*, p. 93.
40 Paul Couch, *Icons of Australian Sport*, p. 93.
41 Paul Couch, *Icons of Australian Sport*, p. 93.

There were no pre-game instructions from coach to defender on how to tackle Ablett's strengths. "That was either naïve by them, or they had some real confidence in me to nullify him. I'm tipping it was the former rather than the latter!" Maginness joked. "I walked towards him thinking that if the supply to him wasn't as good as it could be, or what it had been during the finals, it would make my job a lot easier." Ablett later said Maginness "probably wasn't the right match-up for me from a strength point of view," adding that he "enjoyed the challenge of playing on Chris Langford," a "good solid backman."[42]

In one of the most dramatic openings in Grand Final history, at the first bounce Geelong's Mark Yeates charged at Hawk centre half-forward Dermott Brereton and crashed into him, breaking his ribs. The Cats won the clearance and sent the ball forward where Ablett marked and kicked the first goal inside 30 seconds. "I thought to myself: 'God, this is not the start I wanted,'" Maginness said. "There was chaos in that first 30 seconds. Dermott was on the ground, people were running everywhere and you sensed a bit of panic setting in." The young defender realised "we were in for a really tough day." Ablett soon cannoned into Ayres, then Robert DiPierdomenico, intent on destruction.

Brereton refused to leave the field after Yeates's hit, instead heading to the forward pocket to recover. In Ablett's mind, the decision not to send Yeates on to Brereton was "the biggest mistake Blighty made" that day.[43] Brereton kicked an inspiring goal for his side a few minutes later, as the Hawks recovered from their early shock to open up a 40-point lead at quarter-time. Ablett had failed to add to his opening goal and Maginness was feeling confident heading into the second term. "I went to quarter-time thinking: 'If I can keep him to four goals, that will be good.' Aside from that goal he really hadn't done much else—other than break Robert Dipierdomenico's ribs and clean up Ayresy."

What 'Dipper' did not realise was that Ablett had not only broken his ribs, he had also punctured a lung. That he played out the game was remarkable and inspiring. Of the hit, Dipper recalled: "Ablett's behind me, telling me what he's going to do: 'I'm coming to get you, big fella!'

---

42   Paul Couch, *Icons of Australian Sport*, p. 117.
43   Paul Couch, *Icons of Australian Sport*, p. 108.

I could feel him, I could hear him. I did hear my ribs break, and adrenalin takes you to places that people don't know they can get to. My body was changing; my body was inflating, [and] my voice was really high."[44] Ablett later conceded he would "get some weeks for that now," adding of those ferocious bumps on players blocking his space:

> I used to say to them, hey listen, I'm territorial and I'm not just going to let you do that. It's going to cost ya! That's why there were several times in my career when I was charged for that. I'll tell you, you might do it four or five times only. But it sends a message to a lot of players who won't try it. What amazes me is how did he play the game out with two broken ribs and a punctured lung?[45]

Early in the second quarter, Maginness, playing Ablett from behind, effected a spoil as he continued to keep the dangerman under control. "The ball came down, a contest, and I was holding on and I really retarded his run," Maginness said. "And he turned around to me and he said: 'If you do that one more time, I'm going to knock you out.' And I said, 'Gary, that wouldn't be a godly thing to do, would it?' And I still don't know whether he said, 'I'm not God' or 'I am God!' Needless to say, I continued to hold on as much as I could for fear of getting knocked out."[46]

Shortly after, Bews sent the ball forward and the strength of Ablett won out: he plucked a one-handed mark in the forward pocket and kicked a brilliant check-side goal. At 10 minutes, Ablett proved too quick for Maginness, marking on the lead and slotting a 35-metre goal. "Geelong just looked for him every single time they went forward," Maginness said. "That was their main avenue to goal, and so even if you were right near him they would kick it to him one on one and back Gary in every time. That then put pressure on me."

A minute later, at a boundary throw-in in Geelong's forward pocket, Maginness was alongside Ablett on the outskirts of the stoppage when, in a split second, Ablett burst away, leapt above the two ruckmen and

---

44   *The Final Story: 1989* DVD.
45   *Icons of Australian Sport*, p. 110.
46   Scott Maginness, *The Final Story: 1989* DVD.

plucked the ball from the air, landed and snapped a miraculous goal. "I didn't envisage him doing that!" Maginness said:

> He was edging forward and I was wondering why he was getting so close to the contest rather than pulling himself back. You're thinking about that, then, all of a sudden, he goes up, grabs it and snaps a goal. I thought to myself: "Ah, that's why he did it!"

The Cats trailed by 29 points and Jeans switched Langford on to Ablett. "The runner came out after Gary's fourth goal, and he just did a switch motion with his fingers," Maginness recalled. "From a team perspective, I admit I was relieved, because I felt that 'Langers' was better suited to him than I was." Langford got a reprieve soon after when Ablett dropped a mark he should have taken, just 15 metres from goal. Ablett was Geelong's best player in the second quarter, yet for all his heroics the Cats trailed by 37 points at the half.

In the third quarter, Ablett claimed another scalp when he crashed into Andy Collins. Maginness was back in the frame at seven minutes when Ablett outmarked him again; his fifth goal for the day cut the margin to 30 points. Then he cleaned up Ayres—again—as the zone around Ablett became ground zero for Hawthorn defenders. With five minutes remaining in the quarter, Ablett marked over John Kennedy and kicked his sixth goal. He almost snapped another with two minutes remaining, but his kick just missed. For all their efforts, however, the Cats had failed to narrow the lead. Hawthorn went to the final break leading by 36 points and the game appeared over. Ayres, who had left the field injured during the quarter, remembered "we were six goals ahead, but Geelong had that man Ablett, and what he did, particularly in the last quarter, was unbelievable—he single-handedly kept them in that game."

Many of Hawthorn's players were either injured or out on their feet by the final quarter, and, as a consequence, Geelong charged home. After two fine spoils by Langford in the opening minutes, Ablett found Robert Scott, who in turn passed to Neville Bruns, and his goal cut the margin to 29 points. With 17 minutes left, Ablett goaled from a mark 30 metres out for his seventh goal to reduce the margin to 21 points. A female streaker ran across the field, but so intense was the final quarter that hardly anyone noticed.

With 10 minutes left, Langford had hold of Ablett's right arm, yet the Cat was able to control the arriving ball with his left hand, break free of his opponent and snap a brilliant left-foot goal. Number eight brought his side to within 17 points. Six minutes after that, Bruns sent the ball high to the goal square where Ablett marked from behind Langford and kicked his ninth, equalling Collingwood's Gordon Coventry (1928) for the most scored in a Grand Final. It was 11 points the difference. He had kicked four on Maginness and now five on Langford.

When David Cameron goaled with 36 seconds remaining, the margin was six points. Remarkably, it was DiPierdomenico's courage in the centre that saved the game for the Hawks: he threw himself on the ball to force a stoppage, the clock ticked down and the siren beat the Cats. Dipper then headed off the ground and straight to hospital. The iconic photograph of a dejected Ablett and an elated Langford at the moment the siren sounded summed up one of the most amazing Grand Finals the game had ever seen: Hawthorn 21.18 (144) to Geelong 21.12 (138). Had the match been drawn, both sides would have been forced to make multiple changes for the replay.

Ablett had recorded 12 kicks, three handballs, eight marks, three tackles and kicked 9.1. He became the second player, behind Richmond's Maurice Rioli in 1982, to win the Norm Smith Medal in a losing side, and in his acceptance speech, the born-again Christian thanked God for making it possible. "I was completely deflated," he said later. "The effort that went into that game had left me shattered. It was a long year and we had to do it the hard way while they had a rest. To put in so much and get so close was heart-breaking."[47] He described winning the Norm Smith as a "great honour". But, he added, "that was undermined by the huge disappointment of getting so close."[48]

Maginness said Ablett's performance was "pretty phenomenal" and

---

47 *Icons of Australian Sport*, p. 114.
48 *Icons of Australian Sport*, p. 117.

his nine goals would stand "for a very long time".[49] Blight marvelled at how his mercurial forward "changed games, consistently—more than any other player I've ever seen."[50]

Ablett believes the fallout of his 1989 achievements led to him "suffering from depression very badly" by 1991. He admitted to "crying before games", finding the expectation on him after "becoming the yardstick" too great to handle. He contemplated suicide. "I got to a point where I couldn't keep on going the way I was," he said.[51] Sensationally, he retired before the 1991 season. "A lot of people think football is everything in life but there are so many more important things," Ablett explained in *Icons of Australian Sport*. "I felt under so much pressure to perform and that just magnified everything… People don't know that, they just see this star. They see the façade, not the real person. The invasion of privacy, the pressure, I wasn't coping and didn't know what else to do."[52]

Blight was shocked when Ablett told him he was retiring. "The club did everything possible to talk him around but for me there were two sobering points—we did OK without him in the first part of the [1991] season and he was still on our list if he wanted to come back."[53]

Ablett said that the break away from the game "gave me some breathing space and time to process things. I got to a point where I could lay down a strategy despite the depression and still play football with the hope of eventually overcoming it."[54] He returned to the senior side in round 13, as the Cats went as far as the Elimination Final. The next year, 1992, they returned to the Grand Final. During the season Blight had convinced Ablett to spend more time at full-forward, rather than up the ground, and he scored 72 goals, although the Cats lost to West Coast in the Grand Final by 28 points—the first time a non-Victorian club had won a Premiership. Ablett kicked 3.1, but Ashley McIntosh was able to contain him from causing a 1989-style spree. Blight said Ablett was reluctant to go to full-forward at first "because he still thought he could play on the

---

49 After Coventry and Ablett's nine goal efforts, only Dermott Brereton has kicked eight goals in a Grand Final (1985), while 11 players have kicked seven goals: Coventry (1930), Norm Smith (Melbourne, 1940), Tom Reynolds (Essendon, 1943), Dick Harris (Richmond, 1943), Gordon Lane (Essendon, 1946), Jack Collins (Footscray, 1954), Ted Fordham (Essendon, 1965), Alex Jesaulenko (Carlton, 1972), Kevin Bartlett (Richmond, 1980), Jason Dunstall (Hawthorn, 1988) and Stephen Kernahan (Carlton, 1993).
50 Malcolm Blight, *The Final Story: 1989*.
51 *Icons of Australian Sport*, p. 122.
52 *Icons of Australian Sport*, p. 124.
53 *We Are Geelong*, p. 213.
54 *Icons of Australian Sport*, p. 126.

wing and half-forward."[55]

In 1993, Blight's theory that Ablett, with his speed off the mark, strength in a contest, exceptional leap and accurate kicking could dominate at full-forward proved correct. "I had to learn how to lead from the goal square," Ablett said. "Malcolm helped me because I wasn't a full-forward's backside but I did learn quick."[56] Indeed he did. Ablett kicked 124 goals and 60 behinds in just 17 games—the club's first centurion since Larry Donohue in 1976—yet Geelong missed the finals by percentage. So Ablett-focused was the team when attacking that he kicked 36 per cent of its entire score in 1993, the most by a Cat since Doug Wade (41 per cent) in 1969. In round six against Essendon, Ablett kicked 14.7 and Bomber full-forward Paul Salmon kicked 10.6, in one of the greatest games of all time. Was it his greatest game? Ablett thought not:

> Funnily enough it's not one of the games I rate in the best. Maybe it was the style of the game, maybe because I was at full-forward. I never enjoyed playing at full-forward when I played well as much as I did when up the ground because of the freedom, taking a bounce and kicking a goal. That's what really excited me.[57]

For all his dominance that year, including winning the first of three consecutive Coleman Medals, Ablett still rated 1989 his best year of football:

> I felt 1989 was my best year and the year I enjoyed most because I was up the ground… It annoys me when people class me as a full-forward because I wasn't. People compare me to full-forwards yet I only played the last four years of my career there. I was a winger and a half-forward flanker who loved to use my pace and have a run and a bounce… The only reason I became a full-forward is because I couldn't run all day anymore and by moving there it prolonged my career.[58]

---

55 *We Are Geelong*, p. 213.
56 *Icons of Australian Sport*, p. 137.
57 *Icons of Australian Sport*, p. 140.
58 *Icons of Australian Sport*, p. 106.

During the early 1990s, 3AW radio commentator Rex Hunt became synonymous for his calling of Ablett's exploits. It was in 1989 that Hunt first screamed his famous "Yeeablett!" line:

> It was down at Geelong and, don't ask me why, but my mind went racing back to an old black and white film I had seen at the Mentone Theatre on comedians Bud Abbott and Lou Costello. They were flying upside down in an old Tiger Moth plane, and Costello yelled out: "Abbott!" So, I decided to do that with Gary this day, and my co-commentator, Bill Jacobs, nearly jumped out of the commentary box when I yelled "Yeeablett!" All of a sudden the crowd started getting on to it and it just grew from there.

Hunt would "get the fixture every year and highlight in Texta" when he was scheduled to call Geelong games. "He got to such heights that I called him 'The Pontiff', because the Pontiff (the head of the Catholic church) couldn't possibly do what he could do," Hunt said. "What Gary did was, he allowed me not just to commentate or describe the play, he instead allowed me to *broadcast*, which very few players ever did." Hunt conceded that he was in "total awe" of Ablett's play, and was often caught watching his heroics rather than concentrating on the play around him. "Ablett had so much going for him that it became frustrating to see superior athletes left in his wake," Hunt added.

Ablett kicked 129.79 in 1994. In round eight, against Sydney, he kicked the third 14-goal haul of his career. The week before, at the MCG against Collingwood's Gary Pert, Ablett took what some believe was the greatest mark of all time, leaping over the top of the 187cm defender and clutching the ball to his chest for a spectacular high grab—one of many he took during the 1990s:

> I was caught just behind Perty and never had much room to get a run-up. I thought my only hope was to jump around him and stick my legs around his shoulders. I turned, leaving me with one hand. People say it wasn't a mark but ask the umpire. I pulled it in and controlled it to the ground when it

then spilled out. I hurt my hip and was winded and probably shouldn't have taken the kick, which I missed.[59]

In the Preliminary Final, against North Melbourne, Ablett stuck his hand out in the dying seconds to outmark full-back Mick Martyn, and kicked the winning goal after the siren. "I felt shattered for him the day I took that mark," Ablett said.[60] The following week, however, against West Coast (again) in the Grand Final, he managed only 1.2 in his side's 80-point defeat.

Ablett was named captain of both Geelong and Victoria in 1995 and kicked another century (122.85). However, he was held goalless by Stephen Silvagni in the 61-point Grand Final loss to Carlton. Ayres had replaced Blight as coach at the start of the year, and his relationship with his champion forward was rocky, ultimately leading to Ablett's retirement before the 1997 season:

> My relationship with Ayresy was OK until 1996… When he took over in 1995 I'd kicked two hundreds in a row. Blighty used to make me do two training runs before Christmas. When Ayresy took over he wanted me to do 17 training sessions before Christmas. I said "Why?" because I had gone all right under Blighty's training schedule. Ayresy looked at me and said, "Malcolm Blight is no longer coaching here." I thought then, maybe I'm on the way out.[61]

Ablett kicked his 1000th goal in round 12, 1996, against Fremantle at Kardinia Park, and finished his career with 1030. As of 2018, he has kicked the fifth-most goals in history, behind Wade (1057), Jason Dunstall (1254), Coventry (1299) and Tony Lockett (1360). He won Geelong's goalkicking nine times (1985-86, 1988-90, 1993-96), was a four-time All-Australian (1992-95) and a Leigh Matthews Trophy winner (AFLPA MVP, 1993). He did it all and more, although a Premiership eluded him. For many of his teammates, opponents and observers, Ablett is the greatest player of all time.

Ablett was named on the half-forward flank in Geelong's Team of the

---

59 *Icons of Australian Sport*, p. 213.
60 *Icons of Australian Sport*, p. 192.
61 *Icons of Australian Sport*, p. 184.

Century, and on the interchange in the AFL Team of the Century; and although he was named Geelong's Greatest Player of All-time, his entry into the Australian Football Hall of Fame was delayed due to a number of off-field controversies. He was eventually inducted in 2005, although many believe he will be elevated to Legend status in the future.

Remarkably, Ablett's son, Gary junior (Geelong 2002-10 and 2018, 192 games; Gold Coast 2011-17, 110 games), may have come closest of all players to surpassing his father's breathtaking feats. After taking time to find his feet as a small forward at AFL level, by the mid-2000s Ablett had become a dynamic midfielder. While Nathan struggled with the intense media scrutiny of carrying the Ablett name, Gary embraced it. Both played in the 2007 Premiership side, but Nathan walked out on the club soon after. Their father, having failed in four attempts to win a Grand Final, was overcome with pride and emotion when the Cats finally broke through to end a 44-year Premiership drought:

> I'm still a bit stunned to think the boys played together in a Premiership side for Geelong… It's a great feeling, a fairytale… At the game I was holding back the tears, it was a very personal moment, but the tears flowed on my way back to Geelong that night. I didn't want to steal anyone's thunder after the Grand Final, so I stayed in the background.[62]

Ablett snr continues to shun the limelight in retirement. Those around him seldom speak about him to the media, continuing to shield him from the intense scrutiny that followed him during his dominant days with the Cats. Indeed, many were unwilling to be interviewed for this book out of respect for football's most intriguing character.

Ablett wrote in *Icons of Australian Sport*, "People don't know the price you sometimes have to pay for success, but you pay it because we think that success is where happiness and fulfillment and a sense of self-worth is found." But, he added, "It's a lie."[63]

NOTE: Interviews with Gerard Healy, Scott Maginness, Gary Ayres and Rex Hunt were conducted by the author.

---

[62] *Icons of Australian Sport*, pp. 284-285.
[63] *Icons of Australian Sport*, p. 124.

GARY ABLETT

Statistics

BORN: 1 October 1961

GAMES PLAYED (Hawthorn 1982; Geelong 1984-97):
248 (Hawthorn 6; Geelong 242)

GOALS: 1030 (Hawthorn 9; Geelong 1021—club record)

FINALS PLAYED: 16

FINALS GOALS: 64

GRAND FINALS: 4

GRAND FINAL GOALS: 13

NORM SMITH MEDAL: 1989 (presented by Bill Goggin)

— Norm Smith Voting —

(**JUDGES:** Ted Whitten, Ross Oakley, Ron Carter, Laurie Sandilands and Bernie Quinlan)

The Age votes: **Laurie Serafini:** 3 Gary Ablett, 2 Chris Mew, 1 Darren Flanigan;
Alan Jarrott: 3 Ablett, 2 Flanigan, 1 Mew;
John Hendrie: 3 Ablett, 2 Robert DiPierdomenico, 1 Darrin Pritchard;
David McKay: 3 Ablett, 2 Pritchard, 1 Dean Anderson;
Mike Sheahan: 3 Ablett, 2 Pritchard, 1 Gary Buckenara;
Caroline Wilson: 3 Ablett, 2 Pritchard, 1 Greg Dear;
Steve Perkin: 3 Ablett, 2 Pritchard, 1 Anderson.

TOTALS: Ablett 21, Pritchard 9, Mew 3, Flanigan 3, DiPierdomenico 2, Anderson 2, Buckenara 1.

Tony Shaw

As captain of Collingwood (1987-93), Tony Shaw led the Magpies to the promised land. The image of Shaw and coach Leigh Matthews holding aloft the Premiership Cup after the 1990 Grand Final victory over Essendon—which broke a 32-year drought—remains one of the most iconic of the club's rich history. Shaw was an unlikely champion: he was short, slow and lacked the brilliance of some teammates. But he had heart, a galvanising personality and could run all day. As a leader Shaw was inspiring; his Norm Smith Medal-winning performance in 1990 was a fitting reward for his relentless determination. He won Collingwood's Copeland Trophy twice (1984, 1990), became the club's games record holder, and was named on the bench in its Team of the Century. In the 1990 Grand Final, Shaw played an exceptional first half, and had 22 kicks, 10 handballs, took eight marks and laid four tackles.

We grew up in a housing commission area in Reservoir. Mum and Dad never drove a car, so it meant that we had to walk, run or bike, but we only had one bike between us most of the time. There was Judith, Ray, Christine, Kelvin, myself and Neville, and we all played sport. It was a good upbringing, where the opportunity was

← **SHAW THING** Tony Shaw led from the front in 1990 as Collingwood broke a 32-year drought to win the club's first flag since 1958.

always there for us to play any sport we liked.

We did it all growing up: cricket, basketball, footy. We basically lived at the Coburg Basketball Stadium, and all played basketball. We all played cricket, too. We were really lucky to come up with three great sporting venues nearby: the Coburg Basketball Stadium, Keon Park Stars Football Club and the Keon Park Cricket Club. All us boys played in A-grade Premierships with each sport. Because Mum and Dad couldn't drive, we had other people who would help us out from time to time. The McLeods were one family, Beth and Max, who were like a second father and mother to us. They drove us anywhere we couldn't walk to; plus, they were involved at the basketball stadium and the football club. We were just very lucky, and each sport was super competitive. So that's the environment we came up in, and we probably had to fight for a feed half the time.

My dad, Reg, played for Brunswick in the Victorian Football Association (VFA); my mum, Eileen, played netball and was apparently pretty good at it. But she had six kids, so it became difficult to play sport after that. And Dad worked two jobs to support us all, so his football career was cut short as a consequence.

I never aspired to play in the VFL. I played state basketball up to under-18 level. Now you may look at my height (170cm) and question that fact, but I was used as a defensive guard, much like I was at Collingwood. I managed to play one game with the Coburg Giants, but when I was 17 I had to make a decision between basketball or footy. I tried out with the Collingwood under-19s, as we lived in Collingwood's recruiting zone, but my mate and I didn't get an opportunity at first. Ray had won the Liston Trophy in 1973 while playing for Preston, so that gave me a little taste of what was possible in footy. But all I wanted to do was compete, whatever sport I played; it gave me an outlet that I needed from a young age. Basketball was certainly my main love early on. If I thought I was going to get taller than I was, I probably would have kept going with basketball. But I probably made the right decision in the end.

I went to the 1970 Grand Final as a 10-year-old, and I cried when Collingwood lost to Carlton. Mum was a Hawthorn supporter, Dad was

North Melbourne, but us kids were all Collingwood, having grown up in the club's recruiting zone.

I went to Collingwood at the start of 1977 to try out with the under-19s. The coach was 1953 Premiership wingman Des Healey. After about seven quarters, my mate and I were seeing blokes that we had beaten as 16-year-olds, yet we weren't getting a go, so we left and went back to the Diamond Valley Football League (now the Northern Football League). Nobody had told me I wasn't good enough, it was us telling them we weren't going to waste our time on the sidelines not getting a chance. Poor old Billy O'Keefe was the team manager, and he copped the brunt of our frustration. We said, "You can stick your club up your arse!" then we walked out. I played in the 1977 Premiership with Reservoir-Lakeside, then returned to Collingwood before the 1978 season.

Playing in that senior Premiership with Reservoir-Lakeside, against men, accelerated my development as a footballer. It was a tough competition; there was no order-off rule. I was king hit a couple of times, so you had to be aware of what, and who, was around you at all times.

It's a bit of a blur how I went back to Collingwood. I had had a good year at Reservoir-Lakeside, and Collingwood had recruits out scouting that area as it was in their zone. The Magpies suffered a lot of injuries during the 1978 pre-season, and Ray had mentioned to Ronny Richards that I had had a good year. So Ron tried me with the reserves. I played 12 games with them in 1978, and also played five senior games—three home and away games and two finals—then got dropped. But it was a pretty quick rise after some 12 months earlier having walked out on the club.

I was a Collingwood supporter growing up, but I loved the way St Kilda's Darrel Baldock played. I also liked Collingwood's Richardson brothers, Wayne and Max, particularly Wayne. John Greening was another; I later wore his No. 22, which was good.

My first VFL game was against Footscray. Alby Smedts played in the back pocket, and I played on Alby and kicked a goal. We won the game, so it was a good debut all round. It was exciting more than intimidating.

THE NORM SMITH MEDAL

I never had a lot of nerves before games. I had played a lot of state basketball, played in big games growing up, plus cricket finals, so I had played in a lot of high-pressured games by the time I got to Collingwood.

I viewed being overly anxious as a waste of time, partly due to my lack of ability. It was wasted energy I couldn't afford to spend time worrying about. It didn't happen during my time at Collingwood, I don't know why exactly, but I attribute it to those early big games during my junior sporting career.

Tom Hafey was a fitness fanatic. He'd be doing weights in the gym when you first arrived at training! But he was great for me, because he loved blokes who trained hard. I trained really hard because I had to, but I loved training regardless. I find it interesting that some players last for a long time yet don't like training. Tommy was great for me, gave me an opportunity, as did Ron Richards. Ron gave me a lot of support and opportunity. With their support it all seemed to happen for me.

While it was good having Ray there with me, he let me have my space. I probably got more support from Ronnie Wearmouth, who was a very underrated player for us. Ronnie would give me insights into where to go, and shortcuts to take to get myself in the best position to win the ball. So he was good to me. I didn't want Ray to worry about me too much. He had his own career, and I understood that. But it was good to be able to play with him, and later play with Neville as well.

I didn't feel that the club was haunted by losses in Grand Finals. For me, by 1980 it was all new in a way. In fact, a lot of those blokes weren't brought up in it, guys like Denis Banks, Peter Daicos and myself, for example. Certainly when I had lost two Grand Finals in my first two years it became an issue, but that was history; that's what happened. |Each season brought new challenges.

I didn't believe in that 'Colliwobbles' crap. They had their time, and they had been unlucky on occasions with a few near misses. In 1980, Richmond were just a super team and we weren't good enough. But we got there, and we worked our butts off to get there: we just couldn't go all the way on Grand Final day. I didn't come on until half-time, and by then we were 43 points behind, so that was hard. We got beaten by 81 points, so I joke today that I helped to stem the tide in that second half! But it hurt, no doubt. It was pretty hard to cop at the time. It was a debacle really, but I didn't get a chance to do much. Not that I'm saying I would have made the difference.

If I have one criticism of Tom, he should have made changes earlier that day. We were getting smacked, but we didn't change anything. Michael Woolnough came on about seven minutes before half-time, and I came on at half-time. Now us two weren't going to change the result, but by then we were 40 points down. Things should have changed earlier, to at least see if we could get back into the game. But Tom did it that way at Richmond and they won four flags, so maybe we just weren't good enough. We could get there, but winning it on the day might have been beyond us.

Losing in 1981 was harder again, because we were more competitive that day than we had been in 1980. We certainly had our opportunities going into three-quarter time. Then a couple of things happened in the break with committeemen yelling at players. That put us off. We didn't have control going into the last quarter, which was disgraceful. Thorold Merrett had a go at Ricky Barham, as he thought there was an instance where Ricky didn't go hard enough. It all became a bit of a shemozzle, really, and it took our focus away from what we should have been focusing on: winning the game. I wasn't thinking we were done, but I'm not sure what everyone else was thinking. We still wanted to win the game regardless of where things were at by three-quarter time. We lost and we had to wear that until we, hopefully, got another opportunity. As it turned out, it took another nine years to get there again.

After round 10 in 1982, Tom Hafey was out. He got us to five Grand Finals in five years (including the draw and replay in 1977), so it's not like he was doing anything wrong. What happened was, the senior players felt he trained us too hard, which is right. I was still young then, so I didn't worry about the hard training. But, with great respect for Tom, there was some truth in that. We trained too hard on the Thursdays; we trained an hour and we knew the other mob were doing 10 minutes then going and having massages. But that's how we got there each time—we worked our arses off. Maybe, though, a freshen up at the end of the year might have helped us on Grand Final day.

I think we stuffed up after 1981. First, we brought in John Cahill to replace Tom, and John was good for me because I won my first Copeland Trophy under him in 1984. He was a very offensive coach, which I loved, but he made me into a tagger; he thought I could play defence and, hopefully, get the ball myself. I had a good couple of years under John. But behind the scenes, things weren't great, and it took us a while to work through that. Our administration was all over the shop during the 1980s—we fell about $3 million in debt. Ranald McDonald was president then, and Ranald was a ripper bloke, but things were happening off the field that caused a lot of instability. I never got caught up in that stuff, though. The reason Tom got the arse was because of the senior players—that was it. They had a vote on it. Then they went back to the board, and the board was too weak and didn't tell the players to stick to playing, not meddle in the coaching side of things. Tom had enormous faith in players; maybe too much in the end.

It was an interesting period for me. I'd just come off two losing Grand Finals, then had my best year in 1984, so I was starting to think that I could play at the level; I had belief in my ability to compete. I didn't become captain for another three years, though, so it was still a learning stage in my development.

We had six coaches from 1982 to 1986: Hafey, Cahill, Mick Erwin, Bob Rose for a second time, and then Leigh Matthews came in. Bob was a ripper bloke, but the game had probably gone past him by that stage. With so many coaching changes, it meant that things kept changing for the players and time just flew by as a consequence. For me, I played my first state game in '84, so I was winning a bit of respect. Personally, that probably took the edge off us being bad as a team. But I played to win Premierships, not to win individual awards.

I had an offer to go to Hawthorn. A lot of people don't know this, but when our club secretary, Tony Farrugia, moved across to Hawthorn in 1980 he soon asked me to go to with him. But Collingwood offered me another contract, and they were always good to me that way. In my third year at the club, my wife Deb and I bought our house and they gave me an advance in my pay to help me do that. That was in our bad times, too, when we lost Premierships and started to decline. So that was really good of them, and I wanted to repay them for the faith they had shown in me. How strong the Hawthorn offer was, though, I don't know. Tony might have just been sounding me out to get an idea of where my head was at.

Leigh wasn't impressed with me at first. But that was okay. He had enough faith to soon make me captain, and then it all started to happen for us around that time. I knew Leigh wanted more speed and he didn't think I was quick enough. I was certainly in agreeance with that, it wasn't an issue. But I had to try and win him over, to prove that I could play. I think I did that. Then he saw the other side of me, which was my leadership capabilities. At the start, I don't think he was seeing me as a long-term player in his plans, but it worked out all right for everybody eventually.

I thought I was ready to be captain before they made me captain. From 1984 through to 1987, I felt that I belonged. I was aggressive out there, and I didn't tolerate blokes who didn't work hard. I had no issues with telling them so; the same if they were undisciplined. We all enjoyed ourselves, and would have a beer after the game and so on. But I was married young and had kids young, like Leigh had done, so I found myself in a position where the leadership role suited me. I was ready for it by 1987. It was either myself or David Cloke who was going to be named captain. Mark Williams had had a falling out with Leigh by then, and he had moved up to play with Brisbane. I was chosen in front of Clokey, but I would not have had any issue about playing underneath David, had he been named captain. I don't know how David felt about it, but we had no issues between us afterwards. We got on well then, and we still do.

I got in trouble by saying that I would do anything on the field to get an advantage: verbalising and things like that. But that was a different era. Now we know that it's not to be accepted. Everybody was involved in it back then, it wasn't just me. I needed something to get me into a game.

It's the old saying: touch the ball early and you're into it. If I couldn't touch it early, I wanted to get physical, and I did that by throwing my weight around and getting kamikaze. Then, if that didn't work, that's when I would get verbal. So I had three things to fall back on if I wasn't in the game. If you only have one thing to fall back on, and that doesn't work, then what do you have? It got me involved in games, and got my competitive juices flowing. I picked my targets. Some blokes you don't waste time on because they're too smart; others are too dumb, so you don't waste time on them either. I picked my mark.

My stamina was elite. My speed wasn't, but my stamina was one of my strengths. I would talk to my opponents all the time, and they'd be trying to catch their breath while I'd be yapping away at them. I knew that if I was getting into their heads, yapping away, they'd be thinking: "This bloke won't shut up and I'm buggered!" So that became a way to try and emotionally wear them down. It helped me, and hopefully it hindered them.

I attribute my stamina to the fact Mum and Dad never drove. I used to run from Reservoir to Keon Park; I'd run to training on a Sunday morning from Reservoir to Coburg, then run home after training for an hour and a half. I lived at the Coburg Basketball Stadium, and when I wasn't playing I would referee. I was always running to and from places, so that became a massive bonus when I got to Collingwood.

People are motivated in different ways. My motivation was to not let my teammates down, and to hopefully play in a winning side each week. The glory then comes from wanting to perform each week, and wanting to succeed as a group. Also, my motivation came from the fact I was playing footy at the highest level; I wanted to play it forever, so I knew I had to work to be able to play it for as long as possible. That, and team success, motivated me. I was probably more of a kick-in-the-arse kind of leader; I didn't need a pat on the back from my teammates to feel motivated. You have to have a realism about what it is you're doing.

I was never overly demonstrative on the field when it came to disciplining players; I didn't want to embarrass them during a game. But behind the scenes I did it. Sometimes I would manufacture it by setting it up.

I could do it one on one, but sometimes I would bring in some support to back me up. To me, you can never let those things go if someone has done something wrong, or stepped outside the team rules. But I wouldn't single them out in front of everybody on the field during a game. I never wanted to give the opposition a chance to get one up on us.

I think a couple of times my nephew Heath has been wrong in how he's gone about it. But he knows that. He's got my fiery side in him, and he's a leader like I was, a competitor. Ray, on the other hand, was a lot quieter than I was. But he was a good captain doing it his way. You can't clone yourself on someone else; we all do things differently. Dad was very placid. He had an alcohol problem, and was a good footballer who should have gone further, but he was very placid—particularly in the early days before the drink got to him. Mum was very straight forward, wouldn't take any bullshit. So maybe I got it from her!

What is courage? That's a good question. I've always thought that the time when you have to go back with the flight, that's the scary thing. You know you're going to get hurt, but you're going to go anyway. The time when you don't, the embarrassment you feel afterwards is a lot worse than the pain you're going to have by going. You can't live with that, and it takes a long time to regain respect from that type of situation. The only time Leigh ever questioned my endeavour was after a contest between Melbourne's Rod Grinter and myself, where he felt I didn't go hard enough. I disagreed, but he never questioned me again after that.

Coming from outside, Leigh was able to freshen up the club. It was a different voice and a different way of going about it to what we had been used to. Now, Leigh was not a tactical genius. But he just set the scene, had certain rules, certain things you had to do, things you had to commit to. Who would have thought that our forward line on Grand Final day in 1990 would be Peter Daicos, Gavin Brown and Gavin Crosisca? Leigh did that, and in Browny's case, Leigh knew that his tackling and forward pressure would be important. You knew where you stood with Leigh, which I enjoyed. He was also fortunate to inherit the nucleus of a good team. The under-19s won a Premiership, and six or seven of them played in the 1990 Grand Final. We then got Craig Kelly (1989),

THE NORM SMITH MEDAL

Tony Francis (1990) and Scott Russell (1990) from Adelaide, as well as Michael Christian from Western Australia (1987); things started coming together under Leigh in the late 1980s. But you've got to keep going back to the well year after year. You need to play in finals, and more finals, before you're ready. We didn't win a final until the replayed Qualifying Final in 1990, so it took a while.

Let's not kid ourselves: Hawthorn were our bogey team, and they got put out against Melbourne in the Elimination Final. You need luck, which we got when we drew with West Coast in the Qualifying Final. Leigh was fantastic the week after the draw. Yes, Essendon had a few injuries by finals time in 1990, but they also had the extra time due to the replay to get themselves right. I can see their argument that it killed their momentum, but I certainly didn't worry about all that. Leigh was brilliant, and after we won that replay we began doing a lot of pressure work at training; we trained under pressure all the time. Just touching, not hard physical work that could result in injuries. Every time you went near the ball you had someone touching your back, just letting you know they were there and you needed to make smart decisions with the ball.

After that draw, it was probably the most one-sided finals series a team had played. We belted sides in those finals. Our tackling went through the roof. I think we broke records in those last couple of finals. But we needed a bit of luck, and we got that when Hawthorn were knocked out, then we had the draw, and that may have played on Essendon's mind. Then we capitalised on that luck. It wasn't just the tackling, but our pressure across the ground went up. West Coast came at us, and we came at them, and out of that drawn game we knew we had to up the ante a bit. So we trained for that. I think Leigh deserves enormous credit for that.

After we won the second Semi-Final, I thought we could win the Premiership. We weren't worried about West Coast or Essendon after that. Well, I don't know about the other blokes, but that was certainly my thinking. I hoped they were coming along with me! I was pretty confident, but we still had to have a different game-plan for each of them. I certainly wasn't worried who we played in the Grand Final.

Essendon captain Tim Watson and I were at the MCG a day or two out

from the Grand Final. I got there about 20 minutes earlier than Tim did, which I thought was interesting. He arrived right on time. He had been to three Grand Finals (1983-85), so I found that interesting that he wasn't there early. We had a photo together with the Cup, and then we went and had another photo after the Grand Final Parade. But at the MCG, after Tim had left, I was sitting there with the Cup for another 15 minutes by myself. While I'm not saying Tim didn't place enormous importance on the occasion, or didn't want it more than I did, it was very important for me to have that time alone with the Cup. I just wondered whether, maybe, having been there before, he may not have been as focused as I was. But he had every right, as he'd already been there, done that, and he knew what was involved.

I didn't have nerves and I just embraced the occasion. I knew, along with Leigh, that we were the face of it leading up to the game. But we were pretty organised in our preparation; we knew where we were going all week, and what we were going to do. Alan Richardson trained but was struggling with a cracked collarbone, as did Ron McKeown (who was not selected in the side), then Shane Kerrison and Craig Starcevich came in for those guys. Plus, Brian Taylor was still in the mix for selection as well. So, there were things happening in the background all week. But, overall, we were pretty organised going into the game.

We started our number one ruckman, Damian Monkhorst, at full-forward. He hadn't had good form coming into the game, whereas James Manson had. Both were aggressive players, but Leigh felt he was better off with James starting in the ruck and 'Monkey' up forward. Monkey had the first shot of the game, and it was just something different we tried: adding a big body in our forward line.

We missed a couple of early opportunities, and we dominated for the first seven or eight minutes. Then, Essendon went forward a couple of times and Paul Salmon marked them and kicked two quick goals. Suddenly, we were two goals down having had most of the play. Some people may have been shitting themselves, but I remained confident we could get back into the game on the scoreboard. Then, 'Daics' kicked a brilliant goal that got us going. We started with 'Ned' Kelly on Salmon, then changed to 'Chriso' (Christian), then changed back. Leigh made an adjustment quickly, but we knew we hadn't made the most of our chances when we went forward. We just needed something to go through, which came when Daics kicked his goal. By quarter-time we were back within a couple of points, so no damage had been done.

Daics's goal was unbelievable—no one could kick that! You couldn't even see daylight between the posts. And he didn't do a boomerang kick, he just kicked it as a drop-punt. That's Daics. He would do it at training, and I saw him kick 13 goals in a game once: he was just freakish. I maintain that he's the best player I've seen at Collingwood. I still find it amazing that he kicked 97 goals that year as a small forward. And he didn't win our best and fairest. I'm glad he didn't, because I won it! But 97 goals... that is an incredible amount of goals for a small forward. He may not have had a lot of stats in the Grand Final, but he did a lot of defensive things for us that went unnoticed.

Darren Millane had broken his thumb in two or three places, but played through the finals. He had it injected every time, had it plastered after every game, and played with it strapped; it was just amazing what he put himself through to play in that finals series. He played on Greg Anderson, who was a State of Origin player, and he beat him one-handed. He could use his forearm for extra control, but he couldn't really use his thumb and hand. Whether we got motivation from it, I don't know, but it was bloody gutsy. He was a tough bastard. He was powerful, never shirked the issue, could jump on your head, bullock his way through a pack—he could do it all.

Derek Kickett started in the midfield with me, which I was a bit worried about because he was an enigmatic player. But, I knew that if he stayed in there for too long I was going to run him into the ground. He was a small forward, whereas I knew I could read it better on the ball. We always got on well, but when the blue started I swung and missed him, then he had a go at me, then Michael Long came in. I got thrown out the back, but went in for another go. It was pretty hectic there for a while.

The push and shove started over the boundary line. I couldn't pinpoint one thing, but then it became more heated. Browny ran down to get involved and Terry Daniher belted him from behind. You need to be wary of what and who is around you when you are going into something like that. Browny went down, and the issue then, aside from his wellbeing, was how it was going to impact us after quarter-time. It was all about getting control of the game, and Leigh was magnificent at the huddle.

This is why Leigh was so good: straight away he said to put our heads over the ball, that the umpires will try and take control; he hit it in one. Instead of strategic instructions—although we did have to replace Browny with Starcevich—it was a controlled, unemotional address.

We went out and put our heads over the ball, they gave away two early 50-metre penalties, and within seven minutes we'd kicked five goals and blown the game open. I could see that Monkey and Jimmy were getting a bit edgy after what happened to Browny, but the message at the break was about sucking it in, getting in tight, and letting Leigh tell us about what we needed to do when we went back out there. I didn't need to say anything, we just needed to go out and follow up on his instructions. We had to take any undisciplined acts out of it, and we went out and cracked in and we tackled hard. I remember Scotty Russell getting Alan Ezard in the pocket, then Ezard grabbed his head and they gave the 50-metre penalty to Scotty. He went from being on the angle where he wasn't a certainty to kick the goal, to suddenly being in much closer where he was a certainty to kick it.

Craig Starcevich, for his size, had enormous stamina; his stamina was freakish actually. He was on Terry, who was getting a bit older—a bit like myself and Daics were—but he just kept on the move, ran Terry around. He was agile, and though he got knocked out later on, his role for us after Browny went down was huge. He was a different player to Browny, because he was on the move all the time, whereas Browny would throw himself into the contest and the longer runs weren't really his game. We had a fairly small forward line; we didn't have the giants that Essendon had in theirs, and maybe they were too slow in comparison to our forwards that day. We thought going in that we might get them with the speed factor, then with our defensive pressure when they tried taking the ball from defence. I don't watch the game a lot, but when I do what is obvious is that Essendon smashed balls out of defence under pressure; they kicked the ball out of there, but not to specific targets, and we were able to send it straight back in.

Did I think Browny would come back on? Probably not. But it was different then, we didn't have concussion rules like today. Browny's got a hard head, although Terry got him in the right spot that day. I've seen him get crunched a number of times when going back with the flight of the ball, and you expected him to be out cold, but he had this hard head and was able to play through things that other people couldn't. So, others might not have come back on. To see him come back, it was good, the timing of it was good, but it didn't suddenly change how we went about it. It was brilliant all the same, and when he kicked that goal was huge. He had run straight on and was in Terry's face immediately. I think he was stupid to do it, because Terry could really fight, but Browny was showing him that he was still around. It was pretty gutsy stuff. They wouldn't even think about coming back on today, but that's how it was back then.

Those things can be overrated in the moment. I was mainly thinking, "I hope Browny gets a kick or kicks a few goals," rather than being caught up in the fact he had returned to the field. So, in the moment I was probably more unemotional about it than others were. I was just so focused on getting the job done.

I was very surprised with the match-ups: I had Derek, then they put Bomber Thompson on me when I started to get a bit of the ball. But Bomber was a half-back flanker, plus he had a crook ankle and was limping most of the day. Having said that, when your team is keeping the ball in the forward line for as long as ours were it meant I didn't need to go in there a lot. I wasn't tagging as such. I had Darren Bewick for a while, and I had a good record against Bewick: he was the danger bloke for us. If he had of gone forward the plan was for me to hand him over to a defender. But because we hemmed it in our forward line and kept putting pressure on, I had the luxury of sitting behind the play. That kind of role is bread and butter for anyone who is good at reading the play, and that was one of my strengths.

I hated it when Derek Kickett stood on my head and took that mark in the last quarter. I used to love getting in a marking contest, because I was really confident in my ability to hold my position due to my core strength. It was a good mark, but it wasn't a huge mark because he only took it over me! I was set up beautifully. I had to go back, he had the run up, and we know what happened next. Let's not focus on that. It still gets pointed out to me regularly today.

Leigh always said that if you were more goals up than minutes remaining on the clock, you couldn't lose. The moment I thought we had it won was when I passed the ball to Monkey and he put us eight goals up with five minutes to go. Then, when Leigh came down and reacted how he did, that was another indication that we had the game won. I remember standing next to Tim Watson towards the end, and I said, "Mate, do you reckon we've got you?" He said, "Mate, this is gone!" That's when it hit me, but I was still shitting myself that the game wasn't won. I was so focused right throughout the day that I was determined to play it out until the siren. Monkey's goal was a huge relief though. Then Millane ends up with the ball, which was fitting in a way.

I dropped to my knees in relief, nothing more. I didn't cry or anything like that, it was just pure bloody relief that we weren't losers anymore. Certainly, I felt the excitement later, and it probably comes quicker than what you think looking back. But in that moment when the siren sounded and I fell to my knees, the only emotion was relief. Then you lose track of what's going on, because it's a crazy time after that. That relief came from the fact I had been there a number of times and been on the losing end, as had the club over a long period of time.

Leigh and I embraced on the field after the game. He had shown a lot of faith in me after initially being sceptical. And I think I repaid that in lots of ways, not just on the field, off it as well. We still get on really well today, and that was a special moment that we shared together after the game.

Leigh always said that Michael Voss and myself were the two greatest captains he ever had. But, I remember him saying one time that Vossy was the best captain he had. I heard that and rang him up straight away. I said, "Well, is it me or is it Vossy?" He said, "When I'm talking about you, it's you, and when I'm talking about Vossy it's him!" We joke about that. It was just good to know that I had earned respect in Leigh's eyes.

I was buggered that night. I had a drink but I couldn't go on because, emotionally, I was a wreck. After the build-up during the week, then the emotional energy used during the day, I had nothing left to give by that night. Being the captain of the club, it all built and built, and I was absolutely stuffed by the end.

Tony Peek came up to me after the game and said "You're going to get your medal shortly," and I assumed he meant the Premiership Medal. I already knew I had to go up to receive the Cup anyway, so I said "Oh yeah, the Grand Final Medal?" Then he said, "No, the Norm Smith!" It didn't sink in straight away, and it doesn't sink in until later. I think that night, at the Southern Cross Hotel, with my wife and all the players there, along with all the trainers and everybody, and just seeing the joy on their faces: that's when I sat back and thought, "You're now a member of a winning Grand Final side, you're the captain of that side, and you've won the best on ground which means you can play in the biggest of games." I remember thinking, "Whoa! It doesn't get much bigger than this."

I look at the game, and I had a lot of possessions and I controlled things a fair bit. But at the same time, I thought there were better blokes on the day. Monkey was fantastic for us, Starc was going all right until he got knocked out, Scotty Russell was brilliant as well. I could always accumulate the ball, and I knew what I could do out there. Whether I was awarded the medal or someone else was, I didn't care either way. It was nice to win it, but it wasn't the be-all-and-end-all.

Ray left ten minutes before the final siren. He just couldn't stay to watch the end. We got together the day after though at the club. He played in four losing Grand Finals, plus a draw. He just had no luck. And that's the hardest thing for me, because we played with so many blokes who never got the opportunity. Then there was Banksy and Daics who I had been through everything with, so it was great to share that with them. Then you look at Francis and Russell: they were at the club for one year and they won the Premiership. So, Ray left early knowing we'd won it, and I don't begrudge him that, because he took it hard. And there were plenty of others in that boat. Bob Rose for example.

I took the Cup home that night, then the Sunday morning I took it around to my in-law's house, then went to the club about 10.00am. I got to take photos of the Cup with my family. The club didn't actually know I took it home; we sort of stole it! They thought we went out the front door, but we had snuck out the back to the carpark, so they were shitting themselves wondering where the cup was for a while there.

To go back to Victoria Park for the celebrations, seeing the trainers and everybody just so happy; that was special. I had been there since 1978, yet some of the trainers were 60 years old, so they had been there through all the losses. To see the joy on their faces was unbelievable for me. It was like a rock concert at Vic Park—there must have been 40,000 people there. I had people write to me saying that they can die happy now that they have seen Collingwood win a Premiership. Even people today who you meet for the first time, they say: "Mate, that was the greatest day of my life."

Kelvin committed suicide in 1991. He had played with Collingwood's under-19s and reserves, but never played a senior game for the club. He wrote a note when he died, saying that he felt a bit of a failure, but there were obviously other things involved that he struggled with, unfortunately. I think we all go through depression at times, it just depends whether you get diagnosed with suffering from it or not, and whether you can get access to the right help to work through it. It's not easy, and, in those days, they didn't diagnose it like they do today, which meant a lot of people suffered depression without knowing that was what they needed help with. It was a hard time. I'd just won a Premiership with Collingwood, life was good, and then that happened. It was really hard on my mum and dad: Dad probably drank more, Mum never drank, but she probably smoked more. You do what you need to do to deal with those types of things I guess. You feel guilty for a while, but you try getting on with life. I certainly think about it at times, think about Kelvin, but you need to keep moving forward and that's what I have tried to do.

THE NORM SMITH MEDAL

I made a few mistakes as a coach. I probably should have had a greater apprenticeship by going to Carlton, instead of staying at Collingwood. I had the assistant job at Carlton, I knocked it back. But I had four years to get things right at Collingwood. I know that I didn't identify certain things that were happening in the game. Would I be a better coach the second time around? No doubt, because I now know the mistakes. While I don't have regrets, I'm filthy with it being on my CV because I hate failing at anything. But, I also learned a lot about myself. As a player, I felt like I was in control. If I had my preparation right, I controlled my own destiny. But as a coach, that control was much different, because you suddenly have to make sure 20 players have their preparation right. But I had a go, and as we know, there are plenty of others in my position.

What did footy give me? It gave me an opportunity to live a pretty high level of life. A level that might not have happened otherwise, considering where I came from. It was a hard life early on because Mum and Dad didn't have a lot, but we got through it. They were brilliant in what they did for us. From football, I got so many friendships. We all have our struggles outside of footy, whereas playing footy allowed me to control things. Outside of footy, you can't always control things in the rest of your life. I knew what I was doing when I was playing footy; I knew what I had to do to prepare; and I knew what I did well. I could control that. I've been in the media as well, and I've just started my own real estate business, and all these things stem from what I did as a footballer. It's the greatest game on earth. There are more facets of our game required from a player than in any other game: You need strength, power, speed and stamina. It's been a long ride, but a really enjoyable ride. But it's not over yet. I'd still like to get back involved at club land in some capacity.

It was great to see Heath and Rhyce win Premierships. We had moved Rhyce on from Collingwood after 2008, but it worked out great for him at Sydney. He said after they won in 2012, "Now I'll be the one bragging at the Christmas dinners!" It was so good for the family, so good for Ray. It was bullshit how Rhyce was hung out to dry after the 2003 Grand Final loss. We lost by 50 points, yet he and Richard Cole were made scapegoats. For two instances in a game, they got slaughtered afterwards. I was dirty on coach Mick Malthouse at the time, and we get on well now, but I felt he should have stuck up for those boys. And the club should have as well, but they didn't. But he fought back to win one eventually, which was great.

—— Statistics ——

BORN: 23 July 1960
GAMES PLAYED (1978-94): 313 (Collingwood games-played record holder)
GOALS: 157
FINALS PLAYED: 22
FINALS GOALS: 9
GRAND FINALS: 3
PREMIERSHIP: 1990
NORM SMITH MEDAL: 1990 (presented by Frank Adams)

— Norm Smith Voting —

(**JUDGES:** Ted Whitten, Ross Oakley, Trevor Grant, Ron Barassi and Ian Robertson)

The Age votes: **Mike Sheahan:** 3 Tony Shaw, 2 Scott Russell, 1 Craig Kelly;
Rohan Connolly: 3 Shaw, 2 Kelly, 1 Russell;
Gerard Wright: 3 Shaw, 2 Damien Monkhorst, 1 Kelly;
Caroline Wilson: 3 Shaw, 2 Monkhorst, 1 Russell;
Mark Ray: 3 Shaw, 2 Monkhorst, 1 Craig Starcevic;
Wayne Schimmelbusch: 3 Shaw, 2 Kelly, 1 Russell;
Gareth Andrews: 3 Shaw, 2 Monkhorst, 1 Russell;
David McKay: 3 Shaw, 2 Monkhorst, 1 Kelly.

The Age **TOTALS:** Shaw 24, Monkhorst 10, Kelly 7, Russell 6, Starcevic 1.

Paul Dear

The brother of triple Premiership player Greg Dear (Hawthorn 1986, 1988-89), Paul Dear played in the Hawks' losing 1987 Grand Final, but missed the back-to-back flags of 1988-89. By 1991, he had become one of the AFL's best mobile, pinch-hitting ruckmen, able to also play across half-forward and cause headaches to opposing defenders. He played 23 games in 1991, averaged more than 14 disposals a game and kicked 23 goals. With his large frame (188cm and 105kg), Dear's crash-and-bash style was perfectly suited to the physicality that a Grand Final demands. On the wide expanses of Waverley Park—the first and only time the AFL Grand Final was played at the venue—Dear's mobility was critical to Hawthorn's dominant 53-point victory over the West Coast Eagles. He had 18 kicks, eight handballs, took 11 marks and kicked two goals.

I'm from a family of seven kids. Of the four boys, I'm the youngest. So being the youngest and growing up on a 10-acre (four hectares) farm we would always be playing basketball, cricket and footy after school. I learned pretty early how to handle big bodies, because my big brother, Jim, was six-foot-six (198cm) and well built. Greg (Hawthorn 1985-93, 137 games; Richmond 1994-96, 53 games) was six-six as well,

← **GREAT DAY** Of Hawthorn's late 1980s Grand Finals, Paul Dear had played in only the losing 1987 decider against Carlton, but redemption came when he was a dominant forward in the club's 1991 triumph at Waverley Park.

but he was slimmer, and my other brother Lawry was my height but slimmer, too. We were constantly competing one on one in the backyard.

I was a Richmond supporter, because when I was young the Tigers were one of the top teams. In those days you didn't get the media saturation you do now. You had *The Winners* on ABC-TV on a Saturday night, and you'd see the odd game on telly, but you tended to watch the local footy more than anything else.

I never had the goal of playing in the VFL. We were in Hawthorn's zone, and so Jim went to the Hawthorn under-19s and then on to the reserves. But I just enjoyed playing footy. I went along for the journey and quickly progressed through the ranks. My view was, give it everything and see where it goes.

Most of my junior footy was played either forward or in the ruck. I was playing senior footy at Churchill from 15 years old, and I was generally playing outside my age group. Mum had made the decision early on that I was big and strong enough to follow my brother, who was 18 months older than me, and so I never really played in my own age group. When I got to under-16 level the senior side started showing some interest, and so I started playing seniors.

I came through the Hawthorn under-19s, and because of that hierarchy I didn't really mix with the senior players. You trained at different times, and even though you saw them around the club you weren't really involved with them from day to day. You knew where you were in the pecking order—you were on the bottom rung!—and when I made the under-19 list there were 60 of us on it. I can remember sitting in the gym and senior coach, Allan Jeans, coming in and saying, "We expect two of you guys to make it to senior footy," and so you knew straight away what the odds were—they weren't good! It was hard work. From that under-19s group, only myself, Ray Jencke and Anthony Condon went on to play senior footy. Yabby was spot on, wasn't he?

Allan Jeans was a leader of men. When I was in the under-19s, he would come and sit beside me and his constant message would always be: "Get the best out of yourself; don't walk away from this place being a coodabeen." He wanted you to achieve all that you could while you were there, because that would help to set you up for life. He always said how he had seen too many guys walk away from football and then years later say that they could have been this and they could have been that. He felt that they lived an unfulfilled life, so he made sure that he told us to give it our best, and if that still wasn't good enough then at least we could walk away happy that we tried and didn't give up.

I think Jeansy saw a lot in the way I played. I was a big kid who attacked the ball hard. He would come up and say, "You've got a big body son, use it. If you don't, you're no good to me." So I played a really physical, crash and bash type of game, and he showed a lot of faith in me. He would be yelling and screaming at me on the track, and I'd feel a bit down after it, but he would come up to me later and say, "Son, I know I'm hard on you, but be more concerned if I'm *not* hard on you."

I had a solid core. I was really strong through the hips and the legs, and I had a big arse, so I was naturally strong through the body. I found I needed to focus more on the endurance side rather than the strength side, because I could hold my own against most players, even the big ruckmen. I did a lot of work on my endurance. I'd be swimming and riding a bike, lots of cardio as opposed to weights.

I didn't have to compete against my brother very often at training. I was a fill-in ruckman, as I was only six-foot-one-and-a-half (187cm). We would do a lot of boundary throw-in work together, but in terms of centre-bounce ruckwork we had different methods. My process involved running straight at the opposition's ruckman to try to take him out of the contest, which you were legally able to do in those days. But you certainly didn't try that at training! Greg tended to spend more time in the ruck, and I spent most of my time forward, so we didn't find ourselves competing for the one spot too often. But, of course, there was always a bit of a rivalry between us, being brothers, and when he moved to Richmond in 1994 we played against each other for the first time and that was a bit of fun.

The 1987 Grand Final was surreal. I made my debut in round 13, against Melbourne, and I managed to hold my spot going into the finals.

THE NORM SMITH MEDAL

The Grand Final against Carlton was one of those stinking hot days—something like 29 degrees by eight o'clock in the morning—so we knew we were in for a hot one. We had struggled our way into the Grand Final, and we had a lot of injuries, including our full-forward Jason Dunstall, who missed the game after kicking 94 goals that year. We lost, and I didn't have an impact at all from full-forward, which made it equally disappointing. So that didn't sit well with me, and I've never watched a replay of the game.

It is an interesting scenario when you lose a Grand Final. You're second best, but you are seen as being a complete failure. Whereas if you make a Preliminary Final that's seen as having done okay. Compare it to an Olympic environment where, if you come second, it's still seen as being pretty bloody good. But when you lose a Grand Final, you basically write the year off as a failure.

I was not selected for either the 1988 or 1989 Grand Finals. Then, when we didn't make the Grand Final in 1990, I was starting to wonder whether I would ever get the chance to win one. In 1991, I had such a strong desire to get myself a Premiership Medal, because I thought to myself: "I arrived at the club in 1984, they've played in six Grand Finals for three Premierships, plus they won in 1983, so if I don't win one soon I'm going to be seen as a complete failure." That really drove my commitment to the cause in 1991.

We knew we had an older team in 1991. But we went over to Perth and knocked off West Coast in our first final, and I don't think that they had been beaten over there for a couple of years. That win really set us up for the Grand Final. There's no doubt that if we had lost that game, and had to play every week of the finals, we would have had a different outcome. Having that week's break gave us the opportunity for the older players to freshen up. But we had some superb players like Michael Tuck, Gary Ayres, Chris Mew and Dunstall, so you knew that you could rely on them to get the job done. The break was critical for us.

In the team meeting during Grand Final week, it was made pretty clear that I needed to have a big day. We felt that we needed to get 10 goals out of Dunstall, Dermott Brereton and myself, and that I needed to be running around getting plenty of kicks and causing havoc. That would then force West Coast to bring guys like Glen Jakovich, Guy McKenna or Ashley McIntosh away from their forward line. I was seen as the odd man out, and someone who could give us the upper-hand. As it turned out, I played on Michael Brennan, McIntosh and also Jakovich for a while, so we kept them on their toes.

I had built up a pretty big engine by 1991, but I was also playing at around 110 kilos, so I was big and mobile. I knew that if they put someone on me who could run with me, I could generally out-muscle them, and so when that happened I would try to get into one-on-one's inside 50 with them where I could mark in scoring distance. When they put someone on me who could match me for strength, I would then use my mobility to push further up the ground and take the defender away from their backline.

All Greg said to me before the 1991 Grand Final was just to "go out and enjoy yourself." Having played in the 1987 Grand Final, I knew what to expect. And Hawthorn had a system by then, because they'd been in so many Grand Finals during that period. You knew what was expected of you.

Alan Joyce had taken over from Yabby that year. Alan was so intense and so passionate, and that's how he drove the side in 1991. After a game he'd be fired up; whether that was positive or negative, he would still deliver the same messages. He wasn't as strong a tactician as Jeansy, but he drove the side through his intensity. The problem with Al was that he didn't know when to shut down the intensity, and so after a number of years he started to lose the playing group. And if you look through his history, he is quite successful early on and then he has this drop off. But he was a great coach, and I did really well under him.

I loved playing at VFL Park. It was a great place to play, because you could just run and run and run. It wasn't congested, and I think that helped us in the end because Subiaco, the Eagles' home turf, was quite a narrow ground, and we were able to find space everywhere on Grand Final day. Although the Grand Final was played at VFL Park for the first and only time while the Southern Stand at the MCG was being built, it still felt like a Grand Final. It's a bit of history, being the only Grand Final played there, and I was a part of it, which is great.

I couldn't hear Angry Anderson from inside the change rooms. The Batmobile is always brought up today, but I don't recall seeing it on the day.[1] I do remember the fireworks when we ran out, and I thought that was a bit strange considering it was the middle of the day. You were focused on the task ahead, and all the other stuff was just peripheral. You couldn't afford to take too much notice of that. At Waverley you were right down under the stadium, so you never really heard the crowd.

The Eagles came out of the blocks, but we expected that, being their first Grand Final. We knew it would be a long haul. They kicked a couple of early goals from free kicks, but we kicked a couple of our own towards the end of the first quarter which kept us within nine points at quarter-time. We'd settled into the game, so we weren't too worried.

I had a bit of a purple patch during the second quarter. The Eagles defenders kept kicking the ball out to me, and we were getting goals from their kick-ins; that starts to mentally challenge a side. From memory, they kicked it to me three times in a row and I scored 1.2, so that must have played with their minds a bit. I knew I was up and running and that I was having a good day. The previous Grand Final that I played in I hardly got a kick, so I was pretty motivated to have an impact on the game.

Halfway through the last quarter we knew we had the game won. But we were still trying to make sure that we stuck to the task. All the time I played at Hawthorn I never thought that we were going to lose, and so you just kept focusing on making sure that you were doing everything possible to win. We didn't want to give them a sniff. When the siren went, it was a feeling of absolute relief. It had always been a boyhood dream to play in a winning Grand Final, and so to have been there during their glory years and to finally get one, it was just absolute relief.

---

[1] The pre-match entertainment involved former Rose Tattoo frontman Angry Anderson performing an instantly infamous rendition of *Bound For Glory*, having been transported around the ground in a mock "Batmobile". See: http://tinyurl.com/y7p8f6cm.

Greg was in the rooms after the game and he was pretty excited for me. It would have been great to have played in a winning one with him, especially after we'd played in a losing one together. But he was still happy for me. He was disappointed to have missed out with his knee, but he already had *three* Premierships, so it wasn't like he hadn't experienced what it was like to win one!

My Norm Smith Medal is at the Hawthorn museum. Before that I just kept it in a box. Out on the ground it was a complete shock when I was told I had won it, because all through junior footy I had never won a lot of awards. Winning that medal never even entered my mind. Being known as a Norm Smith medallist has certainly given me recognition. There are 22 Premiership players every year and only one Norm Smith medallist, so you are in an elite club, and it does give you a lot of recognition. I suppose my name stays out there, whereas it may not have otherwise. I quite often joke when I'm standing with my brother and somebody approaches me to talk about the Norm Smith Medal. I say to them, "You do know that this bloke has three Premiership Medals?"

It's interesting winning the Norm Smith. You are singled out for your performance, when it really is a team performance. It's quite different from a Brownlow Medal, because you can win a Brownlow Medal when your team is performing badly, but very rarely can you win a Norm Smith Medal if your team is performing badly.

You didn't need to be a rocket scientist to know that with the salary cap and the draft, Hawthorn's formula for success was basically dismantled by the AFL. And rightly so, because it's not good for the competition to have the same team in the Grand Final year after year. I knew it was only going to get harder to get there, which is why it came as such a relief to win in '91. As history shows, Hawthorn did not make it into another Grand Final until 2008.

Playing the style of game that I played, it took a toll. I received quite a few broken bones, especially in the hands, and I injured my shoulders and needed reconstructions. At one stage, one of my coaches wanted me to get my playing weight down to close to 100 kilos, and I did that over a pre-season, then after the first game I couldn't walk! I realised that if they wanted me to keep playing the physical game then I needed that extra padding.

Like most old footballers now, my back's pretty ordinary. So are my knees; it's taken its toll on my body, that's for sure. I never set out to hurt anyone, but if the opportunity was there, you took it. Football is a physical game and in those days it was expected. You had to make your size felt, and I was a big player so I needed to play my role by making an impact around the ball, which then freed up my smaller teammates. But I'm paying for it now.

—— Statistics ——

BORN: 28 December 1966
GAMES PLAYED (1987-96): 123
GOALS: 80
FINALS PLAYED: 10
FINALS GOALS: 6
GRAND FINALS: 2
PREMIERSHIP: 1991
NORM SMITH MEDAL: 1991 (presented by David Cloke)

PAUL DEAR

— Norm Smith Voting —

(**JUDGES:** Ted Whitten, Ross Oakley, Malcolm Conn, Peter Booth and Don Scott)

Herald Sun **votes: Neil Roberts:** 3 Paul Dear, 2 Stephen Lawrence, 1 Gary Ayres;
Trevor Grant: 3 Lawrence, 2 Dear, 1 John Platten;
Michael Horan: 3 Dear, 2 Lawrence, 1 Platten;
Colin Kinnear: 3 Dear, 2 Lawrence, 1 Platten;
Glen Quartermain: 3 Lawrence, 2 Dear, 1 Anthony Condon;
Glenn McFarlane: 3 Dear, 2 Lawrence, 1 Platten;
Ken Piesse: 3 Dear, 2 Platten, 1 Lawrence;
Scot Palmer: 3 Dear, 2 Platten, 1 Ayres.
Herald Sun **TOTALS:** Dear 22, Lawrence 15, Platten 8, Ayres 2, Condon 1.

Peter Matera

During the early 1990s, West Coast's Peter Matera was one of the most devastating wingmen in the game. With his explosive pace and penetrating kicking, Matera was a 100-metre player—that is, he could dash 40 metres then kick a further 60, giving the Eagles an X-factor that few teams could counter, particularly between 1991 and 1994 when they dominated the AFL. Few players have compiled a finals series to rival Matera's in 1992—he was best afield in the two lead-up finals and turned in another sizzling game in the Grand Final with five goals from a wing to break Geelong hearts.

P eter Matera's father, Michael, was born in Grassano, Italy, and served in the Italian army during World War II. When the war was over, he emigrated to Australia aged 21 with "a few of his mates" because "they thought there was a lot of work," Matera explained.[1] His father bought a horse and cart and made his way to Wagin, 225km south-east of Perth. There, in Noongar country—which has produced many AFL champions including Lance Franklin, Nicky Winmar, Graham Farmer, Barry Cable and Stephen Michael—he met his future

---

1   Sean Gorman, *Legends: The AFL Indigenous Team of the Century*, Aboriginal Studies Press, 2011, p. 155.

← **SUPERB** There have been few more dominant displays by a wingman in any match, much less a Grand Final, than that produced by Peter Matera in 1992.

wife, Jane, an Aboriginal woman, and the couple had eight children—seven boys (Wally, Frank, Mike, Peter, Gino, Phillip and Gerard) and a girl (Carmello).[2]

Matera recalls that his older brother, Mike, almost ended his sporting career before it began. "Mike was mucking around with an axe one day and must have thought my right hand would be a good target. He took a swing and all but chopped off the ring finger." It was hanging by a "strip of skin" and resulted in him losing the top of his finger.[3] Fortunately, it had no negative effect on his football development, which was inspired by his eldest brother, Wally, as Peter recounted:

> Wally, a naturally talented footballer, was my earliest idol. He could do no wrong and I just loved watching him outpace and outsmart bigger and taller opponents. He was what we call a football 'natural' and, in many ways, he was my first coach, even if it was just street football, sometimes with a ball so old it was round as a basketball.[4]

Matera described himself as "sports mad", admitting that his schooling took a back seat to his love for all things sport-related. "I was no dunce," he said, "I could hold my own in all subjects. It simply was a case of being more interested in sport, especially football. My mind tended to wander during class, usually to the next week's matches, or how I had performed in my previous match. If it wasn't football or soccer, it was some other sport or game."[5] He played basketball and was a goalie in soccer.

"The school football side then started getting beaten and the headmaster said, 'If you don't get into footy and play in the footy side you're going to have a hard time,'" Matera said.[6] Having been sold on football, Matera soon won a D-grade best and fairest with the Federals club in Wagin, the earliest sign that he had the attributes to play the game.[7] Two of his favourite players, outside his family, were South Fremantle's Maurice Rioli (who won the 1982 Norm Smith Medal at Richmond) and Stephen Michael.

---

2   Peter Matera and Jim Main, *Waltzing Matera: The Peter Matera Story*, Gary Allen, 1996, p. 9.
3   *Waltzing Matera*, p. 10.
4   *Waltzing Matera*, p. 10.
5   *Waltzing Matera*, p. 11.
6   *Legends*, p. 156.
7   *Legends*, p. 156.

Surprisingly, in light of his speed at AFL level, Matera was not the fastest boy at school, regularly finishing no better than second or third in school sports events. "Although I had natural pace, I did not make the most of it until I was almost a senior footballer," he added. "I then was playing against better footballers and had to extend myself to get past them."[8]

When Wally Matera was chosen as one of the inaugural West Coast players in 1987, it gave Peter the belief that he, too, could play at the highest level. "I reasoned that if Wally could star at senior level, I could do it," Matera said. "This is not knocking Wally, but a mere statement of my belief in my own ability. I was taller than Wally even then (Wally was 170cm, Peter 181cm), I knew I had plenty of pace and there was absolutely no questioning my determination."[9] That year, he made his debut for South Fremantle in the WAFL, playing on a half-forward flank. His form was spasmodic, but as he was "built like a stick insect" knew he had room for considerable improvement. "My pace had to be complemented with strength and this meant plenty of work and the development of physical maturity."[10]

In 1989, Matera was the only non-VFL player to represent WA in the State of Origin clash with Victoria. Although it was clear he was in the sights of Eagles recruiters, Matera said he wanted to be drafted to Fitzroy. "This might sound silly considering that Fitzroy even then was considered the poor relation of the VFL competition, but brother Wally was a Lion [by then] and I was very keen to join him in Fitzroy's maroon, blue and gold."[11] Fitzroy official Arthur Wilson visited Matera and indicated the Lions were considering him in the 1989 National Draft. The Eagles, too, had shown interest, but Matera had his heart set on Victoria. "I almost fell over when I heard the announcement of the fourth overall selection, by the West Coast Eagles, of P. Matera, of South Fremantle," he said.[12]

When the 20-year-old Matera arrived for his first pre-season training session with West Coast, his new teammate, John Worsfold, remembers

---

8   *Waltzing Matera*, p. 12.
9   *Waltzing Matera*, p. 14.
10 *Waltzing Matera*, p. 14.
11 *Waltzing Matera*, p. 18. Wally Matera played 24 games for West Coast (1987-88), then a further 32 games for Fitzroy (1989-90). Their younger brother, Phillip, later played 179 games for West Coast (1996-2005) and kicked 389 goals. He was West Coast's leading goalkicker five times (2000, 2002-05), an All-Australian (2003), and, like Peter, was named in the Italian Team of the Century (forward pocket) in 2005. Wally's son (Peter's nephew), Brandon, played 101 games for Gold Coast (2011-17) before joining Fremantle in 2018.
12 *Waltzing Matera*, p. 19.

having "immediate questions" about the local recruit because he was a skinny wingman with "no weight on him" and "permed hair". But, Worsfold added, he was "obviously quick." The hard-as-nails defender questioned whether Matera "would be strong enough to play AFL footy, or whether he'd get chewed up by the much bigger opponents he would inevitably come up against." Matera recalled entering the Eagles dressing room for the first time:

> When I first went down to the Eagles there were some big names. Johnnie Worsfold, David Hart, Chris Mainwaring, Craig Turley, Dwayne Lamb and then all of a sudden now I'm their teammate. So it was a big shock as I was a rookie. I didn't really care about it much, I just flaunted it a bit. Those guys pretty much put me back in my place a few times and then I started becoming more professional. I knew I had pace so it was more trying to fit in playing in a professional team that had team goals and team structures. I needed to know the players I played against and what their weaknesses and strengths were.[13]

He struggled to keep up during his first pre-season. "I had heard horror stories of VFL players training until they retched but discounted these yarns as exaggerations," he said. "Wally had told me training was tougher than at any WAFL club, but the proof of the pudding was in the eating. I could not believe the amount of work expected of us over the pre-Christmas period … The runs were gut-wrenching … I worked by butt off over the summer of 1989-90, but it was worth it. I could feel myself getting stronger and more durable."[14]

Worsfold considered Matera a good trainer who worked hard in the gym and on the track. "While he was slight in build, he was strong as well," Worsfold said. "I think he was always conscious of not putting too much weight on because he knew that his strength was going to be his speed and agility. But he did get himself stronger in the body, and that helped his game."

Defender Chris Waterman knew that once Matera adapted to the

---

13   *Legends*, p. 159.
14   *Waltzing Matera*, p. 22.

training requirements and got his body ready to handle the rigours of AFL level, he could become a standout player. "I had seen him play in the 1989 State of Origin game, where he was pretty electric, so we knew what we were getting," Waterman said. "We just didn't expect it to come so quick and hard and fast. He took off in 1991 and was All-Australian straight away. From there, there was no looking back." As time went on, coach Mick Malthouse had to force Matera to ease back on his training, to preserve him for match day. "He was getting the ball 30 times in a game and training every session, so during seasons Mick had to get him to give his body a rest in order to manage him," Waterman said.

Unfortunately, like other Aboriginal players of his era, Matera was not immune to racist taunts:

> Once people knew that I had an Italian dad and an Aboriginal mum I used to get it. They would say, "You're not Aboriginal. You think you're Aboriginal but you're not. You're not black. If your mother's black how come you aren't?" All this type of stuff... You couldn't really do much, you couldn't over-react. It was just part of footy until they changed the rules ... [But] before they brought the rule in it was just really bad.[15]

Inside the club, Matera quickly became one of its most popular players, as Worsfold explained:

> He's naturally a pretty shy guy. But when he got comfortable, when he'd settled in, he showed us his great sense of humour. He was very quiet for that first period, but as he got to know the guys he was a good fun guy to be around.

Waterman believes Matera could have been a stand-up comedian. "He was a funny bastard," Waterman said. "He never took anything that seriously, and still doesn't whenever we manage to catch up with him. He was always one of the lads and fitted in well with our team. He's certainly got some character about him, and he loves having a laugh and a beer—when you can get hold of him!"

---

15   *Legends*, pp. 159-160.

Matera had just nine disposals on debut (plus two hit-outs!), in round one, 1990, against Collingwood at Subiaco, and managed just five games due to recurring injuries that season. He believes this lack of senior appearances worked in his favour the following season—his breakout year at AFL level. "I still was a virtual unknown outside WA at the start of the 1991 season," Matera said, adding that "it suited me fine."[16]

When he gathered 25 disposals in the opening round, against Melbourne at Subiaco, his confidence rocketed and, he added, he "started playing as if I felt I could hold my place in the Eagles side."[17] He played 26 of a possible 27 games, including all four of West Coast's finals, and was named All-Australian for the first of five occasions (1991, 1993-94, 1996-97) over his 13-year career.

He and fellow wingman Chris Mainwaring formed the most devastating wing combination in the League. "They were different in styles," Worsfold said. "Although Mainy was still pretty quick, he was one of our best distance runners, more so than a burst player like Peter. We were blessed as defenders to have those two guys on the wings. They complemented each other really well." Although they performed many memorable heroics on the wings at Subiaco, Matera and Mainwaring would regularly push deep into defence to support their teammates.

The Eagles dominated the 1991 season, winning 19 of 22 matches in the home and away rounds to finish three games clear of Hawthorn in top place. But the Hawks caused one of the great finals upsets in the Qualifying Final, winning at Subiaco by 23 points. Matera had 22 disposals and kicked one goal—the only goal he scored for that finals series. He then had 23 disposals in the first Semi-Final against Melbourne and again in the Preliminary Final against Geelong.

The city of Perth was abuzz with excitement the following week, with the home side having become the first non-Victorian team to reach a Grand Final. For the only time in League history, the game was played at Waverley Park—Hawthorn's home ground—due to the redevelopment of the Southern Stand at the MCG. "We had every intention of doing our very best in the Grand Final in an effort to land the Premiership but,

---
16 *Waltzing Matera*, p. 29.
17 *Waltzing Matera*, p. 29.

in hindsight, I believe we already were victims of the disease Malthouse feared," Matera said. "Like so many inexperienced teams that had made the big one, we probably felt that we had already climbed the mountain. We learned, to our bitter experience, that we merely had reached a basecamp halfway up the mountain."[18] The Hawks thrashed West Coast by 53 points, with Matera, who had 23 disposals for the third straight week, one of his team's better players.

The 1992 season was all about redemption. The Eagles won 15 games and had one draw, finishing the home and away rounds in fourth place, only two points off the top three sides, Geelong, Footscray and Collingwood. After 444 disposals in 1991, Matera had just 378 in 1992. However, it was the defensive side to his game, which gets lost amidst his goalkicking highlights and blistering runs, that his teammates appreciated more than the number of possessions he gathered. Waterman described Matera as an outstanding defensive player who "would never lose a one-on-one contest." Waterman said that even in the rare moments Matera was knocked off balance, he was straight back up and throwing himself at the next contest "like a cat on a hot tin roof." "His opponent would think he had a couple of metres on him, but he'd chase them down straight away," Waterman said. "He was very good defensively, because he had that explosive speed which allowed him to cover ground and close someone down."

Fellow midfielder Dean Kemp described Matera as "one of those freak athletes who had the power, strength and ability to keep on his feet." "He didn't get much credit for the defensive side of his game, but 'Roo' [Matera] was an amazing tackler and chaser as well." Worsfold, too, praised Matera's defensive mindset:

> When he tackled someone, he would almost be starting to get the ball into his hand before he completed the tackle, knowing that he was going to take off immediately. Even ground balls, if he tackled someone and the ball spilled out, he'd be that low to the ground and balanced that he would take the ball at top speed and very quickly he'd be away. With some of his rundown tackles, he would catch up with

---

18 *Waltzing Matera*, p. 36.

someone, rather than having to lunge to try and tackle them like most of us. Out of that, he would know "I've caught this bloke, it's going to be holding the ball" and he'd almost have ripped the ball off them ready to go back the other way before they had even realised they had been caught. Some of that stuff, when it happened, I would stand there on the half-back flank and just start clapping. I'd say to the bloke I was playing on, "You shouldn't be able to do that!" It was unbelievable. He did some brilliant things like that.

Waterman described Matera's kicking skills as elite. "Even on his left foot he was way above average," he said. "Everyone remembers Peter's goals, but with his field kicking he could hit a target from 60 metres away. As he was getting the ball between half-back and wing a lot of the times, it only required one bounce and he would be in range of goals—which was 60 metres out for him." Because of those superior foot skills, Waterman said that Matera "never stood out for his handball," adding:

> He could handball well, but he never had to use it much. He was always finding space and getting through traffic. He had that sideways movement and explosive pace off the mark. He probably handballed to himself more times than he handballed to anyone else! If he got tackled, he'd drop that little handball to his advantage, tap it on, lose the tackle and get the ball back.

Worsfold recalled that Matera was quiet before games, "getting himself focused." Part of that preparation involved a decent meal. "I remember he used to have a big pre-game meal in the morning before a game, which was surprising," Worsfold said. "You looked at him and didn't think he would eat that much, but he would load up before games—way more than I would. He'd have four pieces of toast, all loaded up with baked beans or spaghetti, and he would smash it down. I would think, 'This bloke is supposed to be running amok on the wing in a couple of hours time,' but it seemed to work for him somehow."

On the field, Matera was more vocal. "You would always hear his voice out on the field—that was a standout with Peter," said Waterman.

"He was good enough to always get in the right positions, and you'd hear him call for the ball. I'd look up and there he was."

Matera's legend was cemented during the 1992 finals series—he was best player afield in all three of West Coast's finals. In the first Elimination Final, against Hawthorn at Subiaco, Matera had 28 disposals and kicked three goals in a 13-point win. Then, in the second Semi-Final against Geelong at the MCG, he played one of his finest games. He had 35 disposals, seven marks, kicked two goals and laid five tackles in a 38-point triumph. To this day Waterman remains in awe of his teammate's performance against the Cats:

> Had they handed out a Norm Smith Medal in the second Semi-Final, he would have got one then as well. In that Semi-Final, against Geelong, he did it all and won the game off his own boot. He had 35 possessions on the wing. I played on the other wing and had about five disposals because, basically, I just stood there and watched him! He dominated that game on his own, and that game was much better than even his Grand Final performance.

After Geelong defeated Footscray, by 64 points, in the Preliminary Final, Cats coach Malcolm Blight recognised that he needed to nullify Matera's dominance if they were a chance to topple the Eagles in the Grand Final. "Peter Matera had towelled us up in the 1992 second Semi-Final, playing on a young Peter Riccardi," Blight recalled. "In fact, Matera was always a nuisance when we played against the Eagles. Mark Bairstow, our captain, had played on the wing in state games, and so we matched him up with Matera in the Grand Final."

The day before, on the Friday during the Grand Final Parade—which the Eagles attended for the first time, after Malthouse chose to snub the time-honoured event in 1991, something he and a number of Eagles players later regretted—the heavens opened. The Eagles captain, Worsfold, recognised that Matera's running game could suffer if the rain continued during the Grand Final. Therefore, he and his teammates employed their own mind games to keep their star wingman focused and confident:

THE NORM SMITH MEDAL

It was quite wet on the Friday before the 1992 Grand Final—we used umbrellas during the Grand Final Parade. Peter didn't want a wet, heavy track for the Grand Final. After the parade, we trained on the MCG and the surface was quite wet, and we had a feeling that Peter wasn't too happy with the surface, probably thinking it was going to influence his ability the next day to utilise his speed. After we trained, they put the heavy soaking machines on the ground to soak up the water. We were staying at the old Hilton Hotel [now known as the Pullman] across the road from the ground, and during our team meeting that Friday night we could see out the window the lights on at the MCG. So we were all reassuring Peter that they were over there drying the surface out to make sure it would be a fast track the next day. We were really focused on getting him in the right frame of mind, telling him it was going to be ideal for him the next day to get him thinking positively.

The football scuttlebutt during the week was that the Cats would target Matera physically, as they had done to Hawthorn's Dermott Brereton in the 1989 Grand Final—their most recent appearance on the big stage. Matera recalled that, as the players walked from their hotel and down through Yarra Park to the ground that morning, "we came across a multitude of fans, some friendly and many hostile."[19] One comment in particular hit home: "You won't last five minutes, Matera!" Having been cleaned up in the 1991 Grand Final, the comment played on Matera's mind as he prepared for the 1992 decider. "I could not get it off my mind, even as I ran on to the MCG," he said:

> I could not put a face to the voice because of the size of the crowd, but I heard the comment clear enough... I know this should not have worried me as it was probably a Cat fan trying to put the wind up me. But I kept thinking of how I had been cleaned up early in the 1991 Grand Final and

---
19   *Waltzing Matera*, p. 48.

how Geelong tore into Hawthorn at the opening of the 1989 Grand Final.[20]

Again, the skipper was on hand to support his teammate. "There were some whispers that Peter might be physically targeted at the start of the game," Worsfold said. "I think it was all mythical, but it meant there was a tiny bit of anxiety at the start of the game. I was playing on [Geelong's potential match-winner and 1989 Norm Smith medallist] Gary Ablett, but I moved up on to the wing at the start to get close to Peter, as if to say, 'If I see anyone coming at you, I'll get my body in their way.'" Subtly, Matera's teammates sought to calm his nerves by showing him that he was covered should anything untoward happen. Matera later said, "I feared the worst but told myself that if I got cleaned up, so be it. I would be wary, but I was not going to pull out for love or money. If anything I was even more determined to succeed."[21] Fortunately, the pre-game rumours proved false, and it was Matera who delivered the knockout blows.

Seconds into the game, Matera won the first effective kick and took a long running shot for goal, but the ball drifted left for a behind. Ablett delivered early body blows, lining up Don Pyke and Tony Evans with bumps. There were further blows on the scoreboard when the Cats kicked two goals in the opening four minutes. Then, halfway through the term, in a sign of what was to come, Matera roved a ball-up at half-forward, burst clear and bombed a goal from 55 metres out—West Coast's first of the day. However, he missed an easier chance on the run from 25 metres out just seconds before the quarter-time siren as the inaccurate Eagles trailed Geelong by 19 points.

When Ablett kicked a long set-shot goal two minutes into the second quarter, the Cats were threatening to blow the game open. They had been creating better chances when going forward, with their run and carry through the middle of the ground cutting the Eagles to shreds. In contrast, whenever West Coast went forward they were hurried and indirect. With Geelong's key defenders Tim Darcy and Tim McGrath cutting off attacking drives before providing rebound, it took another

---

20 *Waltzing Matera*, p. 48.
21 *Waltzing Matera*, p. 48.

moment of Matera magic to keep his side in the game. At the 10-minute mark he burst through the 50-metre line and kicked over the heads of the Geelong defenders for his second running goal of the game. Waterman believes it was his best goal:

> He kicked a goal in the second quarter which no one ever talks about, apart from his teammates, that is. There was a scuffle of play just forward of the wing in our attacking half. He just walked up, plucked the ball out, dodged a bloke, took a bounce and kicked the goal. Everyone talks about the one on the run in the third quarter, but that goal in the second quarter actually kept us in the game. It was an amazing goal! You rarely see someone simply walk up, pluck it out and go bang. It was out of nowhere, and I think the crowd went: "What just happened?"

Evans, with two late goals, plus a great snap around his body from Sumich helped keep the Eagles within touch at half-time. They trailed by 12 points but were beginning to gain some control. Their pressure had intensified, and they were moving the ball better. Matera's opponent, Bairstow, had been one of his team's best players, and Blight later joked that it was a "genius" move on his part to pit his captain against the attacking wingman. "I thought Mark was our best player to that point," Blight said. "Mark's first half had been crucial in us having a lead at half-time. Could I have done something later in the game? Maybe. But it wasn't only Peter that beat us that day. They had a great side and we ran out of talent."

Worsfold believes that Matera "broke the game open in the third quarter," busting the Bairstow shackles to spark the Eagles with two third-quarter goals. Late in the second quarter, Matera and a number of teammates appeared frustrated with umpires and opponents alike. But after half-time their focus was resolute, although it was not immediately evident on the scoreboard. Bairstow won the first kick of the third quarter, Ablett kicked the first goal (Geelong led by 17 points), Evans then kicked his third goal, Wilson snapped a miracle goal over his head, before Matera entered the conversation at the eight-minute mark. Receiving the ball in front of the MCC Members' Stand, he set sail for goal from outside 50—his third goal of the day giving the Eagles a two-point lead. Kemp thought it inspiring. "When he kicked that big goal in the third quarter and put his arm up in the air and ran off, that was a huge moment," he said. "His game that day was one out of the box, and it was great to have a front row seat to his performance."

With five minutes remaining, Matera gathered at centre half-forward, spun on to his left foot, bounced his way through the 50-line again and drilled a left-foot goal. He was not the sole reason for the dramatic change in the game's momentum—that had already begun to change before he kicked his third goal, thanks in part from a lift by Brett Heady in the middle of the ground—but Matera raised the intensity with his two goals and the crowd sensed that the Eagles were beginning to soar. And he almost kicked a third goal for the quarter, again charging through 50 but hitting the goal post halfway up in the final minutes. It didn't matter; West Coast managed five goals to one for the quarter and led by 17 points at the final break.

One minute into the final term and any hope of a Geelong fightback was killed off by… guess who? Sumich marked 30 metres out and no Geelong defender was standing near Matera. Sumich handballed over the top and the wingman waltzed in and dribbled through his fifth goal of the day to increase the margin to 23 points. The eventual margin was 28 points, 16.17 (113) to 12.13 (85), and the Premiership Cup left Victoria for the first time. Matera had gathered only 15 kicks and three handballs, but his five goals (and three behinds) were decisive in him being named the Norm Smith medallist. During the on-ground euphoria, Matera remembered:

> We were all huddled in the middle of the ground, the happiest men in Australia, when an AFL official marched over to me and said, "You have won the Norm Smith Medal." "Oh, piss off," I told him. I had not even considered the possibility of winning the award for being best player on the ground. I was happy enough just to be in a Premiership team. However, the official refused to "piss off" and told me again that I had won the medal. This time I believed him and told Glen Jakovich, who hugged and congratulated me.[22]

---

22   *Waltzing Matera*, p. 55.

THE NORM SMITH MEDAL

Waterman considers that no one dominated the Grand Final, but Matera's scoreboard damage was critical. "He only had 18 touches, but his five goals were vital in what ended up being a 28-point win for us." Matera said he was in "tears of joy" when he received his Premiership Medallion and "only a little more composed" when presented with the Norm Smith Medal. "I had dreamed for so long of winning an AFL Premiership medal, but to be named best on the ground in the most important match of the year took my joy to a new dimension."[23] Although his Premiership medal remains "a symbol of what we, as a team, had achieved that day", the Norm Smith Medal is "a reminder that I was able to play well when it counted most."[24]

Two years later, in 1994, Matera polled 28 Brownlow Medal votes and finished second to Carlton's Greg Williams (30 votes). In the Grand Final six days later, West Coast (which had finished a game clear on top of the ladder with 16 wins, then won the fourth Qualifying Final by two points over Collingwood and the second Preliminary Final by 65 points over Melbourne) again defeated Geelong. In a far more dominant team performance, the Eagles led for most of the day and won by 80 points, 20.23 (143) to 8.15 (63). Matera had 13 kicks, two handballs and laid five tackles, but did not score a goal. "I had what I considered to be an ordinary game," he said. Having entered the match with a leg injury, he was hampered throughout. "I knew that because of my lack of fitness and the fact I was nursing my leg injury that I would not get anywhere near another Norm Smith Medal, but I at least won a few contests," he said.[25] Waterman recalled Matera trying to kick a goal from the same spot as one of his goals from 1992, "but he put it out on the full!"

"He was serviceable though," Waterman added. "I think he had set the bar so high in 1992 that everyone was hoping and expecting him to do the same again in 1994. He was still a vital part of our team, though, and as a team we dominated that game." Dean Kemp was awarded the Norm Smith Medal. Although Matera may have been quieter in the 1994 decider, the *Herald Sun*'s then chief football writer, MikeSheahan, had no hesitation in saying that Matera "cost Geelong two Premierships":

---

23   *Waltzing Matera*, p. 55.
24   *Waltzing Matera*, p. 55.
25   *Waltzing Matera*, p. 91.

PETER MATERA

> Peter Matera was almost my favourite player at the Eagles during those years. I couldn't believe that someone playing on the wing could be as destructive as he was. The conventional wingers were smallish, clever, and would pinpoint their passes to someone at half-forward. But then there was Matera, who could run like the wind and could kick the ball 60 metres, accurately. Thinking of all the Norm Smith medallists, it's hard to think of anyone who won more decisively than he did in 1992.

In 1996, following a number of injuries to West Coast's defenders, Matera showcased his versatility by moving to half-back. "Peter was not only a great wingman," Waterman said. "When I went down with injury in round one, 1996, then 'Woosha' [Worsfold] and 'Bluey' (Guy McKenna) went down in round three, our half-back line was suddenly gone. So Mick moved Roo to the half-back flank and he was an All-Australian there that year." The following year, as a defender, Matera won his only club champion award.

Matera's final seasons coincided with younger brother, Phil, playing alongside him at the Eagles, at the other end of the ground in a forward pocket, but only after Peter was talked into remaining at the club in 1997, having stated his intention to play for Melbourne. Again, it was Worsfold's intervention that changed his mind and saw him play out his career with the Eagles. He was named vice-captain in 1999 and, in round 20, 2002, became just the second Eagle, behind Guy McKenna, to play 250 games for the club.

In 2005, three years after his last game, Matera was named on the wing in the Indigenous Team of the Century; in 2006 he was inducted into the Australian Football Hall of Fame, then in 2007, he was chosen as a wingman in the Italian Team of the Century. Indeed, Matera remains one of the greatest Eagles. Where does he rank? Says Waterman: "I've always said we could put a blanket over a lot of them."

> We had guys like Dean Kemp, Matera, Glen Jakovich, McKenna, even Woosha in terms of his leadership. Plus Sumich, for his goals in finals, and Ashley McIntosh for

who he played on and beat at full-back. We had at least 10 Hall of Famers in there. Most of us say, though, when push came to shove, there was one bloke who won us more games than anyone else—that was Peter Matera. He was the match-winner who stood out in that sense. Roo could beat anyone.

Worsfold, too, rates Matera. "Peter's certainly up among the top few to have played for West Coast," he said. "A lot of people would have him as the best player that West Coast has had. In his era we had some very good players, such as Jakovich, McKenna, Kemp, and Peter was certainly rated very, very highly among that select group."

NOTE: Interviews with John Worsfold, Chris Waterman, Dean Kemp, Mike Sheahan and Malcolm Blight were conducted by the author.

──── Statistics ────

BORN: 3 April 1969
GAMES PLAYED (1990-2002): 253
GOALS: 217
FINALS PLAYED: 21
FINALS GOALS: 23
GRAND FINALS: 3
PREMIERSHIPS: 1992, 1994
NORM SMITH MEDAL: 1992 (presented by Bruce Doull)

PETER MATERA

— Norm Smith Voting —

(JUDGES: Ted Whitten, Ross Oakley, Mike Sheahan and Rex Hunt)

The Age votes: **Mike Sheahan:** 3 Peter Matera, 2 Ken Hinkley, 1 Ashley McIntosh;
Rohan Connolly: 3 Matera, 2 Brett Heady, 1 McIntosh;
Richard Hinds: 3 Matera, 2 McIntosh, 1 Heady;
Gerard Wright: 3 Matera, 2 Heady, 1 Dean Kemp;
Barry Richardson: 3 Matera, 2 McIntosh, 1 Hinkley;
Gareth Andrews: 3 Matera, 2 Heady, 1 McIntosh;
John Hendrie: 3 Matera, 2 Kemp, 1 McIntosh;
Michael Lovett: 3 Matera, 2 McIntosh, 1 Hinkley.

The Age **TOTALS:** Matera 24, McIntosh 10, Heady 7, Hinkley 4, Kemp 3.

Michael Long

The trail blazed by Essendon's Michael Long on Grand Final day 1993 was matched only by his heroics off the field, where he overcame his natural shyness to take a courageous stand against racism and begin a lifelong campaign against Indigenous disadvantage. Long entered the 1993 decider supremely confident on the back of a stunning Preliminary Final performance, promising himself that he would "run like the wind". The result was not only the Grand Final's defining moment, a solo run and goal in the first quarter that tilted the game Essendon's way, but also 33 disposals, eight marks, two goals and—fittingly in the International Year of the Indigenous Person—the Norm Smith Medal.

Michael Long's influence on the field was often breathtaking. His performances in the 1993 finals series alone—when he ran, bounced, weaved, ran some more, and topped it off with the most memorable of Grand Final goals—ensure that his legacy will be long lasting. Those 1993 finals defined Long's legend as a player, but his contribution off the field, championing the cause of Aboriginal people and taking a famous stand against racism, has been his greatest impact on the game and Australian society at large.

← **ICONIC** The 1993 Grand Final will be remembered forever for Michael Long's speed, courage and purpose. His first-quarter goal remains one of the game's classics.

THE NORM SMITH MEDAL

When Collingwood ruckman Damian Monkhorst racially abused Long at the MCG on Anzac Day 1995, his decision to stand up for his rights helped to set the AFL on the path towards reconciliation.

In 2004, three years after retiring from the field, Long walked from Melbourne to Canberra, determined to meet with Prime Minister John Howard over Aboriginal rights. This journey—*The Long Walk*—is celebrated annually when Essendon plays Richmond in what became known as the *Dreamtime* game. In 2018, the Bombers were to unveil a statue of their inspirational trailblazer at the club's training and administration base at Tullamarine.

Long's understanding of the trauma experienced by his ancestors began on the Tiwi Islands, where he was born on 1 October 1969. His parents were members of the Stolen Generation. "My father, Jack, was stolen from his parents—my grandparents—at Ti Tree in Alice Springs," Long explained in an interview published in *Champions*. "My mother, Agnes, was taken from her mother at Daly River [230km south-west of Darwin]."[1] Long said these events hung "like a black cloud" over his family "because of all the close relationships we've missed out on."[2] Fortunately, he and his eight siblings (Steven, Bruno, Noel, John, Cathy, Chris, Sue and Patrick) were not removed from their parents, but stories of the devastation from forced displacement were taught and ingrained in them from a young age.[3]

Long's earliest football memories occurred on the Nightcliff Primary School oval in Darwin. His father, a tough and rugged footballer who played for St Mary's, coached his son's school team. But it was the daily matches between the Long boys away from school that taught Michael how to thrive on a football field. He described those games as "some of the toughest I played," and "a case of survival" where he worked out that, "If I don't run and use my pace, I'm gonna get hurt!"[4]

Long's brothers may have taught him to protect himself on the field, but his temperament and outlook were defined by his father. "I don't think you'll get anywhere in life unless you have a mix of hardness and tenderness," Long said. "Dad wasn't the most skilful footballer, but

---

1 Ben Collins & Dan Eddy, *Champions: Conversations with Great Players & Coaches of Australian Football*, Slattery Media Group, 2016, p. 181.
2 *Champions*, p. 181.
3 *Champions*, p. 181.
4 *Champions*, p. 182.

his toughness is legendary. But for all his ruggedness on the field, he's probably the most gentle and welcoming person off it. I've tried to adopt those traits myself."[5]

His mother, Agnes, had an enormous influence, too. "If you talk about women in football, you talk about women like my mother," Long said. "Her life was football and her children. Her husband and seven sons all played and she washed our gear, dropped us off at training, dropped us off at games, and picked us up."[6] In December 1983, the family was rocked when Agnes died of ovarian cancer. Long was 14 and the loss of his mother was the most devastating moment of his young life. So much so, as Martin Flanagan explained in *The Short Long Book*, that Michael continues to "share a cup of tea with his mother" every day.[7] Long told Flanagan that, during the 1993 Grand Final—Long's crowning moment as a player—he felt his mother's presence on the ground with him.

Although Long captivated football audiences with his brilliance, he maintains that his brother, Steven, was "the most talented footballer in the family."[8] Steven was "a freakish player who could kick goals from anywhere, and he was so tough he was dangerous."[9] However, when their mother died, Steven "took on the role of a parent" and football became a lesser priority. "Under different circumstances he could easily have played in the AFL," Long said.[10]

As with many Aboriginal boys of the 1970s and 1980s, Long idolised Maurice Rioli, later related to the Long family through marriage (Michael's sister, Cathy—Cyril Rioli's mother—is married to Maurice's younger brother, Cyril jnr). "We used to watch (ABC TV's) *The Winners*," he recalled. "Everyone just barracked for Richmond when Maurice was in his heyday (1982-87). I still remember going around to a good friend, Ted Berry's place, and watching the 1982 Grand Final with the family… everyone followed Maurice."[11]

Rioli won the 1982 Norm Smith Medal that day in a Richmond side that lost to Carlton by 18 points. And it was Rioli who draped Long's

---

5   *Champions*, p. 181.
6   *Champions*, p. 181.
7   Martin Flanagan, *The Short Long Book*, Vintage, 2015, p. 24.
8   *Champions*, p. 181.
9   *Champions*, p. 181.
10   *Champions*, p. 181.
11   Sean Gorman, *Legends: The AFL Indigenous Team of the Century*, Aboriginal Studies Press, 2011, p. 146.

Norm Smith Medal around his neck in 1993. With their nephew, Cyril (Hawthorn's 2015 Norm Smith winner), the trio share a remarkable family connection to AFL Grand Final day. Another nephew, Daniel Rioli (Cyril's cousin), was a member of Richmond's 2017 Premiership side, while Long's son, Jake, made his debut for Essendon in 2016 and his nephew, Ben, for St Kilda in 2017. Their cousin, Willie Rioli, made his debut for West Coast in 2018, and another cousin, Ronnie Burns, played for Geelong and Adelaide (1996-2004, 154 games). The Longs and the Riolis are, surely, football royalty.

Like a number of Norm Smith winners (notably Scott Pendlebury and Simon Black), Long credits his time playing basketball at 14 and 15 years of age as having assisted his "hand-eye coordination, vision, explosive running (and) evasive skills." And just like those fellow winners, there came a time when he was forced to choose between the round and the oval balls. "Dad gave me an ultimatum: either you play football or you don't live here," Long said. "It would never have come to that because it was inevitable that I would get back into football at some stage, but that got the message across and made it happen a bit quicker."[12]

Long said that hunting, too, "played an enormous part in my football career." His father was "regarded as one of the best hunters and fishermen in the Territory," and Long grew up hunting magpie geese. He also fished regularly and caught crabs. He recalled that his father "taught us to use all our senses: hand-eye coordination, vision, listening, smells, touch—general awareness." Transferring those skills to the football field proved vital to Long's game. His senses were "so finely tuned that you only had to hear a voice and you could tell who it was and where they were," he said. "You could handball or tap the ball to them without even looking." But, he conceded, "it was hard work getting to that stage of awareness. You're not born with it."[13]

Through hunting, Long developed his core strength and leg muscles. "We might have to carry five or 10 geese through a couple of kilometres of thick, knee-high swamp back to the car," he said. "In terms of strength and core stability, that was the best training you could do."[14] He said he

---

12   *Champions*, p. 182.
13   *Champions*, p. 182.
14   *Legends*, p. 145.

"never lost a 100-metre sprint in Darwin" because his legs "were probably two or three years older than the rest of my body in terms of strength." When he later arrived at Essendon, despite being "one of the skinniest players on the list," Long's leg strength was superior to that of many seasoned players. "It was already there, without having to go on weights programs to get it."[15]

Like the rest of his family, Long played for St Mary's. Between 1986 and 1988, he played 53 games and won two Premierships, one fewer than his father. Michael's brothers, too, won a raft of Premierships: Noel (won 11), Bruno (eight), John (seven), Patrick (six), Chris (four) and Steven (three). Remarkably, between father and sons they played exactly 1000 games for the club and kicked 1008 goals. Steven and Noel also won the Northern Territory Football League's equivalent of the Norm Smith Medal, the Chaney Medal: Steven in the 1986/87 Grand Final, while Noel won it three times (1989/90, 1994/95 and 1995/96).[16]

In *Legends*, Sean Gorman wrote that before the 1988 Bicentennial Carnival in Adelaide, football was a sport Long played with "a modicum of seriousness" but also for enjoyment. But, he added, "the football landscape changed" when Long represented the Territory at the carnival. Long approached the carnival "a lot more seriously" and, as a consequence, was selected in the All-Australian side.[17] From there came an invitation to join the West Torrens Eagles, where Chris and Noel already played.

Torrens was coached by former Essendon utility and 1984-85 Premiership player Paul Weston (1983-85), a connection that enabled the Bombers to become aware of Long's ability. "Leaving the family for the first time and moving away to Adelaide really opened up a new world for me," Long said.[18] He won the best and fairest award in 1988, but, for the first time, was subjected to racist taunts:

> I was walking down the street one day and someone called me "Black Sambo". It shocked me. I'd never experienced it before. My father's attitude was always: "We are one. It doesn't matter who you are. As long as you're a good person,

---

15 *Champions*, p. 183.
16 For more information on the Long family's extraordinary impact on the St Mary's Football Club, see: http://stmarysfc0.tripod.com/id37.html.
17 *Legends*, p. 146.
18 *Legends*, p. 147.

the door is always open." Racism wasn't part of our dialogue. There was an understanding and a respect of other cultures because we'd grown up together, gone to school together and worked together. But Adelaide was different.[19]

Although shattered by the abuse, Long was determined to endure the challenges of being away from home. "If I didn't succeed, I would have felt like I'd failed my family," he said. "There's no bigger motivating force than that. I had to succeed for them as well as myself. I'd had friends and brothers who'd travelled to different places and states to play football, but I had a vision that I wanted to be more than that. I wanted to be successful at a higher level."[20]

That pathway became clearer when Essendon coach Kevin Sheedy and recruiter, Noel Judkins (son of Richmond's 1930 Brownlow medallist Stan) decided to open the doors at Essendon's then home ground, Windy Hill, to Aboriginal footballers. Only Norm McDonald (1947-53, 128 games including the 1949-50 Premierships) had represented the Bombers before Sheedy's arrival at the club in 1981. But Sheedy, a former Richmond defender (1967-79, 251 games, including the 1969, 1973-74 Premierships), was determined to create a more inclusive Essendon under his watch, and attracting and developing Aboriginal footballers—an untapped reservoir of football talent—was at the top of his to-do list.

Sheedy had played against Carlton's Syd Jackson (1969-76, 136 games including the 1970 and 1972 Premierships), and had seen Maurice Rioli star with the Tigers. He thought, "Why are [more of] these people not getting a chance?" There had been just 28 Aboriginal footballers to play in the VFL before 1988, but Sheedy's recruitment of Long, along with the debut of St Kilda's Nicky Winmar in 1987, became a turning point in the relationship between the premier football competition and the Aboriginal community. "It all basically starts when Long and Winmar come in," Sheedy recalled:

> The tipping point is really the drafting. With the drafting coming in [in 1986], we had toured extensively throughout

---

19   *Champions*, p. 186.
20   *Champions*, p. 184.

MICHAEL LONG

Australia as a club, trying to build our team and our club as a whole. We played everywhere and we got more confident that we could handle recruiting Indigenous players. We had to change our set-up within the club, too—you just couldn't switch on the light. You have to *make* it happen, so you go and get a player and then make a network around him. It's a significant step to take, but 330 [Indigenous players have played in the League] since.

Sheedy—who once wrote, "I don't think I had an Aboriginal friend when I was growing up in Fitzgerald Street, South Yarra"[21]— admits it "was very difficult to implement, because we all knew that some would go home, and some did." He said that developing the right support networks for Aboriginal footballers was "a learning procedure that a club like Essendon had to go through." Of his enormous contribution to football as player, coach, entrepreneur, salesman and philosopher, Sheedy's role in opening the doors to Aboriginal people may be his finest. The annual *Dreamtime at the 'G* game, between Essendon and Richmond, is but one of his many significant contributions to the sport. "We went after Aboriginal footballers like a rat up a drainpipe," Sheedy wrote in *A Touch of Cunning*.[22] Long remains appreciative of the role Sheedy played in shaping his life:

> Kevin Sheedy was all things to me. A father figure and a life coach. It was as much a learning thing for 'Sheeds' as it was for me, but he had vision. Not a blurred, vague vision of what he'd like to create, but a crystal-clear vision of the potential he sees in a footballer. He was a pioneer in a lot of ways, especially in recruiting Aboriginal players. That will be one of his many legacies.[23]

Long was recruited to Essendon with the club's third selection in the 1988 National Draft (pick 23 overall), behind Michael Werner (pick nine, who went on to play 60 games) and Brad Fox (pick 12, 21 games). That Long was still available at pick 23 was a relief to Judkins,

---

21 Kevin Sheedy, *Sheeds: A Touch of Cunning*, Wilkinson Books, 1995, p. 277.
22 *Sheeds: A Touch of Cunning*, p. 278.
23 Long, *Champions*, p. 184.

who later said "we couldn't believe it" that no other club had chosen him earlier.[24] They were not to know it at the time, but as Sheedy later wrote, "The Long family added another dimension" to the club and the game.[25] For Long, however, adapting to the colder weather in Melbourne during his first season was a huge shock to the system:

> I really struggled with Melbourne's cold climate. My first job was on a construction site in the city. I had to catch a tram to work for a 6am start. It was freezing cold. I hated it. I didn't last long in that job. Coming from 35 degrees to 10-12 degrees was a huge shock to the system. And my first year here (1989) was the wettest year I've spent in Melbourne... Sometimes I'd sit in the sauna, fully clothed, before training just to warm myself up.[26]

Despite being one of the skinniest players in the league in 1989—teammate Mark Harvey joked that Long would have made a great jumps jockey—he played 24 of Essendon's 25 games, including its three finals. In the Qualifying Final, against Geelong, he kicked four goals in Essendon's 76-point victory. The Bombers then lost to eventual premier Hawthorn by 36 points in the second Semi-Final, and were belted by a Gary Ablett-inspired Geelong (94 points) in the Preliminary Final. Once the club realised Long could withstand the physical rigours of League football, Harvey said, "they knew we were going to have some kind of a player." The VFL named him its Rookie of the Year.

Long concedes that, in his early time at Essendon, he was "one of the shyest people there ever was," and communicating with teammates was "a major issue." But with brother Chris having journeyed to Melbourne to act as his "security blanket" (and play some reserves games for the Bombers), he was soon able to "overcome a lot of personal barriers." That said, Long admits, "If it wasn't for Chris, I might have gone back to Darwin."[27]

His happiest place during those difficult early days was on the football field. "My best language was football," he said. "I did my talking on the

---

24 Simon Matthews, *Champions of Essendon: Ranking the 60 Greatest Bombers of All-Time*, Hardie Grant Books, 2002, p. 151.
25 *Sheeds: A Touch of Cunning*, p. 281.
26 *Champions*, p. 184.
27 *Champions*, p. 184.

MICHAEL LONG

field. It was the only place I felt comfortable expressing myself. For a while there, the only way I could communicate was through football. It took a while to feel comfortable talking to people on their level, without feeling inferior. Football was my educator, my teacher."[28] He was a quick learner.

In the 1990 pre-season draft, Essendon recruited another Aboriginal player, Derek Kickett, who had played 12 games for North Melbourne. Long played all 25 games for the Bombers in 1990 and was out there on Grand Final day when Collingwood settled better after an ugly quarter-time brawl and humiliated Essendon by 48 points, thus breaking a 32-year Premiership drought. Long managed just 10 disposals and two tackles, but he was not alone in a dismal day for the club. The only highlight was Kickett's high mark over Norm Smith medallist Tony Shaw.

Three years later, in 1993—the International Year of the Indigenous Person—one of the first defining moments in combating racism in sport occurred. In round four, at Victoria Park, Winmar, having been racially abused by the Collingwood crowd, lifted his jumper and pointed to his black skin after St Kilda's 22-point upset. For white Australia, it was one of the first signs that something was amiss on the sporting field.

Due to injury, Long played only two of the first eight games, as the Bombers stuttered through the first half of the 1993 season. He returned in round nine, which coincided with a reversal of form that saw the club quickly rising up the ladder. After falling as low as 11th in round seven, by round 10 it was inside the top six. When it lost to Geelong in round 21, Essendon was second and had the bye in the final round. However, after a remarkably tight season with no obvious standout, top-placed North Melbourne lost its last game, and the Bombers and Carlton claimed the top two positions.

Having played a draw in round two, the two ladder leaders kept supporters on their seats again in the Qualifying Final. In football's first night final, the Blues won by two points and Long, with 27 disposals, was Essendon's best player. He was good again in the first Semi-Final (25 disposals), as the Bombers defeated reigning premier West Coast by 32 points. Having defeated Adelaide by 46 points in round nine, Essendon

---

28   *Champions*, p. 184.

THE NORM SMITH MEDAL

was favoured to repeat the dose in the Preliminary Final and book a rematch with Carlton in the Grand Final. However, in the opening half, the Crows ran the Bombers ragged and led by 42 points at half-time. There were many concerns in the Essendon dressing room during the break, but for Long it was a double worry. "My family was coming down for the Grand Final, but we were being beaten," he recalled:

> I thought: "Hold the bus, folks!" It was the moment I knew I had to do something. And I knew I would do something. It's the moment when you have everything in the palm of your hand. You make things happen. It's moments and spurts in a game that you're in control of. You're making decisions, showing leadership, inspiring your teammates and doing things that you haven't done before but that were always there, within you, waiting to come out.[29]

From the first bounce of the third quarter, Long and Essendon were on a mission. Long won the first centre clearance; moments later, he spoiled an Adelaide kick-in that resulted in a goal to Darren Bewick. At the next centre bounce, Long stole the ball and charged clear again. Minutes later, his bouncing run down the wing ended with Paul Salmon kicking another goal. They were big plays that brought his teammates, and the crowd, to life. The Bombers kicked six goals to one in the third quarter to trail by just 12 points at the final break. The goal spree continued in the last quarter, and when Long tapped the ball cleverly to Tim Watson, who handballed to Gary O'Donnell, his goal put them in front. They held on to win by 11 points in one of the most dramatic finals in history, and Long threw his arms around Bewick (who kicked six goals) in relief. He later said:

> The 1993 Preliminary Final was the first time my skills and flair came out in the AFL. I was at my best in that finals series... Everyone talks about the Grand Final but I played just as well in the prelim against Adelaide. I was just so focused.[30]

---

29 *Champions*, p. 184.
30 *Champions*, p. 185.

MICHAEL LONG

According to O'Donnell, "Longy showed the way through the middle of the ground" and became "the catalyst for the team going all the way." Earlier in the season, Long had confided in Essendon president David Shaw, himself a Premiership player (1962, 1965), that he had dreamed of playing a key role in an Essendon Premiership. It was an ominous premonition that played out in front of millions (and an MCG crowd of 96,862) on Grand Final day against Carlton. "I went into the '93 Grand Final knowing no one could beat me," Long said. "My mindset before the game was: 'I'm gonna run like the wind.' Sometimes you can walk down the players' race full of confidence and for that moment, and moments during the game, you know you're going to do some real damage."[31] He added:

> At those times, whoever your opponent is, your attitude is: "You're putting him on me? Him? He can't beat me." You're driving the ship and, if someone gets in the way, you either drive around them or through them. Nothing can touch you. You do it all on pure instinct.[32]

That instinct was on show at the seven-minute mark of the first quarter when Long kicked one of the great Grand Final goals. Of the moment that has come to define him as a player, Long recalled in *Champions*:

> I don't know why I was so far downfield from the half-forward flank. It was because my man had got sucked into the pack, I suppose. Sean [Denham] gave me a handpass and Tim Watson yelled: "Keep going!" I got around a tall defender and kept going, and not being the biggest kick, I wanted to get closer to the goals… I had to bounce it a fair bit because I was so pumped up and running so fast I was covering a fair bit of ground… When I thought I was close enough to goal, I let fly. It was a long, low, direct kick and I thought it would go straight through, and it did. I know (Carlton full-back Stephen) Silvagni claimed he touched it on the line, but the goal umpire didn't think so, and I charged back down the ground on a real high.[33]

---

31 *Champions*, p. 185.
32 *Champions*, p. 185.
33 *Football Record*, 1998.

THE NORM SMITH MEDAL

It was a scintillating piece of play that brought the crowd to life. Long's childhood friend, Olympic Gold medallist Nova Peris, remembers "screaming so loud! My whole family was. Such a special moment." Moreover, it was because of Long's feats in the No. 13 guernsey that Peris chose to wear the same number during her own illustrious sporting career.

According to assistant coach Neale Daniher, the set-up at the kick-in that opened the door for Long's theatrics had been devised just two days earlier at training. "Everything just worked exactly how we'd planned it," Daniher said. "In the coach's box I was going to say 'What about that, Kev!' but it was too early in the game [to get carried away]." Long's young teammate, James Hird, said the goal was inspirational.[34] Harvey believes it was inevitable Long was going to produce something special because, "he had the ability to embarrass the opposition when he got the ball." Like Hird, Harvey drew inspiration from Long's dynamic display:

> You play in a team with Michael and you see him do things like that, you just find this confidence and belief that you're going to win that game. It was a case of, "They're not going to beat us today because Michael's on."

Long, too, admits to being inspired, albeit for a number of reasons. "I allowed my emotions to inspire me," he said. "The emotions tied up with my family, the hunting skills, the desire, the preparation, the adrenalin."[35] He also said:

> I knew Carlton would be after me. I could see what was coming. I could also see what was going. I had a psychological victory, because they were worried about me and I was only worried about myself and the team. I dictated to them. Anything they did, I had the answer.[36]

The Bombers shocked the Blues in the first quarter and led by 30 points at quarter-time. Daniher deserves much of the credit for Essendon's opening blitz, as he had pored over hours of vision of the Carlton centre square structure and cracked the code to its three-year dominance in that

---

34 James Hird, *Reading The Play: On Life and Leadership*, Pan Macmillan, 2006, p. 52.
35 *Champions*, p. 184.
36 *Champions*, p. 185.

part of the field. Blues coach David Parkin concedes that by the time he realised they had been exposed, the Bombers had the momentum and had opened up a significant lead. That said, the Blues made no inroads on the scoreboard in the second term; Essendon kicked five goals to four and led at half-time by 37 points.

Long continued to run amok. Teammate David Grenvold said, "Long's control of the game was outstanding." In all, he had 20 kicks, 13 handballs, eight marks and kicked two goals; his willingness to bring teammates into the game was a key component of his Norm Smith Medal-winning performance. The Baby Bombers (dubbed as such because of the team's 20 players on Grand Final day, 12 were aged under 25) defeated the more experienced Blues 20.13 (133) to 13.11 (89). Martin Flanagan wrote of Long's memorable finals series:

> There had been great Aboriginal players before him, but none exactly like him. His performances in the 1993 finals series were as dramatic as the advent of technicolour television. There was a new wizardry in the game, an Aboriginal wizardry. His performance in the Grand Final was one of sustained intensity and frenetic pace. No one could go with him, no one could get near him.[37]

After reaching the hilltop in 1993, Long plummeted to the depths of despair the next season when he suffered the first of two severe knee injuries. "My first knee reconstruction cut me down in my prime," he said. "I was 24 and still on a high after winning the Premiership a few months earlier, and the club was grooming me as a leader. They named me captain in a practice match in WA, but all of a sudden—*bang*! I did my right knee and I was out for 12 months. It was a real test of character."[38]

The now not-so-baby Bombers failed to live up to expectations in 1994 and fell away dramatically; they won just 11 games and finished 10th, replicating Collingwood's failure in 1991 (seventh). To that time, no team had finished lower in its Premiership defence than Essendon in '94.

Long admitted that, before his return from injury—in round one, 1995, against Fitzroy at the Western (now Whitten) Oval—he was

---
37 *The Short Long Book*, p. 44.
38 *Champions*, p. 185.

reduced to tears in the dressing room. "I went into a toilet cubicle and started crying," he said. "I knew it was a pivotal moment in my career, and my life. I prayed to Mum for guidance and strength. But I was best on ground that day (25 disposals) and all my doubts disappeared... It was my most consistent season."[39] He was named All-Australian and finished equal fourth in the Brownlow Medal.

Although his performances on the field in 1995 were among his career best, Long's decision after the first Anzac Day clash between Essendon and Collingwood to call out Monkhorst for his racist taunt of "black c---", became his most significant achievement that year. Kickett had departed the club after being dropped for the 1993 Grand Final, but six more Aboriginal players had played for Essendon since Long's arrival in 1988. The Bombers had become one of the League's leading promoters of Aboriginal culture[40] and Long was their spiritual leader.

Flanagan calls Long's public outing of Monkhorst football's "Mandela moment".[41] Despite receiving death threats and hate mail in the ensuing days, Long admits he was determined to proceed for the good of his people. "It was who I was, where I was from, and culture, history, what you believed in and how you were brought up," he said. "It was the right thing to do."[42] He also said:

> I never thought it would have impacted [on] other sports, the workplace and over-the-fence comments of supporters. It changed people's minds, made people think... made players think and realise how much of an impact it had... It was a very hard thing to do because I didn't have all the answers or solutions and I didn't get support until later on.[43]

Because of Long's stand, the AFL introduced Rule 30 to combat racial and religious vilification. Then AFL chief executive Ross Oakley later wrote in *The Phoenix Rises* that the rule was "a groundbreaking code that was the first of its kind in Australian sport" and "second to none in world

---

39 *Champions*, pp. 185-186.
40 After Long and Kickett, Essendon has recruited many Aboriginal players, including: Gavin Wanganeen (first played in 1991), Dean Rioli (1999), Cory McGrath (2001), Nathan Lovett-Murray (2004), Andrew Lovett (2005), Patrick Ryder (2006) and Anthony McDonald-Tipungwuti (2016).
41 *The Short Long Book*, p. 48.
42 Long quoted from www.abc.net.au, 29 April 2015. For more see: http://tinyurl.com/j3s8ntp.
43 *Legends*, p. 149.

sport."[44] It would come to define the final years of Long's playing career and, particularly, since his retirement in 2001. "I got a lot of criticism over it—even some Indigenous players didn't agree with me—but I saw no other way to bring about change," Long said.[45]

His playing career almost ended prematurely in round seven, 1996, against Geelong in the League's Centenary celebration match, when he suffered a second major knee injury. With his knee facing the wrong way, Long was despondent in the dressing room when Sheedy approached him and said, "Only champions come back from injuries like this."[46] Spurred on by his coach's words, Long determined that he would return to the game, although his recovery was not without its struggles:

> As I was being wheeled in for another operation, I looked across at my wife Lesley and my baby son Jake, who was crying, and it hit me like a tonne of bricks. I thought: "I'm black, I'm broke, I've got nothing, and I've got a wife and a child to support. I have to play next year." What I did have was my pride. That was a defining moment for me as a man. When you think you're going bad in life and the only thing that can save you is football, you've got no choice but to work your backside off.[47]

After just 14 games in 1997-98, Long was named co-captain in 1999 (with the injured Hird, who played only seven games) and played 20 matches, including Essendon's heartbreaking one-point loss to Carlton in the Preliminary Final.[48] Then, in the club's dominant 2000 season (the Bombers won 21 of 22 home and away games, beat North Melbourne by 125 points in the first Qualifying Final and Carlton by 45 points in a Preliminary Final) he played 23 games including the 60-point victory over Melbourne in the Grand Final. That day Long had 11 disposals and kicked one goal, but his high, forceful bump on Demons ruckman Troy Simmonds became the talking point. He received a four-match suspension, with the incident one of a number later highlighted

---

44   Ross Oakley, *The Phoenix Rises*, Slattery Media Group, 2014, p. 285-286 and 289.
45   *Champions*, p. 186.
46   *Champions*, p. 186.
47   *Champions*, p. 186.
48   Long had been vice-captain in 1996 and 1998.

by the AFL when they clamped down on unruly behaviour in the game's decider. Hird, who won the Norm Smith Medal, later wrote:

> I spoke to Longy about it after the game, and he felt terrible. He said he wished he hadn't hurt Simmonds. Troy's family were critical of him when they spoke to the media, but these things happen with instinctive play. Longy didn't mean to hurt Simmonds. I think you have to assess it in the context of the game.[49]

It had been a memorable year for Long. He had also been the AFL Players' Association's representative in the 2000 Olympic Torch relay.

In 2001, Essendon returned to the Grand Final again, but Long tore his hamstring at training on the Thursday night and was devastated to miss the game. His cousin, Dean Rioli, laid a game-high nine tackles, but the Bombers lost to the Brisbane Lions by 26 points. For Long, it was an unceremonious ending to a truly momentous career. His impact on Essendon was recognised in 2002 when he was named at No. 23 among the club's top 60 champions, and in 2007 he was inducted into the Australian Football Hall of Fame. A decade earlier, in 1997, when when the Bombers selected their Team of the Century, Long was named on a wing, one of two Aboriginal players (along with 1993 Brownlow medallist Gavin Wanganeen) chosen in the side.

Three years later, Long was working at the AFL when he approached CEO Andrew Demetriou, who later remembered:

> He was terribly angry and upset. He told me that he wanted to walk to Canberra—he wanted to go and see the Prime Minister, John Howard. He wanted to get his message across and raise awareness... It's not often people walk into your office to talk about those sorts of things. And I thought, anyone who tries talking him out of it is not going to succeed. He was determined to do it, and he did.[50]

---

49 *Reading The Play*, p. 136.
50 Andrew Demetriou quote sourced from the documentary, *Ten Years: The Long Walk*, produced by The Long Walk, the Essendon Football Club and AFL Media, 2016.

MICHAEL LONG

On 21 November 2004, Long and cousin John Cusack parked their car at Kalkallo, 40km north of Melbourne, and without fanfare or publicity simply started walking towards Canberra, more than 600km away. "We thought, 'This is probably the place to start the journey,'" Long later explained. "If you look at the surroundings, and the traffic that was coming past, you think, 'Yeah, bloody long way!'"[51] Former teammate Tim Watson was the only one who ventured out to see Long begin his journey:

> I thought there was going to be some sort of organisation out there, and [that] he had a van and all that sort of stuff. I got out there, and he'd really just parked his car on the side of the road and hopped out in his street clothes. And he was just wearing his shoes—not any sort of walking shoes, not any runners. I said, "What are you doing?" He said, "I'm gonna walk to Canberra." I said, "Like that?" and he said, "Yeah." So he just took off...up the side of the freeway.[52]

As had been the case with Canadian amputee and cancer sufferer Terry Fox—who in 1980 embarked on a cross-country walk to raise awareness of cancer—Long's mission soon generated significant publicity across Australia.[53] "It was probably [not] until we got to Albury (330km from Canberra) that we got confirmation of meeting with the Prime Minister," Long said.[54] Howard recalled that momentum built and he thought, "Gee, this is impressive. When he made it plain he'd like to see me, I said 'Certainly.'"[55] As Long recalls it:

> A lot of the politicians came out to walk with us and greet us. But we'd actually said what we'd wanted to say in the media, in terms of the Australian public were going to be the ones who would make the difference. We told the story along the way, along that journey, and that was probably the most important part... He (Howard) was open to discussion...

---
51   Long, *Ten Years: The Long Walk*.
52   Tim Watson, *Ten Years: The Long Walk*.
53   For more on Terry Fox, see: Leslie Scrivener, *Terry Fox: His Story* (3rd Ed.), McClelland & Stewart, 2000.
54   Long, *Ten Years: The Long Walk*.
55   John Howard, *Ten Years: The Long Walk*.

it was really about the things that were burning in our hearts that was probably just as important that he heard.[56]

A shortened version of Long's famous walk continues before every *Dreamtime* game, where a sea of people walks behind Long from Federation Square, in the heart of Melbourne, eastward to the MCG; the significance of his journey is now educating a new generation of Australians. Long remains adamant that football gave him the platform to make a difference:

> Don't underestimate what football has done. It's the greatest ally for Indigenous people. It has fast-forwarded the process. I have seen what football has done and seen how it has changed people's minds and attitudes and lack of insight. I see football as being enormous in reinforcing those messages because of how powerful it is.[57]

Sheedy wants everyone to understand the importance of Long on the country's attitude towards Aboriginal people. "When the next generations of young Aboriginal kids come through, they should occasionally find a spare moment to remember what Michael Long has done for them," he said. "I think all Australians should be thankful."[58]

—— Statistics ——

BORN: 1 October 1969

GAMES PLAYED (1989-2001): 190

GOALS: 143

FINALS PLAYED: 20

FINALS GOALS: 16

GRAND FINALS: 3

PREMIERSHIPS: 1993, 2000

NORM SMITH MEDAL: 1993 (presented by Maurice Rioli)

---

56 Long, *Ten Years: The Long Walk*.
57 *Herald Sun*, 29 June 2011, p. 82.
58 Kevin Sheedy, *Stand Your Ground: Life and Football*, Macmillan, 2008, p. 343.

MICHAEL LONG

FITTING: Michael Long's Norm Smith Medal was presented by the 1980 winner Maurice Rioli. Both were players for Darwin's St Mary's Football Club. Maurice's nephew, Cyril Rioli, would win the Medal in Hawthorn's 2015 Premiership victory. (Photo: a still from the AFL NT's 2016 Team Of The Century, in which Long was named on a wing, with Maurice Rioli half-forward and Cyril Rioli an on-baller.)

— Norm Smith Voting —

(JUDGES: Ted Whitten, Ross Oakley, Tim Lane, Ian Robertson, John McGrath)

Herald Sun votes:
Mike Sheahan: 3 Michael Long, 2 Stephen Kernahan, 1 Mark Mercuri;
Ron Reed: 3 Long, 2 Kernahan, 1 Gary O'Donnell;
Trevor Grant: 3 Long, 2 O'Donnell, 1 Kernahan;
Daryl Timms: 3 O'Donnell, 2 Long, 1 Kernahan;
Geoff Poulter: 3 Long, 2 O'Donnell, 1 Mercuri;
Bruce Matthews: 3 Long, 2 O'Donnell, 1 Kernahan;
Trent Bouts: 3 Long, 2 O'Donnell, 1 Kernahan;
Michael Stevens: 3 Long, 2 O'Donnell, 1 Kernahan;
Tony De Bolfo: 3 Long, 2 Kernahan, 1 O'Donnell;
Paul Gough: 3 Long, 2 O'Donnell, 1 Kernahan;
Nick Bideau: 3 Long, 2 Kernahan, 1 O'Donnell.
TOTALS: Long 32, O'Donnell 18, Kernahan 14, Mercuri 2.

Dean Kemp

Dean Kemp was a lithe, smooth-moving blond wingman with the ability to run all day. In the early 1990s, Kemp along with Peter Matera and Chris Mainwaring formed the AFL's most exciting centreline, carrying the West Coast Eagles to their first Premiership in 1992 and repeating the dose in 1994, when Kemp was named best afield in the Grand Final. In a star-studded team, Kemp shone brightly. He won the club's best and fairest award in 1992 and was named All-Australian that year; he also represented Western Australia and joined Ben Cousins as co-captain of West Coast in 2001. Kemp is a member of the Australian Football Hall of Fame as well as the West Australian Football Hall of Fame and, in 2006, he was selected at centre in West Coast's best team of its first two decades in the league. In his Norm Smith Medal performance, Kemp had 18 kicks, five handballs, took five marks and kicked two goals

My mum, Judith, was an exceptional sportswoman; she was a state runner. I think a lot of my running ability came from Mum. I always enjoyed the running part of pre-season training. I enjoyed pushing myself as hard as I possibly could. It didn't matter how hard I pushed myself, within a few minutes of completing the exercise I was fine again. So I took that thinking into games. I wanted

← **QUIET ACHIEVER** Dean Kemp was the ultimate team player, and gathered possessions at will in West Coast's 1994 win.

to beat my opponent by pushing myself to the absolute maximum that I could go. I knew that by having a better threshold than my opponent, while not letting him know that I was hurting as much as he was, I could try breaking him by making him think that I could go all day.

My dad, Robert, died when I was a young fella. He was a good footballer—an all-rounder who was good at whatever he did. He played all sports, including footy with Kalgoorlie, but didn't stand out at anything in particular. I was 15, and it was football Grand Final day in town. He was down at the wood heap and had a heart attack while chopping wood that morning. It's always stuck in my mind that he died on Grand Final day.

It was hard not having my father around. My older brothers, Wayne and Gary, had left home by then. My older sister, Sandra (twin to Wayne) helped Mum raise my younger sister, Melissa, and me. I also helped my mum out as much as I could. Footy became an important outlet for me; it was the best part of my life at that time. Whether I was playing with my mates, or at the higher level, I just loved the chance to compete by playing footy. It made me very happy.

Growing up in Kalgoorlie was a fantastic grounding for me. I was a little skinny kid playing against men from an early age. You had the old gold miners, for example, and I learned early on to protect myself against those big blokes. It was an awesome place to grow up in; a footy-mad town, who loved their VFL and WAFL competitions.

My brothers used to bash the crap out of me. I'm sure I learned my determination and competitive spirit from trying to survive against them. I always knew I was up for the fight of my life whenever I played against them in the backyard. You just hoped one day you could beat them, and it did come eventually.

I was very small growing up: at best, five-foot-five at 16 years of age. Tim Gepp (Richmond 1983-85, 57 games; Footscray 1986, 14) came down from Perth after his days at Richmond to do some competitive work. He said, "Righto, let's do some competitive stuff," and we all jumped up and he said: "Hang on, little fella, you're not involved in this." Some of the boys spoke up and told him I've got no dramas with the competitive

DEAN KEMP

side of things. He still reminds me of that story whenever I see him!

I played my junior footy with the Railways Football Club in the Goldfields Football League, but was never picked in any of the state or Teal Cup under-18 teams. I remember trying out with the Subiaco Colts one time, but I was a bit small and they didn't really give me a chance to show what I could do; they just left me in the forward pocket. Gary played over 100 games for Subiaco, so he kept a close eye on me as I came up through the ranks, and eventually they picked me up.

I used to love watching Melbourne's Robbie Flower, who also wore No. 2. I was a mad Geelong supporter, though. Former Geelong Premiership player John Watts (Geelong, 1963-65, 52) was best man at my dad's wedding, and Dad was best man at his wedding. So I followed Wattsy closely. I was an East Perth and Geelong supporter. I loved watching Peter Featherby, who played for both of those clubs, the Nankervises as well; Micky Turner was another, and I loved watching them all on *The Winners* on a Sunday night. I'd wear the Cats jumper to school whenever I could.

The West Coast Eagles had their worst year in 1989. I was picked up at the end of that year: the draft went up to selection 116, and I was chosen after that as an additional supplementary player along with Anthony Begovich.[1] I was in the side for the first practice game, played on a wing against Chris Mainwaring, got a few kicks and got picked for the senior team for round one. It all went from there.

Before I was drafted, Geelong coach Malcolm Blight came over and watched Gary and myself play with Subiaco. The week before, we kicked about nine goals between us. But the day he came and watched I only got about three kicks! But I later had some fond memories of playing against Geelong, so it worked out okay.

I definitely hoped I would one day play in the VFL. I think that sometimes your pathway opens up easier than you expect. Before you know it, you're there, like it was meant to be, even though you didn't necessarily plot it out step by step. I loved footy, but I loved basketball as well. It just all

---

[1] Of West Coast's draft class that year, Kemp, Peter Matera, Tony Evans, Brett Heady, Ashley McIntosh, Ryan Turnbull and Peter Wilson all played in Premierships for the club.

happened after I began playing with Subiaco. I played a full year there then, all of a sudden, I was at the Eagles. Some players find the transition pretty hard to take, but for me it all seemed to come naturally. I was lucky I guess. I was able to step up to each level and play all right, and was never too daunted or intimidated by the prospect.

That first pre-season at West Coast was an eye-opener. When I got drafted I was with my mates up at Kununurra, 3200 kilometres north of Perth. I was staying with a local policeman from Kalgoorlie who had moved up there. He said to me, "You know you got drafted today?" I didn't know! He said, "Yeah, you've got to get back to Perth because they're looking for you." We had to sell our Falcon station wagon to afford to get back to Perth in time. He sold that for us, and my mates and I bought bus tickets and headed back to Perth. Within a week I was starting pre-season. I hurt my groin early on, and I had a meeting with coach Mick Malthouse and the doctors. They said: "It looks like you're going to need an operation to get it sorted out quickly." I thought about it over the weekend then, miraculously, the groin came good and I never needed an operation. I played the year and it didn't trouble me at any stage. Mind over matter maybe, I don't know. We all thought I was gone, so it was a miracle of sorts that I came good. I wasn't fond of knives and operations, so maybe that helped me get over it.

I didn't like to get beaten at training. Craig Turley was always a good runner, and Dwayne Lamb could chug along all day. Later we had guys like Drew Banfield, then Ben Cousins. We had a really good core of guys who pushed each other, because no one wanted to get beaten. Chris Mainwaring was a good runner, too, so we had a really good group who prompted and drove that competitiveness. Even though they were your teammates you still wanted to beat them. For me, each session we had I didn't want anyone to beat me. We used to have a lot of dust-ups at training. Nothing nasty, but there were punches thrown. It's natural when everyone is so competitive. That's what we certainly were, and it served us well.

I think Mick Malthouse has got harder as he's got older. I still talk regularly with him today. I'll ring him up from time to time to see how he's going. He was an amazing person for us at the Eagles. He was actually a bit soft with us in those days. I formed a strong bond with him as my coach; maybe success helps to form bonds like we had. He was always very fair with me, we never had any troubles. Mick had that mentality of us versus them, and I think that helped to fire us up. We bought in to what he was doing, and we followed him with anything he said and did. He was a great motivator.

Mick always tells the story that I rolled up at the club at 75 kilograms and finished at about 76 kilos! I don't know why, but I could never put muscle on, and I worked just as hard as everyone else. I was in the gym longer than anyone but I could never put any weight on. I'm still the same size now.

I was always very nervous before a game. It's not a nice feeling being nervous, but once you've experienced it for a long time, then you retire, you actually miss that feeling. You become quite used to it; you look forward to it and you know that it's coming. So, when it's not there, it's like a hole that you aren't filling in your life.

For my first game I lined up on Collingwood's rugged wingman Darren Millane. I was about 68 kilograms, Millane was about 6"2' and about 90 kilograms. I walked over to him and thought, "Gee, I'm going to be fighting out of my weight here." I looked across the ground and saw Paul Peos on the other wing; he was bigger and heavier than me, and he was playing on Graeme Wright. So I zipped around the back of the square and went across to Peo and said, "Peo, Mick wants us to change over. You take the old slow bugger and I'll go on the younger, quicker bloke." He was pretty fired up, so off he went and lined up on Millane. It was a pretty physical game—Tony Francis, also in his first game, got suspended for six weeks for kicking. There were some big blues as well, so it was a big introduction to AFL footy. I left the change rooms after the game feeling pretty happy with myself, and just as I went to walk out the door Malthouse called out to me: "Kempy, back in here!" I turned around and went over to him, and he gave me a decent lecture about never making my own moves out on the field. He said, "I saw what you did, don't let me see it again!" So I was given the big talking down after my first game.

THE NORM SMITH MEDAL

And here I was thinking that I'd got away with it! I never did that again.

I played with some great players in my time at the Eagles, and John Worsfold was an amazing bloke to play with. He wasn't the most skilful, nor was he the fastest, but he was an impressive young leader. He was leading the club at 22, and I know what I was like at that age. He was so much more mature than I was. John led by example. If he was injured, he would be at the club rehabbing harder than anyone. And no matter what was happening in a game, he'd always give 100 per cent of himself. We would have struggled to have been the team that we were without him as our leader; he was just the ultimate warrior for us.

We used to travel as much as four weeks in a row sometimes, and being away from my own bed meant that I wasn't a very good sleeper before games. I had trouble with the time difference, as Melbourne was always two hours ahead of Perth. I was conscious of the fact I needed to sleep, and that played on my mind, so sometimes I was buggered before the game had even started. It was hard to adjust, but what was good about all the travel was that it brought us closer as a group. We grew to enjoy the challenge of being there together as a group, and relying on each other to get the job done. So, travelling became fun in that sense, and putting up good performances on the road became a yardstick of the way we approached interstate games.

It was a long and tough debut season. I remember myself and Brett Heady sitting on the plane after losing the Preliminary Final. We were that buggered, just wrecked, having played 23 and 20 games respectively that season. We said, "If this is how it's going to be every year, we're not going to last very long." That first year was the tough one, certainly. After that, my body started to acclimatise to the rigours of AFL footy.

We gradually worked out our away program. We were getting better in how we were rehabbing after games. For example, after interstate games we'd get in a pool as soon as we could. Then, when we got on the plane we ate different foods, and so our sport science guys were really important to us in that period. For the time, I think we were one of the leaders in that field. There was a large focus on getting the body adapted to the travel, and in ensuring we did the correct rehab to get us right for the next week's game.

My first final was a draw. Bloody Peter Sumich! I can't believe he missed that shot.[2] We played a fair bit out at Waverley: it was a big, open ground that we quite liked playing on. I don't remember a lot about the game itself, other than at the end when it was really tight and 'Suma' just needing to score for us so that we could come back the next week. He didn't kick the goal, but he was lucky enough to at least kick the point, which forced a draw. While it kept us alive, in a way it hindered us because it forced us to travel an extra week. In the end, though, I think that the experience of playing four hard finals in 1990 made us stronger as a group, teaching us what it took to win a Premiership in Victoria.

We got on a roll in 1991. Importantly, we had no major injuries. For any side, if you can have a decent run where you can maintain your momentum, keeping your good players on the field, it makes a huge difference to your Premiership chances. That's what we were able to do in 1991. We had first-class rehab people looking after us, and that allowed us to play as well as we did in 1991 and 1992.

We didn't think that anyone could come to Perth and beat us in 1991. So the loss to Hawthorn in the Qualifying Final blew us away. But, take your hat off to Hawthorn, what a team of champions they had. We admired their players so much, having won so many Grand Finals. All of a sudden, here we were against them in a big final. We weren't scared of them, not at all, but we respected them and knew what they were capable of. They handled that situation far better than us, and maybe we got a bit overawed with the occasion. Then, on Grand Final day, they were just too good, too strong for us.

Mick didn't let us do the Grand Final Parade that year. Not that it bothered us at the time, because we didn't know much about it anyway. But we got to do it in 1992 and 1994 and it was an awesome experience. It was great that we were able to get into a couple more Grand Finals to be able to experience that event. It really makes the week an incredible

---

2   In the replay the following week, Collingwood won by 59 points. West Coast then defeated Melbourne by 30 points in the first Semi-Final, but lost heavily to Essendon in the Preliminary Final. All of West Coast's four finals were played at Waverley Park. It had been forced to travel for six consecutive weeks.

one, and it's not something you want to miss out on. It was the experience of a lifetime.

Perth was buzzing, particularly as we were the only team in town at the time. When we played in the three Grand Finals, apparently there was hardly a car on the freeways in Perth—that's how big it was over there. We had the whole community behind us in whatever we did, and it was an amazing feeling to be a part of that. But it certainly created a lot of pressure. It was hard to adjust to as a young player, because even if we played well but lost, it was never good enough. Once we got on that roll around 1991, playing at such a high level, people expected you to maintain that every single week. But every team has their ups and downs. They were fantastic supporters of our team, but at the same time there was a lot of pressure that we were under to live up to their expectations.

I had a funny year in 1991. After a pretty good debut year, I didn't feel that I did anything special in my second season. I was just in and around the place, without actually standing out, so that became the driving force for me to improve for 1992. I probably thought that, after the good first year, it was all just going to happen or me in '92. But it didn't work out that way.

That became the platform for me to focus on getting stronger and fitter. I worked harder than I'd ever done before. Craig Turley was one of the best runners, and in my first two years I was always finishing just behind him. But in the '92 pre-season I began beating him consistently by running harder and harder all the time. That had been what I was striving for: to get to the level 'Turls' was at, then to try and push past him. He'd won the best and fairest in '91, so I knew if I could outperform him then I could set myself up for a great year. On one occasion we were doing a long run and I was pushing myself really hard, getting in front of him and beating him. I thought, "Right, I have done it, now I need to carry it on from here."

I won the best and fairest in 1992, so that justified the work that I put in over the pre-season. What made it even better was that I had played so well in the club's first ever Premiership season. And that's really special to me, knowing that I contributed in the year when we had our first taste of success.

I didn't need firing up before a game. I was fairly quiet in my preparation; just did my bit without ranting and raving. There were certainly some players in our team that needed that, but I was more focused on what I needed to do. And that wasn't yelling and pushing and carrying on; it was focused solely on what I needed to do to win the ball.

It was quite ironic that Geelong was our opponent in both Premiership victories. They were a champion team during that period, with so many great players. It was an honour to play against those guys, and was a challenge we looked forward to when we met them in the 1992 and 1994 Grand Finals. To get over the top of them was one of the best feelings I've had in my life.

Peter Matera was on fire in the 1992 Grand Final. In fact, Suma is still dirty that 'Roo' [Matera] didn't pass off a couple of those goals he kicked to him instead. Twenty-five years later and he's still going on about it. I remember when Roo kicked that goal and put his arm up in the air as he ran off: that was a huge moment. He was one of those freak athletes who had the power, strength and ability to keep on his feet. He didn't get much credit for the defensive side of his game, but Roo was an amazing tackler and chaser as well. His game that day was one out of the box, and it was great to have a front-row seat to his performance.

The 1993 season was a failure for us. It was the same team as '92, and much was expected of us. We had a couple of injuries that year which didn't help us, but we also dropped away a little bit in other areas. When you're in such a competitive environment as the AFL, if you drop away even slightly your opponents will sense that; they are always looking for your weakness from which to exploit to their advantage. They came at us every week, and we weren't able to perform at the level we had in 1992. The year went by so quickly, and suddenly it was done and dusted before we knew it. That was devastating.

The hardest part is to be the hunted, rather than the hunter. No doubt. And each week is a different challenge because it doesn't matter who you play, you're always the favourite to win. You have to find a way to keep backing up, week after week, against sides who are testing themselves against the best. It becomes a physical and mental battle.

If you have a good year personally, it changes dramatically for you the next year. Suddenly, every time you go out there you have somebody focused on you, constantly at you. But that's just another challenge to meet and work through. You need to look forward to it, because it's going to happen either way. Get used to it and get on with it, so you can help the team.

To beat taggers, my philosophy was to just run, to always be on the move. Not just run at pace, but run *with* pace; short, sharp bursts, back and forward. It obviously takes a fair bit out of you, and it's a skill in itself learning to run like that. You get a method of running when you're playing, but to then up that level to another tempo to try and break the tag can become a real mental battle for you. That was the main thing I tried to do after playing so well in 1992.

Taggers would do anything to try putting me off my game. They would grab me on the 'Niagara Falls' when we were in the packs. Or they would scratch me or belt me, but nothing out of the ordinary that you don't expect from playing footy. I never got into verbalising my opponent. I saw that as being a waste of time and energy. I enjoyed playing against guys like Anthony Stevens, Tony Liberatore and Chris Bond. Every week you'd come up against somebody different, but it was always a good challenge for me. We'd always shake hands at the end, there were never any hard feelings.

I saw Gary Ablett starting on the wing in the 1994 Grand Final. I thought, "What's he doing up here?" Luckily Michael Brennan went to him, which saved me from having to worry about him! The noise when you run out on to the MCG on Grand Final day is just phenomenal; you can hardly hear your mates talking to you. But when the ball gets bounced, all that external noise becomes a blur and your mind focuses on the game—much like if you were playing back home. The game returns to how you always remembered it, and you just get on with it.

DEAN KEMP

In any game, you want to get a couple of early touches. I was able to get a couple of early ones in the '94 Grand Final, and I used the ball a couple of times, so from there my confidence grew. Your teammates see that, also, and they grow in confidence as well.

Our defensive players that day were unbelievable. Guys like Guy McKenna and Worsfold at half-back, David Hart, Ashley McIntosh, Chris Waterman and Glen Jakovich; they were all great players who could use the ball well and could run and run all day—they could do it all.[3] We probably didn't realise how important they were as a group for us, whereas now you watch those games back and you see how integral they were. Those half-backs are like quarterbacks: they really control the play. That's what ours did that day. It made it easy for guys like me to hang out on the wing and wait for them to get it out to me. But don't tell 'Bluey' McKenna that! Waterman was one of those underrated players for us. He could play anywhere and he was bloody awesome to have in our team.

We started to win so much of the ball in the second quarter; it just seemed to be bouncing our way. Things were certainly starting to happen for us. I remember thinking as we were coming into half-time that, while we didn't have total control of the game, we were really getting stuck in at the contest and were running on well. You almost don't feel tired in those moments: you just feel so amped up and excited by the challenge ahead. In fact, you feel as if you can play for more than four quarters.

Billy Brownless's screamer was a beauty! I never forget to remind McIntosh about that one. I tell him he shouldn't be letting guys climb over his back like that. Billy got up so high he almost leapt over the top of McIntosh, but I think he marked it when he hit the ground!

After half-time, things really opened up for us. Our forwards were finding space, and we were getting a lot of drive through the midfield and from half-back. We recognised that we were starting to get on top of Geelong. That quarter was certainly the turning point in the game for us, and we started to wear the Cats down.

---

3   All six players were selected in West Coast's Team of the Decade (1987-96), and only Hart was missing from the club's Team 20, which celebrated its first two decades in the League.

THE NORM SMITH MEDAL

The Cats were attacking, but they couldn't get the score on the board. It's moments like that where something important happens in a Grand Final. Against the flow of play, something out of the ordinary happens. For me, it was when Peter Wilson fired a handball over his head straight to me and I ran in and kicked a goal. That was one of those moments that you look back on and realise was an important moment in the game.

I used to dislocate my finger all the time. It's a bloody terrible looking finger today! It's the middle finger, and it still pops out regularly. I can be putting my shoes on and it will come out. It doesn't hurt, but it looks awkward because it juts out at a 90-degree angle. It was something I always had problems with, and on Grand Final day I had trouble with it.

I always tried to play through injuries. By my last year, my body was buggered, but I didn't miss many games during my career. I prided myself on that, always getting myself up for the next game. I simply did not want to miss. I wanted to be a part of it week after week, year after year, so I was always keen to push myself as hard as I could.

I never passed to Chris Lewis for what was my second goal of the game. But everyone thinks I did! I took a shot at goal and kept it low because of the breeze. I said to 'Lewy', "Just let it go, son!" He applied a good bump for me, to allow that ball to sail through. I went up and said, "Thanks mate, good shepherd!" I drilled it straight through from 50, that's my memory of it! That's when you know things are going your way.

When the game was over, all I was thinking about was getting my hands on a Premiership Medal. The Norm Smith Medal didn't come into it. The excitement, the yelling and the screaming was just incredible. Winning a Norm Smith was not considered in those moments. When I was announced the winner, and I walked on to the podium, I sent a cheer back to my mates in Kalgoorlie. They liked that, the boys! They were all in the pub down there, and, don't forget, I'd only left there a few years earlier. I had gone from Kalgoorlie to the MCG pretty quickly.

You always want to play well in the big games. That was something I prided myself on. I wanted to play well and do my part for the team.

DEAN KEMP

If you get a few more kicks and have a bit more fun, and are lucky enough to win a Norm Smith Medal, then that's incredible and unexpected. To win the Norm Smith was amazing, but to win that first Grand Final in 1992 sticks in my head as the biggest thing we achieved. To have been a part of that success was awesome.

The Medal is on display at home. I've got two boys, Sunny and Robbi, but their mates are more interested in talking footy with me than they are. I think they all come around just to talk footy! Both boys play in the local league down here in Margaret River where I'm living now. They don't have their dad's build, they are more like my wife, Karin; she's six-foot tall and they are similar to her. They are more key position players, unlike me who was better suited to the wing, but it's great to go and watch them play.

The game was definitely a lot harder to play as I got older. There was a huge difference, in fact. I look at Dustin Fletcher (400 games) and Brent Harvey (432) and think, how the hell were they able to do it for so long? They were just freaks to be able to continually adapt to the changes in the game. When you look at our Eagles sides, not many had exceptionally long careers.[4] Our lifespan in the game seemed to be a lot shorter in comparison to some of the long careers of the Victorian based players. I don't know whether it's something to do with the constant travel. I think if you can play 12 years over here, it's probably the equivalent to 14 or 15 years for the east coast players.

I miss Chris Mainwaring.[5] He was our upbeat, bubbly character who everyone loved. No one had a bad word to say about him. He loved everyone, loved having fun, loved a good drink, and he was so much fun to be around. If you were out with him, it was always a good time. To lose him was bloody terrible, a tragedy, and one of the worst times in my life when I heard that he had passed away. It's like losing a family member, because you build up such a bond with your teammates, particularly if you experience some level of success together. Even today I struggle to comprehend that he's gone. He was far too young. He went hard, trained

---

[4] As of 2017, no West Coast player has yet played 300 games. Dean Cox played 290, Glen Jakovich 276, Darren Glass 270, Guy McKenna 267 and Drew Banfield 265. Dean Kemp played 243 games, and sits eighth on the all-time games played list for the Eagles.

[5] Chris Mainwaring died tragically of a drug overdose on 1 October 2007, aged just 41. The outer wing at Subiaco Oval was named the Chris Mainwaring Wing for all Eagles home games.

THE NORM SMITH MEDAL

flat out, wasn't the most skilful guy but worked as hard as anyone in the team. He would inspire you with how he went about it.

It was fantastic when the Eagles won the Premiership again in 2006. I had sort of stepped away from footy after I retired; I didn't watch much footy for a few years. But to see them win that Grand Final was really special. I had watched them get beaten in 2005 (four points), which was heartbreaking to lose by such a small margin. So to see them win it in 2006 (one point) was great. And to see 'Mainy' in the rooms afterwards jumping around with them, that was a fantastic scene.

We're all getting older, and we seem to have a reunion every couple of years! That's always an awesome time when we all come together. When I reflect on my career, it's sharing those moments with my teammates that I hold dearest.

—— Statistics ——

BORN: 17 February 1969
GAMES PLAYED (1990-2001): 243
GOALS: 117
FINALS PLAYED: 25
FINALS GOALS: 19
GRAND FINALS: 3
PREMIERSHIPS: 1992, 1994
NORM SMITH MEDAL: 1994 (presented by Gary Ayres)

DEAN KEMP

— Norm Smith Voting —

(JUDGES: Ted Whitten, Ross Oakley, Sam Newman, Bruce McAvaney and Michelangelo Rucci)

The Age **votes: Rohan Connolly:** 3 Dean Kemp, 2 Don Pyke, 1 Glen Jakovich;
Gerard Wright: 3 Kemp, 2 Jakovich, 1 Pyke;
Richard Hinds: 3 Kemp, 2 Jakovich, 1 Michael Mansfield;
Linda Pearce: 3 Kemp, 2 Jakovich, 1 Mansfield;
Gareth Andrews: 3 Kemp, 2 Pyke, 1 Jakovich;
Barry Richardson: 3 Kemp, 2 Jakovich, 1 Chris Lewis.

The Age **TOTALS:** Kemp 18, Jakovich 10, Pyke 5, Mansfield 2, Lewis 1.

Greg Williams

There are some who suggest that Greg 'Diesel' Williams was one of the most influential players in AFL history. Certainly, with his ability to bring teammates into the play through handball—a la Graham 'Polly' Farmer—he is a worthy nominee. Blessed with neither pace nor height, Williams made up for his deficiencies with precision ball use, summing up situations quicker than everybody around him. He had 38 disposals on debut for Geelong in 1984, hinting at what was to come. Fourteen times he topped 40 disposals; in round 19, 1989, he recorded 53, then an AFL record. His career average was 26.9. He led the League for disposals four times (1985-86, 1993-94), won Brownlow Medals at Sydney (1986) and Carlton (1994), captained Victoria (1989) and is a member of the Teams of the Century of the AFL (interchange), Carlton (centre) and Sydney (centre). In his brilliant Norm Smith Medal performance in Carlton's 1995 Grand Final victory over Geelong,, Williams had 17 kicks and 14 handballs, took five marks and kicked 5.3—making it a 32nd birthday to remember.

L eigh Matthews was my hero. I lived in Essendon until I was 10 and then moved to Bendigo, which was in Carlton's zone, but I always loved Matthews. When I was young, I went to Windy Hill

← **DIESEL** Few players in the game's history had Greg Williams's capacity to bring their teammates into the game with pinpoint hand-passing and superb foot-passes. His Norm Smith Medal and Premiership win was icing on the cake, adding to his two Brownlow Medals.

all the time with my old man (also named Leigh) because he supported the Bombers. But when I went to Bendigo, Peter McConville was at my club, Golden Square, and there were a few others who also went on to play for Carlton. My coach there, Tony Southcombe, played 13 games for the Blues as well (1977), but he only stayed half a year and then returned to Bendigo.

Dad represented Victoria in squash. He also played against Australian squash champion Geoff Hunt, so he was pretty good at the sport. Brenda, my mum, had six kids—Mandy, John, me, Joanne, Leigh and Michael—so there wasn't much time for sport. John was six-foot-two, a big man, and did a pre-season with Geelong, but he didn't get on to the senior list. He did win three Geelong Football League best and fairest awards (1986 at Barwon and 1988-89 at St Mary's), plus one in the Goulburn Valley Football League (1984 at Shepparton United). Leigh kicked 102 goals for Golden Square in 1989, in the Bendigo Football League. He was six-foot-four but was never approached by a VFL club. All us boys were good players; we were all slow though. Dad was pretty fast, so I'm not sure who we blame for our lack of pace.

I did two pre-seasons at Carlton when I was 18 and 19 and played one game in the seconds there on a permit. But I ended up back at Golden Square both times and won the league best and fairest in each of those years (1982-83). I then wrote a letter to Tom Hafey asking if I could do a pre-season at Geelong. Carlton's coach, David Parkin, didn't want me and so, after the second time they sent me back home, I decided there was no point going back down again. As I was zoned to the Blues, they agreed to do a trade with somebody from Geelong to allow me to go there. That same year, Harry Kernahan came to my house and I was going to join him at Glenelg in South Australia, where his son, Stephen, was playing. I was going to go, but I wanted to play in the VFL so my first choice was Geelong. It was Hafey's first year, and he asked me down to do the pre-season, no promises, to just see how I would go.

I wouldn't say I was fat, but I was certainly unfit as a teenager. I did a really good pre-season that first time at Carlton, and it was after that when I started to train harder. Tony Southcombe was a marathon runner and so I ran with him a lot. My old man always said to me that I was a player who walked around the field and gathered 40 possessions. It wasn't that I wasn't trying, but I didn't have to kill myself to get the ball. The higher I went, though, the fitter I needed to be. Those two pre-seasons I did at Carlton changed my approach and helped me to get really fit. There were periods after I went back home where I was running every day, which I'd never done before. When I finished with Hafey after the '84 pre-season I was the fittest I'd ever been. I was so fit I was dangerous.

My ability to read the play was just a natural talent. I always seemed to get the ball a lot, so it was an innate thing I was blessed with. My ability to handball was something that evolved the more that I played. Even as a kid I handballed a lot, particularly compared to everyone else. Back then, handball was not as big a deal as it is today. I always thought that the best way to bring other players into the game was through handball, so that became the best way forward for me. I never thought about it much, but I always seemed to have approximately half kicks and half handballs, and that grew the more I played. It probably became more handballs than kicks as I reached the higher levels. I knew I couldn't run out of a pack because I was too slow, so I worked on getting rid of it quickly by hand.

It was a natural thing to use both sides of my body. I found I had no issue turning left or right. In fact, I probably handballed more with my left hand, because I found it comfortable to hold the ball with my dominant right hand and hit with my left, rather than the other way around. I controlled the ball with my main hand, rather than hit it with that hand like most do. It was comfortable for me to hold with my dominant hand and fend off with the other hand, while also allowing me to remain in control of the ball.

I didn't really aim for target practice. What I did was, I always opted for the hardest handball on offer, whether in practice or in games. If a player ran past me and was just a metre away, I would look for the teammate who was five or 10 metres away instead. If there was someone wider, I would always look for them and hit them out wide rather than take the easiest one each time. I always took the hardest. *Always.*

The good players always adapt, so my teammates got the idea pretty quickly as to how I operated. Sometimes, though, a bloke would run past me thinking they wouldn't get it and I'd hit them in the back of the head with the ball! It was my way of saying, "Don't ever take your eyes off me." When I was at Geelong, in an early practice game I told our captain, Mick Turner, "Mick, just stand over there near the boundary," which was a fair way away. I got the ball and handballed out to him and he ran off and kicked it. So the next boundary throw-in he said, "Where do you want me to stand?" He adapted straight away.

The biggest relief for me was getting that first game; that was the hardest one to get. When Tommy said I was playing (against Fitzroy in round one, 1984), that was a huge moment for me. In the practice games he took our former captain, Brian Peake, out of the centre and played me in there. He not only put me in there, he left me there and, having played well in those matches, he gave me the opportunity to continue on in that first game of '84. I actually ran through Peaky in one practice game and it forced him from the ground. He didn't come back on, so that was significant. I was desperate to make it and I think Hafey saw that.

I really loved my time at Geelong. I played the first 12 games in '84 before doing my knee, which forced me to miss the rest of that year. I won the best first-year player for the League, plus I got 38 possessions in my first game, so it was a really great start despite the injury. I kept fit during that recovery period and, in 1985, I had one of the best years I ever had. I gathered the most possessions in the VFL (675) and won Geelong's best and fairest. Hafey was sacked at the end of the season and then he signed with the Sydney Swans for 1986. The Swans then offered me a heap of money to go up there with him. I said to Geelong that if they could give me at least half of what Sydney were offering, I'd stay. But they couldn't match it; not even half of it. The offer was too good to refuse and so I left.

That was really the start of money exploding in the game. The guys at Geelong weren't getting much in comparison to some of us in Sydney; I doubt many clubs had that kind of money at the time. Swans owner Geoffrey Edelsten gave the Sydney players more than what other clubs could offer. He was unreal at the start, gave us whatever we wanted, but a lot of it was false promises. I got paid everything I was owed, but for some guys it was difficult. I know some had their cars repossessed, so it was pretty tough in that sense. Plus, we had no real home ground to train on, and the ones we did train on weren't great surfaces. Despite that, we finished near the top of the ladder in 1986 (second) and 1987 (third), so the team on the field was going well. But we didn't have home finals back then, so we were forced to play on the road in September, which didn't help us. We exited in straight sets both years.

It was a surprise to win the Brownlow Medal in 1986. I never thought I was going to win it, but I knew I had the numbers to get looked at by the umpires. It wasn't a very high count; I won with 17 votes, the same as 'Dipper' (Hawthorn's Robert DiPierdomenico). Dipper is an extrovert, so it was good he was up there with me that night—I didn't have to say much! I was fortunate to always poll well during my career.[1]

Winning the Brownlow ensured I received more off-field attention. But I was already the highest possession winner in the League, so nothing much changed on the field. I had been tagged from day dot anyway; there weren't many games in my career—at any level—where I didn't get tagged. You don't necessarily get used to it, and it does get hard at times when you're constantly being tagged. I played against Tony Shaw a lot, he was a challenge, as was Shane Heard at Essendon. Also Dwayne Lamb from West Coast, who was bigger and stronger than I was. An opponent like Lamb was always hard to beat when he was blocking or facing me at a contest.

It was all possession-based for me. Always. I know I had games where I played better with 30 possessions than ones where I had 40, but my aim was always to try getting 10 or 12 possessions every quarter.[2] I was fanatical on that and that was all I trained for, to try and achieve that every single week. If I had a quiet quarter, I was pissed off with myself. The only acceptance with that was if I ended up having at least

---

[1] Greg Williams received 154 Brownlow Medal votes during his 250-game career: 34 three votes, 15 two votes and 22 one votes, at an average of 0.64 votes per game. To the end of 2017, he is one of just 13 players to have won at least two Brownlows, and one of five players to have won a Brownlow at two different clubs.

[2] The most disposals Williams ever recorded in a game was 53, in round 19, 1989, against St Kilda at the SCG. He not only had 25 kicks and 28 handballs, he also kicked 6.1!

30 by the end of the day. If I could get to 30 I was happy, but I always tried getting 40. If I was on track by half-time with 15, I aimed to have 20 or 25 in the second half and make it 35 or 40 rather than just 30. I was never happy with 25. My attitude was like that all through my career, even at junior level.

Having that mindset was good in some ways, but a negative in others. I was fanatical towards that aim and I trained to achieve that. At the end of every quarter I wanted to know how many possessions I'd collected. I couldn't count them myself during quarters, so I always asked somebody. I joke that I couldn't count quick enough to keep up!

Stress and over-thinking was a big issue for me. I always worried about the game, but I can't explain why. It all worked out and I was very consistent, but I was a perfectionist. I joke with my mates that it's not that easy being a superstar. It really isn't. There might be other superstar athletes out there who found it easy, but I doubt it. The pressure you place on your own performance is immense. There would be times early in games where I felt pretty ordinary and couldn't find the energy to run; I'd be getting tagged at the centre bounce and I knew there was a guy on the wing who was planning to clean me up. The umpires didn't give me any support either, so it felt like the whole world was against me at times. Then I'd go into the rooms at half-time and Hafey would say, "C'mon Greg, you've got to lift!" That's when the stress got to me and that happened a fair bit. But in most games I think I was able to get through that and respond, hopefully helping us to win while getting at least 30 possessions along the way.

Getting best in the newspaper, that's what I was all about. I always thought about winning everything: the best and fairest, the Brownlow—everything! I know most blokes say they weren't thinking about winning those awards, and that's fine, but I used all that as an incentive to perform every weekend. I'd use anything to get myself up for a game. On those days where I struggled early, I found that by the end of the game I was performing well and would have preferred the game to have kept on going. It was hard to be at my peak all the time, though, mentally and physically; even getting through the week's training, week after week, was tough. Being so driven, it really wore me down.

Playing for and captaining Victoria was one of the biggest highlights of my career. I felt captaining my state was the highest accolade I could get as a player, so I was rapt when the great Ted Whitten made me captain in 1989. I loved playing for the Victorians and I see that as a big hole in the current players' careers. It's difficult today, though, with so many interstate teams in the competition. I watch the Australian team in the International Rules series games against Ireland—which I also played in—and you can tell that the players today play for each other like we used to with Victoria.

I had chances to captain at club level, but it wasn't the be-all and end-all for me. Certainly, to be captain of Victoria was great, but I always felt that I was in charge out on the field anyway, even without the title of captain. I was always talking out on the field and really felt like I was in charge of everything out there. Obviously, the competition you come up against is always difficult, and I certainly didn't feel that I was better than anyone, but I felt that if I played at my best I could be the best out there. I knew how good I was and knew what I was capable of, and I was able to get to a pretty good standard most of the time.

We didn't get the support from the VFL while I was up in Sydney. By 1988, things changed dramatically. Suddenly we were near the bottom of the ladder and there was no excitement looking forward. We nearly folded at one point, so it was shocking during my last years there. The VFL didn't seem interested in helping us, so after 1991 I told the club I wanted to return to Victoria. St Kilda were interested in me, plus a couple of other clubs from memory, but I wanted to go to Carlton. They offered me good money to go there, but it wasn't easy getting there. The Swans tried to keep me, and the VFL ended up suspending me for the first six weeks of the 1992 season for signing dual contracts with the Swans and Blues. Eventually, though, I was able to get to Carlton like I'd hoped.

'Sticks' Kernahan was the first guy I met when I got to Carlton. I knew he was a great player, having played against him in the under-17s, and once I got to Carlton we quickly became close friends. We remain best friends today and see each other all the time. He was really strong around the club, leadership wise. Everyone loved him and they still do. He always had time for everyone, and always managed to play well every week. He was a champion player and is a champion bloke.

I was always aware if somebody, like Kevin Sheedy for example, said through the media that I was no good. When something like that happened and we were playing Essendon next, I'd always use that as motivation to get up and play well against them. If I wasn't finding the ball, I might do something like start a fight to get my adrenalin flowing; whatever it took, I would do it. When I first started, Hawthorn's Terry Wallace was the best possession winner in the League, so I wanted to get more than he did. Most of his possessions were kicks, whereas I would have 20 handballs a game, which was unheard of. The game changed after I started doing that consistently; even Terry started to handball more as a consequence. Teams began handballing more and there's no doubt it was my fault that that change occurred. I could tell that the game was changing more towards that direction, but I still managed to handball more than anyone else.

The 1993 Grand Final against Essendon was a disaster, both personally and as a club. The older I got, the worse my knee became and, by 1993, I was having real trouble with it. In fact, I still have trouble with it now and it needs to be replaced. In '93, my knee would get drained at half-time of every game, yet I still finished second in the Brownlow that season (one vote behind Essendon's Gavin Wanganeen). I had hardly trained and my knee was no good. Each time they drained my knee it would feel so much better in the second half, and I had it drained in the Grand Final. But the day overall was just a disaster for us. It was the most shattering day of my career. Sean Denham played me tightly and was later suspended for the tactics he used: he got two weeks for punching me in the mouth. I hit him, too, and broke his nose. He was a pain in the arse that day. He hit me first and I retaliated, but I didn't get reported. At the tribunal a few days later, chairman Neil Busse said to me: "There were 16 cameras there that day and none of them caught you hitting Sean." I was pretty proud of that effort! I was only retaliating though, and 95 per cent of the times I hit someone were in retaliation. I didn't want to punch anyone, but if they punched me or held on to me, tried knocking me out, what else could I do? Sometimes you have to retaliate to make a statement that you won't just put up with it.

I had 44 possessions in round 10, 1993, against Melbourne, yet didn't receive a Brownlow vote. I kicked a goal, we won by 54 points, and I knew I'd played well. So it was a shock when I did not receive even one vote on Brownlow night. I have looked at the newspapers from that game and every one of them had me best on the ground. It is what it is, but had I received even one vote that day I would have won three Brownlow Medals, so the conversation is different than *just* winning the two.[3]

People don't understand how bad my knee was in 1994. In that pre-season I did bugger all training, and during the season my training was like nothing anybody had ever done before. It was simply go out on Thursday night for half an hour—that was it! I trained as hard as my knee would allow during rehab. Nearly every night I trained with our runner, Colin Seery, though I was unable to train like I had up until then. I just couldn't. But throughout 1994 I would go out and play and do well, despite not doing much during the week. It was ground-breaking in what I was able to achieve that year on such a limited preparation. Everyone else was training their guts out, yet I'm playing better than most of them! I received 30 Brownlow votes to win my second medal, which was a lot of votes, yet I don't think it was necessarily my best individual year. Any of 1985-86 or 1994 would be.[4]

We played Geelong in the 1994 second Semi-Final missing three of their best players: captain Mark Bairstow, Paul Couch and Garry Hocking. I think we all thought we would automatically win, because we went out there and didn't play like we should have and they beat us by 33 points, knocking us out in straight sets. I was thinking I was destined to not play in a Premiership team and that became a big issue

---

3 Williams polled 17 votes, to miss by one vote, finishing second to Essendon's Gavin Wanganeen. Geelong's Garry Hocking also polled 17 votes but was ineligible, due to suspension. Wayne Carey and Jason Dunstall were equal third with 16 votes. Williams polled in seven games: four three votes, two twos and a one.

4 In 1994, Williams was adjudged best afield by the umpires on nine occasions, one of just eight players to have done so since the Brownlow Medal was introduced in 1924. Excluding 1976-77, when two vote-cards were submitted by the umpires after each game, only Dustin Martin's 11 best-on-grounds in 2017 is greater than Williams's return in 1994. Williams became just the third player in the one vote-card system to receive 30 votes, although another eight winners since 1994 have received at least 30 votes.

for me. I needed a Premiership to cap off my career. When Essendon beat us by about 100 points in a pre-season game in 1995, I thought we were in trouble going into that year. It wasn't looking good and time was running out.

Parkin's decision to place ownership of the team on to the players was good for us in 1995. Suddenly, players were having their own meetings to discuss the game and the various tactics we were going to use; all the players were able to have their opinions. We already had a zone set-up to keep the ball in our forward line, but the playing group focused heavily on improving that. We focused on how we set up at kick-ins, like how everyone does it today, except at the time it was pretty ground-breaking. We had our full-back up as far as the centre circle, which was unheard of then but which proved very effective for us. That came from us players driving it, and it made it very difficult for teams to get the ball out of their defence against us.

I look at that team in the mid-1990s and we probably should have won a couple more Premierships. We could have, but we didn't. We had a great group of young and middle-tier players—Matt Clape, Brad Pearce, Anthony Koutoufides, Scott Camporeale—and we had a settled defence, a great defence really: Andrew McKay, Silvagni, Peter Dean, Ange Christou and Dean Rice. They were hard blokes to play on. We had a superstar ruckman in Madden, and with the likes of Craig Bradley, Fraser Brown and Brett Ratten in there it all clicked for us in 1995. We won 16 in a row from round 10 through to, and including, the Grand Final. We even discussed as a group whether we should drop a game to allow us to regroup before the finals. Everyone outside the club was saying we should lose one before the finals to ensure we remained hungry, but we decided we didn't want to lose any games. We just kept powering on, keeping our intensity high, and we kept that going right through the finals.

It's true that I was reluctant to move out of the centre and spend more time up forward. But I knew I wasn't the fittest I had been, so I agreed to play forward more often and that seemed to work well whenever I was down there. We decided I would play up around half-forward, staying in one half of the ground rather than covering the whole field. That certainly worked well in the Grand Final. It was difficult deciding to give up some of my control in the centre. But in the 1993 Grand Final we had been too predictable in there and the Bombers were able to work us out as a midfield. So Parkin wanted to try and be more unpredictable through the centre. He had Ratten and Bradley and other guys he could rotate through there, so his plans worked out well in 1995.

In the Grand Final, I had an early shot on goal but kicked it out of bounds on the full: that was just pure nervousness. I was super nervous early on, even though it was my 219th game. As a kid, I watched Leigh Matthews and thought that he never got tired, never got nervous or missed a goal. But people watching just don't understand that we all get nervous. I told myself to settle down and concentrate. I was constantly on the move and, despite that miss on goal, I helped Sticks get one, then kicked one myself soon after, so I was in the game early which got me going for the day.

My memory for specifics within games and what I know I did largely comes from what I've read or watched since. I don't actually remember a lot from my career. I don't remember running out for the 1995 Grand Final, nor any detail about specific things I did, other than what I've watched of the game since. That's something that concerns me as I grow older. I've watched the game a few times over the years, and Rice's tackling in that first quarter was unbelievable; Clape's pressure, too, really set the tone. Earl Spalding was always strong, even if he fumbled more than any person I know!

We took control of the game early in the second quarter. At half-time we were 40 points ahead. I pushed up the field when I could, and that was a call I was able to make on my own; I didn't need Parkin to tell me to do it, he gave me the licence to make positional moves within games whenever I saw fit to do so.

I never went out that day thinking I was going to kick five goals. In fact, I never aimed to kick a lot of goals during my career. I tried to set them up from the middle of the ground instead. So to kick five in the Grand Final capped off a truly great day in my career. We won

THE NORM SMITH MEDAL

comfortably (61 points), it was my 32nd birthday, and I was awarded the Norm Smith Medal as well—you couldn't get a better day! But becoming a Premiership player was the greatest thing of all. That capped off everything I had done. As a team, it was an awesome thing to do together. We had had our chances in 1993 and '94, so it was great to finally get a Premiership together.

I knew I had played well. I scored five goals, set a few more up for teammates and had 31 disposals, so I thought I could be half a chance to get the Norm Smith Medal. But I didn't understand who else had played well. I always found it hard to know who had played well in the games I played in. I would know whether I played well myself or not, but I was never aware of how other players had gone. I was so focused concentrating on what I was doing that I found it difficult to take in what others were doing out there. Kernahan used to count his marks and kicks during games. So he always knew exactly how many he had, whereas I couldn't do that.

What does it mean to be a Norm Smith medallist? It simply means you played well in a Grand Final. It's great to be recognised for that. Being known as a Norm Smith Medal winner is a great thing. It's a big part of the whole Grand Final experience. The Premiership is obviously the best thing, but after that the Norm Smith is right up there. Being recognised as a big-game player is very important to me. Everyone wants to play well in the big games, so it's great that I was able to do that. Whether a state game or a big final, to come up against the best players and stand out for playing well against them is very satisfying.

Being suspended for nine games for pushing an umpire in 1997 was unfortunate, but I don't think it tainted my career overall. When it happened, there were reasons why I received nine weeks. For example, the usual tribunal chairman, Neil Busse, was away, so they had a different chairman hearing my case. I don't think that helped my cause. I was shocked when he gave me nine weeks, though. Carlton took it to court and I received a suspended sentence in the end, but it was a real downer at the end of my career. I certainly didn't despise umpires, but I felt frustrated with them. It's a tough job they have and they're so important to our game. Like anywhere, you have different personalities and you aren't going to get along with everyone all the time. I'm sure I got on well with most of them…well, maybe half of them! Guys like Peter Carey were great because they would give it and take it, and they seemed more human in the way they operated, which I related to more so than those who were in your face and inflexible.

I didn't find it difficult adjusting to life post-footy. By 1997, I was getting injured more often, so I'd had enough by the end of that season. I'd played for 14 years and was 34 by then, so I was really satisfied with what I had achieved in my career. Winning the 1995 Grand Final helped to cap everything off; if I didn't win that I'd have regrets, so that was great. In the end I was happy to finish because I was mentally and physically done.

Because of repeated head knocks I was stunned a lot during my career. A lot of people ask me today whether I'm all right, and I am, outwardly, for the most part. But I know that inside my brain I'm not right. Things have deteriorated in there due to the effects of repeated head knocks. My anger has gotten worse also. I was always angry out on the ground, which was something I used to motivate me and to protect me against opponents. It's a hard game and that was part of it. But I now can't remember when my kids were born, and can't remember details of the Grand Final, so that worries me. Obviously, I know I was there and I've watched what I did in matches, but in terms of actually recollecting events I don't have that recall. What I'm experiencing—particularly not being able to remember things like the birth of my kids—cannot be normal.

Your brain is protected inside your head for a reason. So it doesn't make sense to be getting hit in the head all the time, no matter how tough you are. If the number one brain surgeon in America is telling young athletes they shouldn't play gridiron again after a serious knock, that's pretty compelling evidence to me. I'm worried for the girls playing AFLW now who haven't had the depth and length of training that the guys have had. They need to be protected. The umpires almost have to be too hard on any head-high contact, to help eliminate it from the outset. Many of the men have been protecting themselves from bumps and tackles since they were

THE NORM SMITH MEDAL

young boys. But some of the women have only been playing the game for a couple of years, so they don't have that experience in protecting themselves yet. We need to be looking at that now in order to protect them as early as possible. And what about kids in schools who don't get the testing that happens at football clubs? It's a serious topic of discussion. Because of my experiences and concerns, it is something I will continue to research and seek advice on, as I don't want others to suffer what I have since retiring from the game.

——— Statistics ———

BORN: 30 September 1963

GAMES PLAYED (1984-1997): 250 (Geelong 1984-85, 34 games; Sydney 1986-91, 107; Carlton 1992-97, 109)

GOALS: 217 (Geelong 10 goals; Sydney 118; Carlton 89)

FINALS PLAYED: 11

FINALS GOALS: 12

GRAND FINALS: 2

PREMIERSHIP: 1995

NORM SMITH MEDAL: 1995 (presented by Bob Rose)

GREG WILLIAMS

— Norm Smith Voting —

(**JUDGES:** Ross Oakley, Malcolm Blight, Kevin Bartlett and Rohan Connolly)

***The Age* votes:**
Rohan Connolly: 3 Greg Williams, 2 Anthony Koutoufides, 1 Ang Christou;
Neil Balme: 3 Peter Dean, 2 Stephen Silvagni, 1 Christou;
Barry Richardson: 3 Williams, 2 Koutoufides, 1 Christou;
Gareth Andrews: 3 Williams, 2 Koutoufides, 1 Christou;
Stephen Howell: 3 Williams, 2 Koutoufides, 1 Silvagni.

***The Age* TOTALS:** Williams 12, Koutoufides 8, Christou 4, Silvagni 3, Dean 3.

Glenn Archer

North Melbourne defender Glenn Archer was one of the most courageous players of his era, never afraid to stand his ground with a charging Tony Lockett or Gary Ablett bearing down on him. Six times the AFL Players' Association voted him the game's Most Courageous Player (the Robert Rose Award, 1998-99, 2002-03, 2005-06). In 311 games for the Kangaroos, Archer lived on the competitor's fine edge, providing heart, soul and backbone for his team, and directing relentless aggression at his opponents. Often he was forced to compete against much taller men, yet was rarely beaten, despite later conceding that he suffered from crippling pre-game anxiety throughout his career. In the 1996 Grand Final he was tasked with filling the hole in front of Lockett, the powerhouse Swans full-forward, a role he performed unflinchingly while also picking up 22 possessions in a game well worthy of a Norm Smith Medal.

A rcher's father, Graham, served in the Vietnam War as a teenager and played football for Oakleigh Districts. He was tough and uncompromising, which clearly rubbed off on his son. That said, when the five-year-old Archer "begged" his father to let him play under-9s football at Noble Park with his older brother, Mark, he eventually

← **SHINBONER** Glenn Archer was consistently rated as the game's most courageous player, and later as the "Shinboner of the Century." He was a great player in North's greatest era.

relented after initially wanting him to wait until he was six.[1]

As a schoolboy, Archer and his friends would sneak into nearby Waverley Park without paying, even slipping into the dressing rooms and helping themselves to the players' food and drink! He was there the night North Melbourne's Kerry Good kicked the winning goal in the 1980 Escort Championships Night Grand Final against Collingwood. Archer, a Magpies supporter, joined hundreds of others who ran on to the field as Good lined up for goal. "He said he was out there yelling at him!" future North Melbourne teammate Jason McCartney explained.

As a junior, Archer was the knockabout bloke who was happy having a kick of the footy with his mates; there were few, if any, thoughts of a future AFL career. "He liked a smoke and a good time," McCartney said. Even when North Melbourne asked him to play with its under-19s, he lacked the dedication that coach Denis Pagan expected of his young players. "He was a wayward young fella back then," Pagan recalled:

> He liked to have a good time. He loved playing with his mates, too, but I don't think he was totally committed to playing AFL football—maybe he didn't think he was capable of it. He came to training, and we trained pretty solidly in the under-19s during those times, and he said, "No, too hard for me." He didn't want to do it. I rode him pretty hard, and he said, "I'm not putting up with this idiot!" So he went back to Noble Park.

Having seen enough of Archer to recognise he was worth persisting with, Pagan refused to take no for answer:

> I rang him again the next year and said to him, "Look, just play one game in the under-19s and see how you go," and he said, "okay, I'll play one game just to get you out of my hair." He played one game, then he said, "I'm going back to Noble Park." I said to him, "We're going to Sydney next week, have you ever been on a plane?" "No," he said. We were

---

[1] Ben Collins and Dan Eddy, *Champions: Conversations with Great Players & Coaches of Australian Football*, Slattery Media Group, 2016, p. 11.

playing Sydney under-19s at the SCG, so he came up and played, went well, and he started to come around after that. He was actually playing centre half-forward in those days. He stuck at it and he grew as an individual. He was still rough around the edges, but everything was getting smoothed off—slowly.

Archer, who started out as a forward before moving to defence early in his career, concedes that, if not for Pagan, "I don't know where I'd be."[2] The coach gave him "a lot of guidance and discipline at a time when I could have gone another way."[3] Having seen his closest childhood friend die of a heroin overdose, Archer feared that he, too, would have made poor life choices if not for football; therefore, Pagan's influence was critical in changing the course of his life. "It would be interesting to see where I would've ended up if I didn't go to North and clean up my act a bit," Archer said.[4]

Pagan worried about Archer's temperament, and the pair "certainly had our moments," but the coach knew if he channelled Archer's energy in a more disciplined way, he could become a force on the field. "His football was always at a top level, but his temperament wasn't," Pagan said.

Archer admitted he had "white-line fever," but in his early days the anger was "on both sides of the white line."[5] At school he had been "a very angry and wild boy."[6] In an effort to calm himself, he even attended anger management classes while at high school. "They didn't have any effect, though," he said. "Something in my head would just snap and I'd go off. I always reacted aggressively. A lot of it was not wanting people to have one over me or get the better of me."[7]

McCartney said, "I've never seen anyone have that on and off switch like Arch has." Although it worked for him in the heat of battle, McCartney said, it "also got him in trouble at times." Teammate Wayne Schwass calls Archer "a rough diamond" but adds that "he would do anything for his teammates and his club." He was "an old-fashioned footballer" who

---

2 *Champions*, p. 12.
3 *Champions*, p. 12.
4 *Champions*, p. 12.
5 *Champions*, pp. 15-16.
6 *Champions*, pp. 15-16.
7 *Champions*, pp. 15-16.

teammates loved playing alongside "because he was a selfless player who had total disregard for his own safety."

Archer's courage was unquestionable. Indeed, Pagan called him "one of the toughest, most courageous players I ever coached." Sometimes he was too courageous for his own good, and crossed the line to recklessness, but Pagan was reluctant to ask him to curb his game. "I never counselled Glenn on being too courageous and risking injuries," he said. "He was the perfect role model for other members of the team to follow. We had people like Glenn, Anthony Stevens, Wayne Carey, even Dean Laidley who was a sack of bones but was prepared to throw himself in front of opposition forwards to take intercept marks. You've either got that in you or you haven't, and Glenn certainly had it in him."

Schwass believes it was "simply in his DNA". It was instinctive, and to curb it would have reduced his value to the team. "You could have warned him a thousand times, but he wasn't going to change the way he played his footy," said Schwass.

McCartney said that, whenever the players partook in boxing training, Archer was not allowed in the ring, not because he could not handle himself, but "because of that short fuse." Boxing coach Jack King protected Archer from himself. "He could only do bag work," McCartney explained, "because if someone had have landed one on him, it would be street-fighting at its best! Arch wore his heart on his sleeve; his emotions ran wild. He was just that fierce competitor who didn't want to be beaten at anything."

McCartney recalled Archer later saying that, early in his time at North, he "did a couple of courageous acts which were highlighted by the commentators." Hearing of their praise, he determined that he was going to keep throwing himself at everything, regardless of the outcome. "That became a trademark of his career—that courage to throw himself at anything and anyone," McCartney said. Archer thinks he was lucky he was never seriously injured:

> People told me, "If you keep playing that way, you won't last too long." But I felt a million bucks most of the time. I had a couple of sore shoulders, a bad hand and an elbow injury. I was lucky not to have any really serious injuries. And it *is*

luck. When you're crashing into blokes and being crashed into, you only have to get hit in the wrong spot and you're in trouble. That's enough to keep your mind on the job and not take anything for granted.[8]

Whenever the ball entered his area, Archer would keep his eyes firmly focused on the ball's flight, not allowing himself to contemplate the consequences of any impending collision. "You often see blokes run back with the flight of the ball and they duck their heads a bit as they take the ball because they're half-thinking about the ball and half-thinking about what's coming at them," he said. "If you're thinking about self-preservation, you're not thinking about marking the ball."[9] It sounds simple but remains the most courageous act a footballer can perform.

Archer's ascension to the senior team, in round four, 1992 (a 15-point loss to Carlton at the MCG), coincided with the inclusion of many players who would be significant in the club's rise as a force. With names like Carey, Stevens, Schwass, Corey McKernan, David King and Adam Simpson, among others, the Kangaroos became the team of the 1990s under Pagan, who replaced club legend Wayne Schimmelbusch as senior coach after the team had been thrashed in a pre-season match in Adelaide, in February 1993. "We had some really strong personalities and characters at North during those years," Schwass said. "Arch's leadership qualities spoke for themselves. He wasn't an outwardly vocal type of leader—he led by actions. And that was inspiring."

While the Kangaroos finished 12th in 1992, the seeds were sown for future success. The following year, driven by Pagan's intensity and relatively simple game-plan, they stormed to third position before losing the second Elimination Final to West Coast by 51 points. After the season, Archer declined an enticing offer from Sydney to relocate to the Harbour City. "I was only on $5000 a year at North when the Swans offered me $450,000 over three years," Archer said. "I thought, 'It must be a prank. Not even the superstars would get that kind of money.' But it was fair dinkum."[10] His loyalty would be rewarded three years later against, of all clubs, the Swans.

---

8 *Champions*, p. 15.
9 *Champions*, p. 15.
10 *Champions*, p. 13.

THE NORM SMITH MEDAL

North was third again in 1994, then played a thrilling draw in the second Qualifying Final against Hawthorn, before kicking away in the first ever extra-time period in a final to win by 23 points, with Carey sublime. Then, just as it appeared the Kangaroos were headed to a second extra-time contest, in the first Preliminary Final against Geelong, Cats full-forward Gary Ablett out-manoeuvred North full-back Mick Martyn as the final siren sounded to mark in the goal square. With scores level, Ablett kicked the winning goal to shatter North's dreams. There was more heartbreak in 1995 when the Roos were soundly beaten by eventual premier Carlton (62 points) in the first Preliminary Final.

During those years, Archer learned the defensive craft against some of the greatest forwards the game has ever seen. "I learned a lot from copping hidings from two superstars—Jason Dunstall (Hawthorn) and Tony Modra (Adelaide)."[11] This was a golden era for forwards. Archer would also encounter St Kilda's Lockett (who crossed to Sydney in 1995), Carlton's Stephen Kernahan, Richmond's Matthew Richardson, West Coast's Peter Sumich, Ablett at Geelong, and, in a different way, Collingwood's Gavin Brown—McCartney's teammate for four seasons.

On the Archer-Brown dual, McCartney recalled: "You could not get two more ferocious competitors playing on each other. It was on for young and old! They were both similar in stature and were kamikaze in the way they went about their footy. It was great to watch." Archer said of Brown that he "loved playing on him because you always knew what you were going to get," adding that "both of us just went flat out at the ball."[12]

Pagan said the arrival of Fitzroy's John Blakey during that period helped to improve Archer's training standards. "They virtually hooked up together at training," he recalled. "John was the perfect role model, who I have no doubt had a very positive effect on Glenn. He just got better and better as a consequence, and, while I won't say he was the *consummate* professional, he was certainly still professional. He became a far more prepared, and fitter, footballer as he went along." Archer agreed that Blakey was significant:

---

11   *Champions*, p. 12.
12   *Champions*, p. 12.

GLENN ARCHER

> John Blakey extended my career by about five years by giving me a love for training. In 1996-97, we were dedicated but not ultra-dedicated like you need to be today. In '97, I moved to Warrandyte and lived only three minutes away from 'Blakes'. We started commuting to the footy together. A few weeks after the season finished, during the time of year I really lived it up, Blakes would be knocking on my door saying, "Come on, mate, let's go for a run." At first I thought, "Rack off!" because the last thing on my mind was fitness work. But I'd go with him. We might run, swim or do weights. Before I knew it, I was loving it—and getting really fit.[13]

For all of Archer's on-field bravado, before games he was riddled with anxiety, so much so that he would vomit moments before the team left the dressing room. "I was aware of it, but we never saw him doing it," McCartney said. "It was due to his fear of failure. That was how competitive he was—he would get so worked up over the thought of failing."

Archer revealed that he was "so terrified of failure I didn't enjoy the build-up to games."[14] The confident Carey played on arrogance, while Archer was motivated by negative thoughts. "I was a bundle of nerves and very anxious before games, even pre-season games, because I didn't want to make a fool of myself on the big stage," Archer said. "On the morning of a game, the last thing I wanted to do was play footy. I'd sit there with a sick feeling in my guts, wishing I didn't have to play."[15] McCartney recalled that the vomiting was an unspoken event that players knew Archer needed to do in order to calm his nerves. "With his white-line fever, he would go into a frenzy before the game, and that must have fuelled his need to throw-up before we ran out to play."

After repeated failure in finals, by 1996 the Kangaroos were a steeled and determined side. They finished second, two points behind Sydney, then belted Geelong by 60 points in the third Qualifying Final. In North's third consecutive Preliminary Final, against a rising Brisbane, Archer

---

[13] Archer, *Champions*, p. 13.
[14] Archer, *Champions*, p. 17.
[15] Archer, *Champions*, p. 17.

was among his team's best in a 38-point victory. The Kangaroos had reached their first decider since 1978's loss to Hawthorn. Their opponent was Sydney, which, thanks to an after-the-siren point by Lockett, had defeated Essendon by that margin to reach its first Grand Final since 1945 (when known as South Melbourne). Both clubs had sentiment on their side: North had last won in 1977, the Swans in 1933.

North's week began in controversy, however, when McKernan tied for first with Essendon's James Hird and Brisbane's Michael Voss in the Brownlow Medal count, but was ineligible due to a controversial one-week suspension for kneeing Cats ruckman John Barnes in round six. Five days after the count, McKernan was one of North's best in the Grand Final. It was not the only controversy the club faced in 1996: North all but merged with Fitzroy mid-season before the rest of the League clubs, fearing the creation of a super team, voted against the tie-up. Brisbane swooped at the death knell and the Lions were swallowed up and off to Queensland instead.

Archer's task for the Grand Final was simple: to stand in front of the game's most imposing forward, Lockett. "I got told during the week by Denis that I was playing on Craig O'Brien in the forward pocket," Archer said:

> And he just said, "Don't worry about what Craig does, just get in front of 'Plugger' (Lockett) and block his leads. Because if he kicks 10, we're in trouble." I said, "Yep, not a problem." So I went up to Mick Martyn and said to Mick, "I've gotta come off Craig and get in the hole in front of you and Plugger, but between the two of you there's probably 240 kilos, so just say something if the ball's in the air and I'm underneath it." In typical Mick Martyn fashion, he said "Yeah, no worries, Arch, no worries." And after about the fifth time of getting Tony Lockett's knee in the back of my head, and Mick not saying nothing, I knew it was going to be a long day. And it was. It had nothing to do with courage, I just had no idea what was going on behind me.[16]

---

16   Archer quote sourced from his induction speech into the Australian Football Hall of Fame, in 2012.

The Swans were relentless in a physical and frenetic first quarter. Lockett kicked a goal in the opening two minutes, then was met by a fired-up Archer who attempted to go toe-to-toe with him (Lockett returned the favour late in the quarter with a hard bump). When Darren Crocker kicked North's first goal five minutes later, Archer proceeded to win the next centre clearance, bullocking through congestion to send his team forward. His opponent, O'Brien, copped a sliding knee to the face from David King two minutes later that sent him bleeding from the field.

Carey was North's best player in the opening term, and with four minutes remaining the Roos led by one point. But a late goal to Troy Luff and two more from Lockett—the last coming after he shoved teammate Shannon Grant out of the way and snapped on his left foot—sent the Swans to the first break leading by 18 points. It could have been more, but Daryn Cresswell missed after the siren. Paul Roos had dominated in defence, Greg Stafford was on top of McKernan in the ruck, Lockett and Luff were dangerous up forward. The warning signs were there for Pagan.

When Jason Mooney goaled 40 seconds into the second quarter, the Swans led by 24 points and had momentum. Had Paul Kelly goaled from his next centre clearance, it would have been a five-goal lead just a minute in to the term. A "Sydney, Sydney" chant was echoing around the stands. At one point, Archer was even forced to compete in the ruck.

The fightback started soon after: North began creating deeper forward entries, and Freeborn found space to snap truly. Schwass and Martyn were providing rebound from defence, Laidley was throwing himself in front of Lockett, and two minutes later Freeborn roved off hands and snapped a second goal. Lockett read the ball best against Martyn to kick his fourth, but Crocker replied. Archer was influential across half-back in the latter stages of the half, and Brett Allison goaled with 45 seconds remaining. It was clear the tide had turned when, 20 seconds later, Freeborn snapped his third goal, then Archer stormed from the next centre bounce but missed a long shot for goal. Now with the momentum, North led by two points at half-time.

THE NORM SMITH MEDAL

It was a tug-of-war at the start of the second half, with both defences making it difficult for either side to score. At 10 minutes, Craig Sholl, with a strong mark and 35-metre goal, broke the deadlock for North. McKernan was now becoming influential around the ground, although Lockett kicked a fifth goal to keep Sydney within 12 points. The Swans came again, but North's defence, sensing the moment, were desperate, preventing a second consecutive shot at goal.

Two minutes later, Sholl kicked a 50-metre goal to open up a handy lead once more. Then Swans defender Andrew Dunkley misjudged Peter Bell's long shot in flight and North had two goals in 30 seconds. Crocker then roved McKernan's palm-down in the forward pocket as North increased the margin. At three-quarter time the Roos led by 25 points and the Swans were on the ropes.

Martyn had been superb on Lockett after quarter-time, and in the opening two minutes of the last quarter he stood firm to out-mark the Swans' matchwinner. He then gave off to Archer, North went forward, and Stevens delivered a telling blow when he kicked truly from 35 metres. When Sydney next went forward, it was Archer who floated across to mark in front of Lockett, one of a number of disposals he gathered in the final quarter, his best period of the game.

Two minutes later Mark Roberts goaled on the run from 50 metres out. When he scored a second goal with 10 minutes remaining, North's supporters (in a crowd of 93,102) began to celebrate. Lockett managed a sixth goal, but there was no coming back for Sydney, the Kangaroos winning by 43 points, 19.17 (131) to 13.10 (88).

Archer rated his own performance as "good, not great", but was conscious of having done enough to meet Pagan's high standards. "Each week Denis would rate us from poor to excellent—in between were average, above average, good and very good," Archer said. "Denis was such a massive influence on me that straight after games I'd think, 'I wonder what Denis thought about how I played today?'" By halfway through the last quarter North had sewn up the match and Archer admits thinking, "I haven't played as well as I can, so I reckon he'd rate me just 'above average' at this stage." He determined that if he could add to his disposal count in the final minutes Pagan might pump up his rating up to "good". Archer said he "did get a few more kicks late in the game, but didn't do anything special."[17]

In the euphoric moments after the final siren, Archer says the Norm Smith Medal "didn't cross my mind at all."[18] When AFL talent manager Kevin Sheehan "tugged at my jumper and said: 'You've got to go to the dais—you've won the Norm Smith Medal,'" he was "dumbfounded". "I said: 'What? There's no way I could have won it.'"[19] A few minutes later, Pagan and Carey accepted a gold, rather than silver, Premiership Cup, specially made in celebration of the League's Centenary season.

Once everyone converged on the victorious North dressing rooms following the presentations, *The Footy Show*'s Trevor Marmalade—a lifelong Kangaroos supporter—saw Archer head in his direction. "I'm standing there and I see Arch making a beeline towards me, with both medals around his neck," Marmalade recalled.

> He got near me and the 'Duck' [Carey] stopped him, had a look at the medals and said, "That's gotta be worth another 100k a year!" Then Arch turned around to me and said, "Mate, got a cigarette?" He knew Trev would have a smoke! So we went and stood in the bowels of the MCG and had a smoke together before we got on the team bus. I loved it. It was surreal looking back: I got to stand there having a 'dart' with the bloke who was wearing a Premiership Medal and a Norm Smith Medal, just moments after our team had won the Grand Final. A special memory.

In just five seasons, the kid from Noble Park, who initially didn't want to play in the AFL, had become a Norm Smith medallist. He had gathered 14 kicks, eight handballs and taken eight marks. Archer was also selected in the All-Australian team for the first of three occasions (1996, 1998 and 2002); his confidence, as a consequence, soared, and over the next few seasons he emerged as one of the game's most consistent defenders.

After losing the 1997 second Preliminary Final to St Kilda, the

---

17 Archer, *Champions*, p. 13.
18 Archer, *Champions*.
19 Archer, *Champions*.

THE NORM SMITH MEDAL

Kangaroos finished a game clear on top of the ladder in 1998 and returned to the Grand Final, where they were heavy favourites to defeat reigning champion Adelaide. By half-time the Crows were barely hanging on: North led by 24 points and only shocking inaccuracy (6.15 to 4.3) had kept Adelaide within reach. But the pendulum swung a full 180 degrees after the main break: Andrew McLeod dominated and Darren Jarman hit the scoreboard repeatedly (five goals) as North was overrun to lose by 35 points. With 16 disposals and three marks, Archer battled valiantly in defence and was his team's best player again.

Having dominated for much of the decade, but with only one Premiership Cup in the trophy cabinet to show for it, the Kangaroos were on a mission in 1999. They won 17 of 22 home and away games to finish second, four points behind Essendon. They then beat Port Adelaide in the third Qualifying Final, and the Brisbane Lions in the Preliminary Final, with Archer among the best players.

Grand Final week started badly for the club when centre half-back McCartney (having crossed to North, his third club, after missing out on Adelaide's 1998 triumph) was suspended for striking Brisbane ruckman Clark Keating, and was ineligible to play Carlton in the Grand Final. Martyn had an incident with Simon Black investigated as well, but was cleared to play. Another concern for Pagan during the week was the broken ankle suffered by Stevens, his key midfielder, in the Preliminary Final. On the other hand, the Blues were riding a tidal wave of emotion heading into the game, having shocked Premiership favourite Essendon to win the second Preliminary Final by one point.

Miraculously, Stevens declared himself fit to play, while Archer was given the task of filling McCartney's boots and playing on Carlton's centre half-forward, Lance Whitnall. "I hardly slept before the 1999 Grand Final because I was scared Lance Whitnall would destroy me and it would cost us the Premiership," Archer said. Leading into the game, the Blues' 20-year-old key forward had kicked 53 goals and taken a League-high 184 marks; he was pivotal to Carlton's prospects. "I played it over and over in my mind," Archer said, adding that it "did my head in. I was wide awake and vomiting at 4am." By mid-morning, feeling lethargic and anxious, Archer thought to himself, "How the hell am I going to beat Whitnall today?" Despite this less-than-ideal preparation, on reflection Archer conceded, "those thoughts probably helped me because I ran on to the ground thinking, 'I don't want to feel like that.'"[20]

The Blues were competitive, but North won comfortably by 35 points, 19.10 (124) to 12.17 (89). Whitnall was held to two goals, and although Archer had only seven disposals and three marks, he was one of his team's most important players, along with Peter Bell and Shannon Grant, who won the Norm Smith Medal. Pagan said, "In typical Glenn style, he made it hard for all the Carlton forwards that day." Looking on from the players' race, McCartney admired Archer's performance, saying: "I was just hoping he did his job for us down there, and he certainly did that."

What heightened Archer's feats during North's mighty era (three Grand Finals and four Preliminary Finals 1994-2000) was that he was often opposed to taller and heavier forwards. "He was always battling out of his weight division," McCartney said. "Many a time he played on much bigger opponents and it was that competitive streak in him that allowed him to frighten the life out of the opposition, therefore allowing him to hold his own and thrive." Archer said, "An opponent's size is only a disadvantage if you allow it to be."[21]

Essendon centre half-forward Scott Lucas locked horns with Archer during those years. "Glenn was a really tough opponent because he was such a competitor," Lucas said, echoing Archer's teammates. "But not only that, he would also keep you constantly thinking about the game. He would go and help his teammates out in order to get separation from an opponent so that they couldn't influence the next contest either." Bomber full-forward Matthew Lloyd said that North's entire backline made it tough for opposing forwards. "North was an arrogant side and a very good side," he said. "Their backline of Archer, Martyn, King and Martin Pike was a tough, aggressive and experienced group. They were always tough to play against."

---

20   Archer, *Champions*, p. 17.
21   Archer, *Champions*, p. 23.

McCartney felt fortunate to play alongside, rather than against, North's defenders. "I was surrounded by so many great players who were all super competitors," he said. "Rarely was I caught one-out, because I knew help from Arch or one of the other defenders was not far away. Having Arch come in third-man-up was tremendous, and it gave me great peace of mind." McCartney joked that it was "lucky Arch was there, because Mick Martyn wouldn't help you!" Archer's ex-teammate, Schwass, who moved to the Swans at the end of 1997, found it tough whenever he played in the forward line against his former side. "Arch was one of the only blokes who ever shirt-fronted me," Schwass said. "I spent the next three quarters trying to get him back, but I couldn't!"

His on-field strength became legendary, but it was Archer's role off the field following captain Carey's controversial departure at the beginning of the 2002 season—following an extramarital affair with the wife of close teammate Stevens, which came to light after a March gathering at Archer's house—that enhanced his standing in the football world. The club was in turmoil, Stevens was shattered and Pagan shocked, yet the leadership and public solidarity of all three was important. Days after the event was made public, all three sat together at a press conference, their teammates standing united behind them.

"Glenn was absolutely outstanding in the way he supported Anthony," Pagan said. "We were very lucky at North to have great leaders through that period. Arch played a terrific role in supporting his good mate, 'Stevo', all through that difficult period and was a great leader for us." McCartney echoed his coach when he said, "Arch was unbelievably strong after the Carey drama. You reflect back and think the club could have shut down—it was that critical a point in its history. He galvanised the whole group during that period." Archer lamented the entire saga and credited Stevens, who was named captain in Carey's place, with leading the team through the hardest stages:

> It was very well documented and it was getting out of control. I had people, journos, camped outside my house for days at a time. Helicopters following me and Stevo up the bush; it was really hard to comprehend. I was thinking, "This is just never going to end." And emotionally, it just, obviously,

> drained the hell out of Anthony and myself in the end, to the point where I thought, "That's it for me, I don't want to play anymore." I just couldn't see myself playing footy anymore. But it was Stevo, he was the one who basically told me to pull my head in and said, "If I can get through it and play, I think you can play." I thought, "Yeah, that's a pretty good point!" So he was the one who dragged us through that, which shows how tough that bloke is; to go through what he did, then become the captain and pull everyone together when everyone wanted to fall apart. He was the glue—along with Leigh Colbert and John Blakey—that held the place together.[22]

North's first game post-Carey was round one, 2002, against Port Adelaide at Football Park. In an emotional night, and in Archer's 200th game the Kangaroos recorded a memorable 10-point victory. Afterwards, Archer and Stevens were chaired from the field. They finished seventh by season's end and lost the Elimination Final to Melbourne, but Archer's on-field leadership and consistency was rewarded with a second-place finish in the best and fairest (he had been third in 1998 and was third again in 2005) and his third All-Australian honour.

Just weeks after North's dramatic 2002 season ended, McCartney suffered life-threatening injuries in the Bali bombings that rocked the popular tourism destination on 12 October. During his challenging but inspiring recovery, McCartney appreciated the kindness and support of Archer and his teammates:

> Arch was certainly a huge support for me after Bali. All the boys were, but Arch and Anthony Stevens in particular were really good at supporting me. Even more so when I returned to the club to try and play again in 2003. I played a VFL game on the Sunday, and at training on the Monday—we were scheduled to play Richmond that Friday night—they were both in the gym and I felt they were acting a bit funny around me. I think they knew I was going to be selected—

---

22   Archer quote sourced from his 2012 interview with Mike Sheahan for *Open Mike*, courtesy of Fox Footy.

coach Dean Laidley (who replaced Pagan after 2002) must have pre-told them—and I didn't find out until half an hour later. They were great for me during such a difficult period in my life, which I'll always be grateful for.

Archer's loyalty to family, friends and teammates is one of the defining features of his character. When North played Adelaide in round six, 2003, five rounds before McCartney's famous comeback game against the Tigers, Carey was pitted against his former teammates for the first time since departing the club. In one of the most emotion-charged, dramatic games of the period, Archer and Carey tussled on a number of occasions, his support and concern for Stevens obvious for all to see. McCartney admires Archer's loyalty to this day, describing him as "genuine, authentic and caring."

In round 21, 2007, the teenager who, in the early '90s had wanted to play with mates at Noble Park rather than commit himself to North Melbourne, ran out for the 307th time, breaking Wayne Schimmelbusch's games-played record (1973-87, 306, including the 1975 and '77 Premierships).[23] Four games later, in the Preliminary Final against Port Adelaide, any dreams of a fairytale finale were eliminated following an 87-point belting by Port at AAMI Stadium (previously Football Park). Yet again, in his last game, Archer was one of his team's best players.

According to Geelong's Paul Chapman (who won the 2009 Norm Smith Medal), even at the end Archer remained an intimidating opponent, as Chapman found out personally in the Qualifying Final that year:

> 'Moons' (Cameron Mooney) decided to whack into a North player, as Moons does. I moved forward to break it up when 'Arch' came at me, eyeballing me. The look in his eye was bloody scary. He was angry. I thought, "I'm dead here." I seriously thought, "Glenn Archer is going to knock me out before they have even bounced the ball." He put the fear in me and flew the flag for his team but didn't whack me. Arch wasn't a dirty player. In fact, he was one of my favourite players and I loved playing against him, even watching him

---

23 Archer's record 311 games for the Kangaroos has since been overtaken by Brent Harvey (Round 12, 2011, 432 games in total) and Drew Petrie (Round 16, 2016, 316 in total at North and a further 16 for West Coast).

on television. His courage was inspiring but if you were open in front of him, good luck![24]

> It was the first time I was genuinely scared on a football field. There had been a bit going on during the game, and I found myself in a tussle in the goal square with one of the Kangaroo boys. He grabbed me from behind, and when I turned around and saw who it was, my heart sank. Glenn Archer was universally regarded as the toughest player in the AFL, and here I was going toe-to-toe with him. The first thing I thought was, "Don't let go." I knew if I let go he was likely to jumper-punch me one more time and probably knock me out. I hung in there, trying desperately not to show Archer how scared I was, counting down the seconds before my teammates came to the rescue.[25]

Pagan coached Archer in 212 senior games (1993-2002), and he remains appreciative of the sacrifices the defender made during that time. "Glenn more than played his part in so many of the games that I was involved with," he said. "I'll be forever indebted to the role-model example he set, plus his courage, and his ability to perform under pressure."

In 2001, Archer was selected in the back pocket in North's Team of the Century. Four years later, on 18 March 2005, he was afforded the highest honour the club has yet bestowed on a player: "Shinboner of the Century", a tribute to not only his courage and competitiveness, but also to the significant role he played off field in typifying the club's "shinboner" attitude. In 2008, North and Essendon established the Archer-Hird Medal for the best player in matches between the clubs. Both champions had famously swapped guernseys after their final on-field meeting, in round seven, 2007. In 2012, they were inducted together into the Australian Football Hall of Fame.

---

24 Paul Chapman and Jon Anderson, *Chappy: Believe It Or Not*, Hardie Grant Books, 2015, e-book version.
25 Luke Hodge and Scott Gullan, *Luke Hodge: The General*, Michael Joseph, 2017, e-book version.

THE NORM SMITH MEDAL

Archer wrote in *The Shinboners*, "It's not a fantasy to suggest that the North Melbourne Football Club changed my life, not just in a sporting sense, but in a whole-of-life package." Indeed, his love for the club that shaped and moulded the boy into the man remains absolute. "It's safe to say that North formed me, and so many of those who came before me, who played with me, and have followed me to Arden Street."[26]

NOTE: Interviews with Denis Pagan, Jason McCartney, Wayne Schwass, Scott Lucas, Matthew Lloyd and Trevor Marmalade were conducted by the author.

—— Statistics ——

BORN: 24 March 1973
GAMES PLAYED (1992-2007): 311
GOALS: 143
FINALS PLAYED: 24
FINALS GOALS: 12
GRAND FINALS: 3
PREMIERSHIPS: 1996, 1999
NORM SMITH MEDAL: 1996 (presented by Bob Pratt)

---

[26] Nick Bowen, Dan Eddy and Andrew Gigacz, *The Shinboners: The Complete History of the North Melbourne Football Club*, Slattery Media Group, 2017, p. 6.

GLENN ARCHER

— Norm Smith Voting —

(**JUDGES: Ross Oakley, Leigh Matthews, Ron Barassi** and **Mike Sheahan**)

Herald Sun votes: **Mike Sheahan:** 3 Glenn Archer, 2 Wayne Carey, 1 Paul Roos;
Ron Reed: 3 Roos, 2 Archer, 1 Wayne Schwass;
Trevor Grant: 3 Corey McKernan, 2 Archer, 1 Daryn Cresswell;
Geoff Poulter: 3 McKernan, 2 Carey, 1 Archer;
Tony De Bolfo: 3 McKernan, 2 Carey, 1 Archer;
Scott Gullan: 3 Archer, 2 McKernan, 1 Carey;
Daryl Timms: 3 McKernan, 2 Archer, 1 Carey;
Bruce Matthews: 3 Archer, 2 McKernan, 1 Cresswell.

TOTALS: Archer 17, McKernan 16, Carey 8, Roos 4, Cresswell 2, Schwass 1.

Andrew McLeod

Has there been a more watchable player than Adelaide's Andrew McLeod? What McLeod did with ball in hand—moving effortlessly between players, seemingly at his own casual pace, cutting midfields to shreds and turning defence into attack in a heartbeat—was football at its artistic best. He was devastating when weaving through the midfield for the Crows during his club-record 340-game career (1995-2010). And he hurt teams on the scoreboard, his goals from outside 50 bringing Adelaide fans to their feet. McLeod's performances in both the 1997 and 1998 Grand Finals catapulted him to superstardom, his deeds in the two biggest games in the Crows' history now the stuff of legend.

McLeod's father, Jock, played for Waverley in the Victorian Football Association (VFA), but it was with the Northern Territory Football League's Darwin Buffaloes where he carved out his own fine career after moving there in 1964. He played against the likes of Maurice Rioli, who became the first Aboriginal player to win the Norm Smith Medal, at Richmond in 1982. Jock more than held his own among Darwin's finest: he represented the Northern Territory, played "over 250 games" with the Buffaloes and was a member of "five or six

← **DOUBLE UP** Andrew McLeod could do it all: in the midfield, up forward, and late in his career, as a rebounding defender. His two Norm Smith Medals show what a great player he was on the biggest stage.

Premierships" during the club's golden era in the late 1960s and early 1970s.

His free-wheeling style of play typified the Buffaloes approach at the time. "I played all over the ground because I was pretty quick," he said. "I was a running player, a half-forward who moved to defence, like Andrew did. But I got injured and started having a lot of knee trouble." He blames genetics for the "McLeod knee", an affliction that affected Jock and his two sons, Jonathan and Andrew. Jock later coached Katherine to the 1982-1983 Northern Territory Football Association Premiership, and was an assistant to legendary Palmerston coach Russell Jeffrey, among numerous off-field roles during a 50-year involvement in the game.

McLeod senior's running ability was aided by the advice and training he received from his uncle, Norman, who trained professional runners in Melbourne. "There's no doubt my uncle made me a better runner because he found all the faults that I had—and I had plenty of them," Jock said. "I wasn't a quick starter, but once I got going I was all right." Andrew did not require the same amount of tutoring as his father—he was a standout in Little Athletics in Katherine and Darwin; his running ability, fostered during those years, propelled him to his extraordinary success in the AFL. He also credits time spent hunting and chasing pigs and geese as having aided his running. "You're so scared you run faster," he joked.[1]

McLeod's mother, Marie, played hockey and basketball, representing the Northern Territory as a hockey goalkeeper. Andrew's Aboriginal heritage stems from his mother's side: Marie's grandmother was a Wardaman, from the Katherine area of the Territory; Andrew's grandfather was a Wargamaygan, a Torres Strait Islander. From his father's side he inherited Celtic blood. "I don't know whether it's a good mix he's got behind him or not," Jock joked, "but we've gotta make the best of it!" McLeod's great-grandfather was one of Darwin's first registered Aboriginal footballers. "His name was 'Put' Ahmat and those gates at Marrara (Stadium) are named after him," Andrew said. "So it was inevitable I was going to play footy at some stage."[2]

Importantly, McLeod's parents welcomed people of all backgrounds, something he, too, later embraced. He described himself as "a unique

---

[1] Ben Collins and Dan Eddy, *Champions: Conversations with Great Players & Coaches of Australian Football*, Slattery Media Group, 2016, p. 209.

[2] Sean Gorman, *Legends: The AFL Indigenous Team of the Century*, Aboriginal Studies Press, 2011, pp. 205-206.

manifestation of the divine," believing he was "just like everyone else—one of a kind. A lot of people get caught up in judging others, but the reality is we're all unique in our own special way."[3] From a young age, McLeod's uniqueness was evident in his sporting pursuits. "I was pretty lucky as I got to play different sports from an early age," he said. "There was soccer and both [rugby] union and league. I [also] did some boxing. My mum's brother was a boxer so I spent a bit of time doing that."[4]

Jock believes Andrew would have played A-grade rugby league had he not pursued football. All three of their children were sporting standouts in their junior years: Jonathan (born 1972), sister Juliette (1973) and Andrew (4 August 1976). "Whatever they turned their hands to, they were all good at," Jock said. "You couldn't stop them playing something. They'd always be off together doing stuff, particularly the boys. Then they'd come home and want to clean each other up in the backyard!"

It was in the sporting arena, particularly the football field, where Andrew felt most comfortable to express himself. "I spent many hours observing my idols," he said. "I was the kicker and played five-eighth in most rugby teams, so I loved watching Wally Lewis (rugby league) and Michael Lynagh (rugby union), and later Brad Fittler (league)."[5] His football heroes were Rioli, Michael McLean (Footscray/Brisbane 1983-97) and 1993 Norm Smith medallist Michael Long (Essendon 1989-2001). "There was also a fella named Greg Bruce, who was an awesome half-back flanker for the Darwin Buffaloes, where Dad played," McLeod said. "Greg was a great resource, and someone who always had time for me. I spent countless hours watching those boys do their stuff, and then I'd grab my older brother and mimic their moves in the backyard."[6]

Jock believes Jonathan also deserves credit for his younger brother's development. "Jonathan's got a lot to do with why Andrew got to where he did," Jock said:

> Jonathan pushed him all the way with his fitness and competitiveness. Johnno was always into fitness and weight

---

[3] *Champions*, p. 210.
[4] *Legends*, p. 206.
[5] *Champions*, p. 209.
[6] *Champions*, p. 209.

training, running, anything to improve his own levels. And because Andrew idolised his older brother, he would always be doing stuff with him. Johnno was playing A-grade footy at about 19 and Andrew was already making his NTFL debut at 15. In fact, Johnno was a bit of a mongrel, because he was always telling Andrew how soft he was!

Having progressed through the junior ranks (including playing fullback in the NT schoolboys side on occasions), Andrew was on what he believed to be a stopover in Adelaide with his father—after playing in a representative game in Victoria for the NTFL versus a Victorian Football Association team, in which he was judged best on ground. Jock informed Andrew, to his shock, that he had arranged for him to board with an Adelaide family and to play for Port Adelaide's colts. The seniors were led by Jock's friend and 10-time Premiership coach John Cahill, who was keen to develop young McLeod into a future senior player.[7]

"My old man tricked me into coming down to Adelaide," McLeod said. "I was only 17 and thought I'd only be here a couple of weeks. Little did I know I'd be here for good."[8] Jock explained that his son "thought he was coming back to Darwin with me, but I had other ideas!" He added:

> I just thought that if he came back with me, I'd never get him back to Adelaide again. I was driving back to Darwin this day, and I got up early that morning and said to him, "You're staying, mate. Stay here and play footy." I think he thought he was only going to be there for a couple of weeks! When I told him he wasn't coming, he had this horrible look on his face and I felt as if I'd betrayed him; I felt really bad about it, and when I was driving home I got sad a few times. In fact, my mates still joke today that I abandoned Andrew all those years ago!

Fortunately, the unexpected change of environment for McLeod was managed well by Cahill and his team at Port Adelaide. When the coach

---

[7] John Cahill played 264 games for Port (1958-73, SANFL), kicking 286 goals. He played in the 1959, 1962-63 and 1965 Premiership teams and won four best & fairest awards. He then coached 624 games (Port Magpies 1974-82, 1988-96, 2005, 444 games, winning the 1977, 1979-81, 1988-90, 1992, 1994-95 Premierships; Collingwood 1983-84, 47 games; West Adelaide 1985-87, 69 games; Port Power 1997-98, 44 games; South Adelaide 2008, 20 games). The Port Adelaide Power's best player award is named the John Cahill Medal.

[8] *Champions*, p. 209.

felt the teenager needed a break from his training, Cahill would send him home to Darwin for a few days to refresh his mind and spend time with his family. "John understood those kids and what he needed to do with them to get the best out of them," Jock said, appreciatively.

Despite soon feeling comfortable in the City of Churches, McLeod's path to the Adelaide Crows later that year (1994) was far from a *fait accompli*. "I put my name in the draft and Fremantle picked me up as a pre-concession," he said. "They could pick two players from South Australia and they picked myself and Darryl Wakelin."[9] Neither would play for the Dockers.

Fremantle was entering the AFL in 1995, and coach Gerard Neesham was busy recruiting players for its debut season. The AFL's draft system was in just its ninth year and far removed from the combination of scientific analysis, draft combines and accessible vision of potential draftees that clubs have at their disposal today. Therefore, remarkably but perhaps not surprisingly, none of the key figures at the Dockers had seen McLeod play when they invited him and Jock to Perth for a meeting, on 19 October 1994.[10] Neesham later conceded, "We just didn't know who he was, had never been briefed on him or his ability, had never seen him play, for even a second."[11] Jock explained what took place:

> It wasn't a very good set-up the club had at the time; as a new club they were operating out of relocatable buildings. We sat there and football manager Gerard McNeil came in, pulled a contract out and put it on the table. I thought, "Gee, they're producing a contract straight up?" He went through it and said, "This is what's happening." We looked through the contract and pretty soon we realised Andrew was getting more money at Port Adelaide than what he was going to get at Fremantle. Port had already made a pretty good offer for Andrew to stay there, so we had that in our minds when we saw the Fremantle offer. We just sat there and waited. Neesham came in with McNeil and, as soon as they walked in, Neesham said to Andrew, "Can you please stand up?" Andrew looked at me and I looked at him and he said, "What for?" "I want to see how

---

9   *Legends*, p. 207.
10 Les Everett, *Fremantle Dockers: An Illustrated History*, Slattery Media Group, 2014, p. 41.
11 Gerard Neesham, *Fremantle Dockers*, p. 42.

tall you are." And, virtually, that was the end of it. Afterwards, when Andrew and I spoke about it, he said, "Gee Dad, they pulled me halfway across Australia, I'm virtually one of the top draft picks, and they don't even know how tall I am?" So, it was a bit amateurish.

McNeil later confirmed the story: "We did ask him to stand up, but he didn't really want to engage. His dad did most of the talking...it was a very quick meeting, 20 minutes at the most."[12] Jock felt the club was uninterested in his son's thoughts or needs. "Gerard didn't ask Andrew anything about himself—it was all about what he was going to do as coach, as if Andrew was already on board. That didn't sit well with Andrew or myself...We decided it would be better for Andrew to spend another year in Adelaide with Port."

Soon Jock was courting offers from clubs around the country, including Collingwood, but the care and interest shown by Adelaide (Port Power did not enter the AFL competition until 1997) convinced McLeod to sign with the Crows. Jock recalled:

> The club's recruiter, Tim Johnstone, made the effort to visit us in Darwin, but they weren't pushy or anything. They just said, "How would you like to do this, this and this?" They were really good. Andrew wanted to play AFL, and of course they wanted him, but they were more prepared to take it slowly, slowly and develop him as a person and as a player. We appreciated their approach and how they went about things.

There were more negotiations required between Fremantle, the McLeods and the Crows, but, eventually, the deal was done: the Dockers received former Crow forward Chris Groom (who played just seven games and kicked 18 goals in his one season at Fremantle, after playing 12 games for Adelaide), while the Crows secured a future games-record holder, dual Norm Smith medallist and Premiership player, triple best and fairest winner (1997, 2001, 2007) and five-time All-Australian (1998, 2000-01, 2006-07, the latter as captain).

Jock said it was a stressful time acting as negotiator for his son.

---
12   *Fremantle Dockers*, p. 42.

Fortunately, he was supported by Andrew's then young girlfriend, Rachael, who helped her future father-in-law to send faxes, in the days before mobile phones and email made communication easier. "At one stage we had three or four phones all connected at once as we tried to swing the deal," Jock recalled. "The only person who wasn't getting stressed out about it all was Andrew."

Crows defender Mark Bickley (McLeod's captain from 1997-2000), recalled that he had "heard lots of reports from our recruiters" about McLeod's potential, and that after a "pretty quiet start" the youngster soon showed that he had special qualities. Bickley compared McLeod with a "Rolls-Royce", so impressive was his ball use at training. "He was always a shy kid, a bit reserved and didn't say much," Bickley added. "But most people who saw him train and play early on could tell that he had some special traits."

Bickley admits to some doubts as to whether McLeod was going to be able to apply himself at AFL level, because "he was a little bit chubby and had a few rough edges." But those concerns were soon shelved. "The more things he was able to achieve the more professional he got, and he went on to become a star," Bickley said. Key forward Matthew Robran (1993-2001, 130 games) said the shy McLeod "let his footy do the talking." Bickley saw that McLeod's competitive nature emerged during intraclub games at the start of 1995. "Whenever we played a game between us, that's when you saw the best of him."

The football world became aware of McLeod's talents in round nine, 1995, against Hawthorn at Football Park in Adelaide. In just his second game, McLeod kicked the winning goal in an exciting two-point victory. "From there, everyone started to take notice," Bickley said, "and he started to believe in himself. It was like a self-fulfilling prophecy: the more he believed in himself, the better he got, and the more he then expected of himself. From there, he just progressed so quickly."

Former Crows defender Jason McCartney (1995-97, 37 games) still marvels at McLeod's game-winning goal that night. "He played on Ray Jencke (then playing his 160th game) and he turned him inside out on the boundary line, forward pocket, dribbling it along the ground for a goal," McCartney recalled. "It was unbelievable! We knew we had a player on our hands then."

McLeod was initially played as an "elusive half-forward" because, Bickley said, "he didn't have the engine then to play in the midfield." It took the arrival of Malcolm Blight as coach in 1997 (replacing Robert Shaw) for McLeod to improve his aerobic ability. "He had a really good role model, who doesn't get a lot of credit for what he did," Blight revealed, "and that was Mark Ricciuto." As a consequence, Blight added, McLeod began to "knuckle down and get his body right, and as soon as he started working harder all bets were off." Robran also credits the arrival of Neil Craig as fitness coach for McLeod's rapid improvement:

> Neil got us all super fit so that we could run out games, and Andrew certainly benefited from that. Then, because he had the fitness to stay competitive for an entire match, Andrew took his game to the next level. He became the match-winner that we saw during the 1997 and '98 finals series after that.

Blight soon moved McLeod to half-back, a masterstroke that gave the Crows an attacking element from defence and through the midfield that was unrivalled across the competition. Bickley said of the move:

> Malcolm's philosophy was, he liked to leave himself some room to improve the side if things weren't going well. He'd say, "We'll start off one way, but if we're losing I always want a little switch that I can flick to help us get better." In the 1997 finals series that switch was Andrew, where Blighty would throw him into the midfield. So he became a star overnight, all because of that ability to go from defence into the middle when we needed him to.

Bickley described half-back as "the perfect scenario" for McLeod to utilise his elusiveness and creativity. "In those days, forwards didn't really pay much attention to their opponents—half-backs were meant to be players who played on the forwards," he said. "Andrew had the ability to defend, but he also had the ability to play off his man because his pace would always get him back to his man if he needed to." If his opponent did not get the ball, McLeod became "like a dog off the leash; he'd just go to where the ball was and invariably get it, then he would attack," Bickley said.

As he became more prominent on the field and in the media spotlight, McLeod conceded that it "took me a while" to adjust to life as a Crow. "You had to change everything, your lifestyle gets thrown out the window and the worst thing is you live in a fishbowl," he said. "You become public property. Everyone wants to speak to you. Everyone wants a piece of you. Everyone wants to know about you and everyone wants to poke and prod you."[13] Jock said his son "didn't really struggle with fame." He never courted the publicity, but it didn't alter his persona. "He doesn't like publicity and he doesn't like fame. Even today, if he's out, he'll wear dark glasses and a cap so he doesn't get recognised. But it never altered who he was."

The game did not consume him the way it did some of his teammates, and he appreciated a more balanced lifestyle where family was always his first priority. "I was different because of my upbringing and who I was," McLeod said. "A lot of those blokes, all their life was about the club. They'd sorted out where they wanted to be. Football was number one for them whereas for me, and still to this day, football is number two."[14] That said, Robran is adamant that McLeod understood his value to the team. "It wouldn't have taken Andrew too long to realise he was an integral part of the squad, and that his best footy was as good as anyone else's in the side," he said. "I would think he realised at a young age that he would be a valuable member of the side for many years to come."

Separating McLeod from the pack was his clean ball-handling, balance, vision and decision-making. Blight knew if they could get the ball in McLeod's hands, the game would open up. "Clean hands are crucial, especially at ground level," McLeod said. "You have to keep practising running flat out and taking the ball one grab. It's a bit like chasing geese in the bush; either you grab them by the neck in one grab or they bite you."[15] Robran believes that what set him apart was "his ability to read the ball off hands, whether from a marking situation or a spillage." His teammates admired McLeod's "uncanny ability to know whether the ball was going to fall to the left or the right" of a contest.

Often Robran was the recipient of McLeod's fine work down field. The dashing defender was also at the big man's feet at marking contests,

---

13   *Legends*, p. 207.
14   *Legends*, pp. 207-208.
15   *Champions*, p. 210.

sweating on the loose ball if Robran failed to mark. "A lot of times, I would be the one competing, and if it fell to ground he would be the one scooping it up, and he'd do it at pace. I loved how clean he was with the footy at ground level," Robran said. He added that, of all the attributes McLeod had at his disposal, it was his ability to read the ball off hands and then, if forward, kick a goal on the run, that he enjoyed most. Adelaide's supporters agreed.

Bickley described his skills as "sublime", adding that McLeod "had a sixth sense" and would regularly kick the ball to space, rather than directly to his teammate, thereby forcing them to run into the opening to receive his pass:

> I can remember so many times when he would kick the ball to an area, yet the forward wasn't leading to that area—that's just where the space was. Then, once the ball was kicked that direction the forward reacted and, all of a sudden, he's leading out marking on his chest! Andrew was basically saying, "Mate, run here and you'll get it." He directed his teammates where to go, and that happened a lot.

This was possible because, as Robran explained, McLeod "had a beautiful leg and could kick well on both sides." When McLeod gathered at half-back, Robran would "make a beeline to lead towards his leg" where, "99 times out of 100" he would receive the pass on his chest. "His left foot was just as clean as his right," he added. "It's a strength all footballers need these days, but for back then he was terrific on both sides of his body when not everyone else was."

There were two players, however, that McLeod preferred to kick the ball high above rather than see them lead: high-flying forwards Tony Modra and Brett Burton. He told his father that he did so because "I wanted them to take the hanger of the year!"

McLeod revealed that, when he was at his best, the game moved in "slow-motion" and he was "on cruise control." He could "see things unfold before the actual event."[16] Bickley recalled the club undertook some decision-making experiments that enlightened them to McLeod's exceptional decision-making process:

---

16   *Champions*, p. 210.

> Players would wear cameras on their heads and we'd film vision [at training], then we'd put it on a big board and players could practise picking the ball up, then looking up and seeing a giant movie screen of teammates leading and they'd kick the ball to what they thought was the best target. We were able to see what they saw, and why they made the decision they did. With Andrew, he wasn't looking at the players that were leading, he was looking at where the space was, and he would invariably hold on to it and wait until a player led into that space. Whereas other players—and I put myself in this category—would look up and simply look for where the forward was leading to. If they were leading into congestion, we would still kick the ball to them. So that showed us that Andrew saw it differently from everyone else.

McLeod credits his clear thinking for those decision-making strengths. "Good decision-makers are very clear thinkers," he said. "They can think their way through situations and they don't get flustered by any pressure that's around them. Generally, the more pressure there is, the clearer they think. That's how I feel."[17]

He played 26 games in 1997, the most he managed in a season from his 16 years at Adelaide. All his strengths were on show as the Crows put together a 13-9 record in the home and away rounds (finishing fourth). They then won the first Qualifying Final against West Coast (33 points), the second Semi-Final versus Geelong (eight points), and came back from 31 points down at half-time to beat the Western Bulldogs (two points) in the Preliminary Final. McLeod was one of his team's best in all three.

As he prepared for the club's first Grand Final, McLeod did what he always did: he called his father. "Throughout Andrew's AFL career, I spoke to him every day of the week," Jock recalled:

> He'd ring me or I'd ring him and we'd talk about stuff—not always about footy. It was just what we did. When he went into that 1997 Grand Final, he was still like a kid in his approach. Yes, he was concentrating on the game and

---

17   *Champions*, p. 210.

he was nervous, but he wasn't overly nervous where some players burn too much nervous energy before the game. He was more excited about playing in a Grand Final.

Jock believes one of the keys to his son's achievements and consistency was his ability to not play the match in his head before he ran on to the field. This differed from the previous year's Norm Smith medallist, Glenn Archer (North Melbourne, 1996), who was known to vomit before games due to his anxiety. "I don't think he ever played the game in his head before he played," Jock said. "He's a pretty casual bloke at the best of times and he likes his own space." McLeod told Jock that the only time he felt overawed on Grand Final day was when he ran on to the field. Said Jock: "He later said to me, when he ran out he thought, 'Gee, there's more people here than in the whole of Darwin!'"

On Grand Final day 1997, it seemed as though Victoria had been overrun by South Australians, many making the trek across to cheer their team to victory. Adelaide's opponent was hoping to create its own piece of history, however: St Kilda had not won a Premiership since 1966 and entered the game as favourite to win and break that 30-year drought.

McLeod, opposed to Matthew Lappin, was busy from the outset, twice cutting off St Kilda attacks at half-back. It was a sign of what was to come. For Jock, watching his son's composure, it was reminiscent of his junior days in Darwin. "He reminded me of the young kid running around in the backyard," Jock said. "He was carefree and was out there just playing footy. He got the ball plenty of times and Malcolm put him in a few different positions. He made some really good footballers look pretty ordinary that day."

Despite McLeod's early form, the Saints settled quicker; their key forwards Jason Heatley with two goals in the first five minutes and Barry Hall were imposing themselves on the game. It took makeshift forward Shane Ellen, a surprise move by Blight at the start of the game, to kick the first goal for the Crows. McLeod's foot skills were on display for the 98,828-strong crowd when he drilled a long pass to Troy Bond a few minutes later; his run and carry was an important factor in his team not only withstanding the Saints' early dominance but then, halfway through the quarter, edging in front. Late in the term, commentator Bruce McAvaney said, "What a game McLeod is playing—he's got the ball on a string." St Kilda coach Stan Alves switched Rod Keogh on to McLeod in the final minutes, with Lappin having struggled to negate his drive.

With 1997 Brownlow medallist Robert Harvey dominating in the middle, and Hall kicking three early goals, the Saints took control of the game in the second term. As St Kilda swarmed across the ground in waves, on one occasion McLeod gathered the ball between two opponents, broke both tackles, maintained his footing, then shook off another tackler before clearing the ball. His clean handling was a standout as the Saints applied the pressure.

Bickley said that McLeod, who spent more time in the midfield in the second quarter, "had an extra gear" that enabled him to free himself from congestion. "There were times when he'd be running and gliding and someone would be about to tackle him, yet he just had another gear to be able to go to," Bickley said. "Then he would use that electric pace. Very rarely can I recall him being tackled or caught holding the ball—it simply didn't happen. And that was because of the awareness he had of what was going on around him."

The Crows trailed by 13 points at half-time, but in the third term—the so-called Premiership quarter—dramatically swung the game their way. In an intense and crucial period of the match, Bond kicked the first goal, then Chad Rintoul, followed by Ellen. Darren Jarman put them in front at the halfway mark, then McLeod cannoned into Harvey, rattling the key playmaker as he hit the deck. McLeod stayed upright. Ellen goaled again, playing the most unlikely of cameos, and a high snap by Peter Caven made it six goals to two for the term as Adelaide took a 10-point lead into three-quarter time. If all that was not enough to ignite the Adelaide faithful, late in the quarter McLeod launched himself skywards from the middle of a pack at half-back to take one of the marks of the day.

The final quarter was the Jarman show: positioned one-out in the forward line, he kicked five of Adelaide's eight goals (to St Kilda's four) as the Crows charged to their first Premiership in just their seventh season in the AFL. Starting his attacks on the defensive side of stoppages, McLeod repeatedly streamed through the centre of the ground as he completed his four-quarter dominance. Adelaide won by 31 points: 19.11 (125) to 13.16 (94). Despite Jarman's late heroics, McLeod was Adelaide's best player and deserved his Norm Smith Medal. He had 18 kicks, 13 handballs (10 disposals more than the next best Crow, Kane Johnson), 11 marks and three tackles, a tally eclipsed only by Harvey (36) and Nathan Burke (33).

"Andrew basically dominated and set up so many goals for us," Robran said. Moreover, "he had a couple of decent opponents in the middle" in Harvey and Burke, "so he performed on the biggest stage against some real quality opposition." For all his flashiness, Bickley preferred to praise McLeod's composure when the Saints appeared to have control of the game in the first half:

> We were under the pump at various stages, and what stood out for me was Andrew's calmness in those situations. He was unflappable, so when things weren't going well for us in both games (1997 and again in 1998) Andrew was still getting the footy. So, it wasn't like we didn't see him in the first half. Then, once we got on top, he started joining the party. He was doing it when it was tough, though, when the ball was coming into our forward line regularly.

McLeod appreciated the adage that a player's worth is gauged by how he performs in big games. He was "always conscious" of those who performed great deeds when it mattered most. "But wanting to do it and actually believing you can do it are two completely different things," he added. "You need to have that belief, and I always have."[18] Although he never played for individual awards, having admired two other winners in Rioli and Long, McLeod recognised there was "a bit to live up to."[19] He appeared humble and emotional when receiving the Norm Smith Medal from Fitzroy's 1969 Brownlow medallist, Kevin Murray.

The 1997 result was one of two proud highlights for Jock McLeod that year. The other? Older son Jonathan was also judged best afield in the victorious St Mary's team that won the NTFL Grand Final.

Having become just the seventh team to win from fourth position in

---

18   *Champions*, p. 210.
19   *Champions*, p. 210.

1997,[20] the following year the Crows became the first team to claim the Premiership from fifth place. The task looked beyond them when they lost the first Qualifying Final, to Melbourne, by 48 points. However, with McLeod leading the way (17 disposals and three goals in wet conditions) and Peter Vardy kicking six goals, Adelaide defeated Sydney at the SCG in the second Semi-Final, by 27 points. According to Jock, his son should not have played against the Swans, as he was carrying an injury that affected his capacity to run. "He had a lot of injuries through the finals series," Jock revealed. "At one point, before they went to Sydney, I didn't think he was going to make the team."

That McLeod carried an injury into the Preliminary Final, against the Western Bulldogs again, adds weight to what he was able to achieve that day. It was, arguably, a finer performance than either of his Grand Final games. Despite being tagged by 1990 Brownlow medallist Tony Liberatore, McLeod kicked seven goals from 19 disposals as the Crows completely outplayed the Bulldogs and won by 68 points. As of 2017, it remains the most goals kicked by a Crows player in a final.

One Bulldogs insider (who asked to be anonymous) later said the decision by coach Terry Wallace to pit Liberatore against McLeod was a mistake and had raised eyebrows in the pre-game team meeting. But 'Libba' was not alone with the task: Robran recalled that at least three players tried to negate McLeod's influence, all to no avail. Describing it as "a great solo effort," Robran was aware his teammate was injured:

> He almost did it on one knee. In the third quarter he burst out of the middle and kicked a goal and his knee virtually locked on him. Immediately, and with a very noticeable limp, he headed towards the bench to ask to come off for a rest and get his knee checked. But they said, "No, stay out there." Then he's gone on to kick a bunch more goals and finish with seven! It was just a magnificent individual effort; the complete, all round performance.

The 1998 Grand Final was eerily similar to 1997. North Melbourne dominated early, as had the Saints the previous year, but its inaccuracy

---

20   The others to come from fourth and win the Premiership were Fitzroy (1916), Carlton (1945), Essendon (1949), Essendon (1965), Richmond (1969) and West Coast (1992).

to half-time kept the Crows in the game (6.15 to 4.3). Then, in the third quarter, Adelaide kicked five goals to two and took a two-point lead into the final break. Jarman performed his goalkicking heroics again, kicking five, and the Crows kicked six goals to none in the last quarter to win by 35 points, 15.15 (105) to 8.22 (70).

Hampered by his injured knee, McLeod was forced to play a different role from his all-ground heroics of 1997. "He played a completely different game," Jock explained. Rather than the run and carry of 1997, McLeod "got the ball and brought other people into the game." Blight told Jock immediately after the game, "Whenever Andrew got the ball, we got it our way, and he was responsible for eight or nine of our goals." Later, Blight said:

> When people ask me about Andrew McLeod's game in those two Grand Finals I call him the *sweetest* player I've seen. The way he moved and glided around the footy ground, and the way he understood the game, he was the sweetest-looking player you'd ever see. He is one of my all-time favourite players, and of course I take a lot of credit for his success! Only joking.

McLeod was matter of fact about his twin achievements. "It's every player's dream to play well in a Premiership side, and I was just lucky that I was judged best on ground because they could have given those two Norm Smiths to a number of blokes."[21] But Bickley said that, when the time came for someone to stand up and lead the club, McLeod grasped the moment, not once but numerous times throughout the 1997 and 1998 finals. "When the big games came around, he was the one who got the best out of himself. We measure blokes, give them a few extra ticks, if they play well in the big games, because that's what people remember, and it's what matters most for a team to have success. Andrew stood up in our four biggest games during that period."

In the years following his back-to-back Norm Smith Medals, McLeod was forced to endure greater attention from opponents, particularly after Gary Ayres (the first dual Norm Smith medallist) replaced Blight as coach of the Crows at the end of the 1999 season. Bickley recalled:

> Andrew had enormous success across half-back and drifting

---

21   *Champions*, p. 210.

through the middle in the late 1990s, then, when Gary Ayres took over as coach in 2000, Andrew was playing as a midfielder every week. That's when the taggers and the scragging by opponents started happening. He would admit himself that while he didn't struggle with it as such, he didn't enjoy it as much having someone hanging off him every week. I don't think he enjoyed the Gary Ayres era (2000-04) all that much, partly because of that. He went back to half-back under Neil Craig (2005-10) and played some good footy again back there.

McLeod's consistency during the 2000s was remarkable. Until his last season (2010), he rarely missed a game. In 2000 he finished third in the Brownlow Medal, then was runner-up in 2001 and won the AFLPA's Leigh Matthews Trophy as its MVP. He led the Brownlow Medal count after round 19 (with 21 votes) but did not poll in the last three games—despite collecting 35 disposals in round 20 and 37 in round 22. Brisbane midfielder Jason Akermanis overtook McLeod in round 21 and, despite also not polling in the last game, held on to win by two votes. McLeod then led the 2003 Brownlow count until round 15 (with six best-on-grounds, the most of any player that season), before failing to poll in the latter rounds and finishing equal-fourth.

In 2005, McLeod was named captain for the International Rules series against Ireland, one of his greatest personal honours. He was coached by Essendon's Kevin Sheedy, a figure McLeod "loved", according to Jock, having followed the Bombers keenly as a child. Sheedy was also on the selection committee that, in 2005, chose the Indigenous Team of the Century. One of five Norm Smith medallists in the team, McLeod was named ruck-rover.[22]

That he won the Jim Stynes Medal as best Australian player in the 2005 International Rules series also showed that McLeod could adapt to a new code—one with a round ball and different rules—and excel. Two years later he captained the Indigenous All-Stars team that lost to Sheedy's Bombers and was awarded the Polly Farmer Medal as best player afield—

---

[22] The others were Peter Matera (wing, 1992 Norm Smith winner), Maurice Rioli (centre, 1982), Michael Long (wing, 1993), and Byron Pickett (interchange, 2004).

THE NORM SMITH MEDAL

yet another example of his affinity with the big stage.

McLeod was and is a champion for his people. His determination to inspire young Aboriginal people has continued post-football through his work with the 'Andrew McLeod Indigenous Program' at the Crows. There he works alongside wife Rachael and the club's first Aboriginal player, Eddie Hocking (1991, 11 games). "Andrew's out and about all through the middle of Australia, visiting kids, they run scholarships for them, so the work they are still doing is fantastic," Robran said. "The club is lucky to have him still involved around the place and heading up these programs. He is so passionate about these kids, and about Indigenous culture in general." That passion extended to the club's AFLW team, for which McLeod was an assistant coach in 2018.

McLeod considers himself to have been lucky on his journey. "Not only have I been able to play the game I love on the biggest stages, but I've also gone on a journey, finding myself as a person while also being a role model for young Indigenous boys and girls. That has been the biggest thrill—to know you have done something to help other people."[23]

The last word went to the man who knows McLeod best, his father Jock:

> I'm such a fan of the way he conducted himself on the footy field. I worked all around Australia and people always came up and asked me about him. I know many people—some who were really good footballers—who would go and pay their money to watch Andrew play football. The thing about him was, whenever you went and watched him play, he always did something memorable. He rarely had an off day and he played the game as it should be played. He wasn't a dirty footballer at all, and he didn't have to be. I would simply sit and admire how he played. I even felt sorry for some of the blokes they sent out to tag him, because he made them look stupid!

NOTE: Interviews with Jock McLeod, Malcolm Blight, Jason McCartney, Mark Bickley and Matthew Robran were conducted by the author.

---

23   *Legends*, p. 204.

ANDREW MCLEOD

—— Statistics ——

BORN: 4 August 1976
GAMES PLAYED (1995-2010): 340 (Adelaide record)
GOALS: 275
FINALS PLAYED: 22
FINALS GOALS: 23
GRAND FINALS: 2
PREMIERSHIPS: 1997, 1998
NORM SMITH MEDALS: 1997 (presented by Kevin Murray)
and 1998 (presented by Keith Greig)

— Norm Smith Voting —

1997: (**JUDGES:** Wayne Jackson, Leigh Matthews, Patrick Smith and Tim Lane)

The Age votes: **Rohan Connolly:** 3 Andrew McLeod, 2 Darren Jarman, 1 Shane Ellen;
Stephen Howell: 3 McLeod, 2 Shaun Rehn, 1 Jarman;
Ian Cockerill: 3 McLeod, 2 Ellen, 1 Kym Koster;
Jake Niall: 3 McLeod, 2 Jarman, 1 David Pittman;
Alan Shiell: 3 McLeod, 2 Jarman, 1 Ellen;
Mick Atkins: 3 McLeod, 2 Ellen, 1 Rehn;
Paul Daffey: 3 McLeod, 2 Jarman, 1 Simon Goodwin.
The Age **TOTALS:** McLeod 21, Jarman 9, Ellen 6, Rehn 3, Koster 1, Goodwin 1.

— Norm Smith Voting —

1998: (**JUDGES:** Wayne Jackson, Leigh Matthews, Mike Sheahan and Eddie McGuire)

Herald Sun votes: **Mike Sheahan:** 3 Peter Caven, 2 Andrew McLeod, 1 Ben Hart;
Bruce Matthews: 3 McLeod, 2 Kane Johnson, 1 Shaun Rehn;
Michael Stevens: 3 McLeod, 2 Darren Jarman, 1 Johnson;
Trevor Grant: 3 McLeod, 2 Jarman, 1 Rehn;
Michelangelo Rucci: 3 McLeod, 2 Johnson, 1 Rehn;
Andrew Capel: 3 McLeod, 2 Johnson, 1 Rehn;
Mark Robinson: 3 McLeod, 2 Jarman, 1 Caven;
Damian Barrett: 3 McLeod, 2 Johnson, 1 Jarman;
Daryl Timms: 3 McLeod, 2 Jarman, 1 Johnson;
Scott Gullan: 3 McLeod, 2 Jarman, 1 Johnson;
Geoff Poulter: 3 McLeod, 2 Johnson, 1 Jarman;
Tony De Bolfo: 3 McLeod, 2 Caven, 1 Rehn.
Herald Sun **TOTALS:** McLeod 35, Johnson 13, Jarman 12, Caven 6, Rehn 5, Hart 1.

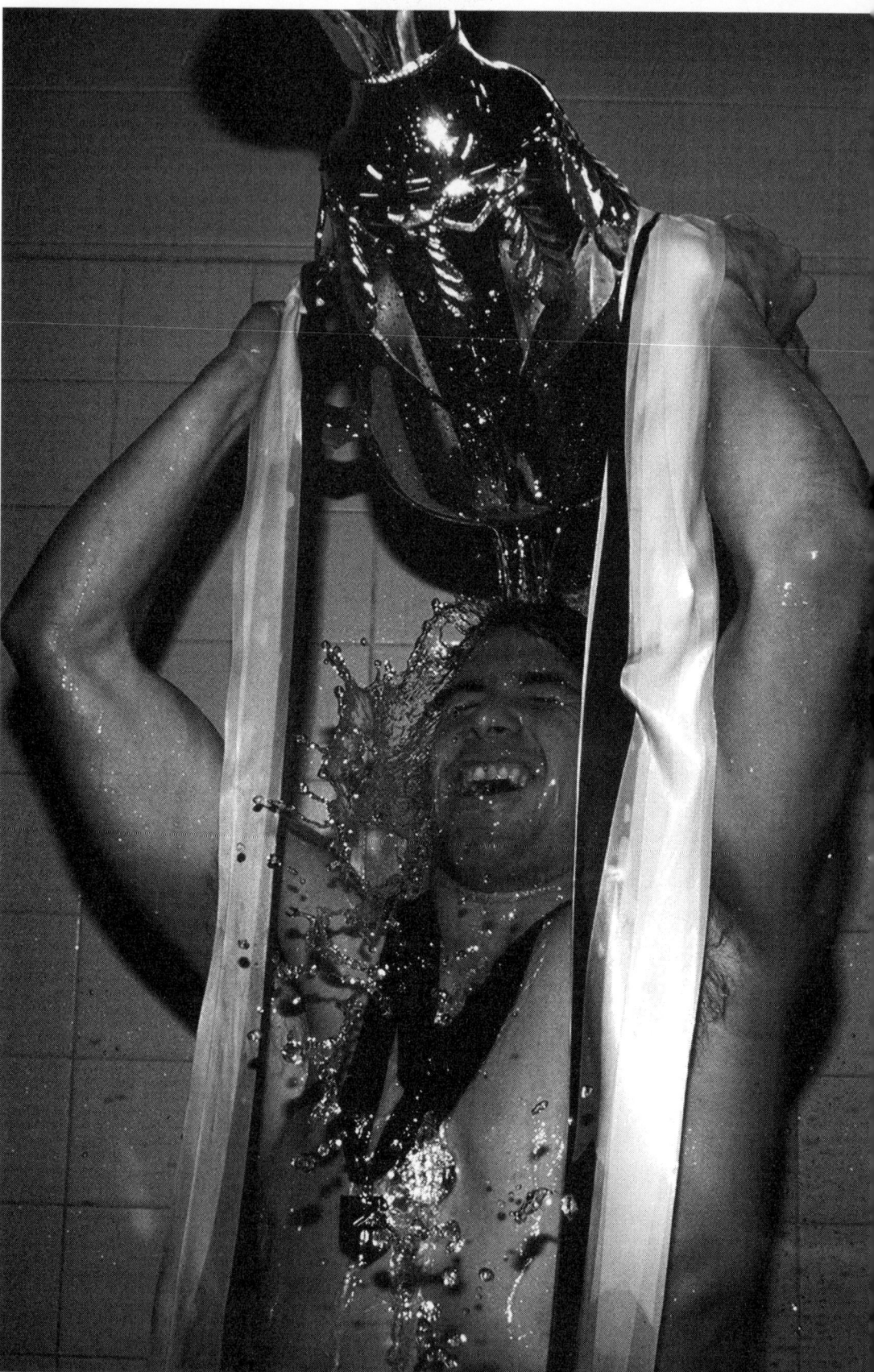

Shannon Grant

It took Shannon Grant two failed Grand Final attempts before he tasted Premiership success. As a 19-year-old Grant was a member of Sydney's losing 1996 Grand Final team against North Melbourne, then, in 1998, having crossed to North, he was part of a Kangaroos side that kicked itself out of the Grand Final before being overrun by Adelaide. But in the 1999 decider against Carlton, Grant turned in a best-on-ground display to help North claim its fourth Premiership Cup. Grant's four goals were a microcosm of his 301-game career: he always seemed to hit the scoreboard in crucial moments. He was consistent, too, winning North's best and fairest (the Syd Barker Medal) in 2001, coming second in the award three times and third once, and was an All-Australian in 2005. In his Norm Smith Medal-winning performance, Grant had 15 kicks and four handballs, took five marks, and kicked four crucial goals in North's 35-point win over the Blues

My parents were pretty sporty. My mum, Dianne, played a lot of netball, and my dad, Robert, played amateur footy at Elsternwick. With five of us in the family (Stewart, Brad, Tara, Shannon and Nicholas), they were pretty tied up in all their kids' sporting endeavours, and were a great support for all of us during our formative years.

← **SWITCHED** From a Sydney loser in 1996 and a scapegoat in North's 1998 shocker, Shannon Grant became a big winner at North Melbourne in 1999—North's best in a stunning victory over Carlton.

THE NORM SMITH MEDAL

When you have older brothers, you learn to work for your wins in the backyard. It's an interesting one, isn't it? Of the groups of brothers who go on to play in the AFL, it's the third or fourth down the line who seems to have the greatest career. For example, I can think of the Selwoods (twins Adam and Troy, plus Joel and Scott), the Clokes (Jason, Cameron and Travis) and, to a lesser extent, the Motlops (brothers Shannon and Daniel, plus cousin Marlon). I guess I was the same in that sense. You learn to fend for yourself from a young age, especially in the backyard, but it's fun doing it.

Most of my junior footy was played forward or on the ball, much like my AFL career. I was centre half-forward early on, but I stopped growing around 13-14 years old; everyone kept getting bigger around me, so my role changed as I got older. By under-18 (TAC Cup) footy I was playing on the ball and up forward for the Western Jets. I played a bit at half-back during my three years with the Sydney Swans, but at North Melbourne it was predominantly midfield and forward.

I loved Hawthorn. I was a big Tony Hall fan, and loved Darren Jarman, too. But I also enjoyed watching how Chris Mew and Chris Langford went about it down back. They were such strong defenders. Hall and Jarman were exciting up forward, but the older I got the more I appreciated what the key defenders did. They weren't flashy, but were great in their positions. I went to a lot of Collingwood games as well, because Mum was a Collingwood fan—Dad was Hawthorn—and I loved watching Gavin Brown play for the Magpies. What a star he was.

I went to most of Hawthorn's Grand Finals between 1983 and 1991. It was a good period to be following them! We'd catch the bus out to Waverley, from our home in Flemington, to watch them play. I'd also go to Glenferrie Oval and watch training when I could. I loved my footy from a young age, and was fortunate that, between my parents and older brothers, we could attend lots of VFL then AFL games.

I didn't plan a path to the AFL, but it was always something I wanted to do. I just worked hard, trained hard, started doing okay in representative sides and, from there, I was fortunate enough to be drafted by the Sydney Swans at the end of 1994.

Being selected by Sydney, and having to move up there, was all part of the lottery of the National Draft. I had spoken with quite a few clubs, but Sydney had picks two and three and so they were in the box seat to take me. Fremantle selected Jeff White with pick one, then the Swans took Anthony Rocca with two and me with three. Essendon (pick four), Hawthorn (eight) and Collingwood (nine) were after that, and I had spoken with all those clubs, so I wasn't sure they would select me. Sydney general manager Ron Joseph and coach Ron Barassi came to my house in the lead-up to the draft, so I had a strong inkling I would be going to Sydney.

It's an overwhelming thing to do, moving interstate as a 17-year-old. But I was very fortunate in going to the Swans, because they were a great footy club who looked after me and my family. That certainly made the move up there an easier transition than it could have been otherwise.

I consider myself fortunate and lucky to have had a year under Ron Barassi. He was such an icon of the game, a greater fella, and I loved training and playing under him during 1995. He was also great company to be around; always good with us young blokes. I built a great relationship with Ronny Joseph, as well, during those couple of years he was there before he started his own management business. I remain great mates with him today, and he managed me my entire career. Making it to the AFL was one thing, but the friendships that came out of my three years at Sydney have endured to this day.

Barassi was big on the fundamentals. For me, it was a case of head down, bum up. I was only a teenager, and while I played 10 games that first year I didn't play under him that much. I was injured mid-season and missed about eight games, but in the time that I did train under Ron he worked me pretty hard. He was old-school in his approach, which I think was a good lesson for me as a young player. It instilled a strong work ethic in me, which I carried throughout my career.

Our captain, Paul Kelly, was an absolute star. Just so humble and down to earth. But a workhorse, too. I learned a lot from him by the way he prepared and the way he trained. 'Kel' was a terrific role model for a young kid coming up. Being 17, I didn't have a driver's licence, so a lot of the time Kel would pick me up in the morning then drop me off at night on his way home. Apart from being a great role model (he won the Brownlow Medal in 1995), those little things made him such a great leader. He was always available to lend a hand to us young kids, and always had time for us. I have nothing but admiration for the bloke. I loved him as a leader, and was inspired playing under him.

Early on, it was a bit daunting training and playing alongside Tony Lockett. He was such a famous figure. But like with Kel, he was an outstanding guy to be around, just so decent. He had a lot of time for the younger blokes. Sometimes, after training, he would take the young blokes out for dinner, which we all really appreciated. That he invested that time into us was great. That's probably a side of 'Plugger' [Lockett] that the public didn't see. To play alongside him was great. He was full-forward and I was forward pocket, so I was next to him on the ground a fair bit. He always made you walk taller out there, and you were confident whenever he was around because you knew he had your back. Plugger had an amazing footy brain, knew the game so well. But back then it was a case of getting up the ground and leaving him one-out with his opponent—there wasn't a lot of science to it. There weren't the plus-ones behind the ball like today. Everything was so open and one on one, so he had a field day down there. But he instructed us, and was terrific in the way he helped us out; not just on game day, during the week as well.

Rodney 'Rocket' Eade's biggest strength as coach was on game day. Tactically, he was exceptionally good, and was one of the earliest coaches, during that mid-1990s period, who started practising different things, approaching the game a different way. On game day he was able to read the flow of the game really well, see things as they were happening and adjust accordingly. He had a great footy brain, and that showed in the results we had in 1996. We were 12th in 1995, then in his first year as coach we finished first after the home and away rounds and played off in the club's first Grand Final since 1945. That shows how capable he was as a coach.

We were building momentum both on the field and in the media. Crowds were bigger, and in general there was a lot more interest in the Swans. That's what happens when you start winning in a non-traditional football state. It was a great time to be around the place. We were winning, we were playing some good footy, we had players like Plugger, Kel, Paul Roos, Andrew Dunkley and Mark Bayes, who were all having a big influence on the club, and we also had a group of talented kids coming through. It was an exciting time, and playing finals added to that excitement.

We had two tight finals victories: six points over Hawthorn (in the fourth Qualifying Final) and one point against Essendon (second Preliminary Final). Just to get into the Grand Final was an amazing achievement. We put in a hell of a lot of work, but on Grand Final day we came up against a pretty good team in North Melbourne who were going to be tough to beat. Although we lost the game, I think that group, that year, started to set the club on the path to sustained success. Success isn't just about winning Grand Finals. It's about always being competitive, and having a strong, sustainable culture that can last from one generation to the next. And that's what Sydney developed during the 1990s, and it's what continues with the Swans of today.

It was phenomenal being in a Grand Final at 19 years old, but quite overwhelming, to be honest. It was a big moment, and it was hard keeping the energy levels at the height they needed to be at for the entire game. A few of us younger blokes had played the game over in our heads before we'd run out, so that was a great learning curve to go through. I think it helped us to grow. It certainly helped me to become a better player for the rest of my career. I hoped that, should I ever get another opportunity, I would prepare better than I did for that game.

By the end of 1997, I was looking at my options regarding a move home to Melbourne. The Demons had the first pick in the 1998 pre-season draft, and they were pretty keen on me. But I had some good friends at North Melbourne, and coach Denis Pagan, footy manager Greg Miller, and some of the players came up to Sydney to meet with me. I had a good feeling about the club. They were a good, strong footy club during the '90s. Plus, I had grown up in the North Melbourne area, they were consistently playing finals footy, and I wanted to play finals and, hopefully, win a Premiership. For those reasons, North was a good fit for me and so I chose to go there. It worked out well for both clubs in the end: I played my best footy at North, and Wayne Schwass did well up in Sydney. There aren't a lot of trades that are win-wins, but that was probably one of them. The Swans certainly tried to retain me, but my mind was made up that I wanted to go home, and they were great in helping to facilitate that. It was hard, because they had been phenomenal with me, but the pull back to Melbourne was pretty strong at the time and I knew I needed to go home.

Denis Pagan was an outstanding coach. He worked us hard, but that's AFL footy. If you didn't work hard, you wouldn't have made the grade. He was hard, but extremely fair, and he had a really good relationship with his players; he took the time to get to know them. He also knew what motivated them, and which ones he could push to get more out of. That was one of his strengths. He had a really good sense of humour, too, which no one saw outside of the club. He has kept that sense of humour today whenever we catch up. I was lucky. After Barassi and Eade, Denis helped mould me into an even better player, installing a stronger work ethic. As a result, he got the best out of me. He pushed me pretty hard, and because I had so much respect for him it was easy to respond when he asked more of me.

My role didn't change much. I was playing defence more regularly at Sydney, and I spent more time on the ball and up forward at North, but the fundamental aims were the same. Working week in, week out with Anthony Stevens, Adam Simpson, Peter Bell and Anthony Rock, I was learning more and more each week. I particularly learned a lot off watching 'Stevo' go about it. Having good role models around me, guys playing in similar positions to me, it helped me to get better, quicker. If you didn't compete, or play the right way, Denis would put you in the reserves. It was as simple as that! And if he thought you didn't do enough in the Friday night game, he had you doing one-on-ones on the Saturday morning, regardless of how sore you were. You did not want to be singled out on the Saturday morning, so you put even more into your Friday night performance.

It was amazing to play alongside Wayne Carey. He and Tony Lockett are two of the best players I played with, both exceptionally good players in their positions. Wayne was strong and competitive, and you always walked taller around him. He oozed confidence, arrogance even, but a good arrogance. He was just confident in his own abilities, and he played that way. He got that way because of how hard he worked; he was one of the hardest workers I have seen on a training track, a great athlete, so to play alongside him was amazing. He was a terrific captain and a great player to watch at full flight. I was lucky to play with both those guys. You probably appreciate it more after you retire. When you're in each other's pockets every day, you are not only teammates but mates as well. So you don't look at them as revered figures at the time. But reflecting on it, to have played with so many good players, and to have had some success with them, is something I'm pretty proud of.

The 1998 Grand Final was a bad day. We were hot favourites against Adelaide, and the game should have been over by half-time. But we kicked ourselves out of it. We led by 24 points at half-time (6.15 to 4.3) but, for whatever reason, the whole team just stopped after the break. Unfortunately, we got steam-rolled. Darren Jarman and Andrew McLeod—the stars of the 1997 Grand Final victory over St Kilda—turned on some more magic, and we picked a bad day to play our worst game of the year. It was frustrating, because we'd done so much right; we just couldn't pour on the scoreboard pressure. The Crows of that era were a great team, so when they got hold of us in the third quarter we couldn't stay with them. They ran away with it, winning by 35 points. It wasn't much fun watching one of my childhood heroes in Jarman turn it on to beat us!

I had another poor day personally. I had now played in two losing Grand Finals. Our team was smashed in 1998, and I was one of the players who had a poor day. You obviously sit down and go through it, but you know where you stand within the group after a poor game like that—you don't need to be told. I knew. It was a bad day for the footy club overall, because we had gone in as hot favourites, and it was equally as bad for me on a personal level.

The 1999 season was my best to that point. I came third in the best and fairest, so I was consistent. I had a good finals series, which was my main aim. It took me three or four years to feel physically and mentally ready to perform consistently. It's hard when you're a teenager, because you're coming up against guys with eight or nine pre-seasons under their belts. They are bigger, stronger, more experienced, whereas you're still developing, finding your way and getting taught how to play the game, so it takes time. When you get to about the 50- or 60-game mark, that's when you feel comfortable that you can maintain your spot in the side. It doesn't happen overnight. By 1999, I had played 83 games and was entering my peak years as a footballer. I was ready for that finals series, physically and mentally.

I went into the 1999 Grand Final just trying to prepare the same way I had all year. We didn't make a big song and dance about it, just treated it like any other game. We knew how disappointed we were after 1998, and our whole year was about making amends for the opportunity we had stuffed up the year before. We were determined not to change our regular routine, or do anything different, and we all knew what was at stake on Grand Final day.

I usually slept pretty well before games. On game days, there were four or five of us who joked around too much in the rooms, which upset a few of our older teammates at times. Myself, 'Duck' (Carey), 'Simmo' and 'Belly' all liked to have a joke and muck around to lighten the mood. That helped us to settle. Whereas, Robert Scott, Stevo and John Blakey couldn't be ruffled up because they were all regimented in their routines. I found that I played better the more relaxed I was, so entering that Grand Final I made sure I remained relaxed and didn't get too strung up.

Jason McCartney missed the Grand Final through suspension, for striking Brisbane's Clark Keating in the Preliminary Final. It was such a shame for Jase. He had come across from Adelaide when I did, at the end of 1997, and had established himself at centre half-back. He was one of our gun defenders and was integral to our success. Our defence was as good as there was in the League, so it was sad for Jase, and for us, that he was forced to miss that game.

I started on a wing against Carlton's Ben Nelson, drifting forward whenever possible. Then Stevo got injured in the second quarter, and

I replaced him in the midfield. He had entered the game with an ankle injury, which was absolutely stuffed. He could hardly run during the week. How he got up for that game I don't know, because it was a three-month injury normally. He played, but during the game he tore his pectoral muscle—he just had a bad week! It shows you the strength, the resolve of the bloke, to get up and play through all that. And when he was out there, he was contributing really well. I was just glad that I could contribute and pick up the slack after he succumbed to his injuries.

The Blues had the ball in their half early, but our defence stood up. They were awesome! 'Arch' was great on Lance Whitnall, Mick Martyn was terrific, as was Byron Pickett. They just stood up for us, particularly in the critical 50-50 moments. Their ability to keep us in the game early was crucial to the eventual outcome.

To kick a goal in the first quarter was great for my confidence. The earlier you can get involved in a game, the more settled you become, so to have some important touches was great. I felt like I was beginning to have some influence by halfway through that quarter, and I put that down to my work rate. I had become a lot fitter in that 12-month period, part natural progression and part having another pre-season under my belt. I was finding space at important moments, and could use the ball well when I had it.

It was midway through the second quarter when we started controlling the midfield battle. We were winning more of the footy around the ball. Corey McKernan kicked a couple of big goals, Simmo had some important touches, as did Matty Capuano in the ruck. Getting on top in the midfield was the main reason we began to take control, and, unlike the year before, we made the most of our chances when we went forward. I found the scoreboard a couple of times, too, one coming from a lucky bounce. You appreciate those when they bounce the right way, because many don't. Nelson had tagged me early, but then he got moved off me and when I went into the midfield; being in and under, my tag was broken and I found more space. Having said that, whoever my opponent was got plenty of space as well. I was lucky to make the most of my chances when I did have the ball.

THE NORM SMITH MEDAL

We were 20 points up at half-time, and knew what we had to do in the third quarter. The resolve within the group was such that we never felt we were going to lose that day. You just sensed that everyone was ready. We knew we wasted the opportunity the year before, and we had to make up for it. There were moments in the third quarter where they came at us, but we steadied and started getting on top late in the quarter. Plays like the one of Micky Martyn, who won a 50-50 ball and bounced his way out of defence, plus some big wins by Arch were huge for us to halt their momentum and send the game in our direction. By winning those critical contested balls, we could shape the way the game went.

We weren't an arrogant team, but sometimes to be successful you need to have a bit of arrogance to the way you play. But it has to be the right arrogance. You can't be over-confident, yet need to be confident enough in your own ability to perform when it matters. We were certainly a confident, strong team, and that only came about because of how hard we worked. We had a lot of talent, but gee we worked hard during the week and over summer. It didn't just happen, and that's why we had the success we had. That, and a strong game-plan that stood up in finals footy under Denis.

The defensive side to my game wasn't my strongest attribute growing up, nor was it when I first entered the AFL system. Denis was really strong on you being able to contribute to the team when you didn't have the ball. As I got older, I feel I got a lot better at that, and that was evident through my play in the '99 Grand Final. It didn't come natural to me. When I was coming up through junior footy, I wasn't taught what to do when I didn't have the ball, nor where to run or any specific tackling techniques, those fundamentals of the game. I worked at them, though, and I think by 1999 I was much stronger in that aspect of my game.

Halfway through the last quarter we were on top and still kicking goals, so that's when I started to realise we were going to win the Premiership. But you remain focused on where the game's at, rather than thinking about the final siren. Wayne took a one-handed mark and goaled towards the end, and that's when I could look at the scoreboard and think we were home. You're that focused until then, though, that you don't get caught up in the outcome until it becomes obvious.

Somebody from the AFL lets you know straight away that you've won the Norm Smith Medal. So I knew before it was announced on the stage. You obviously don't play the game for those things, but it was nice to be recognised as having contributed and played well on the day. It was just such a great feeling to finally win a Premiership, and to be a part of the winning team cemented, forever, a special bond with my mates.

Being a Norm Smith medallist doesn't necessarily mean more to me now than it did then. The thing that means more as I get older is being part of a Premiership side. We had so many good players that day who all contributed to the result, and that's what you play for: to play finals and to win Premierships. So that stands out as more significant for me than being recognised as a Norm Smith medallist: that I contributed to my team winning a Premiership.

You don't think you will be back in the Grand Final every year, because you know how hard they are to get into. You need a bit of luck along the way. But with the team we had I thought there would be more appearances before my career was finished. We got close in 2000 (lost the Preliminary Final to Melbourne), then things happened within the club that broke it apart. All of a sudden, the team you had won with so often was no longer the same team. We played a few more finals, including a prelim final (2007, 87-point loss to Port Adelaide), but never got back to the Grand Final after 1999. It made me value how hard they were to get into and then win.

When the Wayne Carey controversy happened in 2002, it wasn't a great time around the club. But it was also a period where other leaders rose to the fore. Guys such as Stevo, Arch, Blakey, Simmo and Mick Martyn were the fabric of the joint; they were good senior players who made the place tick during that difficult time. The heart and soul were Stevo and Arch, though; they were warriors and exceptional leaders, and they took ownership of the team after Wayne left, as difficult as it was for Stevo in particular. We were lucky to have those guys to lead us through that.

It got harder for me. My body wasn't the same. It was taking me longer to recover and prepare for the next game. I was having some knee and back issues, which wore me down. But the hardest thing for me was that the game continually got quicker. I was struggling to keep pace with the increase in tempo. By 2008 it was getting too quick for me. I was never quick anyway, but as my body was breaking down more often it became harder and harder to get up each week. I was slowing down as the game was getting faster, so I knew my time had come to retire. I was lucky though. I got to play with two really good footy clubs, and over a long period of time. I played 301 games, and feel fortunate to have done it for as long as I did.

I still marvel at Brent Harvey's ability to have performed over such a long period. 'Boomer' was a freak athlete; just an amazing player. To play so well, for so long (432 games over 21 seasons) at that level was phenomenal. Even when he finished up he was still playing great footy. Boomer has been one of those ones out of the box, who will go down as one of the game's greats. I know how hard it was for me to keep my body healthy, so what he did was remarkable.

In 2017, my daughter, Anderson, started playing Aussie Rules football. She loves her footy, and if she wants to continue to play it as she gets older we will see where it takes her. I'm rapt my three kids—Anderson (13), son Archer (10) and daughter Claudia (2)—all love playing sport. And I think it's great that girls now get so many opportunities to advance in sports such as footy. It's great for the AFL, but it's also great for society.

—— Statistics ——

BORN: 19 April 1977
GAMES PLAYED (1995-2008): 301 (Sydney 58 games; North Melbourne 243)
GOALS: 361 (Sydney 38 goals; North Melbourne 323)
FINALS PLAYED: 19
FINALS GOALS: 27
GRAND FINALS: 3
PREMIERSHIP: 1999
NORM SMITH MEDAL: 1999 (presented by Simon Madden)

SHANNON GRANT

— Norm Smith Voting —

(JUDGES: Wayne Jackson, Jason Dunstall, Anthony Hudson and Caroline Wilson)

Herald Sun **votes: Michael Stevens:** 3 Shannon Grant, 2 Peter Bell, 1 Byron Pickett;
Geoff Poulter: 3 Grant, 2 Pickett, 1 Bell;
Mark Robinson: 3 Grant, 2 Archer, 1 Bell;
Bruce Matthews: 3 Adam Simpson, 2 Archer, 1 Mick Martyn;
Trevor Grant: 3 Pickett, 2 Archer, 1 Grant;
Jason Frenkel: 3 Bell, 2 Grant, 1 Pickett;
Mark Stevens: 3 Pickett, 2 Bell, 1 Grant;
Scott Gullan: 3 Grant, 2 Bell, 1 Pickett;
Grantley Bernard: 3 Bell, 2 Grant, 1 Martyn;
Mike Sheahan: 3 David King, 2 Bell, 1 Pickett;
Daryl Timms: 3 Grant, 2 Pickett, 1 Bell;
Elissa Hunt: 3 Bell, 2 Grant, 1 Pickett.

Herald Sun **TOTALS:** Grant 24, Bell 20, Pickett 15, Archer 6, Simpson 3, King 3, Martyn 2.

James Hird

A third-generation Essendon footballer, James Hird eclipsed the playing careers of his father Allan jnr (1966-67, four games) and grandfather Allan snr (1938-47, 154 games, Hawthorn, Essendon, St Kilda, including Essendon's 1942 Premiership; his name adorns a grandstand at Windy Hill). Injury bedevilled Hird's first two years at Essendon, but in 1993 it all started to happen. He won a Premiership at 20 years of age, in just his 20th game. A Brownlow Medal followed in 1996, before a recurring foot injury almost ended his career. Hird made an inspirational return in 2000; not only did he captain the Premiership side, he was awarded the Norm Smith Medal. Hird's influence on matches was decisive, and his courage undoubted, never more evident than in the weeks after he suffered severe facial fractures in a collision with teammate Mark McVeigh in 2002. Hird fought back, and in 2003 won the fourth of five best and fairests (1994-96, 2003 and 2007). By then Hird had been named at No.3 among the 'Champions of Essendon' and at half-forward in the club's Team of the Century. After retiring in 2007, Hird returned with much fanfare in 2011 to coach the Bombers; this stint became the darkest in Essendon's, and Hird's, story. His contribution as a player, however, ranks him among the finest to wear the red and black. In 2012 he was inducted into the Australian Football Hall of Fame. His crowning moment was the 2000 Grand Final, when he won 24 kicks and five handballs, sent the ball inside 50 on 10 occasions, and kicked two goals.

← **IN THE ZONE** James Hird reckoned he was so much in the zone in the 2000 Grand Final that he felt there were times he was outside looking in. It was a great view, as his performance was dominant.

THE NORM SMITH MEDAL

My passion for Essendon Football Club runs deeper than most people realise. Both my father (Allan Hird jnr) and grandfather (Allan Hird snr) played for Essendon. The family connection gave me a real love for the club, and football in general, and gave me respect for tradition and what the club means to a lot of people. It's important to me that Essendon supporters understand I was once one of them. When the Bombers win or lose, it means as much to me now as it did when I was a kid.[1]

Dad would wake me up at 6am for private training sessions. I was about 14 at the time. Three or four mornings a week, we'd go to the park across the road. We'd run around the park two or three times—it was about 1km around—and kick the footy for about an hour; then Dad would go to work and I'd get ready for school. It would be freezing... and we'd be rugged up in clothing you'd wear to the snowfields. Half the time I couldn't even feel my fingers. The ball would be like a rock and would hurt your foot when you kicked it. I didn't like it much at the time—who would?—but I can see how much it helped me. Apart from learning how to control the ball in the wet, it was very beneficial from a psychological point of view.

I adopted Dad's simple philosophy: "There are plenty of skilful players who don't make League footy. If you want to make it, no matter what happens, keep your eyes on the ball, win it at all costs, and win it as many times as you can." There's a lot more to it than that, but when you boil it down that's the most important thing. Win the ball first and see what happens after that. If you win the ball, you control the game.

I was probably lucky to be drafted (in 1990). That year the Sydney Swans could pick up the best two players from the ACT. I had some talent, but I wasn't outstanding, which was highlighted by the fact the Swans overlooked me. There wasn't a lot of interest in me. Sydney, Hawthorn and Essendon each had quick chats with Dad, and I'm grateful Essendon drafted me [with its sixth selection, No. 79 overall].[2]

---

1   Some of James Hird's quotes are sourced from his interview with Ben Collins in *Champions: Conversations with Great Players & Coaches of Australian Football*, Slattery Media Group, 2016, pp. 95-103. Quotes on Hird's 2003 facial injury were also sourced from his 2002 diary, *Challenging Times*, Slattery Media Group, 2002, pp. 114 and 118. All other quotes are from Hird's 2018 interview with Dan Eddy.

2   Those drafted ahead of Hird were Todd Ridley (pick 13, 25 games for Essendon, 48 AFL games), Richard Ambrose (pick 21, 0, 3), John Fidge (pick 24, 0, 59), Glenn Hoffman (pick 37, 0, 0), Jarrod Carter (pick 51, 0, 0), and Steven Fry (65, 0, 0).

It was a controversial decision at the time. They almost drafted someone else instead. Some people at the club thought, "This kid's no good; he'll never make it." But apparently 'Sheeds' (coach Kevin Sheedy) said: "No, we'll give him a go. I think he's got something." I moved to Melbourne only a month after finishing school (aged 17).

Sheeds put me on the spot at my first training session. My parents drove me down from Canberra and dropped me off for my first day at the club. He took us for two laps of the 'Tan' [the 3.87km running track around Melbourne's Botanic Gardens]. When we finished, Sheeds asked me: "Which player at Essendon do you play like most?" I didn't know what to say, so I said: "Mark Thompson." I was hoping like hell Sheeds didn't think I was too brash. He said: "Well, if you play like him you'll have a good time here."

I started the first intraclub practice match (in 1991) in a back pocket. I got a couple of kicks, but I didn't set the world alight. I did my knee a few weeks later and only played a handful of under-19 games in my first season at the club.

In my first two seasons I was worried I'd be sent back to Canberra. It took me a whole year—until round one, 1992—to break into the senior side. But then I did a medial ligament and missed seven or eight games, played a couple of reserves games, and copped a punctured lung. I wasn't having much luck, but I stuck at it and ended up playing in the reserves Premiership under Denis Pagan. A lot of the young blokes like 'Mercs' (Mark Mercuri), Joey (Misiti), Steve Alessio and a few others played in a senior flag the next year.

Denis Pagan was my reserves coach for only one season, but he left a huge impression on me. He was fantastic the way he constantly drove and challenged us. It was exactly what I needed at the time. After senior training had finished, he'd take five or six young guys aside and really work them. Denis's message was very simple, but very effective. Anyone who played under him had to be 100 per cent accountable for their actions and giving their all.

I was a bit scared of him. He ripped through me a couple of times after games about the way I played. Some of the sprays he gave me, or teammates sitting beside me, have stuck in my memory. It hadn't happened to me before, but it was a good thing because it woke me up to the realities of what was required. I thought, "I'd better do what he wants me to do because he's going to stay on my case until I do."

(St Kilda captain) Danny Frawley called me soft. It was round eight, 1993, against St Kilda at Waverley—Tim Watson's comeback game after being retired for a year. I was playing on Danny and I took my eyes off the ball in a contest. I squibbed it. Danny didn't have a go directly at me, but he kept reminding Tim, with whom he'd played state footy, about how weak this young bloke playing alongside him was. He went on and on about it, saying, "How can you play with this weak so-and-so, Timmy? He won't even have a go. He's soft. He's got no heart." It was a real kick in the guts. Here I was copping a verbal pasting from one of the game's most respect players via my idol, Tim Watson.

The worst thing a footballer can be called is soft, because it reflects upon his character. It was then I decided, "I'm going to go hard at the ball every time from now on." It was an inspiration to go hard all the time—not just when it suits you. To say I didn't pull out after that would be ridiculous. There are always times when you can go harder. Every player would be the same in that regard. If they had their time again, they would have approached certain situations a bit differently. You regret when you let that happen, but if you go as hard as you can on the majority of occasions, you'll earn the respect of your teammates.

I wasn't the most aggressive player—I didn't crash into blokes—but I prided myself on being hard at the ball. It's for others to judge whether someone is courageous. I wasn't the fastest, the strongest, the fittest, most naturally gifted athlete or physical specimen. I wasn't the most talented or the best kick, either. I had to work hard on every aspect of my game, and I had to do certain things to get the ball that other players probably didn't have to do. My game was built around winning the ball, and plenty of players seemed to win the ball a lot easier than I did. I had to put my body on the line to win it; if I didn't, there mightn't have been a spot for me.

If you're not quick, you need quick hands. I worked a lot on my reflexes and taking the ball with one grab, which was my greatest skill. It's not something you're born with; you have to keep practising it. I worked on that at different times with my father and (former Essendon assistant coach) Mark Williams. I always worked hard on my football, and I always worked hard with a football. I worked a lot on my own as well. You can do plenty of things to improve your game when it's just you and your footy. Just handling the ball, throwing it against a wall, kicking it to myself, constantly touching the ball and putting myself under pressure. Use your imagination and, if you can, try to simulate a match situation.

I was very hard on myself. Whether it was self-doubt or a lack of confidence, I always felt the need to work hard to maintain a standard. When I felt that standard dropping, rather than have a rosy attitude and think everything will be fine, I quickly did something about it to regain that focus. I'm all about being focused and intense about everything I do.

Work ethic, and my love for the game, got me where I was. I was introduced to footy when I was very young and, after a while, it became natural. But a lot of work went into it. You'll only work hard at something if you love it and it means a lot to you. As a kid, all I wanted to do was play footy for Essendon. When you've got that goal and you're so passionate about it, it's hard for someone to stop you from doing it.

Being a bit unorthodox probably helped me. When I got the ball, opposition players might have expected me to do something in particular, and when I didn't it gave me a bit more time. Half the time I didn't know what I was going to do with it, so how was the opposition going to know?

Follow your first instinct because it's the right one 95 per cent of the time. I played a lot on instinct—get the ball, spot the first option and give it. Sometimes that lets you down, because if you held on to the ball for a split-second longer you might have chosen a better option. Young players are great athletes, strong marks and great kicks, but they let themselves down with their decision-making. It's the old thing of natural footballers versus natural athletes. Joe Misiti was a classic example of that. He would never have made the Olympic running team, but when he got the ball he always seemed to make the right decision. I saw myself a bit like that, too.

THE NORM SMITH MEDAL

A thing that distinguishes great players is the ability to concentrate and maintain intensity. As you get older, it becomes increasingly difficult to play out four quarters, do all the training and maintain the intensity you once had, but your ability to concentrate never leaves you. If you want to be a good, consistent player but can't concentrate for 120 minutes, you're kidding yourself.

I had more coaches try to teach me how to kick properly than I've had hot dinners. My kicking style was the main topic of conversation with my coaches over the years. Just about every (specialist/skills/assistant) coach who came to the club said: "We need to improve your kicking technique." I even had a specialist kicking coach come in to try and iron it out. Sheeds was always on to me about it, but he eventually gave up. I'm the first one to admit my kicking style was far from copybook standard. I didn't guide the ball on to my boot like you were supposed to—I dropped it from a great height in comparison to most players—but I must have dropped it on to my boot okay because it generally went where I wanted it to. That doesn't mean it's the correct way, but I did thousands of kicks and was comfortable with it. For a kid who kicked the footy every day, it's strange I didn't have a better technique. But the bottom line is accuracy, and it really doesn't matter how ugly a kick you are as long as you hit the target more often than not.

They're right when they say you don't fully appreciate your first Premiership—unless you've toiled for it your whole career. The senior players deserved it (in 1993), but us 19 to 21-year-olds didn't because it was well before our time. When we won in 2000, I was 27 and, after coming back from a serious injury, disappointments and uncertainty, I savoured that Premiership a lot more because I appreciated the enormity of what we'd achieved.

Sheeds gave me a licence to use my own intuition. A couple of years before I became captain [in 1998], he took me aside and said: "If you feel like the game is getting away from us, put yourself behind the ball or go on the ball for a few minutes and see if you can get the ball out of the middle and change it up." I took that on, and took it a bit further later on. Sheeds liked having tall midfielders who could run and take a mark, so he was never afraid to put me on the ball.

When I was at my best, I played on autopilot. It was pretty special. You know what's going to happen; you know where the ball is going to go; you know you're going to get it, and you know what you're going to do with it. You know all that without actually having to think about it. You're playing on pure instinct, and all your instincts are spot-on.

Foot injuries nearly finished me. I broke my foot for the third time in a night game at the MCG at the start of '99 (round two against the Kangaroos). A few months later, in July, I wanted to start training again. The side was going really well and I wanted to be part of the finals campaign. But a scan showed the crack hadn't healed at all. Retirement was never mentioned, but I couldn't see the club putting up with a recurrence of the injury. I had an operation but I was concerned I wouldn't get back. After missing only three games in three years (1994-96), I hardly played in the three years from 1997-99 (22 of 69 games). It was getting desperate. I thought, "What am I doing to myself? What am I doing to my family? What am I doing to the club? I can't keep going on like this for much longer."

I had a modified pre-season for two or three years. I was the guinea pig for a program developed by our fitness coach John Quinn. I did about 20 sessions a week, only 30-45 minutes a session, never training two days in a row, with a lot of swimming and running in water and cross-training. 'Quinny' was phenomenal during that period, devoting a lot of time to work one-on-one with me to get me up to play. Many of my skills sessions were simply standing there and kicking the ball with one of our trainers, Colin Hooper.

I had to work a lot harder to play well after my foot injuries. In '96 (when he won the Brownlow Medal in a tie with Brisbane's Michael Voss), I felt I could get 25 touches and kick four or five goals most weeks, whereas after my foot injuries it took more self-motivation to do it. In some ways, that was more satisfying when you played well because it was a far greater challenge.

I played my best footy when I played 70 per cent at half-forward and 30 per cent on the ball. It was my ideal role. I did that in '96 and 2000, which were my best two years from an individual perspective.

THE NORM SMITH MEDAL

My lead-up to the 2000 Grand Final was less than ideal. We used to train around 3pm on the day before a game, and on the Friday afternoon before the Preliminary Final against Carlton, we had just finished the warm-up and were doing the first drill when football manager Matthew Drain came over and said, "Your daughter's been rushed to hospital, here's the phone to call the hospital. Get in your car and go straight to the Epworth." Stephanie had suffered a febrile convulsion, and they had to put her into an induced coma so that her brain didn't overheat. She was in intensive care from Friday night through to about lunchtime on the Saturday, so it wasn't the ideal preparation for a Preliminary Final. Luckily I received a call during the day saying she was out of intensive care, so I decided to play that night. I can't remember anything of the game, and after we won (by 45 points) I jumped straight back in the car and went back to the hospital. She was in hospital until Monday, but she remained pretty sick right up to the Grand Final. Fortunately she got through that period and returned to full health.

I didn't go to the Brownlow and we didn't do all the normal Grand Final Week things that you usually do. I basically trained and then went to the hospital or home. It kept a lot of the hype away, but I don't recall much of the week because it was such a blur. My wife, Tania, was incredible during that period; she stayed by Stephanie's bedside the whole time and was incredibly strong. Both of us were young, first-time parents, so it was all a great unknown. When Stephanie was in intensive care, the doctors didn't know what was bringing on her fever, and we had nervous waits while they tested for all kinds of possible causes. It took a while for all those results to come back, so it was a very distressing week.

Growing up an Essendon supporter, I went to the 1983, '84 and '85 Grand Finals that the Bombers played in. I was there to see Billy Duckworth win his Norm Smith Medal in '84, which was an amazing performance going from half-back to half-forward and kicking goals. Then Simon Madden in '85 was spectacular again. I also vividly remember Gary Ablett's game in 1989—an incredible performance. And, having played in the 1993 Premiership, I have fond memories of watching from close range the games of Norm Smith winner Michael Long as well as Gary

O'Donnell, who were our two best players that day. I don't think anyone goes out to win a Norm Smith Medal, but you certainly want to play well on the biggest stage. That was all I was thinking about going in to the 2000 Grand Final.

(Ruckman) John Barnes should have taken the mark early in the game that resulted in my first goal. We didn't really get the ball into our forward line at the start. It was a funny day; the wind was quite bad, so no one was kicking the ball well. Melbourne captain David Neitz missed a couple of shots early, then after a while Blake Caracella kicked it in to Barnsey, who dropped a mark he would have taken 99 times out of 100. [Melbourne's] Guy Rigoni picked it up and I tackled him, forcing a stoppage. Out of that I grabbed the ball and was fortunate enough to get it on my boot quickly and kick the first goal of the game.

All year our young players were great for us. Particularly Justin Blumfield, Caracella, Chris Heffernan and Dean Solomon, and they were all terrific for us early in the Grand Final. Caracella and Solomon dominated early when we were struggling to get our hands on the ball. It wasn't like the rest of the year when our team usually dominated the game early on and set up our victories. In the Grand Final it took us a while to get a hold of the game. I felt we were missing goals we should have kicked, so to go to quarter-time with 4.8 (to Melbourne's 3.3) could have come back to haunt us.

Late in the quarter I put myself in the middle to help get the ball going our way. It was something I enjoyed doing, particularly before I injured my foot in 1997, when I had a lot more power. After injuring my foot, I lost some of that power in my leg, which you need in the forward line, and I needed to play in a position where it was constant running, which was the start of me playing on the ball a lot more. Throughout 2000 I would regularly go on to the ball at different times in matches. The plan was always—depending on who opposed me—to try to work up the ground to stoppages. When Alastair Nicholson came on to me early, I decided it was a chance to get up the ground, rather than stay deep, and try using my running ability as opposed to just relying on my one-on-one marking.

Whenever I went on to the ball during a game, I would have a different player pick me up, different from my forward line opponent. The secret in that situation is to try playing in between the two of them, to have them think you're doing one thing, then do the other thing. That opens up a bit of space for you as a consequence. Also, having a team like ours that was super dominant, where they were all getting their hands on the ball regularly—as well as the fact Matthew Lloyd and Scott Lucas had defenders trying to drop back on to them—meant that all through that year I was able to find a bit of space. That was also the case at times during the Grand Final.

I kicked a second goal during the second quarter. When I first started out in the early 1990s, I wasn't a great set shot at goal—my teammates would still say today that I *never* was! They reckon I floated them all through. But in 1995 and 1996, I did a lot of work on my goalkicking, and from then on I think I became more consistent in that area. When you're kicking at the MCG, you need to try to keep the ball lower rather than kick it up high where the wind can get hold of it. The more you play there, the more tricks you learn about kicking at the 'G. The wind higher up is not necessarily the wind it's going to be in the goal-face, so having that experience of kicking there probably helped me in those big games.

Longy's bump on Troy Simmonds in the second quarter was pretty brutal. These days it would likely be dealt with much more harshly than it was back then (Long received a four-week suspension). Longy certainly never had intent to hurt Simmonds, but he would always try and make an opponent earn their possession. In the ensuing WWE wrestling match that took place immediately afterwards between myself and David Schwartz, if it had have continued much longer I would have been KO'd in about 30 seconds!

We were 57 points up at three-quarter time, but we certainly didn't think we'd won the game. We were always confident that year that we would win games of footy, but Sheeds was a pretty tough taskmaster around finishing games off; he always drove us to finish games strongly, no matter the scoreboard. So he made sure we kept going hard in that final quarter and kept our eye on each contest, rather than looking up at the scoreboard. Obviously, we were very confident, but the game wasn't over. It was not until the last three or four minutes where we were able to sit back and say, "They're not going to come back from here." We had been determined to finish off the year in a really strong way because of the near-perfect season we'd had.

The siren sounds and all you think is, "We've won a Premiership!" To be captain of that Premiership is something that's really special; special that the club has put the faith in yourself and your leaders to lead the team to the Holy Grail. It's a tremendous honour. Holding the Cup up with Sheeds that day remains my best memory in footy.

The Norm Smith Medal didn't enter my head at all after the final siren. It was more relief then, as it had been such a build-up for us, not just that year but for three or four years. Personally, I'd hardly played any footy for three years, plus, because of the way we went out in '99 [losing the Preliminary Final to Carlton by one point] and the criticism we received from losing that game, we were determined to win in 2000. We all went to the '99 Grand Final as a team and watched North Melbourne beat Carlton, then the dinner we had after that set down the foundations for the Premiership we built in 2000. We really sacrificed a lot, so it was a sense of great relief when we finally achieved what we set out to achieve.

The first thing I wanted to do after the game was go and find Tania and Stephanie and give them a big hug. It was a hugely emotional moment for the three of us. In the photo taken of us embracing over the fence, you can see that Stephanie still doesn't look very well at all, but having them both there to celebrate with me was really special.

Whenever you have a good game you think you're a chance to be named best on the ground. But I knew that Blumfield had played a great game, Caracella, too, as did Solly and a number of others. When you win convincingly like we did, the Norm Smith voting can go in any number of ways. I was probably fortunate that it went my way that day.

There were so many great stories that came out of winning that game. John Barnes had played in three losing Grand Finals with Geelong. Myself, Lucas and Jason Johnson had missed out on the 1999 finals series through injuries, plus Dean Wallis had been through many injuries himself. It was Sheeds's fourth Premiership, joining the great Dick Reynolds as a four-time Grand Final-winning coach of the club. So it was a huge celebration for everyone, an enormous relief, and the end of a difficult week for my family.

Over time, what's become most significant from that day is winning the Premiership. The Norm Smith is certainly great, and you want to know that you performed well on the big stage on Grand Final day—and that you did it in a winning team. I'm very proud that I've won the Norm Smith, but when I reflect on that day, it's more about the wonderful team we had. It was an incredible year, to only lose one game and to play with that group of players; to walk out on the ground having such confidence in your teammates was a wonderful feeling that season.

My major regret from the 2001 Grand Final was losing [to Brisbane]. On a personal level, the regret ran a lot deeper because I played so poorly and let everyone down. It's no excuse, but I played injured. I had a groin strain and didn't train at all in Grand Final week. That said, I wouldn't have pulled out unless I had it forced on me.

Brad Scott towelled me in the Grand Final. I played a dog of a game. They say once you cross the white line you're 100 per cent fit, but that's not always the case. I wasn't able to give 100 per cent and I didn't perform to the standard I or the club expected.

It would be ludicrous to say we should have won more Premierships in that three-year period (1999-2001). We had a great side and we won a lot of games (62 of 74), but that would do a terrible disservice to the Kangaroos, who were the team of the '90s, and the Brisbane Lions, who went on to win three successive flags and become one of the greatest teams of all time. We won two in my time, and for that I can count myself lucky because a lot of great players never won one.

It's not a great feeling knowing the Bombers haven't won another Premiership for 18 years. It would be great to see this current crop of players keep building this year and win another one for the club in the near future. I think they've got a definite chance over the next three years; if they can get back to playing at top form, they could end the drought for us. A club like Essendon needs to be winning Premierships, and 18 years is too long to have waited for another one.

There was pain before the injury [at Subiaco, in round six, 2002]. Pain at the way we were playing. We needed to beat Fremantle. I started on Matthew Pavlich and he gave me a hiding in the first half, running off me and creating play deep into their forward line. I really had no answers for him. I felt tired, I couldn't run; I couldn't keep up with him. At half-time Sheeds gave me a bit of a spray. About 10 minutes into the third quarter he (Pavlich) runs down the field. Suddenly I'm running back with the flight of the ball ... my head was looking back for the ball. Next thing I know, I've slammed into the heaviest contact of my life. It felt like the whole pack had hit me. Later, when I looked at the TV coverage, it was only Mark McVeigh's knee. But oh, the *pain*. I have never felt pain like it. I knew straightaway there was something seriously wrong.

"This is a prick of a game; I don't want to play it anymore." That's what I said after I had my face caved in. I was lying on a table in the hospital and they hadn't given me any painkillers. I was in the worst condition I ever felt and I said a few things I didn't mean. But after I was given some morphine, I thought, "What was I saying? Of course I want to play again."

I had seven fractures of the face. They told me they would cut away the top of my head, peel back my face to my chin, and re-sculpt my face with metal plates, eventually getting it back to what it had looked like before the smash. I think if I had not been so high on drugs I would have freaked out!

It's actually harder coming back from a finger injury than a head injury. Every time you grab the ball you can feel your finger, whereas your head is such a solid thing and it takes a freak accident, as happened to me, to be seriously hurt. After the operation, the surgeon said, "The plates are in so you'll be fine." When I'd recovered, I wasn't sore; I could cop knocks to my head and it wasn't any worse than it would normally be.

I don't regret the injuries I suffered. They taught me a lot about myself, other people, and the value of hard work. Every time I've had a serious injury or a disappointment, I came back a better player, a better leader and a better person. If I had gone through my whole career without an injury and playing good footy every week, I probably wouldn't have as much understanding for players who do it tough. You certainly learn more when things go wrong.

I was adamant I wouldn't ever coach, but (then Essendon chairman) David Evans was pretty influential in convincing me. He outlined how it would all work, why it was necessary, and that the club needed someone with an Essendon identity to come back and coach, who would also bring some Essendon people back with them. He played on my heart strings and there was no doubt that there was some romanticism there for me in coming back. Unfortunately, it didn't work out how we all wanted it to.

By the end of my playing days, I knew I needed a break from football. But when I looked at the situation, I understood that I had watched a hell of a lot of footy, I talked about it a lot and I analysed it quite closely—something I had always done. So, in some ways, it was a natural progression. When you play at such an intensity, and you're living it and you're in it like I was, you need a break, so coaching didn't seem like something that was going to happen at the end of my career. However, it soon felt like there was a big hole there by not having football in my life. But I had to convince Tania first! There were a lot of conversations around the dinner table; she needed a lot of convincing, but eventually she said yes.

The main thing I took from Sheeds' coaching into my own approach was his positivity and his relationship with players. You can have the best game-plan and all these great ideas, but if your players aren't playing for you and they don't believe in what you're doing it doesn't work out well. I admired the way Sheeds could always find a way to motivate his players and sell hope that we could win, while also building a good team—it was something that I found intoxicating. I wanted to follow that philosophy every day. He was also a great tactician and has an astute football brain, but the main thing I drew from his coaching was his ability to sell hope to his players that we were going to be a great team.

Some would say I didn't have any strengths as a coach. I think my relationship with my players was the highlight for me; I certainly worked very hard on that relationship, because it was one of the things I identified as being most important. Not that I had to be their best friend, but that we were in it together and that they believed in the game-plan. Also, setting up a structure where every player was educated on how they needed to play each game, so that when they walked out on to the ground they had a very clear knowledge of what our game-plan was, and what their role was within that plan.

You still get nervous before games like you did as a player, but overall you feel helpless as a coach. As a player you'd sit there and think, "I'm not sure how I'm going to play today, but I've at least got control of my performance." Whereas, as a coach, you are paranoid about whether your players are ready to play or not. I always thought that, if the team I was coaching was ready to play—in terms of their intensity, motivation and feeling—that we were going to be in with a good chance; we'd either win or go close. But there were days where maybe I overtrained them or they were flat, and it didn't matter what you were doing you just couldn't get through to them on the day. So there is a lot of anxiety in coaching because of all the things you can't control.

When you go into coaching for the first time, you think it's all about match-day in the coach's box. The reality is that, yes, there is a bit about that, but you have got to be so well prepared during pre-season, leading up to the season, and then during the week between games. What happens match day doesn't come about just because someone's magical in the coach's box. There are certainly advantages to being really good in the box, but if you're not a great preparer and don't have the game-plan set up, and you don't have your players fit and ready to play throughout the year, well, you can be the best magician in the box and it simply won't work.

When everything happened in early 2013, one of the things I said to myself and talked a lot about with Tania was that "this is going to be a tough period ahead." But my priority was always to do my job first and foremost. Yes, there were going to be periods away from the club where I needed to deal with everything going on. But, at training, on game day and after the game, I was determined to do the job at hand and not let the other stuff come into it. Sometimes I managed that better than other times, but after a game I thought it was important to stay pretty calm. There was a lot of chaos going on around us, but I wanted to try staying as calm as I could and to be as clear-headed as I possibly could be.

The game against Fremantle (round three, 2013, at Subiaco) was both the lowlight in my coaching career and the highlight, too. Going into that game, the media was suggesting I was going to be sacked, or had been sacked, so to win that night was simply incredible. How we won that game, I've got no idea! But we did (by four points), and what everyone saw afterwards in the change rooms was just raw emotion from the players and myself. We won again against West Coast over there (in round 14, by seven points) after Jobe Watson had been highly criticised that week, which again was an amazing feeling. That 2013 season was an amazing one overall. Despite what was happening, we played some fantastic football and really, as a team, from round one in Adelaide when we beat the Crows through to the end of the season, we put in some remarkable performances. Unfortunately, there wasn't much to celebrate after that.[3]

I still watch four or five games each week. I also enjoy watching my boys play footy, so my love for the game remains strong and always will. It's a great game. I now do a podcast with [former Hawthorn captain and 1999 Brownlow medallist] Shane Crawford, and we love talking footy. Not that we talk much footy—we talk a lot of rubbish, too!

Stephanie (now 18) plays football, and she tells us she's going to be the next big star. She's kicking a footy with Essendon's VFLW team and she loves it. I really love watching the women play football. They play with an attitude that says "this is the greatest thing in the world." Their passion for the game is obvious and it's a refreshing and wonderful thing to see. Stephanie asks my advice from time to time, but she doesn't take it, like most kids her age! I could be the great Leigh Matthews giving her advice, but as her father there's no way she'll take it on board. She works hard, though, so it's great to see from a father's perspective.

---

3   Essendon won 14 games in 2013, good enough to finish seventh. However, the club was banned from competing in the finals as part of the punishments handed down by the League after the joint AFL-Australian Sports Anti-Doping Agency investigation of 2013 that rocked the game and devastated the Bombers, leading eventually to the suspension of 34 players in 2016 after a ruling by the Court of Arbitration for Sport. Ninth-placed Carlton replaced Essendon in the top eight. Having coached 66 games to that point, Hird was suspended for 12 months, returning in 2015 to coach another 19 games before resigning after Essendon's 112-point loss to Adelaide in round 20, 2015. In all, he coached 85 games (2011-13, 2015) for a winning ratio of 48.8 per cent.

JAMES HIRD

The game's given me a lot. If you had asked me five years ago, I'd have said that the game allowed me to be the person I am, and that it created a number of wonderful opportunities for me and my family. It really has. But it's also now given me a greater perspective on life, and has taught me a lot about how the world works.

—— Statistics ——

BORN: 4 February 1973
GAMES PLAYED (1992-2007): 253
GOALS: 343
FINALS PLAYED: 20
FINALS GOALS: 26
GRAND FINALS: 3
PREMIERSHIPS: 1993, 2000
NORM SMITH MEDAL: 2000 (presented by Lou Richards)

— Norm Smith Voting —

(**JUDGES:** Wayne Jackson, Garry Lyon, Stephen Quartermain and Malcolm Blight)

Herald Sun votes: **Damian Barrett:** 3 James Hird, 2 Dean Wallis, 1 Blake Caracella;
Rod Nicholson: 3 Hird, 2 Wallis, 1 Paul Barnard;
Amanda Buivids: 3 Hird, 2 Justin Blumfield, 1 Mark Johnson;
Scot Palmer: 3 Hird, 2 Barnard, 1 Wallis;
Mark Harding: 3 Hird, 2 Caracella, 1 Blumfield;
Ken Piesse: 3 Hird, 2 Blumfield, 1 Damien Hardwick;
James Weston: 3 Hird, 2 Blumfield, 1 Wallis.
TOTALS: Hird 21, Blumfield 7, Wallis 6, Caracella 3, Barnard 3, M Johnson 1, Hardwick 1.

Shaun Hart

Shaun Hart was small in stature but had a heart to match Phar Lap's. Having begun as a Brisbane Bear in 1990, Hart became a spiritual leader of the Brisbane Lions during the late 1990s and early 2000s. Therefore, it was fitting that he was awarded the Norm Smith Medal in 2001, having battled dutifully during the lean years as a Bear. A dedicated trainer, Hart's aerobic capabilities allowed him to play forward, in defence, or in the midfield. Indeed, he was never far from the action, and the Brisbane forwards licked their lips whenever Hart kicked the ball in their direction. He played 273 games, kicking 177 goals, and was a valuable member of the club's three consecutive Premierships (2001-03). Later, he mentored the young Gold Coast Suns players, drawing on his early experiences with the Bears as an example of how, by never giving up, anything is possible. In his Norm Smith Medal-winning performance against Essendon, Hart had 14 kicks, nine handballs, took three marks and had five inside-50s.

My love for footy was born out of growing up in a state where footy was the thing people did. From 1978-81, I lived in Corop, a town of 200 people near Rochester in country Victoria. We were passionate Richmond supporters—Mum, Fran, was a Sydney supporter, but all us boys were Tiger fans. I loved the Richmond

← **BALL MAGNET** Shaun Hart's career started slowly, as did that of Brisbane, but when the riches came they came in droves.

players, particularly Dale Weightman, the 'Flea', and I wanted to emulate him and his teammates. Richmond won the 1980 Premiership when I was nine years old, and I remember thinking to myself that I would love to be there one day myself. We had one of the only businesses in town, and the night before the 1980 Grand Final Collingwood supporters sprayed shaving cream all over our windows. They wrote "RIP Richmond". Fortunately, the next day we gave them a good old touch-up to the tune of 81 points.

From the ages of seven to 10, I lived at Corop. Then, when our business didn't work out, we moved to Shepparton and I was there until I got drafted, at 18, by the Brisbane Bears. I'm the middle of two brothers, Craig and Glenn. It was always competitive in the backyard—we had a few blues through bad sportsmanship, as brothers do. I remember the first day we played cricket in the backyard in Shepparton, and one of the balls cracked a window. We weren't too popular that day!

Dad, Ian, played in the fourths for Richmond at one stage. He was born at Clematis, near Emerald, while Mum was from Coburg way. She was a teacher, and quite sporty as well. I played cricket all the way through the junior grades, then a bit of senior cricket in Shepparton. But apart from that and footy, I've never been great at other sports.

I mainly played on the ball, plus spent some time forward in my junior days with Shepparton United. I played one season of senior football with United, on a half-forward flank, which resulted in a Premiership, in 1989, as an 18-year-old.

God definitely gave me the gift of being able to run. That was the one thing that gave me the opportunity to play League football. I certainly didn't get the height gene! (Hart stands 175cm). I never felt I was an elite reader of the play, but certainly my running ability and my willingness to work hard early on helped me to get involved in games.

My dedication to training was the key to my career. I've always been quite disciplined, which, again, comes from what's been put in me through family. I've always been team focused—I liked to serve others more than myself. I was always taught to do that, and that helped me with my work; to know that I was a part of the bigger picture and wasn't in it for selfish reasons. And that comes back to the values my mum and dad put into us kids from a young age. In your first couple of years at AFL level, you are just trying to survive and get a kick. But from the time I arrived at the Bears, I was already as good a runner as any player there. That was purely because I loved training; I wanted to be the best athlete I could be in order to give myself the best chance of playing AFL footy. And I knew I was doing it not just for me, but for the team as well. I thank my parents for helping me to see the bigger picture.

When I speak to groups of young guys, I talk about the importance of the pipe dream. Back as a nine-year-old watching Richmond and Collingwood, I did seriously think that I wanted to be there one day— that's a strong memory I have. It was a pipe dream all through my junior footy. But even though you're playing okay in the competitions you're in, the dream of playing AFL still seems so far away. When I was 16-17, I made the Vic Country Championships for my age level, got in the squad of 70 or so, but never got near the Teal Cup (under-18s) team itself. When it came to recruiting time, it was really only the fact I had played some senior footy that year that nine AFL clubs contacted me leading up to the draft. That was when I first started to think it was a reality, that I had a decent chance of being picked up by someone. It was by no means a certainty, but much more of a reality than previously. I was playing some pretty good footy in a very good team, and I felt it was going to help me to get a chance to be looked at. Little did I know I would be moving to Queensland, though.

I was studying in Albury-Wodonga, then travelling back to play with Shepparton United on the weekends. I was training during the week with the Wodonga Bulldogs, under Jeff Gieschen (Richmond coach 1997-99). On draft day I'd dropped my mate off and was heading home to Shepparton, and when I was about 40km from Shepp, listening to the radio in the car, they announced that there was a massive 15 people drafted from the Goulburn-Murray region. They were listing where guys had been drafted to, and at this stage I had heard nothing, then they said, "Shaun Hart's been drafted to the Brisbane Bears." It took me about five minutes to come out of shock! I stopped the car and called my parents on a nearby phone and asked, "Have you heard the news?" Mum said, "Yeah, we have. What do you think?" and I just burst into tears. Going to Brisbane wasn't supposed to happen; it was something I had not even imagined was possible. I was away on a footy trip in Wagga Wagga when the Bears' recruiters, Shane O'Sullivan and Brian Kinder, had visited my parents, but I never understood their interest at the time as I had missed out on chatting to them. I was shocked when I heard my name, and it quite literally led me to tears.

When I got to Brisbane they had a house for us young guys. I was one of 11 who rented a six-bedroom house in Carrara (near Brisbane's home ground at the time), and that was an experience in itself. Paul Cronin was involved in the club and Christopher Skase was the owner, but a short while later Christopher nicked off overseas and there were suddenly no finances left for the club. The reality for me was that, early in my career, living away from home, I had to get a job working on the roads in the heat of a Queensland summer—we simply didn't earn enough money by just playing footy. There was a guy from Shepparton who owned a roadworks business, so I worked for him during the heat of the day before heading off to training that evening. I did that for a month or two before I found some other work. I was earning a decent income away from footy, and 'Skasey' had nicked off, so of the 11 in our house there was only myself and another guy, Joe Wilson from Wangaratta, who actually had any money. For a number of weeks we paid the whole grocery bill for the house—there were no funds from the club. I spent $460 on three trolleys full of groceries one time! Eventually, in the August of that first year, we all got the money back that we were owed from the club, but it was a struggle in those first few months. I later reflected on that period and thought, "Gee, the dream must have been pretty important, because if not you probably would have jumped on a plane and went back home." I stuck it out, and it was an amazing educational year for my introduction into the AFL.

There is no doubt that my early experiences with Brisbane helped me when I later mentored the Gold Coast Suns players. It's incredible to look back and see how you got through certain things. We finished on the bottom of the ladder a few times (1990-91 and 1998), but we worked through those bad times. Today players are inclined to move to a club where they are more likely to have some success. But you didn't do that as much back then. By my second year, despite the lack of success, I felt comfortable in Queensland; it was where I wanted to be. Yes, we finished on the bottom three times, but we later won three Premierships. So sometimes you have got to go through some discomfort and you can get your rewards in the end. Recruiter Scotty Clayton did a really good job in the early '90s, bringing in the likes of Justin Leppitsch, the Scott brothers (Brad and Chris), Michael Voss and Darryl White, so we started to build a fantastic team. It was then a case of sticking it out, which, thankfully, I was able to do.

It was like a carnival at our games when we were based on the Gold Coast (1987-92). It was quite bizarre. We had demountable rooms to change in, which was a joke compared to what some clubs had. But at least we had a reasonable gym and some decent facilities to train in. I'm working back at the Gold Coast Suns now, and the set-up they have there, and with the Commonwealth Games based out of there in 2018, the Carrara from my time is very much different. Back then, it was hard to feel like the club was a genuine AFL club, certainly not if you based it on the supporter numbers we had, plus the whole atmosphere of game day. We knew it was going to change as time went on, so we just needed to stick it out.

Robert Walls's arrival as coach for 1991 was a massive eye-opener for me. He came with a real intention to toughen us up, in order to help us become mentally strong footballers. Yes, he taught us the game, but he also taught us how to get uncomfortable and then how to deal with that. The appointment was really well received at the time, but in hindsight Wallsy was quite brutal in his approach. He was certainly effective in developing a strong mindset among the players, although he also pushed a few over the edge on occasions because of his hard-nosed approach. He knew he had a role to play in getting the group ready to go into a space where they could start to think about finals. Funnily enough, just as he chose to give the job away, in 1995, we played finals for the first time, coming from four wins and 11 losses (14th after 15 rounds) to win six out of the last seven and finish eighth.

I was fortunate to play in the club's reserves Premiership in 1991. I hurt my ankle in the second quarter and missed the rest of the game. But being a part of it was fantastic. I had missed a few games during 1991, I was struggling for consistency and fitness, but we were lucky that the club at reserves level was really strong. We had a number of older guys who qualified for the reserves in the finals, so they were all playing in that Grand Final, which was a big part of the reason we were so successful that year. Rodney Eade was the coach, but while the older guys helped us win that game, it didn't set us up for ongoing senior success, unfortunately.

Wallsy almost sacked me after 1991. I didn't know it at the time, though, he told me a long time after that how close he came. I had gone backwards in my second season, and the club made a decision that, of three players—Lachlan Sim (21 games to the end of 1991), Brenton Phillips (61) and myself (17)—only one would survive. Lachlan and Brenton didn't play after that year, so he was true to his word. It's amazing the machinations that occur within footy clubs, and what can happen for some players and not for others. When he later told me, it made me realise that you can get a little bit of luck sometimes. I think it was my ability to run and work and get uncomfortable—plus my youth—that helped me be the one who was chosen. At the time I didn't sense that I was that close to getting cut. I knew I had only managed to play six games in 1991, but, being a young guy, I wasn't sure what the expectations were on me from the club and the coach. I had played 11 games in my first year, most of which were gifted to me because we had an older squad that needed replenishing. But I really struggled to get going in my second year. So I can understand why they felt I was on the cusp. Wallsy was the type of guy that would have wanted to see blokes who were showing improvement, showing hardness, and I'm not sure how tough and resilient a player I was at that stage.

I was not the type of person to not do something about it. I was always someone who pushed myself extraordinarily hard in the off-season, in order to come back better and fitter. I did that in 1992, plus I had a new role in defence, so I was eager to impress down there. Being a disciplined player, I was keen to get a job done for the team. That was why I later moved into tagging roles as I matured as a player.

Moving to the Gabba in 1993 was very important for us as a club. It took a little bit of time for them to restructure the oval for us, but I think it was a major move considering what we had at Carrara. It helped us to begin to feel like a real footy club. Considering we were the *Brisbane* Bears, it was a logical and significant move to relocate to Brisbane. It felt like, all of a sudden, someone decided we needed to get serious and do something about becoming a bigger footy club, with a proper home and proper facilities.

In 1994, I had major burnout and desperately wanted to give the game away. It was only because of the support and encouragement of my beautiful wife, Linda, and our club chaplain, Dean Davis, that I got through it. Things would be very different, in terms of football success, if it wasn't for those two in particular.

Funnily enough, by 1994 we were starting to see some growth on the field. Then we made the finals in 1995, and you started to feel like we were getting somewhere. We were starting to compete week after week, we had Alastair Lynch by then, plus the young guys were starting to play well, so it was beginning to look a lot better than a couple of years earlier. There was a sense that some talent was coming along, some genuine AFL players like Michael Voss and Nigel Lappin. It was different from when I arrived. We had an older squad then, and most of the guys had come to the Bears for the cash towards the end of their careers. So by the mid-90s we were a new group and it was exciting times.

It was exciting to play finals for the first time. We came up against the eventual premier, Carlton, in the fourth Qualifying Final, when it was the one-versus-eight system. Despite that anomaly, we got quite close to them that day, only losing by 13 points, so that was a good effort. The Blues dominated their other two finals (beating North Melbourne by 62 points in the first Preliminary Final, then Geelong by 61 in the Grand Final), so that gave us hope that we were on the right track. It was an exciting time; we were playing some really good footy and competing well against the top teams. To have the opportunity to play in a big final on the MCG was a real thrill.

Wallsy was a teacher by trade and coached us that way. He demanded pretty stringent standards. Then John Northery came in after 1995, and John was an us-against-them type of coach. He tried approaching games as a form of trench warfare, which was very different from Wallsy's way, who was more the dictating teacher in his approach.

After moving to the back pocket in 1992, I had started to play some really good footy. I think I received one vote in the best and fairest in 1991, then ran equal third in 1992. Soon after that, I began play more up the field as well, and I started to believe that I could have a decent AFL career. That said, it wasn't until Leigh Matthews came along in 1999 that I felt I truly understood how to play the game. Then I began to play at an even better and more consistent level.

'Vossy' was an extremely confident young bloke. From an early age you could tell through his contesting work and the way he played all parts of the game that he was going to become a fine leader. A lot of young guys have half an appetite for defence, preferring to win more of their own footy, getting into space and running, whereas Vossy was a guy who immediately hit bodies, he loved the contest, and he would do every part of the game, particularly defence. He was a unique creature in terms of what he set himself to do. The way he led through his actions, in terms of courage on the field, was inspirational.

I wore a helmet all through junior footy, but when I got to the Bears they said I would be a target for the opposition if I wore the helmet in games, so I ceased wearing it. In 1996, I had an appointment with my optometrist and he told me I was losing part of my vision. He said, if you rate vision five out of five, then yours is a three out of five and it is affecting your night vision. Night games were becoming more prevalent, and he said, "Firstly, you will lose your ability to drive at night, and then you likely won't be able to play night footy either." It had come about because of a lot of little head knocks; that was the reason my vision was decreasing. So I opted to put the helmet back on and, funnily enough, my sight hasn't decreased at all since then.

The merger with Fitzroy, in 1996, was a time of anxiety. We became the Brisbane Lions, and people were unsure of where they were in the big scheme of things. All of a sudden the best six or seven players from another club had landed at our club. Although it was heathy for competition, there was a lack of time to align our group with the new group. The reality was, the Fitzroy boys were coming, not necessarily under sufferance, but they didn't really have a choice in relocating. So it was a significant challenge during that time, for the players as well as for coach John Northey.

I don't think it was the marriage that the AFL wanted for the new team. It was clunky, I reckon, in terms of the way players came together. There was also some stuff happening at board level. There was a falling away of people being able to operate under authority, so people were going off in their own directions. John Northey was starting to lose the players' faith to a degree, and it all disintegrated really badly by 1998, even though we had some quality players at the footy club.

Leigh Matthews was intimidating even before he arrived at Brisbane! His reputation, from a distance, was an imposing one, and I think that made everyone stand up and take notice from the word go. He had clearly been informed of the environment from the year before, that it was a bit toxic. So he needed to make some clear statements about the unity of the club and what it would look like. Guys such as the Scott boys were licking their lips at the prospect of Leigh coming in. He was a smart coach who really demanded that we were united.

The first meeting we had with Leigh, he said that he demanded two things from us. He demanded courage at all times, and he demanded that we work with the same energy in defence as we do in offence. He also said it didn't matter what your reputation was as a player, he was going to put the same demand on the best player as he would with the rest of the group.

After finishing last in 1998, we reached the Preliminary Final in 1999 (losing to North Melbourne by 45 points). Our rapid rise was on the back of Leigh teaching us to defend and play the percentages really well. It was similar to Richmond in 2017. Our success came about because of the defensive pressure our team applied, particularly our small forwards. Leigh brought a strong tackling and defensive philosophy from coaching at Collingwood. I believe he had a conversation before the finals in 1990 with a police officer who told him how they named their investigations "Operation something or other". From that, Leigh devised the theme for the 1990 Grand Final: "Operation Tackle". From the success he had at Collingwood, he knew that if we embraced a defensive intent, which included high tackle numbers, then we, too, could become a team capable of winning Premierships.

Leigh was brilliant in 2001 when he said, "If it bleeds, we can kill it." That came about when we were four wins and five losses after nine rounds, and we were playing Essendon—the seemingly invincible team—at the Gabba in round 10. He had watched the movie *Predator* that week, and when he explained his plan in our team meeting he was talking about how to take down the seemingly invincible. He spoke of how the guys in the film had defeated the predator, which gave him the revelation about where we needed to go as a team. It came down to clearly knowing your role, accepting your role, and playing your role.

Leigh then implemented a "Role Appreciation Award", which would go to the player who, each week, we thought had played their role the best. We would all vote on who that was each weekend, and the best player from that game would receive the signed game ball. That was so inspirational for players, who could see that they were being rewarded for stuff that may not have been seen from outside the club. They were then motivated to keep doing it, because of the appreciation from teammates and coaches. Leigh was a genius at being able to recognise, reward and motivate players, internally, to do the right things by their teammates.

After losing the 1999 Preliminary Final, Leigh began describing us as "millionaires" for the way we tried to play in 2000. He felt we got ahead of ourselves that year, after such a good season in 1999. That can happen to teams that have a little bit of success and suddenly think it's just going to happen. We eventually lost the second Semi-Final in 2000 (to Carlton by 82 points), then we were four and five in 2001 and facing the best team of the past 18 months. We knew we were in dire straits if we didn't beat Essendon that week. There was an uncertainty around whether we would even be a chance to play finals again if we lost that game, even though we believed we had a strong squad. The *Predator* example was a realisation for us of what it takes to make great teams, and, adding in that award became a significant piece of the puzzle to force us to understand the way we had to go forward from that week onwards.

We built incredible momentum after winning that game against Essendon (by 28 points). We won 16 straight to finish the season, including a run of 10 games where the average winning margin was about 60 points. It was a ridiculous run of form! It came on the back of us destroying teams mentally before we even played them. Most times by half-time we had our opponents beaten. Leigh was amazing at making every week seem like round one, creating a level of excitement that helped drive the players' energy for each contest, game after game.

After beating Geelong by 43 points, in Geelong, in round 21, we had our review where Leigh brought up an edit of Jason Akermanis taking a risky kick through the corridor. We didn't get punished by it during the game, but Leigh asked 'Aker' in the review whether he would take the kick again, and he said yes, he would. Leigh said, "I want to make sure we're all aware that I don't think that kick is on. Because, in a close final, if we think that type of kick is okay, it could cost us a crack at a Premiership." After a big run of wins, he had zeroed in on one specific detail that would enable us to survive the pressure of a close final. It was a pivotal moment, because we were in a dangerous period and were feeling quite invincible ourselves, thinking it was just going to happen. We needed those little reminders about getting the detail right, so that we didn't get ahead of ourselves.

Winning our first Grand Final was a serious case of incredible relief. It's a funny emotion: you're exhilarated, but also relieved. I almost didn't think it was ever going to happen; I didn't think I would ever experience what it felt like to reach an AFL Grand Final. For me, it had been 12 years in the game. I calculated there had been approximately 3000 sessions of training, gym, in- and out-of-season practice, as well as games in that time. A lot of blood, sweat and tears to be able to get there, which is why I was so relieved. And then I thought of what the start was like to my career, and I recognised that I had become a competent AFL player.

THE NORM SMITH MEDAL

In the Grand Final, I started as a forward. We had a plan to go after Essendon defenders Mark Johnson and Damien Hardwick, just to stoke their fires, because we knew they would both explode if we got a hold of them mentally and emotionally. Luke Power had been on an Ireland tour with Damien, and while over there he found out that Damien hated the nickname 'Astro Boy' because he had these big calf muscles! So we got into him that day, calling him "Astro Boy" every chance we got. Mark Johnson wasn't hard to fire up, either, so we went after him verbally as well. We challenged him, and he just wanted to fight all day as a consequence. So we got a couple of key players off their games, forcing them to play below their best. We got some ascendency early, and being a 27-degree day we knew that the conditions would play into our hands more so than Essendon's. They gained a bit of control just before half-time, but I felt confident we would be okay by day's end. Our approach was like Operation Tackle that led Collingwood to the Premiership in 1990: the belief that, if we could execute our defensive game all day, we would eventually run over the top of the Bombers.

We had six or seven guys in our group who ran late-14, even 15 beep tests—which was a ridiculous level of running power for the game at that time. I don't think anyone could match us in that aspect; our midfield for that time had some incredible players who could run through there, including Vossy, Aker, Lappin, Simon Black, Power, Brad Scott, Robert Copeland, Tim Notting, myself, and a few others. And they all worked both ways just as hard, which was critically important for us. We knew that if we got our defensive game right then Essendon would have to be pretty good to beat us.

We used to get hydrated at half-time in a different way to drinking fluid—we used saline drips. It was no different from going to the hospital when you're dehydrated and the nurses putting fluid back into your system through a drip. During the year the AFL decided it was not a great image for the game; not that it was illegal in any way, it was more to do with it being a poor image to send young kids. So we had to stop doing it at about round 14. In the Grand Final, Essendon deliberately wore black tape around the areas of their arms where we used to have bandages after half-time from the drips. They wore them to have a dig at us, and I remember a funny moment late in the game where one of our blokes made a gesture towards them to signify we didn't need them to win the game. I think there had been a feeling that we were pushing the limits of what was legal, and while we certainly weren't, I think it was great by the AFL to determine it wasn't a healthy look for the game. And it wouldn't have looked good had we kept doing it and won the Grand Final, because there would have been questions around the benefits of it.

There was a moment in the third quarter when the ball went end to end; it was scrappy, but we kept winning it and getting the ball forward. We scored a goal, the noise was massive, and you just felt then that the momentum was starting to roll our way. As a player you get a feel for when things are changing; people's body language changes. It only just edged us in front, but it was a moment where we felt we had broken them, we had the momentum. It was hot, and Essendon was out on its feet. By the end of that third quarter, there was almost no doubt that our run, our capacity to just keep going, was overwhelming Essendon.

The last 15 minutes of the game was really special. Early in that last quarter we knew the game was still up for grabs, but we were really confident with the heat that we had the capacity to run the game out and we didn't think the Bombers could. We wore teams down all year that way. By halfway through the term we knew we'd won, and it was really enjoyable after that.

I had no thought that I could win the Norm Smith Medal. That game was just a whirlwind. If someone had asked me straight after, "How do you think you went in the game?" I only would have been able to recall two or three things I did—it was all a blur otherwise.

It was certainly a shock when someone from the AFL approached me and said I was about to be announced as the Norm Smith medallist. They said, "You will have the chance to say something in about a minute's time." Mal Michael was one of our real practical jokers, and my first thought was that Mal was playing a practical joke on me! I thought, "That can't be right? Someone's not saying that to me, surely?" Then just before they read my name out I realised it was real, that I'd won it, which was amazing. I realised I had had an impact on the game at times, but I hadn't kicked a goal or done anything spectacular. Later, when I watched the game back, I recognised that there were some parts early in the game where I won the footy and kicked the ball into our forward line, so I had an impact early, which was good to know. But overall it was such a whirlwind three hours that I couldn't recall much at all of what I had done. Then, after the siren, I was in a state of euphoria having won a Premiership, so I wasn't even thinking about my own performance.

I thanked Jesus when I accepted my Norm Smith Medal. I had come to the belief during my football career that the person of Jesus Christ, who He is and what He has done, gave me meaning and purpose in life. He had rescued me from doubt and anxiety by giving me identity and purpose. It was because of his influence that I was receiving the recognition of the Norm Smith Medal.

What I learned during my career was that life is about relationships and a cause. I don't believe in evolution, because if we've evolved then we don't have any meaning or purpose to our lives. After about two years of my career, I was searching and wondering about the purpose of my life. Because, I had built it to that point on being a rich and famous footballer, but the reality was that one day that would all fade away, and it could have faded away very quickly early in my career had Wallsy cut me when he had considered doing so. I met Linda during that period, who I have now been married to for the past 25 years; she was a Christian lady who I fell in love with, and I realised that there was something in her life that gave her meaning and purpose beyond what she did for work. That made me realise I was missing something in my life. To me, we're all three-dimensional people, and yet we live two-dimensional lives; we don't necessarily consider who we are as spiritual beings. The power of the heart is who we are. We think about the mind and how smart we are, but when it comes to sport and family and relationships, that's where the essence of joy in life comes from. Now I truly believe that God gives us life with a purpose and meaning. Since putting my faith in Jesus, I've realised there's no other way to go. I realised that my faith is my true identity. I'm created by God to love Him and love others. Great relationships are God's design for our lives. He has given me freedom I never knew before, which is why I thanked Him when I received my Norm Smith Medal.

After winning in 2001, I personally felt willing to do whatever it took to experience winning finals again. With the team we had, it was still a pretty exceptional group—there weren't going to be many changes over the next couple of years. We all had an appetite after 2001. Leigh set the scene at the first meeting of the next pre-season. We watched the last two minutes of the 2001 Grand Final, then Leigh switched the lights back on, turned the game off, rolled the whiteboard down and said: "I've got two words for you—hungry actions. I want to fill this board with the actions I hope to see you do in order to show me that you're prepared to go back to the top of the mountain again in the heat of a Queensland summer." He wanted us to produce a checklist of actions that we would then demonstrate over pre-season to prove to him we were hungry enough to go again in 2002.

Our run of 20 consecutive wins ended in round five, 2002, but we got back to the Grand Final again. We were red-hot favourites against Collingwood, but the Collingwood defence was unbelievable in the Grand Final—they tackled us 73 times, but it felt more like 173! Somehow, we managed to hold on in the slippery, wet conditions that day, winning by nine points to go back to back. Then, 2003 was a different story again. Collingwood was the favourite in the Grand Final, having beaten us at the MCG in the second Qualifying Final (by 15 points). But we put the acid on them early in the game, asked the question of them, and they couldn't answer us. We won our third consecutive Premiership (by 50 points), the first team to have done so since Melbourne (1955-57).

I was responsible for Nigel Lappin being injured before that game. In the first Preliminary Final against Sydney, I jumped up with the flight of the ball, Nige came the other way, and I cannoned into his ribs. It was a significant blow, and I was so thankful that he got up and played in the Grand Final. Him playing that day was one of the most courageous things I've ever witnessed, because the injury he had, and the risk he took just to run out there, was extraordinary. He was equal to any worker in our team, particularly as a defensive runner—he would run for the team like no one else. He was a magnificent all-round player for the Lions. He may have appeared to have been a stylish, receiving player, but he wasn't; he was as tough as they came.

While it was shattering to miss the 2004 Grand Final with a facial injury, I had been playing the worst footy of my career leading in. I had experienced issues with my back during the previous four years, and by 2004 I had come to a grinding halt; I played some really average games. Despite playing in the Preliminary Final, I still wonder today whether I would have been selected had I not injured myself in that game. I was in such poor form leading in, and with Port Adelaide having three tall forwards I doubt they would have retained me, preferring a taller player in my place—who knows? With my face fractured, I was stuck in Melbourne all week—I couldn't fly—so I was sitting around waiting for the team to arrive. The club was very good to me, flew my family down to watch the game with me. It was a sad way to end my career, but I'd been very fortunate in the previous three years. You can't win them all.

It has been a blessing to have experienced all that I have in the game; a privilege to be involved in something I just love doing. Yes, there were challenges, but I think it's given me great discipline, great resilience and a deeper understanding of leadership, that I likely would not have obtained if I hadn't played footy. Throughout my career I came to the significant understanding that my identity is not in what I do and how well I do it, an issue that remains prevalent for young people these days. For instance, if a guy loses his job, and his whole identity is tied up in what he does and how well he does it, he can end up taking his life, which is a tragedy. It's ridiculous, but it's happening too much. I've realised that my identity is well beyond the sporting arena. I was blessed in footy, by God, to have a platform to be able to speak life into other people; to speak life into their relationships, their meaning and purpose. So, overall, football, and the rollercoaster ride that it was, taught me the ability to step out of footy, into life, and to know what's really important.

SHAUN HART

Statistics

BORN: 17 May 1971
GAMES PLAYED (1990-2004): 273
GOALS: 177
FINALS PLAYED: 22
FINALS GOALS: 11
GRAND FINALS: 3
PREMIERSHIPS: 2001, 2002, 2003
NORM SMITH MEDAL: 2001 (presented by Jack Clarke)

— Norm Smith Voting —

(**JUDGES: Damian Barrett, Stan Alves, Tony Shaw** and **Tony Morwood**)

The Age votes: **Caroline Wilson:** 3 Michael Voss, 2 Shaun Hart, 1 Jonathan Brown;
Melissa Ryan: 3 Hart, 2 Chris Johnson, 1 Voss;
Greg Baum: 3 Hart, 2 Voss, 1 Brown;
Rohan Connolly: 3 Hart, 2 Voss, 1 Johnson;
Greg Denham: 3 Johnson, 2 Hart, 1 Voss;
Stephen Rielly: 3 Johnson, 2 Hart, 1 Brown;
Linda Pearce: 3 Johnson, 2 Hart, 1 Voss;
Karen Lyon: 3 Hart, 2 Johnson, 1 Voss;
Geoff McClure: 3 Voss, 2 Hart, 1 Johnson;
Charles Happell: 3 Johnson, 2 Hart, 1 Brown;
Mark Fuller: 3 Voss, 2 Hart, 1 Johnson;
Jake Niall: 3 Hart, 2 Johnson, 1 Voss;
Len Johnson: 3 Hart, 2 Justin Leppitsch, 1 Scott Lucas.

The Age **TOTALS:** Hart 32, Johnson 21, Voss 18, Brown 4, Leppitsch 2, Lucas 1.

Nathan Buckley

Nathan Buckley was the ultimate competitor, a warrior who ceded nothing in his quest for greatness. Indeed, the image of a focused and resolute Buckley leading his Collingwood team down the race and into battle remains etched in our memories. He could cut sides to pieces by foot or by hand, and was equally adept on both sides of his body. Despite never winning an AFL Premiership, Buckley is one of the game's most decorated players. Among the many accolades he won during his 280-game career for Brisbane and Collingwood were the 2003 Brownlow Medal (tied with Mark Ricciuto and Adam Goodes), six Copeland Trophies as the Magpies' best and fairest, and seven All-Australian guernseys. He captained the club and was named on a half-back flank in its Team of the Century. In his Norm Smith Medal performance, in Collingwood's nine-point loss to Brisbane, Buckley had 28 kicks and four handballs, took two marks, laid four tackles and kicked a goal. Four years after retiring in 2007, he was appointed coach of Collingwood.

I saw footy as a way to fit in. As a kid I was never in the in-crowd. But very early on I identified footy as a vehicle to perhaps become a bit more popular among my peers because it was a respected sport. I put a lot of effort into it, and it gave me a lot of self-worth during those

← **CHAMPION** Nathan Buckley tucked away the Medal after his team had lost a tightly-fought Grand Final. He ranks with Collingwood's greatest players, with six Copeland trophies, a Brownlow and a Norm Smith Medal.

formative years. If I felt I had failed on the footy field, I thought it was a reflection of my qualities as a person, or my status at school or among my circle of friends. One of the first instances of that was when I was overlooked for selection in the Northern Territory primary schools side. I was angry and felt hard done-by, and I copped a lot of flak for whinging about it, too. They say I cried—I'm not sure that's true—but I was upset.[1]

I put a lot of pressure on myself to succeed—probably too much. But it helped form my tunnel vision and drive to succeed as a teenager. Without it, I wouldn't have achieved as much.

I struggled for distance in my kicking because I was a small kid. I started kicking around my body to bring my glutes and hip flexor into my kicking action to help my quaddies and, as I became stronger in my legs, I stuck with the same technique because I was comfortable with it.

Coaches always tried to change my kicking technique. They tried to get me to run straight at the target. Even when I had a set shot at goal, I would veer slightly to the right in my last couple of steps—it's just my natural kicking style. I don't necessarily believe in a perfect technique, just basic fundamentals. You need to be comfortable with your own style and that only comes with practice.

I was a receiver. I only enjoyed the skilful side of the game. I avoided packs and didn't want to get involved in physicality because I was built like a stick and I was worried about getting hurt. I started turning away from footy because it was too tough, and started playing tennis instead. Dad was very hard on me during that period and, without his insistence, I might have quit footy.

I played three years of non-stop footy. After finishing high school (1989), I played in Darwin over Christmas (the NTFL season spans October to March), then with Port Adelaide (SANFL) in 1990, and continued to play alternate seasons until the end of 1992. I was footy-fit all year round, which gave me an edge over other players my age.

Dad wanted me to further my footy at Port Adelaide. During his playing

---

1   A number of Nathan Buckley's quotes are extracts from interviews conducted by Ben Collins and Dan Eddy for *Champions: Conversations with Great Players & Coaches of Australian Football*, Slattery Media Group, 2016, pp. 45-55. Buckley's recollections of the 2002 AFL Grand Final are sourced from an interview with Dan Eddy in September 2017.

career at Woodville, he admired Port Adelaide as a strong club with a culture of success, good role models and, importantly, an emphasis on developing young players. Dad wrote to the club and they agreed to let me train with them. I'm certain his choice of club was crucial in my pursuit of an AFL career.

Port Adelaide could easily have given me the axe. In my first year (1990), I played mostly off the pine in the under-19s and struggled, and they must have been close to giving up on me in '91. I reckon I had osteitis pubis, but I was told I had a groin problem and that I'd be okay to run through it. I stopped training for a while and I'm sure they thought I was dogging it.

In my first game back I was best on ground in the under-19s, and then they put me in the reserves and I kicked 5.5 from a forward pocket. I was promoted to the seniors for the last seven games and didn't look back. It goes to show you need a little bit of luck to play AFL footy.

Always strive to widen your comfort zone. In other words, if you're prepared to do a little bit extra, you'll be better able to cope with the next step up in strength, speed or endurance because you've pushed yourself beyond the level you're at. You have to keep pushing and testing yourself if you want to keep improving. Once you have that mindset you see things as a challenge, and an opportunity to improve, rather than a chore.

You could have all the football ability in the world and still not play in the AFL. I reckon 25 to 30 per cent of the game is talent; the rest is work ethic and maintaining competitiveness.

I seriously considered not going to Brisbane (in 1993) and staying with Port Adelaide for another year. I hadn't made it to Collingwood, my club of choice, and I was undecided. But I thought: "Why wouldn't you play AFL footy while you've got the opportunity?" When I arrived in Brisbane, I immediately shut off all the stuff that had happened in the lead-up. In the six months I was there, I was committed to playing my best footy for Brisbane.

Tagging was football for me. Apart from when I was given a designated role, there were only a handful of games in my career where I wasn't tagged. I was tagged in my first three AFL games. I had Anthony Stevens (North Melbourne) in my first game, (Richmond's) Tony Free and then (Melbourne's) Todd Viney. Early in my career, the actual tagging didn't bother me; it was more about adjusting to the speed of the game and finding space. I found that if you focus solely on the ball, your tagger doesn't exist. If you allow yourself to be sucked into a wrestling match, you're doing his job for him. But if your first focus is the ball, and his first focus is you, you'll get to the ball before him. It can be difficult at times when someone is constantly in your face, but after a couple of years of you maintaining your composure and discipline, they realise it's just a waste of time.

(Brisbane coach) Robert Walls challenged me about my lack of tackling and defensive pressure early in my first AFL season. In front of the player group, 'Wallsy' pulled out stats from the previous four weeks and said that I'd only laid four tackles in that time—an average of one a game. He said it wasn't good enough if you had fewer than four a game—one a quarter. He then pulled me aside and said: "You're not doing enough to put pressure on the opposition. I understand that you're being tagged, but you can't play all one way (offensive)."

I was challenged to improve and I've always thrived on a challenge and was ready to do whatever I had to do to rectify it. If I didn't make that transition, I wouldn't be playing.

People who branded me a mercenary for leaving Brisbane were ill informed and short sighted. I gave my all for Brisbane in '93, and when the season was over I was still pretty keen to get to Melbourne—the Mecca of football—and the opportunity existed to go to Collingwood, which was still my first choice.

The true test of my loyalty came in my third season at Collingwood (1996), when I was 24, and Port Adelaide was recruiting players for its first season in the AFL. I've never forgotten the opportunity Port gave me, but I wanted to stay at Collingwood because I felt a strong sense of loyalty to the people I'd been involved with. It's about loyalty to people, rather than loyalty to a club or organisation.

Consistency is a product of work ethic. The most consistent players are the ones who, after they've had a few great games in a row, don't drop off in their training or run around like bigheads. They're looking for the next opportunity to gain an edge.

I was a better runner in a game than at training. It's the adrenalin and the love of the game—I just wanted to get the ball. It's that competitive edge to get the best out of yourself, which the best players have.

If you take shortcuts, you'll be exposed. You might get away with certain things for a couple of weeks, a month, maybe even a season, but it catches up with you. If you don't make the sacrifices and consistently take care of the little things, you'll let yourself and your team down.

When I became Collingwood captain (in 1999), I demanded the best from myself and others—and it backfired. Early on I thought: "Everyone needs to work as hard as I do. If it's good enough for me, it should be good enough for everyone." That approach worked for me personally because I'd lived it my whole life, but placing those demands on everyone else and expecting them to adopt it all within a month or two was unrealistic. It stemmed from honourable intentions, wanting the group, and all the individuals within the group, to play to their potential. But I developed more empathy for my teammates and I came to understand everyone has their own way of doing things. Instead of trying to drive the group with my motivations, I tried to find out what theirs were.

Leadership is about making things easier for people by showing them the right way, but I know at times I made it harder for teammates to make the right decisions. But I think I eventually created an environment where it was easier for them to make the right decision.

The criticism levelled at me about my on-field leadership—from people outside the club—revolved around a perceived selfishness on my behalf because I didn't get the ball passed to me or whatever. But that was more related to disciplines, team rules and expectations the coach was trying to enforce. Part of my job was to ensure the coach's demands were met and occasionally that meant having a word to a teammate, and you can't always take a bloke aside in the heat of battle. If you're not willing to play the way the coach wants for four quarters of a match, you're going to break down as a unit.

If you're honest with yourself, you can be honest with others. Honesty is the key ingredient that underpins any plan to get the best out of ourselves. If you're honest, you'll make the right decisions, the right sacrifices, and you'll be in a better position to judge where you sit in relation to your ability, your team and the competition. In my experience, the difference between playing in a team environment that has been fairly successful and one that hasn't has been the honesty factor. It's such an important quality in the game.

The fear of failure was always there. In the early 2000s, it was a huge motivator for me. I held a real fear of not capitalising on the opportunities that were being presented to me. That drove a lot of my work ethic. In many ways, it was probably unhealthy. You'd rather be motivated by a positive than a negative but, at the same time, it formed a crucial part of my make-up, particularly in my younger days. I was very conscious of not letting myself down, and I never forgot the people that rely on you to do well—teammates, family, friends—so then it becomes a fear of failure not only for yourself but for the people who are close to you.

"The zone" is a crystal-clear state of mind where you know you can do whatever you want to do, whenever you want to do it. You think totally about the game itself, and nothing—nothing—can shake your focus. Things happen instinctively. You run to a position and the ball just comes to you, partly because you've read it well, partly due to luck. You know you're in control of the contest. My best personal experience of it was when we beat Brisbane by three points at Etihad Stadium in 2002. My first three quarters that night were the best I've played. It seemed like I got the ball every time I went near it. But you can't reach that elevated mental state without the right preparation. Confidence is a by-product of hard work.

We'd had some strong performances through 2002. We were a dour side; we only had three or four top-enders, but we were an even side who believed in being really hard competitors. We were a strong tackling side, a good contested ball side, and the evenness of our effort was one of our strongest attributes.

(Coach) Mick Malthouse brought great experience through being involved in finals at West Coast. That gave us some real confidence around the way we were led. We also had a pretty strong leadership group. We finished fourth in 2002, and even though we were well beaten by the Western Bulldogs in the last round (by 41 points), we were able to draw a line through the season and shift our focus towards the finals.

No-one gave us a chance against Port Adelaide in the first Qualifying Final. I was injured and missed the game, but the team went in with a clear game-plan to try and break down Port's midfield run, making it a real contest wherever we could. 'Licca' (Paul Licuria) played a crucial negating role in the middle for us, yet still gathered 40 disposals—that was a big win. Late in the game, Ben Johnson laid a great tackle on Peter Burgoyne in the goal square when it looked as though he would score a certain goal, and that really epitomised our attitude. It didn't matter what the odds were, we were going to put our best foot forward and see what happened. It was a good win (by 13 points), and the feeling in the rooms afterwards was as good as I can remember. It was also the first final the club had played since 1994, and the first winning final that the club had played since the 1990 Grand Final, so it had been a fair gap between victories. We weren't that conscious of the history, though, we were just conscious of the potential of our group and of the future.

The crowd when we ran out for the Preliminary Final against Adelaide was the loudest crowd I ever played in front of. As you gain experience, you lose that feeling of hairs standing up on the back of your neck, but that day was different. There were two teams playing, but Collingwood just dominated the crowd that day. To play in that game, and to win that game, was huge. Our mentality was really narrow, though. We were focused on what we were doing, and we had a really strong belief in how we were going to go about it. But I was certainly able to take a step back and recognise that we were building some serious momentum throughout that finals series.

I think we managed the hype pretty well. The Grand Final Parade was a great experience, and to immerse ourselves in that was terrific. The crowds at the last couple of training sessions at Victoria Park were huge, also. The stands were full and the feeling around the club was one of excitement. Your feet don't touch the ground. They are the exciting moments to be involved in during your career. It's what you play for: to be in those situations, in those moments. It was a great week and I loved it. I couldn't wait for the game to start.

Glenn Freeborn had been through it at North Melbourne (in 1996 and 1998), so he'd been there, done that. He was the only player on our list who had been in a Grand Final, so he was pivotal to our preparation. The leaders arranged for Glenn to step up that week. He's a pretty quiet bloke, Glenn, but he had great respect from his teammates and we valued the way he saw the game. He never got too wound up, and certainly never sought the microphone to speak to the group, but his role that week was really important. He had two messages that stuck with me. The first was to shop early by sticking a tackle, laying a block or getting some body on body. He said, "Don't worry about getting a touch, or getting your first kick, just worry about getting physical early in the game." I'm sure that was a message that his former coach, Denis Pagan, would have got through to the group in North's Grand Finals. The other message was to keep coming back to your teammates; to not worry about the uncontrollable happening around you. I think he was really important for us during the lead-up.

We valued our tackling game. Mick's philosophy was defence first, and we were fine with it being a nil-all draw rather than a shoot-out. The scoring in '02 was pretty frugal, not just in the opening quarter but throughout the game. But we were never concerned about that because of our defensive focus as a team. There was some feeling out there early on. I remember Martin Pike was up and about early, and Michael Voss and Scott Burns clashed at one point, but the game was a real arm wrestle with plenty of courageous efforts on both sides.

I knew I was going to be sat on (tagged) in some shape or form, yet the plan was for me to spend some time opposed to 'Vossy'. Heath Scotland was going to share that role with me throughout the game. But from the outset I was getting tagged. Mick didn't want that match-up to continue, and so he swung Heath on to Vossy pretty early. The way the midfield match-ups worked, a player would be tagged from both teams and the other two midfielders would go head to head. We had Burnsy, Heath and Licca going through there—Licca was looking after (2002 Brownlow medallist) Simon Black for the most part because the Brisbane midfield was pretty powerful during that era. The critical match-up for the Lions was in the ruck, even though they lost Beau McDonald to injury early. They always got a lot of momentum out of those stoppages under Clark Keating, so that was a worry because it meant that he was a chance to give his midfielders first use. We needed to be really strong in the clinches to negate that strength. As we saw in the 2003 Grand Final, we weren't able to do it and they smashed us that day (by 50 points), but in '02 we were able to hold up for the most part.

Anthony Rocca kicked a huge goal for us just before quarter-time. 'Pebbles" (Rocca's) 2002 Grand Final was massive. Had he been paid that contentious goal late in the game[2], that would have given him five goals for the day—that's five goals out of the 10 we would have scored; that's a fairly significant contribution. His impact on that game was profound, and he was worrying Brisbane as much as any of us was. To kick that first goal, and to have been the focal point for us, we really relied on him playing well. He was an underrated player right through his career. We loved him, loved having him in the side, because he was always looking out for what was best for the team. The fact Brisbane's two key defenders, Justin Leppitsch and Mal Michael, were struggling to contain him that day says plenty about his role for us.

Vossy and I were ball players, and we would go wherever the game took us. In that second quarter, they had a fair bit of territory for a while and we defended pretty well against a heap of inside-50s. I felt our ability to absorb that gave us a real chance to win the game. I spent a fair bit of time on Vossy in that first half, then from early in the third quarter Brad Scott came and tagged me for the rest of the game. There was a swing in momentum our way in the third quarter, not so much on the scoreboard but in general play, as both teams tried to gain the upper hand.

---

2   Collingwood fans swear the Rocca shot was a goal. This was before the goalposts were extended. Certainly it could have gone either way.

There was a significant moment in the game just before three-quarter time. Brad Scott got away on the wing, passed it to Jonathan Brown and he kicked a huge goal from outside 50. Then Vossy charged out of the centre and kicked another goal. We went from a few points up to suddenly being a few points down. We had been controlling the game up to that point, and if not for those passages of play we would have led at the final change. It had happened late in the second quarter as well. That's why they were such a good side; they were so hard to hold down for a full 30 minutes, and they could always find a way to kick a couple of late goals when they needed to. You worked so hard for your scores, and then they would go bang, bang: they just seemed to have an awareness of the big moments. They were able to put themselves back in the contest, not that we were disheartened going into three-quarter time.

We were happy to grind out the last quarter, and it was a grind. It was only the late goal by Jason Akermanis that broke the deadlock. Otherwise, we were in the game right up to the final siren. I was so engaged in what was going on, and so determined to find that next break for us to score. It was like being in an arm wrestle with two evenly matched guys, where both of you knew you couldn't afford to give an inch because you knew if you did you would lose. So you're pushing against the other side, trying to find that breaking point, and at no stage did either side give in. Time ran out for us, and they were ahead when the siren went. It was marginal (the margin was nine points). They defended really well in that last quarter and we found it hard getting the ball out of our back half. We missed a couple of chances, which didn't help us and which made it a tougher pill to swallow when the siren blew. But it certainly wasn't for a lack of effort that we fell short.

You're pretty numb straight after the game. As a group, we were just gutted. It was such a close result, and while you didn't feel it in those initial moments, there was an element of pride in what we had done as a team that day. It was hard to handle, really hard, but everyone knew that we could look each other in the eye and know that we'd all had a crack. You are trying to reconcile and work out your own emotions in those few minutes after the game. You're consoling each other, and no-one's thinking about the Norm Smith Medal. So it came out of the blue when it was announced that I had won it. Burnsy said to me afterwards, "I always wanted you to win a Norm Smith Medal, because I knew if you had won one then we'd all have Premiership medallions." That was generally the way it went: the winning side usually contained the medallist. In a sense, it was a microcosm of my entire playing career. I would have much preferred the team success over the individual accolades, but that success eluded me as a player.

Embarrassment is pretty close to how you feel when you accept the Norm Smith Medal in a losing side. It's the fact you haven't achieved what you set out to achieve. As captain of the team, I was not going to go back to the group wearing a medal when my teammates didn't have one as well, so that was why my instinctive reaction was to take it off straight away. Funnily enough, I was handed the medal by Peter Knights, and back when I was 10 years old Peter did a handball clinic at a shopping centre in Darwin which I won. The prize was a signed Hawthorn mirror, and it was handed to me by Peter, so it's funny how things play out in footy. It was amazing to be handed a Norm Smith Medal from a bloke I had held up on a pedestal since that day in Darwin as a 10-year-old. But removing the medal was an instinctive action, it wasn't something I thought too much about. I took it off, held it in my hand, and accepted the congratulations of everyone there, but it was cold comfort for how we were all feeling at the time.

Ultimately, what winning a Norm Smith Medal means is that you were able to perform on the big stage when it mattered. But there's only one Norm Smith Medal, and it doesn't mean that only one bloke stood up on the day. There were 22 other medals that the Brisbane boys walked off wearing that I'm sure they were pretty happy to have. The significance for me is that it says that I was able to stand up when it mattered. You don't get medals for being best on ground in the other big finals, or the big matches in home and away games (aside from Anzac Day). It's the big games, no matter when, where you want to test yourself. That's why you do all the work, so you can contribute to your team as best you can.

THE NORM SMITH MEDAL

Do you get over losing a close Grand Final? You do until someone starts asking you questions about it! The days tick on for all of us. It's 15 years ago now, it's a lifetime ago. I can't get yesterday back, I can't even get this morning back. Time keeps ticking away, so you need to keep making the most of your opportunities; keep putting your best foot forward. It certainly taught me a lot about myself, taught me a lot about the group we had. It hardens you. It makes you realise that there are plenty of elements to success. There are always things you could have done differently, both individually and as a team. But when I think about that team in '02, I feel that was the definition of success: getting the very best out of yourself.

I'm a winner, I prefer to win. But who's to say that our performance against Brisbane that day wasn't the absolute best we could have done as a group. You know of instances where you could have done better, or things could have panned out differently, but that team didn't die wondering. We left it all out there, we just fell short at the end. I know that if other teams I had been involved in had had the same attitude as that team did, we would have had much more success. It's fleeting, though. The next year, in the Grand Final, we didn't roll out, execute or perform with the same intensity and we paid the price for that. You've got to appreciate things for what they are at the time. That team during the 2002 finals was a team that found its absolute best, and that deserves to be acknowledged.

Your reaction to losing is important. You're always taught to be a good sport and a good loser and appreciate that you can't win every time. When I talk to kids, I tell them: "It doesn't matter if you win or lose, as long as you do your best." But I don't mind seeing a kid who's disappointed when he loses because you know somewhere deep down inside him lies a hunger to win. I liked seeing that in my teammates. The players who hurt the most when things don't go well are generally the ones who work hardest to ensure it doesn't happen next time. They're the teammates I loved playing alongside.

The Americans celebrate successful seasons better than we do. What they do really well is they have divisional champions and conference champions. If you lose the NFL Super Bowl, for example, you have still been a conference champion. If you don't win the Grand Final in our sport, you're an also-ran—it's boom or bust. We don't even acknowledge teams that make finals. Yes, we talk about those teams that get there, but if they don't make it to the Grand Final, or win the Grand Final, we almost speak of their finals result in derogatory terms: they have failed is the overwhelming view. What isn't taken into account is how many consecutive years that team might have made the finals, or what a great effort it was in that particular season. Even making it all the way to a prelim doesn't count if you lose. It's an interesting difference in our psyche compared to the American way of doing things.

Coaching now is very different from what it was years ago. When we draft kids and they step in the door, it doesn't matter whether they were pick one, pick 100 or a rookie player, they've all got equal opportunity when they come in. It's what you do with it once you get in. When you become a coach, what you've done before is largely irrelevant: whether you were a good player, ordinary player, struggled through, haven't played at the level, it doesn't matter because it's a totally different skill set. Have you got the capacity to develop and to build, and can you impart it on a coaching team, a playing group and a club? There are a lot of layers to coaching that go far beyond what you could do as a footballer.

I think being a successful coach is how much you trust people, and where and when you give that trust. Being a senior coach can make you a cynic really quickly. If you strip me back to my core I believe in the good of people, and so that resonates with the way that I coach. But there'll be times when I have to remind myself that I need to give space, and trust that the goodwill comes out. While I'm getting better and better at that, it still comes back to experience because you can't just hand it over.

We are more managers now than just coaches. It's dynamic and once again it comes back to the people around you. That's what footy is all about. You can take your eye off the individual and get caught up on tactics, but then you miss out on the medical or physical side. Underneath all that is the players' personal life, and the emotional and stress responses that emerge as a consequence. It's the most enjoyable thing about coaching.

I consider that it's my job to be there for every person in the footy department, and if there's any way that I can support them better and make their life easier then I'll do it. I think there's a lot of demand in care. I can be caring for a player but still be delivering a really strong message to him about what he might have just done, or the way he's responding to a certain situation. I see that as caring for him, because if you don't give him that feedback he doesn't grow and doesn't learn. Care is a basic element of my management style and I think it's fundamental to everything else that I do. We are trying to build a program that wins games of footy as well as developing good people.

I'm quite process driven and always was as a player. It's easy to look at the win-loss as a coach, or the stats sheet as an individual player. But I've always been a believer that if you get your preparation right, and you work hard at it, that's when you give yourself the best chance to succeed. So even as a coach I go back to that process. And that's relevant whether you're a coach, or even a parent, you need to see what needs to be done and give yourself a chance of success by consistently sticking to that process.

I missed playing in a flag as a player. But for my growth as a person, my experiences as a player and the opportunities to play in two Grand Finals were invaluable. In the first half of my career we were nowhere near it. There are no guarantees in footy. I would love to share in success as a coach with this footy club and this group of players, and I'd love them to feel the ultimate by being part of a Premiership team and be acknowledged as Premiership players. Alongside that endeavour is the drive to provide a really solid environment in here, where people grow self-esteem and remember their experiences at Collingwood favourably, because it helped them to become a better person.

I'm hungry for a flag, and if we do win one, why stop there? True success is actually living your life to the fullest. Footy is just one part of who these young men are and we'll celebrate all of them in their own way as we go along. I'd love to set up the club for a sustained period of success.

NATHAN BUCKLEY

Statistics

BORN: 26 July 1972

GAMES PLAYED (1993-2007): 280 (Brisbane Bears 1993, 20 games; Collingwood 1994-2007, 260 games)

GOALS: 284 (Brisbane 21; Collingwood 263)

FINALS PLAYED: 10

FINALS GOALS: 6

GRAND FINALS: 2

NORM SMITH MEDAL: 2002 (presented by Peter Knights)

— Norm Smith Voting —

(**JUDGES:** Mark Duffield, Dwayne Russell, Geoff Slattery, Patrick Smith and Robert Walls)

Herald Sun votes:
Damian Barrett: 3 Michael Voss, 2 Nathan Buckley, 1 Clark Keating;
Rod Nicholson: 3 Voss, 2 Buckley, 1 Nigel Lappin;
Scott Palmer: 3 Buckley, 2 Voss, 1 Anthony Rocca;
Jackie Epstein: 3 Buckley, 2 Voss, 1 Rocca;
Glenn McFarlane: 3 Voss, 2 Buckley, 1 Lappin;
Mark Harding: 3 Voss, 2 Buckley, 1 Lappin;
Ken Piesse: 3 Buckley, 2 Voss, 1 Scott Burns.

Herald Sun **TOTALS:** Buckley 19, Voss 18, Lappin 3, Rocca 2, Keating 1, Burns 1.

Simon Black

Simon Black, the West Australian who became the Brisbane Lions' games-record holder (322), was one of football's most decorated players. Indeed, he is one of just 10 men to have won a Premiership (2001-03), a Brownlow Medal (2002) and play 300 games (1998-2013).[1] Black made up for a lack of pace with his quick reaction time, aerobic capabilities and deft skills by hand and foot. He was a key member of Brisbane's famous 'Fab Four', along with Michael Voss, Nigel Lappin and Jason Akermanis, the midfield that under coach Leigh Matthews propelled the Lions into four consecutive Grand Finals (2001-04). In a team of champions, Black's consistency and durability set him apart; this despite the fact that as a teenager he suffered from Scheuermann's disease, a spinal complaint that he feared would finish his sporting career. He won three Brisbane best and fairest awards (2001-02, 2006), was a three-time All-Australian (2001-02, 2004), captained the club (2007-08), and was one of the most admired players of his era. In his defining performance, against Collingwood in the 2003 Grand Final, Black had 16 kicks, 23 handballs, nine tackles, nine clearances and kicked a goal in Brisbane's 50-point victory. His 39 disposals are the most by any Norm Smith medallist.

---

1   The others are: Dick Reynolds, Gavin Wanganeen, Shane Crawford, Mark Ricciuto, Jason Akermanis, Adam Goodes, Jimmy Bartel, Sam Mitchell and Gary Ablett jnr. Bartel (2011) also won the Norm Smith Medal.

← **HAD IT ALL** Three Premierships, a Brownlow and a Norm Smith Medal made Simon Black one of the greats of Brisbane, in its finest era.

THE NORM SMITH MEDAL

I grew up in Perth and I have special memories of walking to primary school with my brother, Ben, who's two years older than me. I started playing footy because of him, when he was 10 and I was eight. He and his mates started playing junior footy at that time, so I tagged along with them. My parents, Ray and Fran, were both active people, too. My dad was from New Zealand, so Ben and I played rugby before we played Aussie rules. Dad was a good tennis player and a scratch golfer. I wish he had grown up in Australia because footy would have been a good game for him to play. It was foreign to him when he first moved across from New Zealand, when he was 18-19, and I later asked him if he played a game; he said he never did. With our involvement in footy, he always kept a keen eye across the game. We taught him a lot as we went along, so he enjoyed watching the game throughout our junior days. We are originally from Kaitaia, at the top of New Zealand's North Island. We still have cattle farms there today, which my dad inherited when his father passed away.

I was good at middle distance running during junior athletics—I won a couple of state titles when I was 15. I also played a lot of basketball and soccer. I played soccer to the age of 11 and basketball from then through to about the age of 17. I think basketball is such a great game for footballers to play. Being an inside midfielder, basketball was so important for developing my awareness and decision-making. Scott Pendlebury has a basketball background and he's amazing in his awareness and decision-making as a consequence. I think any young, aspiring footballer should play basketball in their off-season to help develop their awareness for footy.

I dreamed of playing at AFL level. But, that said, I used to think of the AFL players as football freaks that you just watched on television, who were far superior to anything I could ever possibly achieve. It was always a distant dream rather than a reality. I knew I wanted to, but I didn't think I would be capable of making it. I've always been a self-doubter, so that was probably my natural way of thinking about it.

When I was 15-16, I had Scheuermann's disease in my spine. It was quite painful for 12-18 months. I was in Year 10 at school and was unable to play much sport. The vertebrae in your spine don't form correctly and it causes a lot of pain. During that time I wasn't sure whether it would last forever and hinder my chances of continuing in sport. Fortunately it came good after about 18 months. It was the year when the state under-16 carnival was happening, and I had to pull out of that because of my back. I think what it did, though, was increase my determination to work harder on my footy if I ever got healthy again. It was really just rest and time that fixed the problem. When I was at Brisbane, I used to require physio four to five times per week to manage it, because it would throw out my hip alignment and lower back. I was very lucky to have access to such a level of care by being at an AFL club, because I needed to constantly monitor it. Even today it still causes me some problems.

I was a West Coast supporter. My heroes were Chris Mainwaring and Peter Matera, the two wingmen. Chris came to my primary school once, and as he was my favourite Eagle it was a huge thrill for me. He took us for a training session and I think I just tagged him for the hour-and-a-half that he was there!

I loved the football as a kid. Mum always says that I used to sleep with the footy; I loved the smell of the leather; loved playing with a football, kicking a football. I would find targets between trees, or I'd try predicting how the ball would bounce when it landed after being kicked in the air. I loved kicking the ball with mates, fighting for the ball—it really caught my imagination from an early age and I was hooked. And that went for other balls, too, such as a basketball, a cricket ball—you name it. I was one of those kids who loved having a ball in my hand and loved playing with it, no matter the shape or size. When I was 14, we moved to a place called Langford, about 20 minutes out of Perth, where we had a couple of acres. We had a big backyard with a lot of trees, so I spent a lot of time running around, either by myself or with Ben and Dad. Kicking the ball around in the yard was always a lot of fun.

I think you accidently develop your skills when you're always carrying a footy around with you. It's not so much deliberate practice; it's more about having the ball in your hand as often as possible. I was always working on my handball and my kicking, purely because I enjoyed having a ball around me all the time. Over hours and hours of doing that, it naturally develops you. For any young person who's serious about their footy, it's so much easier for your development if you have a ball with you wherever you are, and you play with it constantly. It comes back to the 10,000 hours rule, which Malcolm Gladwell wrote about—that is, 10,000 hours of practice to perfect your craft.

I find it staggering today, even at AFL level, the number of guys who can't use their opposite feet. That so many haven't been taught to use both sides of their bodies, by hand or foot, is quite amazing. So many footballers are entering the AFL system who aren't competent on both sides. I'm very big in training sessions with kids to help them develop both sides, because at some point in a game you will be forced to use the opposite side. Even if you just need to kick it 20 metres sideways to someone, you've got to be able to do that competently.

I think what stood out at draft time was my ability to make it to contests. The knock on me was always my lack of pace, but my endurance was a strength; that and my decision-making. I was a left-footer, too, which added a point of difference. I played in a national under-18 carnival as an inside midfielder, but with the East Fremantle colts side, in the WAFL, I played predominantly on the wing. I think my decision-making helped set me apart at draft time, despite my lack of pace.

It was a huge shock when I was selected by Brisbane at pick 31 in the 1997 National Draft. Unless you are likely to be drafted in the top few selections, you don't really know if and when you are going to be selected, or by whom. I never really knew how interested the clubs were in me leading up to the draft, so when they called out my name it was a case of mixed emotions. I remember shedding a few tears and thinking, "Wow, I have to pack up and move all the way over there." I was pretty comfortable at home, so it was a big life change I needed to make. But it was a dream come true to have the chance to play AFL footy, so I was quickly excited at what lay ahead.

My parents were certainly surprised. We have always been a very close-knit family and had, only a few months earlier, moved into a new home. My dad had sold his transport business, so because I had been drafted by Brisbane they decided to move there with me. I didn't live with them, but they were nearby as a support during the second half of my first year. My brother moved across as well, and so my parents then decided to move over permanently because their boys were both living there. I've been very fortunate to have had them around most of the time. I lived with an older couple whose kids had recently moved out of home. They were Lions fans, John and Judy Monsens, and they were a great support for me early on and really helped me to settle into Brisbane in that first year. My cooking was done for me and I was very well looked after, so I was lucky.

The humidity during my first pre-season was a shock to the system! That 1998 summer in Brisbane was a scorcher, so doing all the running in that tropical heat was a challenge. That, and backing up session after session. I was always tired, always fatigued. I was trying to build some muscle mass, because I was pretty thin, but it was hard to do so when I was so active and was sweating it all off. Every day there was some training to do, so getting used to that while trying to recover between sessions was difficult. We used to train at the University of Queensland and John Northey was our coach. One day he said, "Righto boys, find yourself a partner, pair off and have marking contests with each other one on one." I was paired with Daniel Bradshaw! I was about 74 kilos, Daniel was about 95, and if we had 20 kicks he marked 19 of them, and the other one he spilled because it fell off his fingers. I always struggled with losing at anything, but after that humiliation I thought, "I don't think this is for me, I'd better go back to Perth!"

The club also wanted me to bulk up, because I was really skinny. I was lucky to be selected in the first six games that first year. During that period I remember thinking, "Gee, I'm going to get snapped in half out here against these big blokes." I had to focus on the weights and on my nutrition in order to increase my size. I was always a fanatical trainer. I wanted to always make sure I got something out of every session, and I always pushed myself really hard.

It was a great experience that first year, lots of fun. Because we had so many injuries throughout 1998, I played senior footy before I probably should have. A lot of our senior guys were injured that year, so younger guys like myself, Luke Power, Shane O'Bree and Beau McDonald all managed to play senior footy. That was a real positive out of that year, despite the poor results.[2] Being a young player I didn't realise what was happening off the field, though. There were some disgruntled people within the club and seeing John Northey lose his job during the season was a shock. It stuck with me that it was someone's livelihood that was affected. It made me appreciate that this was professional, the real deal, and that footy is a cut-throat industry.

There were concerns within the club that players were involving themselves with off-field issues, and vice versa with some of the officials. When Leigh Matthews arrived I remember him saying, "Players play, administrators administrate, and coaches coach." His big mantra was: know, accept and perform your role. He had a bit of a cleanout of some of the off-field staff, and some players left during his first couple of years. Leigh's great strength was his ability to make the complicated sound simple. He provided us with real clarity, which you see in his commentary today. Among his moves he put Justin Leppitsch and Jason Akermanis down back, and we went from last to third in his first season. Although we had finished last in 1998 we did have a lot of injuries during that year so it wasn't as bad as it seemed. With a healthier list in 1999 we were far more competitive.

By 2001 guys were coming into their own as players. During the Premiership years we had many guys who were all at the peak of their powers at the same time, plus we had some really experienced guys like Shaun Hart and Marcus Ashcroft. We had a great core group of 15-16 players, so we just needed to ensure everyone was fit and healthy to give us our best chance of experiencing success. Leigh also had the great ability of knowing where to put guys in certain positions to enable them to flourish.

During the first eight weeks of 2001, we couldn't seem to get much going our way. It was starting to frustrate Leigh. We played Carlton at Princes Park, in round eight, and they absolutely walloped us (74 points), with Anthony Koutoufides playing one of the greatest individual performances I'd ever seen. Leigh kept us in the rooms for a

---

2   The Lions finished on the bottom of the ladder with five wins and a draw.

good 90 minutes afterwards, and he went through individuals and told them where they were at. He said, "Some of you guys are okay on the Gabba, on your home patch, but as soon as you jump on an aeroplane you give us nothing!" He really went through us individually. What stuck out to me was when he named three guys in the Carlton side: Anthony Franchina, Scott Freeborn and Darren Hulme. He said, "Guys, what are they for Carlton?" It took us a minute or so, then someone said, "They're just role players." He said, "Bingo! That's exactly what they are. They are role players and don't get much recognition in the media or outside the four walls of the Carlton footy club, but you know that every time they go out and play, they play their roles for the team." He said, "I don't know how good you blokes can be, but at the moment you're not going to see your full capabilities because you're not playing your role for the team. Until you guys start playing your roles, you're not going to fulfil your capabilities as a group."

The next week we played Adelaide at the Gabba, who were a good side. We narrowly lost by five points after the siren, then the week after that we played Essendon, the reigning Premier, who had lost just once in 12 months. That was the week he came out and said, "If it bleeds, we can kill it," a line he had taken from the movie *Predator*. We won by 28 points, and that was because we had managed to *play our roles* for the side. It took until that point, though, for us to realise what was required as a team and as individuals. Suddenly, the guys started to own it and drive it themselves. If anyone wasn't doing their role for our team, the other guys were starting to demand a certain standard, as Leigh had talked to us about. Our leadership group under Michael Voss was strong, and they really drove it. We went on to win 16 games straight to finish the year, won our first flag, and it all took off from there.

The media dubbed us the 'Fab Four'—Vossy, Nigel Lappin, Akermanis and myself. We had a great blend of inside and outside players in the middle during that period. Aker's left and right foot were exceptional. Whenever you won the ball, he would always be around for a handball! Nigel could do both, inside or out, as could Vossy. They were all such skilled players, and so hard and tough. Nige played the 2003 Grand Final with a broken rib and a punctured lung, which was one of the toughest things I've ever seen. And Vossy's toughness was legendary. So it was a real treat to play with those guys. The more you play together, the better you intuitively know each other's games. It's a bit like brothers, when you grow up playing together over a long time in the backyard—you just know where the other is going to be and what their strengths are. You hear their voice and it resonates with you. I feel very fortunate to have been drafted to the Lions, which enabled me to be a part of that group.

We ran really deep across the field. It was amazing in that sense. So it was unfair that they singled us four out, because we had several other guys who contributed just as well as we did. I was always a bit uncomfortable when they used to say the 'Fab Four' because we had so many players who were crucial to our success.

It was amazing to win the 2002 Brownlow Medal—I didn't expect it! Recently someone pulled up vision of my Brownlow speech, and I was cringing at the amount of "umms" and "ahhs" I said on the night. We were playing in the Grand Final five days later, so my head was spinning. It was surreal. We had stayed in Brisbane rather than attend the Brownlow function in Melbourne. Late in the count I started getting all these votes; suddenly I was thinking, "Wow, I'm a chance of winning this!" I was really overwhelmed, to be honest, which was evident from my speech afterwards. When you're in the middle of your career, you're so focused on the next thing you need to do, or the improvement you need to make as a player, so it isn't until you reflect on things later on that you are more able to appreciate the significance of something such as winning a Brownlow Medal. Of course, it was great winning one, but my good fortune was to be able to play in such a great side, because that opportunity doesn't come along every day.

After winning the Brownlow, I started getting close attention from guys with whom I would go on to have 10-year battles. Close-checking guys like Brett Kirk, Cameron Ling, Kane Cornes—I started getting tagged by those up-and-coming run-with players. Getting used to someone trying to stop you getting the ball took a while, particularly as I wasn't a big guy. I had to utilise my running abilities to counter their tactics.

I tried to stay on the move around stoppages, be quick with my hands and anticipate things as quickly as possible, and react before they did. Although I wasn't fast over a long distance, I could react really quickly and therefore make fast decisions. My first five metres were quite quick, though, which was because I had reacted quicker to a certain situation.

To counter negating tactics I focused on what I did well, what my strengths were, and I tried to use them to get on top of taggers. When the opposition focus heavily on you, it forces you to think more about your own game; that then brings out your competitiveness. I had a willingness to fight and scrap, because I knew I could either concede and let the opponent do what he wanted to do, or I could build some resilience and turn it into a real one-on-one battle. Leigh said to me, "Blacky, you don't need to get the ball 30 times. Just make sure, if you get it 15 times, your opponent doesn't get it 20." Ling and Kirk and Cornes were good at knowing their starting point, and then working off you to get their own ball, so I needed to be conscious of them not racking up the footy at the same time. My number one strength was wanting to not get beaten.

I was always a nervous type in the lead-up to games. I really internalised things pre-game. The fear of failure drove me a lot throughout my career. With that, you tend not to enjoy the lead-up to games because you've got that sickly feeling where you are anxious and overthinking things. Through time and experience I learned how to handle nerves, but even after 300 games I still used to get wound up and nervous before the games. That was how I prepared for the battle ahead.

We went into the 2003 Grand Final with a number of injuries. Vossy's knee wasn't great, Nige (Lappin) had his ribs and there were a number of other guys who were struggling to get up. It was an enormous effort from our physios to get a lot of our guys in shape to take the field. I was unsure how we were going to go. We were able to get on top of Collingwood early and play some really good footy in the first half. We went into half-time leading by 42 points, so we had our tails up. They had beaten us three weeks earlier in the Qualifying Final (by 15 points), so we went in expecting one hell of a game, particularly because we had guys going into the game carrying injuries. I knew I would have to play more minutes through the midfield than usual, so I really set myself to spend most of my time in there that day. As it eventuated, it turned into one of the most enjoyable games I ever played.

Our ruckman, Clark Keating, was enormous throughout our Premiership era. In the 2002 Grand Final, also against Collingwood, our other ruckman in Beau McDonald went into the game with a bad shoulder. At his first ruck contest he dislocated his shoulder and was out for the rest of the game, so it was left to Clark to ruck the whole day. He was a mountain of strength for us, and critical to us winning by nine points. Then, in 2003, he was again super for us; he was superb in the Grand Final. He lives around the corner from me now and we catch up regularly. Everyone still calls him "Mr September"; he's very proud of that.

We used to have a good understanding with our rucks, such as how hard and where they would hit the ball. We were famous for our ruckmen hitting the ball forward and us midfielders running on to it. By doing that, the Lions were able to change the game. Sides started loading up defensively at stoppages, because we used to bang the ball forward so hard and then run on to it. On the back of that we saw sides start to employ sweepers on the defensive side more often. Clark was a big part of that tactic for us; he was such a competitor.

I remember the game pretty clearly. I just felt like I was in the zone, as they say. I was seeing the ball really clearly and, importantly, I was getting to where the ball was. The longer the game went on, the more I felt I was in tune with the game. It's a beautiful feeling, it really is. I was just so confident that day. It's hard to explain, but you feel so in tune with the game, and your movements are almost instinctive. Such an amazing feeling. Those days don't happen too often, so I wanted to make the most of it.

After the desperate finish in the 2002 Grand Final, we were able to enjoy the last quarter of 2003 a lot more. I remember at three-quarter time Leigh said, "It looks like we're going to win the game, guys. Make sure you enjoy it, but finish the game off really strong." And it *was* pure enjoyment. It felt like I was a kid in a candy shop! I remember having a laugh with my teammates in those dying minutes, that's how enjoyable it was for us.

SIMON BLACK

MEMORIES "Dad took me to the MCG to watch the Eagles play Geelong in the 1994 Grand Final. He took a photo of me down by the fence that day, when the reserves were playing before the seniors. He said, "It would be cool to play out there one day mate, wouldn't it?" I said, "Yeah, Dad, it would." Photo courtesy of Simon Black.

As a kid there was no way I could ever have imagined winning a Norm Smith Medal. Dad took me to the MCG to watch the Eagles play Geelong in the 1994 Grand Final. He took a photo of me down by the fence when the reserves were playing before the seniors. He said, "It would be cool to play out there one day, mate, wouldn't it?" I said, "Yeah, Dad, it would." He passed away three years ago, but he always used to remind me of that moment. After we won the 2003 Grand Final he reminded me of it again, so that was a really special memory. He was such a great mentor for me, and a great mate as well.

Patrick Keane from the AFL told me I had won the Norm Smith Medal. I knew I had played reasonably well, because you have a feel as a player for when you have performed well in games. To be honest, though, I was so caught up in winning the game that I didn't even consider they were about to announce a Norm Smith Medal winner. Then it clicked and, all of a sudden, my name was called out—so it happened really quickly before I had a chance for it to sink in. I was lucky to win a couple of individual awards, but when people ask me what's better, the individual awards or a Premiership, I always say the Premiership. The reason being, they are so hard to win together as a group, and you've experienced it with all your mates. It's not just one year you win a Premiership, you really need to build up to it as a group, over years, just to get there. You need to know each other well on and off the field, that's why it's so special when you win a Premiership together.

Every player wants to be known for playing well on the biggest stage. I certainly had finals and big games where I didn't play as well as I could have, but over the journey I'm reasonably proud with how I played in most finals. To be known as a Norm Smith medallist is great for what it represents, that you had played well on the big stage of a Grand Final.

After losing the 2004 Grand Final to Port Adelaide, we had a few guys who retired due to age or injury. I don't think we managed the list well during that period. Leigh has said since that we deliberately had a crack at winning four Premierships in a row. It would have been incredibly special if we had achieved it, and we almost did. You look at Hawthorn, Geelong and Sydney over the past 15 years, how they've been able to manage their lists and remain competitive, and we weren't able to do that. We made some poor decisions with who we brought to the club, which meant we lost draft picks in order to obtain those guys. So we shot ourselves in the foot as a club in the years after those Grand Finals.

I was lucky with injury that I was able to play more than 300 games. Being a smaller bloke helped, and I never ran fast enough to tear any muscles! You need to look after yourself, and I learned what professionalism was all about, such as recovering correctly after training sessions or games. Having to constantly manage my back issues meant I was probably more diligent than I may have been otherwise. But to get to 300 games you also need a truckload of luck, and I think I was very fortunate to have played for as long as I did.

I was always keen to do some kind of football academy after I retired. I was approached by some people in Brisbane, around combining an educational element to the football side and I really liked that idea.

Initially it was going to be with the upper end of the talent pool, but there were plenty of those types of programs tailored to those players. So with the Simon Black Academy we've taken the approach of developing kids off the field as well as on it. Most of our guys in our program are not elite footballers but they love football and it provides them with an opportunity to play matches of football at university level.

It's a rounded approach, rather than purely a football approach. We run leadership workshops, they learn about nutrition and goal-setting, giving them life skills as well as football opportunities. I've found that a really enjoyable experience because it's focused on trying to make a difference to people's lives. Some of our kids had never set a goal in their lives, so they now strive to implement plans to achieve something special in their lives. Having given my name to the academy, I decided to step away from assistant coaching with Brisbane in order to be present with what we are doing. It's been great fun.[3]

Statistics

BORN: 3 April 1979
GAMES PLAYED (1998-2013): 322
GOALS: 171
FINALS PLAYED: 20
FINALS GOALS: 9
GRAND FINALS: 4
PREMIERSHIPS: 2001, 2002, 2003
NORM SMITH MEDAL: 2003 (presented by Darrel Baldock)

— Norm Smith Voting —

(JUDGES: Gerard Healy, Bruce Eva, Mark Stevens, Robert DiPierdomenico and Dennis Cometti.)
TOTALS: Simon Black 15, Clark Keating 7, Jason Akermanis 6, Mal Michael 2.

---

[3] For more on the Simon Black Academy, see: www.australianrulesacademy.com.au/.

Byron Pickett

Across a decorated 11-year AFL career, Byron Pickett dished out hip-and-shoulder bumps with devastating effect, terrorising opponents with his cannonball attack on anything in his path. Pickett burst on to the AFL stage and was crowned the League's Rising Star in 1998. That year he was also a member of North Melbourne's losing Grand Final team. In 1999, the Kangaroos avenged that defeat with Pickett— who was also named All-Australian that season—one of his team's best players in the 35-point victory over Carlton. After six seasons at Arden Street, Pickett returned home to South Australia and was a part of Port Adelaide's first AFL Premiership side in 2004, when the Power famously halted the run of the Brisbane Lions (2001-03). He finished his career with two seasons at Melbourne, for an overall tally of 204 games and 177 goals between 1997 and 2007. In his Norm Smith Medal-winning performance for Port, Pickett had 19 kicks and one handball, took eight marks, had nine inside-50s from a game-high 11 running bounces, and kicked three goals.

I **was born in Kellerberin (200km east of Perth).** My three siblings—Rebecca, Olivia and Marcus—and I lived in a number of places when we were growing up, including Tammin. My mum, Christine, is from

← **TOUGH** There were none harder at the ball than Byron Pickett, a trait he showed from his earliest games. In 1998 Pickett won the AFL Rising Star award while at North Melbourne. In 2003 he switched to Port Adelaide, and was a significant performer in the club's breakthrough flag. Pickett is pictured (left) at the front, with (clockwise) Warren Tredrea, Damien Hardwick, Gavin Wanganeen (obscured), Peter Burgoyne, Josh Carr, and Chad Cornes.

Mount Magnet, so we were back and forth between places. My dad, Byron senior, is from a little place called Quairading. My parents are from different mobs: Dad is a Baladong-Noongar man, my mum a Budimia-Yamatji woman. The Noongars alone have produced many fine footballers over the years, including Graham 'Polly' Farmer, Barry Cable and Stephen Michael, plus two of my childhood heroes in Nicky Winmar and Peter Matera.

My father was my first hero. Dad played footy for Tammin and he also played in the Western Australian Aboriginal state team, plus he played in Port Lincoln for Mallee Park Football Club. Then, as I began watching the VFL, my heroes became guys like Winmar and Michael Long, but particularly Matera and Chris Lewis, as I was a West Coast Eagles supporter back then. Later I was fortunate to play alongside some truly great players, including Wayne Carey and Gavin Wanganeen.

I started playing footy in the under-10s at Port Lincoln. We moved back to Geraldton for a year, though, and I played with my cousins for the Towns Football Club in the under-12s. We moved around a lot due to our family being spread out across different areas. We'd spend some time with Mum's mob, then move down to stay with Dad's family, but once I started high school we stayed put in Port Lincoln.

I played all over the field in junior footy. I even rucked in the under-17s for Port Lincoln. As I grew older, though, I played more in the backline. When I used to watch Dad and my uncles play, they did all the physical stuff that I later became famous for. You could do that back in those days. I started doing those types of bumps and throwing my weight around once I reached under-17 level. I had good teachers who taught me how to perform bumps correctly; they didn't specifically teach me what to do, I just learned off watching them do it. I don't think it's the size that matters, it's all about the timing. It's a lot different bumping in today's game. You can still get away with the hard bumps, but they protect the head a lot more than they did when I was coming through the system. I always had confidence in my technique to not hit them high. I never elbowed someone in a dirty way, either; I'd always try to tuck my shoulder in when bumping. There might have been a couple of accidental ones, but none that were intentionally high or reckless.

I was a good trainer when it came to the skills side, not so much the running side, though. The fitness side wasn't a strength of my training, but it had to be done if I wanted to achieve what I wanted to achieve. I knew I had to put in the hard yards. But I never really dreamed I'd play in the AFL. I was playing under-19s at Port Adelaide and I just wanted to play senior footy in the SANFL. But that didn't actually happen until after I had been drafted by the Kangaroos, lived in Melbourne, then came back to Port in 2003. I injured my shoulder early in 2003 and had to play one SANFL game to get my touch back after a six-week layoff. That, finally, was my first senior SANFL game.

I never turned down an offer to play with Port Adelaide in their first AFL season in 1997. What happened was, I got approached by Essendon, then the Kangaroos, but Port never spoke to me before the 1996 National Draft. I just put my name into the draft to see what would happen, but wasn't seriously thinking I could play in the AFL. Suddenly, however, the opportunity came up with North and so I took it. Being in the draft, you went wherever you were drafted, so I didn't have any say about going interstate. Essendon had pick 66 and redrafted Paul Hills, then the Kangas took me with pick 67, but my belief was that Essendon had been really keen on drafting me, so I'm not sure why they didn't.

Denis Pagan was an old-fashioned coach. He told you how it was, straight down the line, which I believe is the best way to be. He was honest, which I liked. While it was difficult to adjust to the step-up in training, I was young, had a lot of energy and just wanted to perform and impress, so it didn't worry me too much. It was difficult, but you got used to it. When I arrived, the support I received from the club's leaders was first-class. Guys like Carey, Anthony Stevens, Glenn Archer, Mickey Martyn and Wayne Schwass were great from the first day I walked in the door.

At every club I played at, I built good relationships with the coaches and the players. That really helped me with my development. It made me feel a lot more comfortable knowing I had mates who I could talk to and who would support me. Coming from living in mostly small country towns, going to a city like Melbourne was daunting. But with a lot of support I soon learned how to deal with it. What also helped was having my parents move over to Melbourne for the first 18 months. Once they felt I was stable enough they went back to Port Lincoln, but would come over to Victoria for any big games such as finals and Grand Finals.

Every time I played footy I wasn't playing for myself. I was playing for my family and my country and where I come from. My elders. That's where I got my motivation every year. It was about my community.[1]

My first game was a night game, against Geelong (round 15, 1997). I played the last five minutes, at most, in the forward pocket. I think Denis just wanted to get me out there, to get me amongst it for the first time. It was a memorable experience, albeit a short one! Back then, the guys didn't want to go off the ground at all, whereas these days they're always running on and off the field. The reliance on rotations has changed a lot since I started in 1997.

My biggest memory of the 1998 Grand Final is of us kicking points. I was down in the backline watching the guys kicking point after point. Then Adelaide's Darren Jarman and Andrew McLeod did what they did and we couldn't stop them. When you're young you want to impress in big games like that, so I had been eager to get out there and impress my peers by playing well on the big stage and hopefully helping my team win. It was disappointing we couldn't do that.

It was awesome to be a part of a Premiership team in 1999 when we beat Carlton by 35 points. I had watched Grand Finals on TV, then played in a losing one, so to be out there playing in a winning one was surreal. I consider myself lucky to have been selected by the Kangaroos while they were in their prime as a team. To play in a Premiership alongside those great players was pretty special.

I wasn't satisfied, though. My opponent, Matthew Lappin, had kicked two goals. Sure, our backline did all right overall and I played some good patches; some even tell me I played pretty well that day. But as a defender you mark yourself on whether your opponent kicks goals on you, so two for 'Matty' was too many.

I never got too nervous before games. Players have their routines, which

---

1   Matt Zurbo, *Champions All: A History of AFL/VFL Football in the Players' Own Words*, Richmond: Echo Publishing, 2016, e-book version.

they try keeping the same from week to week. I know a couple of my teammates used to throw up before every game because they were so nervous. But I wasn't too bad. Once the ball was bounced and you had that first contest, it was game on, no matter whether it was round one or a Grand Final.

It took until about halfway through my career before I really started to grab the ball and run with it. Playing in defence, you tried not to do that too much, but I had become confident enough to take the game on by then. I liked to zone off in the backline, although clubs worked me out after a while and so Denis had to move me into the forward line where I utilised my tackling pressure to lock the ball in.

After 2002 I asked the Kangaroos if they would allow me to go home to Adelaide to be closer to my family. I had been at North for six years, won a Premiership and been an All-Australian (in 1999), so they were happy to let me come home. They felt I had done my bit for the club by then and had represented the club to the best of my abilities. It was a thrill for my family when they learned I was coming home. It was also a surprise for my friend at North, Stuart Cochrane, who was also traded to Port Adelaide. He didn't know who the other North player was that had been traded with him; we were good mates, so when he found out it was me it was a pleasant shock for him.

Mark 'Choco' Williams was a very similar coach to Denis Pagan. He would tell you how it was, straight down the line. We had a good relationship, Choco and I, as did all the other brother-boys in the team. We had the Burgoynes (Peter and Shaun), Gavin Wanganeen and Che Cockatoo-Collins, which was awesome. I used to spend a lot of time with Che and his twin brothers, David and Donald, when I was living in Melbourne. We would all go to barbecues at Mickey Long's house every couple of weeks. Jeff Farmer would be there, too.

Gavin was one of the greatest players I played footy with: he and Wayne Carey. I remember Gav's game against St Kilda in the 2004 Preliminary Final. I had a quiet game and he says he did, too, by his standards. But he kicked two very important late goals that night (Port won by six points). I still get goose bumps when I watch vision of him kicking his great goal from the boundary line. I was always in awe of playing alongside him. He's undoubtedly one of the greatest Aboriginal footballers to have played the game.

We went into the 2004 Grand Final really confident. We felt we had nothing to lose; we had no pressure, whereas Brisbane had all the pressure since they were going for their fourth straight Premiership. We took the approach that they had all the pressure on them, so in our minds we were the underdogs.

It was heartbreaking for Matthew Primus when he missed out on playing because of a knee injury. We all had a good relationship with 'Matty'. He was our captain, so we felt for him before and after that game. He had played such a big part in helping us to get there, so it was pretty emotional for the boys. But we all had happy tears at the end after we won.

My role was to win the ball and then run with it, using it well and trying to take them on every time I got it. I took advantage of that, knowing that my opponent and the other defenders would be worried about our tall forwards in (replacement captain) Warren Tredrea, Toby Thurstans and Brendon Lade. They were zoning off me to focus on them and since they weren't paying me any respect I took advantage of it whenever I got the chance. I had quite a few bounces that day and they came about because I had taken advantage of my opponent giving me too much space.

We were really aggressive early on. We took it up to Brisbane, who were renowned as a physical team. We wanted to match them in that area, which I think we were able to do for most of the day. That helped us to get into the game early and I think it surprised the Brisbane players just how physical we were.

I always liked kicking a goal, especially having played a lot of footy in the backline. Kicking goals inspires your teammates, too, so I loved it. I was able to kick three in that Grand Final, which was certainly a thrill.

Shaun and Gav kicked crucial goals late in the third quarter, which helped us to gain the momentum after an arm wrestle for most of the term. That had been a focus coming out after half-time—to start the second half how we had started the opening half, by being physical and attacking.

When Gav kicked his second goal of the last term—his fourth for the day—was when I started to think we were going to win the game. We ran away from them in the last quarter and won comfortably in the end (by 40 points). There are a lot of emotions running through you once you know you've won a Premiership. You're constantly looking at the scoreboard and the clock, counting down the minutes to the final siren. It was really special in that last quarter.

I didn't see Mark Williams do his choking action with his tie at the end of the game. I was on the bench at the end and he did that on the other side of the ground. It wasn't until I saw the highlights after the game that I knew he had done it. It's become almost as famous as the game itself!

It's special being part of any Premiership side. But to be a member of Port Adelaide's first in the AFL was extra special. And to be awarded the Norm Smith Medal was even more special. I had played under-19s at the club, played a game in the reserves and then been in their first AFL Premiership team, so I was pretty lucky. It's something I'll never forget and my grandkids will look back on, too, when they get older. It's something I'm sure they will be proud of.

I don't know what it was like for the other winners of the Norm Smith Medal, but I never went into the game thinking I could win the award. I had so many great players around me, with so much ability, so I didn't expect I'd be in the running to win it. Normally the majority of winners are midfielders and we had some really good midfielders that day, including Peter Burgoyne, Kane Cornes, Josh Carr and Roger James, plus Gav, so anyone could have won it. Just before they presented the Premiership medallions, an AFL official came up to me and told me that I'd won the Norm Smith. My reaction was, "Are you serious?" I didn't believe it at first. Then they called out my name. That was amazing.

Every game I played, I always tried to go out and give my all. That day was no different. I still tried sticking to my usual routine. I had a sandwich before the game and prepared how I always had. I got a massage and had a kick of the footy in the rooms. Back then, we didn't have any earphones like you see players wearing today. Most of the teams have music playing in the rooms now, but, certainly at North, Denis Pagan would never have allowed us to do that.

I didn't want to move back to Melbourne at the end of 2005. But my manager at the time was asking Port for too much money. I had left it to him to sort out my contract. I trusted him to get it done while I was back in my mother's country at Mount Magnet. I didn't want to move back to Melbourne again because the reason I left North for Port was to be closer to family and friends. Suddenly I hear I'm going back to Melbourne for another two years! I think he put too big a price on my head. Port didn't want to take his offer, then Melbourne said they would. If I had been in Adelaide when the deal was being done, I would have let Port make me an offer and I would have taken it because I was happy there. My manager stuffed that up. But, in saying that, I've certainly got no regrets about playing with the Demons. They were really good to me and my family. We even played finals in my first year there, so that was special to be a part of.

Today I work part-time with Port Adelaide and their Aboriginal programs. We go all over the country, doing visits to really remote communities. There are lots of hours spent travelling the dirt roads, but we love doing it, love seeing the kids' faces when we get there. They don't see many AFL players in their little communities, so it's great to go in and see them be so overjoyed that we are there. I'm enjoying imparting my knowledge and experience on to them. It's so rewarding inspiring them to want to achieve all that they can in their lives.

The programs the AFL do with the boys, the Indigenous camps, that's the sort of stuff that is really important. Aboriginal kids, most of them are so shy. They get the boys up in front of the group, yarnin', telling them where they're from. Then they do some leadership programs and stuff, which is good. It helps with their footy, and, y'know, their lives. When someone brings the Norm Smith up among my family and friends, I think about the blokes who won it before me and the blackfellas who won it, the Aboriginal blokes … It's something to tell my grandkids, when that happens. I'm still in awe a bit. One day it will sink in.[2]

My wife Rebecca and I have five kids: Mikayla, Shawanah, Lakeesha, Byron and Kayde. All the girls are netballers. Shawanah has won many medals for netball, while Lakeesha is going to be a really good netballer as she grows up. She plays in the Australian Indigenous Schoolgirls' netball team—they are called the 'Budgies'—and has represented South Australia in state carnivals, so she's going well in sport. The boys play footy for Port Districts. Byron won the under-12 best and fairest in 2017, while Kayde loves to tackle, just like his dad. He's a real team player. I tell him to pass it off when he thinks he should, but if he's ever in range of the goals then go for goal. That's what I did!

——— Statistics ———

BORN: 11 August 1977

GAMES PLAYED (1997-2007): 204

(120 North Melbourne 1997-2002; 55 Port Adelaide 2003-05; 29 Melbourne 2005-07)

GOALS: 177 (North 81; Port 80; Melbourne 16)

FINALS PLAYED: 20

FINALS GOALS: 14

GRAND FINALS: 3

PREMIERSHIPS: 1999, 2004

NORM SMITH MEDAL: 2004 (presented by Wayne Harmes)

— Norm Smith Voting —

(JUDGES: Clinton Grybas, Digby Beacham, Roger Vaughan, Bruce Abernethy and Michael Turner)

TOTALS: Byron Pickett 10, Gavin Wanganeen 7, Kane Cornes 6, Peter Burgoyne 5, Roger James 2.

NOTE: The AFL published the totals in 2004, but not the breakdown of votes by the judges.

---

2   Pickett, *Champions All.*

Chris Judd

Chris Judd was one of the most dynamic players in AFL history. Indeed, Judd's signature burst from congestion left many an opponent grasping in his wake during a stellar 279-game career. As a member of the dominant West Coast midfield, which included Ben Cousins, Chad Fletcher, Andrew Embley and Daniel Kerr, Judd won a Brownlow Medal in his third season (2004), claimed two best and fairests (2004, 2006) and was twice All-Australian (2004, 2006). He was one of the Eagles' key players in the 2005-06 Grand Finals against Sydney and, having replaced Cousins as captain at the start of '06, held the Cup aloft after West Coast's one-point victory over the Swans. At the end of 2007, after 134 games, Judd returned to Victoria and played a further 145 matches for Carlton. He captained the Blues, won a second Brownlow Medal (2010), was a three-time best and fairest winner (2008-10), and added another four All-Australian honours (2008-11) to his bursting resume. He retired in 2015 as one of the game's most decorated players. In winning the 2005 Norm Smith Medal, Judd became the fourth player to have done so in a losing side. That day he had 14 kicks, 15 handballs and, typically, a game-high 11 clearances in the Eagles' four-point loss to the Swans.

← **TRUE CHAMP** Chris Judd had everything required of a modern champion: speed, skill, courage, and durability. At West Coast, he won the Brownlow in just his third season, and the Norm Smith in his fourth, albeit in a losing team. He capped his career with a second Brownlow, with Carlton, in 2010.

It was always a really clear dream that, one day, I would play in an AFL Grand Final. I remember my dad telling me that Essendon's Tim Watson played VFL footy when he was 15 years old (and 305 days), so my dream was always to become the youngest Premiership player. As a five-year-old I was hoping that 13 would be a good age to achieve that. I only underachieved by 10 years!

My mum, Lisa, was a really good netball player, very competitive, but not at an elite level. And my dad, Andrew, was always interested in sport, but he wasn't as competitive as Mum was. He did some reasonable running at school level, but you wouldn't describe him as a great sportsman.

My parents were great, really easy-going. They couldn't have cared less whether I played sport or did music, just as long as I was engaged in something positive. So that meant there was never any pressure, inferred or otherwise, on me becoming successful in any particular vocation.

My older sister, Lauren, wasn't into competitive sport like I was. She participated in Little Athletics when she was young, but once she reached an age where she could make her own decisions, she wasn't interested in pursuing sport.

My heroes weren't set in stone. I was a Melbourne supporter, so Garry Lyon and Jim Stynes were the two Melbourne players I followed the closest. But I also liked watching Tony Lockett play—Dad was a Sydney supporter—as well as Paul Kelly. I also liked watching anyone whom I felt a small connection with, particularly if they had gone to my school or played at the same footy club as me. One was Rupert Betheras (Collingwood 1999-2003, 85 games), who had been at Caulfield Grammar. But I certainly didn't have any one player who was a God-like figure.

We used to go to the MCG quite a bit, my old man and I. We didn't just watch Melbourne; it was whoever happened to be playing on the day. But I had never attended a Grand Final before I was drafted. Since being drafted, however, I don't think I've missed one.

My competitiveness definitely came from Mum. But I also inherited some physical attributes from my old man, such as my height and my endurance capabilities. He's also technically skilful at sports, loves his tennis, so I picked up some useful things from him in that area. But the competitiveness definitely came from Mum.

Without sounding arrogant, I was always a naturally talented athlete. I never tried a sport that I wasn't good at. But I worked at that. In summer I would spend every spare minute hitting a tennis ball against a wall and hitting it back time and again with a bat. Then, in winter, I spent every waking minute with a football in my hand. I found that working hard and being good at something was mutually connected. I always found sport really interesting. I loved playing with people and loved to compete.

I didn't play much TAC Cup-level football. Over two years I played only four or five games with Sandringham Dragons, purely because I had so many injuries. I really enjoyed the pre-season training the TAC system offered though. At school, it was largely mandated that you had to play a summer sport and a winter sport, but by the time I was 16 I had lost some interest in playing cricket; I really wanted to focus on playing football and trying to pursue my AFL dream. It took some negotiating with the school before they allowed me to focus more on footy over cricket during the summer months.

Like a lot of elite footy players, I had an obsessive, compulsive side. So to be able to do something where I could train three nights a week, which could be full-on for a 16-17-year-old, really suited me. And although I didn't play a lot of football during those two seasons, completing those two big pre-seasons with Sandringham was something I really enjoyed.

I first popped my shoulder out when I was seven. At the time, I didn't really understand what had happened, other than that I'd hurt my shoulder. The next time I seriously injured it I was 16. That said, I never got overly attached to it. Some people, when something goes wrong in their lives, they become completely attached to it and it ends up defining a large part of their personality. I knew football was a contact sport and I'd been injured, as most people do who play a contact sport. That was just par for the course. Looking back I can see how it could have created bigger issues for me, but at the time it just felt like that was what happened when you played football and so I just got on with it. There probably should have been fears that it could affect my AFL opportunities, but there weren't because I had that positive mindset.

When I was getting to draft age, the AFL rules were that you could be drafted as a 17-year-old if your birthday was in the first half of the year. My birthday was in September, so I couldn't get drafted as a 17-year-old, but a lot of the players with whom I played junior football, or who had been in the AIS Academy programs with me, had already been drafted as 17-year-olds. That made me believe that I was ready to take the next step, because I was watching players I felt I was comparable to as a player, or even a better player than, and they were already playing AFL football. Like everyone I was nervous and was curious as to just how hard it would be to play in the AFL. But seeing those guys from my age group, those I knew intimately on a football field, being able to cope with it gave me a lot of confidence about what lay ahead.

I was ready to get stuck into it. Yes, I was a little apprehensive about moving to the other side of the country when the West Coast Eagles drafted me with their first selection (No. 3 overall) in the 2001 National Draft, simply because of my close network of family and friends in Melbourne. I was keen to spend more time with them now that school was over. But, aside from that, I was just eager to get stuck into it with the Eagles, work hard and try to prove myself.

I definitely have a connection with those other two guys from the so-called "Super Draft" of 2001, Luke Hodge and Luke Ball. I played footy with 'Bally' at the Dragons, and I had crossed paths with 'Hodgey' over the years, too. We were all managed by Paul Connors, so we had a connection through him. We're all aware of the journey we shared, and the similarities we experienced over our careers. But that connection is also felt with everyone who played in my era, as I'd say it is for most players of the different eras.

John Worsfold was a great coach for me. He was incredibly honest, someone I looked up to in terms of how he went about preparing the players. He has an elite ability to manage people, giving them the right amount of autonomy while also having high expectations on what he wanted us to do. I felt like he was a great fit for where our group was at. He was also a great fit for me, individually, and I was able to learn a lot from him, both as a player and as a person. That is the common characteristic of most really good coaches; they are able not only to teach people things to do within their chosen sport, they also can teach them things about life.

I didn't find adjusting to the AFL training standards difficult at all. I had an athletics background from school, and the middle-distance training I did for that was harder than the running required in the AFL. It certainly wasn't as constant as the AFL, though. That is one of the biggest challenges for a new player who hasn't done much running before he gets drafted; to suddenly be exposed to an AFL running program, twice a day, can be really difficult. But, for me, having that athletics background meant that the adjustment wasn't very difficult to make.

The first-year draftees back then were only doing about 60 per cent of the overall training load. I found that to be more frustrating, more challenging, than the actual body of work. I was always keen to do more.

I knew Daniel Kerr from junior footy. We toured Ireland together with the under-16 AIS/All-Australian Academy as 16-year-olds. So it was great to have him at the club when I arrived. I was very fortunate to also have someone like Ben Cousins to model my behaviours on. Ben was a professional in how he prepared to play. He put a lot of thought into his training and in a lot of ways was ahead of his time. He was also quite sophisticated in the types of training he did, plus the weight he wanted to perform at. It was an era when the Brisbane Lions were the dominant force, they were really heavy, big and powerful in their bodies, but Ben was very clear in that he wanted to be able to outrun those types of players. So, I certainly learned a lot from a player like him at the club during my formative years.

The striking thing with West Coast was, nobody trained to impress the coaches. They were training hard because they wanted to get better and contribute more to the team. I couldn't count the number of blokes who came back after eight weeks off and immediately ran personal best times, or did extra training sessions by themselves during the week. It didn't matter what was laid out in the program, the guys were going to train as hard as their bodies would allow them. That, again, is quite rare to have in a team environment. When you have that many players who are self-driven, you are bound to improve as a consequence, both individually and as a group.

Cohesion in football is an area that we are still developing in our understandings. When you train really hard for an extended period of time, sharing the sorts of experiences you do together on a football field in big games, that understanding you develop is very rare in any part of your life. You learn to understand what a person's thinking, even without them saying something. That's the sort of understanding that develops in really good sporting teams when they play together for a long time. You are really lucky if you get to experience that. It's hard to articulate, but you know when it's happening. To be able to understand what a player's going to do, almost at the same instant they are thinking it themselves, is a lot harder to build than I probably realised at the time. If you're an athlete and you get to share that with other people, it's really special.

I don't remember a lot from my first game. It was at the MCG, against Collingwood (round two, 2002), and having been there before as a supporter I was excited to be making my AFL debut there. I do remember wondering how hard it would be, how strong AFL players were, and how fit they were. I had a realisation, about halfway through the third quarter, that they weren't superhuman and that I was going to be able to play at that level.

I picked up the ball at one stage and Nathan Buckley—a player I had always looked up to—tackled me, bringing me to ground. I remember thinking that the force was no bigger than what I was expecting it to be. Most times that day I was able to stand up whenever I was tackled. So the more instances like that which happened, the greater my confidence grew (Judd had 15 kicks and four handballs). It was a close game. Brodie Holland kicked eight goals for the Magpies and we lost by a point.

Your first game is probably the only game in your career where the result doesn't matter. You're just so excited to be able to take that first step in achieving your dream that the result is superfluous to that moment.

I was able to rationalise where I stood, even before my first game. I had been training all pre-season with the West Coast players. I had been running with them and doing weights, so I was pretty clear on everyone's physical characteristics. I was able to say to myself— rationally—that I was ready to play AFL football. But until you're actually out there on the field you're not certain that you haven't missed something. By two or three quarters into my first game, I thought, "I'm fine here." But, that said, during my first season I knew I was only ever two or three games away from being dropped. That's what I was telling myself early on. I certainly didn't think after that first game, "okay, I'm good for 279 games now." But I did feel that if I kept working hard I was going to be able to have a good career.[1]

I was pretty nervous before games. I look back now and recognise that I was really highly strung, permanently, throughout my career. By nature, when you are an elite athlete, you need to be very focused in terms of what you eat and what you do. My whole life was incredibly structured and really focused on football first and foremost. My routine was similar from week to week, although I was always trying to work out new things I could do to help me improve. Leading into games I was always nervous about whether I was going to be able to play my role and also whether we were going to win the match.

My ability to break away from a stoppage was just good fortune. I didn't train for it. That was simply down to good genetics. I certainly focused on leg weights, which helped me to an extent, but essentially it was from my mum's athletic genes.

I always felt like I could feel what was happening within a game. I could feel how the movement patterns were decided, all by subconscious decisions rather than by consciously remembering specific rules or running patterns. It's hard to explain, but I found that, in those moments, the less thinking done the better.

Being tagged was challenging, but I really enjoyed it. It felt good to take on that responsibility. There was always one player who got tagged back then, so if you could win that battle it usually meant there were some other midfielders who were off the hook and hopefully doing significant damage for our team. When I was driving to games I made a point of hoping I would get tagged. If you were tagged in those days, it was usually

---

[1] This was the only season in 14 that Judd didn't score a Brownlow vote.

by the one person, unlike today where it is a rotating group of people. I really liked that competitive nature of being up against the one person all day, and of trying to get on top of them throughout the game.

There were a couple of times where it got the better of me, though. I whacked St Kilda's Steven Baker once, which wasn't one of my prouder moments. Plus there were a couple of other notable incidents in which my emotions took over. But I think that what I copped on the football field compared to what I dished out left me well and truly in the red.

I still have fond memories of the round 12, 2003 game against Brisbane. It was good fun! That game is spoken about most when people talk about my career, even today. It was my second year (34th game) and I had a bit of a cold on the day. Funnily enough, I often played my best football when I had a cold, almost as if I went in thinking the game would be even harder than it was in reality. I must have tried to compensate for that by forcing more out of myself. I had a day out, the ball bounced my way a few times and I kicked five goals. But what was most special about it was that we had beaten Brisbane, in Brisbane, and by 69 points. In my first year when we played there (round 20, 2002), we lost by 47 points. We were all bashed up by the bigger-bodied Brisbane players, then our flight was delayed on the way home and we were forced to stopover in Kalgoorlie. So my memories of playing Brisbane that first year were highly unpleasant. It was nice for our group to be able to win up there in 2003.

That win showed us we were on the right track. It did wonders for our mindset. A lot of clubs were trying to get bigger, in their belief that they needed to do so in order to compete with Brisbane. Whereas, our approach of running further, and quicker, than those bigger-bodied guys. had proven successful. It showed us that it could be a powerful weapon for us.

We lost three consecutive Elimination Finals, the third being to Sydney in 2004. We had a terrible start to that year, then won nine of our last 11 games. During that period we also implemented a new approach to taking the ball around the wing and creating space for each other. So it felt like it had been a year of significant growth, even though it was the third year in a row that we were bundled out of the finals in week one.

CHRIS JUDD

Most teams that have success can point to where it all started for them. Sometimes that can be one, two or even three years earlier. For West Coast, that second half of 2004 was when it really started to come together for us. Plus, when you are 21 years old, it's different from when you're 31 and you get bundled out in week one. At 21, when you look around and everyone else is of a similar age, you feel like you still have a lot of time to achieve success.

I never thought I would win a Brownlow Medal. I always thought of Brownlow medallists as being great players, and at that stage I was only in my third year and had turned 21 in September. Never in my wildest dreams did I compare my name to a Nathan Buckley or an Adam Goodes, a Michael Voss or a Mark Ricciuto. It was really strange to suddenly be in that company at that age. But I look back on it now as something to be particularly proud of.

By the time I won it again in 2010, I realised that everyone was just a person; they weren't superheroes. I was still particularly proud of winning, it was really special, but there wasn't that same level of discomfort that came with the first one where I didn't feel worthy of it.

Luke Ablett tagged me at the start of the 2005 Grand Final. He was a good player, good runner, nice and strong. But I was lucky in that I had Dean Cox tapping it down my throat right where I wanted it, and I also had an elite midfield to support me. The big challenge for us early on was when Daniel Kerr got injured in the opening quarter. That added an extra challenge to our midfield plans.

Sydney was really good at clogging the game up in close, and putting you under constant pressure. I remember that I was able to get my hands on the ball, but I couldn't get the same space that I had in the home and away season, the kind of space I was looking for in the Grand Final. That's what those Sydney teams were famous for, giving you something that you didn't want.

It's incredibly hot early on in a Grand Final. The pressure is on, it's loud, and there is just no time to execute your skills. But I remember thinking, "It's the same for everyone out here." It is such a huge build-up before a Grand Final, but everyone out there has had the same experience. We were all dealing with the same noise, all dealing with the same nerves and thoughts of what would happen if our team didn't win, so I kept harking back to the fact that I wouldn't be unaffected by those emotions. I just needed to be affected a little bit less than my opponents.

I had this funny analogy in my head that day. I used to skateboard as a kid, and often, if you were going to do a trick down a set of stairs, the first time you attempted it you didn't really try to land it. You just went through the motions, did a test run, then bailed out. Then, often, when you had a crack at it the first time around, you nailed it. So I remember being conscious of not wanting to treat the game as a test run, to be clear in mind that I wanted to stick it the first time. I had watched players in their first Grand Final where, like with their first game, they were waiting to review it and then realise too late that they could have done it on the day. So that's why I was really conscious of wanting to stick it at my first attempt.

We missed chances early. It felt like we played really poorly for the whole game yet almost won. Then, contrast that with the next year, where it felt like we were quite dominant yet we only just won. That was how closely those two teams were matched. We had our chances early in 2005, then chances late as well. I remember Drew Banfield hitting the post, and Drew played a great game for us. Plus a couple of other opportunities went missing. We had enough chances, but we couldn't nail them when it mattered.

It never felt like the game was slipping away from us. The thing about that Sydney team was, they were such a good team and they defended so well—they were always very hard to score against—but they didn't blow you off the field. That came back to their defensive mindset. So even though they were dominant in the second quarter, and we had only scored two goals by half-time, they hadn't put us to the sword on the scoreboard.

There was no one instance that turned things around in the third quarter. But it did feel like we were starting to come into the game, and that feeling continued in the first half of the last quarter. When Luke Ablett kicked across his defensive goal and Ben Cousins marked the ball and goaled for us, it was a big moment in the game. It felt like we were really coming then, felt like we were a good chance to run away with it.

But it wasn't to be.

I've never watched the replay. That game and the one the year after seem to mould into one. I do remember some poignant moments from the 2006 Grand Final, but what stands out from 2005 was how it was a really hard slog all day long. I certainly remember Leo Barry's match-saving mark, but aside from that I couldn't tell you much of what happened. I do recall other games, some of the unimportant ones if you like, but with Grand Finals there is so much stress involved, it's the culmination of so many people's dreams. Not just the players, but the fans too, plus the staff and coaches. There is so much riding on it and so, when it's done—particularly when you lose—part of the disappointment of losing, and it is perhaps your body's way of coping with it, is that it washes away your recall of specific moments.

The Norm Smith Medal was something I wasn't expecting. I wasn't even thinking about it, to be honest. I don't remember feeling embarrassed, but I did feel like I just wanted to get off the ground and move on. That was my overriding emotion.

My Norm Smith Medal was unique because it was won in a losing side. Without being flippant towards the award, it doesn't hold a huge place in my heart because it doesn't signify that we did what we were there to do that day, which was win the game. The Brownlow signifies recognition of a great season, and the Norm Smith recognises that you played a really good game in the Grand Final, but the reality is that we lost that day as a team.

When you play well in a losing Grand Final, you are just as disappointed as everyone else. But you don't feel the shame that comes when you are one of the people who lets the team down in a big game. So, in that sense, I got to avoid that feeling of shame for the next few months leading into round one of 2006. But winning a Norm Smith Medal wasn't what we were there to do on the day, so it was bittersweet.

I rate it a good game, personally, but not the best game I ever played. I don't know if it would be different had we have won. But it was a good game. I couldn't have worked any harder or prepared any better for it. It was just a good, solid game, without being an exceptional one.

THE NORM SMITH MEDAL

I don't spend a lot of time evaluating what any of my awards mean. It was good that I was able to contribute on the day, and was able to control my nerves, so I'm proud of that. There's not as much disappointment about losing that game now when I reflect on it, knowing that we won the year after. The two teams were really evenly matched, so winning one each feels like a fair outcome.

My performance in the 2006 Grand Final is skewed by the fact we won the game, that we did what we set out to achieve as a team. My memories of the day are pretty good, right up until I hurt my shoulder in the third quarter and didn't have any influence for the last 45 minutes. Until I got injured that game was probably better, personally, than in 2005, but I was ineffectual after the injury.

I had replaced Ben as captain that year, so I was given the honour of holding up the Premiership Cup. Ben had been such a special person and such a driving force of our football club. He was particularly important when we were young players just starting out. I had only been captain since the start of the season, under some pretty extenuating circumstances due to events off the field. It only felt right to have him up on stage with me when we received the Cup. John Worsfold discussed that idea with me beforehand and I thought it was a great idea. So I invited him up and it was great to share that moment with him on stage.

My decision to leave West Coast was essentially unrelated to football. All my family was in Melbourne; it was always going to be where I set up my life post-football. So, at 24 years of age, I felt it was a good time to move back home, while I could still make a contribution to another club. I also felt that if I stayed in Perth, it would become harder to leave later in my career. So that was why I left the Eagles. It was hard to leave, though, having gone through so much with that group of players. It was a big decision. But now I live around the corner from my folks, my family is settled in Melbourne, so it was the right decision for me.

I enjoyed my time at Carlton. We didn't achieve what I and others at the club set out to achieve, but I'm comfortable I couldn't have squeezed anything more out of my time there. Although we didn't achieve Premiership success, it was still great to play for a big Melbourne-based club, playing matches on the MCG in front of all the Carlton faithful. Some of those big games against Collingwood, Essendon, Hawthorn and Richmond are treasured memories from my time at the Blues.

When I look at my footy career now, I feel fortunate to have met so many great people. I formed some really good friendships that will last me forever. But it doesn't feel important anymore. I've got four kids now, so trying to keep them fed and healthy means that life moves on. But it feels special to be able to share what I did with so many great people.

Our oldest son, Oscar, is six, and our daughter, Billie, is three, plus we have 14-month-old twins, Tom and Darcy. It's still early days, and the statistics suggest they won't be elite sportspeople, but my wife Bec and I are happy to wait and see what they are interested in as they grow up. Oscar is playing Auskick now and he's enjoying it, so that's great. And Billie will start to get involved in more organised sport in the next year or so as well. Who knows what the future holds, but I'm looking forward to watching them grow and develop in their own unique ways.

——— Statistics ———

BORN: 8 September 1983
GAMES PLAYED (2002-2015): 279 (West Coast 2002-07, 134; Carlton 2008-15, 145)
GOALS: 228 (West Coast 138; Carlton 90)
FINALS PLAYED: 17
FINALS GOALS: 11
GRAND FINALS: 2
PREMIERSHIP: 2006
NORM SMITH MEDAL: 2005

— Norm Smith Voting —

Graeme Bond: 3 Amon Buchanan, 2 Chris Judd, 1 Lewis Roberts-Thomson;
David Reed: 3 Judd, 2 Brett Kirk, 1 Leo Barry;
Mark Robinson: 3 Judd, 2 Kirk, 1 David Wirrpanda;
Michelangelo Rucci: 3 Nic Fosdike, 2 Ben Cousins, 1 Judd;
Stephen Quartermain: 3 Fosdike, 2 Judd, 1 Buchanan.

TOTALS: Judd 11, Fosdike 6, Kirk 4, Buchanan 4, Cousins 2, Wirrpanda 1, L Barry 1, Roberts-Thomson 1.

Andrew Embley

West Coast's Andrew Embley was a member of one of the most talented and hardest-working midfields the game has seen. Dubbed the 'Fab Five', Embley, along with Brownlow medallists Ben Cousins and Chris Judd plus All-Australians Daniel Kerr and Dean Cox, were aerobic beasts who could run all day. Embley, whose father had migrated to Australia from Myanmar, played 250 games for the Eagles (1999-2013), was vice-captain (2004-06), represented the country in International Rules (2004), and was part of West Coast's 2006 Premiership team that defeated Sydney by one point. In a Norm Smith Medal-winning performance that day, he had 14 kicks, 12 handballs, took six marks and kicked two goals.

My dad, Maurice, was born in Myanmar to an Anglo-Burmese mother and an English-Burmese father. They migrated to Australia in 1964. He had obviously never seen an Australian football before then, but when he got here he was in his fourth year of schooling and playing footy was a way to integrate into Australian society, so he started playing footy at school. By all reports he ended up becoming a pretty solid player. He played with Peter Bosustow (Carlton 1981-83, 65 games including the 1981-82 Premierships),

← **VERSATILE** Andrew Embley was disappointed with his form in West Coast's loss in the 2005 Grand Final, but not so the following year, when he worked hard at both ends of the ground in the Eagles' thrilling win.

who later played with Carlton, and Peter has told me a few times that my old man was a really talented player. Dad ended up playing reserves football with Perth in the WAFL in the early 1970s, but in his first or second game he did his knee. They didn't have the medical treatment for injuries that they do today, so that injury ended his career.

Mum's family was a sporty family. My mum, Anne, was born in Ballarat in Victoria, part of a really big family, and they were all pretty sporty growing up apparently. Dad, being Burmese, is not the tallest man, but Mum had the height that myself and my brothers have.

I was obsessed with sport. My earliest footy memory is of playing in the backyard. Having spoken with Mum and Dad about it, they tell me I was obsessed with anything to do with a ball. I would always be playing cricket or football, kicking a soccer ball or shooting a basketball. My brothers and sister had toys in their cots, while I had balls in mine. I was the eldest of four, we had no iPads back then, no computer games either, so I spent my childhood in the backyard, playing sport outdoors.

I am the oldest of four siblings. My sister, Jacinta, didn't want to kick the football with me. My brothers, James and Michael, would play with me, but being younger than I was it never got too competitive. It was more about me kicking the ball to them and teaching them how to play, purely because of the age difference.

I was a Swan Districts supporter. I lived near Bassendean Oval, the home of the Swan Districts Football Club, so I used to go and watch them play all the time. I grew up a really big supporter of the club. We went to a few West Coast Eagles games, but we weren't members and didn't go every week as we did with Swan Districts. You couldn't run around and kick the footy as much at West Coast games, so that was another reason we loved going to watch the Swans play. My heroes were also probably more the Swan Districts players, because we watched them more regularly than the Eagles. Guys like Troy Ugle (West Coast 1988-93, 43 games), for example. But I certainly idolised all the West Coast players, too: John Worsfold, Glen Jakovich, Chris Mainwaring, Peter Matera, Dean Kemp and Drew Banfield. I loved watching all those guys.

We moved to Victoria in 1991. I was living in Robinvale that year, 90km south-east of Mildura, near the Murray River. There weren't many West Coast supporters at my school! I had to fly the flag for them there, so it was great to see them in the Grand Final for the first time in 1991. Mum had a couple of sisters married to farmers in Victoria, so my parents wanted to give us a different cultural experience by living in Victoria for a year. That was a great learning experience for me.

I went to the 1991 Grand Final. West Coast played Hawthorn out at Waverley Park. I would have seen Angry Anderson performing in the Batmobile, but my main memory of the day was West Coast losing and the disappointment of that. It was exciting that they were there, though. West Coast was basically Western Australia's representative in the AFL at the time, so of course we all barracked for West Coast.

I played in most positions as a kid. In my junior football career with Bassendean Football Club, I started in the under-9s and worked my way up the ranks. I was never left in the one position. Instead they threw the kids around a fair bit, so I played midfield, forward and down back at various times. Like anyone I just wanted to be around the football.

My running was something I had to work on, rather than coming naturally to me from a young age. I was reasonably fit as a kid, but it's not until you get into the AFL system that you realise it's something you need to keep improving on. I always felt that I was an okay runner, but I didn't work on it as hard as I should have in those early years. That meant that in my first three or four years at the Eagles I played mostly forward. It wasn't until I got a kick up my backside, and started working on my fitness so that I could play in the midfield, that I realised I wasn't working as hard as I could be. I certainly wasn't a natural runner like some of the other guys in the League. But, by the end of my career, my running ability was a real strength of mine.

It was pretty surreal walking into the West Coast Eagles Football Club for the first time. I had just come out of school footy, and was fortunate enough to be drafted to the Eagles in the 1998 National Draft. I would have gone anywhere to play in the AFL, though, and you mentally prepare yourself to go to Melbourne as that's where most of the teams are. I knew Fremantle was taking either Des Headland or Justin Longmuir with their pick No. 2. At that time, there was a rule in place where only one 17-year-old could go to any one club each year. So, being 17, I had a one in 16 chance of getting drafted.[1] Brisbane took Headland with pick one, Fremantle chose Longmuir, while other guys drafted that year included Mark McVeigh (pick nine, Essendon), Lenny Hayes (pick 11, St Kilda) and Brendan Fevola (pick 38, Carlton).[2] I ended up at West Coast at pick 57,[3] Mick Malthouse was my first coach, and just to be able to sit in the change rooms with all those guys who were my heroes during the 1990s was surreal; they were like superheroes to me.

I debuted in a derby. It was round one, 1999, against Fremantle. I had a good pre-season, and Mick came to me on the Thursday night before the first game and asked me if I was ready to play AFL football. It was an unreal moment; a dream come true. Being the derby, it was even bigger. There weren't the rotations like there are today, so I sat on the bench for most of the game, but just to be playing in the AFL was an amazing experience. Playing a derby was always big, as close to a final as you can get. The early intensity in each game was right up there. They were great games to be a part of, and there was always extra interest in Perth the week leading into the game. They were certainly always tough and hard encounters between the two clubs.

I didn't work hard enough early in my career. I got comfortable. I was enjoying the external things that come with playing in the AFL, rather than focusing primarily on making the most of my opportunity. It took me three or four years to understand what it takes to play at AFL level. The easy bit was to get drafted, the hardest bit is then making the most of the opportunity you have been given. You can have all the support around you, but I believe that it comes down to the individual actually committing and making it happen.

---

1 At the time there were 16 AFL clubs; the Gold Coast Suns and Greater Western Sydney Giants entered the competition in 2011 and 2012 respectively.
2 Other notable players taken in the 1998 National Draft included Jude Bolton (pick eight, Sydney), Adam Ramanauskas (pick 12, Essendon), Brett Burton (16, Adelaide), Nick Davis (father-son selection, 19 overall, Collingwood), David Wojcinski (24, Geelong), Steven Baker (27, St Kilda), Heath Scotland (44, Collingwood) and Shannon Motlop (85, North Melbourne).
3 The other players drafted by the Eagles that year were Brandon Hill (pick 10), Michael O'Brien (26), Scott Bennett (69), Joel Duckworth (89), while Scott Cummings (from Port Adelaide) and Chad Rintoul (Adelaide) arrived via trades. Laurie Bellotti and Chad Fletcher were elevated off the Rookie List.

ANDREW EMBLEY

You couldn't hide from the attention on being a footballer in Perth, but it was something you soon became used to, because you didn't know it any other way. We were scrutinised really heavily, and people would always be coming up to chat with you and have photos taken with you. But because I was used to that from the beginning, it was normal for us players. People in WA love their football, so having just the two AFL teams means there's a lot of focus on the players from those two clubs.

When John Worsfold became coach, he gave me an ultimatum to knuckle down. He was great about it, and gave me the chance to do the work, and that motivated me. When I finally showed the commitment he was asking of me, it became a huge stepping stone in my career. It was the end of the 2002 season, and I had come to a crossroads. John said, "Listen, if you want to be a part of this club you have got to show your teammates the commitment; show them that you truly want to help this team to get to a Grand Final and win one. If you're prepared to do that, and prepared to put the work in, then we'll keep you at the football club. If you can't, then we'll either delist you or help you get a trade somewhere else." I was scheduled to fly out to London on a football trip three days later, so I cancelled the trip. I got myself a personal trainer and I trained all the way through the off-season in 2002. Then I turned up to the start of pre-season in really good shape. I had a terrific pre-season, and suddenly went from playing in the forward pocket, kicking a goal a game and maybe having 10 touches, to playing through the midfield all throughout 2003 in what was a real breakout year for me.

There's no secret to success. You have to put the work in. Everyone who gets drafted to the AFL is really talented, but talent can be a scary word. You need to make the most of that talent to become a good player. If you don't, then your career can wind up finishing pretty quickly.

'Woosha' was a great leader as a player, and became a great leader as a coach. He put trust in you and really backed his players in. He allowed us to go out there and be ourselves, as long as we put the work in. He was like a father figure to me in the early days, and I ended up spending 12 of my 15 years at the Eagles under him, so he had an enormous influence over my career.

My running ability was definitely a strength of mine. Being able to cover the ground, plus push forward and kick goals, was a real attribute. What made me the player I was, was the ability to be able to work hard both ways, pushing back deep into defence when required, but also taking the game on, running and carrying and providing a goalkicking option. Every year we seemed to be doing more and more running, and it wasn't until the end of my career when the science of it started to become prevalent. Then we started to run a bit smarter as opposed to just running a few kilometres at a time for the sake of it. There was more method to the programs later in my career, and they became very individualised as well.

I got to play one game with my brother, Michael. He was at the club from 2004-06, which was great for our family. He was a raw kid, underdeveloped physically, was lanky with not much weight on him. But what held him back most was his terrible run with injuries. He broke his pelvis while playing with Swan Districts, which was a really bad injury. He did get to play one Wizard Cup pre-season game, against Collingwood in Darwin in 2005, so that was a great experience for our family. Ben Cousins had the week off, and Woosha asked me if I wanted to be captain. So I captained the team and Mick played his one and only game with the club. We had a good win, and Mick even kicked a goal, which was great. It was an experience that our whole family were really proud of.

We were blessed with a lot of talent in our team, but you need to make the most of that talent. It was really inspiring to watch Ben Cousins, Chris Judd and Daniel Kerr train. How they prepared themselves at training really set the example for guys like myself. We all recognised that, alone, we were never going to be a successful team. By watching those guys train, they set the benchmark for us all to aspire. They really dragged us along with them, and during that period we trained the hardest we ever had, and I dare say as hard, if not harder, than most other sides during that era. We all pushed each other, trying to regularly raise the bar in terms of what we could do, and that was certainly integral to our success as a team.

Ben was inspirational in the way he led the team. The way he would train, pushing himself to the limit with his fitness, was really inspiring. On game days he was the type of leader who spoke a lot to the group, motivating them that way. It was no surprise to us, seeing how he trained, that he was able to go out there on match day and perform as well as he did. He had a good relationship with all the players, and we all admired, respected and loved him. He was as big as it got over in Perth. He had the movie star looks, was the best player in the competition, and was idolised by everyone.

The West Coast-Sydney rivalry was extraordinary. It was two teams that had enormous belief in themselves. I think the Swans had a lot of characteristics that were similar to ours. You always knew when we came up against Sydney, regardless of the score during a game, it was going to be close at the end because both sides never gave up. The games were always so tight and tough, and both sides had an enormous amount of respect for each other. We matched up really well against each other, so they were great games to be a part of.

The 2005 Grand Final happened so quickly for us. We hadn't won a final as a group leading into the 2005 finals: we were knocked out in straight sets in 2002, 2003 and 2004, so we had a bit of pressure on us as a group. We had a good year in 2005, and before we knew it we were into a Grand Final. Sydney got away from us, then we fought back. At three-quarter time it felt like we were coming on strongly because we were all over them. But we couldn't get there in the end, and Leo Barry took that great mark right at the end which now gets shown all the time. It was really disappointing to fall short, because it's never a given that you are going to play in another one. We knew we had no right to think we were just going to get back there again the next year, so we felt that we had let a big opportunity slip by.

I didn't have a great game. I had a good third quarter when the game was on the line, but over the four quarters I wasn't as consistent as I would have liked to have been. That was disappointing on a personal level.

THE NORM SMITH MEDAL

We had to put that behind us and move on. Although the hurt of losing the Grand Final was an unspoken thing throughout the pre-season, we all knew that deep down we were hurting. But as a group we sought to put it behind us pretty quickly, and we did that by going hard at training. We were a hard training group, and we knew we had to do everything we possibly could to give ourselves another chance to get there again.

Chris Judd was another really good leader for us. I think he was reluctant, at first, to take on the captaincy after 'Cuz'. But he was certainly the best person for the job. He left a lot of the things like pre-game speeches to Cuz, which I thought was really good. He didn't try and take over from Ben as such, and in fact they worked in well together that year. Ben was more the ranter and raver, and would fire you up that way, whereas Juddy was more introverted, and was quieter in the way he motivated the group. It was more through the way he played that he led us during 2006-07, and the impact that he had on the group during that period was enormous.

It was a tough loss against Sydney in the 2006 first Qualifying Final. I didn't play, neither did Daniel Kerr or Ashley Hansen. I had hurt my shoulder against Fremantle in round 21, then missed round 22, and I was hoping we would win the Qualifying Final to earn an extra week off. I knew that I'd then be right to go for the Preliminary Final. But we lost by one point to Sydney, it became do or die, and so I had to play the next week. We came up against the Western Bulldogs, the only Victorian team to beat us in Perth that season, so I was really nervous going into that game. If we had gone out in straight sets then we would have really underachieved. But we came out and put the Dogs to the sword, we had a really good game as a team, and suddenly we were into another prelim.

My shoulder felt good once I returned. It was pretty banged up when I first injured it, but I had it strapped for the Bulldogs game and I was confident that I could get through the remainder of the finals series. I was already booked in for surgery at the end of the season, so I knew it would be getting fixed eventually. In hindsight, having those few weeks off with the injury was the best thing that could have happened to me. I spent the best part of three weeks not playing or doing any physical work at training, but I was able to do a lot of running and really topped up my fitness. So, when I returned, I felt like I was running on top of the ground.

I felt really confident heading into the 2006 Grand Final. We had a strong win over Adelaide in the prelim, the team was feeling good, and, having missed a few guys when we last played Sydney, we were all returning to strengthen the side. We had only lost by four points a year earlier, so I felt that the returning players could more than make up for that difference. We started the game really well, which is important in Grand Finals. That scoreboard pressure is everything early on, so we were off to a good start.

It took me a while to get into the game. I was sitting on the bench by halfway through the first quarter. I hadn't had a touch! I remember sitting there thinking, "It's the biggest day of my life and I haven't got involved yet. As soon as I get back on the ground, I'm going to go and impact the next contest." I went back on, attacked the pack, didn't get the football, but I had done what I told myself I was going to do, which was get in and get involved. It was a small moment, but for me it got me back into the game. From there I started to get my hands on the ball and was involved, and my game grew from there. I started covering the ground much better. I didn't have a match-up as such, and by the second quarter I started to get my share of the football. Sean Dempster came to me in the second quarter, but that was okay because I had the licence to get up the ground and run him around, which suited me. I decided to use my running ability to get up high, then push back towards our goals.

It was like the two Grand Finals were played in reverse. We felt we were coming home the stronger in 2005, while in 2006 we were hanging on for dear life in the last quarter. They had made a surge in the third quarter, and then Adam Goodes kicked a goal in the first 10 seconds of the last quarter. From there, it was game on. I had been told at three-quarter time to start on the wing, then drift into defence at the bounce and play

THE NORM SMITH MEDAL

a kick behind the ball. We knew that Dempster was going to stay close to me, so by me going down into defence it meant an extra pair of bodies in their forward line. That suited us, because their forward line had been quite open and they were looking pretty dangerous. I played most of the last quarter behind the football, and it was really tight and tough. The thought of winning and losing didn't enter your mind, because you were so focused on the next contest, then the next contest. The longer the quarter went, you were just waiting for that siren to sound, hoping that you were in front.

In the last quarter I touched the ball in the Ryan O'Keefe goal.[4] He snapped it around the corner, it went through Sean Dempster and my hands, and I definitely heard the noise of our fingers touching the ball as it went through our hands. But I need to have a chat with Sean about it one day to see whether he agrees with me or not.

I took a crucial mark late in the game. Sydney was coming. I had cleared the ball from defence, but it quickly came back in. I had eyes only for the football, wasn't thinking about anything else. Sometimes in defence you need to spoil, but I realised I was a good chance to mark the ball, so that's what I did. In those moments it's important to back your instincts.

You don't think that you're a chance to win the Norm Smith Medal. It's just pure relief in those moments after the final siren. We had played in two Grand Finals in a row, had the heartbreaking loss the year before, so you just wanted to celebrate winning with your teammates. It's a wonderful moment, and the thought of winning a Norm Smith Medal did not even enter my mind. Then suddenly my name was called up, and I'm walking up there thinking "what am I going to say?" About a month before, I was diagnosed with a paralysed vocal cord, so I had spent the whole finals series unable to talk properly. I had received a whack to the throat in round 20, against the Brisbane Lions. During Grand Final week my voice was the best it had been for a month. Until then I was forced to do a lot of clapping around stoppages to let

---

4   The Ryan O'Keefe goal came with 6.40 remaining on the clock. He gathered the ball in the right forward pocket at the city end, turned on to his favoured left foot and snapped a goal that brought Sydney within one point. Andrew Embley and Sean Dempster jostled for the ball in the goal square, just two metres from the goal umpire, yet the ball was immediately paid a goal, despite the Eagles defenders claiming the ball was touched.

my teammates know where I was; I couldn't yell out to them. So, when I spoke on the podium, my voice didn't sound very good, and I lost it completely a week or two later.

I'm extremely proud of being a Norm Smith medallist. Now whenever I get introduced anywhere it's: "Norm Smith medallist Andrew Embley." So it's certainly special in that sense. But, it's not something I think about too much day to day, to be honest. I received my Medal from another Western Australian in Billy Duckworth, the great Essendon player who won the Medal in 1984, and that was a special moment. The Duckworths are a well-known family in WA, so to get up and receive the Medal from him was a proud moment.

Did we underachieve as a team? It's a tough one. We had our shot at winning a couple of Grand Finals, then we went out in straight sets in 2007, so it was a small window when you look at it that way. Our time went quickly: Cuz got hurt in 2007, and there were other off-field issues regarding him before that; Juddy was on one leg by the end as well, so things weren't happening for us at the end of 2007. Grand Finals are not easy to win, they're not even easy to make it into. Sure, it would have been nice to win another one, but at the same time we're really grateful to have won one.

Despite the history, our Premiership reunion in 2016 was a great occasion. Ben, unfortunately, couldn't make it due to his health issues, but everyone else was there. A lot of us regularly catch up, but there are some we don't see that often. So it was a really good weekend to get together and reflect on what we achieved as a team. We had a lot of good times together, and we remain a really tight group, so it was the perfect weekend to celebrate what we worked so hard to achieve.

Some say that our 2006 Premiership is tainted. But I don't read too much into the argument that there is a black line through that season. You only had to come and watch the way we prepared and trained ourselves through that era to know that we deserved to win that Grand Final as much as anyone. It was a lot of hard work, and took a lot of dedication just to get to a Grand Final, let alone to win one. We're really proud of what we achieved in 2006, and nobody will be able to take that away from us.

I never dreamed that I would have the career that I had. You've got dreams to play AFL; then you get drafted and you hope to play one game; then when you play one game you get a taste for it and you want it more and more. I've been very fortunate to have spent 15 years at West Coast; they became a family to me. I'm a life member there, and I can walk into that football club whenever I want. When I reflect on my career, those are the things I'm most proud of.

—— Statistics ——

BORN: 27 June 1981
GAMES PLAYED (1999-2013): 250
GOALS: 216
FINALS PLAYED: 15
FINALS GOALS: 15
GRAND FINALS: 2
PREMIERSHIP: 2006
NORM SMITH MEDAL: 2006 (presented by Bill Duckworth)

ANDREW EMBLEY

— Norm Smith Voting —

Mike Sheahan: 3 Andrew Embley, 2 Tadhg Kennelly, 1 Beau Waters;
Mark Maclure: 3 Daniel Kerr, 2 Brett Kirk, 1 Dean Cox;
Ray Wilson: 3 Cox, 2 Kirk, 1 Embley;
Jenny McAsey: 3 Embley, 2 Kirk, 1 Cox;
Rohan Connolly: 3 Embley, 2 Kirk, 1 Cox.

TOTALS: Embley 10, Kirk 8, Cox 6, Kerr 3.

Steve Johnson

Geelong and Greater Western Sydney's Steve Johnson was the type of player who caused headaches for opposition coaches. He was unpredictable, able to use both sides of his body, seemed to see the game one step ahead of his opponents, and had the knack for scoring a freakish goal when his team needed one. Conversely, Johnson could also drive his own coaches bonkers trying to do too much rather than playing it safe. Add it all together and you had one of the game's most watchable stars. It was why, in Geelong's all-conquering 2007 Premiership side that defeated Port Adelaide by a record 119 points, 'Stevie J' was awarded the Norm Smith Medal. Johnson (who also won Premierships in 2009 and 2011), had 18 kicks, five handballs, nine marks, and kicked 4.2—the first Norm Smith medallist to kick four goals since Shannon Grant in 1999.

I'm not too sure where my sporting genes came from. My parents weren't standout sportspeople, as far as I know. My uncles on my mum's side played some under-19 football at Geelong, but my old man, Terry, was hit by a car when he was 19 and that finished his sporting career. He tells me he wasn't a bad footballer, though, before the accident. Dad is pretty good at lawn bowls and billiards, so maybe that's where I get my concentration from.

← **SOMETHING SPECIAL** Steve Johnson had more tricks than any player in the modern era. His legacies are twin: having fun on the field, and bequeathing the round-the-corner set shot to the next generation.

THE NORM SMITH MEDAL

I grew up barracking for Collingwood. My idol was Peter Daicos. When I first started playing footy I was one of the smaller guys, and I usually played in teams with my older brother, David. Playing two or three years above my age group meant that I needed to be smart about how I found the footy. I had to be that sneaky player on the outside, who roved the ball off the pack. That's what Daicos did, so I loved watching how he went about his work. Then, when he retired, my idol became Nathan Buckley because he was by far the best player at Collingwood at the time.

I can see how there are similarities in the way Daicos played and how I played. In his day he was clearly the best in the AFL at the snapshot kicks for goal, and the banana kicks and all those different tricky attempts on goal; I have no doubt that I tried to emulate him, and that carried through to AFL level. I would kick the footy at school during lunch time, then I'd kick it after school, and I trained at Wangaratta Football Club as much as I could as well, so I was always working on different ways to win the ball and score goals. The junior coaches I had were never big on you playing an individual style of game, but they did put a big emphasis on us all enjoying our footy and trying to get the best out of our teammates. They never pushed for individuals to be match winners, which I think was great for my development and for teaching me to have faith in my teammates and to not worry solely about my own game.

The motivation for me to improve came from within. I was so determined to play in the AFL. I'm a very competitive person, so I was always wanting to be the best at what I did, and it is that competitiveness that got me so far in my career. Having an older brother helped in fast-tracking me as a junior player, because I was always determined to beat him and his mates in the backyard. I think that is important, having brothers or peers to drive you on. Look at the Selwood brothers—Adam, Troy, Joel and Scott—who, I have no doubt, pushed each other in the backyard to be the best that they could be. They have all gone on to achieve great things at AFL level as a consequence.

There's a myth that I was a natural left-footer as a kid, but that isn't true. I'm not sure where that came from. I was good on both sides of my body, because I listened to all my coaches growing up who all told us to be good on both sides. Funnily enough, my coaches at AFL level liked us to go on to our preferred foot, which for me was my right, as much as possible. But I see it as an advantage to be equally adept at kicking the ball with either foot, and I'm glad that I worked on those skills as a kid because it gave me more options during a game. I always had a footy in my hands, and was always keen to learn more and more about the game.

I would have gone anywhere to play AFL footy. But when I was selected by Geelong I was as happy as I could possibly be, because Geelong is just like a big country town. I could walk along the streets in Geelong and I knew everyone, as I did in Wangaratta. They didn't necessarily stop and talk to me just about footy, and it was a pretty relaxed environment. There were golf courses close by, and the beach wasn't far away, so I always had other things that I could get away and do that weren't footy related.

The players became part of the furniture in Geelong. People down there were so used to seeing me that it wasn't a surprise when they bumped into me in the street. I was just 'Steve' to everyone there, not 'Stevie J' as the media referred to me.

Since 2006, Geelong has led the way, on and off the field. Before that we were just a middle-of-the-road team who didn't know our potential. Then we introduced a new leadership program, and our senior players really drove the improvement of the group. As a young player at the time I had no other choice but to follow along by watching and learning off them. Our standards were raised enormously from then on. When I became a senior player, that was something I then tried to carry through to the next generation of players coming in, both at Geelong and later at the Greater Western Sydney Giants.

The well-publicised internal review at the end of 2006 set us up for sustained success. Coach Mark 'Bomber' Thompson didn't change a lot after the review though. The way he taught us to play footy, collectively and as individuals, was brilliant. That, and the way he went about structuring training. Bomber was already recognised as being a pretty good tactician on match days. What *did* change was the buy-in of the players to what Mark and the club were trying to do.

THE NORM SMITH MEDAL

What was noticeable entering 2007 was that Bomber was desperate for us to improve. We didn't start the season too well, but his messages never changed. He told us that we were going to play really attacking footy; when the opposition had the ball, we were to put a lot of pressure on them. He wanted us to play risk-taking football, but in the first five games the results weren't coming. He told us that if we continued to do what he was asking of us we would see the results. He said that when we did get better at it, no one would be able to stop us. And that's exactly how it turned out.

The turning point for us came in round six, at Etihad Stadium against Richmond. The game went as perfectly as you could get and our attack was flawless, so we got a lot of confidence out of that. It was a build-up of what we had been training for over a long time, and as Bomber had predicted, once we found that belief there was no stopping us.

Once we found our confidence, it was an amazing run to the Grand Final. The biggest factor was that everybody in that team knew they each had a role to play; they didn't have to be best player on the ground for us to be successful. We had a tough game in the Preliminary Final against Collingwood (Geelong won by five points), which could have gone either way. I would much rather play and win a tough Preliminary Final than have a really easy win, because it prepares you more in a physical and mental sense for the next week.

In a Grand Final, you are full of nervous energy. You want to play well as an individual, because it's the big stage and so many people will be watching. But you also need to remind yourself that the reason you got there in the first place was because you had been a part of the best *team* throughout that year. Bomber reiterated the fact that each player needed to play his role in order for us to win.

Things went as perfectly that day as they possibly could in a Grand Final. Early on, ruckman Brad Ottens had a chase-down tackle—which was a miracle in itself!—and it showed us that we were all extremely committed to winning. By half-time we were able to really enjoy that game. While the club hadn't won a Premiership since 1963, the playing group didn't feel those scars of past defeats because most of us were too young when that all happened. We felt the pressure to perform because we felt that we were the best team. You don't need external motivation to help you win Grand Finals, that motivation needs to come from within.

I kicked a couple of goals early in the game, and from there I just had fun all day. I was playing on a half-forward flank, and the ball was moving down the ground so swiftly, and so often, that I would have hated to have been a Port Adelaide defender that day. Every single guy in our team contributed, and the Norm Smith Medal could have gone to any number of players. Although I was awarded the Medal, I was just so relieved to finally get a Premiership.

Every player would like to say that they performed well on the big stage of a Grand Final, and I am certainly no different in that regard. But until you get there, you just don't know how you're going to handle it. The more big games you can play in, the more comfortable that you get in that environment. You learn to embrace the energy that comes from big games in front of big crowds. You worry less leading into those games when you know that you have done the preparation. If you can perform your role then the outcome is generally going to be good for you, and hopefully your team.

I had a lot of belief in my own ability. I knew that if I could get my fitness to an acceptable level, I could play some good footy. I was drafted with Jimmy Bartel, Gary Ablett and James Kelly, and we all drove each other to improve from the word go, which fast-tracked us. We were thrown into senior footy from a young age, which was a plan of Bomber's to get games into his young players. We were all confident players, but we didn't know then how to get the best out of ourselves. But by Bomber showing faith in us, and with the competitiveness of us young blokes, it was just a matter of time before we knew we could be a good team. Then when you do start winning you just want to win more and more, so there becomes a new motivation of craving success and craving that feeling of being part of a winning team. And that never stopped driving me to be the best that I could be.

I made a few well-publicised mistakes early in my career. The hardest thing for me during that time was trying to manage injuries at the same time that I was trying to improve my fitness and my overall game. I was labelled inconsistent during that period, but I always felt that the inconsistency came from me not being able to put regular sessions together on the training track. I was playing a game then missing a week of training because of injury, then playing a couple of games, and it was a vicious cycle that I couldn't seem to break out of. I had no continuity.

I also knew that I needed to make some changes off the field in regards to my behaviour. Those standards were set for me by the likes of captain Tom Harley, his replacement Cameron Ling, as well as Cameron Mooney. Although they were very direct with me about where I was going wrong, I knew that what they were telling me was not because they didn't like me, it was because they all wanted me to get better as a person. Their feedback was the key reason for me turning things around, on and off the field. I was forced to take a good, hard look at myself at the end of 2006, and I began to prepare myself the best that I possibly could. I also learned how to look after my body better, and how to recover correctly between matches.

Gary Ablett and I were like two bulls, always trying to one-up each other. Gary is as competitive as any footballer I have ever known. When he was at Geelong we used to bet on a fly going up the wall, that's how competitive we were against each other! In between training sessions, we would go out and play 'footy golf'. We would set up challenging holes, such as a par three where there was a bin in the property steward's room and we would have to kick the ball into the bin from our change rooms. Silly little competitions like that helped us to improve our bond with each other, but also improve our footy. We were always putting ourselves under pressure to try and do things, and it held me in good stead for being able to do things under pressure in big games.

Once we tasted Premiership success we were hungry and driven to win more. But in the 2008 Grand Final things didn't go our way. Hawthorn took their chances and that's what it takes to win Grand Finals. You have to be the best team on the day and, unfortunately, we weren't.

I don't think the disappointment of losing that game will ever leave me. It was very hard to cop, and I used to hate turning on the TV and seeing footage of Hawthorn celebrating up on the podium. It stung us all, and it made us so motivated to get back there again.

It was a gutsy performance to win again in 2009, although I had a pretty poor game myself. I not only battled a hip injury going into the game, I also battled Steven Baker who tried some dodgy tactics on me in order to stop me going near the ball. He was hard to play against, because he was such a good tagger. I had gone in injured; at the time I thought I was close to 90 per cent, but looking back it was probably the wrong decision to play. Although Baker took the points against me, we won the Grand Final, so I was happy.

When I inured my knee in the 2011 Preliminary Final, I thought I would miss the Grand Final. The pain was excruciating, and I could see my kneecap sitting a couple of inches away from centre. By the end of the week I could still hardly walk, so the doctor put three injections in my knee, and immediately I felt the happiest I had ever felt. I passed the fitness test, but once the injection wore off the knee felt really sore again. I woke up Grand Final morning still not knowing if I was playing.

Of my three Premierships, that one is the most enjoyable and rewarding, because I thought I had lost the opportunity to play in it. The fact that it was against Collingwood, who I had supported as a kid, made it all the more enjoyable. It was also rewarding to win our third flag because, given the success we had over a five-year period, I felt that we deserved a third Premiership.

I love footy so much that I can't see my passion for the game ever leaving me. I intend staying involved in footy long after I finish playing. There are lots of players from that Geelong side who could become very good coaches, because they have all learned off guys like Mark Thompson and Chris Scott, not to mention some of the great assistants we had at the club.

I tried imparting my knowledge on to the GWS players. The team lacked experience in the forward line. They had recruited Heath Shaw (from Collingwood) and Joel Patfull (Brisbane Lions) for the backline, and Ryan Griffin (Western Bulldogs) and Shane Mumford (Sydney and Geelong) in the midfield, but the forward line was still relatively young. Imparting some of my knowledge was something I really enjoyed. And the fact that the players seemed to enjoy having me around was also a good feeling.

They were all extremely competitive, which I loved. I took a backwards step from my earlier days, though. At Geelong I used to have bets with anybody that I could do something better than they could. But around the GWS guys, and as I was a bit older, I tamed it down. Jeremy Cameron is unbelievably talented, and as competitive as I was. He can do everything. He'd walk past with a soccer ball and drill it in a net from 50 metres away. He's good at cricket, too. Even fishing he takes seriously. I went out with him a few times and he was always wanting to catch the next fish. Gary Ablett and I were like that at Geelong.

Statistics

BORN: 4 July 1983
GAMES PLAYED (2002-17): 293 (253 Geelong, 2002-15; 40 GWS, 2016-17)
GOALS: 516 (452 Geelong, 64 GWS)
FINALS PLAYED: 26
FINALS GOALS: 44
GRAND FINALS: 4
PREMIERSHIPS: 2007, 2009, 2011
NORM SMITH MEDAL: 2007 (presented by David Rhys-Jones)

STEVE JOHNSON

— Norm Smith Voting —

Danny Frawley: 3 Steve Johnson, 2 Matthew Scarlett, 1 Paul Chapman;
Steve Butler: 3 Johnson, 2 Chapman, 1 Scarlett;
Josh Francou: 3 Chapman, 2 Johnson, 1 Scarlett;
Jake Niall: 3 Chapman, 2 Johnson, 1 Scarlett;
Daryl Timms: 3 Johnson, 2 Scarlett, 1 Chapman.

TOTALS: Johnson 13, Chapman 10, Scarlett 7.

Luke Hodge

When Luke Hodge departed Hawthorn for Brisbane after the 2017 season he joked that, if not for the Hawks and coach Alastair Clarkson, he may have been no more than a garbage collector in his hometown, Colac. When Hawthorn selected Hodge with pick No.1 in the 2001 'Super Draft', he was a chubby, knockabout country teenager who carried enormous expectations. Although it took him a few seasons to adapt to the rigours of the AFL, when he finally dedicated himself, Hodge became one of the most admired leaders in the game's history. They called him 'The General', and his 'quarterback' role in the Hawthorn defence was critical to the club's four Premierships between 2008 and 2015. Hodge played 305 games for the Hawks (2002-17), won two Peter Crimmins Medals (2005 and 2010), and captained the club from 2011-16, through the triple Premiership run from 2013-15. Hodge was a man for the big moments, and two Norm Smith Medals are evidence of his greatness. Against Geelong in the 2008 Grand Final, he had 20 kicks, six handballs, took nine marks and kicked one goal in Hawthorn's 26-point upset. In the 63-point victory over Sydney in 2014, Hodge had 21 kicks, 14 handballs, took 12 marks and kicked two goals.

← **BORN WINNER** Luke Hodge was the number one pick in the 2001 'Super Draft', and twice he was the number one choice of the judges of the Norm Smith Medal. He also captained the Hawks to its three-peat of 2013-15, and is considered one of the game's all-time great leaders.

THE NORM SMITH MEDAL

When I was young my dad, Bryson, was always the umpire or the trainer at the local footy club, and he also played cricket there. Mum, Leanne, played netball at the club, so from a young age all I can remember is hanging around the club. There was training during the week, running the water for the juniors and seniors on weekends, and I would run the boundary as well; it was second nature. Whatever I did as a kid revolved around sport; whether footy, basketball, you name it, I was always at the oval around the corner from home.

There's something special about growing up in a country town. It's a community where all your friends are in the same school or sporting team, they live just a bike ride away, and so you are never stuck inside playing video games. My parents always kicked my sister Bianca and me (Dylan was born 12 years after Luke) outside and said, "Off you go! Make sure you're back for dinner."

When Dad started playing footy, he was always taught to kick on both sides. Me being a left-footer, and as most left-footers are predominantly left and don't like to change it up, Dad wanted me to kick with my right. Whenever he'd get home from work I'd want him to go to the oval and have a kick. He would give me competitions where my next 10 kicks had to be on my right foot. I'd crack the shits and wouldn't want to do it, but, over time, as you become better at it, you recognise that he was doing it for the right reasons. At the time I just thought he was being mean. That said, I was never blessed with pace, so I wasn't quick enough to run away from an opponent and get onto my favoured left foot very often. That's why I clearly needed to use my right foot.

I was in grade eight when my parents separated. If I had been a little older it might have affected me more. I know Bianca took on more of the responsibility when it happened, because she was in year 11 and doing her VCE. I coped with it by taking any opportunity I had to be out playing sport, whether umpiring basketball, playing basketball, footy—anything!—my outlet was sport. I found, after the separation, I had more freedom to do more of that and so I focused my energies on my sport rather than sitting at home and worrying about the situation.

LUKE HODGE

I was a Richmond supporter. In 1995, round four, Richmond played North Melbourne at the MCG. The Kangaroos had Wayne Carey and they were the strongest team during the 1990s, whereas Richmond was just coming up with a younger team after having not played finals since 1982. The traffic coming in that Monday night was terrible, so it was a long haul down from Colac. When we finally parked and walked in, the Tigers were already about eight goals to one in front, and they went on to win comfortably by 49 points. No one expected them to beat North that night, there was a big crowd in (62,606), and when they were singing the Tigers' theme song at the end—which is a pretty catchy song— I really fell in love with it. I had always loved football, but that night the thought of one day playing at the 'G in front of a big crowd really hit me. I thought, "How good would this be?"

I was a 17-year-old kid when I was selected with the No. 1 pick in the 2001 AFL Draft. When all you've ever wanted to do is play football, I couldn't pack my bags fast enough and move to Melbourne! But it is a big change when you've lived in the country; it's not all bells and whistles at the start. You realise training's a lot harder than what you were used to, and I had a few injuries early. I was forced to miss friends' birthdays back home, particularly 18th parties, which you really want to go to. So I missed my mates, and I missed Colac. But, saying that, I had a lot of friends and people back home who said, "Your mates would give up anything to be in your situation, so even if you miss a few birthdays here and there, you will still catch up with them." I had some good advice from lots of people, but I certainly missed friends and family back home in those early years. I wouldn't trade it for anything, though, it's been great.

My first coach, Peter Schwab, realised that there was a lot of pressure on me early on. I struggled with osteitis pubis early in my career, and I had stress fractures in both feet, so I had a limited training base. I was still coming to terms with what I needed to do to play in the AFL. Chris Judd (the No. 3 selection at the 2001 draft) had an impact straight away; he was top three in West Coast's best and fairest in his first year, won the Brownlow Medal in his third year, and captained the Eagles to a Premiership in his fifth year—it was quite the start to his career!

THE NORM SMITH MEDAL

I was only under Schwabby for the first three years. During my second and third years particularly he helped me to focus on what I could do to become a better player, rather than worry about the external stuff. He would say to me, "How's your body going? How's your training? How's your recovery?" He was basically teaching me that I would get out of my career whatever I put into it, and to not worry about what other people were doing.

It was challenging. Your mates are everything to you when you're a kid, and, yes, you form new mates at your footy club, but the mates I grew up with and went to school with, they were like a relief to me. I knew I could go back home to them because they were only two hours down the road. Fortunately, the scrutiny on high draft picks wasn't as full-on as it is today. We've now got radio stations and TV stations that run 24/7 coverage of footy, plus all the talk shows. But I felt the pressure all the same. I came from a small town of 13,000 people, and next thing there are people reviewing and analysing every little thing you do. It was more pressure than I was expecting, and I concede I didn't handle it that well.

A country footy club is a bit different to the city clubs. When I was 12, I played under-17s, and at 15 I started playing seniors, so I grew up playing footy with older people. I was always taught, from being around older people, that if you see something on the field or the training track, you've got to say something—don't hold on to it just because you're a younger player. That gave me confidence from a young age that if I saw something in a game, I would yell out and try to instruct the people around me on what it was I was seeing. I didn't recognise that as showing leadership qualities; I just saw that as how you were meant to play football.

It was not as if I ever thought, "I want to be the best leader that I can be." I just went out there and played football how I knew to play the game. What I was taught through Alastair Clarkson, Sam Mitchell, Richie Vandenberg and Shane Crawford was that the best way to play football is to try and teach the other guys where to go. I never have a focus to go out there and be the best leader; I go out there to be the best player I can be and to help the guys around me as well as I can. And that's happened more as I've got older. When I was younger, like all kids, you just want to go and play football and try getting a kick. It's not until you get more experienced that you put the team on a higher priority.

When 'Clarko' arrived as coach at the end of 2004, everyone thought, "What's *he* doing here?" But, right from the start he was all about making everyone think about the team first. We had a talented list, but he wanted to make sure the players were thinking more about their teammates than themselves. By taking us to Kokoda in that first pre-season, and everything else he did around that time, it was about trying to get everyone thinking about others more than yourself. As a young kid, you are always taught to think about yourself. When you're playing football, you're thinking about trying to get drafted, so the focus is on what *you* can do. But Clarko had seen it all: he'd played with North Melbourne (1987-95, 93 games) and Melbourne (1996-97, 41), and had coached at Werribee (VFL, 2000) and in Adelaide (Central Districts 2001-02, including the 2001 SANFL Premiership; Port Adelaide midfield coach in the club's 2004 AFL Premiership year). He was determined to educate us towards playing as one team and being the best group of players that we could possibly be.

Because I had been injured and had osteitis pubis when I was drafted, I had never done a full pre-season before Clarko arrived. Before then I only started training towards the end of pre-season. So his was the first pre-season I did, and I was like a kid in a candy shop—I was ready to go, ready to get fit, and that helped me handle that first pre-season under him. It was the first full year I felt comfortable, and I was able to go into the midfield and have an impact, all due to having that first full pre-season under my belt.

There was no wariness when Trent Croad returned from Fremantle in 2004. The decision to trade him out of Hawthorn in order to gain the No.1 draft selection in 2001 had nothing to do with me personally. From day one when he came back, he was fine. He said to me that he went away for a couple of years to make the club a better place. When he came back we became great mates and were able to play in a Premiership together in 2008. The club benefited greatly by him going to Fremantle; we were able to not only recruit me, but Sam Mitchell, too.

THE NORM SMITH MEDAL

What developed in our backline at Hawthorn was similar to what we are creating at Brisbane now. We had a group of guys who were able to play a lot of footy together. Croady came back, then I started playing mid/half-back around that time as well. We also had Brent Guerra and Grant Birchall. We were lucky that we very rarely got injured during those years—not until Croady hurt his foot in the 2008 Grand Final—so it allowed us to develop a consistency and understanding within our defence. Rick Ladson was also part of that. By playing together over a number of years, we developed a great understanding and trust.

We knew we had some good kids coming into the club, such as Lance 'Buddy' Franklin, Jordan Lewis and Jarryd Roughead, but you didn't know how far everyone would develop. We were all still learning. I was only 20 when Clarko was appointed coach, and we had a number of similar-aged guys coming through, such as Brad Sewell and Sam Mitchell. We were just young kids who loved playing footy. As we played and trained more together, we began to understand each other's games, and that allowed us to have the success we had in 2008.

The older you get, and you aren't playing finals, you start to think of how much you want to be a part of it. Early in my career, it wasn't as difficult when we missed out. In truth, I looked forward to my holidays at season's end, because I missed seeing my friends throughout the year. But by 2006, when we won the last four games of the season (for a total of nine wins and an 11th-place finish), then the next year we won our first final and lost the second one, it was starting to get a bit frustrating. Luke Ball (St Kilda's No. 2 selection in the 2001 draft) had played in finals with the Saints, Juddy had won the flag in 2006 and played in the losing Grand Final in 2005. But when I looked at the group we had, I felt confident we would get our chance for finals success at some stage.

We played some good footy in 2007, although we lost the last game and fell from fourth to fifth. In the first Elimination Final we played Adelaide, who were a pretty experienced team, and they jumped us. But we kept sticking at it. When you've got a big fella down forward in Buddy who was just emerging as a player—he kicked seven goals that day including the winning goal inside the last minute. It was an amazing feeling to win that game by three points. We had the high of that win and were still on cloud nine that next week, and we came up against North, who had been cleaned up by Geelong (106 points) in their first final. North went into the game with a better mindset than we did, and was hungrier and more determined than we were and towelled us up (33 points). What it taught us was, whether you win or lose you need to remain consistent from week to week; you can't be too high after a win or too low after a loss.

Clarko moved me to defence in 2008. I was pretty keen to stay in the midfield, where I had been since the middle of 2005. I was playing some really good footy through there, so I thought the best thing for our team was having me in the midfield with 'Mitch', 'Sewelly' and 'Lewy'. I was still young then, so I didn't know whether me going to defence was the best thing for us or not. But Clarko sat me down and explained that I might not get as much of the ball, but I could have just as much impact on a game playing across half-back. I was to provide more rebound for us from half-back, which he felt would fit the team better. When he explained it to me that way and said that he felt this was the way we could have success, I was pretty determined to give it a crack. I think it worked quite well for us.

The issue Hawthorn had with Mitch and I both being nominated for captain at the end of 2007 was that the footy club had only ever had the one captain at any one time. Our president, Jeff Kennett, is a pretty powerful man, and he wasn't taking no for an answer. As soon as we walked into the room after he told us to sort it out, I think we all knew that Mitch was better suited to the role. I was 23 going on 20, and Mitch was 25 going on 30, so he was what we needed at that time. Joel Smith had left, Richie (Vandenberg) had retired, Ben Dixon retired as well, so we were left with a very young list. We all felt that Mitch was the right person because of how professional he was. He had been knocked back early on and had to do everything he possibly could to get drafted, so he was better prepared for the captaincy than I was.

Mitch's strength was in how he understood the game, and how he explained the game to his teammates. How he got the message across was second to none. The way he trained was exemplary; he was a durable player, very competitive, and that was the type of captain we needed at that stage. Mitch always said to me, though, "When your time's right, when you're ready to lead the team, I'll be happy to step aside and let you lead. Whether that's two years, four years, five years, we'll wait and see." We won the flag under him in '08 and he had another couple of years as captain, then we spoke about it after 2010 and the decision was made then for me to take over.

From 23 to 26, people develop differently, physically and professionally. By the end of 2010, I was married to Lauren and we had a little boy, Cooper. I knew how to treat my body right and knew what recovery I had to do each week. Mitch had a baby by then, too, and was expecting twins, so it wasn't only perfect timing for me, it was perfect for him and his family as well.

In the 2008 second Preliminary Final against St Kilda, I went across to the outer wing to spoil and Justin Koschitzke kneed me in the ribs. At quarter-time I spat out some blood and the cameras captured it, which made it a bigger deal than it was. The doctor assessed it early in the week, but he felt that with a low-key preparation I would be fine to play in the Grand Final.

There are different forms of courage. There's courage to do the right thing in the pressured situations—blokes can try being heroes when they don't need to be, and we've all been through that. Then there's courage to put your head over the ball or go back with the flight. There's also courage to screw your guts up when you are absolutely buggered and to give that little bit extra when you think you've got nothing left. Plus, there's the courage to speak up. So, in football, there are five or six different versions of courage that you can use to describe different acts in our game.

There are certainly times I've been scared on a footy field. Whenever you get a ball kicked over your head and you're going back with the flight, you don't know what's coming at you—that's always tough. One time, I heard Jonathan Brown's voice telling me that if I stayed in front of him he was going to put his knee through my spine—that's pretty scary! But when you are playing footy with your teammates, if you expect your teammates to do something then you need to be willing to do it as well, whether that's to give off an easy handball and then sprint 100 metres to cover a bloke because your team will get a goal, or to go back with the flight, you're going to have to do those actions yourself before you can expect your teammates to do the same. We had a group at Hawthorn who were willing to do just that. I think of Mitch's performance in the 2013 Grand Final against Fremantle. He just sat there in the hit zone and got peppered from pillar to post for the entire game, yet he was prepared to take the hits in order to help his teammates.

Mathew Stokes started hitting me in the ribs before the 2008 Grand Final. I thought, "If I start hitting him and fighting back, the Geelong players will realise I have something wrong and they will all start targeting me." So I made the decision—I was wearing a guard around my ribs—that I would let them have a crack at me, and if it hurt I'd try my best to pretend that it didn't, so as to not show weakness. I put my arms up as if to say, "Have a crack, there's nothing wrong with me!" Cam Mooney ran through me a little bit later, and I knew I had to do the same thing—I couldn't show weakness, so I couldn't grimace or have a go back at him. I didn't want to give them that mental edge. It must have worked, because they didn't target me after that.

It doesn't matter whether it's your first game, your last game, or a Grand Final, if you can get your hands on the ball early it helps you to relax. That then takes the pressure off and allows you to just play football. I was able to get a couple of touches early in that Grand Final, which got me into the game.

Clarko drew a picture of a shark on the whiteboard before the game and asked us, "What does this symbolise?" We were all sitting there with dumb looks on our faces thinking, "Where's he going with this?" because coaches have a history of making a point but it not sinking in. His analogy was, "What happens to a shark if it can't go through the water?" and one of the boys piped up and said, "It drowns. If a shark gets stopped, it dies." He said, "Spot on! That's Geelong. Geelong want to get the ball through centre half-forward and run in numbers. So our job, in order to kill Geelong, is to get as many numbers in front of them as possible, push them back, and don't let them get their ball movement going. If we can do that, if we can hold their run, that's the key to us winning this game." He was saying that the way to kill Geelong was the same way you kill a shark: halt their momentum, slow them down, deny them what enables them to survive. I think were able to do that for most of the game.

Whenever you played against that Geelong team, you were always wary that they could take the game away from you if it was played on their terms. Throughout 2008 they were clearly the best team. But in the last five games I reckon we were the best team. Our closest game during those last five was the Grand Final. You are always on edge when you play against a quality team like they were, especially on Grand Final day when they are getting shots on goal and they have players like Gary Ablett, Cameron Ling, Tom Harley and their dangerous forward line— plus a young Joel Selwood. However, there were a few instances where we thought the pressure was starting to get to them. Little things like Brad Ottens not squaring the ball up to two Geelong teammates in better positions, and Cam Mooney missing a couple of easy goals. We realised that our pressure was starting to affect them late in the second quarter. But, that said, we knew they weren't going to roll over; they were going to come hard at us in that second half. We had a patch of about 10 minutes in the third term where we were able to apply some significant scoreboard pressure, and that turned the game our way.

Stuart Dew's third quarter burst was the most important five minutes of my entire footy career. Yet I didn't actually do anything other than sit back and watch! He was moved to the forward pocket because he was buggered and needed a rest as we already had two injuries on the bench (Croad and Clinton Young) and didn't have the rotations. So for him to have three or four major efforts to produce those two goals for us showed how valuable an astute footy brain is to a team. Having played in Port Adelaide's 2004 Premiership, he was calm and knew what to do when he had the ball. His five-minute burst definitely set the game up for us.

I knew how easy and how fast Geelong could score, so although in the final minutes you knew they weren't likely to come back, I was still unprepared to leave them any chances. I remember Crawf running past saying, "Just relax, mate," but I said to him, "Bullshit! It's not over yet."

When that siren went it was just a massive relief. I concede I was probably still too on edge in those last moments, despite the margin, but it was because I was so determined to ensure we got the desired result.

Winning the Norm Smith Medal was the last thing on my mind. It was more the thrill of being part of a team that no one thought could beat Geelong. Winning an individual award wasn't on my radar at all, and it wasn't after the game, either. It was all about celebrating with my teammates for what we'd achieved.

I never aspired to win the Norm Smith Medal. When I watched Grand Finals as a kid, it was because it was the biggest day on the footy calendar and I was admiring the fact they were playing in front of 100,000 people. The older I've become, the more aware of history I am and the more aware I am of the Norm Smith winners, but it wasn't a significant award I was thinking about when I first started playing.

What I learned from repeated failures between 2009 and 2012 is that you can't just rest after winning and expect that it will continue to happen. We were a young team that was expected to play finals for a lot of years and to play in more Grand Finals. And I think, due to our ages, we expected that as well. But in the AFL, if you don't try to stay ahead of the game it's going to bite you on the backside. In 2009 we had a lot of injuries; I think we had about 16 operations after the Grand Final. But that said, the attitude and the hunger wasn't there as it had been in 2008 after we had been kicked out of the 2007 finals by North; nor how it was in 2013 after we lost the 2012 Grand Final to Sydney.

There was always excitement the night before a game, but I always got a decent sleep. I tried not to think much about the game; all that had been done in the week leading up to the game. After the final team meeting the day before the game, I would spend a lot of time playing with my kids. When I woke up on game day, I wouldn't turn the TV on or read the newspaper because it was all about the Grand Final. I would just go out for a light run, have a kick and a bit of a jog around, just trying to stay fresh as I would for any other game. Lauren was good at picking up whenever I was a little edgy. I always thought I was okay, but she may beg to differ! She was really good before Grand Finals and would take the kids for a walk to the park for that hour before we had to leave home. We had a good understanding of what we both needed to do. Then, once we were in the car—and the 2013 Grand Final is a good example—we had a rather different pre-game routine from some of my teammates. My old teammate, Daniel Elstone, came with us to the game and on the way in we were playing *The Wiggles* on the stereo. He said, "What the hell are you doing listening to *The Wiggles* as your pump-up song going in?" But that was just what we always did when driving in to a Grand Final or any big game. To keep the kids quiet in the car, you put *The Wiggles* on! That became our routine, because while it was my time once we got to the ground, during the lead-up it was all about keeping the kids happy.

Playing across half-back against Freo, I just had to do my role. I had an impact early, but then was able to sit back and watch 'Gunners' (Jack Gunston, four goals) and 'Lakey' (Brian Lake, Norm Smith Medal winner) do their jobs. We built an early lead and just had to maintain it. I thought I played a solid game but nothing special. Like my teammates that day, we just did what we had to do to help the side win.

By 2013 it was getting to the stage where we were being touted as 'chokers'. We had lost the 2011 Preliminary Final to Collingwood (three points) after leading late in the game, then the 2012 Grand Final to Sydney (10 points) when we had been expected to win. So winning in 2013 was a relief to finally get a positive result on Grand Final day—it had been a long break since 2008!

It was challenging for us when Clarko first got sick with Guillain–Barré syndrome in 2014. I had seen him walking from his office and he almost tripped over, so I started laughing and hanging shit on him. But he said, "No, mate, it's not funny, I can't feel my feet." That was the first sign something was wrong. Then, against Port Adelaide in round 10, he was running down the steps from the coach's box and he was worried about tripping over because he couldn't feel his feet again. We soon learned how serious it was when he was put into hospital. What we did while he was away (rounds 11-16) was what he had told us to do previously: if you lose someone on the football field you just have to replace him with someone else. We did that all through 2014. We lost Mitch to a hamstring, 'Gibbo' (Josh Gibson) to a pectoral injury, Cyril and Lakey were injured, too, yet we were able to replace them with other players. So when Clarko went down we took it as (assistant coach) Brendon Bolton coming in to do his role for the team. I think everyone stood up, not just me as captain. 'Bolts' and the assistant coaches stood up in their roles, and we as players did what we had to do to help out as well. We made sure that everything tightened up a little bit, because Clarko usually oversaw everything, so we didn't want our standards to slip in his absence.

The 2014 Grand Final against the Swans was about revenge for 2012. That was our mindset. Being my 250th game, it was a personal highlight to be able to run out on to the ground with my kids, Cooper and Chase, and to be able to celebrate that moment with my family. The thing with football is, it's a passionate and emotional game, and we still had a lot of players in the side who had lost to the Swans in 2012. Clarko pulled on our heart strings, our emotional side, in the build-up to the game saying, "What these guys did to us you will never forget, so make sure you get them back." The other thing was that Buddy had played on our side in 2013, but now he was at Sydney and was trying to take the Premiership away from us, so that was another motivation we took in.

It was a physical opening. We had a strong, hardened group by then, and when you add passion and emotion to the mix you get a result like we produced in the opening half (11 goals to five). Someone said to me afterwards, "I can't believe how you targeted Dan Hannebery?" But I said, "We weren't targeting Hannebery, it was purely the fact that he was in the road of a few of our guys when we were trying to achieve what we wanted to achieve." I think Roughy got him, Luke Breust got him and David Hale did, too—all in the first quarter! But he was certainly not targeted. Our approach was to take ball and body, and he was just in the unfortunate position on three occasions of being on the end of it.

In the second quarter Sydney defender Gary Rohan kicked the ball in after a behind, I cut it off and kicked a telling goal. But that only came about due to a play by my teammate, Paul Puopolo. We had a play on the left-hand side of the oval that resulted in a point, then they had a release kick-in to the outside pocket. 'Poppy' sprinted 50 metres to cut off that exit; he shut that one down and so Rohan went to kick it to the bloke that Poppy had just left alone. I was then able to read and intercept and hurt them on the scoreboard. After the game, what we showed wasn't the mark and goal, it was the effort that Poppy did to set it up for us. That was the mindset we took into all three of those Grand Finals: you play your role to help your teammate and the success will follow.

I don't know what I was thinking when I gave Buddy a kiss in the third quarter. When we played them in round 18, I ran into him and corked him pretty well—not on purpose, though. After the game I spoke with him and he said: "You flushed me, but next time we play you I'll get you back!" He got me a couple of times early in the Grand Final, all clean, nothing untoward. But then we came together in the third quarter, and neither of us was going to do anything stupid, so I pecked him on the cheek and he had a bit of a grin and we moved on. I didn't realise, though, that all the cameras were on us at that stage!

I was able to enjoy the last quarter much more than I had in 2008. We were all a bit older and recognised that Sydney couldn't come back from so far down by midway through the last quarter. It was relief like the year before, as well as excitement for, one, what we'd been through having lost in 2012, and, two, having won back-to-back flags. And we had stopped Buddy from taking one off us! It was a rewarding day for all those reasons.

Being so focused on what we were doing, I didn't even think about who would win the Norm Smith Medal. Someone from the AFL came up and said, "Don't swear, thank your sponsors, be polite," and I assumed he was talking about my captaincy speech. I said to him, "Yeah, I've got it all in my notes, mate," not realising what he was talking about. So when my name was read out, it was a shock, but also a huge honour to be recognised again. You look at the stats from that game and Mitch had high numbers (33 disposals), Lewis (37) and Gibbo (32) too, and Roughy kicked five goals. When you beat a great team like Sydney by 63 points, you can throw a blanket over eight or 10 blokes who could have taken the Medal. I was more satisfied in what we had achieved by going back-to-back to be worried about the Norm Smith.

It had been a big build-up. Jason Dunstall had sent a video to Clarko pre-game just saying how the achievement, if we could win back-to-back, would be even greater than the 1988-89 teams that were the first Hawthorn sides to do so. There are now 18 clubs (compared to 14 in 1989) and, with equalisation, you're not supposed to win multiple Premierships. So we were rapt to have achieved the feat that day. That was most important to me after the game.

It's wonderful to have won two Norm Smith Medals, but I'm most proud of being one of only a handful of blokes to have won four Premiership Medals. In 2018 we have our reunion for the team that won the 2008 flag; you don't have reunions for the Norm Smith Medals. Premierships are why you play football. Yes, it's a huge honour in receiving the Norm Smith twice, and it's something I'll be proud of when I finish playing, but the reunions are why you play footy, because it signifies that you had some success with a bunch of blokes along the way.

Resilience was something that Clarko had spoken about for years. We had demonstrated that resilience throughout 2014 with everything that happened that season. So with everything that occurred in 2015, Clarko kept reminding us of the resilience we had shown in the past. He said how we didn't shy away from anything we were confronted with as a group, and that was how we approached everything that happened in '15. With Roughy's cancer scare, assistant coach Brett Ratten tragically losing his son, plus other obstacles we were faced with, there was the possibility for it to derail our season on a number of occasions. What helped was having so many of the guys having played together for so long; we knew each other's strengths and weaknesses.

We lost to West Coast (32 points) in the second Qualifying Final, in Perth, and everyone wrote us off. It was a remarkable achievement to convincingly beat Adelaide in the second Semi-Final (74 points), then go back over to Perth and win again. People hate playing over there once, but to go there twice in three weeks and beat Freo in the first Preliminary Final (27 points) was pretty special. When we came home after winning that we were supremely confident we could beat the Eagles in the Grand Final. They were playing with the "West Coast web", but we believed that, because of the width of the MCG as opposed to Subiaco, we could pick our way through it easier. Once again, as we did in 2014, it was our intensity both in defence and offence that set us up for a pretty relaxed and enjoyable last 20 minutes of the Grand Final.

Because of my team-first attitude, my second-quarter goal from the boundary line was intended to be kicked to the top of the goal square. That's what I told people afterwards... but it's a blatant lie! In all seriousness, though, if I had kicked it to the top of the square and West Coast made a big spoil towards the other side of the ground, we would have had no chance of defending it and they could have taken it the length of the field. So I did the team-first thing and either tried to rush a point or kick a goal. What happened was, we had switched the ball around the outside, then gave it to Poppy, and when I picked it up I had a clear view of the goals. I knew there was a pretty strong wind going from right to left, so I thought if I sat it out there the breeze might bring it back. Some things just go your way. If I did it another nine times I'd miss it every time, but fortunately that time was at a key moment in a Grand Final, so I was pretty happy about that.

The AFL wants every club to win a Premiership once every 18 years. So for our Hawthorn group to achieve what we did, playing in four consecutive Grand Finals and winning the last three was extremely satisfying. I'm certainly looking forward to celebrating that whenever we have reunions in the future, and for the rest of our lives.

My family and I have really enjoyed the move to Brisbane. As far as any coaching aspirations in the future, I'll see what eventuates over the next 18 months while I'm still playing. When I moved up here, I wanted to get to know the players and become a trusted and reliable teammate before anything else. I wanted to understand how they play as a team, and how I could help them to get better. Over the next 18 months coach Chris Fagan will give me more and more responsibility as far as tapes and coaching tasks go, in order to help me develop personally on the coaching side of things.

How do I want to be remembered as a player? I had a tape shown to me when I left Hawthorn, and a lot of teammates said on the tape that I was a pretty selfless captain who did a lot of things out on the field for the benefit of my team, whether by putting my body on the line, or just what

I did to make sure my team always came first. I've spoken with the blokes up here in Brisbane, and they say that when they played against me they thought I was a jerk for what I did against them! I guess if it made my teammates better and was the best thing for my footy club, then I did my role. Being a team-first player and a selfless teammate is how I want to be remembered when I finish up.

—— Statistics ——

BORN: 15 June 1984

GAMES PLAYED (2002-current): 316 (Hawthorn 305, Brisbane 11)[1]

GOALS: 193

FINALS PLAYED: 23

FINALS GOALS: 19

GRAND FINALS: 5

PREMIERSHIPS: 2008, 2013, 2014, 2015

NORM SMITH MEDALS: 2008 (presented by Tony Shaw) and 2014 (presented by Glenn Archer)

— Norm Smith Voting —

2008: Leigh Matthews: 3 Luke Hodge, 2 Joel Selwood, 1 Stuart Dew;
Gilbert McAdam: 3 Brad Sewell, 2 Gary Ablett, 1 Hodge;
Mark Williams: 3 Hodge, 2 Ablett, 1 Sewell;
Luke Darcy: 3 Ablett, 2 Hodge, 1 Sewell;
Brian Taylor: 3 Hodge, 2 Ablett, 1 Shane Crawford;
Emma Quayle: 3 Hodge, 2 Ablett, 1 Sewell.
TOTALS: Hodge 15, Ablett 11, Sewell 5, Selwood 2, Dew 1, Crawford 1.

2014: Nathan Buckley: 3 Jordan Lewis, 2 Sam Mitchell, 1 Josh Gibson;
Chris Johnson: 3 Hodge, 2 Mitchell, 1 Will Langford;
Cameron Ling: 3 Hodge, 2 Lewis, 1 Mitchell;
Anthony Hudson: 3 Mitchell, 2 Hodge, 1 Lewis;
Craig O'Donoghue: 3 Lewis, 2 Hodge, 1 Mitchell.
TOTALS: Hodge 10, Lewis 9, Mitchell 9, Langford 1, Gibson 1.

---

1 Statistics correct to round 13, 2018 season.

Paul Chapman

Geelong's Paul Chapman was a man for the big moments. Versatile, cunning and as tough as teak, Chapman always seemed to make a defining play whenever his side needed it—such as in the final minutes of the 2009 Grand Final, when he kicked the go-ahead goal to help secure the Cats their second Premiership in three years. He was a key factor in Geelong's emergence as a football powerhouse in the early 2000s alongside fellow Norm Smith medallists Steve Johnson and Jimmy Bartel, and played in all three of the club's winning Grand Finals (2007, 2009 and 2011). He also won a 'Carji' Greeves Medal (2006) as Geelong's best and fairest, was twice All-Australian (2009-10) and played for Victoria (2008). Although he finished his career at Essendon (2014-15), Chapman will always be remembered fondly by the Geelong faithful; a warrior among a cavalcade of champions.

Born on 5 November 1981, Paul was the youngest of four children (Brett, Karen and Glenn) to Barry and Paula Chapman. "To me we were a normal family," Chapman wrote in *Chappy*. "I think people look at where you come from (Fawkner, in Melbourne's northern suburbs) and like to label you—well-off, not well-off, middle class, that

← **HARD NUT** Paul Chapman was the go-to man whenever Geelong needed a special moment. In the 2009 Grand Final his goal late in the game sealed the win for the Cats.

sort of thing. I never thought like that so didn't consider myself one way or another."[1]

He "hated football as a kid", he says, and whenever it was on television at home "wouldn't want to watch it."[2] That changed, however, when he turned six and was asked to play alongside Glenn in the North Fawkner under-9s. "I played under-9s for a few years. Then by the time I reached age nine, I was also playing under-11s," he explained. "Undoubtedly, playing against older boys helped me."[3] When Chapman turned 12 he played for North Coburg, where he remained until he joined the Calder Cannons. The Chapmans were a sports-loving family, and Paul participated in an array of sports:

> I was also into athletics and made it to state level, finishing fourth in the 100m when I was 13. I made it to state for discus, too. I would sometimes do athletics and then fill in for Glenn's tennis team or play cricket in the afternoons. Sport was my life and I couldn't be stopped. We were all sports-oriented. Brett trained with Carlton under-19s and Karen was a great high-jumper. Glenn played footy but decided to pursue umpiring.[4]

Paula Chapman remembered that Paul was "the sort of kid who was good at most things." One Christmas he sat at his sister-in-law's piano and began playing. He had received no lessons yet managed to finger a tune. "That was Paul," Paula said. "If he put his mind to it, he could do it."[5]

The Chapman household was rocked on 12 October, 1998, when Glenn was killed in a car accident. "I remember going to school and hearing that someone had been killed in an accident," Chapman recounted:

> I got to school and it was just a normal day until lunch when my name was announced over the PA ... Nobody told me what was going on, except that I had to wait by the front gate for Mum ... She was sitting in the passenger seat sobbing ... I kept asking her, "Mum, what's wrong, what's

---

1 Paul Chapman and Jon Anderson, *Chappy: Believe It or Not*, Hardie Grant Books, 2015, e-book version.
2 *Chappy*, e-book.
3 *Chappy*, e-book.
4 *Chappy*, e-book.
5 *Chappy*, e-book.

> wrong?" "Glenn has been killed," she said. I was shaking and my nose started bleeding... It was the worst day of my life. I hope nothing ever comes close to it and I can't imagine anything ever would... When it happens to you, it tears you apart. I lost a part of myself that day.[6]

As a 16-year-old Chapman's world was instantly turned upside down, the loss of his brother having a significant effect on him as he approached adulthood. "There was just this pain that I can never properly explain—I was utterly heartbroken. The pain and grief eventually turned to numbness, which in time, turned to anger."[7] Chapman said that Glenn's death "stripped me bare". "There was nothing to hide behind and I could only be the person that I was. Without question, it made me more honest, if not at times blunt, towards others."[8]

Just over 12 months after Glenn's death, Chapman was drafted to Geelong with its fifth selection at the 1999 AFL Draft (pick 31 overall). Recruiter Stephen Wells described Chapman as "a hard nut who had fantastic skills."[9] During one of Wells's meetings with the Chapman family in the months after Glenn's death, "Paul expressed to me that he was really going to appreciate the opportunity" if drafted by Geelong.[10] Before reading his name out on draft day, the Cats had chosen Joel Corey (pick eight), David Spriggs (15), Ezra Bray (17) and Daniel Foster (23), and after Chapman they took Cameron Ling (38), Corey Enright (47) and also traded for North Melbourne's 1999 Premiership player Cameron Mooney (1999, 11 games). Five of the '99 crop of draftees would play in the 2007 Premiership side. Wells added more Premiership-calibre talent in the seasons ahead, complementing Matthew Scarlett, Darren Milburn, David Wojcinski and Tom Harley, who were all at Geelong before Chapman's arrival.

Geelong's 177-game defender Tim McGrath remembered Chapman when he arrived at the club as being "like a two-year-old colt, half mad."[11] He was raw and confident, but his training standards were a long way off

---

6   *Chappy*, e-book.
7   *Chappy*, e-book.
8   *Chappy*, e-book.
9   Scott Gullan, *The Mission: The Inside Story of Geelong's 2007 AFL Premiership*, Weston Media & Communications, 2008, p. 33.
10 *The Mission*, 2008.
11 *Chappy*, e-book.

AFL level. "His training habits weren't great and every bloke that ran past him he wanted to belt because he was so frustrated," McGrath said.[12]

McGrath had been a member of Geelong's exciting teams that over a seven-year stretch played in four losing Grand Finals (1989, 1992, 1994-95). Under innovative coach Malcolm Blight, and with superstar forward and 1989 Norm Smith medallist Gary Ablett among others, the Cats played a run-and-gun brand of football that almost won them the '89 Premiership. But their all-out attacking game did not stack up to the defensive strengths of West Coast and Carlton on Grand Final days. The old adage "defence wins Premierships" proved accurate and, by the fourth defeat (under Gary Ayres, who replaced Blight after 1994), it seemed the Cats were destined not to add to their six Premierships, the last of which came in 1963.

Chapman's arrival at Kardinia Park in the summer of 1999 coincided with that of Ayres's replacement as coach, Mark 'Bomber' Thompson. A courageous defender for Essendon (1983-96, 202 games), Thompson played in the 1984-85 Premierships, then captained the 'Baby Bombers' to the 1993 title—all under Kevin Sheedy. Thompson later wrote in *Bomber* that Geelong was "a mess" when he arrived as coach; its young captain Leigh Colbert had just walked out and joined North Melbourne, it had an ageing list and the club was $7.5 million in debt.[13]

It was a dire situation, but Thompson and Wells set about regenerating and developing the playing stocks, while president Frank Costa and CEO Brian Cook began the daunting task of returning the club to being profitable off the field. These four, and others, not only saved the club from possible extinction, they turned it into one of the greatest sporting clubs in Australia. But at the start of 2000 when Chapman walked through the door, success and financial certainty seemed a long way off, as he explained in *Chappy*:

> In the early 2000s we weren't that close and we didn't appreciate each other. In the end, you don't need to be great friends, hanging out all the time, but you do need to buy in. Looking back, it is plain to see that we weren't respected by

---

12   McGrath, *Chappy*, e-book.
13   **Mark Thompson and Martin Blake**, *Bomber: The Whole Story*, Michael Joseph, 2016, p. 101.

other teams and by the football world. Our energy was spent worrying about the teams up the highway and interstate, whereas we should have been concerned about getting ourselves right.[14]

Chapman concedes he was one such player who did not mix regularly with his teammates: "On reflection, I missed out on a lot of things, in particular the closeness of the Geelong boys," he wrote. "Yes, I feel close to them, but I don't share that same bond that they have with each other. I was never a part of their boys' club, which was probably good in some ways but overall I wish I had been more involved."[15] Thompson believed that Geelong's culture when he arrived was "about each to his own", a philosophy he was determined to change.[16] To do that, he needed to regenerate the list and also give games to recruits early in their careers.

Chapman's debut came in round 12, 2000, against Collingwood at the MCG. The Cats managed only one goal to half-time to trail by 30 points but charged home in the second half to win by three points. Chapman recorded just three kicks, two handballs and two marks. In all, he played four games in season one, including the club's nine-point first Elimination Final loss to Hawthorn, at Docklands, where he kicked the first of his 366 goals. At the 2000 AFL Draft, Geelong selected Josh Hunt (pick 44), then the following year, in what was later dubbed the 'Super Draft', it added Jimmy Bartel (8), James Kelly (17), Steve Johnson (24) and Gary Ablett (40, father-son)—all of whom would become champion players.

Chapman said that, during his first two years at the club, the side went through a transitional period where "Bomber definitely gave some of the younger players gratuitous game time" but, by midway through 2001, "we were told that games could only be earned."[17] Having played 29 matches to the end of 2002, he experienced another life-changing event during an end-of-season holiday to Bali:

> Our last night was 12 October and the guys were keen to get out again, but I didn't have the motivation or the spirit. It was

---

14 *Chappy*, e-book.
15 *Chappy*, e-book.
16 *Bomber*, p. 105.
17 *Chappy*, e-book.

the anniversary of Glenn's death four years earlier... Then we heard a massive "BOOM!" I jumped across [teammate] Peter Riccardi. We had no idea what had happened and I'm still not sure whether I was trying to protect him, or I just crapped myself. The water in the pool emptied on one side and swept over like a wave. All the windows in our hotel rooms shattered and an enormous mushroom of smoke lifted into the sky. We were only a couple of hundred metres from where the bombs went off. It ripped through me like nothing I've ever felt before.[18]

Amid the chaos, fear and carnage, Chapman felt helpless, something that he struggled with for a long time:

> Unless you were there and experienced the atrocities firsthand or as a bystander, it's impossible to fathom the fear... I wanted to help but I felt completely helpless. The consensus in our group was that we were to stick together. None of us were medically trained but we did help people with wet sheets and water and helped put them into vans ... I still struggle with the thought that we didn't do enough to help the night the bombs went off... I think Glenn was watching over us that night in Bali; he still had his little brother's back.[19]

Weeks after Bali, at the 2002 National Draft, Geelong selected Andrew Mackie (7) and Tom Lonergan (23), and also elevated Max Rooke from the rookie list. During 2003, with the building blocks beginning to take shape, Scarlett emerged as one of the best defenders of his era, and Chapman enjoyed his best season to date. At the end of the year, the Cats added ruckman Mark Blake (38, father-son). In 2004, Geelong charged back up the ladder, finishing fourth and going within nine points of Brisbane in the Preliminary Final. At the draft the Cats selected Nathan Ablett (48, father-son), Matthew Egan (62), elevated Shannon Byrnes from the rookie list and, significantly, traded for Richmond ruckman Brad Ottens.

---

18 *Chappy*, e-book.
19 *Chappy*, e-book.

Expectations were that the young and exciting Cats were on the cusp of a successful era. In 2005, Chapman missed the finals through injury, but Geelong defeated Melbourne in the second Elimination Final (55 points). Then, in the second Semi-Final at the SCG, the Cats led Sydney by 17 points at three-quarter time before some Nick Davis heroics in the last quarter (four goals) lifted the Swans to a dramatic three-point victory. Chapman said, "It was a difficult lesson learned but it shone a light on our capabilities."[20] Travis Varcoe (pick 15) and Mathew Stokes (61) joined the club. Most in the football world saw the heartbreaking loss to Sydney as an aberration, and when Geelong defeated Adelaide to win the 2006 pre-season Grand Final, the Cats entered the regular season as one of the Premiership fancies.

They won their first two games by 77 and 69 points respectively, but from there the wheels fell off. They won just eight more matches (plus a draw), and finished 10th, some two-and-a-half games outside the top eight. Thompson dubbed it "the year from hell."[21] Despite the mounting pressure inside and outside the club, Chapman enjoyed his finest season. He played all 22 games, kicked 31 goals and won his first, and only, 'Carji' Greeves Medal. "We were a group of players with enormous talent aged between 23 and 26 and we were ready," Chapman said. "So what happened in 2006 was a massive shock and a rude awakening. We didn't really fire a shot that year."[22]

Cook undertook an internal review of the club at season's end after which, many assumed, Thompson would be sacked. Chapman later wrote that, despite the poor results, he believed Thompson was "the perfect man for the job" but that as coach Thompson "wanted to take control of the whole football club. I think that's what eventually broke him down in 2006."[23] During the review, Scarlett spoke with the *Herald Sun*'s Mike Sheahan, declaring that he would quit the club if Thompson was removed. "Scarlo didn't speak much but when he spoke everyone listened," Chapman wrote.[24]

Thompson survived, and to assist him off the field the club hired

---

20   *Chappy*, e-book.
21   *Bomber*, p. 127.
22   *Chappy*, e-book.
23   *Chappy*, e-book.
24   *Chappy*, e-book.

former Richmond Premiership forward (1973-74) and Melbourne coach (1993-97) Neil Balme as general manager of football. "I only discovered that Bomber had survived the review and kept his job by reading about it in the paper," Chapman recalled, adding, "I was pumped."[25] The club also introduced the Leading Teams program, which forced the players and coaches to become more open and honest in their peer feedback. Sydney had used the program to great effect over the previous few seasons. "In 2006 we just didn't seem to care for each other like previous years," Chapman said. "While there were no obvious problems with the playing group, we all seemed to be waiting around to flick the switch."[26]

Another two vital pieces of the Premiership puzzle, Joel Selwood (seven) and Tom Hawkins (41, father-son), arrived via the draft a few weeks later.

Out of the Leading Teams program new leaders emerged, including Harley as captain. Reputations weren't spared, with stars Scarlett and Ablett among those who were advised to become more professional. One of the first examples of the new approach came when the players' leadership group suspended Steve Johnson for poor off-field behaviour, forcing him to miss the opening rounds of the 2007 season. When the Cats then stuttered through their early games, Chapman vented his frustration in the hope his words would motivate his teammates:

> It wasn't all doom and gloom but we were struggling and something needed to change urgently. I had an idea to use the media as a forum to voice my thoughts and opinions—to put it out there but let the media do the hard work. I have always been fairly reserved and more inclined to shun the spotlight than bask in it. So I knew my comments might attract more attention and if I let the media run with the story and perhaps make it more exaggerated than it really was, it would carry more weight.[27]

He explained that he "wasn't so concerned with what others outside the club would say, as I was about rousing spirits internally."[28] After round

---

25 *Chappy*, e-book.
26 *Chappy*, e-book.
27 *Chappy*, e-book.
28 *Chappy*, e-book.

five, Geelong was 10th with two wins and three losses, although it had a healthy percentage. Then, in round six at the Docklands against Richmond, and with Johnson playing his first game of the season, the Cats from Sleepy Hollow suddenly awoke. They kicked 10 goals to one in the opening term, repeated the effort in the second, and eventually won by a staggering 157 points—Richmond's greatest loss. Chapman, who was one of four Geelong players to kick four goals, recalled:

> The feeling going into the Richmond game in round six was very good, but you never think you are going to win by 157 points. From then on, we realised that the more we gave in to a team ethos, the better we would play. For a player like me, that meant not trying to snap goals from the boundary line. We learnt in time that everyone benefited from that philosophy.[29]

As the Cats steamrolled over the competition for much of 2007—their only loss after round five came against Port Adelaide, at Geelong in round 21, by five points—Chapman missed a number of games due to ongoing groin injuries. They were so debilitating that he struggled to get out of bed in the mornings. "Mentally it stuffed me more than physically," he said. "My body was rooted, but mentally I couldn't do anything. I was shot, I was over it. I was hardly training, once a week if I was lucky, and when someone would say do this or do that, I was like, 'I can't do it because I'm too sore.'"[30]

Having missed rounds 17-19, Chapman returned in round 20 and was managed through the rest of the season. In Geelong's 106-point demolition of North Melbourne in the first Qualifying Final, he (along with Mooney) kicked five goals. Thompson was unsurprised that Chapman had lifted his output in a big final. "He was a big-time player, Chappy, along with Jimmy [Bartel]," he said. "A big final actually gets those guys into a head space where they are at their best ... Chapman just naturally went to the ball, and in the big games he and Bartel would stand up."[31]

---

29   *Chappy*, e-book.
30   Chapman, *The Mission*, p. 119.
31   *Bomber*, p. 158.

THE NORM SMITH MEDAL

In a much tighter Preliminary Final, Geelong defeated Collingwood by just five points. Chapman had 15 disposals and kicked a goal, but was disappointed with his performance, labelling it "disgraceful". "I was stuck in the goal square and I couldn't run, I was rooted," he said bluntly. He did, however, feel confident that he would perform better in the Grand Final. "I knew that meant I would play well in the Grand Final. I think one of my attributes has been that if I play bad one week, I am going to step up the next week. I just knew."[32]

Geelong's opponent was Port Adelaide, which had won the 2004 Grand Final and defeated the Cats just five weeks earlier. "I thought if Port Adelaide was smart they would go around and attack the young blokes and try to get them early," Chapman said.[33] Instead, there was surprisingly little fight by the Power: Geelong jumped from the blocks and led by 23 points at quarter-time, then blew the game open with seven goals to two in the second term. After half-time they proceeded to kick 13 goals to two and post the greatest Grand Final winning margin of 119 points, winning 24.19 (163) to 6.8 (44).

Johnson won the Norm Smith Medal in a remarkable transformation after being suspended earlier in the season, while Chapman's inkling regarding his own performance proved accurate: He had 17 kicks, four handballs, seven marks, eight inside-50s and kicked four goals to be one of Geelong's best. Plus he took the mark of the day. "I just leapt and it came off," he wrote. "You dream of taking a massive hanger on the big day so I was pretty happy about it."[34]

The following year the Cats dominated the season, losing just one game, but were stunned by Hawthorn on Grand Final day. The Hawks won by 26 points against an inaccurate Geelong (18.7 to 11.23; although 11 of those behinds were rushed by the Hawthorn defence, leading to a rule change), and Chapman (who missed the Preliminary Final through injury but returned for the Grand Final) had 22 disposals and kicked a goal. In the aftermath, Hawks president Jeff Kennett boasted that Hawthorn never lost to Geelong in big games. In response Chapman declared his team would never suffer defeat to Hawthorn again. The "Kennett

---

32 *The Mission*, p. 169.
33 *The Mission*, p. 204.
34 *The Mission*, p. 216.

Curse" was born. Of Chapman's next 10 games against Hawthorn (covering the remainder of his time at Kardinia Park), the Cats won every time. Hawk midfielder Brad Sewell was regularly opposed to Chapman during the period:

> I remember early on Chance Bateman was trying to get under his skin one day and was winding him up. I had to tell him, "Don't, leave him alone, because he likes being antagonised as it gets him up and about." He was hugely influential forward of centre for the Cats, whether as a high half-forward or as a stocky, strong, robust midfielder who could kick goals. He became one of the most important barometers for Geelong, yet somewhat unheralded during that period when the club dominated.

That year Sydney offered Chapman in the range of $2 million over three seasons, which was "a hell of a lot more" than he was receiving at Geelong.[35] Like a number of his notable teammates, Chapman declined the lucrative offer, choosing team success over personal gain (although, Sydney, too, was a perennial Grand Final contender during his career). "There were definitely players at Geelong, me included, who sacrificed money to stay together to keep the club in Premiership contention," he later wrote.[36]

As Geelong set out to go one better in 2009, and Hawthorn suffered a dramatic hangover that resulted in the Hawks missing the finals, a new force emerged: the Ross Lyon-coached St Kilda. The Saints won their first 13 games, the same as Geelong, and the two teams met in round 14 in what appeared to be a Grand Final preview. In one of the great home and away matches, St Kilda won by six points, despite Chapman collecting the most disposals (39) of any player on the ground. It was the seventh of nine occasions throughout 2009 when he passed 30 disposals, including a best of 41 against Melbourne in round six. He also kicked a career-best six goals against Adelaide, at Kardinia Park, in round 18. Chapman made his first All-Australian team (he was selected again in 2010) and at 27, having played 172 games, he was at the peak of his powers and primed for a big finals series.

---

35 *Chappy*, e-book.
36 *Chappy*, e-book.

In the second Qualifying Final against the Bulldogs, he had 16 disposals and kicked 2.3 in Geelong's 14-point win. Then, with 26 disposals and five goals in the second Preliminary Final, he was one of the best afield in a 73-point belting of Collingwood.

On a wet Grand Final day against St Kilda, Chapman won his first kick inside the opening minute on the southern wing. The first inspirational act of the game came from teammate Max Rooke a minute later, when he chased down Saints defender Raph Clarke, won a free kick, then bombed a 50-metre goal. The Saints looked shaky early with Geelong's pressure forcing some uncharacteristic mistakes. Cam Mooney kicked a second goal seven minutes in. Geelong's early majors would prove telling by day's end. That Adam Schneider missed a simple snap from 15 metres out only exacerbated the Saints' early problems.

Chapman was one of his team's busiest players in the opening quarter (seven disposals), getting in and under to win contested possessions and then dish the ball out to teammates. Lenny Hayes was the Saints' standout, his 11 first-quarter disposals and goal helping to turn the tide his team's way during the last 10 minutes. At the break, with the Cats trailing by two points, Thompson moved his team's leading disposal winner Bartel (nine) on to Hayes in a tagging role—a match-defining decision, as Bartel kept the gritty Saint to just 13 disposals in the last three quarters and had 10 of his own.

After an early goal to Sean Dempster, St Kilda was nine points in front four minutes into the second term and had dominated much of the previous 15 minutes of play. Chapman had a long snap touched on the goal line before the Saints missed three gettable chances that would have given them at least a four-goal buffer; instead, the margin was 10 points.

Chapman clutched at his right hamstring and left the field halfway through the quarter (returning with five minutes remaining, his hamstring wrapped in tape), just as Shannon Byrnes was left alone in the square and cut the margin to four points. The rain had gotten heavier, and had St Kilda finished accurately its lead may have been telling in the wet conditions. It had dominated the inside-50 count 29-12 but could not convert those opportunities. Ablett went deep forward and won a free kick three minutes later, giving Geelong a one-point lead against the flow of play. Chapman later revealed that, after his early injury, he had doubts he could see out the game:

> Physically I don't know how I got through the game. I copped a corky just before quarter-time that sent a spasm up my leg. They put some ice on it to get the swelling down. Close to my first contest in the second quarter, I lunged and pulled my hammy. The physio, Mike Snelling, told me it was a decent 10cm tear. I wouldn't have got up for the following week. They said because it was still warm it helped, but I could only play effectively up forward after that.[37]

There was controversy with four minutes left when Zac Dawson kicked straight to Hawkins in the goal square, who snapped a 'goal' despite replays later showing the ball had deflected off the goal post. Geelong went forward from the next centre bounce, and Varcoe handballed to Chapman who snapped a second goal in 30 seconds to suddenly open up a 12-point lead. Remarkably, in the last minute, St Kilda scored *three* late goals: the first to Clint Jones, then Justin Koschitzke, and Koschitzke again before the ball had returned to the centre due to Milburn being penalised for remonstrating with the umpire. The Saints suddenly led by six points.

Chapman started at full-forward for the third quarter, but was soon up marking at half-forward. Geelong led by two points when Mooney goaled five minutes in, but Nick Riewoldt, starting to impose himself, put the Saints back in front. It was a scrappy term, with neither side able to gain the ascendancy. If there was a standout for the Norm Smith Medal by the halfway mark of the quarter it was St Kilda's Jason Gram, who was involved in most of the Saints' attacks. Chapman ensured he was back in the judges' thoughts, however, when he snapped a clever goal from the pocket with nine minutes remaining. Four minutes later he was up clearing the ball from half-back.

A late goal by Leigh Montagna helped the Saints lead by seven points at the final break, meaning Geelong would need to become the first team

---

37 *Chappy*, e-book.

since Essendon in 1984, when 23 points behind Hawthorn, to come from behind at three-quarter time and win a Grand Final.

Chapman's best quarter was the crucial last; in the opening minute he drilled a pinpoint pass to Hawkins, who goaled. In a tightly fought, tension-filled game that recorded the most combined tackles ever in a Grand Final (118 to St Kilda, 96 to Geelong), there were no more goals scored until the 24-minute mark, when, again, Chapman was pivotal. With scores level, the ball was centred to Ablett in the middle, Dawson spoiled and the ball spilled loose. Scarlett instinctively toe-poked the ball to Ablett, who drove it long to a contest in the goal square. Varcoe roved, flicked out a handball to Chapman standing alone, and his high left-foot snap put Geelong six points ahead. "I knew I had to get it high to get it over (Jason Blake's) hand," he said. "I thought straight away it had enough on it, but I was worried Jason might do the old 'touched it' cry. He didn't. That put us six points up."[38] Thompson was not surprised that Chapman was in position to kick the defining goal:

> That is what Chappy does. He *wants* the football right then, he has no nerves, and he *wants* that kick for the win, just like Stevie Johnson does, and Jimmy Bartel. Funnily enough, he had Jimmy Bartel wide open for a handball if he needed him, and he probably should have given the ball up, too, given that he was on his non-preferred side. But it was all perfect, really.[39]

The Saints went goalless in the last quarter, with an after-the-siren goal from Rooke giving the Cats a 12-point victory, 12.8 (80) to 9.14 (68). With nine last-quarter disposals, and 26 for the day (17 kicks and nine handballs, plus four marks, four tackles and three goals), Chapman was voted best on the ground by three of the five judges (nine votes in total). However, Gram (30 disposals, five marks) received votes from all five judges to also record nine votes. For the only known time since the Norm Smith Medal was first awarded, Chapman won after a countback due to his superior number of three-vote cards.

Chapman said that winning the medal was satisfying "because it meant

---

38   *Chappy*, e-book.
39   *Bomber*, pp. 203-204.

I had played well in an important game for my team."⁴⁰ Of learning he had won the Medal, he recalled:

> Sometimes after games players start guessing as to who will win the individual award on offer. But 2009 was too tight to be making those sorts of guesses. I was standing with 'Otto' (Brad Ottens) and some random bloke just came up to me. He must have been from the AFL. I didn't really hear what he said at first and just remembered him saying, "Make sure you thank the sponsors and don't swear." I said "What?" and then looked at 'Otto' and he said, "I think you may have won the Norm Smith," and he gave me a hug. Two minutes later I was named. It was just weird that this random had come out of nowhere to tell me. And he was funny the way he did it.⁴¹

On the "tie" with Gram, he joked that the three judges who voted for him—John Worsfold, Nathan Buckley and Jason Dunstall—deserved his thanks. "'Bucks' was one of my favourite players when I was growing up so to be voted by him was extra special," he wrote, adding, "I kept the medal on when we were on the ground then took it off as soon as we got off the ground and gave it to Mum and Dad."⁴²

Harley retired after the Grand Final, and Chapman was discussed as a potential replacement for him as captain. McGrath said, "A lot of the Geelong supporters wanted Chappy as captain. That was never going to happen, but if it was a popularity contest he would have got the job for sure."⁴³ Instead the job went to another fan favourite in Cameron Ling.

The Cats finished second in 2010. Against St Kilda, in the second Qualifying Final, Chapman's reputation as a ruthless competitor led to him being falsely accused of belting Adam Schneider behind play, as former Saint Rob Eddy explained:

> Chappy was playing midfield-wing and he was running alongside Schneider. The ball went out for a stoppage and

---

40 *Chappy*, e-book.
41 *Chappy*, e-book.
42 *Chappy*, e-book.
43 McGrath, *Chappy*, e-book.

> I knew those two were behind me, and that they'd been arguing at each other. I turned around and 'Schneids' was on the ground, so I assumed Chappy had decked him. I ran over to stick up for my teammate and we got into a massive wrestle—we had each other by the throat and were exchanging words. Then we got broken up and were jogging back to our positions when Schneids came over and said, "Thanks, man. He didn't actually touch me, I was just playing for the free kick!" I was so exhausted, having wasted all my energy wrestling with him for no reason!

Despite perceptions that Chapman was an angry player on the field, Eddy said this was not the case:

> He was a big bull of a guy, but he was a really nice, quiet sort of a guy, too. He wasn't angry towards you on the field, which is different from the perception. He was hard at it, but he was placid, a good leader, and you could always hear him talking and directing his teammates.

The Cats fell four points shy of the Saints, then beat Fremantle in the second Semi-Final (69 points), but lost the Preliminary Final to eventual premier Collingwood (41 points). Thompson then stood down as coach, to be replaced by Chris Scott, and Ablett—having finished second in the Brownlow Medal count—departed to captain the newly established Gold Coast Suns.

Despite the changes, the Cats (with yet another important recruit, James Podsiadsly, up forward) finished second again in 2011, returning to the Grand Final where they went in as slight underdogs against Collingwood. The match was tight for three quarters, but in the final term the Cats kicked five goals to none and won by 38 points. Bartel won the Norm Smith Medal, while Chapman, as in all three of Geelong's finals that year, was among the best players. He had 14 kicks, 10 handballs, five clearances and took four marks.

Describing his game as "serviceable," Chapman felt he "played my role but never really got into it the way I wanted to."[44] He was being a touch

---

44   *Chappy*, e-book.

harsh, as due to recurring injuries he had seldom trained at more than 70 per cent and had struggled mentally as a consequence:

> It's a physical thing but after a while it becomes a mental battle. There were times (in 2011) where I just got so frustrated with it that I wanted to chuck it in because I wasn't playing to the level I wanted to. You lose your love of footy when all you're ever doing is worrying about your body.[45]

With its third Premiership in five seasons, Geelong had cemented its reputation as one of the greatest teams of all time. Between 2007 and 2011, Geelong won 105 matches and lost just 20, including winning 12 of 15 finals. After coming close to shutting the doors at the end of the 1990s, the players, coaches and administrators had turned the club around substantially, to the point that it now regularly contended for finals, had a state-of-the-art stadium, and was admired throughout the sporting world as one of the best-run organisations in Australia.

Chapman's last game for the Cats came in the 2013 second Semi-Final, against Port Adelaide. Geelong won by 16 points and, with four goals and 20 disposals, Chapman was best afield. Injury forced him to miss the losing Preliminary Final against, of all clubs, Hawthorn. Considering the Hawks had not defeated the Cats since the 2008 Grand Final, had Chapman played the result may have been different—the Hawks came from 20 points down at three-quarter time to win a thriller by five points, on route to the Premiership the following week.

After years of sacrifice and remarkable success from Geelong's Premiership champions, Scott had the unenviable task of phasing some of them out of the team in order to regenerate the list and remain competitive. Johnson went to Greater Western Sydney, while Kelly, Stokes and Chapman joined Essendon during the club's darkest period following the controversial supplements investigation. There they were reunited with Thompson, who worked alongside coach James Hird, replacing him for 12 months in 2014 when Hird was serving a year's suspension from the game. Chapman recalled his time with the Bombers:

---

45   Scott Gullan, *Greatness: Inside Geelong's Path to Premiership History*, Weston Media & Communications, 2011, p. 117.

> I went to Essendon thinking that we could just focus on playing football and let the other stuff sort itself out in the background. But as human nature would have it, they couldn't shake it and they carried the burden with them every day—out on the field, taking it home after a long day on the track. They were probably even dreaming about it. And if it wasn't eating them up from the inside, the media would throw a few punches. There were never any positive articles written about Essendon. It was all just doom and gloom.[46]

Although the wins were few and far between during his two seasons and 29 games at the club, the three Geelong players' mentoring roles with some of Essendon's youngsters was critical in helping them to develop. "I didn't expect it, but I made some great friends at Essendon," Chapman said. "In fact, it was the best part of the move. I wish I could have done more to help Essendon. It didn't end the way I wanted it to."[47]

In all, Chapman played 280 games in 16 seasons, his transformation from fiery youngster to respected veteran and ultimate team player one of his finest achievements:

> At the start of my career I was selfish. I was worried about getting a game each week and if I did play it was about kicking that spectacular goal. Then I learnt about trust and self-sacrifice and how far it could take you and the team. I learned to restrain myself at the times that mattered so I would be more predictable to my teammates and I stopped trying to snag them from the boundary.[48]

Harley was full of praise for Chapman's role in Geelong's greatest era:

> He possibly didn't have the external profile of Jimmy (Bartel) or Gaz (Ablett) but won a best and fairest before those two, and the supporters just loved him as a player. You could argue he was Geelong's most popular player of his era,

---

46   *Chappy*, e-book.
47   *Chappy*, e-book.
48   *Chappy*, e-book.

a view that was elevated even further when he started playing big finals and he became such an obvious big-game player. He certainly played with a chip on his block and you could argue he lived life sometimes with a chip on his block. He played like he was always trying to prove things to people. He was a backs-against-the-wall, me-against-the-rest kind of player. When you walked down the race in big games and looked across to see Chappy there, you knew things were going to be OK.[49]

NOTE: Interviews with Rob Eddy and Brad Sewell were conducted by the author.

——— Statistics ———

BORN: 5 November 1981

GAMES PLAYED (2000-15): 280 (2000-13 Geelong, 251; 2014-15 Essendon, 29)

GOALS: 366 (Geelong 336; Essendon 30)

FINALS PLAYED: 22

FINALS GOALS: 36

GRAND FINALS: 4

PREMIERSHIPS: 2007, 2009, 2011

NORM SMITH MEDAL: 2009 (presented by Paul Dear)

— Norm Smith Voting —

John Worsfold: 3 Paul Chapman, 2 Jason Gram, 1 Joel Corey;
Gerard Healy: 3 Gram, 2 Jimmy Bartel, 1 Gary Ablett;
Nathan Buckley: 3 Chapman, 2 Darren Milburn, 1 Gram;
Gerard Whateley: 3 Harry Taylor, 2 Max Rooke, 1 Gram;
Jason Dunstall: 3 Chapman, 2 Gram, 1 Ablett.

TOTALS: Chapman 9 (won on countback due to more 3-votes), Gram 9, Taylor 3, Milburn 2, Bartel 2, Rooke 2, Ablett 2, Corey 1.

---

49   Harley, *Chappy*, e-book.

Lenny Hayes

Draw

One of the most admired players of his era, Lenny Hayes was the beating heart of the St Kilda Football Club during 297 selfless games (1999-2014). Indeed, Hayes typified the team-first approach that became synonymous with the Saints under coach Ross Lyon. He was relentless in his attack on the ball and a committed tackler—a skill aided by having played rugby league and union as a child in Sydney—but he was also fair; his sportsmanship earned him universal respect throughout the football community. Hayes captained the Saints (2004, 2007), won three best and fairest awards (2003, 2010, 2012), was a three-time All-Australian (2003, 2005, 2009) and a driving force in St Kilda's Grand Final appearances in 2009-10, particularly in the 2010 drawn Grand Final against Collingwood, which earned him the Norm Smith Medal. That he fought back from two knee reconstructions, and also played with a heart condition that required surgery in 2012, only added to his legend. In his Norm Smith Medal game, Hayes had 18 kicks and 14 handballs, took five marks, laid 12 tackles and kicked a crucial late goal.

← **FORGOTTEN MAN** When you win the Norm Smith Medal in a drawn Grand Final, it's a small consolation and a reminder of what might have been. Lenny Hayes's long kick in the final moments drew the match, but had it bounced more kindly, the Saints would have won.

THE NORM SMITH MEDAL

I became interested in Aussie rules in Sydney through my dad, Chris, who was originally from Victoria. He met my mum, Elizabeth, while they were both travelling overseas. She was from Sydney, so when they returned to Australia they chose to settle there. Dad was a big North Melbourne supporter and when they first moved in together Mum thought he was a little bit crazy because he would yell at the TV whenever footy was on. Mum didn't know much about the game at that stage, so it was a bit of a culture shock to her. Dad influenced my interest in the sport by taking me to see the Sydney Swans regularly and he eventually joined me up with our local footy club, Pennant Hills.[1]

Dad played local footy in Melbourne, but I don't think Mum played much sport. I know her brothers played some rugby union up in Sydney. They had four kids: Eleanor, myself, Gillian and Duncan. We played more rugby league and cricket in the backyard than we did footy and it was always competitive between us all. Being six years older than Duncan, I had to let him have a few early wins so he didn't run indoors to Mum all the time!

I didn't know it at the time, but looking back now I'm sure my early years playing rugby at school helped me with my footy later on. We never played kick-to-kick at school, it was all touch rugby. I wasn't the quickest, so I developed a side-step to get around opponents. I used that during my footy career to wrong-foot opponents and get around them. I've no doubt my tackling technique was crafted through the way I had to tackle for rugby league and union whenever I played contact rugby. Tackling like a rugby player certainly helped me when playing AFL.

I admired Sydney Swans captain Paul Kelly. As I grew older I loved watching how St Kilda's Robert Harvey went about things; Shane Crawford at Hawthorn, too—all those champion midfielders of the era. I played all over the field as a junior: half-back, half-forward and then, when I advanced to the under-18 competition, I played more through the midfield.

The pathway to the AFL has changed since I was drafted by the Saints

---

1   Lenny Hayes's great-grandfather, Vin Maguire, played 43 games for Geelong (1915, 1917-19).

[at pick 11 in the 1998 AFL Draft]. Now the Swans and Greater Western Sydney Giants have their own academies to enable them to develop players. Back in my day I would likely have fallen into the Swans' academy system. What helped me reach the AFL was that when I turned 15 the NSW/ACT Rams joined the TAC Cup under-18 competition and they played games weekly. Before then, if you were under 18 in New South Wales you had to try and impress recruiters at annual carnivals; there wasn't the weekly competition against the Victorian under-18 teams back then. With the introduction of the Rams, we were suddenly exposed to guys playing with the Northern Knights and Gippsland Power, among others. So the timing of their introduction was perfect for my development. It afforded me the opportunity to test myself against my peers in Victoria, and it put me in front of the eyes of AFL recruiters.

I finished at my local school after year 11, because I moved to Canberra to play with the Rams. I did year 12 down there, which was a ballsy decision at the time—there were no guarantees I would go anywhere in footy. I had seen a couple of guys I knew get drafted, so I wanted to give it my best shot. I was 17 when I moved to Canberra to pursue my dream and I lived with a host family while I was there. The Rams were a combination of guys from Sydney, Canberra, Wagga and the Riverina area. As Canberra was central to that, it became the club's home. Canberra has a strong footy history, with guys like Alex Jesaulenko (Carlton, St Kilda), James Hird (Essendon) and Aaron Hamill (Carton, St Kilda) coming from there. The region is still producing quality players today, such as Josh Bruce (GWS, St Kilda) and Jack Steele (GWS, St Kilda), so it's a great region for footy.

That I had lived away from home for two years helped me when I was drafted to St Kilda. But it was still daunting walking into the club for the first time. Mum drove me down from Sydney and as soon as we hit Melbourne it poured with rain, then we had to find our way out to Moorabbin. I entered the club rooms and Jason Cripps was doing a bench press and was benching about 130 kilos. I felt way out of my depth when I saw him do that! To then meet and train alongside Robert Harvey, a hero of mine, was terrific. Plus, the Saints had played in the 1997 Grand

Final, losing to Adelaide, then finals again in 1998, so I was entering a club that had some terrific players and role models there to learn from. I certainly had self-doubts early on, but once I began training and the boys got around me I was able to find my way.

It was tough early on. While I was rapt to be playing AFL footy, the club was being belted week after week. Tim Watson was my first coach, but he was gone after 2000; Malcolm Blight was only there for a few months in 2001 before he left, then Grant Thomas took over. So within a couple of seasons I was on to my third coach! My good mate, Mark McVeigh, went to Essendon and in his second year he was an emergency in their 2000 Premiership team, then played in their losing 2001 Grand Final, so we were on very different journeys early on.

Grant Thomas brought the group together when he became coach. He sensed that the club was a little disjointed and that work needed to be done in bringing everybody together. He would have us all around at his place quite often; he would have the barbecue going and he used that as a means of getting everybody to mix together. He also demanded that we give 100 per cent effort as a team, 100 per cent of the time. That was his mantra, and if you weren't doing that you would be told so. Eventually the players started demanding that effort from each other, and that's when we started to go somewhere as a club.

When you're getting belted it forces you to grow up quickly as a player. But I'm glad that I went through that early in my career, then had some success later on, because it made me appreciate it more. Had we experienced immediate success, being young I may have taken that for granted. But having gone through those hard times (last in 2000, 15th in 2001 and again in 2002) it made us appreciate the winning years.

I didn't feel comfortable at AFL level until my fourth year. I was getting regular senior games, but I didn't feel like I was contributing much to the side. I felt I had more to give. I was drafted as a midfielder, but it took me more than three years to earn consistent midfield time because we had guys in there like Nathan Burke, 'Harves', Andrew Thompson and a few others—it was hard to break in there. But that was good for my development as it forced me to improve my overall game in order to earn a start in there. It wasn't until my fourth year, when I had a pretty consistent season, that the penny dropped for me and I went to another level. I had missed a few weeks of my third year with a shoulder reconstruction, and sitting out during that time I was able to appreciate that I definitely had more to give as a player. That next pre-season I had my best preparation and was able to turn in a pretty good year as a consequence.

We were able to bring in a lot of talented young players who were impressionable and eager to learn. I sensed that we had been through the darkest times and were on the verge of coming out the other end. Bringing in younger players gives everybody else at the club a boost. We knew that we needed to play 30-50 games together as a group, and once we achieved that we would be in the mix contending for Premierships. That's the great thing about the National Draft, it can turn the club around pretty quickly if you get some good talent in.

We played finals in 2004 but came up against the Brisbane Lions. The Lions were the dominant team of that era. I'm sure they saw us as young upstarts, and they certainly stamped their authority in the second Qualifying Final. They absolutely bullied us in that game, which was a good lesson for our group. They got after us physically and verbally, winning by 80 points, and it showed us that finals were a different season to the home and away rounds; a different brand of footy was required. It was a tough lesson to learn at the time, but it made us realise that we had a fair way to go on our journey. We were able to turn things around a week later and beat Sydney by 51 points in the second Semi-Final, then we almost defeated Port Adelaide in the Preliminary Final, falling six points short. We had a really good team then and, although we lost the prelim again in 2005 (to Sydney by 31 points), I think the 2004 prelim was the time we felt we could have gone on and played in a Grand Final.

I did my knee in 2006. It was against North Melbourne (round nine) when I tackled someone and got swung around. I felt something in my knee, but at half-time the doctor said it appeared structurally sound and so I played the second half. It didn't feel right, but I certainly didn't think that I had done serious damage to my knee. It swelled up overnight at home, and when I had it checked the next day it was confirmed that I had injured my anterior cruciate ligament, which was a surprise.

It is such a long process coming back from a knee injury. Most injuries you can return from within a few weeks, or a couple of months, but there's an extra mental battle with a knee injury because you know you will be out of the game for up to a year. Plus, the muscles in your quad and through your leg all waste away because you can't strengthen them for quite a while. So getting that strength back—that and regaining your confidence—are the two biggest things you deal with after a knee injury.

I came back and played after just nine-and-a-half months. But after I suffered a second knee injury, in 2011, then returned after 12 months, I found that those few extra weeks of training gave me more confidence to feel that I was right to go. I had more continuity in my training after the 2011 injury. In 2007 I was probably too heavy when I returned; I was doing a lot of upper-body weights while I was out and I put on a couple of extra kilograms which, when coming back from a knee injury, is not the smartest thing to do.

A lot of different things define courage. In the face of adversity, continuing to push through regardless would be how I would describe courage. It's a tough one to answer, though. Not many guys could go back with the flight of the ball like a Nick Riewoldt, could they? There are different types of courage on the footy field.

I believe you can learn to win the mental battle within yourself. It's something I talk to guys about now that I'm an assistant coach at the Giants, about that little voice in your head telling you you're tired. If you can control that voice, you can likely push yourself to places you didn't think possible. I did some mental visualisation training around controlling that when I was playing, which was something Robert Harvey was big on, too. It was Harves who introduced me to that technique. Grant Thomas was big on visualisation as well, on training the mental side of your game, so we focused heavily on that during those years.

I was always pretty focused before games. We used to talk about taking care of your Monday to Friday. If you had done the work throughout the week, prepared correctly and done your mental visualisation, you were willing to accept what came your way on the weekend. So I didn't get too nervous before games; I always felt confident in my preparation. But there were certainly guys throwing up in the toilets before matches, so it can be different for everyone.

I tried to lead through action. I was never one for giving a big motivational speech. I led by example and on the occasions that I did speak it was never a big, overbearing speech; it was more about willing my teammates to take ownership of the team's direction.

Ross Lyon came to us from Sydney after 2006 and, tactically, he was a really strong coach. So with the combination of the talent we had and Ross coming in and providing a really strong game-plan, we felt we were going to be a strong chance to compete for Premierships. Ross is a great man-manager as well, although it wasn't something he was great at early on. It was something he got better at the longer he was in the job. He was great for us. He's different from the person you see on TV. He could be pretty ruthless, but he could also be someone you could have a chat to. That's why he's such a good coach. Once he wins the trust of his players, which he builds pretty quickly, he can then be ruthless but maintain the respect of the group.

It was a great feeling finally making a Grand Final in 2009. We had been to the prelim a few times and fallen short (2004-05 and 2008, a 52-point loss to Hawthorn), so to get over that hurdle by beating the Western Bulldogs by seven points was a relief. The prelims are probably the toughest games to win, because a Grand Final berth is at stake while, for the loser, you go home empty handed. Having had the year we had in 2009 (20 wins and just two losses), it was pure relief that we made it through. It was then exciting to be able to experience Grand Final week.

The match was really intense. Play was up and back all through that opening quarter, very physical, and I remember feeling exhausted by quarter-time. I was thinking, "Gee, I've got another three quarters of this!" It was the most intense game I ever played in. There were more than 200 tackles between us and Geelong that day (a Grand Final record, 214). It was one of those tight games played between two pretty even sides throwing everything at each other, almost like a heavyweight boxing match where both combatants were trading blows the entire time. Unfortunately for us, the Cats just found a way to win at the end.

Looking back on my career, that loss was the one that hurt the most because throughout the game I felt like we had Geelong beaten. In most statistical areas we were on top, yet we couldn't manage to put the score on the board. If you give good sides an opportunity—and Geelong was a very good side—they will punish you on the scoreboard, which is what happened at the end of that game. It was devastating after the year we had had. To be beaten by just 12 points was pretty hard to take.

Playing against Collingwood during 2010 was like playing against ourselves. Like us, they had a pretty strong forward press. We beat them in round three (28 points) when Nick Riewoldt injured his hamstring—ripped it off the bone, in fact—and didn't play again until round 15. It became very different from other years. Nick missed all those games, plus we had some off-field controversies at different times, so the path to September was very different compared to 2009. Somehow, we found a way to put ourselves in a good position to contend, and once we booked our place in the Grand Final we felt full of confidence that we would give ourselves a great chance to win. Having been there before gave us confidence, too, knowing that most of the Collingwood players hadn't. But they were always going to be tough as they had a great year as well.

My role was to play as an inside midfielder. With the amount of rotations in the game by 2010, you didn't go in with any specific match-ups as a midfielder. I knew I'd be opposed to former teammate Luke Ball at times, and at other times Scott Pendlebury, plus a couple of other Magpie mids at different times.

It wasn't a great start for us. Darren Jolly scored the opening goal after just 23 seconds, then they scored another couple of early ones before we hit the scoreboard. It was the worst possible start you could get to a Grand Final! Even walking in at half-time, they led by 24 points (7.8 to 4.2) but should have been a couple more goals in front. They had blown some chances, including two late ones missed by Travis Cloke.

It was pretty quiet and sombre when we first entered the rooms at half-time. It was either Nick (Riewoldt) or our fitness guru, David Misson, who said a few things which sparked everyone. Then Ross made some positional moves, including switching Sam Gilbert to the half-forward line and Farren Ray to a tagging role on Dane Swan, which then released Clint Jones for us. We felt that if we could score the first couple of goals they would start to feel the pressure, particularly as it was their first Grand Final as a group.

We got on top, and 'Gilbo' kicked a goal that made Ross's move a genius one. We also started tackling better and took control around the ball. After kicking a couple of goals, you could feel the Magpies start to tighten up a bit. That last half was a real arm wrestle.

I don't remember anything Ross said at three-quarter time. My memory for specific speeches is not great. I do remember thinking, "We're a massive chance here," and there was a lot of that optimism around the huddle. We knew they were exhausted—we were too!—and because we had been there the year before, we had the confidence that we could go the distance.

Brendon Goddard was everywhere that day. In those matches, when you know your teammate's in the zone, you try to get them the ball as much as possible. I kicked one to him where he flew for a huge mark, and after he kicked the goal I started to think that we might actually win the game—we started to believe. Brendon was magnificent for us that day.

Everyone was pretty spent in that last quarter. I was conscious of not staying on the ground too long, as I felt I had done that in the last quarter in 2009. So I wanted to make sure I came off and had a rest. After Goddard's goal, I went to the bench but then Collingwood scored a lucky goal to put them in front and so I went back on. You watch that last quarter and it looks like no one is moving very quickly, which was because we were all stuffed. Grand Finals are like that, you have nothing left in the tank by the end of the game.

Everyone thought I was outside my scoring range when I lined up for goal in the last quarter. My dad tells the story that I was 65 metres out into the breeze—it gets further out every year! I was just outside 50 and felt confident I could get the journey. I was lucky enough to get onto it and as soon as the ball hit my boot I knew it was a good strike. If I was one metre further out it probably would have been touched on the line. But, lucky for us, I was right on my distance and it went through for a goal.

I can still remember the play that tied the scores. We brought the ball out of defence and 'Rooey' [Riewoldt] took an amazing mark over about three blokes on the wing. I looked up and there weren't too many guys up the field for him to kick to, so I told him to hold on to it so that three or four of us could run up to our half-forward line. He kicked long and the ball was brought to ground, where it sat up perfectly for me. That moment is one I have played through my mind repeatedly since: could I have done something extra? Watching it back, somebody was there to block for me but I thought I was under pressure and so I just banged it on my boot. Maybe I could have laid it up short to Stephen Milne for him to run on to it? I wasn't thinking about the consequences in that split-second when the ball bounced out of Milney's reach and through for a point to tie the scores; I was solely focused on finding my opponent. You don't have the time to stand still and think, plus we had no idea how much time was left in the game. It's a moment that will stay with all of us forever.

When the siren went, signalling a draw, it was disbelief. We weren't too sure what was going to happen next, whether it was extra time or we were to come back the next week. The officials came onto the field and told us we'd be back next week. Everyone was exhausted. There was silence in the crowd, no one knew what to do. I'm sure the fans were all thinking, "We have to somehow find another ticket for next week now." There was plenty going on.

It was a shock to win the Norm Smith Medal. The AFL's media manager, Patrick Keane, came up and told me I had to accept the Medal. I warned him that I couldn't talk, my voice was gone, but he said to just do my best. I still cop it for that today! I had been accidently elbowed in the throat by Dale Thomas in the first quarter, and struggled to talk after that. At quarter-time I was trying to tell the midfielders something but they were all looking at me wondering what I was saying. Even today I can't make a high-pitched scream. If I ever strain my voice, I lose it for a day or two, so I likely did some damage that day. It's not as bad as rugby champion Darren Lockyer's voice, but if I have a big night out or yell too much at training I find that I still lose my voice.

After the presentation, we had to go to a different dressing room because our original rooms were flooded. So that was just another layer of drama during the chaos at the end of that game. We went into rooms on the other side of the ground, and all our gear was there but no one knew where anyone's stuff was at first—it was all over the place! We decided not to attend the after-match function that night so that we could immediately focus on our recovery.

We had a couple of guys who were cooked from the first game. Although we got ourselves up to play again seven days later, some of the guys had spent so much energy in the first game that Collingwood got the better of us early in the Grand Final rematch. They were too good for us, which was devastating. It was hard to take, losing like we did (by 56 points). Early in the last quarter Collingwood knew they had it won and their fans were going berserk, so I was getting pretty angry in that last quarter when the game was out of reach.

I don't think you ever fully get over it. Each time I have been to watch a Grand Final since 2010, I find I'm okay until the last 10 minutes but then all the emotions start coming back. I doubt I'll ever get over it. But it doesn't consume me either. I don't think about it every day. But certainly in the last 10 minutes of each Grand Final those feelings rush back.

Being a Norm Smith medallist is a funny one for me. I'm sure when you ask other guys they give you a very different answer. I appreciate the history around the Medal but, to me, it's a bit of a hollow experience because we didn't win the Grand Final. It's something that, one day, I'll be able to tell me kids, Hunter and Jacob, about—that I actually did something okay when I was younger. I think it's an award that you would enjoy a lot more if you had won the Grand Final that year as well. You don't have a reunion to go and celebrate winning a Norm Smith

Medal, not like you do with a Premiership. It's a team game we play, but I certainly appreciate the history and significance of winning the Norm Smith all the same. It's just that I went home without a Premiership Medal, which took the gloss off it.

People ask me if I have my Medal hanging up on display. I don't. I don't even know where it is! It's in a shoebox, buried in another box from when my wife Tara and I moved from Melbourne to Sydney after I finished playing, so it's somewhere in our garage. I'm sure that one day I'll pull it out and show my boys. Just not right now while they're so young.

My heart scare came at a strange time. I missed 2011 with my second knee reconstruction, then, just after Christmas, I had a routine ECG test done where it was found that I had an abnormality in my heart. I did some follow-up tests during 2012 and then, halfway through the season, they told me I would have to have surgery. It was tougher on my family than it was on me, to be honest. When you're in the middle of it, you are a little oblivious to the full impact, whereas they see you with all the tubes coming out of you, and have to sit through the surgery. But it was certainly a challenge for me. I couldn't do anything for a few months, then pre-season came around and I turned up to train. The club hadn't seen anything of that nature before, so they weren't too sure what program they should give me. I had lost a lot of my fitness, so it was a grind getting back to play again. Thankfully it's all good now and there are no ongoing issues with it, which is a relief. I remember one time having to walk laps with a group of 70-year-olds. I was supposed to be this elite footballer, yet I felt pretty stupid with where I was at with my fitness. I was very thankful I was able to work my way back and play a few more games after that.

In my final season I was taken aback with all the fuss towards me. I didn't see myself as that sort of popular player. I just felt I was someone who got the best out of himself. I wasn't overly quick, couldn't jump high, didn't kick heaps of goals; I was just good at what I could do. That was to put good pressure on, be strong in close, things like that. The biggest thing for me was: was I a good teammate to play with? That was all I aspired to be and I reckon that I probably was in the end.

LENNY HAYES

Statistics

BORN: 14 January 1980
GAMES PLAYED (1999-2014): 297
GOALS: 95
FINALS PLAYED: 15
FINALS GOALS: 5
GRAND FINALS: 3
NORM SMITH MEDAL: 2010 draw (presented by Peter Matera)

— Norm Smith Voting —

Brad Scott: 3 Brendon Goddard, 2 Dale Thomas, 1 Lenny Hayes;
Matthew Lloyd: 3 Hayes, 2 Goddard, 1 Thomas;
Chris Grant: 3 Hayes, 2 Nick Maxwell, 1 Goddard;
Michael Gleeson: 3 Hayes, 2 Thomas, 1 Goddard;
Steve Rielly: 3 Hayes, 2 Sam Fisher, 1 Thomas.

TOTALS: Hayes 13, Goddard 7, Thomas 6, Fisher 2, Maxwell 2.

Scott Pendlebury

Replay

Through his decorated career, Collingwood captain Scott Pendlebury has been one of the game's elite midfielders; his five Copeland Trophies as Magpie best and fairest (2011, 2013-16) are evidence of his consistency over a long period. Always balanced and composed, Pendlebury appears to have an extra second whenever he has ball in hand. Indeed, with his junior basketball background, Pendlebury's ability to "read and react"—as he puts it—in a congested situation has allowed him to flourish around stoppages. He is a five-time All-Australian (2010-14), an International Rules representative (2008), a two-time Anzac medallist (2010-11) and, in 2014, replaced Nick Maxwell as Magpie skipper. In the 2010 Grand Final replay against St Kilda, Pendlebury had 20 kicks, nine handballs, took seven marks and laid 11 tackles.

As a kid, I didn't love playing footy. I loved watching and supporting it, though. I was an avid Melbourne supporter and I remember going along to the local footy in Sale, where we lived, and sitting in our car with my grandpa listening to Melbourne play on the radio. I was always more interested in that than in the game we were

← **BIG GAME PERFORMER** Scott Pendlebury's Norm Smith Medal was no surprise as he continually produces his best in the biggest moments.

watching. I was fascinated by the AFL, the big crowds and all the games. But I didn't enjoy playing it as much as I did watching it. I played it a little bit as a kid, but I was more interested in following Melbourne than playing locally.

I've got an older brother, Kris, and a younger brother, Brian. Growing up in Sale, as with any country family, we tried our hands at every sport we could—tennis, basketball, footy, cricket, golf, roller-blading, skateboarding, BMXing—whatever we could do outdoors, we did. We were lucky in that where we lived was 500 metres away from the basketball stadium and the local footy ground. We could walk there whenever we wanted.

My dad, Bruce, played footy and cricket. My mum, Lisa, played basketball, so they were very outdoorsy. I saw Dad play basketball twice, but he played it like it was a game of footy—he was that rough! My love for basketball came from Mum. From a young age I always loved basketball. It was the opposite to footy in that I loved playing it but didn't enjoy watching it. As basketball was an all-year-round sport, you could always play it. That was one thing I liked about it. Whereas, with footy, you would fall in and out of love with it depending on the time of year.

I enjoyed watching Melbourne's David Schwartz and Jeff Farmer. When I played footy as a kid, I always had Farmer's No. 33 on my back. Then, as I got older, I began following Shane Woewodin, Adem Yze, Cameron Bruce, Brad Green, all those sorts of guys. I didn't go to the 2000 Grand Final where we (Melbourne) lost to Essendon. Instead, I watched it at my best mate's place in Stratford. It wasn't a great day to be a Melbourne supporter, but I was pretty pumped that we were actually in a Grand Final. During that finals series, no one gave us a chance. We knocked off Carlton in the Qualifying Final and North Melbourne in the Preliminary Final. No one had given us a hope of beating North, so it was an exciting time. Kris was an Essendon supporter, so he had the wood over me for a while after that game.

Basketball was where I saw my future. There was a guy in Sale, Rhys Carter, who was four years older than me and he went to the Australian Institute of Sport (AIS), in Canberra, for basketball. I remember growing up and watching him. You were looking up to guys who grew up in your local area, and he was one I looked up to because he was an awesome basketballer. As he had been to the AIS, it made me think that maybe I could do that, too. So when I was 11 or 12, that's when I knew I was going to take my basketball seriously and have a real crack at it. Rhys went to the AIS at 16, and whenever he came home he had always improved, so I figured it must be an amazing program they run up there in Canberra. He was awesome with me; he would always let me know when he was back in Sale and we'd go and work out together.

As a teenager I had thoughts of representing Australia in basketball. In my bedroom at home I had this A4 piece of paper with the world championship year for my age-group in the under-20s on it (2008). Rhys's team had the likes of future NBA star Andrew Bogut in it and they won a Gold Medal. So that was one of my goals, to make that team. That piece of paper was in my bedroom for years. I only took it down in 2007, a year after I began playing in the AFL. I had moved back home for a couple of weeks at the end of the season and I told myself, "I don't need this anymore. It's time to take this down." By that time I had new ambitions in football, but it took me that long to finally put the basketball goal to bed.

I went to the AIS a number of times. Whenever their team had tournaments, or they travelled internationally, they would need guys to go up and help fill out their teams for the local competition up there. I would go and live there for a while and play basketball. Then, when I was up there for the under-18 All-Australian camp, I was playing with guys all my own age and I was offered a scholarship. But I soon felt really lonely and isolated up there. A lot of the guys on scholarships were two to three years older than me. Plus, myself and one other guy were required to go to school, whereas the others had all finished their schooling. I decided to go back to Sale after a few weeks.

My original plan was to come back to Sale for a year, finish my schooling, keep playing basketball, then move back to the AIS at the end of that year to focus on the World Championships with a new intake of guys. I was fortunate that my basketball coach in Sale was the All-Australian under-18 coach, David Mowbray. David remains one of the best coaches I've had in my sporting career. Although I was training for basketball, I don't know why but I had this itch to play footy again. Probably because my older brother played.

I made a phone call to Gippsland Power in February 2005. By then, their year was pretty close to being sorted out. I asked if I could go down and do a pre-season with them. Power's talent manager, Peter Francis, knew my older brother as Kris had played at Power for two years. Peter said, "We can't promise you anything. Come down for a run, we've got a practice match on Saturday which you can play in. It's probably more unlikely than likely, but we'll have a look at you." I played in that game and I think I went okay at centre half-back. Before I knew it, I had made the Gippy Power team and was playing in round one. I found it fun playing with that group of guys. There were 20 of us who, every Wednesday, would jump on a minibus in Sale and go up to Morwell to train. We won the flag that year, barely lost a game and I found this real passion for footy. Myself and Rob Eddy were bottom-aged guys in that team—Rob went on to play for St Kilda against us in the 2010 Grand Finals—and Paul Hudson was our coach.

The biggest challenge for me was understanding what the coaches wanted me to do. I played on a wing, so it was pretty simple. Picking up the terminology of footy was a challenge, though. I spoke with 'Huddo' about it and told him, "I've got no idea about any of this terminology, so after the meetings I'll need to ask you some questions, if that's all right?" He was awesome about it and made it so simple for me. I played wing-defence, as we used to call it. My role was to play from our forward-50 all the way into our defence. I wasn't required to go inside our forward-50 arc. That was all they wanted me to do. Nice and simple. It made my development an easier transition than it could have otherwise been due to my limited footy background.

What I was able to bring from basketball to football was my professionalism and work rate. I feel that, in the AFL system right through the TAC Cup, certainly in comparison to basketball, young players are given everything. Everything is paid for. Whatever you want as you are coming through those representative teams, you get it. Whereas in basketball there is no one there to help you and you have to do it all yourself. So I was pretty mature as a 17-year-old kid trying to enter the AFL system. In basketball, I had to learn to do a lot of things myself, and it allowed me to mature at a young age. It gave me a strong work ethic, which I utilised as I started to develop my way through the TAC Cup system.

Playing basketball as much as I did growing up, it was all about read and react. As a point guard, which I was, you have got to learn which option is the right option to take; you've got to think a lot more when you play basketball. Whereas, in footy at the under-10s and under-12s levels, if you're the best player it's simply about going to get the ball. You take marks and you don't really think about the game as much—it just happens. But basketball is very much a decision-making game. When I first started playing in the midfield, I recognised that it was a read and react game. If you saw someone free you might give a quick handball, whereas if he's under pressure you might hang on to the ball for that extra half a second. Or you might see a better option out of the corner of your eye, and by letting the play unfold for half a second you can then open the game up.

I didn't feel the pressure of being a No. 5 draft pick. I didn't play much early on and was just stoked to get drafted. What really helped me was having 'Daisy' Thomas get selected at pick two before me. He was the club's first draft pick, whereas I was just another one of the guys the club drafted, albeit at No. 5. So having Daisy as the pin-up boy of Collingwood's 2005 draftees made it easier.

Another blessing in disguise was getting glandular fever in December of my first pre-season. I missed a couple of months and the expectation, the pressure to play senior footy, was gone. By the time I was back, fully fit and ready to go, there were no expectations or timelines on when I would play senior footy. I spoke with assistant coach Alan Richardson and the plan was to play VFL reserves at Williamstown and work my way up through there. There was no pressure to perform. I also didn't have high expectations going into my first year about trying to play in the seniors.

THE NORM SMITH MEDAL

I was happy just getting into the AFL system and then trying to work it out from there.

Daisy's early senior games in 2006 lit a fire within me. Watching him, I thought that, considering I had played with him the year before, then I, too, could surely play at AFL level.

When I was playing at Williamstown under Brad Gotch, Collingwood coach Mick Malthouse would pull me aside and instruct me on things I could be doing better. One time, against Werribee at Werribee, 'Gotchy' put the team board up in front of everyone and Mick walked over and moved my name from the wing into the centre. Mick grabbed me after that and said, "You need to learn how to make it as a midfielder, because you won't make it as a wingman." That was fairly honest feedback for an 18-year-old to hear! It was great, though, as it was another challenge for me to take on; to try figuring out how to play in the midfield. I needed to get used to the physicality in there, that and the ruckman's hit zones. I felt a lot more comfortable being in the midfield, rather than out on the wing where you're just running up and down. If the ball came out to you on the wing, great, but if it didn't you found yourself kicking stones and being out of the action.

I started working closely with 'Richo'. We watched guys like Lenny Hayes, Ben Cousins, Daniel Kerr and Chris Judd, and we would go along to different games to watch those guys play, trying to follow their different running patterns. We'd talk about things they did well, things that worked, things that they could have done differently. It was a great education for me.

My debut against Brisbane (round 10, 2006) was a weird night. Blake Caracella injured his neck, Dane Swan pulled his hamstring and someone else went down as well. I remember being the lone guy on the bench and thinking, "I'm bound to get some field time tonight because there are a few injured guys out there." My first kick was a goal, so that was memorable. But it feels like a long time ago now.

Everything about Collingwood is cool. When you don't barrack for Collingwood you don't really like them. But once you get to the club, your eyes are opened to how huge the club is. They've got the biggest supporter base, the training facilities and the location of the club in inner-Melbourne are ideal, your president is one of the most outspoken people in football, Mick (Malthouse) was an iconic figure in the game, Nathan Buckley was one of the best players to ever play. The whole club is set up really well. If you want to be great, it's the perfect place to be.

I almost played in a Grand Final in my second season. Although I don't remember a lot about the Preliminary Final against Geelong in 2007, I do remember Scotty Burns right at the end getting a clearance on the half-forward flank and then the siren sounded—we lost by five points. I could see how gutted the older guys were. As a younger player, I probably wasn't as gutted about the loss as they were. What I took away from it was the fantastic opportunity I had to experience such a game in what was just my 32nd match. It gave me a massive hunger to try and get back there, particularly because everyone was telling me those opportunities don't come around often. Having that experience so early showed me that they were right. We had worked so hard to not get the reward we were striving for. I was certainly shattered it didn't happen for us, and it hung in my mind throughout 2008. We didn't get there that year (lost the first Semi-Final to St Kilda by 34 points), nor in 2009 (lost the Preliminary Final to Geelong by 73; Pendlebury was injured), so we were desperate to do it in 2010.

I latched on to Paul Licuria during those early days. Mick and Richo said that Paul was the best trainer and prepared the best, so they suggested I try and emulate what he was doing. I worked extremely closely with him early on. Having 'Bucks' and 'Burnsy' there was great also. I would look at them and I just knew that they were Collingwood through and through. Everything they did, the way they lived, the way they prepared, they were always great role models. And if you ever needed anything, they were both very approachable. But they were at a stage in their careers where they couldn't train every single session, couldn't lift weights in the gym flat-out every session either, because they had to manage their bodies and be a bit smarter. So that's why 'Licca' was great for me early on. He taught me where to go, when to pace myself and how to mentally challenge myself. I took so much from Licca's lessons.

THE NORM SMITH MEDAL

I never really get nervous. I'm pretty relaxed going into games. I'm a big believer that, if you do the work you won't go into the game nervous. I know nerves play a part in what everyone does—we all get them—but the more nervous you get can stem from when you know you haven't done all the work beforehand. I always try doing all the work and preparing as best I can—both physically and mentally—and from there I know I'll be right to go on game day.

We played St Kilda in round three, 2010, and they restricted us to 41 points. I remember thinking St Kilda was the best side in it and we had a bit of work to do to catch them. I knew we were a good side, but I didn't then know just how good we could be. The next time we played them, in round 16, we beat them by eight goals. It was then that I thought, "We're a big chance here if we can have a good run with injuries." We had a team that was really clicking, and we were playing a great brand of defensive footy. We could attack, but we could restrict really well also. So that was when I first got excited; when I first thought that, "If this all falls into place, this is going to be exciting."

Grand Final week was a very different experience. It's hectic, it's busy, it's exciting, and if you go and get a coffee down the street everyone is talking about the upcoming game. Suddenly your face becomes very recognisable when you're out anywhere. Mick Malthouse was awesome immediately after that Preliminary Final victory over the Cats (by 41 points). We had a fairly young side and Mick was all about us embracing the week. He'd been through a few Grand Finals himself—one as a player with Richmond (1980) and five as a coach (West Coast 1991-92 and '94, and Collingwood 2002-03) to that stage—so he wanted us to embrace everything about the week. He said, "If you go to get a coffee and people are coming up and wishing you luck for the game, say thanks and how you're looking forward to it." Even the Grand Final Parade was a fun, rather than a daunting, experience for us.

I was one of the players who was lucky that we had a draw. It gave me a chance to make amends for a fairly quiet game; I played just an average game in that first Grand Final. I didn't win my position, didn't play my role as well as I could for the side, and I was part of a midfield group that was well beaten by the St Kilda midfielders. So, for us guys, we felt pretty fortunate after the draw that we got another chance the following week.

Straight after the game, Eddie McGuire, Mick and (fitness coach) David Buttifant made the call that we should still attend the after-match function. Jason Gram is a good mate of mine, and he told me that St Kilda didn't go to their after-match function—they cancelled it to focus on their recovery and preparation. Looking back on it, I think that was one of the best things we did that week. It allowed us a chance to get together with all our families and talk about everything. Mick and Eddie got up and spoke about it being half-time in the Grand Final, so that helped our mindset to go from one of disappointment at not winning, to suddenly thinking that the job was half done. Then our thinking switched towards the fact we had an opportunity to play in another Grand Final. That helped my mindset, and I'm sure it helped the mindset of my teammates. We then had a really fun week. We didn't dwell on the what-ifs of the draw. It was a case of: let's get at them again next week.

Both Grand Finals started the same way. On both occasions, we came out and went forward from the first bounce. In the draw, Darren Jolly scored an early goal. In the replay, we got a clearance, it went sideways, Chris Dawes knocked it to me and I kicked it to Travis Cloke in the goal square. Unfortunately, Dane Swan had given away a free kick in the middle of the ground for decking Clinton Jones, so Clokey wasn't able to kick the goal.

I don't have clear memories of the game. It's just a blur. If I sit down and watch it I can recall what happened, but overall it remains a blur in my memory.

The thing I remember most is Heath Shaw's smother on Nick Riewoldt. That smother has become an iconic moment in Grand Final history. It was inspiring! We had dominated play, yet they were about to score a goal in typical St Kilda fashion—they were expert at holding up, holding up, then scoring a goal on the counter attack. If Riewoldt kicks that goal, it's 20-7 and suddenly, despite dominating play, we are only two goals in front. It was as if that moment was the event that broke St Kilda. We went up the other end and Brent Macaffer goaled for us. They may disagree, but for me it felt like that was their little chance to get back into the game early on and we were able to take it away from them.

Darren Jolly was super for us. Bringing such an experienced player down from Sydney was great for our team. He was a stable guy in our midfield; we could lean on him after his finals experience at the Swans—he had played in their 2005 Premiership side. 'Joll' performed really well for us in those Grand Finals, sliding forward and kicking goals as well as competing so hard in the ruck. He was such a great athlete that he was also like an extra defender for us at different times.

Our pressure all day, and particularly in that third quarter, was the trademark of Collingwood all year. We could attack and score heavily against sides, but we never got into shootouts because we made sure that we restricted their ability to score. We were great at applying forward pressure, and I recall one instance where Alan Didak applied a smother and then snapped a right-foot goal. We knew then that it was party time, to a degree.

In that final quarter, I remember thinking that I couldn't believe I was about to be part of a Premiership. It was the best feeling. Then the siren sounds and everyone goes nuts. There are so many people involved: trainers, staff, it's so much bigger than just the 22 guys who play the game. It was great to celebrate over those next few hours, have some beers with the staff and to see the smiles on everyone's faces. It was such a reward for the whole footy club: the fans, the guys who didn't play but who had been involved throughout the year, the staff. It was an unbelievable experience.

The Norm Smith Medal didn't enter my mind. I was just trying to celebrate and get around to all the boys. Before you know it, the ground is full of people. I had mates who didn't play that day but were on our list, so I was celebrating with them as well. You get over to the St Kilda boys and shake their hands, so your mind is all over the place in those moments after the final siren. I remember an AFL staff member tapped me on the shoulder and said, "Scott, you've won the Norm Smith Medal." I didn't even really take it in when he said it! A few seconds later it sank in, but I still didn't know what to think. Due to the strength of our side that day, we had five or six guys who would have been worthy Norm Smith medallists. We played such a good brand of footy and I was probably on the receiving end; I received a few handballs here and there. Winning the Premiership was enough for me. The Norm Smith Medal was a little bit of icing on the cake. The Premiership alone was unbelievable.

Former North Melbourne forward Arnold Briedis got my name wrong when he presented the Medal to me. He couldn't say my name and instead mumbled "Scott Embereem." I still cop flak from the boys for that today.

It's funny being recognised as a big-game player. Because I think that in the big games you need to do the simplest things well. You often see a dropped mark or a fumble in a big game, and I think that guys get caught up in the size of the crowd, the emotion, or in trying to do something they don't normally do. For me, in big games—or any game for that matter—I like to focus on going out there and executing the basics as well as I can.

What went wrong in the 2011 Grand Final? I don't know! It's a funny one to try and find reasons for why we lost (by 38 points). In my mind, we were a better side in 2011 than we were in 2010—we dominated games. In fact, I think some sides doubted they could get near us, let alone beat us. Geelong, though, was the one side that could get us—all three games we lost that season were against the Cats. In the Grand Final we started really well and were a couple of goals in front early. But in the last quarter, when the game was there to be won, they kicked a couple of important goals and from there the floodgates opened, particularly so once we realised we were too far back to win. If it wasn't for Geelong, it would have been the perfect season.

As captain I'm all about trying to pass down the lessons I have learned from Bucks, Burnsy and Nick Maxwell. Prepare really well and make sure you're hungry; that you're a competitor. To make the most of the opportunity we've got, because we live a fortunate life to be playing in the AFL. So, make the most of the opportunity and don't take it for granted. In the way you train and the way you play, just give everything of yourself. That's what I try to do as a player, and what I've tried doing as captain.

THE NORM SMITH MEDAL

It's hard to explain the coaching differences between Mick and Bucks. Because Bucks learned a lot of his football lessons from Mick. Tactically they have their differences, as every coach does. Mick liked to play wide around the boundary, minimising risk; and Bucks is a bit like that, but he also doesn't mind us taking the game on a little bit more and playing with more flair. I know a lot of people say they are very different, but for me I don't think they are all that different in their philosophies. I can see that Bucks has been moulded by Mick. With evolution, the game constantly changes and you can't always do the same things from year to year. For me, as I want to get into coaching when I finish playing, they have both been fantastic to learn from. Just different things, like how you motivate your players and staff, how you delegate. They are both a wealth of knowledge.

I had a little taste of coaching in 2017 when I broke my finger. I really enjoyed that experience. Although I hope it isn't something I need to think about any time soon, I need to begin looking at life after footy and coaching is where I'd like to stay involved in the game. Bucks and the coaching staff are willing to educate me, and I'm always asking them questions which they are happy to help me with. But I've got more to achieve as a player before I worry about that.

──── Statistics ────

BORN: 7 January 1988
GAMES PLAYED (2006-Current): 263[1]
GOALS: 163
FINALS PLAYED: 17
FINALS GOALS: 7
GRAND FINALS: 3
PREMIERSHIP: 2010
NORM SMITH MEDAL: 2010 (presented by Arnold Briedis)

---

1   Statistics correct to round 13, 2018 season.

SCOTT PENDLEBURY

— Norm Smith Voting —

Tom Harley: 3 Dale Thomas, 2 Scott Pendlebury, 1 Dane Swan;
Danny Frawley: 3 Pendlebury, 2 Steele Sidebottom, 1 Nathan Brown;
Dermott Brereton: 3 Pendlebury, 2 Swan, 1 Thomas;
Martin Blake: 3 Sidebottom, 2 Pendlebury, 1 Darren Jolly;
Stan Alves: 3 Sidebottom, 2 Luke Ball, 1 Jolly.

TOTALS: Pendlebury 10, Sidebottom 8, Thomas 4, Swan 3, Jolly 2, Ball 2, Brown 1.

Jimmy Bartel

Jimmy Bartel is one of the game's most decorated players. Indeed, he is one of just nine men to have played 300 games, won a Brownlow Medal and played in a Premiership;[1] add a Norm Smith Medal and Bartel is one of just two players, with Brisbane's Simon Black, to have produced that quartet of accolades. He was courageous, durable, fair, reliable and competitive, attributes that endeared him not only to Geelong supporters, but also to the wider football community. In Geelong's three winning Grand Finals (2007, 2009, 2011), Bartel was called upon to play three different roles, and was among the best players in each. In his Norm Smith Medal performance against Collingwood, which the Cats won by 38 points, Bartel had 15 kicks, 11 handballs, took six marks and kicked three goals.

I didn't have the older or younger brother to compete against when growing up. But I had two older sisters, Olivia and Emma, and my mum Dianne, who were all sporty themselves. They were super-competitive in everything we did. We'd have a family game of tennis and my older sister and myself would play against my middle sister and Mum,

---

[1] The nine are Dick Reynolds, Jason Akermanis, Simon Black, Sam Mitchell, Gavin Wanganeen, Mark Ricciuto, Adam Goodes, Shane Crawford and Bartel.

← **STAR PERFORMER** Jimmy Bartel was another player who produced at superhuman levels when the chips were down. With Brownlow and Norm Smith Medals, he can claim to being one of the best of the best during Geelong's golden run.

and everything was competitive, right down to every point. Even if we were playing cards, or a board game, we all wanted to win. Mum was pretty good at field hockey, and could hold her own in any sport because she had really good hand-eye coordination.

Mum was massive on me playing sport. There was never too much sport we could play, as it meant that you were outside being active. Not only were there the sporting benefits, but the great people you would meet as well made sport worthwhile. There was nothing wrong with being competitive, and there would be goal-setting that took place as well, trying to challenge yourself against people, constantly. That's what she always encouraged. To never take the easy approach. I was lucky that, because she encouraged me so much, I actually enjoyed training from a young age and all through my career.

Mum being a primary school teacher was great for my development. Every school holidays we would tell her what sport we wanted to play and she would bring home the school's sports equipment. One time we set up a mini Olympics in our backyard, as Mum brought home the shot put, the discus, and even a couple of hurdles that she had strapped on to the roof of the car. One year she brought home the high jump mat and poles! We were encouraged to be competitive, but never in a bad way. You were always expected to shake hands at the end of it, knowing that whatever the outcome you had given your best.

Cricket was my first love. I played in the under-17 national carnival for Victoria, then not long after that I was drafted to Geelong (pick 8, 2001 AFL Draft[2]); so that certainly helped me to make my decision to choose footy over cricket. What I enjoyed about football was the team environment, where you rely on each other to get the result. I know cricket is a team sport, but it's only you batting and only you bowling. Having said that, if the growth we have seen in T20 cricket had been taking place when I was young, things may have been different for me. I always preferred bowling because, if you made an error when you were batting you were done, whereas if you were hit for a four when bowling you always had the next ball to make up for it.

---

[2] This was the so-called Super Draft: the first 10 were Luke Hodge, Luke Ball, Chris Judd, Graham Polak, Xavier Clarke, Ashley Sampi, David Hale, Bartel, Luke Molan and Sam Power. Bartel was recruited via St Joseph's, Bell Park and the Geelong Falcons.

I loved footy, but it picked me as much as I picked it.

I was a Richmond supporter, and was captivated by the Tigers during 1995 when they had a real run at the finals. I think everyone in the team, bar Matthew Knights, had long hair! I loved Duncan Kellaway as a player. There was a period there where Kellaway played on Jason Dunstall and Tony Lockett, both great full-forwards, then he went into the middle on James Hird and Michael Voss, then he went to centre half-back and played on the likes of Wayne Carey. I thought it was ridiculous how he was able to do all those roles! I even enjoyed his unfashionable kicking skills. He was a terrific player. My grandfather was a Richmond supporter, and that was a common bond between us. Growing up in Geelong, I loved the Cats, too. At three-quarter time they used to let you into Kardinia Park for free, so we would go and stand in the outer and watch the last quarter before kicking the footy on the oval after the game.

For some reason, Gary Ablett snr loved playing against Richmond; he always kicked stacks of goals against them. I ran on to the ground the day Ablett kicked his 100th goal, and again when he scored his 1000th goal. I didn't get close to him, I pretty much just stepped on the ground so that I could tell people I ran on. Who would have thought that I would end up playing with his sons, Gary and Nathan?

I loved watching Kenny Hinkley play, too, because I wore long sleeves as a kid like he did. Kenny would baulk everyone on a half-back flank and was great to watch. He later coached my local footy club, Bell Park, so I started forming a bond with him there. Then I got to Geelong and he was the assistant coach, so we kept crossing paths all through my career. He coached the seniors at Bell Park, but I would jump in and train with the older guys and Kenny would always take the time to say hello. I remember seeing the Geelong players around town and just thinking that they were enormous. They were like monsters when I was a kid.

I never put a lot of thought into being drafted. I was one of those kids who, when footy finished, I would go to the cupboard and get out my cricket gear straight away. All through my junior career, that was my mindset. I was never a kid who, at six and seven years old, said I was going to play AFL footy. I grew up also playing basketball and I played golf on weekends with mates, so I was never playing footy thinking that it would lead me to be drafted.

I felt out of place when I first arrived at Geelong in 2001. Earlier that year, I had gone and watched Richmond play Geelong and Brad Ottens kicked a few goals, as did Steven King, and I was in awe of how well they played, particularly Steven. Then, just a few weeks later, I'm trying to kick to him on the lead; I didn't know what to call him! I wondered whether it was rude for me to call him 'Kingy', should it be 'Steven' instead? Or 'Mr King'? So I felt like I didn't belong. What helped to put me at ease was the fact I was one of eight draftees that year, so it was almost like we got to hold each other's hands through that first period. You certainly feel the pressure because you want to justify why they would take you with their first pick (eighth overall in the 2001 National Draft), so you wanted to do well to return the favour. Also, coach Mark 'Bomber' Thompson would ride me pretty hard about it, saying things like: "We used pick eight on you, so you better perform well." He was always pretty tough on the first pick each year, guys like Joel Corey (pick eight in 1999) and Andrew Mackie (pick seven in 2002), he always held you accountable in that sense. But we were also told the first day we got there that it didn't matter what number you were drafted, everyone was now at zero and all had the same opportunities if they worked hard enough.

The club, through recruiter Stephen Wells and coach 'Bomber' Thompson, targeted competitive, aggressive players. Yes, they had to have talent, but they were big on the character of the player they were recruiting. They wanted a massive group of super-competitive blokes, which is what they got. There would be training drills where blokes would lose their temper and be fighting amongst each other. I couldn't count the amount of times Steve Johnson wanted to wrestle Paul Chapman! What all that created was an ultra-competitive environment where everything was a competition. And Bomber was the ring leader for all us young kids who wanted to compete all the time. Training was all about competition. When guys came in from other clubs, they were always surprised at the amount of match practice we had. I think that type of training stood us in good stead later on for the big games.

I felt pretty comfortable with the physical aspect of AFL footy from the start. It was the pure running aspect which took time to adjust to; that endurance and power needed to play full games. The really good players had had five or more good years of pre-seasons, so I was finding that they could get to more contests than I could. It was about different types of running. I was used to jogging most of the time, with the odd sprint each quarter. When I got to AFL level I was expected to go flat out then have a rest; it was high speed, repetitive efforts that took a lot of adjusting to.

My first game was unbelievable. We played a powerhouse Essendon, it was round one, 2002, and they were a mature side. My first kick was smothered, so there was no glory in being in the first-kick-first-goal club. I'm a member of the first kick smothered club instead! I was coming up against guys like Joe Misiti, Matthew Lloyd, James Hird, just big bodies everywhere, and we were this young side in comparison. I got crunched a couple of times, and looking back I probably got concussed as well because I was seeing stars for a while that day. It was hard first up, but I loved the speed of it. I could see things unfolding before they occurred, and I knew that if I didn't make a good decision they would hurt us on the rebound. It was a great lesson, despite the fact we got belted.

I needed to improve my all-round game. I had come from playing predominantly in the midfield in under-18 footy, where I would accumulate possessions and be free to play my own game. So I needed to learn about the different transitions in an AFL game, going from attack to defence, as well as the correct positioning for different phases. They wanted me to go back to the seconds and work on those technical things. They really pushed the message into all of us to value every second of our time in the AFL; they would always speak with us about the privilege we had playing AFL footy.

Playing in my first final, in 2004, was a bit like the first quarter of round one each season. It's all about intensity, bodies going everywhere, and plenty of mistakes. But unlike round one, it was like that for the full four quarters. Relentless. It never died off, and sides were willing to try different things to get an edge during the game, being a knock-out situation, so it was mentally draining as well as physically taxing. I had played in an under-17 Premiership with the Geelong Falcons in my first year. Myself and Luke Hodge were in the side. Then the second year we made it to the Preliminary Final. Damien Christensen was coach, and he had played in a lot of local Grand Finals, so he would talk to us about the experiences of that. Then I played in the VFL finals series in 2002 when Geelong won the Premiership. Although it was nothing compared to an AFL final, the preparation that went into it, and the lose-and-go-home factor helped you to prepare for those experiences at AFL level.

Sometimes a player beats you off his own boot. That happened to us in 2005, against Sydney, when Nick Davis dominated the last quarter. Nobody gave us a chance before the game, but we built together a good game-plan and Sydney was just hanging on going into the last quarter. Then Davis played the best 15 minutes of his life. It was unbelievable. Everything was going on for him. There were no tougher losses than that, but the good thing about our group was, whenever we took a tough beating we all fronted up to it. I remember being in the meeting room afterwards, and not one player was singled out for blame; it was the whole team. And it was all about positioning. "If we ever get into that situation again, this is what's going to happen," Bomber said. It was the hardest way to learn it, but when we later played in big games I think everyone was calm because we all knew what we had to do.

The much-publicised internal review at the end of 2006 wasn't as disastrous as people believed it to be at the time. We had injured guys during pre-season and so a lot had entered the season underdone. But we still won 10-and-a-half games, so it wasn't a complete disaster. Certainly not to the level everyone was saying it was. Yes, it was a failure that we didn't make the finals, but we didn't finish last either. What we did know was that we had to make some changes; that what we were doing wasn't working. We needed Bomber to be focused on coaching, and so the club brought Neil Balme in to help him. Neil was a steady hand who provided great balance. In the past we would ride a win really high, then suffer a loss really badly, to the extent that we would almost drag our tails into the next game. But Balmey had that calming influence, where he would say "You're not going that great, but you're not going that bad." That was what we needed to gain greater balance and perspective as a group.

We changed our strength and conditioning program. The summer before, having seen how big the Brisbane side was, we tried to copy them. But we were almost too big and we couldn't run. So we trimmed it all off the next pre-season, and we went back to playing the "Geelong way". It was what Geelong as a club had been famous for during its successful period in the 1990s, and also in the 1950s and 1960s when the Cats last won Premierships, that free-flowing attack. Yes, you still defend hard, but then you launch your attack. Bomber recognised that everyone was trying to follow the Sydney and West Coast model of shutting games down, but that wasn't in our nature, not when you have players like Gary Ablett, Steve Johnson, Matthew Scarlett and Corey Enright. They were naturally attacking players, so we decided to play to our strengths.

I still struggle to comprehend being a Brownlow medallist. When I won it in 2007, we were playing in the Grand Final a few days later, so my focus was solely on the upcoming game and I didn't get to celebrate winning it at the time. What blew me away was, when you go to a Brownlow they have montages of the previous winners like Simon Black (2002), Mark Ricciuto (2003, tied), and Paul Kelly (1995) who I loved watching when I was a kid. Then suddenly, a couple of hours later, I'm standing on stage as one of them. I still don't believe it.

We were confident going into the 2007 Grand Final. Andrew Mackie and I often stood down one end of the line during the National Anthem, and we were both pretty laid-back guys. Before the 2007 Grand Final, he looked at me and said, "We've got this today, don't we?" I said, "I think we're a good chance." We had a bit of a giggle about it. There was no tension in it. I remember Brad Ebert having a shot early for Port Adelaide and missing, and you could almost see everyone take a deep breath because the adrenalin had been pumping in those first few minutes. That miss seemed to allow us to finally get our second wind and to settle into the game.

We led by 52 points at half-time but the game wasn't over. With the nature of footy, despite being so far ahead at half-time, you knew that if

Port kicked the first couple of goals in the third quarter they were back in the game. But by halfway through the third quarter we were still pouring the goals on, so we knew by three-quarter time that we were going to win. It meant that we got to play a whole quarter of a Grand Final having the luxury of taking it all in. It was one of the few times where we got to play football purely for the enjoyment. That doesn't happen much at AFL level.

I got excited before big matches. How cool was it that I got to go to the MCG, in front of 90,000 people, and play my games of football! I was always reflecting on that. It was the whole reason I trained, to get prepared for those moments. I always took the view that I could sleep more comfortably at night having had a crack at it than if I had stood out of the play. It was about trying, maybe failing, but always doing anything other than *not* trying.

I was always taught that, the bigger the game, the more the fundamentals become important. It almost sounds boring or repetitious, but it really is about doing the simple stuff over and over again that is most important in big games. Coaches always told me to control the things I could control. I couldn't do anything about the crowd. When I was lining up for goal, it was the exact same action I needed to take if I was kicking in the park, it's just that there are 90,000 people watching what I'm doing. The action doesn't change, so it's important that you stick to what you can control in those situations. What other people think about your performance is none of your business, it was never something I worried about. Thinking about what people will think if I miss isn't helping me to kick the goal, so why worry about it? The only thing that was going to help me was catching my breath and making clean contact with the footy.

Courage comes with focus. When you think of the focused players, like Joel Selwood and Glenn Archer, they lock their eyes on the footy and you could shoot fireworks off around them and they wouldn't even know. It's the single-mindedness of someone like a Robert Harvey, who could be battered from pillar to post yet could still get himself up and keep running. So I put courage with focus and determination. But you also need the skills to execute it. There was a time early in my career where

I wasn't realising how reckless I was, going into contests. A couple of times I was even put on report purely for coming into a contest clumsily and causing front-on contact. Or, conversely, I would come back with the flight for a mark and come out of it with sore ribs or concussion. I needed to work on my technique, to protect me from myself. I spent hours with assistant coach Brendan McCartney, working on my technique to get better at the skill.

I've never watched any of the four Grand Finals I played in. I maintain good thoughts of each game, so I haven't needed to sit down and watch them again. I will one day, though. I look at the 2008 Grand Final a little bit different to how others do. Yes, I was shattered that we lost, but I'm big on giving the opposition its dues. They're entitled to play well, and Hawthorn during that finals series out-performed us. We scrapped our way past the Bulldogs in the Preliminary Final, and were pretty lucky to beat them. In the end we learned so many lessons out of losing in 2008 that we might not have won in 2009 had we won in '08. In 2009, it was still burning in the guys' guts, and that Grand Final was a hot one. So having guys on our team who were refusing to let go because they didn't want to allow 2008 to happen again worked in our favour. Bomber mentioned it to us at three-quarter time. He said, "You're not coming off the field as a loser." It had been mentioned at the start of pre-season that year, and he had made the point that things would be changing in the sense that we would not be taking injured players into games anymore, something that had happened at times during 2008. We needed fully fit guys, all the time, so that we could put the foot down when we needed to.

I played every Grand Final in a different position. I started 2009 at half-forward, and was winning a fair bit of footy early on. We used to play one of our forwards as another midfielder. You would start at half-forward and just move up after the bounce. On that day, I remember Bomber came flying down from the coach's box at quarter-time and said to me, "Are you on Lenny Hayes?" I said, "No, I'm at half-forward." "Well, you've got him for the rest of the game! Don't let him touch it again." Lenny had been going bananas in the first quarter. Late in the year there were a couple of times where Brendan McCartney had swung me on to an opposition player because, although we had Cameron Ling stopping someone, the good sides had more than one quality player so sometimes we needed to clamp down on more than one. There were times where Brendan would ask me to spend 10 minutes on someone to try to curtail their influence. So I had some practice before the Grand Final. It was pretty clear that Lenny was going to beat us single-handedly if he kept going the way he was, so my plan was to stick as close to him as I could. In that situation, Bomber didn't care if I didn't get the ball, he just didn't want Lenny getting it. I had to have total trust in the coach, because we didn't want '08 to happen again. So if he thought it was the move we had to make, then I just had to do it. If I do it, and we still lose, I've done everything I can for the team. And I had the trust in my teammates to be doing the same.

Criticism of Tom Harley as captain didn't sit well with me. I have always loved celebrating my teammates' success, and I think Tom was undersold on how good a player he was. He was an All-Australian centre half-back (2008), so he was no mug. He was a great intercept mark, would often take the opposition's big forward, and he was perfect for our team at that time. He had a really good understanding of how to communicate with the coaches as well as with the players. We had some different personalities in our team. We had footy nerds, we had footy larrikins, and we had everything in between. He was really good for me, personally. He was in locker number two, and I was in number three, so from my early days he was like a big brother to me. We had some really good conversations, and he was the perfect leader for our team at that time and a great captain for us.

Tom Harley and Cameron Ling had similarities as leaders. They were both smart and articulate. But they probably drove things in different ways. 'Harls' was a bit more subtle, whereas 'Lingy' was louder and more vocal. They were similar in their styles, though, and ruthless on values. They wanted you to be an individual, but on three or four key values they would never budge or compromise, and that made them great leaders.

My two senior coaches had different styles, too. Bomber was big on teaching the fundamentals and game style whereas Chris Scott used a lot of video and technical teaching. When Chris came in after 2010, we already had a pretty mature list, so he was able to take some edges off some stuff we had been doing, then add some new layers to it. So I think it was a great time for him to come in when he did. Collingwood had cracked us in 2010, and it took someone from outside the club to see that. And he was really astute in explaining to us how we could work our way back to beating Collingwood again.

Football is a test, and people think losing is a great motivator, but winning is, too. I always liked being the challenged team, because it meant you got to play in a big game every week. Every game had meaning, because every team wanted to test themselves against the best, so we were getting the best of everyone. And that brought out the best in us. When you get physically tested over and over again, then you come through the other side, it builds a confidence, a belief, in your side that you can stand up to anyone in any situation.

I was pretty crook the week before the 2011 Grand Final. I had been sick, and then I had my wisdom teeth break through. They felt pretty bad, and I couldn't eat much, so we were contemplating pulling them out before the game. I decided not to in the end, but I know that there were also rumours that I was taking broken ribs into the game. That was never the case, but I was certainly crook all week leading in. In fact, I struggled through the Preliminary Final because of that. I came off numerous times in the prelim, and had to go and stand down the race just until I composed myself. But I was never not going to play the Grand Final.

Travis Varcoe kicked a goal before anyone had a chance to move out of position. He kicked it that quickly, it felt like it was part of the pre-game! It was lucky he scored those two early goals in the Grand Final, because it was the Travis Cloke show for the next half an hour. It looked like he was going to kick eight or nine goals the way he was going. But the change happened when Tom Lonergan went on to him. Tom just seems to play well against the very best. He's super-disciplined, and was playing for his first Premiership. When we think of unbelievable comebacks, it's extraordinary to see what Tom has done to fight back. He's got the longest arms in the world, which is ideal when playing on the best forwards. His role on Cloke was enormous for us.

I always felt I was in the game that day. Some players start a bit slow and they get worried, but from the outset I felt I was always around the play and was feeling good physically. Starting on the wing, I was able to get myself into the contest early. Then I moved to half-forward after James Podsiadly went off with an injured shoulder in the second quarter. Me going to half-forward was for team structure. There were lots of contests around the ground, and I knew Joel Selwood, James Kelly and Paul Chapman would never give up and would show Collingwood that we weren't going to go away. Me going to centre half-forward, despite being a short-arse (Bartel stood 187cm) was okay because I had played a lot of school footy there. In my time at Geelong I got shifted around everywhere, so the coach making a move in-game was not an issue.

I kicked a crucial goal in the second quarter. I remember there was a ball-up near the boundary line, and in my mind I was thinking that the ruckman would try hitting the ball towards the boundary as that was the safe option. I wanted to tempt him to try hitting it past me, knowing full well that if he hit it out on the full it would be called deliberate and we would get a free kick. As soon as he hit it towards the boundary my instinct was to let the ball go out. That's what happened, so I suddenly had a free kick. After every training session, I loved to kick barrels and snaps for goal, and I would stand up against the fence with assistant coach Blake Caracella, and we'd go through the way guys held the footy to kick snaps. So I reckon I had kicked that snap goal 200 times in training. I knew what to do, and I went through the cues I learned with Blake. I wanted to aim for the far goal post, because I knew the ball would arc a certain way. I flushed it, and kicked the goal.

Repeatedly training for different scenarios is critical to performing them in big games. Nothing is a fluke, and with the amount of hours Tom Hawkins spent on short leading patterns and body work, during and after training, it was only a matter of time before he would succeed at AFL level. In fact, the work he did with Harry Taylor and Tom Lonergan probably helped all three of them long term. They did so much work after training that they all built confidence. It was like they were all preparing for that Grand Final. Tommy's game up forward was a real break-out performance.

It was on all day. There were big contests, but there were free-flowing contests as well. Once we got our nose in front at three-quarter time (by seven points), you could feel the team lift again. We had finished putting the brakes on Collingwood and were moving the tide our way. Hawkins started to lift, Brad Ottens was getting involved, Allen Christensen took a crucial mark on the wing between two guys; you could just see that we were running better across the ground by then.

When I had the ball outside 50 in the last quarter, I knew how much time was left. As soon as I marked it, I took some time off the clock and took it upon myself to take the shot. I had the trust in myself that I'd get it done, and I did. I knew I could get a little more distance by taking a couple of steps out and hooking it, and I also knew that I could still kick it straight by doing that. I didn't waste a lot of distance by blasting the ball high in the air; I kicked it flat and hard, something I had trained for countless times in my career.

I was too busy dishing out hugs to be thinking about winning a Norm Smith Medal. In that euphoric moment after winning a Grand Final, you get a burst of energy and think you could play another game. It's amazing! An AFL official came up and told me that I'd won the Medal, but even then I didn't appreciate that I'd won it. In fact, I'd forgotten about it straight away as you are too caught up with hugging and celebrating with everyone. Then Michael Long read out my name. I was still shocked! Matthew Scarlett gave me a big hug, and Andrew Mackie did too. I was still dealing with the fact I had won another Premiership, so being announced winner of the Norm Smith Medal didn't really sink in.

There is something special about winning a Norm Smith Medal. With no disrespect for the Brownlow, the Norm Smith is significant in that it signifies that you helped your team win a Premiership; that's what sets it apart. It is reinforced when you have a Premiership reunion, where you know that you have helped to contribute to that moment and you can share it with your teammates, whereas you can't do that with a Brownlow.

THE NORM SMITH MEDAL

I'm certainly not denigrating the Brownlow in any way, it's just the reality of the achievement that winning a Premiership—with or without the Norm Smith Medal—is something you can celebrate forever with your mates.

To be a Norm Smith medallist is unbelievably special. Now, every time the Grand Final comes around, I think that not only did I get to play in four of them and win three, but I actually had a significant impact on that particular day as well. As I've got older, and now experiencing the build-up to Grand Final week from afar, I feel a part of it in a different way. Not only have I won Premierships, but I've won a Norm Smith, and I can genuinely say that I helped significantly in Geelong winning a flag. That's pretty cool.

I thought I played pretty well in all our Premierships. I played such different roles in all of them that it's hard to rank which was my best game. At least the coaches must have felt that I was useful in their plans, getting me to play such different roles each time.

In 2016 I made a big statement about domestic violence. I took it upon myself to create my own campaign. It was obviously a very personal issue for me growing up, having witnessed it with my parents and siblings. I spoke up when I did because I finally felt ready to do so. It was uncomfortable, but I understand that if it's uncomfortable for me, yet it helps others, then that's beneficial and worthwhile. As an AFL player towards the end of my career, I understood the platform that players have, and how lucky we are to have that platform. My son, Aston, had just been born, plus I have nephews who are impressionable, so I felt it was important to be a good role model for my own family. It bothered me that I could still pick up a newspaper, or listen to the news at night, and domestic violence remained so prevalent in our society. We claim to be a modern and progressive society, yet two women die *every* week from domestic violence. That's unacceptable! One in four women will suffer some form of abuse from a partner or loved one. There have not been enough men who have stood up and said, "It's not right." I now ask them, "What if this was happening to your sister or your mother? Why then, would you do it to your own partner?"

The reason I grew my beard out was simple. Footballers all care about how they look, so I wanted to find a fun angle for a difficult subject. I didn't want to ram the message down people's throats, because that's when they tune out. So by growing my beard out it allowed people to open up a conversation around why that player had such a horrible beard and long hair. Then the conversation is away, and they can shape that conversation however they feel comfortable. Hopefully, in some small way, I was able to make a difference.

──── Statistics ────

BORN: 4 December 1983
GAMES PLAYED (2002-16): 305
GOALS: 202
FINALS PLAYED: 28
FINALS GOALS: 22
GRAND FINALS: 4
PREMIERSHIPS: 2007, 2009, 2011
NORM SMITH MEDAL: 2011 (presented by Michael Long)

— Norm Smith Voting —

Rodney Eade: 3 Jimmy Bartel, 2 Joel Selwood, 1 Scott Pendlebury;
Matt Granland: 3 Tom Hawkins, 2 Selwood, 1 Bartel;
Garry Lyon: 3 Bartel, 2 Selwood, 1 Pendlebury;
Bruce Matthews: 3 Bartel, 2 Selwood, 1 Cameron Ling;
Matthew Richardson: 3 Bartel, 2 Hawkins, 1 Selwood.
TOTALS: Bartel 13, Selwood 9, Hawkins 5, Pendlebury 2, Ling 1.

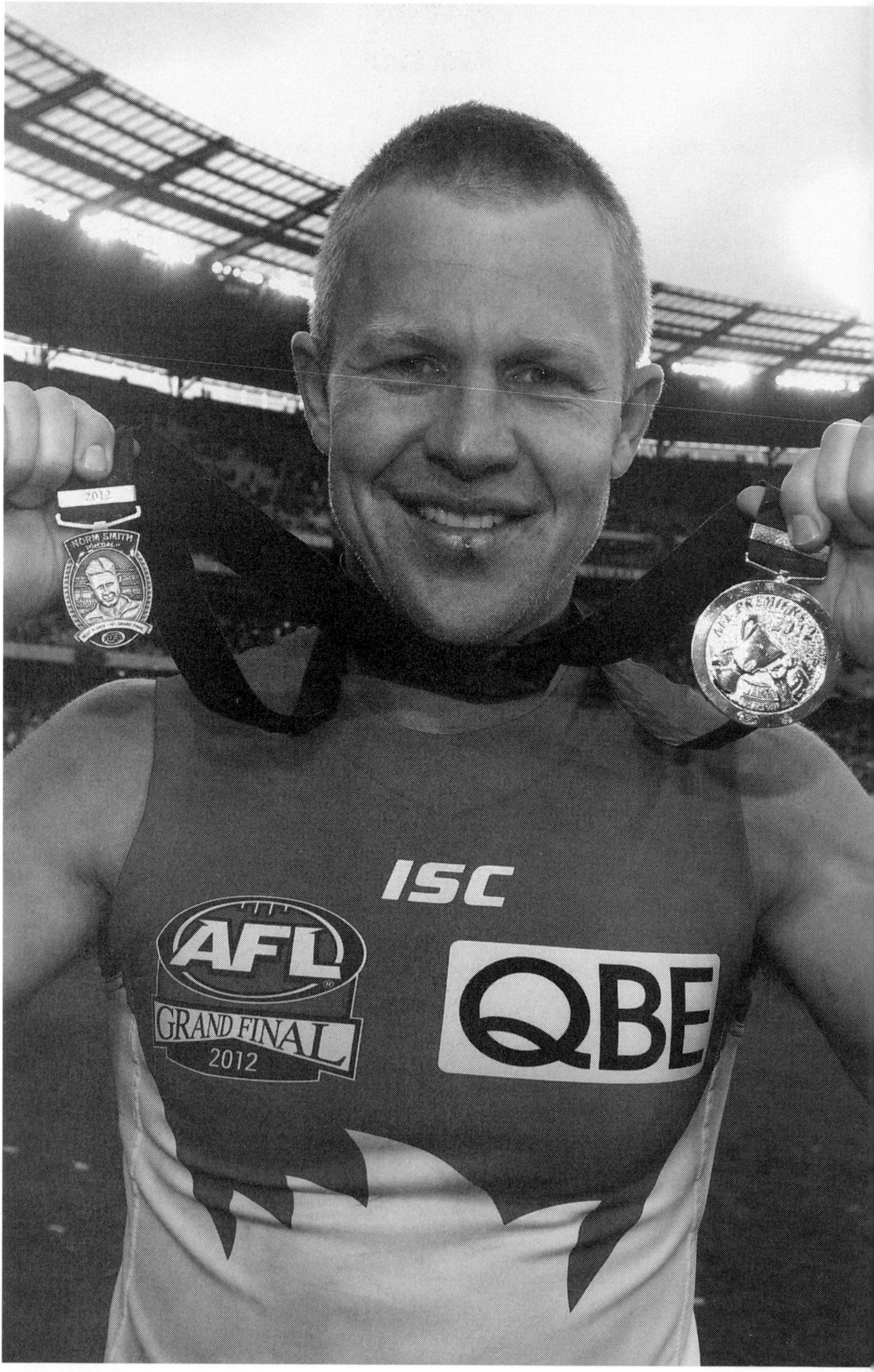
2012
NORM SMITH
ISC
AFL
GRAND FINAL
2012
QBE

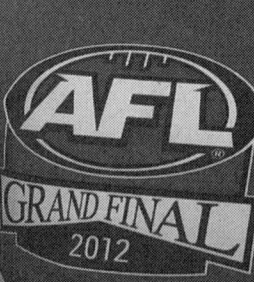

Ryan O'Keefe

Ryan O'Keefe was a strong-minded, hard-working midfielder for the Sydney Swans during their rise as a football power. He could do it all: run, tackle, mark overhead and kick goals. After a slow start to his career, O'Keefe blossomed under coach Paul Roos, becoming one of the club's most consistent performers. He played in the drought-breaking 2005 Premiership side, and was a member of Sydney's losing team the following year. After rejecting an offer from Melbourne in 2008—and overtures from Hawthorn—he won the Swans' best and fairest in 2009. O'Keefe's 2012 finals campaign was dominant, culminating in him winning the Norm Smith Medal in Sydney's thrilling 10-point victory over Hawthorn. He had 15 kicks, 13 handballs, took three marks, won seven clearances and recorded a game-high 15 tackles.

I **was a Fitzroy supporter.** I liked watching Paul Roos, he was someone I looked up to as a kid. But I also enjoyed watching Gary Ablett senior and Tony Lockett, who were both stars in the late 1980s and throughout the 1990s. I was at Fitzroy's last game in Melbourne, played at the MCG against Richmond. That was a big occasion, knowing that they were merging with Brisbane at the end of the season. Although I supported the Lions, I was never a diehard supporter. I just loved footy in

← **PRESSURE PLAYER** Ryan O'Keefe was a great performer on the inside of stoppages. When the pressure was at its highest, in the 2012 decider, he was at his best.

general; loved playing the game even more than I did watching it.

My dad, Brian, played with the under-19s at Fitzroy and then played with Footscray (1980, three games). My grandfather, Lionel Ryan, also played with Footscray (1954-57, 32 games, 12 goals). He was an emergency in the Bulldogs' 1954 Premiership side. I am the oldest of five siblings: there's me, Aaron, Dane (who died of sudden infant death syndrome when Ryan was five), Bridie and Mason. Aaron was certainly sporty like me, whereas Mason wasn't. We were all a bit different in our interests. There were plenty of competitive sporting contests between Aaron and myself, whether in the backyard or against the neighbours in the street. You could safely play cricket or kick the footy in the street back then, so we did that a lot. We lived at Hoppers Crossing, then moved into Moonee Ponds when I was 11.

I played everything growing up: cricket, footy, basketball, athletics, I rode my bike everywhere, tennis, plus I played a fair bit of golf. I was always outdoors playing something because I just enjoyed playing sport.

I played cricket and football at St Kevin's College. My cricket coach wanted me to spend more time on my cricket, but I had begun training with the Calder Cannons by then and felt that I should concentrate solely on football. So at about 15 years old I began dedicating myself to football. I was vice-captain of the St Kevin's first XVIII, then our captain got injured during the season which meant I became captain in his absence.

Dad was supportive of my footy. But he wasn't an overly possessive dad and placed no expectations on me. My granddad probably had more influence in teaching me, but again, he wasn't overbearing. They just supported me and let me do it in my own way.

I was beginning to play well and was making representative sides. I went to watch a match at the MCG, and I can remember it being a moment where it hit me that playing footy is what I want to do, to commit myself to seeing how far football could take me. I was probably 14 at the time. From then on, I concentrated on that goal, continued to work hard, and things seemed to fall into place for me. I just wanted to play in the AFL, wanted to be drafted by anyone and couldn't care where I went. In the

RYAN O'KEEFE

1999 National Draft, the Sydney Swans selected me with their 56th pick. I had made it to the AFL, and a new phase of my life was beginning.

I was pumped to go to Sydney. So much so that I was on the plane the next day and was out of there! I was a pretty independent kid, so it didn't faze me having to move interstate. I never got homesick. I was just glad to get the opportunity, because I had put a lot of hard work into reaching that point. I simply packed my bags and away I went.

I was fortunate when I got to the Swans that they had some great players at the club. Guys like Paul Kelly, Wayne Schwass and Andrew Dunkley, who were really good role models. Tony Lockett then came back in 2002 and played a final season, plus another of my childhood heroes in Paul Roos was around then, too. Those guys probably had more of an impact on me early than what coach Rodney Eade did.

Paul Kelly was great at setting the example. He's an amazing person, loved his footy, and the way he attacked it set a great example for everyone. I feel privileged to say that I played with him.

My first game was against the Bulldogs, on Mother's Day in 2000 (round 10, after the early start to the season because of the Olympics). We lost the match and I didn't get much game time. It was a time where rotations weren't a huge part of the game, so if you started on the bench you didn't see a lot of playing time. There were a few games under Rodney Eade where I spent 90 per cent of the day on the bench, but that's how it was back then.

It took me a couple of years to feel comfortable at AFL level. Probably when Roosy replaced Rodney as coach in 2002. Roosy immediately showed faith in me and believed in what I was doing, giving me the confidence to show what I could do. With that added belief, my career took off from there. So I can thank Roosy for helping me to become the player that I did. Roosy's strength was being able to get the best out of people. The way he manages people sets him apart.

My brother, Aaron, died in a car accident in 2002. It was a very difficult time for me and my family and it took me a little while to get used to him not being around anymore. It was hard to deal with at first, but once I did, I didn't look back. In fact, what happened to Aaron helped to motivate me in regards my outlook on life. I would think, "What would Aaron want me to do? What would make him proud?" Things like that. I was in my early 20s, so it was certainly tough.

When something tragic like that happens you have a choice. You either think, "How bad is this? Poor me," and give up. Or you make the choice to move forward. I determined that it was a part of life, and that I needed to use what happened to Aaron to help me to grow and develop as a person. I wanted to make the most out of life. What it did was make me appreciate everything. From that day on, I didn't want to waste a single day, wanted to get the most out of myself every day and have no regrets. Life's too short to dwell on the negative, so why not use difficult circumstances to grow and learn from. His death taught me to not waste this precious gift of life, live every day and get the best out of myself.

By 2003, I could sense we were entering a good period as a team. We had a core group of players, maybe a dozen of us, who were starting to play a fair bit of footy together. There was a real bond between us which is hard to describe. Basically, we all wanted to play for each other. From 2003 onwards, we started to enjoy some success as a team. We all remain close to this day, all because of that bond we formed around that time.

We lost finals in 2003 and again in 2004. But I didn't find it hard to keep positive. Losing a game of footy was nothing compared to Aaron's death. For me, it's not the victories that define me, it is what people do when they get knocked down, or they've lost something or someone. How do they bounce back? That is what defines a person.

In 2005, the make-up of our team was very consistent. I think we only had one change to the line-up for that whole back half of the year. Having that stability, and having played a lot together, we had formed a strong bond. We were a really good team, and I emphasise the word *team*. It was always said that we weren't as talented as every other squad, but believe me, we had some very talented players in our side. But our whole ethos was: teams might have more talent than us, but we know we are the best *team*. And as long as we remained a team and played as a team, that would be a strength of ours. We didn't want to play as individuals.

They said we played ugly footy. But it was winning games, so if winning is ugly then that's what we did! Beauty is in the eye of the beholder, isn't it? But it wasn't a style of game where we kicked lots of goals and generated a lot of commercial breaks, so certain people probably saw it as ugly if they were coming at that view from a marketing angle.

The 2005 Grand Final was a typical West Coast-Sydney game of that era. It was hard and close and went down to the wire, so it was exciting to be a part of. We played a number of close games during that period, because both sides matched up really well against each other. All players went full bore at each other every time we played.

I was a bit off that day. I was badly concussed in the Preliminary Final against St Kilda, so it wasn't my best game in the Grand Final. But it wasn't about individuals, it was about playing your role. So I just remained focused and played my role. The Eagles tagged me pretty heavily most of the day, but doing that created an opportunity for one of my teammates, so that was the way I looked at it. I was never not going to play, though—it was a Grand Final! The Swans had not won a Premiership in 72 years, so I was never missing that game.

I was interviewed after the one-point loss to the Eagles in the 2006 Grand Final where, again, I put the result into perspective. Yes, it was devastating to lose, and was something we had all worked so hard for—a lot of effort went into it—but I didn't let it define me. There was a moment, however, in the final quarter where I had a kick in defence smothered that resulted in a goal to the Eagles. I blamed myself for contributing to the loss.

That moment spurred me on in the 2012 Grand Final. Before the 2012 Grand Final, I looked back at that moment from 2006 and determined that, whatever I did, I was going to make sure I, and we, didn't lose the game. I wanted to do everything possible to help my team win.

I'm a competitor, I always want to win. I love winning! So, after 2006, I had full confidence in our team, and our coaches, to get back to another Grand Final. I knew we were doing absolutely everything possible to get there, so I had no doubt we would get another opportunity eventually. As it turned out, it took us six years, but I never lost heart. If you ever go into a season thinking you're just there to make up the numbers, you might as well not bother turning up.

My biggest strength as a player was my mental toughness. My drive to achieve was my strength, and it still is now that I am an assistant coach with the Adelaide Crows. I was competitive when I was a kid, hated losing anything, no matter whether it was a game of marbles or a game of footy, I was always competitive. Through things that happened in my life I built a resilience, which was aided by my internal drive to succeed. When I wanted something, I was always prepared to do anything to achieve it, and I left no stone unturned to get there.

I almost went home to Victoria in 2008. Free agency was beginning to come into the game, and I had an offer from the Melbourne Football Club to leave the Swans and return to Victoria. But it couldn't get finalised, a trade couldn't be arranged, and I happily chose to stay at Sydney.[1]

John Longmire had been an assistant under 'Roosy' for nine years, so him becoming coach in 2011 was a seamless transition. I had worked closely with John for a long time by then. Roosy's strength was his people-management and his defensive philosophies. What John added, aside from his people skills, was an added layer of tactical stuff to how he wanted us to defend. The game was evolving and John was evolving with it. That's what happens, the game is continually evolving from year to year, even half-way through a season the game changes slightly. John was a really smart coach in how he saw that evolution and was able to adapt accordingly. The proof of his ability as a coach is in the pudding. By his second year we had won another Premiership, and the club has been in two more Grand Finals since then (2014 and 2016). I rate him one of the best coaches I've had.

In the 2012 Grand Final, I was one of our key generals in the midfield. My job was to take care of the most dangerous Hawthorn mids. I was to play a two-way game on those guys, allowing my teammates in there to be able to play their games. I played on Sam Mitchell for a while, then in the last quarter Shaun Burgoyne started to get going. John got a little itchy about that, so he moved me on to him. My strength as a

---

1 According to journalist Mike Sheahan, Hawthorn also showed significant interest in obtaining O'Keefe at that time. See the *Courier Mail* online, 10 October 2008.

midfielder was my running power. I prided myself on being that two-way midfielder who could defend and tackle, turn the ball over, then once we won possession I could turn and provide an option going forward.

I just loved working hard. If I didn't come off the ground after a game feeling absolutely cooked, I was disappointed in myself.

The game ebbed and flowed. Hawthorn got going early, then we dominated the second quarter, then they came back at us in the third, then we came back again in the last quarter. It was a tight arm wrestle all day long, which is what you want from a Grand Final. You want to see two heavyweights going blow for blow, and that's what it was like that day.

At no point did we lose faith that we were going to win that game. At three-quarter time we led by one point. As we left the huddle, I remember the guys saying, "We've got this," we were so confident we would win. That comes back to the belief we had built in each other. I remember telling myself, "Righto, I'm going to make sure we don't lose this game. I'm going to do everything in my power to make sure we win."

What stood out that day was the pressure we applied on Hawthorn. Our attack on the ball and on the body was relentless. We were constantly crashing in. Every time a Hawthorn player got the ball, bang, there was a Sydney player on him. During the year, Hawthorn's kicking efficiency was in the high 70s, but in that game it was in the low 50s. We were relentless, even possessed, in how we applied immense pressure on them at every contest. That's what wins big games of footy: whoever wins the contest controls the game.

I had 15 tackles that day. My approach was: if I see a Hawthorn player with the ball in his hands, I'm going to jump on him. I wanted to put pressure on them every time they got it, and I suppose I was able to put myself in the right positions to do that. I was able to win the ball off them, but also win plenty of ball myself. In big, high-pressure games, it's those little moments that keep adding up. It might be a big tackle or a big smother, a spoil or a mark at a crucial time—those key moments can all define the game. They all add up. So if you can string a few of them in your favour, like we did in that last quarter, you're more than likely going to end up victorious.

THE NORM SMITH MEDAL

I remember Nick Malceski's winning snap for goal well: he nearly kicked my head off! It came off the back of some good pressure, and he got the ball and snapped it and I had to duck or he would have kicked me in the head. We didn't have time to celebrate, though, because there were still seconds remaining. On the field we didn't know how much time exactly, so we quickly focused on getting back. If you watch the footage, everyone is calling for us all to get back behind the centre for that next centre bounce.

I knew I had played all right that day. In fact, if you go through my whole finals series that year—the Qualifying Final against Adelaide, the Preliminary Final against Collingwood, then the Grand Final against Hawthorn—I played the best patch of footy in my career. I averaged 33 possessions, 11 tackles and eight clearances over the three games. So I rate that September as the most influential and best footy of my career.

I put my success in the 2012 finals series down to my interrupted start to the year. That pre-season, Ted Richards ran across my leg and I cracked my fibula, so I didn't play until round two that year, and hadn't played at all during the pre-season. I had done everything up until early January, though, so I was fit before the injury. I then missed eight to 10 weeks of training, plus all those early games. I had a slow start to the season, and it took until the Hawthorn game in Tasmania (round five) for me to start getting going again. What it meant was, by finals time I was feeling really fresh. In other years, by the time finals came around I found I was just hanging on. But in 2012, because of that slow start, I was feeling really good by September and that showed in my performances. I also knew that there was no guarantee that we would get another opportunity to be in a Grand Final, so I was in a really good head space and was pumped to make that finals series count.

I was celebrating the win, thinking "how good's this?" Then the AFL's media manager, Patrick Keane, came up and said, "Look, Ryan, just get ready, mate, you've won the Norm Smith Medal." I said, "What?" Then they called my name out and I found that I was quite overwhelmed with emotion. It was a bonus winning that Medal. Whether I won it or not didn't bother me; I was all about winning the team thing, the Premiership Cup. Team success is the ultimate. Individual awards are more a note of recognition that you had done your role for your team, or, in the case of the Norm Smith Medal, that people appreciated the role you played for your team that day.

Everyone wants to be a good player in big games, don't they? When those games come along, there are plenty of players who played well during the season, but under the pressure and higher stakes they crumble. You don't want to be one of those people. I'm pretty proud of my finals record overall, I feel it was pretty solid. I'm proud that, the higher the pressure, the higher the stakes, my mental toughness came to the fore. I backed myself to perform when it mattered, and I feel I was able to do that.

Since retiring in 2014, I have been able to look back on my achievements. I'm pretty proud to be a Norm Smith medallist. There are not too many of them. It's probably harder to win a Norm Smith than to win a Brownlow, just because not many players make it to a Grand Final in the first place. So to have that recognition is great. And being Sydney's only winner of the award makes it that extra bit special.

Statistics

BORN: 24 January 1981
GAMES PLAYED (2000-14): 286
GOALS: 261
FINALS PLAYED: 24
FINALS GOALS: 25
GRAND FINALS: 3
PREMIERSHIPS: 2005, 2012
NORM SMITH MEDAL: 2012 (presented by Dean Kemp)

— Norm Smith Voting —

Brett Ratten: 3 Brad Sewell, 2 Ryan O'Keefe, 1 Lance Franklin;
Mick Malthouse: 3 O'Keefe, 2 Sewell, 1 Dan Hannebery;
Drew Morphett: 3 O'Keefe, 2 Franklin, 1 Hannebery;
Neil Cordy: 3 O'Keefe, 2 Franklin, 1 Jarrad McVeigh;
Tim McGrath: 3 Hannebery, 2 Brad Sewell, 1 O'Keefe.
TOTALS: O'Keefe 12, Sewell 7, Hannebery 5, Franklin 5, McVeigh 1.

Brian Lake

A self-professed larrikin, Brian Lake was from a breed of footballers gradually phased out of the game in the professional era. As was the case with Essendon's 1984 Norm Smith medallist Bill Duckworth—one of the game's great larrikins—when the ball was in Lake's area something interesting, or unusual, often happened. He was a key, if at times controversial, defender for the Western Bulldogs through three successive deep runs deep into September (2008-10) that fell desperately short before a string of injuries had a deleterious effect on his form and motivation. It took a late-career move to Hawthorn at the end of 2012, after 197 games with the Bulldogs, for the versatile defender to rediscover his focus. A superb pack mark, Lake flourished under coach Alastair Clarkson during the Hawks' triple Premiership era (2013-15). He won the 2013 Norm Smith Medal and was one of the Hawks' best again in 2014. When he retired after the 2015 Grand Final, having secured a third Premiership in three seasons, he was widely recognised as one of his era's most durable defenders.

Born out of wedlock, in Adelaide on 27 February 1982, Lake was initially given his mother Chesel's maiden name, Harris. But in December 2007, following the birth of his own son, Cohen, he

← **THREE-TIME WINNER** It looked a big gamble when Hawthorn traded for Brian Lake from the Bulldogs at the end of the 2012 season. What a payout it turned out to be: Lake was a brilliant full-back through an era in which the Hawks won three flags; his highlight, taking the Norm Smith Medal in his first season at Hawthorn. Lake pictured here with son Cohen and daughter Mylee.

THE NORM SMITH MEDAL

legally changed to his father Brian's surname, Lake. He explained that he "had the chance to change to Lake when Mum and Dad (Chesel and Brian) married when I was 10 or 11, but I decided not to ... With school and footy, I decided to put it off." However, as he was their only son, and with only aunties on his father's side of the family, "it was a [last] chance to carry on the Lake family name."[1]

It was a credit to Lake's innate determination, durability and on-field awareness that he was able to even be considered by an AFL club. Playing for Woodville-West Torrens in the SANFL, Lake suffered from sleep apnea, which hindered his ability to meet recruiters; he also struggled to stay attentive in team meetings. With little money and living in a rundown house, he was doing it tough. Indeed, he was a "pudgy" 19-year-old, had a part-time job at an abattoir that required him to start work in the early hours, and had been overlooked during his under-18 draft year.[2] He admitted in 2016, "Before I got drafted, I'd get in trouble like some other kids would—I probably got in trouble a little bit more than I should have."[3]

Enter Western Bulldogs recruiter Scott Clayton.

Lake was being managed by Brenton Hart, the father of Adelaide defender Ben, when Clayton inquired as to his client's background and wellbeing. "Brian had shown a fair bit in his 18th year, but he didn't get drafted," Clayton recalled in 2018. "As it turned out, he had this sleep issue which totally affected his performance, meaning he was really inconsistent. He would fall asleep in meetings, then he'd wake up and they would ask him a question and he would say something stupid which they'd all laugh at. It was like he was a bit of a joke, simply because he had this undiagnosed condition."

Lake ran a "pitiful beep test" in front of the League's recruiters at the 2001 Draft Combine. However, Clayton had been "really impressed with his footy" at Woodville-West Torrens. With the assistance of Hart and Clayton, Lake received medical treatment for his apnea, as well as for an adenoid "the size of a golf ball". "His doctor couldn't believe how he had managed to play professional sport," said Clayton.

---

1 Whitten Oval Online Forum website, 11 January 2008. For the full article, see: https://tinyurl.com/yamuulc6.
2 *The Age* online, 29 September 2013.
3 *Open Mike* interview with Mike Sheahan, *Fox Footy*, 27 September 2016.

> He was clearly a terrific intercept mark, it was just his inconsistency that held him back. He couldn't run far enough for long enough, all due to his condition. He needed a break to go his way, and he needed some love, to be honest, because he'd had a pretty tough old go of it growing up.

The Bulldogs took a punt on Lake with their fourth selection (71 overall) at the 2001 AFL Draft, later dubbed the "super draft" due to the extraordinary crop of players it produced. Others selected before Lake included Luke Hodge (pick 1), Luke Ball (2), Chris Judd (3), Jimmy Bartel (8), Nick Dal Santo (13), James Kelly (17), Jason Gram (19), Steve Johnson (24), Sam Mitchell (36), Leigh Montagna (37), Gary Ablett (40, F-S), Jarrad Waite (46) and Dane Swan (58). Five players from this draft—Hodge, Judd, Bartel, Johnson and Lake—would later win Norm Smith Medals; toss in seven Brownlows, and "super" may not be a sufficient descriptor! According to Clayton, the Bulldogs were confident Lake would still be available late in the draft:

> I was always confident he would get through the draft to our selection, because there were some inconsistencies in his testing. If you didn't do some research into his condition, you wouldn't know that there was something that could be fixed which would make a huge difference to him. So we were lucky to find that out when we did. I don't think anyone else was going to draft him, so I felt we could have taken him with any of our picks.

When Lake arrived at the Bulldogs, he initially lived in Kealba in Melbourne's western suburbs. During his first two weeks in Melbourne, following a night out and perhaps a few too many beverages, he forgot his home address so chose to get a cab to the Whitten Oval and sleep in the grandstand. "That was back in the day when you could have a get-together, and could enjoy a few beers and some drinking games," he explained in 2015:

> I had been in Melbourne for a couple of weeks, and I didn't know the suburb I was living in ... I forgot where

> I was living. I looked at my licence and it still had my South Australian address. I knew we had training the next day, a recovery session, so I thought, "Well"—it saved me a cab fare as well! —"I'll just go to the club and sleep there."[4]

His one-night "stand" was the first of numerous weird and wacky events that became synonymous with Lake's career. Coach Terry Wallace was unimpressed with the sleepover, however, and called Lake into his office that morning. Lake recalled:

> He said, "Brian, can I please have a meeting with you?" I was a little bit nervous; I thought, "Gee, I'm out the door, I'm back to South Australia straight away." He sat me down and he slammed the door, to an extent, behind me—not too bad, just enough to make me a little bit [more scared]. [We] probably had about a minute's pause, he just made me sweat on it a little bit more. Then he just looked me in the eyes and he said, "Brian, work out where you bloody live! Now, get out and go and do some training." That was just a relief. It's amazing, the sweat was just pouring off me; that just evaporated, and I went out there and all the boys were looking at me and laughing.[5]

Under his first two coaches at the Bulldogs, Wallace (2002) and Peter Rohde (2002-04), Lake managed 31 games for just five wins. His debut came in a round 21 loss to Carlton (two points) at Docklands in 2002, in which he recorded just one kick, one handball and one mark. He then played 13 games in his second season (and kicked six goals), and 17 in his third as he became a regular in the team. But it took the arrival of former Sydney coach Rodney 'Rocket' Eade at the end of 2004 for Lake's career to finally take off.

"I didn't know a lot about Brian before I arrived as coach," Eade explained in 2018, "and he was a little bit overweight when I got there." Having been an elite runner as a player for Hawthorn (1976-87, 229 games, including Premierships in 1976, 1978, 1983 and 1986) and

---

[4] Lake's retirement speech, 6 October 2015. For the full press conference, see: https://www.youtube.com/watch?v=nWrDEeNfN8U.
[5] *Open Mike.*

the Brisbane Bears (1988-90, 30), Eade set high training standards for his players; standards that Lake initially failed to meet:

> His training standards weren't high. Brian was more of the old-style football mentality where he was more dependent on playing—he wasn't one for a big pre-season or a big session on the track. He just did what he had to do to get by. He was a unique character in many ways. He believed in himself, but it was always a bit of a battle to convince him to do what we needed him to do in order to prepare himself as best he could.

Lake credits Eade as the coach who "probably got the best out of me" during his time at the Bulldogs.[6] Theirs was a "sort of love-hate relationship" along similar lines to that between Ron Barassi and Brent Crosswell during the latter's 15-year career at Carlton, North Melbourne and Melbourne (1968-82). Both players, Lake and Crosswell, repeatedly and sometimes publicly pushed their respective coach's buttons, but more often than not they also delivered in big matches. "A lot of it was getting a message across to me on a personal level," Lake said of Eade. "We probably had a fair few guys there who couldn't accept too much criticism... so he used me a lot to get a point across, if he needed to, to the group."[7] Eade laughed when asked whether he lost any hair as a consequence of coaching Lake:

> He was a terrific player who, at heart, was a low-key, free spirit who was casual in his approach. He's just a casual guy who, every now and then, needed a cattle prod, which he reacted to in the right way. That would get him on board and he would play exceptionally well. Just that sometimes he would get comfortable after a purple patch of form, and then he'd drop away a little bit. But that wasn't a big issue.

Eade added that Lake "would always make me laugh" because he had "a really good sense of humour which I enjoyed." Noted as a highly strung coach on match days, Eade would occasionally be forced to

---

6   2015 retirement speech.
7   *Open Mike.*

THE NORM SMITH MEDAL

chuckle at some of Lake's comments in team meetings and at huddles. "He'd make you laugh at the most inopportune times and you'd have to tell him to bugger off," Eade said. "He was quite funny, Brian, in his own way. He certainly added some levity to the situation, which was good." Lake conceded that he "lived and died by the sword," and that "Rocket used to get into me a fair bit." But he also said that Eade "gave me the confidence to back myself."[8] The coach understood what it took to ensure his defender was in the right headspace for game day.

> Under Rocket, I probably got away with a lot. For me, if I was performing on game day, then whatever I was doing during the week must work. If that's not training the day before a game, or the last session, because I wanted my body to freshen up a little bit more, Rocket would let me do that because he knew I'd be able to perform on game-day. That got a lot of people's noses out of joint at the football club… I got away with a lot because, at that stage, we were pushing so much for a Premiership. Because we needed to win the next week, I got away with it.[9]

Lake would have revelled in the 1980s, when Eade played, because he was an old-school footballer who preferred to play rather than spend time in the numerous team meetings that players are expected to attend and participate in as professional footballers. Eade recalled that Lake "wouldn't say a lot in team meetings," adding:

> It was always a challenge to keep his attention. He'd be looking at the ceiling and all around the room, so I'd probe him with questions and force that interaction. He certainly had some good opinions and good thoughts, but he wouldn't volunteer them too often. But in situations where I offered him one-on-one advice, he would have strong opinions about how he thought he needed to play or where the team could improve. I always took that on board when he offered it. There were times, however, where he could be counter-

---

[8] 2015 retirement speech.
[9] *Open Mike*.

intuitive, where you'd want him to do a certain thing and he was stuck in his old ways. But most of the time he was pretty good.

The Bulldogs finished half a game outside the top eight in 2005, and Lake, with new-found belief and having taken ownership of the full-back position, played every match of the season for the first time. According to Eade, as Lake's confidence and consistency grew, so, too, did his teammates' trust in their 195cm defender:

> He developed quickly into being one of the better full-backs in the competition. His ability to judge the flight of the ball was a real strength, as was his marking, which was as good as anyone in the competition. From there, our team gained a lot of confidence around him for the way he played.

That season Eade's former club, the Swans, broke the longest Premiership drought in football (72 years) when they defeated West Coast in the Grand Final. Their famous four-point victory meant that the Bulldogs became the new holder of the longest span without a Premiership (since 1954). The Swans' Premiership captain, Barry Hall, was a physical, explosive focal point, and, of all the decade's key forwards, it was Hall who troubled Lake the most:

> I've always said Barry Hall [was my toughest opponent]. Just his speed and power, you weren't able to get too close to him because he was just able to push you off. And when you're too far off him, [with] his explosive power in his legs, he was able to get that 10-metre gap on you reasonably easily. He's the standout player, but you had [Nick] Riewoldt, also Matthew Richardson—just with their fitness and their athletic ability.

Fortunately for Lake, Hall joined the Bulldogs in 2010. Of playing on the key forwards, Lake said, "I always loved that challenge of one-on-one … you always loved those battles. You start on 'em at the start of the game and you finish on 'em."[10]

---

10   *Open Mike.*

THE NORM SMITH MEDAL

In 2006 the Dogs played finals for the first time since 2000, and again Lake played every game, including the victorious Elimination Final (41 points over Collingwood) and the losing first Semi-Final (West Coast, 74). While the team slumped to 13th in 2007, Lake had his best year to that point, winning the Charles Sutton Medal as best and fairest, his one and only best-player award. One of his standout performances came in round 18 at Docklands, where Lake held St Kilda's dual-Coleman medallist (2004-05) Fraser Gehrig to no kicks, no handballs and just one mark, while collecting 15 disposals and 10 marks himself.[11]

The Bulldogs charged back up the ladder in 2008. They won 15 games to finish third, Lake's close friend and teammate Adam Cooney won the Brownlow Medal, and the team went deep into September. In the Qualifying Final the Bulldogs fell 51 points short of Hawthorn but Lake (22 disposals and 11 marks) was one of his team's best. He kicked a goal in the second Semi-Final as the Dogs defeated Sydney by 37 points, and was prominent in the 29-point loss to Geelong in the Preliminary Final with 22 disposals.

There was more heartbreak in 2009 when, having again finished third, the Bulldogs lost a nail-biting Preliminary Final by seven points to St Kilda. At 27 years old, and seemingly at the peak of his powers, Lake was selected in the back pocket of the All-Australian team for the first time (Geelong's Matthew Scarlett was named full-back). In 2010 he was chosen as the All-Australian full-back. That year the Bulldogs suffered a third consecutive Preliminary Final defeat, this time at the hands of St Kilda, by 24 points. The club's Premiership drought was now 56 years.

Despite the triple disappointments, Eade—who, in round three, 2010, Lake's 150th game, had accused him of deliberately defying instructions, berating him in the rooms afterwards[12]—said that Lake's performances in defence from 2008-10 were a critical factor in the club's ability to compete against the best sides. "He held the defence together in many ways during our finals runs," Eade said. "His ability to beat a player one on one, then his ability to intercept mark and rebound the ball, was terrific for us."

---

11 *Open Mike.*
12 *The Age* online, 12 April 2010.

By then, the position of the full-back had evolved from being focused on negating to one where defenders were expected to cut off the opposition's forward entries by going third man up, playing a floating intercept role in the back half, and then providing rebound and run from defence. Lake's ability to read the play set him apart. "He was able to judge the flight of the ball while also using his body to position himself against an opponent, which was an extreme skill," Eade said. Against North Melbourne in round nine, 2010, Lake grabbed 22 marks, two shy of his remarkable career high of 24 against Brisbane in 2007.

Lake's struggles with injury and form—which came to define his latter years at the Whitten Oval—began after the 2010 season when he underwent operations on his knee, hip and shoulder. "I just couldn't recover after the three surgeries I had at the end of 2010," he said in 2015. "To go through that (next) season with the body not right was hard, and I ... copped it from everywhere."[13] He played just five senior games in 2011, as the Bulldogs missed the finals by two-and-a-half matches. Cooney, too, struggled with a knee injury (13 games), the two mates spending much of the season together in rehab. As questions surrounding his return grew louder, he feared his career could be over:

> Me and Adam Cooney had the same sort of experience in that 2011 season, where everyone was turning on us and we weren't playing good football. The side was struggling as well, so you always had in the back of your mind that this could be your last year ... I'm a reasonably positive sort of a person, so I kept the head up and still had confidence that I could get back to playing good football.[14]

During a period of heavy criticism, when some questioned Lake's dedication to his teammates, coaches and the game, fellow defender Dale Morris spoke out in defence of his teammate. "Brian's one those proud guys," he said, adding that Lake was "doing the extra things that he can" to return to his best. "I think people underestimate how big those operations were," Morris said.[15] Eade conceded at the time that

---

13 2015 retirement speech.
14 2015 retirement speech.
15 *The Australian* online, 10 June 2011.

Lake had lost confidence in his body, which in turn affected his form. He said "Brian's struggling for confidence," and what he faced was no different to a player attempting to return from a major knee reconstruction.[16]

On the most difficult season of his career, Lake said: "Those sorts of days you learn a lot about yourself and people around you, and how quickly some people can turn on you."[17] Former Hawthorn captain Shane Crawford wrote in the *Herald Sun* during 2011 that Lake and Eade needed to "sit down and mend the rift that seems to exist between Lake and the Bulldogs' coaches," adding that it was "sad to see such a good player so badly out of form and fitness."[18] A few weeks later, following a 49-point loss to Essendon in round 21, and with the team having failed to qualify for the finals, Eade was sacked. He was replaced in the interim by his assistant, Paul Williams, before Brendan McCartney was hired at season's end.

The new coach was determined to play Lake purely in defence, after Eade had switched him forward on occasions during 2011. On the eve of the season, Lake said, "The plan is, I've had some good years in the backline, so most likely I'll be staying there."[19] The plan was short-lived, as Lake was went forward again halfway through the season, a move he was unimpressed with. "I just thought, my position in the AFL level was (as) a defender," he told Mike Sheahan on *Open Mike*. "I guess when you're 31 years old and they're trying to change you into a different position, you sort-of know you're potentially out the door the next year."[20]

The Bulldogs slumped to 15th in 2012, although Lake was able to play 20 of 22 matches. "My form was up and down in that year, very similar to the football club as well—we were fairly struggling."[21] Enjoying a few beverages at the MCG on Grand Final day, when Sydney defeated Hawthorn by 10 points, Lake could not help but wonder whether he would ever experience the high of a Premiership. Less than two weeks later, on the first day of the trade period, the 197-gamer signed with the Hawks, and those Grand Final ambitions suddenly moved a step closer.

16 *The Australian* online, 10 June 2011.
17 2015 retirement speech.
18 *Herald Sun* online, 12 June 2011.
19 *The Age* online, 2 March 2012.
20 *Open Mike.* Lake was 30 years old, not 31.
21 *Open Mike.*

BRIAN LAKE

Hawthorn received Lake (who was overseas when the deal was done) and pick 27 in the draft (ultimately 28, Tim O'Brien), and the Dogs gained picks 21 (Nathan Hrovat) and 43 (Josh Saunders).[22]

"I spoke to Marty [Pask], my manager ... and [said I] thought that my days were numbered at the Bulldogs," Lake said in 2015. "I thought I needed a change to go and strive to win a Premiership—that's what every AFL player wanted to do."[23] Greg Baum later wrote in *The Age* that, "Leaving clubs for less money is not the done things these days. But Lake was happy to take a [pay] cut, and happy to do everything that came with proving Hawthorn had done the right thing."[24] Lake said that arriving at Waverley Park, Hawthorn's training base, at 30 years of age for the 2013 pre-season allowed him to "press the reset button" on his career.[25] However, by January, Lake had tested the trust of his new teammates and his career was clinging to a cliff's edge.

Following a boozy evening at a Portsea Polo after-party at the Sorrento Hotel, Lake and wife Shannon were arrested and spent four hours in the police lock-up. Given a final warning by the club that any further indiscretions would result in his contract being terminated, a humbled Lake said: "I've worked my butt off to get my body right. To have too many drinks on the weekend, I've taken a step back ... From here I want to move on and gain respect. It was a very embarrassing incident."[26]

Hawthorn's then captain, Luke Hodge, joked in 2018 that it "only took Brian to about round 18 of his first season for him to settle into our system!" Teammate Brad Sewell agreed, while conceding that it was a challenge for players to walk into a new club:

> It's really difficult for any player to come into a new system and into a new side, least of all a mature, experienced player who's relatively set in his ways. I think it took us as a playing group, and as a backline, a while to get used to Lakey, and vice-versa. I think it started to jell in the latter part of the

---

22 Martin Blake, *The Mighty Fighting Hawks: A Celebration of Hawthorn's Three Premierships in the Clarkson Era*, Michael Joseph, 2014, p. 232. In a great trade deal for the Hawks, not only did they pick up Lake (three Premierships and a Norm Smith Medal), they also traded Stephen Gilham and pick 27 for Jed Anderson. Lake effectively replaced Gilham in defence. Anderson was then traded for pick 19, which became Ryan Burton, and with pick 28 (originally 27) they selected Tim O'Brien, a long-term key forward prospect.
23 2015 retirement speech.
24 *The Age* online, 29 September 2013.
25 2015 retirement speech.
26 *Herald Sun* online, 14 January 2013.

> year, the last weeks of the season. By then we had a better understanding of what made Lakey tick, and he certainly got a better understanding of what the boundaries were, and of what the team's expectations were of him. And also, we better understood, as did he, what he could and couldn't do.

Hodge said that, in Lake's defence, "he played in an era where, as a full-back, you were expected to punch or mark or stay in the defensive 50." The Hawks' system when Lake arrived was, according to Hodge, "all about squeezing up the ground and making sure you kept the ball in your forward 50. So a lot of times early on, everyone would be squeezed up and you'd look across to the spot where Lakey should have been, but he'd be 50 metres behind!" Lake agreed that it had taken him a while to feel comfortable in the Hawks' system:

> I guess the way they play football, the defensive structures, it took me a while to understand it. Coming from the Dogs, there's always been one-on-one [with] me always taking the key forward, so my role was just locking down on him and nullifying as much as possible. Coming into Hawthorn and learning team defence at the age of 31 is not easy, because you do have habits that you fall back into. I had a lot of issues in 2013…You come in and out of games; when the pressure's on you fall back into your old ways. So it's just getting that out of your mind as quick as possible… they'd always be reminding you, "Brian, just team defence," and bring you back on track.[27]

According to Sewell, the senior players were consulted before the club recruited Lake. "That was, and still is, the Hawthorn way," he said. "It wasn't a group decision as such, but we were certainly consulted and were well aware of what was happening. So in that sense we played a part in the club getting him." Sewell said the players "had a pretty good idea of what type of player we were getting" as Lake had "matched up really well on 'Buddy' (Franklin) in the past." But, he added, "I don't think we could have appreciated the impact he was going to have, not just in

---

27   *Open Mike.*

his first year, but in the two years after that. During that trade period, if someone had said that 'this is what you will get out of Lakey over the next few years,' you would have taken that in a heartbeat."

Lake was fortunate that Hawthorn, under Clarkson, had proven successful in recruiting experienced players who were able to integrate seamlessly into Hawthorn's system and structure: Stuart Dew (Port Adelaide), Brent Guerra (Port/St Kilda), Shaun Burgoyne (Port), Josh Gibson (North Melbourne), Jack Gunston (Adelaide), David Hale (North), plus Lake, all became key players during the club's four Premierships in eight years. And although it may have taken him a few months to find his feet in the Hawks' defence, Lake was appreciative of the players and coaches for aiding his transition into the team during 2013:

> Playing in the back six with so many good players, with 'Gibbo' (Josh Gibson), 'Stratts' (Ben Stratton), 'Birch' (Grant Birchall), Shaun (Burgoyne), Luke Hodge in stages as well [was invaluable]. To come and slide into a side like that, just knowing you don't have to do anything extraordinary in the game, you've just got to play your role and in the structure of the back six, [was comforting]. And when you've got that, and a clear role in what you have to do, it makes your job easier.[28]

Lake said he felt like he had "just jumped on the back of the peloton" when he began playing for Hawthorn.[29] In his 19th game for his new club, the first Qualifying Final against Sydney, he was one of Hawthorn's best in its 54-point win. Two weeks later, his difficult decision to leave the Bulldogs was justified when the Hawks won a heart-stopping Preliminary Final by five points over Geelong. After 217 games and 12 seasons, Lake had realised his ambition of reaching the game's biggest stage. Their opponent was Fremantle, in its first Grand Final appearance, meaning Lake would be matched up against one of the finest forwards of the modern era, Dockers captain Matthew Pavlich. It promised to be a match-defining contest.

---

28 2015 retirement speech.
29 *Open Mike*.

THE NORM SMITH MEDAL

In the opening minutes, the Grand Final was all Hawthorn, trapping the ball in its forward half and creating repeat entries. Jack Gunston kicked the first goal at the three-minute mark. When Fremantle went forward two minutes later, Nat Fyfe, who started well, juggled a mark but missed his set-shot, spraying it out of bounds. The Hawk defenders, particularly Lake and Gibson, were reading the play to intercept and rebound, but Fyfe looked threatening when he marked again at the 12-minute mark. His kick, however, again sprayed wide for a second out-of-bounds result. Both were gettable opportunities and would have exerted some early scoreboard pressure. Instead, Fremantle trailed by six points. Four minutes later, Franklin was paid a 50-metre penalty that took him to the goal line, and the Hawks led by 11 points. The Dockers were goalless at quarter-time.

Gunston goaled three minutes into the second term, then Rioli kicked another 90 seconds later; leading by 24 points, Hawthorn's pressure all over the field in the opening minutes of the quarter was telling. Tendai Mzungu finally kicked Fremantle's first goal at the 10-minute mark. For all of Hawthorn's dominance, the margin was just 18 points. The game's tempo had lifted, with Ryan Crowley, Fyfe and Michael Barlow bringing the Dockers back into the game. Once again, Gunston proved decisive: his third goal, at 14 minutes, came during Fremantle's best period.

Lake was quiet in the second quarter; instead, it was Birchall who was Hawthorn's best defender. Lake, nevertheless, had kept Pavlich goalless—the 'Pav' doing Lake a big favour when he missed a simple set-shot from 20 metres out. Fyfe then missed his third scoring attempt of the game with three minutes remaining in the half. In the last 90 seconds, Lake stood firm to mark on the last line of defence; Hale then did the same, as Hawthorn took a 23-point lead to the main break.

Just 20 seconds into the third quarter, Lake held on too long to Pavlich, who goaled from the free kick and cut the margin to 17 points. But Jarryd Roughead responded for Hawthorn. Pavlich kicked a second goal six minutes in; he and ruckman Aaron Sandilands were willing their team back into the game. Gibson was moved on to Pavlich, with Lake released as the deep, floating defender, but he was in no-man's-land when

Walters marked and his goal cut the margin to 10 points. Fremantle had dominated the clearances in this quarter, and the Hawk defenders were under constant attack. Chris Mayne's long goal at the halfway mark cut the margin to just three points. Clarkson looked concerned in the coach's box, the Fremantle chant rang out in the stands, and the game reached a critical juncture.

Lake's telling spoil on the wing, with eight minutes remaining, resulted in a goal to Roughead. He then belted the ball away from Zac Clarke in the back pocket 30 seconds later. Three minutes on, Lake out-marked Walters. However, Walters goaled soon after, cutting the margin to three, but Gunston quickly replied with his fourth goal. The Hawks led by 10 points at three-quarter time and, during the break, Hodge was forced to discipline his key defender:

> I remember telling Lakey to shut-up at three-quarter time! We'd changed a lot of structure, and he was babbling on about something that had nothing to do with what we were about to do. I told him to "shut the hell up", and I recall him looking at me as if he wanted to kill me! That was the good thing about Lakey: he would go off on a tangent and his mind would be a million miles away, but if you gave him a spray you at least knew you were going to get a good response out of him.

With Hodge, Lake, Gibson and Birchall building an impenetrable wall in defence from the beginning of the last quarter, Isaac Smith kicked a huge goal from outside 50 metres at the four-minute mark to increase Hawthorn's margin to 17 points. Luke Breust roved and kicked another four minutes later. The ball had spent 90 per cent of the time in Hawthorn's half because of the work of Lake and his comrades in defence. Lake, in particular, took some monumental marks in the final quarter, standing his ground to intercept whenever Fremantle threatened to score. Halfway through the term, when Brad Hill goaled to push the margin to 30, it was all but over—even Clarkson appeared to celebrate.

Fremantle wasn't done with, however, and if not for two bad misses by Haydn Ballantyne, plus missed attempts by Pavlich and Crowley, it could have been within a goal. Hawthorn's attack had been the most potent in the League all year, but during the season's defining minutes it was the pressure and composure of the defence that ensured the Hawks won the Premiership. The final margin was 15 points, 11.11 (77) to 8.14 (62), in front of 100,007 fans, with Lake and Hodge embracing in relief on the siren. The latter had just become a Premiership captain for the first time. In 2018, Hodge said of Lake's performance:

> That last quarter of the 2013 Grand Final, where he took six or seven intercept marks, was over and above what we expected from him. But he was more than capable, and he took his opportunities when he could. One thing you need in Grand Finals or big games is reliable people around you. On the big days, Lakey was reliable.

Interviewed on the ground by Channel Seven's Matthew Richardson moments after the final siren, Lake said that, one year earlier, he was "probably blind [drunk] up in the second level with a few mates"; his disbelief at what he had just achieved was clearly evident. Sam Mitchell then told 'Richo' that Lake was "a great pick-up" who did "a lot of things you probably see, but a lot of things you won't."

In a fairytale game for Lake, he had recorded 16 kicks (the most he had in any game all year), six handballs, 10 marks and five rebound-50s. With 12 Norm Smith Medal votes, he finished one vote ahead of Gunston, and when Lake was announced as the Norm Smith medallist the cheer of the Hawthorn faithful said it all. *Fox Footy* commentator and 1988 Brownlow medallist Gerard Healy was overjoyed:

> Lakey has a special place in my heart for Grand Finals, because I backed him at 80-1 for the Norm Smith Medal! It was a bet we did on radio (3AW) on the Thursday night beforehand, so I followed him intently that day. His intercepts, his spoils and his impact on that game started to accumulate into what was clearly going to be a pretty solid performance. You started appreciating Brian's performances even more as he got older, but what was special about his Norm Smith Medal performance was that it put a stamp

on how good a player he was. He had a couple of terrific years at the Bulldogs, but he let himself flounder there for a period of time. However, under Alastair Clarkson he elevated his game to an exceptional level through his spoiling, intercepting, distributing—he was just a fantastic full-back during those Hawthorn Premiership years. The Norm Smith Medal will remind people forever that he was an A-grade defender in a darned good side, and he played a hell of a game in that Grand Final.

Hodge believes that Lake, much like Crosswell during the 1970s, saved himself for the big matches. "He was always someone you wanted on a big stage," he said. "It could be round one or round 15, and he could be a space cadet; he'd be looking up at the crowd, might look like he doesn't give a stuff." But, Hodge added, "you get to a big game or a Grand Final, and you knew exactly what you were going to get from him. He would back himself to take the big marks, and you knew he was going to kill the ball and be physical when he had to."

If Good Brian was on show on Grand Final day, then Bad Brian made an appearance in round 16 the following season. Against North Melbourne at Docklands, Lake applied what *Channel Seven*'s Dennis Cometti labelled a "sleeper hold", and what fellow commentator Leigh Matthews called a "choker hold", on Kangaroo forward Drew Petrie.[30] The case was sent to the Tribunal, where Lake received a four-match suspension. Recalling the incident in 2016, Lake said:

> Petrie was probably getting on top of me by that stage. I tackled him and brought him to the ground—I just wanted to tackle him really hard ... I didn't deliberately try to strangle him, or anything like that ... For me, it was just that idea of not losing—I wasn't going to lose that wrestle ... I understand that now, that it's not a good look for the game.[31]

After his month-long layoff, Good Brian remerged for the final three games of the home and away season and then all three of Hawthorn's

---

30 *The Age* online, 5 July 2014.
31 *Open Mike*.

THE NORM SMITH MEDAL

finals. In the Grand Final, against Sydney, he had 10 kicks, 10 handballs and took seven marks as the Hawks dominated from start to finish to win by 63 points. Hodge claimed his second Norm Smith Medal, while Lake was again named among the best players. Having played just 32 matches for the club, he now had two Premiership Medals.

Twelve months and 22 games later, he claimed a third when Hawthorn defeated West Coast in the 2015 Grand Final. Rioli won the Norm Smith Medal, while Lake, in game 251, had 14 kicks, three handballs and took 11 marks. In the last quarter, in one of the game's memorable moments, Lake lingered in the goal square while Eagle Josh Hill ambled towards goal—Lake appeared in two minds as he attempted to cover two loose West Coast players, while also trying to force Hill to kick under pressure. The result: Hill's low shot on goal was sensationally smothered by Lake and, as the match was well sewn up, even Clarkson marvelled at the play from his vantage point in the coach's box. After the game, Lake said of the smother: "I played with Josh for a while [at the Bulldogs] so I knew what sort of player he was—I knew he was going to go for goal, to be honest with you."[32]

For his role in one of the greatest teams of all time, Lake had played a major part in Hawthorn's hat-trick of Premierships. Indeed, he had more than justified the gamble Hawthorn took on him at the end of 2012. Rejuvenated by his late career heroics, he was keen to continue playing in 2016, but the club had other ideas and, just days after the Grand Final, Clarkson sat at a press conference with Lake and David Hale to announce their retirements. Lake told the media that football "changed me, not just on the field, but off the field as well, into a better person."[33]

He later conceded that, although his body was willing to play on, the "mental side of football is reasonably draining." He said, "I was probably a person who's never lived an elite lifestyle," and that he "got away with not being that ultimate professional" for most of his career.[34] Lake's remarkable run of success continued with Caroline Springs in 2016, when he played in a fourth consecutive Premiership. According

---

32 2015 retirement speech.
33 2015 retirement speech.
34 *Open Mike.*

to the man who had shown him the "love" way back in 2001, Bulldogs recruiter Scott Clayton, Lake had exceeded all of his initial expectations:

> Did I think he would turn into the player that he did? The easy answer is no. But you don't draft someone because you don't think they'll turn out to be any good. You see something. But the degree of success you never know. It was a long bow to think he would play to the level that he did over so many games. He was brilliant for the Bulldogs, and then to go and finish it off how he did at Hawthorn was amazing.

NOTE: Interviews with Scott Clayton, Rodney Eade, Luke Hodge and Brad Sewell were conducted by the author.

Statistics

BORN: 27 February 1982
GAMES PLAYED (2002-2015): 251 (Western Bulldogs 2002-12, 197; Hawthorn 2013-15, 54)
GOALS: 34 (Western Bulldogs 32; Hawthorn 2)
FINALS PLAYED: 21
FINALS GOALS: 2
GRAND FINALS: 3
PREMIERSHIPS: 2013, 2014, 2015
NORM SMITH MEDAL: 2013 (presented by Greg Williams)

Norm Smith Voting

Brendan McCartney: 3 Jack Gunston, 2 Luke Hodge, 1 Brian Lake;
Tony Shaw: 3 Lake, 2 David Mundy, 1 Gunston;
Glenn McFarlane: 3 Lake, 2 Gunston, 1 Mundy;
Adam McNicol: 3 Lake, 2 Gunston, 1 Mundy;
Karl Langdon: 3 Gunston, 2 Lake, 1 Nat Fyfe.
TOTALS: Lake 12, Gunston 11, Mundy 4, Hodge 2, Fyfe 1.

Cyril Rioli

Of the many superlatives used to describe Hawthorn forward Cyril Rioli, Bruce McAvaney's "delicious" has been the most exceptional, and most quoted. Indeed, for the man known simply as Cyril, whenever the ball enters his area we lick our lips in anticipation of what's to come. Whether it's kicking a miraculous goal, leaping over taller opponents or providing an exhilarating chase-down tackle, Rioli—dubbed 'Junior' to distinguish him from his father, Cyril 'Senior'—has kept fans of all persuasions on the edge of their seats. In his first season, 2008, Rioli played every game including the victorious Grand Final victory over Geelong. He ran second in the best and fairest in 2009, before hamstring issues forced him to alter his running patterns. He was awarded the first of three All-Australian jackets in 2012 (claiming the other two in 2015-16) and added three more Premiership medallions during the club's three-peat (2013-15). In the 2015 triumph over West Coast, Rioli continued a remarkable family record on the game's biggest stage, joining uncles Maurice Rioli (1982) and Michael Long (1993) in earning a Norm Smith Medal.[1] In the 46-point 2015 triumph over West Coast he had 14 kicks and four handballs, took a game-high 12 marks, and kicked two goals.

---

1   Cyril Rioli's cousin, Daniel, also played in Richmond's 2017 Grand Final victory.

← **FAMILY AFFAIR** It seemed like destiny that Cyril Rioli would join his uncles, Maurice Rioli and Michael Long, with a best on ground performance on Grand Final Day, adding a bonus item to a trophy cabinet containing four Premiership medallions.

THE NORM SMITH MEDAL

My whole family played footy, so I enjoyed it growing up. My cousins played, and it was really the only sport I knew—that and rugby. On the Tiwi Islands, where I grew up, footy is the number one sport. I loved watching it. I was able to watch my dad, Cyril, play; he was my favourite player. I always wanted to be like him.

Dad played in Darwin and won 12 Grand Finals with the St Mary's Football Club.[2] I really looked up to him, I still do, and he's someone who I hold very high in life. He's someone I always turn to. He went to school in Perth and played for South Fremantle, then he played over 200 games for St Mary's. He was a small back pocket, so I'm at the opposite end of the ground to him.

When I was growing up, my uncle Maurice Rioli was away, either in Perth or Darwin. I'd see him a few times each year. But I certainly knew what he had done in the VFL (Richmond 1982-87, 118 games), and he was someone I looked up to. When he moved back to the Island, I had moved to Darwin, then I went to Melbourne. Although we weren't around each other that often, I knew what he had done in football and he was someone I wanted to be like. Whenever I used to see him, everyone would come up to him—he had a big impact, not only on our family but on Northern Territory football, as well as the people at South Fremantle [1975-81, 1988-90, 168 games] and the Tigers.

My mum, Kathy, did athletics growing up. It's funny, we joke about it now. Dad was quick, but Mum was just as quick, so we joke to Dad that I got my speed from her. I don't know if she participated in other sports but, like Dad, she is one of the main people who has helped me greatly along the way.

Mum's brother is Michael Long (Essendon 1989-2001, 190 games). I was fortunate to see him play football, and he was around a lot more than uncle Maurice was in those early days. I would see him whenever he was up on holidays, then, once I moved to Melbourne for school, I would go to his house over the weekends. I spent a fair bit of time with him in those early years in Melbourne. He was always there to help me,

---

2   Cyril Rioli senior won the St Mary's best and fairest award twice and also captained the club. Like his son (forward pocket), Rioli senior is a member of the AFLNT Northern Territory Government Team of the Century (interchange). Maurice Rioli (half-forward) and Michael Long (wing) are also in the team.

but he also let me go about my business. If there was something that needed to be corrected in my game, he would be there to guide me. I was very fortunate he was down here when I moved down, because I found it really difficult to be away from home. He was someone to lean on who was more than happy to help me out.

You think moving away from home will be easy. I had been to Melbourne a few times for holidays, but it was a big eye-opener when I actually moved here to live and go to school at 14 years of age. I found it really hard. It would have taken me more than a year to get my head around the fact I was going to be here for a very long time. I was fortunate I had a lot of support from a lot of people; that's what got me through. My cousin, Dean (Essendon 1999-2006, 100 games), and some other cousins were all down here, plus uncle Michael. Then there was another cousin, Steven Rioli. Steven was one of my idols growing up—I put him up there as one of the best footballers I've seen. I loved watching him play. He came down with me initially, but he left after a week and went back home. For some reason I chose to stick it out, and the rest is history.

We were both at the school and we were hating it; hating being away from home. It was all very new to us. I remember us talking about it in those first few days and me saying, "Let's go home, I hate it here." Steven took off and I found it really hard being there by myself. I don't know why, but I remember thinking: "I'll give it a go, I've got to try this. I don't want to let people down. Who knows what's going to happen, but I need to try." Fortunately, I had a lot of support at that time, which helped me to get through it. They helped me to look at the possibilities I had in front of me. Not many kids get the chance to do what I was trying to do. I thought, "What's the worst that could happen if I stick it out? I'm a chance to be drafted by an AFL club if I can stay here." I would tell myself things like that all the time, to help me get through the hard periods.

My uncle, Sebastian, was down living with Dean, and he—'Sibby'—was a great support. Derek Kickett (North Melbourne/Essendon/Sydney 1989-96, 152 games) came and saw me, too. He said, "The hardest thing you did was get on that plane. The easiest thing now is just to go to school." That stuck with me. It was only a few words but they made a huge impact on me and helped get me through. Having so many relations down here I was able to go and hang out with them on weekends. When it used to come around to Sunday night, knowing I had to leave them and go back to school the next day, it made the Sundays pretty tough each week. I got through, thankfully.

I went and watched Dean play a few games with Essendon. I was at the game in round 11, 2004, when Hawthorn and Essendon had their famous fight—I was sitting on the wing at the MCG that day, right in front of the action. Uncle Michael would take me to games as well, and everyone used to notice him wherever we went. I used to think "Wow!" Now it's me going through that stage—who'd have thought? Michael took me to *The Footy Show* and various other events, things that you wouldn't otherwise get the opportunity to do. So that really opened my eyes to a whole new world. I used to look forward to the weekends, getting out of school and being around family and going to different events. I barracked for Essendon because of the family connection. Everyone on the Tiwi was Bombers, which is why I started going for them.

Despite carrying the Rioli name, I didn't have any expectations or pressure that I placed on myself. For people looking in from the outside, I'm sure there were some who thought, "He's a Rioli, he should be good at footy." But that never worried me. I just loved playing the game. I'm proud to be a Rioli, but I didn't feel any pressure to go out there and be the best footballer. I wasn't too fussed about it, but I understand other people see the Rioli name and get excited. I just always tried to play my normal game, and that's all I've ever done.

I'm sure opponents noticed me a lot more because of my name. But I went okay at school footy. I may have been targeted a couple of times, but it was very rare that anyone went after me. I just played. We had a lot of other good footballers in our school team, so I'm sure I was the least of their worries.

It's hard to explain my on-field awareness. When I played footy on the islands we never had a structured game. We would play different games, including one played in the 50-metre arc. You would kick out, and you had to get the ball to the 50-metre line, then take it back—a bit like half-court basketball. There was no structure though, we just played. We would kick the ball up and, subconsciously, you started to notice the players around you while the ball was in the air: who you had nearby and what was going on around that area. That may have played a part in my awareness. I use it in everyday life, too. If I go to the shops, I feel my awareness for what's around me is pretty good. That must transfer to how I see things on the field.

When I train, I get to know my teammates a lot better, get to know what their strengths are, where they'll be running and so on. Being in that group environment constantly, and understanding each other's traits, helps you a lot out on the field. It's hard to explain, though, it just seems to come naturally to me.

I get asked about my overhead marking a lot. It's funny, during my early AFL years I rarely jumped. I guess, though, when you're playing with a player like Lance 'Buddy' Franklin (Hawthorn 2005-2013, 182 games; Sydney 2014-current, 89 games) there's no room to jump! But as the years went on, and the more games I played, I felt more confident to do those things. When I was young, I would think, "If I jump, I might get in trouble; just stick to the game-plan." But now it's like second nature to me: if the ball's there I'm going to jump for it. Looking back to my junior days, I felt like I had a good jump, but now my timing is a lot better. Being that bit older, I feel more confident to jump for and take those grabs that people ask me about. I'd like to have a better answer for everyone, but I think it's just the confidence within myself to know I can take those marks.

There was no structure to learning goalkicking growing up. Being on the Tiwi Islands, there might be two balls between 10 or more of us. We'd all be walking along, and someone would say "Hit that sign," or you'd try kicking it between two trees. We were always testing ourselves to try and kick to a certain target, or between something. They were only little things at the time, but I'm sure they helped me kick the way I do today. There has been a lot of practice, plus the confidence to take those shots because you know within yourself that you can do it.

THE NORM SMITH MEDAL

The Kokoda Track was really hard. It was one of the toughest things I had done to that time, and my first real test as a Hawthorn player. No sooner had I arrived at the club and they said, "You're doing the Kokoda Track." I thought, "This will be easy, I love the bush," but little did I know, it was a bit more involved than just a bush walk! The first day was all flat terrain, and I thought, "Yep, I can get through this easy enough." But it got much tougher. I was carrying more weight on me back then, a chubby little kid, and I returned from there much skinnier. I remember Dad and other people being pretty shocked when they saw me after we returned from Kokoda. While it was tough, really tough, it was such a great experience to do it first up when I arrived at the Hawks.

Alastair Clarkson was very approachable, easy going, a real family man. I felt really comfortable going up to speak with him, even from the start. He can be pretty cruisy, and then he cracks the whip when the time is right. But I found him overall to be pretty easy going and free-flowing from the beginning. The more you learn about him, the more respect you have for him.

What sets 'Clarko' apart is his ability to stay ahead of the game. He's always looking at trends, at other sports, and bringing in different tactics such as the zone defence seen in soccer. When he first introduced it I thought, "This is crazy! What does soccer have to do with footy?" But when I thought about it, and saw what he wanted to do, I realised pretty quickly that it was going to help us be successful. That's his strength—he's always thinking about new things, about new ways to win, always thinking to the future. From when I first started under him, it's amazing the amount of coaches that have gone through the system under him.[3] He loves seeing those guys reach their potential; loves helping them to do that. His vision for the game, its trends and its people is as good as anyone's. If he ever has an idea he'll call a meeting and tell us about it, then he'll ask the players and coaches their opinions, always wanting to find ways for us to get better as a team and as a club.

I played every game in my first year. I was fortunate that the team was

---

[3] At the beginning of 2018 no fewer than seven of the League's 18 senior coaches learned all or some of their trade under Alastair Clarkson: Chris Fagan (Brisbane), Brendon Bolton (Carlton), Leon Cameron (GWS), Damien Hardwick (Richmond), Adam Simpson (West Coast) and Luke Beveridge (Western Bulldogs). Stuart Dew (Gold Coast) played under Clarkson at the Hawks.

winning more often than not—I had arrived at a pretty good time in 2008. I certainly put no pressure on myself, and never felt I had pressure on me to perform from day one. I had a good pre-season, received a lot of help from my teammates, and I was fortunate that my body held up throughout that whole year. Going from school footy, to nationals, from playing 15 games of footy a year to 25 at the top level in one season, it was a big adjustment. The club managed me really well through that first year, knowing my loads throughout games and throughout training. They kept a close eye on me and it all came together for me.

Midway through that first year, I was mentally drained. The club gave me the opportunity to go home to Darwin for a few days, and that—both mentally and physically—helped me a lot, enabling me to handle the requirements on body and mind in the second half of the year.

You don't expect too much in your first year. We had guys like Shane Crawford, for example, who had been there since 1993 and had never played in a Grand Final. So to make the Grand Final in my first year I probably took it for granted and didn't enjoy the result quite as much as 'Crawf' who had waited so long to get there. Certainly I found I enjoyed the few we won later down the track a lot more, because I was more experienced myself by then. That said, in 2008 I was certainly excited to be playing in the Grand Final. I got to spend it with my parents, my girlfriend (now wife) Shannyn, my sister Kahlisha, and my other family members. So that was awesome. I remember thinking that why I moved to Melbourne in the first place was for moments like that, so it was an unreal feeling to be playing finals footy, then to play in a winning Grand Final, all in my first year.

When we won in 2008, I thought we had a pretty good young team, so I expected it would happen again for the next few years. I wasn't cocky about it, but I felt we were a good chance to win a couple more with that group. Then we suffered some injuries and we fell away, missing finals the next year. From a personal point of view, maybe I didn't come back in the best shape. But I felt I was able to back up my first year with another good season, finishing second in the best and fairest. So while it was a poor year for us, missing finals, I felt I had a good year personally.

THE NORM SMITH MEDAL

Over the next few years we changed a few things and we returned to the finals pretty quickly. But it took us until 2012 to reach another Grand Final.

It was tough to deal with injuries during that period. It's funny now, but the week before I hurt my hamstring for the first time, we were talking about it at the club. They said, when I have one I'll feel it—I'll know I've done it. Sure enough, that week I felt it and I knew straight away that I'd done my hamstring. Dad had a lot of hamstring injuries when he played, as did some of my cousins. I look at it as a part of the game—it happens to some players more than others. But it took me a while to get on top of it.

We changed my running style. One of my problems was running at full speed and picking up the ball—that was a big part of my game. But understanding my body, and knowing how my hamstrings are, I can't do that anymore. When I play, I just play, but now I know not to put myself in certain situations because my body can't handle them. I think about it when I'm playing now, and I know if my hammys feel a bit sore at training we can back things off to protect them. As you get older, you tend to know your body a lot better, and you feel more comfortable telling the physios and coaches that you don't feel right. We then modify my program accordingly. Over the last three or four years we've been really good at managing that aspect of my body.

Losing the 2012 Grand Final to Sydney cut deeply. We went in as favourites and had been very good all year, so that was something I took very hard when we lost. But as much as you don't want it to happen, I look at it now and say that, who knows, but if we had have won that one would we have won the next three in a row? Because that drove us on to winning those next three. It was embarrassing losing on the day. I didn't want to be around anyone, didn't want to go out and show my face anywhere. I was embarrassed with what happened and how I played, so it cut me up a lot losing that game.

I suffered another hamstring injury in 2013 (round five) and didn't know whether I would be right for the finals. But losing in 2012 was a big motivation for me to get back. And not only for 2013, it remains my motivation and will until I retire. We worked really hard in that 2013 pre-season, so to be struck down by another hammy injury was very frustrating. I wanted to be out there to prove to myself, prove to the AFL world that Cyril Rioli was still around. Winning in 2013 was such a huge weight off our shoulders. That put to bed the question of, "Will they win another one?" When we won, it was such a huge relief for myself and for the whole club.

I had huge doubts in 2014. I suffered another injury (round 15), although, initially, I felt confident I would make it back. But then we realised how serious it was, so all my time was spent trying to get it right, getting fit again, and I was pretty scared I wouldn't get back in time. We were having another good year, so I wanted to be there with them in the finals. Entering Preliminary Final week I remember thinking, "Am I going to be able to come back and play?" It was nerve-racking. But I was fit, and I played my first VFL game that week. The coaches said to me, "Play your heart out and prove to us that you can play. If you get through and prove it to us, you will be a chance to play in the Grand Final if we get there." It was exciting to know they would give me every chance to play.

Not many people know, but 'Sibby' passed away in 2012 and it hit me hard. From then on, I had made a personal commitment to have a good year for him. When we lost that year's Grand Final to the Swans, that was something I struggled with—that I wasn't able to do it for him. So when we beat Sydney in the 2014 Grand Final, he was, in a sense, my driving force to get back and play that day, and to win for him like I had promised when we played the Swans in 2012. When I got subbed out late in the game, and the television camera showed me crying on the bench, the reason was more for Sibby than anything else. I just hoped he knew that I had done that for him. The emotion of that was overwhelming. Like with the 2013 Grand Final, the relief by beating Sydney in 2014 was huge for me. I had been carrying that for a long time, so to beat the Swans after they beat us two years earlier was an enormous weight off my shoulders.

For our club, the 2015 season was pretty messed up. We had a lot of things happen off the field: Jarryd Roughead was diagnosed with cancer, assistant coach Brett Ratten lost his son in a car accident, and I also had some personal issues I was dealing with. But we held tight as a group, and we all looked after each other, so that made us a lot closer and united as a club. We learned more about each other, and it made us more resilient. Then, we lost our first final to West Coast in Perth (32 points), so that made the task even harder. But we hit that head on. We knew if we lost again our season was over, but we held tight and learned a lot from that game, which drove us on for the rest of that finals series. We had so many things to motivate us from that year, and it drove us to win the next two games and reach another Grand Final.

We went along to watch Box Hill and Williamstown in the Grand Final. Box Hill was losing, the game was all but over, yet I remember sitting there with Shannyn and saying, "I'm not leaving. I want to watch this game, because I want to witness that feeling of losing; of the hurt, the pain of losing a Grand Final." Box Hill lost by 54 points, but from that Sunday on I was all business. I put everything into that last week. I switched into footy mode the second I arrived at the club on the Monday, wanting to mentally prepare myself to play well in the Grand Final. My role was to play my normal game. We had studied West Coast since that first final, and had learned a lot from how they played against us in that game.

There was a bit of everything in my first quarter performance. I kicked a couple of goals, gave a couple away, went for marks, even kicked one shot out on the full. Any footballer wants to start well in a Grand Final, and I was no different. Having studied the opposition, I felt I knew what their defenders were like. They liked to sit off you, so I felt that if I could get easy hit-ups, easy marks, it would work against them because of how they set themselves up in defence. We were playing amazing footy that day; our guys were running hard, sharing the ball well, which made things easier for me. I was just lucky enough to get on the end of some of their good play.

I modelled my game on defensive pressure, on trying to turn the ball over. And that was my mentality going into that game. All I wanted to do was lay pressure, and I would let the rest take care of itself. So to be able to get on the end of the ball as well meant I was in the play regularly.

A lot of the guys were making it easier for me, they were predictable to me, and that came back to me knowing my teammates, knowing the way they played. That made it a lot easier for me to read the ball and read the play. Up in our forward line we were pretty happy with what the guys were doing down the ground to give us those opportunities.

I told 'Roughy' it was pretty selfish of him to mark that kick of mine on the goal line in the last quarter. No, that said, he gave me my first goal… but he wasn't having a shot for goal, was he! We joke about that now. In all honesty, I was actually kicking him the ball, but it was going through so he could have done the decent thing and let it go! All I really cared about was winning the game, so I didn't mind who scored the goals.

Going into the last quarter, I'm not going to lie, winning the Norm Smith Medal did cross my mind. I know Sam Mitchell was having a very good game, Isaac Smith was, too, as was Shaun Burgoyne. I looked at all those guys and knew they would be in the running. But I also thought to myself, "I could be in with a chance here!" But winning the game was my priority, particularly considering we lost the first fight against them in the opening round of the finals. To win the return bout (by 46 points) was the best thing of all. Then, afterwards, to hear my name called out as the Norm Smith winner was still a real shock, despite me sort of hoping I would win it. They called my name and I was like, "Oh, really? Okay!" It was an unreal moment. As I said, I've never put too much pressure on myself to be best on the ground, or that because my uncles won Norm Smiths I had to win one, too. I just wanted to go out and play—still do—and whatever happens from me playing, happens.

I don't sit and reflect on winning the Norm Smith Medal too often. I still feel like I've got a job to do as a player. But when I finish football I can grab it and show my kids, and that will be great. I certainly hold it close to my heart, though. Of all my footy accolades, having a Norm Smith Medal is up near the top. And it's special knowing I achieved something that Maurice and Michael also achieved, two guys I looked up to growing up.

I considered quitting before the 2018 season. When Dad suffered a heart attack in late 2017, footy was a long way from my mind. I've only

THE NORM SMITH MEDAL

got one dad. Plus, I've been away from home for such a long time now. The only thing going through my mind during those weeks of his recovery was making sure he was my number one priority. I started to think that I wanted to move back home to be around him, and be around my family, because I've missed out on a lot of special family moments since being away. And, without sounding cocky, I've been lucky with what I've achieved during my time at Hawthorn. I've got Premiership medallions, a Norm Smith Medal, been named All-Australian three times—I feel like I've achieved a lot in footy, so if I did pull the pin and move home I would have no regrets about not getting the best out of myself. But with Dad recovering, I reassessed my goals. I'm close to playing 200 games. I had a pretty bad year in 2017; I was injured and I also played some pretty poor football. So I want to prove to myself that I can still play. I don't want to go out that way. Yes, I really miss home and I enjoyed being home for an extended period between seasons. I love it in Darwin, love it on the islands. I had so many things going through my mind, and at the lowest point when Dad was quite unwell, I began rethinking a lot of things. Fortunately, I had my wife alongside me, there were a lot of people supporting me through it, including the football club who were great in allowing me to have time off. For any footballer, you need to be in the right headspace to play at your best. I had a lot of time to think, and I'm glad that I made the decision to come back for 2018.

——— Statistics ———

BORN: 14 July 1989
GAMES PLAYED (2008-current): 185[4]
GOALS: 273
FINALS PLAYED: 19
FINALS GOALS: 22
GRAND FINALS: 5
PREMIERSHIPS: 2008, 2013, 2014, 2015
NORM SMITH MEDAL: 2015 (presented by Andrew McLeod)

---

4 Statistics correct to start of 2018 season.

CYRIL RIOLI

— Norm Smith Voting —

Peter Bell: 3 Cyril Rioli, 2 Sam Mitchell, 1 Shaun Burgoyne;
Dermott Brereton: 3 Mitchell, 2 Rioli, 1 James Frawley;
Mark Thompson: 3 Mitchell, 2 Rioli, 1 Isaac Smith;
Guy McKenna: 3 Rioli, 2 Frawley, 1 Mitchell;
Peter Lalor: 3 Rioli, 2 Luke Hodge, 1 Frawley.

TOTALS: Rioli 13, Mitchell 9, Frawley 4, Hodge 2, Smith 1, Burgoyne 1.

Jason Johannisen

South African-born Jason Johannisen is one of the most exciting runners the game has seen. With his shock of fuzzy hair and energetic dashes from defence, Johannisen quickly became a fan favourite at the Western Bulldogs. Aged six, he migrated from Johannesburg to Perth with his parents and younger sister, and before long took to the indigenous game of Australian football—a sport he had not heard of before arriving. Johannisen attracted the attention of the Bulldogs, who rookie-listed him in 2011. He now has the distinction of being not only the first former rookie-lister to win the Norm Smith Medal, but also the first foreign-born winner. In helping the Bulldogs break a 61-year Premiership drought by defeating Sydney by 22 points in the 2016 Grand Final, Johannisen had 25 kicks and eight handballs, took seven marks, had seven rebound-50s, and nine inside-50s.

I grew up in Johannesburg, South Africa. My childhood was no different from that of Australian kids. I remember playing out on the street with neighbours, riding my bike to the shops, the usual stuff kids do. I was six when I moved out here with my parents, Eldrid and Sonya, and younger sister Simone, who's three years younger than me. Mum says she played a bit of netball in school when she was growing up, while my dad was also sporty. He loved all sports and played soccer and baseball in South Africa.

← **JJ DAY** Travelling further than anyone to claim the Norm Smith Medal, Johannesburg-born Jason Johannisen produced a 33-possession rebounding masterclass in the Bulldogs' miracle win of 2016.

I played rugby when we first moved to Perth in 2000. Coming from South Africa, I knew nothing about the AFL: rugby and cricket were the only sports here that I knew. Dad was from Durban, so he went for the local Super Rugby team, the Sharks. I was torn between going for them or for the Lions, who were based in Johannesburg. But then the Western Force started up in Perth and I began following them. As a kid I also followed the Springboks whenever they played internationally.

Fitting in at school in Perth was pretty easy for me. My cousin, Keagan, was a year older than me and I had enrolled in the same primary school, so hanging out with him made it easier. It didn't take me long, though, before I began to feel comfortable enough to make friends in my own year level. All the kids were very easy going and nice to me. That's how I started to play Australian football, because each day at recess and lunch time that was all they played. It was through playing with them that I started to fall in love with footy.

The Fremantle Dockers (formed in 1995) were still a fairly new team when we arrived. Dad liked barracking for the underdog, so we all followed Freo rather than the more successful West Coast Eagles. We became members and went regularly to watch the Dockers play. Matthew Pavlich was one of my favourites, as were Jeff Farmer, Paul Medhurst and Peter Bell. They had a pretty good team and so it was always fun to go along with Dad and Mum and watch them play.

What I loved about footy was how exciting the game was. Playing rugby, everything's forward of you so I found it a bit boring compared to footy, which is so electrifying and high scoring. You need a lot of skill and a lot of athletic ability to play footy, which is what initially drew my eyes towards it.

I was blessed to run the way I do. It is something I was born with. I don't think I'd be anywhere near the player I am today without that ability to run and break the lines. I began to show improvement in the under-14s and under-15s, under a coach called Murray Glaskin; he fast-tracked my development, encouraging me to take the game on as much as possible. I played in the midfield a lot in the juniors, and also spent time up forward. I had to use my pace out of stoppages, then sneak forward and try to find space to kick goals.

The dream of most Aussie kids is to become an AFL player. For me, it got serious in the under-15s when I was invited to a development squad at South Fremantle. That was the first time it hit me that I could perhaps make it to the AFL one day. That is also when I started taking the game more seriously. Unfortunately, though, the next year I got cut from the under-16 squad and I thought my dream was done and dusted. I went back and played junior footy with my mates at Willetton.

It was shattering when I was cut, because I felt I hadn't had the chance to prove myself. I was one of the first cut from the squad and it was upsetting that I couldn't go out and show people what I had to offer. Murray had connections at East Fremantle and he told them I had potential. He then arranged for me to obtain a transfer from South Fremantle to East Fremantle. Former Hawthorn and West Coast Eagle player Steve Malaxos was coach at East Freo and he invited me to do a one-on-one training session with him. After that, he determined I would be good enough to play under-18 footy with the club; the following year I received an invitation to join the under-18 colts team at East Fremantle. I missed the first 10 games due to injury, but played the rest of the season, culminating in the under-18s Grand Final victory. Later that year (2011), I was picked up in the rookie draft by the Western Bulldogs. I went from thinking I could make it, to then having a big setback, then working my way back into contention through the opportunity presented to me by East Freo. I am thankful that Murray recognised there was something in me, then did what he did to help me get to East Fremantle.

I didn't think I was going to get drafted when I did. I still had another year of my under-18s footy to play and we were on a family holiday in the United States. I had spoken with the Western Bulldogs a couple of weeks beforehand; they told me they were looking at selecting me. Because of that conversation, I was in my hotel in the States, on my laptop, watching the rookie draft happening live. When I saw my name pop up I was just so happy and then, when I told my family, Mum started crying. That was a really awesome experience, and I remain thankful for the opportunity the football club gave me. Better still, they let me remain on holiday and I didn't have to start my first pre-season until January!

I'll be honest: I wasn't the best trainer going around. I wasn't the fittest guy when I first arrived at the Bulldogs, so I really struggled in my first pre-season. The training loads were so different from what I had been used to. When you arrive at an AFL club it's day to day, whereas in the under-18s you might train twice a week. At AFL level you have to back up day after day, so that's what shocked me the most. That and the high standard expected of you at every training session.

The scrutiny of being an AFL player has never fazed me. I'm a pretty relaxed and laid-back guy and I try not to let anything get to me. When you have a bad performance, or train poorly, you are your own worst critic. The only feedback I listen to is from the people close to me at the club, my coaches and teammates.

I have Lindsay Gilbee to thank for my debut. In 2012 the coaches asked him if he wanted a farewell game, but he said: "No thanks, play the young kids instead, give them some game time." In round 19, I was the one lucky enough to get the call-up. It was a surreal experience. You always dream of playing one AFL game and when it comes around you find you have no emotion; you're numb to the moment, in a way. My family flew over from WA and, although we lost to North Melbourne by 54 points, I'll never forget making my AFL debut.

Brendan McCartney was senior coach during a crucial time in my development (2012–14). Brendan had achieved success as an assistant coach at Geelong, working alongside Mark Thompson during their Premiership era. His style of coaching was that of a teacher. I picked up a lot from him and learned plenty. He moulded a lot of my game you see today, so I appreciate the massive role Brendan has played in my journey.

The period that saw Brendan leave the club was tough to handle. It was a position I had never experienced before, so it was shocking to me. Our captain, Ryan Griffin, left to join Greater Western Sydney, and other senior players such as Brownlow medallist Adam Cooney also left. Then Brendan left, so it was a weird feeling at the end of 2014. I was thinking, "What's going on?" But I also knew the club had made decisions based on what they felt was best for the football club. Out of that, we were lucky to bring in Luke Beveridge and from there things turned around quickly.

JASON JOHANNISEN

'Bevo's' strength as a coach is his ability to bring the best out from everyone. He's got a different philosophy as to how he thinks the game should be played, and that was refreshing for us players. He drove us to be a lot more attacking and free-flowing, which, as it has turned out, is how we play our best footy. On top of that, he is great at building relationships with people. When he arrived, he was all about knowing the individual, instead of just knowing the player. I think that was a critical element in bringing the group together. It certainly helped to build closer relationships between the players and coaches, which set us up for the success that followed.

My role changed when Bevo came in. Under Brendan, I had been a more defensive player who didn't take the game on. But Bevo immediately saw my attacking flair and said that we needed to use that to our best advantage. I started becoming a more attacking defender, using my assets to get the ball quickly into our forward line, therefore putting the opposition defenders under pressure.

It is always great running with the ball in front of a packed crowd. In a way, the crowd helps you in those moments: when you do something good it exhilarates you; you to want to do more. If someone's chasing you while you bounce out of defence, the roar of the crowd helps to get you up and about and really engaged in that moment when someone's pursuing you at top speed. There's no better feeling when you perform a great play, or do something good, and the crowd appreciates it. You can really feel it out there and it helps give you more momentum to want to attack the next contest.

We didn't know how far we could go in Bevo's first year. We didn't have any expectations, we just went out and played. So to make the finals in his first year, and for heaps of young players to get a taste of finals, that early really launched us into 2016. I missed out playing that second Elimination Final against Adelaide through injury, so for myself, as well as the others, that seven-point loss gave us added drive to approach the next pre-season with momentum. Making finals in 2015 gave the group a lot of belief that, if we played at our best, we could beat anyone.

In round four, 2016, I suffered a serious hamstring injury. Thankfully, I received good results from the scan that week, because for a day or two

THE NORM SMITH MEDAL

I felt my year was over; if I had required surgery on my hamstring, it would have meant season over for sure. Thankfully, the tendon remained in place just enough for the surgeon to suggest we take the precautionary approach of allowing it to heal by itself. That meant a three-month layoff and that was hard, because I'd started the season quite well. It was massively deflating at first, but I also knew that I was a good chance to come back and play in the back half of the season. I wanted to do everything I could to ensure my body was in the best condition possible when the time came for me to return to the side.

I was supposed to return through our VFL reserves team, Footscray. But they were playing at Coburg and I felt the surface wasn't ideal for my return game, not in comparison to an AFL ground anyway. A couple of weeks before, I was joking with the coaches that I wasn't going to play VFL and that they instead had to find me a seat on the plane for the round 15 trip to Sydney. I didn't think it would actually happen that way, but I put in a good two-week training block before the Sydney game and felt like I was match-ready. I had a chat with Bevo that week and we both felt I could get through the match.

I got to live every child's dream when Marcus Bontempelli passed to me in the last 35 seconds of that game. To kick the winning goal was unreal! I was out of breath, tonguing it by that stage, as I wasn't match fit having missed so many games. When I marked the ball, I thought we were one point down. But when I glanced up at the scoreboard I realised we were two points behind. Suddenly, I realised that if I missed we would lose the game, rather than a worst-case scenario of it being a draw. No pressure! I just had to calm any nerves and focus on the routine that I practised every day at training. It's a cliché, but that's all you can do in that moment. I focused on my momentum and ball drop, watched it on to my boot and, thankfully, I flushed it. I couldn't have kicked it any better.

The bye weekend that was introduced by the League for the week before the finals definitely helped us. We had a few players coming off serious injuries and, without that bye, I doubt we would have had them playing at 100 per cent. Especially considering we had to travel to Perth to play the West Coast Eagles in the first final. That's a hard trip, so we needed our best 22 available to give ourselves the best chance of beating the Eagles. That bye certainly allowed us to achieve that and it set us up for the entire finals series.

Nobody outside the club gave us a chance of beating the Eagles. But we thought our form was good going in and we pulled off a great win. The club had never won an interstate final before then, so that victory propelled us through the rest of that finals series. It gave us so much belief.

Beating Hawthorn, the reigning Premier, was another boost for us. Going into that second Semi-Final, the boys were really confident we could match them; we certainly weren't scared or intimidated about playing the three-time champs. We were all saying, "We've got this! We've got what we need to beat them." It was an up and down first half, but then we broke it open as we thought we could, eventually winning by 23 points. We were building and building.

The Preliminary Final against GWS at Spotless Stadium in Sydney was an awesome experience. With so many of our fans there, it felt like a home game for us; so many had driven up or found any possible means of transport to be there. Knowing that if we won we were going to a Grand Final only added to the excitement. It was an amazing game to play in; probably the best game I'd been in to that point. The intensity was at a premium, and there were so many talented players out there. It was a game of back-and-forth momentum shifts, a crazy night. To win by six points was amazing.

Having been involved with Hawthorn and experiencing so much success there, Bevo was all about us players in Grand Final week. His message was: "It doesn't come around very often, so you just have to fully enjoy it. Don't put any extra stress on yourself. Just embrace the excitement of the week and being around your teammates and your families." I think we handled that week pretty well as a consequence.

It's funny how I approach games. My parents think I'm too relaxed pre-game! I don't get nervous or struggle to sleep and I'm so chilled beforehand. I listen to music and have a laugh in the rooms. But once it's time to focus solely on the game, I never want to let down my teammates,

THE NORM SMITH MEDAL

I always try to go out and play my role. Before the Grand Final, my family flew over and I went and chilled with them in their hotel. They found it strange that I was so relaxed before such a huge game. Even during the pre-game warm-up on the ground, it was such a sunny day and everyone was having a kick, but I sat on the ground and took in the sun, tried to get a tan and chill out.

Every player wants to get involved in a Grand Final early because it sets them up for the rest of the game. That first quarter was the hardest quarter I've ever played in. It was up and back, no one was scoring, you were running non-stop. To touch the ball and collect a few possessions myself (an equal game-high 10 in the first quarter) was great for my confidence. It allowed me to remain in the game, knowing that I was finding the ball okay under that intensity.

In the second quarter, Josh Kennedy took over the game for the Swans. He had 12 disposals and kicked a couple of goals. His dominance helped them to gain a two-point lead at half-time. At the break we talked about needing to quell his influence and Bevo sent a couple of players to do roles on him in the second half. I thought Tom Liberatore and Jack McCrae were able to limit his influence after half-time (22 disposals in the first half and 12 in the second), which was really important to the outcome.

I was getting enough of the ball, but turning it over a lot as well. It's frustrating when that's happening, particularly when you do it as much as I did! The Sydney defenders were so good at reading the ball. They were watching my eyes and then getting two players to the drop of the ball each time I disposed of it. Heath Grundy alone intercepted quite a few of my plays; he just read the ball so well. Although it's frustrating when it happens, you need to tell yourself to get ready for the next contest, rather than dwelling on the turnover for too long. If you dwell on your mistakes it will only bite you on the backside. So each time I chose to forget about it and worry about the next opportunity.

It may have appeared that I didn't have an opponent, but that wasn't the case. I had Gary Rohan at times, Tom Papley, too, but what I tried to do was be aggressive and push up the ground every chance I got. That tactic worked for me for most of the day and helped me to find space. That's the way I had played all season, so I didn't intend changing my approach for the Grand Final. In the end, I was lucky enough to get a few touches (33) which was great.

There was a patch in the last quarter where we had a lot of momentum but we just couldn't finish off the Swans. We couldn't score the goal that would have broken the game open. I kicked a goal, but after a review it was ruled a touched behind, one of a number of points we kicked. The fact we had been scoring repeat behinds meant we were able to set a wall up across half-forward, allowing us to keep the ball locked in. We *finally* scored a goal, a result of keeping the ball in our half for much of the last quarter. When Tom Boyd and Liam Picken kicked their goals, that's when we knew we'd won the Premiership and broken the long drought.

It was such an even spread of contribution from the whole team. I thought our defence held strong. Joel Hamling's role on Lance 'Buddy' Franklin was great. Yes, Buddy was injured early in the match, but Joel still did an amazing job on him. Easton Wood was good in the air, Dale Morris laid a great tackle and Matty Boyd played great down back as well. Every player around the ground had his moment—all playing a part in such a great win.

There was so much emotion when the final siren sounded. Toby McLean was having a shot at goal and I was setting up as the last man in defence, so when the siren sounded I had no one around me. I looked around to hug someone but there was no one there! Instead I had to turn to the crowd and raise my hands in triumph. I saw all the Bulldogs supporters jumping up and down, going crazy, which was such a good feeling. Everybody knew how long we'd waited to win one (since 1954), so to see the pure joy on the fans' faces was amazing. I've never felt happier than in those few moments after the final siren.

Winning the Norm Smith Medal was a complete shock, because so many players had played well. An AFL spokesperson worded me up just before they announced it and I was in disbelief—I didn't know what to say! Winning that award is such an honour. I look back at all the players who have won it before me and I struggle to see myself at that level.

THE NORM SMITH MEDAL

It hasn't really hit me yet, but I'm sure it will when I retire. At the moment, while I'm still playing, the emotion of winning the Premiership overrides everything else. In those moments immediately after the game, you're too busy celebrating with your teammates because you've all worked so hard together as a group; they've been a part of your journey and you in theirs. But once I retire and reflect on everything, I know I will appreciate winning the Norm Smith Medal a lot more.

When the big games come around, you always want to be that player who gets involved and makes an impact. That was the mindset of a lot of our players that day, and that year, which is why we were able to get the victory on Grand Final day and lift the Premiership Cup. That I was awarded the Norm Smith Medal was a bonus for me, but a number of guys could have won it.

When we arrived at Whitten Oval on the Sunday, we couldn't see a blade of grass on the ground because it seemed every Bulldog fan had turned up to celebrate. We presented the Cup to the fans and all sang the club song. It was extra special because winning doesn't mean as much without the supporters to celebrate it with. To be walking down the street, even today, and have people pulling you up to thank you for making their life complete, that's an awesome feeling.

I'm not sure whether winning the Norm Smith Medal was the reason I was targeted by the opposition in 2017. I had a really good pre-season after the Premiership and felt I started the new season off well, which is the likely reason they started putting more attention on to me. When it started, I didn't handle it as well as I would have liked; I went into my shell a bit and didn't know how to cope with it because it was a new challenge and one I hadn't faced before. But as the year went on I started to find ways to get involved and have more of an impact. Things like changing positions or changing my running patterns, trying to make two-on-ones to help my teammates out, anything that broke up the heavy tagging that I found myself under.

In those first few difficult games, I felt I had let down my teammates. It was mainly Bevo and our backline coach, Steven King, who helped me through that period. I had been selfish in thinking I could handle it myself, when in reality I was struggling with it. I started asking my teammates what would work if I ran this way or did that block, trying different things to not only help myself but help my teammates too. Bevo and Kingy deserve a lot of credit for helping me through that, as do my teammates.

Despite the hysteria surrounding my unsigned contract in 2017, all the players and coaches knew I was staying on at the Bulldogs. It was just the finer details that needed to be worked through before I signed on the dotted line. There was lots of outside noise, but I was always going to remain committed to the club because they had given me the opportunity to play in the AFL. They had taken a gamble on me as a rookie and have given me so much since. They have not only allowed me to become a Premiership player, they have made me into a much better person just by being able to be around everyone at the club. So it was easy for me to decide to sign on for at least another five years.

——— Statistics[1] ———

BORN: 8 November 1992
GAMES PLAYED (2012-CURRENT): 96
GOALS: 30
FINALS PLAYED: 4
GRAND FINALS: 1
PREMIERSHIPS: 2016
NORM SMITH MEDAL: 2016 (presented by Shannon Grant)

— Norm Smith Voting —

Michael Voss: 3 Jason Johannisen, 2 Liam Picken, 1 Josh Kennedy;
Wayne Carey: 3 Tom Boyd, 2 Picken, 1 Kennedy;
Jay Clark: 3 Kennedy, 2 Johannisen, 1 Picken;
Brad Johnson: 3 Johannisen, 2 Kennedy, 1 Boyd;
Emma Quayle: 3 Boyd, 2 Johannisen, 1 Kennedy.
TOTALS: Johannisen 10, Kennedy 8, Boyd 7, Picken 5.

---

1   Jason Johannisen's statistics are correct to round 13, 2018 season.

Dustin Martin

As individual seasons go, Dustin Martin's 2017 performance for Richmond was one of the finest in the game's history. Whether fending off an opponent with his tattoo-covered arms—which he did regularly—or bursting out of the midfield and bringing his teammates into the play, or going forward to provide an imposing presence near goal, Martin dominated all over the field. He was near unstoppable! In a season in which the Tigers broke a 37-year Premiership drought, Martin was its lead actor; his influence provided a significant impetus for Richmond to will its way to victory time and again during a season, and a September, to remember.
He won the Brownlow Medal, a second consecutive Jack Dyer Medal (Richmond best and fairest), was All-Australian, AFLPA MVP, AFLCA Player of the Year, and took home a string of media awards. He simply did it all. Ominously, at just 26 years old, Martin's career is only just getting started.

It all began in Castlemaine on 26 June 1991. Martin is one of three boys (Tyson, Dustin and Bronson) to father Shane, a New Zealand-born Maori, and their Australian-born mother Kathy. From as early as five, Martin always had a football in his hands. Kathy said she

← **TIGER TIME** Cutting an unprecedented swathe through the competition in Richmond's stupendous 2017, Dustin Martin added the Norm Smith Medal to his Brownlow, AFLPA MVP award and Premiership medallions from the same campaign; he is the first to achieve such a feat in one season.

"knew he was going to play AFL" even then.[1] Martin remembered, "I was like any young kid—loved his footy. Mum and Dad introduced me to Auskick when I was five or six and I [have] loved footy ever since."[2]

Shane and Kathy purchased a property just out of Castlemaine, at Yapeen, so their three active boys could have "their own football oval."[3] Kathy explained that, on their 1.2 hectare property, the boys would play football, cricket and ride motorbikes. "They'd have all their mates around and they'd make up their own football teams and I'd let them write their football numbers on their old T-shirts," she said. "They used to run out off the back veranda and run out on to the field."[4] In the cold of winter, Kathy let the boys play football in the hallway of the house. "I didn't care about the walls, they can be fixed, and boys have to burn off some energy [somehow]."[5]

Martin's childhood friend, Cory Adamson, remembered that he, his brother Josh and the Martin boys would play football all day. Then, when they had worn themselves out and gone inside, "Dustin would always stay out by himself, practising kicking goals. That's all he wanted to do. Just play AFL. There was no other option."[6]

Martin's idol was hard-running St Kilda ruck-rover and 1997-98 Brownlow medallist Robert Harvey. Like Martin, Harvey was all-but impossible to tackle, an accumulator of possessions and could run all day. Martin's under-12 coach at Campbell's Creek, Steve Adamson, recalled that they "could not get Robert Harvey's jumper off him," adding that Martin "trained in it, he went to school in it, he slept in it."[7]

After the divorce of his parents in 2005, Martin moved to Sydney with his father. He left school after year nine and worked alongside his father in his transport business. While there, Martin played football with the Ingleburn under-16s, then with Campbelltown's under-18s, despite being just 15. A year later he returned to live with his mother and played football for Castlemaine, where, again, his dedication to—and passion for—his craft was evident to all observers. Before long he was playing with the Bendigo Pioneers in the TAC Cup.

---

1 *Herald Sun*, 16 September 2017, p. 6.
2 2017 Brownlow Medal speech.
3 *Herald Sun*, 16 September 2017, p. 6.
4 *Herald Sun*, 16 September 2017, p. 6.
5 *Herald Sun*, 16 September 2017, p. 6.
6 *Herald Sun*, 2 September 2017, p. 83.
7 *Herald Sun*, 2 September 2017, p. 83.

DUSTIN MARTIN

Castlemaine teammate Luke Walters recalled, "We'd be sitting here having beers and the lights are virtually off and he'd be there check-siding goal after goal after goal."[8] After kicking all the balls at his disposal, Martin would fetch them and go back for more practice. "It was bizarre," Walters added. "You'd actually sit there and have bets—'All right, he'll get four out of five.' Most times he'd get five out of five."[9]

In one game for Castlemaine, Martin kicked eight goals from centre half-forward against the reigning premier, Eaglehawk. He was just 16. Teammate Nick Churchill soon made contact with Western Bulldogs recruiter Dale Bower, and said, "Mate, I've just seen this gun who's going to play AFL."[10] Martin's eight-goal performance had been the only highlight from his team's display. "He was the only player at Castlemaine who was getting a kick," Churchill added. "We lost by about 15 goals."[11]

Following the 2009 AFL Under-18s Championships, Martin, who starred for Country Victoria, was named centre in the All-Australian team. He was a sought-after commodity, as Richmond recruiter Francis Jackson explained:

> I remember his power, his ability to surge, and his skills on either side of the body. It seemed there was nothing he couldn't do. He had that ability to keep his feet, but even more so playing against boys. He just had so many modern-day attributes.[12]

The Tigers' national recruiting manager, Matthew Clarke, said that what set Martin apart as a junior was exactly what audiences see today:

> Natural size, ability to kick the footy, strength. He said he was born to play AFL, and he's shown that. He always had the tools. His running wasn't super but it was good enough, and by the end of the year he went to the Draft Combine and ran a 14.3 beep, which is excellent for someone who hadn't been in the pathway system long.[13]

Clarke conceded it was "the only time we've told a kid we were going to pick him," so determined were the Tigers to obtain Martin at the end of

---

8   *Herald Sun*, 2 September 2017, p. 82.
9   *Herald Sun*, 2 September 2017, p. 82.
10 *Herald Sun*, 2 September 2017, p. 82.
11 *Herald Sun*, 2 September 2017, p. 82.
12 Konrad Marshall, *Yellow & Black: A Season with Richmond*, Slattery Media Group, 2017, p. 433.
13 *Yellow & Black*, pp. 433-434.

THE NORM SMITH MEDAL

2009. "It's funny, but he hardly said anything," Clarke added. "You tell some kids and they give you high fives or they break down in tears. He was like, 'Yep, that's good, no worries.'"[14] Melbourne had the first two selections at the 2009 AFL Draft and chose Tom Scully at one, and Jack Trengove at two. True to its word, Richmond then selected Martin with pick three.

For all Martin's obvious football strengths, there were questions surrounding his dedication. During his early years at the club he was involved in a number of well-publicised events away from the club that had some suggesting the Tigers should cut ties with him. "I was just a young bloke who liked to play up every now and then," Martin conceded. "I'm sure (manager) Ralph (Carr) and my old man were sick of it, and the club too, probably. So they sat me down and told me to pull my head in or they won't help me anymore."[15]

After one particular incident, Martin and Richmond reached a fork-in-the-road moment. "They'd told me the same thing 100 times before and I didn't really listen, but I could tell they were serious this time," Martin explained, in 2018. "So I went away and had a good hard think about things and decided to take things more seriously. I've always taken my footy seriously but it was more the off-field things getting in the way. I've just found a better balance in my life now."[16]

The football field had always been a sanctuary, but with the support of his family, Carr, coach Damien Hardwick, assistant coach Mark Williams, and captain Trent Cotchin—who had become a close confidant—Martin was able to gain greater control of his life away from the game. And from there, his football soared. "The coach and Trent, they have been great for me, great support—always stood up for me," Martin said. "But [also] everyone involved at the club; it is a great club and I really love it there. I love all my teammates as well."[17] Hardwick said of Martin:

> He's got that hard exterior. Chiselled. Tattooed. He looks like he means business. But as time went by, the real Dustin came out. I'll be sitting on the couch at 10pm after a win, watching the TV, and he'll send me a picture of him with a

---

14   *Yellow & Black*, p. 434.
15   Martin, 2017 Brownlow Medal speech.
16   Ben Jhoty, 'Roar Power', in *Australian Men's Health* magazine, April 2018, pp. 25-26.
17   2017 Brownlow Medal speech.

beer and the words "I love you, coach." You wouldn't think he would be that guy, but that's who he is. It makes me feel better just knowing he's around.[18]

Tigers chief executive Brendon Gale is another who stood by Martin during his early years and is proud of having seen him grow as a young man. "He's really matured in the last few years," Gale began:

> He was always a great competitor, but in the early days it was about coming to terms with what was required in the whole of his life and the whole of his preparation. That might have been a bit challenging. He's got a real independent streak. He's a self-starter, self-motivated. And he's got a really strong sense of who he is. Not everyone has that. It's a form of intelligence. He's got a different set of friends, but when he comes to the football club he's the uber pro.[19]

Richmond's previous superstar, Matthew Richardson (1993-2009, 282 games), said Martin's early indiscretions deserved context. "Any kid 17 to 23 is going to go out and probably muck up a little bit and that's what happened with Dustin," he said. "But as you get older you get a bit more mature and you realise what's important and what isn't. Footy's obviously pretty important to him."[20]

It is no coincidence that Martin's ascension to AFL superstardom has come on the back of his dedication to training. According to Peter Burge, Richmond's physical performance manager, Martin "hates missing training. There are times we have to tell him to have a light session. We should do it more often, because he won't come to you if he's tired—he'll want to please everyone. We have to say, 'You're due, mate. Take a rest.'"[21] Football manager Neil Balme said Martin had conditioned himself to play well every week because he was "very disciplined and very organised" and "knows what's good for him."[22]

Martin's reluctance to engage with the media has become legendary, giving the impression he is aloof and lacking in footy 'smarts'. However,

---

18   *Yellow & Black*, p. 438.
19   *The Age*, 30 September 2017, Good Weekend section, p. 13.
20   *Australian Men's Health* magazine, p. 25.
21   *Yellow & Black*, p. 439.
22   *Australian Men's Health* magazine, p. 28.

according to those at Tigerland, this perception is inaccurate. Assistant coach Andrew McQualter was surprised with Martin's football intellect and eagerness to learn when he arrived at the club in 2014. "What I've learned with Dusty is that I can tell him something once—in this scenario, if this happens, you need to do this—and straight away he goes, 'Yeah, got it,' and the next time he'll do it perfectly," McQualter said. "He's as smart as anyone I've seen in that regard. I probably didn't realise he had that nous about him."[23]

Cotchin said, "Dusty is what he is. He doesn't care what people think. He's taught me the value of that. But sometimes I wish he would do some media, because I'd love people to know the real Dusty, which is this genuine person who wants the best for everyone that he loves."[24] The skipper conceded that, from the outside, "you might suspect that he's quite simple in his approach to footy." However, Cotchin added, "while he does just go out there and play, I think he sees the game a lot better than people imagine."[25]

Part of Martin's approach to football is centred around channeling his mind and sharpening his focus. Meditation, he says, is "awesome", adding that it keeps his head "clear and calm, and gets rid of all the bullshit."[26] Richmond's peak performance mind coach, Emma Murray, revealed that "Dusty has got three things in his mind the whole game. *Strong. Aggressive. Unstoppable.*" If things are not going his way on the field, he says "strong", if he "does something that's weak" he says "aggressive", and if "he tries to do something and someone blocks his way", he says "unstoppable".[27]

Murray added that Martin has "an impressive connection with his own emotional intelligence," and that his self-awareness is "incredible". So much so that she considers him "more in tune with himself than any athlete I've ever worked for."[28]

Balme played 159 games for the Tigers (1969-79) and was a key figure in their 1973-74 Premierships. He coached Melbourne (1993-97) and later worked alongside Geelong coach Mark Thompson during the

---

23   *Yellow & Black*, p. 437.
24   *Yellow & Black*, p. 438.
25   *Yellow & Black*, p. 437.
26   *Australian Men's Health* magazine, April 2018, p. 26.
27   *Yellow & Black*, p. 441.
28   *Yellow & Black*, p. 441.

DUSTIN MARTIN

Cats dominant era (2007-13) which included the 2007, 2009 and 2011 Premierships. He knows football inside out, and recognises that there are many influences on the modern footballer, including the opposition, the crowd and the weather. But Martin, he said, "works hard to put all of that out of his mind and just concentrate on the simple stuff like how to get the next footy."[29]

Despite finishing second in Richmond's 2013 best and fairest, third in 2014 and second again in 2015, it was 2016 when Martin truly emerged as one of the Tigers'—and the AFL's—top performers. He had career highs in disposals (684), clearances (114), Brownlow Medal votes (25 and third overall) and won his first Jack Dyer Medal as Richmond's best player. He was All-Australian for the first time. His team, however, produced a horror season, winning just eight games to finish 13th, after finishing fifth in 2015 then losing yet another final. There were calls for Hardwick's head, Cotchin's leadership was questioned, and all indications were that the club, as it had done in the past, was on the cusp of imploding.

Instead, it was the low point in what became a famous turnaround. Gale and president Peggy O'Neal showed faith in Hardwick, Cotchin accepted he needed to become a stronger leader, full-forward Jack Riewoldt became more team-focused, they recruited mature bodies in ruckman Toby Nankervis (Sydney Swans) and midfield/forwards Josh Caddy (Geelong) and Dion Prestia (Gold Coast), and a number of fanatical and talented youngsters emerged, such as Kane Lambert, Jack Graham, Jason Castagna, Jacob Townsend, Daniel Rioli (cousin of 2015 Norm Smith medallist Cyril, and nephew of 1982 winner Maurice) and Dan Butler—plus they still had the finest defender of the era in Alex Rance—and the Tigers stormed back up the ladder in 2017.

They finished third after the home and away rounds, their highest finish since 1995. Having lost three Elimination Finals under Hardwick (2013-15), they smashed that hoodoo against Geelong in the second Qualifying Final (by 51 points) and, suddenly, as the Western Bulldogs had done on route to their drought-breaking Premiership in 2016, the Tigers began a run through the finals that captured the imagination of the football world. And at the centre of that whirlwind was, of course, Martin.

---

[29] Neil Balme, *Australian Men's Health* magazine, pp. 26 & 28.

THE NORM SMITH MEDAL

Only twice during the season did Martin have fewer than 20 disposals, while he had 30 or more on 12 occasions, and 40 or more twice. His ball-winning was impressive, but it was his ability to hit the scoreboard far more than in 2016 (32 goals and 23 behinds compared to just 9.9 in 2016) that made him a force to be reckoned with. With the scoring influence of the game's key forwards having fallen away in recent seasons, players such as Martin, Geelong's Patrick Dangerfield and Fremantle's Nat Fyfe (the last three Brownlow winners) have given their teams an X-factor—and opposing coaches nightmares.

That Martin had consistently performed at such a high level throughout the season was remarkable in light of the almost weekly questioning, speculation and innuendo surrounding his contract situation. As had been the case with Gary Ablett jnr, Lance Franklin and Dangerfield before him, the longer Martin held off putting pen to new contract, the more rumours circled Punt Road that he, like those other champions, would depart his original club for greener pastures. On the eve of the finals, Richmond supporters breathed a huge sigh of relief when Martin declared his intention to remain at the club for the next seven seasons.

He later conceded that the negotiations were stressful and that he was "sick of everyone talking about it, sick of my ugly face being in the paper every day."[30] Through all this noise, AFL great Wayne Carey marvelled at Martin's ability to block out the distractions and perform at such a high level, week after week:

> I don't think there's been a player in the history of the game who's been under that sort of pressure. You think of (Patrick) Dangerfield when he was in Adelaide, but that was the Adelaide media compared to Melbourne media. How he handled the year, and didn't sign until just before the finals, and to be able to perform under that pressure, and then sign and have the hoo-ha about signing and still perform maybe even better—there's not too many athletes, not just in footy but I think in the world, that can cop or handle that pressure and still perform.[31]

---

30   2017 Brownlow Medal speech.
31   *Herald Sun*, 22 March 2018, p. 60.

Having swept up almost every media award on offer during the 2017 season, Martin cemented his legend at Punt Road with a dominant finals series. It was reminiscent of some of the other great finals series previously played by Gary Ayres (1988-89), Gary Ablett snr (1989), Peter Matera (1992), Michael Long (1993) and Andrew McLeod (1997-98). In the Geelong victory, Martin had 28 disposals and was best afield, despite being held goalless for the first time in 10 weeks. Then in the Preliminary Final against Greater Western Sydney at the MCG, he had 20 disposals and kicked three goals in Richmond's 36-point triumph that sent the club to its first Grand Final since 1982. The Tiger Army had awoken, and Grand Final week was like nothing seen before in Melbourne—at least not since The Beatles rocked the city in the winter of 1964.

Two nights after defeating the Giants, Martin was again the centre of attention when he received a record 11 best-on-grounds for a final total of 36 votes, the most recorded in the one-vote-card system, to win the Brownlow Medal by three votes from the 2016 winner, Dangerfield. His mother, Kathy, said that she had predicted Dustin would win the Brownlow. "I sent him a text message before the start of last season and I said to him this season or next you'll win the Brownlow," she revealed before the vote count. "I call him my warrior," she added. "That's what his name, Dustin, means."[32]

In seven seasons that warrior had evolved from a clean-skinned, immature recruit into one of the calmest yet most destructive forces the game had ever seen. Richardson, for one, marvelled at Martin's ability to remain on his feet despite constant physical attention—much like Harvey had done for St Kilda. "He's able to get out of tight situations and then he's got that bit of explosiveness that enables him to burst out of traffic. Not many players can do that," Richardson said.[33]

Burge explained that Martin "has a great ability to transfer force from the ground through his body and then use this to accelerate or hold his position when competing with an opponent."[34] Never is this more evident than whenever he produces one of his trademark fend-offs. Murray saw

---

32 *Herald Sun*, 16 September 2017, p. 6.
33 *Australian Men's Health* magazine, p. 28.
34 *Australian Men's Health* magazine, p. 28.

THE NORM SMITH MEDAL

"magic on the field", a player who has tapped into "a white, bright, light of energy."[35] The AFL's chief executive officer, Gillon McLachlan, described Richmond's No. 4 as simply dynamic.[36]

It goes without saying that five days after winning the Brownlow, Martin was the hot favourite to win the Norm Smith Medal against Adelaide in the Grand Final—this despite the fact that no Brownlow winner had achieved the double in the same season. But that was the last thing on Richmond minds when the Crows jumped from the blocks and opened up a 10-point quarter-time lead. Martin had been busy (eight disposals) and had assisted in Richmond's second goal, from Bachar Houli. But with late goals conceded to Adelaide's Rory Sloane and Hugh Greenwood, it was Adelaide, the League's highest-scoring team, that looked ready to blow the game open.

Three minutes into the second quarter, however, Martin had a hand in Riewoldt's first goal. Richmond began to gain the ascendancy just before half-time, and when Martin marked and goaled not long before the siren, the Tigers led by nine points and had held the Crows to just six behinds for the quarter. By the time Adelaide's skipper, Taylor Walker, goaled midway through the third term, the Tigers had kicked seven consecutive goals and led by 26 points. The surprise packet in their goal spree was Jack Graham (three goals), and when Martin handballed to Castagna for a late goal, a 34-point lead had opened up at the last change.

When Richmond kicked the first two goals of the final quarter, Seven commentator Bruce McAvaney declared it "Tiger time", and the roar of the 100,021-strong crowd was deafening. Gale was in tears after Dan Butler goaled from the forward pocket with seven minutes remaining; Hardwick, too, was elated in the coach's box as the realisation sank in that the Tigers were going to win their first Premiership since 1980.

The crowning glory came two minutes later. Riewoldt centred the ball to the top of the goal square, Martin juggled the mark, played on and snapped a high right-foot kick around his body for a goal. The final margin was 48 points, 16.12 (108) to 8.12 (60), and, despite fine displays by Houli, Prestia, Rance and Nick Vlastuin, it was Martin—with

---

35 *Yellow & Black*, p. 441.
36 *The Age*, 30 September 2017, Good Weekend section, p. 11.

14 kicks, 15 handballs, six clearances and two goals—who was declared the Norm Smith medallist. In his understated way, Martin later said, "I was just trying to play my role" and "it did not even bother me" whether he was judged best afield or not. He wasn't thinking about it.[37] Hardwick described Martin's performance as "incredible".[38]

Halfway through the final quarter, former *Herald Sun* chief football writer Mike Sheahan was asked who he thought would win the Norm Smith. "I wanted to go with Bachar Houli, and probably at half-time Houli was in front," he said, but added:

> Dusty had to win it, because of his influence on the game after half-time. While both were worthy contenders, I wasn't surprised when Dusty won. With players like Martin, they can be the victims of their own high standards. Houli would have been a brilliant, romantic story had he won it, because of his (Muslim) background, but I think Dusty actually *won* the game for them. No-one else in that game could give the impression that he could in the key moments; that they were the big kid from grade six coming down to play with the grade three kids. And that's what Dusty did.

Fox Footy host and 1988 Brownlow medallist Gerard Healy praised Martin's entire finals series, describing it as "exceptional". Healy said, "It seemed like the whole finals series was played through Dusty; like he's Superman," adding that "there is no natural force that can stop him at this stage of his career."

Richardson echoed the superhero tag when he said, "Whenever I see a young kid with a Richmond jersey and I ask who their favourite player is, 98-99 per cent say Dustin Martin … He's captured the imagination of a lot of people. He's like a superhero."[39]

North Melbourne's dual Premiership captain, Carey, believes only injury will slow Martin in the coming years. "He's in rare form and his frame of mind is, he goes out there knowing that if he's anywhere near his best, no one will get near him," Carey said. As one of the greats himself,

---
37   Post-game press conference following the 2017 Grand Final.
38   Post-game press conference following the 2017 Grand Final.
39   *Australian Men's Health* magazine, p. 25.

THE NORM SMITH MEDAL

Carey knows all too well that it is "a good frame of mind to be in."[40]

Fox Footy's Sarah Jones believes Martin will eventually emulate Carey and enter into football's pantheon of champions. "I hope this is just the beginning, that we're going to be talking about Dusty in years to come as being right up there with the greats of the game like Wayne Carey, Leigh Matthews, James Hird and the Abletts," Jones said. "I hope that we have just seen the beginning of the Dustin Martin dominance, because he is such an incredible player to watch."

Hardwick said the question would now be asked,: "How does Dusty Martin get better after the season he had?" The two-time Premiership player and now Premiership coach then answered his own question:

> Dustin's one of those players that every year that he's come back he's improved one facet of his game. His handball was probably an area that we feel he could get better at. [But] he probably doesn't need to handball because his fend-off is so strong. His ability to do that (increase his handball) will open up teammates even more, [as] his unselfish nature is really improved in the way he plays the game.[41]

Kathy Martin is adamant that her son will continue to dominate the competition for the foreseeable future. "We all knew he was born to play AFL. He's just getting better and better and better, and he's only going to get better again next year. He blows my mind away, he really does."[42] And finally, Gale has an ominous thought for Martin's future opponents:

> You look at images of footballers—action shots, getting the ball, anticipating contact—and you know how they've got that startled, panicked look? You look at Dustin's eyes in those moments and they give nothing. They reveal nothing. He's like a shark. Like a great white, just cruising through the water. And then he strikes.[43]

NOTE: Interviews with Gerard Healy, Sarah Jones and Mike Sheahan were conducted by the author.

---

40 *Herald Sun*, 22 March 2018, p. 60.
41 *Herald Sun*, 7 March 2018, p. 79.
42 *Herald Sun*, 16 September 2017, p. 6.
43 *Yellow & Black*, p. 442.

DUSTIN MARTIN

Statistics

BORN: 26 June 1991

GAMES PLAYED (2010-current): 190[44]

GOALS: 204

FINALS PLAYED: 6

FINALS GOALS: 6

GRAND FINALS: 1

PREMIERSHIPS: 2017

NORM SMITH MEDAL: 2017 (presented by James Hird)

— Norm Smith Voting —

Chris Judd: 3 Dustin Martin, 2 Bachar Houli, 1 Jack Graham;

Terry Wallace: 3 Houli, 2 Shane Edwards, 1 Martin;

Daisy Pearce: 3 Martin, 2 Houli, 1 Dion Prestia;

Mark Maclure: 3 Martin, 2 Alex Rance, 1 Houli;

Jake Niall: 3 Martin, 2 Houli, 1 Prestia.

TOTALS: Martin 13, Houli 10, Rance 2, Edwards 2, Prestia 2, Graham 1.

---

44   Statistics correct to round 13, 2018 season.

Acknowledgements

I grew up fascinated with Grand Finals, particularly in the players who perform great deeds on Grand Final day. Watching Essendon's Michael Long run Carlton ragged in the 1993 Grand Final remains the highlight of my time watching football. The Norm Smith Medal has always held a special place in my heart, and it was a privilege to be asked by my publisher, Geoff Slattery, to interview the Norm Smith medallists for this wonderful, and long overdue, publication.

There have been 37 Norm Smith Medals awarded since the Medal was introduced in 1979 to recognise the best player on Grand Final day, and, of the 36 surviving recipients, I was able to interview 26 of them—the other 10 proved as elusive off the field as they were on it. To those who shared their journeys with me, thank you, it was wonderful to learn about why you all did what you did, and the challenges you faced along the way. In order to understand the winners more intimately, particularly those I was unable to interview, I conducted a total of 78 interviews and their recollections and stories were greatly appreciated; particularly Jock McLeod and Phil Egan. Jock's insights into his son, Andrew, were invaluable and enlightening, while Phil's recollections of the late Maurice Rioli enabled me to understand what drove him as a player with the Tigers.

Many other people helped me to piece this book together, and if I forget anyone I apologise—there simply isn't the room to thank you all! Those I remember are: Kate Slattery, Gabrielle Storrs, Jeff Sickert and Russell Jackson (SMG), Patrick Keane, Tony Peek, Col Hutchinson and Cameron Sinclair (AFL), Brad Smith and Tom Dullard (Fox Footy), Kall Burns (Gold Coast), Tony De Bolfo (Carlton), Ross Glendinning (West Coast), Leigh Meyrick (GWS), Lucy Mills (The Lighthaus), Gregor McCaskie and Natalie McGregor (Essendon), Kevin Diggerson (Geelong), Josie Fielding, Karlee Slinger and Greg Swann (Brisbane Lions), Peter Haby, Hannah Greasley and Amber Wayn (Hawthorn), Adrian Ceddia and Katie de Haer (Western Bulldogs), Paul Connors and Georgie Gardiner (Connors Sports), Les Everett, Karen Buckley, Ryan Smith and Ian Shuttleworth (Adelaide), Jeremy Moore and Greg Ryan (North Melbourne), Ross Oakley, Scot and Lorraine Palmer, Stephen Rielly and Sarah Allen (Collingwood), Vincent Formosa (Cash's), Keir Reeves (Federation University), Joel Reynolds, Simone and Barbara Cheatley, Scott Appleton and Nova Peris, Dean Rioli, Shane Paterson and Timothy Boyle.

Thanks, also to Rhett Bartlett, Sean Gorman, Konrad Marshall, Ashley Browne and Jon Anderson, who kindly granted me permission to draw on some of their fine work. This enabled me to source quotes from some of the medallists I was unable to interview. Theirs were some of the many secondary sources I drew from when researching this publication (books, newspapers, magazines and the AFL Record), all of which are cited in the footnotes in each chapter. I am indebted to all my fellow authors and journalists who have documented the game. As my personal library contains every Grand Final DVD from 1961 onwards, I was able to re-watch every Grand Final from 1979 to 2017 in order to document each Norm Smith winner's performance. *YouTube*, too, was a valuable online resource, as was *Fox Footy's Open Mike* program. Again, each audio-visual source is referenced in the footnotes. Many websites were accessed for information, the most visited being AFL Tables (www.afltables.com), a must-see site for any keen football researcher.

The thrill of writing this book has coincided with one of the most difficult periods of my personal life, and the support, love and kindness shown to me from so many people is something that has been unexpected but which I will always be grateful for. Again, too many to list, but I particularly want to thank Geoff Slattery (again) for going above and beyond in his care, patience and support. Also, my large and loving family, of which Mum (Heather) and Dad (David) are worthy of their own Medals for their repeat performances in the big moments. Hugs and kisses also go to: My three siblings, Kristen Elliott and Nick and Adam Eddy, aunt Yvonne Appleyard, Scott and Nova (again), Keir Reeves (again), Tony De Bolfo (again), Peter Haby (again), Bec Suckling, Meg and Kev Fitzgerald, Robyn Colwill, Jan and Rob Mortlock, Cathy Matthews-Abood, Leah and Adam Laidlaw, Brad Sinclair, the wonderful staff at 3MFM, my coffee makers at Henrietta's café in Leongatha, Melanie Eastwood, Leon Rice, Brad Koetsveld, Shea Kemp, Matt Fleet, Trinity Ouk, Luba Pavlovic, Sarah Price, John Holmes, Vivian Carroll, Jess Appleyard, Jess Lomas and Michael Wilkinson.

And a special thank you to Rose Vagilli…you know what you did.

To Dennis, you've been my best buddy and kept my feet warm throughout the writing process. And Ernie, my *Little Big Boy*, I hope Dad's book inspires you to create your own chapter one day.